Lesbian Health 101

A Clinician's Guide

SCHOOL OF NURSING
UNIVERSITY OF CALIFORNIA SAN FRANCISCO
UCSF NURSING PRESS

Lesbian Health 101
A Clinician's Guide

Suzanne L. Dibble, RN, DNSc
Patricia A. Robertson, MD

SCHOOL OF NURSING
UNIVERSITY OF CALIFORNIA SAN FRANCISCO
UCSF NURSING PRESS

Design/Production: Patricia Walsh Design, Mônica Lacerda
Text Editor: Paul Engstrom
Index: Michael Ferreira

For information, contact:
UCSF Nursing Press
School of Nursing
University of California, San Francisco
521 Parnassus Avenue, Room N505
San Francisco, CA 94143-0608 U.S.A.
Phone: (415) 476-4992
Fax: (415) 476-2373
Internet: www.ucsfnursingpress.com

ISBN: 0-978-0-943671-25-3
First Printing, 2010
Printed in U.S.A.

Disclaimer:
The authors and editors of *Lesbian Health 101: A Clinician's Guide* and the University of California, San Francisco disavow any responsibility for the outcomes of the patients to whom any information in this publication is applied, including general assessment and treatment/management, and in the case where specific drug therapy has been delineated. It is the individual practicing clinician who shall remain fully responsible for the outcome of the evaluation and management of the patients to whom any clinical guidelines in this publication are applied, including instances in which specific drug therapy has been set forth. For additional information concerning specific drugs and drug therapy, health care providers should consult the drug package insert and/or a clinical pharmacist.

We dedicate this book to lesbian patients who have dared to "come out" to their health care providers and share their health concerns, to health care providers of lesbians who strive to learn more about lesbian health issues, and to lesbian health researchers who despite the lack of funding have made lesbian health research a priority in their lives and have now made it possible to start to develop best practices in lesbian health care.

Contents

Acknowledgements

We thank our chapter authors for their evidenced-based writing as well as their patient cooperation and flexibility with our many queries.

We thank Dean Kathleen Dracup at the School of Nursing at the University of California at San Francisco for her encouragement and support of this groundbreaking and interdisciplinary project. In addition, we thank Paul Engstrom for his detailed copy editing; Mônica Lacerda and Patricia Walsh for their creative cover design and reader-friendly layout; and Yvette Cuca for her work coordinating the project. We especially thank Sue's spouse, Jeanne DeJoseph, PhD, CNM, for her thoughtful editorial assistance, and also our families, friends, and colleagues for their support during this challenging project.

Lesbian Health 101
A Clinician's Guide

Suzanne L. Dibble, RN, DNSc
Patricia A. Robertson, MD

Reflections on Lesbian Health

SUZANNE L. DIBBLE,
DNSc, RN

PATRICIA A. ROBERTSON,
MD

WHY *publish a book on lesbian health? Don't lesbians and heterosexual women face the same health issues? The answer to this well-meaning query is a resounding "No!" That is why this book is a synthesis of the latest information from lesbian health researchers and clinicians about all aspects of women's health. Our purpose is to help readers—clinicians, students, and/or lesbians—increase their understanding of lesbian health issues.*

More than 10 years ago, the National Institute of Medicine reported that the U.S. health care system does not adequately serve the lesbian population. The institute strongly recommended that research grants be awarded to determine the absolute and relative magnitudes of risks and protective factors that influence lesbian health.[1] However, due to the conservative national political climate during the subsequent 8 years, federal funding for such research was minimal. There were few clinical trials to explore, modify, or support lesbians' health behaviors. Given the minimal funding and the lack of evidence-based guidelines to direct clinical care for lesbians, health organizations that provide lesbian-specific care, such as Lyon-Martin Health Services in San Francisco (www.lyon-martin.org), the Mautner Project in Washington, D.C. (www.mautnerproject.org), the Howard Brown Health Center in Chicago (www.howardbrown.org), Fenway Health in Boston (www.fenwayhealth.org), and the Atlanta Lesbian Health Initiative (www.thehealthinitiative.org), struggled to survive.

In 1999, the Lesbian Health & Research Center (www.lesbianhealthinfo.org) was established at the University of California, San Francisco, as an interdisciplinary collaboration between the School of Nursing and School of Medicine, with the two of us as the founding co-directors. Over the following 8 years, we held research and clinical conferences that focused on lesbian health issues, mentored lesbian health researchers, and advocated for change and additional research funding, with some success. We also sponsored an e-mail service called "Ask the Doc." Anyone could submit questions about lesbian health; a program coordinator would put them in touch with a clinician or researcher somewhere in the country. Lesbians and sometimes clinicians who wanted to know more about specific lesbian health issues submitted questions from around the globe.

The new administration in Washington, D.C., has requested input on women's health issues in order to set a related research agenda. In 2009, Vivian Pinn, MD, director of the Office of Research on Women's Health at the National Institutes of Health, conducted four town hall meetings across the United States to discuss emerging issues of importance for women's health research in the coming decade. At the meeting in San Francisco, we presented priorities for lesbian health research funding based on our survey of 345 accomplished lesbian health researchers and experienced lesbian clinicians. In order, these priorities were depression, quality of life, internalized homophobia, hate crimes, homophobia, resilience, aging, alcohol abuse, weight management, the coming out process, intimate partner violence, smoking prevention/cessation, parenting, cancer, youth, and social support.

However, research alone is not enough to significantly impact the health of lesbians. Findings must translate into clinical practice. Additional key priorities are educating clinicians about lesbian health issues and culturally appropriate care, and developing practice-based guidelines for lesbian health care. The health care environment must support diversity, including acceptance of different sexual orientations, so dismissive or judgmental interactions at the front desk and in the exam room do not discourage lesbians from returning for follow-up screening or visits.

Better access to health care services for lesbians is imperative. Multiple studies have revealed that lesbians access the health care system less frequently than do heterosexual women, a major reason being the lack of health insurance. Although 70% of lesbians are in partnered relationships, most of them, unlike married heterosexual couples, do not have insurance benefits through their partner's employer. In some domestic partnerships and civil unions, lesbians do have health care benefits through their partner's employer, but, unlike married heterosexual couples, the one with benefits pays additional taxes on the benefits because these are viewed as income. For the same reason, the employer must pay higher payroll taxes for that employee.[2] Equity between partnered lesbians and partnered heterosexual women in terms of health benefits could be achieved through federal recognition of same-sex marriage. All lesbians, partnered or single, should be able to access healthcare without barriers related to their sexual orientation.

It is critical that policymakers, clinicians, researchers, and students learn about the lesbian population and the health issues we encounter. Advocacy by all clinicians to help lesbians obtain culturally appropriate health care services is essential, be it recommending lesbian-friendly breast cancer support groups or speaking up about inequities. By reading this book, you are making a commitment to this underserved population. You will make a difference in our health care and quality of life. Thank you.

Gratefully,

Suzanne L. Dibble, DNSc, RN
Professor Emerita
School of Nursing
University of California, San Francisco

Patricia A. Robertson, MD
Professor and Endowed Chair of Obstetrics and Gynecology Education
Department of Obstetrics, Gynecology & Reproductive Sciences
School of Medicine
University of California, San Francisco

REFERENCES

1. Solarz, A. L. (Ed.). (1999). *Lesbian health: Current assessment and directions for the future*. Washington, DC: National Academy Press.

2. Badgett, M. V. L. (2007). *Unequal taxes on equal benefits: The taxation of domestic partner benefits*. Center for American Program & Williams Institute. Available at www.law.ucla.edu/williamsinstitute/publications/UnequalTaxesOnEqualBenefits.pdf.

ABOUT THE EDITORS

Suzanne L. Dibble, DNSc, RN is Professor Emerita at the Institute for Health and Aging, Department of Social and Behavioral Sciences, School of Nursing, University of California, San Francisco (UCSF). She has been an active researcher for much of her career. She has conducted numerous funded studies, written more than 100 articles, and co-wrote a recent book, *LGBTQ Cultures: What Health Care Professionals Need to Know about Sexual and Gender Diversity*. In addition, she has co-edited two books—*Culture & Nursing Care* published in 1996, and *Culture & Clinical Care* published in 2005. She co-founded the Lesbian Health & Research Center at UCSF in 1999 and co-directed the Center until 2007 when she retired from her full-time position at the University. She is currently working part-time on a research grant to develop a screening tool that measures substance abuse, trauma, and mental health issues. In addition, she is founder and president of Dibble Consulting Corporation, where she assists clients with health care research.

Patricia A. Robertson, MD is Professor and Endowed Chair in Obstetrics and Gynecology Education in the Department of Obstetrics, Gynecology, and Reproductive Sciences at the University of California at San Francisco (UCSF). She has been a long-time activist in lesbian health care, co-founding Lyon-Martin Clinic in San Francisco in 1978 (which currently provides primary health care to lesbians and other women), publishing about sexually transmitted diseases and delayed Pap smears in lesbians in the early 80s, co-founding the *Women in Medicine* conference in 1984 (an annual scientific meeting and social support venue for lesbian physicians and their families), and co-directing the Lesbian Health & Research Center at UCSF from 1999 until 2007. She is Director of Medical Student Education in her department, and is also a perinatologist who provides clinical care to women with high-risk pregnancies.

CHAPTER 1

"But I'm Not Sick. Why Should I Get a Check-up?"

HEALTH SCREENING FOR LESBIANS

AUDREY S. KOH, MD

CHARLENE, *58, had been menopausal for 7 years. She had weathered hot flashes with a hormonal yam cream purchased from a health food store. Her high-deductible insurance policy covered catastrophic illness. This served her purposes because, as Charlene said, "I'm healthy and I use homeopathic remedies, which aren't covered by my insurance anyway." She did not see any reason to visit a doctor in the absence of an obvious, severe sickness. She also was afraid to face a doctor uncomfortable with, or even hostile to, her same-sex orientation. In the aisles of the health food store,* she has heard plenty of stories about problems other women have had with the patriarchal medical system.

When Charlene mentioned to her new lover that she had been having vaginal spotting unresponsive to a "female toner" remedy, she was urged to seek more formal medical attention. With trepidation and her lover in tow, Charlene went to see her lover's gynecologist, having been assured that the doctor was lesbian-friendly. On exam, Charlene was 64 inches tall, weighed 192 pounds, and had a body mass index (BMI) of 33. Her external genitalia, vagina, and cervix were hypotrophic; indeed, her cervix was stenotic, making Pap smear sampling of the cervix difficult and sampling of the endometrium impossible. Transvaginal sonography showed that the endometrial lining was abnormally thick—12 mm wide. While Charlene was under anesthesia, the gynecologist sampled the endometrium after using agents to soften and dilate the cervix. The biopsy revealed well-differentiated adenocarcinoma. Charlene underwent a laparoscopic-assisted vaginal hysterectomy, bilateral salpingoophorectomy, and pelvic and para-aortic lymphadenectomy. Her endometrial adenocarcinoma was stage IA. She is now undergoing close surveillance of her cancer.

CASEY had a hysterectomy at age 36 due to a large fibroid uterus with heavy, painful menses and no interest in childbearing. Freed from her monthly misery, she had not seen a physician for more than a decade. At age 48, she was bothered by pronounced growth of facial and body hair. This had progressed over 5 years, but she thought it was due to her Mediterranean origins. Dark hair was growing not only on her chin, upper lip, and sideburn area, but also on her arms and torso, surpassing that of her female family members. Casey's partner, Lois, did not mind this extra hair and in fact found it to be interesting and *attractive. Despite Lois's reaction, the rate of hair growth worried Casey, so she sought the only type of doctor she had ever seen as an adult: a gynecologist.*

On exam, she was 66 inches tall, weighed 278 pounds, and had a BMI of 45. Her blood pressure was 150/100. She had extensive male-pattern hair growth compatible with virilization. She also admitted that her skin had become somewhat more oily and acneiform. The clitoris was of normal size. The bimanual pelvic exam was extremely limited by her obesity. Casey did not report hot flashes. Laboratory exam for androgen excess revealed a serum total testosterone of 378 ng/dL (normal being 14–76 ng/dL) and free testosterone of 15 pg/mL (normal being 0–2.2 pg/mL). Serum levels of luteinizing hormone, follicle-stimulating hormone, dehydroepiandrosterone sulfate, 17-hydroxypro-gesterone, and thyroid stimulating hormone were all normal. A fasting lipid panel showed elevated triglycerides of 293 mg/dL, very-low-density lipoprotein of 59 mg/dL, low-density lipoprotein of 144 mg/dL, high-density lipoprotein of 38 mg/dL, fasting glucose of 109 mg/dL, and hemoglobin A1c of 6.3.

The high testosterone level prompted a CT scan to rule out adrenal pathology. The adrenal glands were normal. The ovaries were described as slightly prominent with a suspicion of stromal hyperplasia. Pelvic ultrasound showed that the ovaries were normal and did not appear to be polycystic. The working diagnosis was virilization and hyperandrogenism due to ovarian hyperthecosis. Laparoscopic bilateral salpingoophorectomy was performed. The pathology report indicated a normal left adnexa and a right ovary with a Leydig cell tumor.

Postoperatively, Casey's serum total and free testosterone levels normalized at 43 ng/dL and 1.0 pg/mL, respectively. She underwent laser hair reduction for the extensive hirsutism, began taking antihypertension medication, and started an exercise program to treat the hypertension.

JANE, *a 44-year-old realtor, had signed on with a primary care physician years earlier through her HMO insurance, although she had not previously met the doctor. But severe headaches that interfered with her ability to run back-to-back open houses prompted Jane to visit this physician for the first time. The headaches had recently worsened due to the financial stress of her partner losing her job. (The partner, a teacher at a private school, had recently "come out" in her workplace.) The physician did not inquire about her partner status or sexual orientation, and Jane did not disclose this information. In fact, she was secretive about her sexual orientation at work and with her family, having only come out to a small number of friends. She was worried that coming out would adversely affect her career as a rising-star realtor.*

On the forms she filled out before the visit, Jane affirmed that she smoked. The physician talked with her about the health risks of smoking. With the physician's encouragement, Jane chose a quit date and also started taking bupropion (Wellbutrin) for 6 weeks to help her stop. The doctor referred her to Web resources and local support groups, and did a Pap smear, as Jane had not had one for several years. The test revealed atypical cells of undetermined significance, suspect high grade. She was referred to a gynecologist for a colposcopy.

Cervical biopsy of an abnormal area showed carcinoma in situ and the endocervical curettage was positive for cervical intraepithelial neoplasia 2. A curative loop electrosurgical excision procedure (cervical conization) was performed.

Upon questioning by the gynecologist, Jane said she had not previously had Pap smears because she "wasn't sexually active." However, upon further questioning and only after assurances of confidentiality, Jane disclosed that she was in an 8-year relationship with a woman. She also said she had had a few sexual encounters with men in her twenties, but had not gone to a doctor "once I didn't need birth control." Her long-term female sexual partner had not had a Pap smear in a decade.

Despite the doctor's advice to quit smoking, Jane did not stop initially. But when told that smoking could hasten the advance of her cervical dysplasia, she quit and encouraged her partner to do the same.

■   ■   ■

These scenarios illustrate problems encountered by lesbians who have not received regular health care due to ignorance about the importance of routine check-ups, seemingly good health, or fear of heterosexist providers in the health care system. Delays in seeking care enable risk factors to cause serious health conditions, leading to increased morbidity and mortality. Preventable factors cause 70% of all illnesses and 40% of yearly mortality in the United States.[1]

Preventive medicine involves identifying conditions that cause the greatest burden of suffering for patients, and providing preventive services that are demonstrably effective in improving patient outcomes. There is a wealth of evidence-based information on preventive health recommendations that seek to reduce morbidity and mortality. (See, for example, Office on Women's Health, U.S. Department of Health and Human Services.[2]) To the extent that lesbians are less likely to have a physician or feel safe entering the health care system, fewer opportunities are available to them for the preventive health assessments and interventions appropriate for all women.

Should preventive health care guidelines be applied differently to lesbians? This chapter discusses general barriers to health care for lesbians and how the prevalence of diseases among them may differ from the prevalence in heterosexual women. Health conditions in lesbians that contribute differently to risk are overweight and obesity (and the attendant cardiovascular risk), breast cancer, cervical cancer, smoking, alcohol consumption, depression, and intimate partner violence.[3] Table 1.1 shows screening recommendations for women in general.

BARRIERS TO HEALTH CARE

Lesbians access health care to a lesser degree, and at a later stage after they experience health problems, than heterosexual women do.[4-6] Lesbians may not realize the importance of health screens in the absence of bothersome symptoms. They may have fewer routine encounters with the health care system because they might not routinely seek

TABLE 1.1. CLINICAL SCREENING SCHEDULE FOR WOMEN

PROCEDURE	AGES 18–39	AGES 40–49	AGES 50–64	AGES 65+
GENERAL HEALTH				
Full check-up, including weight and height*	Discuss with health care provider (HCP)			
Thyroid test (thyroid stimulating hormone)*	Start at age 35			
HEART HEALTH				
Blood pressure test*	At least every 2 years			
Cholesterol test†	Start at age 20, discuss with HCP	Start at age 45, then every 5 years	Every 5 years	
BONE HEALTH				
Bone mineral density test*		Discuss with HCP	At least one test. Talk with HCP about repeat testing.	
DIABETES				
Blood glucose test*	Discuss with HCP	Start at age 45, then every 3 years	Every 3 years	
BREAST HEALTH				
Mammogram†		Every 1–2 years	Yearly	
Clinical breast exam‡	Every 3 years	Yearly		
Breast MRI‡		MRI screening not recommended for women whose lifetime risk of breast cancer is < 15%		
GYNECOLOGIC HEALTH				
Pap smear and pelvic exam†	Begin at age 21, every two years until age 29. At age 30, women who have had three normal Pap smear results in a row should get screened every 2–3 years.	Every 2–3 years after three consecutive normal Pap smear results and discussion with HCP		Discuss with HCP. Women 70 years old or older who have had three or more consecutive normal Pap smear results in the last 10 years may choose to stop cervical cancer screening.
Chlamydia test*	Yearly until age 25 if sexually active with men. Women older than 25 should undergo this test if they have new or multiple male partners.	Women should undergo this test if they have new or multiple male partners		

(cont.)

TABLE 1.1. CLINICAL SCREENING SCHEDULE FOR WOMEN (cont.)

PROCEDURE	AGES 18–39	AGES 40–49	AGES 50–64	AGES 65+
Sexually transmitted infection (STI) tests*	Both partners should get tested for STIs, including HIV, before initiating sex			
MENTAL HEALTH SCREENING†				
Yearly				
COLORECTAL HEALTH (using 1 of the methods below)†				
Colonoscopy (preferred if patient is willing and able to undergo the test)			Every 10 years	
Patient-collected fecal occult blood test (FOBT)			Yearly	
Flexible sigmoidoscopy			Every 5 years, preferably with a yearly patient-collected FOBT	
Double contrast barium enema			Every 5–10 years	
EYE HEALTH				
Complete eye exam*	At least once between 20–29 years old and at least twice between 30–39 or whenever there is an eye problem	Every 2–4 years		Every 1–2 years
EAR HEALTH				
Hearing test*	Starting at age 18, then every 10 years	Every 10 years		Every 3 years
SKIN HEALTH				
Mole exam*	Monthly self-exam and then by HCP every 3 years starting at age 20	Monthly self-exam and by HCP every year		
ORAL HEALTH				
Dental exam	1–2 times every year			

Adapted from:

* Office on Women's Health, U.S. Department of Health and Human Services. (2009). *Screening tests and immunizations guidelines for women.* Available at www.womenshealth.gov/screeningcharts/general.

† ACOG Committee on Practice Bulletins – Gynecologic (2009). ACOG Practice Bulletin No. 109: Cervical cytology screening. *Obstetrics & Gynecology, 114,* 1409–1420.

‡ American Cancer Society. (2008). *American Cancer Society guidelines for the early detection of cancer.* Available at www.cancer.org/docroot/ped/content/ped_2_3x_acs_cancer_detection_guidelines_36.asp.

contraception or prenatal care. There may be socioeconomic barriers to care access, including an unmarried partner's lack of health insurance.

Additionally, lesbians may avoid the health care system altogether because they fear, or have experienced, discrimination based on their sexual orientation. Lesbians who are not open with family members, coworkers, and friends about their sexual orientation are less likely to disclose it to their health care providers, yet they often would do so if asked directly.[7] Lesbians who disclose their sexual orientation to their providers are more likely to receive appropriate screening tests than are lesbians who do not.[5] Providers can improve the accuracy of patients' social and health histories by training themselves and their staff to be culturally sensitive and open to all sexual orientations.

■ ■ ■

In the scenarios above, Charlene, Casey, and Jane all delayed their use of the health care system. Charlene trusted nonallopathic remedies, feared homophobic reactions from physicians, and had a high-deductible insurance policy. She only sought traditional health care after homeopathic tinctures failed and her partner strongly supported and reassured her.

Casey did not see any reason to consult a physician because in middle age her uterus was removed; in her view, the hysterectomy left nothing to check. Also, the increased hair growth may have been more acceptable in her lesbian community, which, compared with heterosexual settings, less rigidly adheres to stereotypical gender appearance. Her partner did not view Casey's hirsutism as either a health or cosmetic concern.

Finally, Jane was wary of exposing her sexual orientation to anyone. She only sought care after her headaches became debilitating, even though she had employment-based health care coverage. She had never seen her primary care physician and, upon meeting the doctor for the first time, did not feel comfortable enough to disclose her sexual orientation. The physician diagnosed and treated Jane, but, unaware of her sexual orientation, may have overlooked a factor contributing to her headaches: stress. Fortunately, the physician did some catch-up preventive screens, even though Jane did not think she needed a Pap smear. She and her partner were under the dangerous misconception that lesbians who do not have sex with men cannot get cervical cancer.

OBESITY

Excess body weight is pandemic in the United States; 66% of adults are at least overweight (BMI > 25) and 31% are obese (BMI > 30).[8] Obesity and physical inactivity are associated with hypertension, diabetes, hyperlipidemia, cardiovascular disease, degenerative joint disease, thromboembolic disorders, and cancers of the breast, gallbladder, esophagus, kidney, uterus, ovary, colon, and rectum,[9] and with higher all-cause mortality.[10] Weight loss and more physical activity can reduce these risks. Women with additional risk factors such as cigarette smoking, heavy alcohol consumption, glucose intolerance, hyperlipidemia, or a family history of premature cardiac disease should especially be targeted for risk-reduction measures.

Cardiovascular disease is the leading cause of death among women in the United States, greatly exceeding the mortality caused by all cancers combined.[11] Curbing overweight and obesity is an important factor in reducing cardiovascular disease.

Three large, population-based studies analyzing BMI by sexual orientation convincingly showed that lesbians have a higher prevalence of excess body weight than heterosexual women do. In the National Survey of Family Growth, which comprised nearly 6,000 adult women, the odds ratio (OR) was 1.40 for overweight and 2.6 for obesity in lesbians compared with heterosexuals.[12] Analysis of the Nurses' Health Study II, which included 694 lesbians, revealed an OR of 1.2 for overweight and 1.5 for obesity compared with heterosexual nurses.[13] In the Women's Health Initiative, the largest randomized trial to date of women in the United States, lesbians and bisexual women had an OR of 1.25 for obesity compared with heterosexual women.[14]

A study of 324 California lesbians and their heterosexual sisters found that the lesbians had significantly higher BMIs and greater abdominal/visceral adiposity—that is, larger waist circumference and waist-to-hip ratio.[15] In a study of overweight lesbian and bisexual women in Los Angeles County, higher BMI was correlated with older age, worse health status, lower socioeconomic status, relationship cohabitation, and lower frequency of exercise.[16]

Reasons posited for this higher prevalence of overweight and obesity include the possibility that large body size is more acceptable among lesbians. They may reject the dominant culture's aesthetic of thin women. The lower incidence of eating disorders in lesbians compared with bisexual or heterosexual women[17] supports this hypothesis. Research on the large social networks in the Framingham Heart Study identified the social or cultural spread of obesity: a person's chances of becoming obese increased 57% if a friend became obese in a given interval and increased 37% if a spouse did.[18] This type of culturally induced obesity may be occurring in lesbian communities.

Just as obesity may spread in social networks, the same social influences may help health care providers instill healthier eating and exercise habits, and reverse the obesity trend. The obesity pandemic and the related morbidities and mortality highlight the need to counsel overweight lesbians on effective ways to reduce and maintain their weight.

■ ■ ■

Charlene's obesity, with its attendant peripheral adipose conversion of androstene-dione to estrone, probably contributed to her endometrial cancer. Now that the cancer has been treated, she should have routine health screens and targeted screens for cardiovascular disease, diabetes, and other cancers. Although Casey sought health care for hirsutism, her work-up revealed metabolic syndrome. Had she been getting periodic health exams, her obesity and metabolic syndrome could have been treated before they became so severe. She can receive treatment for metabolic syndrome and undergo complete preventive screening now that her hyperandrogenism has been cured. Given her normal testosterone levels, Casey's lipid abnormalities may eventually improve.

BREAST CANCER

Excluding skin cancer, breast cancer is the most common malignancy and the second most common cause of cancer death among U.S. women. A woman's lifetime risk of developing breast cancer is 12.7%. Detection of breast cancer when it is not yet palpable—that is, when lesions are smaller than 1 cm in diameter—is associated with a lower mortality rate and improved quality of life relative to lesions diagnosed at a later stage.[19]

In women younger than 40, screening mammograms have a higher false-positive rate due to the higher incidence of dense breast tissue and the lower incidence of breast cancer. In women 40 to 49 years old, screening every 2 years and annual screening reduce mortality by 13% and 36%, respectively.[20] Screening mammograms and, if available, digital mammograms should begin by age 40 and continue every 1 to 2 years. At age 50, women with increased breast density should receive annual screening and, if available, digital mammograms. At ages 70 and older, comorbidities, diminished life expectancy, and the greater incidence of ductal carcinoma in situ (which may not increase the mortality rate) alter the risk/benefit ratio of screening mammography.[21] Women 70 to 79 years old can continue to receive biennial screening mammograms if they have a life expectancy of at least 10 years.

Clinical breast examination is effective for breast cancer screening. A large analysis by the National Breast and Cervical Cancer Early Detection Program showed a sensitivity of 59%, a specificity of 93%, and a positive predictive value of 4%. In addition, 7.4 cancers were detected per 1,000 women who received such exams, despite their normal results from screening mammograms.[22]

A critical review of breast self-examination research found insufficient evidence for or against this practice. Breast self-exam consistently has a low sensitivity of 20% to 30%.[23] Nevertheless, it can potentially find breast cancer and may be recommended.

Some studies have shown lower rates of mammographic screening in lesbian and bisexual women. In a study of subjects already in a health care setting, lesbians had an OR of 0.53 for previous, appropriate mammographic screening compared with heterosexual women in the control group.[6] Women in a population-based study in New York City who had sex with women were less likely to have received a mammogram in the previous 2 years than were other women (53% vs. 73%). Even after adjusting for health insurance coverage, they were four times more likely than the other women not to have received appropriate mammographic screening.[5]

Of the many theorized breast cancer risk factors, most do not differ according to a woman's sexual orientation. However, several of the weakly associated risk factors may be higher among lesbians compared with women generally. Nulliparity is associated with a relative risk (RR) of 1.3 for breast cancer and is higher in lesbians compared with heterosexual women.[13,14] Delayed childbearing (older than age 30 vs. younger than 20) is associated with a RR of 1.9 to 3.5 and is also more common in the lesbian population.[13,14] Consumption of two to five alcoholic drinks daily compared to no alcohol has a RR of 1.4; lesbians may have a higher rate of heavier drinking compared with women generally.[13,24] Urban residence has a RR of 1.1 to 2.0. Rothblum and Factor found that lesbians more commonly reside in cities than their heterosexual sisters do.[25]

Lesbians have a lower rate of lactation, which is a protective factor against the development of breast cancer ($RR = 0.73$). Postmenopausal obesity is weakly associated with breast cancer. Having a BMI < 22.9 compared to a BMI > 30.7 has a RR of 0.63 for breast cancer; lesbians have a lower rate of this mildly protective factor.[13] Hormone replacement therapy is associated with an increased breast cancer risk that rises with duration of treatment ($RR = 1.40–2.86$). Lesbians may undergo hormone replacement at a lower rate than heterosexual women do.[26]

Given that lesbians have a higher rate of some risk factors for breast cancer, public health policymakers, physicians, and community health educators should try to reduce the obstacles that prevent lesbians from receiving appropriate screening. Physicians should also counsel their patients about risk factor modification. Lesbians can lower their breast cancer risk by reducing postmenopausal hormone replacement, alcohol consumption, and obesity; increasing physical activity; and maintaining a diet that has fewer than 25% of calories from fat.

All three patients in the scenarios at the beginning of this chapter had not received any of the recommended breast cancer screens until they visited their doctors for other reasons. It is appropriate for health care providers to review patients' overall health care—especially for those who underutilize the health care system— even though the review may be unrelated to a patient's chief complaint. This can be challenging, given today's shorter appointment times and specialized health care.

However brief the appointment, a patient who has a positive experience may be more likely to follow up on recommended health screens and treatments.

REPRODUCTIVE TRACT CANCERS

Cervical Cancer

Guidelines for cervical cancer screening apply to all women, regardless of sexual orientation. The guidelines vary according to patient age and risk factors. Pap smear screening (cervical cytology) should start at age 21 and continue every two years until age 29. Women age 30 or older who have had three consecutive normal Pap smears, in consultation with their health care provider, may be screened every 2 to 3 years. Those older than 30 may have a human papillomavirus DNA test as well as a Pap smear. If the results from both are normal, these women should not be rescreened more frequently than every 3 years.[27]

Squamous cell carcinoma of the cervix is a disease in sexually active women. It develops in response to infection by high-risk types of the human papillomavirus (HPV), particularly in adolescence, when squamous metaplasia begins. Most lesbians have been sexually active with men, particularly in earlier stages of sexual identity exploration, such as adolescence. Fifty-four percent to 80% of lesbians have had sex with men during their lifetimes, 3% to 23% within the previous year.[4,28,29] Lesbian sexual behavior has sometimes been associated with risk-taking; it is unknown if women who take risks are more likely to have sex with women and/or if women who had sex with women are greater risk-takers generally. In some settings, women who had sex with both women and men may exhibit more risk-taking behaviors than do strictly heterosexual women, thereby increasing their likelihood of acquiring a sexually transmitted infection.[30] Among U.S. college students, women who had sex with both women and men were more likely to report multiple sexual partners than were their peers who had partners of the opposite sex only.[31]

Risk factors for higher rates of HPV infection include early onset of intercourse, multiple sexual partners over time, and sexual partners who themselves have had multiple partners. HPV infection can be transmitted between women; both HPV and cervical neoplasia have been found in lesbians with lifetime same-sex contact.[32] Cigarette smoking and immunosuppression increase the risk of cervical cancer.[33]

Researchers have reported lower rates of appropriate Pap smear screening in lesbians compared with heterosexual women in urban centers across the United States[5,29,34] Lesbians have cited several reasons for not getting tested: cost and lack of health insurance, prior adverse experiences with the test, not knowing where to get it, and believing that the test is unnecessary if they were not sexually active with men.[34]

Astoundingly, even some of their medical providers believed that lesbians do not need Pap smears.[29]

Half of women in the United States who develop cervical cancer have never had a Pap smear, and another 10% have not been screened within the previous 5 years.[35] This should be a clarion call to promote routine cervical cytology screening for all women regardless of their perceived or actual sexual orientation. It also highlights the need for educational outreach to both women and their health care providers that stresses the importance of routine Pap smears for lesbians. Consideration of HPV vaccination should be the same for lesbian, bisexual, and heterosexual women.

■ ■ ■

Jane was in a long-term monogamous relationship with a woman, but she had previously had casual male sexual partners and had not had a Pap smear since then. It is unclear whether she contracted from men and/or women the HPV that led to cervical dysplasia. Her case illustrates the need for all women to receive cervical cytology screening, regardless of their sexual partners' gender.

Endometrial Cancer

A woman's lifetime risk of acquiring endometrial cancer is 2.6%, making this the most common female reproductive cancer. Risk factors for uterine corpus (endometrial) cancer that differ between lesbians and the general population are the greater likelihood of lesbians being nulliparous ($RR = 3.0$) or obese ($RR = 2.0–5.0$) and the smaller likelihood of having used long-term oral contraceptive pills ($RR = 0.3–0.5$). Lesbians are more likely to smoke; those who do not have a reduced risk for endometrial cancer ($RR = 0.5$).[36]

Ovarian Cancer

Although ovarian cancer is the second most common female reproductive cancer, more women die from it than from cervical and endometrial cancer combined. Risk factors that are more prevalent among lesbians compared with heterosexual women include low or no parity, later child-bearing, less use of oral contraceptives, and lower rates of breast-feeding.[37]

Due to limited sensitivities and specificities, there is no effective screening test for ovarian cancer in low-risk, asymptomatic women. An annual pelvic exam is recommended for all women. They and their physicians should pursue the evaluation of symptoms commonly associated with ovarian cancer—increased abdominal size, abdominal bloating or pain, fatigue, indigestion, inability to eat normally, urinary frequency, pelvic pain, constipation, back pain, recent urinary incontinence, or unexplained weight loss—even though these symptoms are nonspecific.

SUBSTANCE USE

Cigarette Smoking

Several large, population-based surveys have revealed higher rates of current cigarette smoking among lesbians compared with heterosexual women. These studies are the Women's Health Initiative sample ($OR = 2.58$),[14] the Nurses' Health Study II ($OR = 2.0$),[13] and the California Health Interview Survey ($OR = 1.95$).[38] A population-based study of lesbian, gay, and bisexual adults in California further delineated these differences: 28.7% of lesbians and 26.9% of bisexual women currently smoked compared with 12.2% of the general population.[39] Avoidance and cessation of smoking could reduce the mortality from lung cancer by 90%.[40] At every patient encounter, smokers should be counseled about quitting, and adolescents about not starting.

■ ■ ■

Jane's physician did not counsel her about quitting until she already had cervical carcinoma in situ. Smoking probably contributed to this pathologic process. Sometimes a particular message or particular messenger will have a greater impact than another. Jane did not heed the advice of her primary care physician, with whom she did not develop a rapport, to stop smoking. In contrast, the bond she developed with her gynecologist plus her personal fear of cancer, which exceeded her fear of cardiovascular disease, finally impelled Jane to quit.

Alcohol Consumption

Lesbians consume more alcohol than heterosexual women do, regardless of whether alcohol consumers are defined as "nonabstainers" (57.5% of lesbians vs. 44.6% of heterosexual women[41]) or as those who engage in "heavy drinking"—60 or more drinks per month (4.5% of lesbians vs. 2.3% of heterosexual women[13]). Some of the reasons posited for lesbians' higher consumption include socializing with alcohol in bars and at parties, and self-medicating with alcohol due to the stress of homophobic surroundings.[24] Rates of alcohol abuse are higher among single and childless women than they are among women who live with their children,[42] an association that may also contribute to higher drinking rates among lesbians.

Light to moderate alcohol consumption (one to six drinks per week) in middle-age or older women has been associated with lower risk of coronary heart disease. On the other hand, higher consumption increases breast cancer risk. Risky or hazardous drinking (for women, more than seven drinks per week or more than three drinks per occasion) is associated with higher rates of motor vehicle accidents, suicide, violence, hypertension, mental disorders, and alcohol dependence.[43]

Health care providers should screen all adults and teens for alcohol and other substance abuse problems. Short questionnaires such as the Rapid Alcohol Problems Screen (Table 1.2) can help detect such problems. Clinicians can effectively reduce alcohol consumption by means of brief interventions, including feedback, goal-setting, and follow-up.

TABLE 1.2. RAPID ALCOHOL PROBLEMS SCREEN

1. During the last year, have you had a feeling of guilt or remorse after drinking?

2. During the last year, has a friend or a family member ever told you about things you said or did while you were drinking that you could not remember?

3. During the last year, have you failed to do what was normally expected of you because of drinking?

4. Do you sometimes take a drink in the morning when you first get up?

A "yes" answer to at least one of these four questions suggests that the patient's drinking is harmful to health and well-being.

Source: Cherpitel, C. J. (2000). A brief screening instrument for alcohol dependence in the emergency room: The RAPS 4. *Journal of Studies on Alcohol, 61,* 447–449.

MENTAL HEALTH

Depression

All women should be screened for depression. Short, simple screening questions help detect patients who need further evaluation. Many studies have found higher rates of severe depression, including suicidality and suicide attempts, in lesbian teenagers compared with heterosexual female teenagers.[44,45]

Among adults, several studies with valid comparison groups have shown equal rates of anxiety and depression in lesbians compared with heterosexual women.[26,46] The Women's Health Initiative found that lifetime lesbians, bisexuals, and adult lesbians are more likely to be depressed (16%) than are heterosexual women (11%).[14] Another study with internal comparison groups of lesbian, bisexual, and heterosexual women found higher rates of depression and suicidality only among the lesbian and bisexual women who had not disclosed their sexual orientation.[45]

One theory is that societal stigmatization of and discrimination against sexual-orientation minority groups contribute to higher psychiatric morbidity rates in these populations.[47,48] However, lesbians who disclose their sexual orientation have less anxiety and higher self-esteem, and are more likely to have social support, thereby diminishing the likelihood of psychiatric disorders.[49]

Regardless of whether there were equal or higher rates of depression among lesbians compared with heterosexual women, lesbians in all of these studies utilized psychotherapy and other mental health services at a higher rate than their heterosexual counterparts did.[25,45,46]

Screening all women for depression is appropriate. It may be particularly fruitful when women do not present as lesbian or bisexual—that is, they have not disclosed their sexual orientation—and may be experiencing more stress and isolation than those who have disclosed their orientation. Sensitive inquiries about sexual orientation and behaviors may be a woman's entrée to coming out to her physician, followed by appropriate support and perhaps subsequent disclosure to others.

■   ■   ■

Jane may benefit from counseling about her lesbian identity. Coping and stress-reduction skills might reduce her headaches and make it easier for her to quit smoking.

DOMESTIC VIOLENCE

Intimate partner violence affects women in all socioeconomic and ethnic groups, and women in same- and opposite-gender relationships. Estimates of the prevalence of domestic violence in lesbian relationships vary, but research suggests that the rates do not differ significantly from those in the general population; it occurs in about 25% of lesbian and heterosexual couples.[50] As with heterosexual couples, domestic violence is associated with drug and alcohol abuse and with prior exposure to violence.[51]

Domestic violence is underdiagnosed because patients often conceal that they are in abusive relationships and the signs and symptoms of abuse may be subtle. Abuse in lesbian relationships may be especially underreported due to internalized homophobia and social isolation of the victim, leading to reluctance to report domestic violence. Officials in law enforcement and the judicial system may falsely assume that abuse in lesbian couples is a fair fight between equals and not respond appropriately. All women should be screened for domestic violence, but questioning of trauma victims, emergency room patients, women with chronic abdominal pain or chronic headaches, pregnant women, women with sexually transmitted infections, and injured elders is particularly warranted.

IMMUNIZATIONS

Routine immunizations have reduced many infectious diseases in the United States. Lesbians should be immunized according to the recommendations for all women (Table 1.3).

TABLE 1.3. BASIC IMMUNIZATION SCHEDULE FOR WOMEN

VACCINE FOR	AGES 12–49	AGES 50–64	AGES 65+
Influenza	Discuss with health care provider (HCP)	Every year	
Tetanus, diphtheria, pertussis (Tdap/Td)	Every 10 years. Substitute one dose of Tdap for Td in ages 19–64.	Every 10 years (Tdap)	Every 10 years (Td)
Human papillomavirus	Three doses at 0, 2, and 6 months in ages 12–26 years	—	—
Meningococcal infection	For ages 19–49, discuss with HCP if attending college or living in close quarters (one or more doses)	Talk with HCP	
Herpes zoster (shingles)	—	—	Starting at age 60 (one dose only)
Varicella (chicken pox)	If no immunity, two doses at 0 and 4–8 weeks	Talk with HCP	
Pneumococcal infection	Talk with HCP		One time only, but talk to HCP about need for revaccination
Measles, mumps, rubella	Talk with HCP (one or two doses)	Talk with HCP (one dose)	
Hepatitis A	Talk with HCP (two doses)		
Hepatitis B	Talk with HCP (three doses)		

Source: Advisory Committee on Immunization Practices, Centers for Disease Control and Prevention. Recommended adult immunization schedule—United States, October 2007–September 2008. *Morbidity and Mortality Weekly Report, 56,* Q-2.

CONCLUSION

A patient's sexual orientation and sexual behaviors are intertwined with her general health. Lesbians often access the health care system later than heterosexual women do for screening and preventive care, and therefore have health conditions that place them at higher risk. Obstacles to entering the health care system should be modified and preventive health care instituted whenever possible, with special attention paid to health conditions that may increase lesbians' risk of morbidity.

REFERENCES

1. Fries, J. F., Koop, C. E., Sokolov, J., Beadle, C. E., & Wright, D. (1998). Beyond health promotion: Reducing need and demand for medical care. *Health Affairs, 17,* 70–84.

2. Office on Women's Health, U.S. Department of Health & Human Services. (2009). *Screening tests and immunizations guidelines for women.* Available at www.womenshealth.gov/screeningcharts/general.

3. Mravcak, S. A. (2006). Primary care for lesbians and bisexual women. *American Family Physician, 74,* 279–286.

4. Diamant, A. L., Schuster, M. A., McGuigan, K., & Lever, J. (1999). Lesbians' sexual history with men: Implications for taking a sexual history. *Archives of Internal Medicine, 159,* 2730–2736.

5. Kerker, B. D., Mostashari, F., & Thorpe, L. (2006). Health care access and utilization among women who have sex with women: Sexual behavior and identity. *Journal of Urban Health, 83,* 970–979.

6. Koh, A. S. (2000). Use of preventive health behaviors by lesbian, bisexual, and heterosexual women: Questionnaire survey. *Western Journal of Medicine, 172,* 379–384.

7. Van Dam, M. A., Koh, A. S., & Dibble, S. L. (2001). Lesbian disclosure to health care providers and delay of care. *Journal of the Gay and Lesbian Medical Association, 5,* 11–19.

8. Hedley, A. A., Ogden, C. L., Johnson, C. L., Carroll, M. D., Curtin, L. R., & Flegal, K. M. (2004). Prevalence of overweight and obesity among U.S. children, adolescents, and adults, 1999–2002. *Journal of the American Medical Association, 291,* 2847–2850.

9. Renehan, A. G., Tyson, M., Egger, M., Heller, R. F., & Zwahlen, M. (2008). Body-mass index and incidence of cancer: A systematic review and meta-analysis of prospective observational studies. *Lancet, 371,* 569–578.

10. Peeters, A., Barendregt, J. J., Willekens, F., Mackenbach, J. P., Al Mamun, A., Bonneux, L., et al. (2003). Obesity in adulthood and its consequences for life expectancy: A life table analysis. *Annals of Internal Medicine, 138,* 24–32.

11. Mosca, L., Jones, W. K., King, K. B., Ouyang, P., Redberg, R. F., & Hill, M. N. (2000). Awareness, perception, and knowledge of heart disease risk and prevention among women in the United States. American Heart Association Women's Heart Disease and Stroke Campaign Task Force. *Archives of Family Medicine, 9,* 506–515.

12. Boehmer, U., Bowen, D. L., & Bauer, G. R. (2007). Overweight and obesity in sexual-minority women: Evidence from population-based data. *American Journal of Public Health, 97,* 1134–1140.

13. Case, P., Austin, S. B., Hunter, D. J., Manson, J. E., Malspeis, S., Willett, W. C., et al. (2004). Sexual orientation, health risk factors, and physical functioning in the Nurses' Health Study II. *Journal of Women's Health, 13,* 1033–1047.

14. Valanis, B. G., Bowen, D. J., Bassford, T., Whitlock, E., Charney, P., & Carter, R. A. (2000). Sexual orientation and health: Comparisons in the Women's Health Initiative sample. *Archives of Family Medicine, 9,* 843–853.

15. Roberts, S. A., Dibble, S. L., Nussey, B., & Casey, K. (2003). Cardiovascular disease risk in lesbian women. *Women's Health Issues, 13,* 167–174.

16. Yancey, A. K., Cochran, S. D., Corliss H. L., Mays, V. M. (2003). Correlates of overweight and obesity among lesbian and bisexual women. *Preventive Medicine, 36,* 676–683.

17. Siever, M. D. (1994). Sexual orientation and gender as factors in socioculturally acquired vulnerability to body dissatisfaction and eating disorders. *Journal of Consulting and Clinical Psychology, 62,* 252–260.

18. Christakis, N. A, & Fowler, J. H. (2007). The spread of obesity in a large social network over 32 years. *New England Journal of Medicine, 357,* 370–379.

19. Ries, L. A. G., Harkins, D., Krapcho, M., Mariotto, A., Miller, B. A., Feuer, E. J., et al. (Eds.). (2006). *SEER cancer statistics review, 1975–2003.* Bethesda, MD: National Cancer Institute. Available at seer.cancer.gov/csr/1975_2003.

20. Feig, S. A. (2002). Effect of service screening mammography on population mortality from breast carcinoma. *Cancer, 95,* 451–457.

21. Mandelblatt, J., Saha, S., Teutsch, S., Hoerger, T., Sui, A. L., Atkins, D., et al. (2003). The cost-effectiveness of screening mammography beyond age 65 years: A systematic review for the U.S. Preventive Services Task Force. *Annals of Internal Medicine, 139,* 835–842.

22. Bobo, J. K., Lee, N. C., & Thames, S. F. (2000). Findings from 752,081 clinical breast examinations reported to a national screening program from 1995 through 1998. *Journal of the National Cancer Institute, 92,* 971–976.

23. Humphrey, L. L., Helfand, M., Chan, B. K., & Woolf, S. H. (2002) Breast cancer screening: A summary of the evidence for the U.S. Preventive Services Task Force. *Annals of Internal Medicine, 137,* 347–360.

24. Drabble, L., Midanik, L. T., & Trocki, K. (2005). Reports of alcohol consumption and alcohol-related problems among homosexual, bisexual and heterosexual respondents: Results from the 2000 National Alcohol Survey. *Journal of Studies on Alcohol, 66,* 111–120.

25. Rothblum, E. D., & Factor, R. (2001). Lesbians and their sisters as a control group: Demographic and mental health factors. *Psychological Science, 12,* 63–69.

26. Valanis B. G., Bowen, D. J., Bassford, T., Whitlock, E., Charney, P., & Carter R. A. (2000). Sexual orientation and health: Comparisons in the Women's Health Initiative sample. *Archives of Family Medicine, 9,* 843–853.

27. ACOG Committee on Practice Bulletins – Gynecologic (2009). ACOG Practice Bulletin No. 109: Cervical cytology screening. *Obstetrics & Gynecology, 114,* 1409–1420.

28. Koh, A. S., Gomez, C. A., Shade, S., & Rowley, E. (2005). Sexual risk factors among self-identified lesbians, bisexual women, and heterosexual women accessing primary care settings. *Sexually Transmitted Diseases, 32,* 563–569.

29. Marrazzo, J. M., Koutsky, L. A., Kiviat, H. B., Kuypers, J. M., & Stine, K. (2001). Papanicolaou test screening and prevalence of genital human papillomavirus among women who have sex with women. *American Journal of Public Health, 91,* 947–952.

30. Marrazzo, J. M., Koutsky, L. A., & Handsfield, H. H. (2001). Characteristics of female sexually transmitted disease clinic clients who report same-sex behaviour. *International Journal of STD & AIDS, 12,* 41–46.

31. Eisenberg, M. (2001). Differences in sexual risk behaviors between college students with same-sex and opposite-sex experience: Results from a national survey. *Archives of Sexual Behavior, 30,* 575–589.

32. O'Hanlan, K. A., & Crum, C. P. (1996). Human papillomavirus-associated cervical intraepithelial neoplasia following lesbian sex. *Obstetrics & Gynecology, 88,* 702–703.

33. Mitchell, M. F., Tortolero-Luna, G., Wright, T., Sarkar, A., Richards-Kortum, R., Hong, W. K., et al. (1996). Cervical human papillomavirus infection and intracervical neoplasia: A review. *Journal of the National Cancer Institute. Monographs, 21,* 17–25.

34. Matthews, A. K., Brandenburg, D. L., Johnson, T. P., & Hughes, T. L. (2004). Correlates of underutilization of gynecological cancer screening among lesbian and heterosexual women. *Preventive Medicine, 38,* 105–113.

35. National Institutes of Health. (1996). National Institutes of Health Consensus Development Conference statement on cervical cancer. *Gynecologic Oncology, 66,* 351–361. Available at consensus.nih.gov/1996/1996CervicalCancer102html.htm.

36. Viswanathan, A. N., Feskanich, D., De Vivo, I., Hunter, D. J., Barbieri, R. L., Rosner, B., et al. (2005). Smoking and the risk of endometrial cancer: Results from the Nurses' Health Study. *International Journal of Cancer, 114,* 996–1001.

37. Dibble, S. L., Roberts, S. A., Robertson, P. A., & Paul S. M. (2002). Risk factors for ovarian cancer: Lesbian and heterosexual women. *Oncology Nursing Forum, 29,* E1–7.

38. Tang, H., Greenwood, G. L., Cowling, D. W., Lloyd, J. C., Roeseler, A. G., & Bal, D. G. (2004). Cigarette smoking among lesbians, gays, and bisexuals: How serious a problem? (United States). *Cancer Causes & Control, 15,* 797–803.

39. Gruskin, E. R., Greenwood, G. L., Matevia, M., Pollack, L. M., & Bye, L. L. (2007). Disparities in smoking between the lesbian, gay, and bisexual population and the general population in California. *American Journal of Public Health, 97,* 1496–1504.

40. Peto, R., Darby, S., Deo, H., Silcocks, P., Whitley, E., & Doll, R. (2000). Smoking, smoking cessation, and lung cancer in the UK since 1950: Combination of national statistics with two case-control studies. *BMJ, 321,* 323–329.

41. Aaron, D. J., Markovic, N., Danielson, M. E., Honnold, J. A., Janosky, J. E., & Schmidt, N. J. (2001). Behavioral risk factors for disease and preventive health practices among lesbians. *American Journal of Public Health, 91,* 972–975.

42. Hughes, T. L., & Wilsnack, S. C. (1997). Use of alcohol among lesbians: Research and clinical implications. *American Journal of Orthopsychiatry, 67,* 20–36.

43. Sheridan, S., Pignone, M., & Mulrow, C. (2003). Framingham-based tools to calculate the global risk of coronary heart disease: A systematic review of tools for clinicians. *Journal of General Internal Medicine, 18,* 1039–1052.

44. Garofalo, R., Wolf, C., Wisso, L. S., Woods, W. R., & Goodman, E. (1999). Sexual orientation and risk of suicide attempts among a representative sample of youth. *Archives of Pediatrics & Adolescent Medicine, 153,* 487–493.

45. Koh, A. S., & Ross, L. K. (2006). Mental health issues: A comparison of lesbian, bisexual and heterosexual women. *Journal of Homosexuality, 51,* 33–57.

46. Cochran, S. D., & Mays, V. M. (1999, August). Are lesbians more at risk for psychiatric disorders? Evidence from the 1996 National Household Survey of Drug Abuse. *Proceedings of the National Conference on Health Statistics.* Washington, DC.

47. Krieger, N., & Sidney, S. (1997). Prevalence and health implications of anti-gay discrimination: A study of black and white women and men in the CARDIA cohort. Coronary Artery Risk Development in Young Adults. *International Journal of Health Services, 27,* 157–176.

48. Committee on Lesbian Health Research Priorities, Institute of Medicine. (1999). *Lesbian health: Current assessment and directions for the future.* Washington, DC: National Academy Press. Available at www.nap.edu/openbook.php?record_id=6109&page=17.

49. Oetjen, H., & Rothblum, E. D. (2000). When lesbians aren't gay: Factors affecting depression among lesbians. *Journal of Homosexuality, 39,* 49–73.

50. Burke, L. K., & Follingstad, D. R. (1999). Violence in lesbian and gay relationships: Theory, prevalence, and correlational factors. *Clinical Psychology Review, 19,* 487–512.

51. Schilit, R., Lie, G. Y., & Montague, M. (1990). Substance use as a correlate of violence in intimate lesbian relationships. *Journal of Homosexuality, 19,* 51–65.

ABOUT THE AUTHOR

AUDREY S. KOH, MD is an obstetrician/gynecologist in private practice and Assistant Clinical Professor at the University of California, San Francisco, School of Medicine. She conducts lesbian health research and writes on women's health issues, with a focus on gynecology as well as preventive health. Dr. Koh volunteers for a variety of LGBT civil rights organizations.

CHAPTER 2

"Just Ask Me."
CLINICAL CARE FOR LESBIAN ADOLESCENTS

ELIZABETH LORDE-ROLLINS, MD, MSc

STEPHANIE, 14, *also known as Stevie, was helping her cousin reroof her aunt's home when she fell off the roof. But she got up immediately, saying she was OK except for her arm. The cousin called Stevie's mother and they all met in the local urgent care center. After the mother saw that Stevie was alright, she became angry and asked, "Why do you have to be such a tomboy?" Just then, a nurse led Stevie into an exam room. The nurse wanted Stevie, who was dressed in her cousin's flannel shirt, to change into a hospital gown, which Stevie obviously did not want to do. Why she resisted was unclear.*

Clinical care for youths who are lesbian, gay, bisexual, or transgender (LGBT) has much in common with care for heterosexual adolescents. Indeed, research shows that sexual minority youths value many of the same qualities of care that telegraph competence to all patients, regardless of their age or sexual orientation: a clean environment, a well-educated and informative clinician, and respectful exchanges with the clinician and office staff.[1] However, it takes more than a tidy waiting room and an attentive provider to make lesbian and women who have sex with women (WSW) adolescent patients feel at home. When surveyed, sexual minority youth say they often do not feel safe enough to disclose their sexual attractions or behaviors unless the clinician first broaches the subject.[1,2] Therefore, clinicians who care for LGBT adolescents must reinforce the office's confidentiality policy, train staff to avoid heterosexist behavior, and, in all spoken and written communications, use language that is not heterosexist or judgmental and that does not convey any assumptions. These steps may be even more crucial regarding two groups: adolescents who are attracted to the same sex and/or behave like others of the same gender but who do not self-identify as sexual minorities, and youths who identify with a particular sexual minority but have not disclosed their orientation to family members, friends, or health care professionals.

BACKGROUND

Although research on sexual orientation and sexual minority health has increased significantly in the last 20 years, many knowledge gaps remain. There have been very few longitudinal studies of adult lesbians and WSW, which could shed more light on adolescent sexual minorities. Despite racially based health care disparities, there have been even fewer studies of African American, Latina, and Asian sexual minorities. Furthermore, most early studies subsumed lesbian participants under the heading "LGB" (lesbian, gay, or bisexual).[3] While a sexual minority designation encompassing many different identities may be useful politically, investigations of these separate categories demonstrate that gay, lesbian, and bisexual adolescents are not a monolithic group. Characteristics such as culture, race, class, and age may be stronger gauges than sexual orientation of lesbian youths' health risks and strengths. Health disparities among sexual minority youths are well-documented.[4]

In addition, research on sexual minorities lacks standard definitions of the people it targets. Nonheterosexual youth seem to increasingly resist labels that researchers once used; instead, they prefer identities such as "unlabeled," "queer," "boi," and "bisexual" that more accurately describe their attractions and relationships, and a philosophy that embraces noncategorical, nongender-based models of sexuality.[5,6]

Complicating matters, several studies have demonstrated that sexuality in the general population, particularly among women, may be much more fluid than previously thought. For example, a young woman who identifies as bisexual at age 16 may identify as lesbian or unlabeled 10 years later, or vice versa.[5]

Development of Sexuality

In the last two decades, researchers have also gained a much better understanding of female sexual development. Gender variance typically develops before the preschool period.[7] In a recent study of 25 girls diagnosed with gender identity disorder in childhood, 72% identified as heterosexual, 16% as lesbian, 8% as bisexual, and 4% as asexual on follow-up (14 years later, on average). None identified as transgender. Three of the adolescents (12%) were gender dysphoric—they reported distress with their gender identities. Of these three, one self-identified as asexual and reported neither sexual fantasies nor behavior, one identified as bisexual and reported fantasies involving both sexes and current sexual activity with a female partner, and one identified as heterosexual but reported sexual fantasies and current sexual behavior involving women only.[8]

How woman-loving identities—lesbian, bisexual, queer, or unlabeled—develop in women is far from clear. Diamond's longitudinal study of sexual minority women offers some insight. Participants, who initially included 38 lesbians, 27 bisexual women, and 24 unlabeled women between 16 and 23 years old, were assessed five times over a 10-year period regarding their sexual identities, attractions, and behaviors.[9] Among the 79 who were still participating on follow-up, 83% of those who first identified as unlabeled and 73% of those who first identified as bisexual changed their identities, compared with 48% of the women who first identified as lesbian, although there was fluidity in all three groups. After 10 years, 67% of participants had changed their sexual identities at least once since the study began and 36% had changed their identities more than once. There were no group differences in recollected age of first same-sex attraction, which averaged just under 15 years old, and on the last assessment, even participants whose identities changed still reported same-sex attraction.[5] The fluidity of sexual identities is such that "lesbian youth" may be a misnomer. Table 2.1 defines some common, sexuality-related terms.

CREATING SAFE SPACE FOR LESBIAN AND WSW ADOLESCENT PATIENTS

Whether they know it or not, clinicians with young female patients are providing care to lesbians and WSW. The prevalence of particular sexual orientation groups, especially among young people, varies widely depending on how researchers define

TABLE 2.1. SEXUALITY-RELATED DEFINITIONS

TERM	DEFINITION
Sexual minority	Lesbian, gay, bisexual, transgender, questioning
Gender variance	A behavioral pattern of intense, pervasive, and persistent interests and behaviors characterized as typical of the other gender[5]
Lesbian	A female who identifies her primary sexual and loving attachments as being predominantly female, whether or not she has had any sexual contact or only opposite-sex contact
Gay male	A male who identifies his primary sexual and loving attachments as being predominantly male, whether or not he has had any sexual contact or only opposite-sex contact
Bisexual	A male or female who identifies his or her primary sexual and loving attachments as being with both sexes, regardless of sexual contact history
Transgendered male	An individual, born female, whose identity is male and who may or may not undergo medical treatment and/or procedures to transition his body so it aligns with that identity
Transgendered female	An individual, born male, whose identity is female and who may or may not undergo medical treatment and/or procedures to transition her body so it aligns with that identity
Women who have sex with women (WSW)	A female who has sexual contact with other females, whether or not she identifies as lesbian or has sexual contact with males
Men who have sex with men (MSM)	A male who has sexual contact with other males, whether or not he identifies as gay or has sexual contact with females
Butch	Masculine in appearance and manner
Femme	Feminine in appearance and manner

them. For example, if the definition of "lesbian youth" is young women who experience same-sex attraction, prevalence ranges from 14% to 21%.[10] But if the definition is same-sex contact, it ranges from 2% to 7%.[10,11] Even fewer adolescent females would define themselves as lesbian. In querying more than 36,000 public high school students, the 1987 Minnesota Adolescent Health Survey found that 1% of females identified themselves as bisexual or lesbian and 9.6% said they were unsure.[11] Because the survey lacked detailed questions about past sexual behavior, a quantitative analysis comparing the number of students who defined themselves as lesbian with the number who had experienced female-to-female romantic involvement and/or sexual contact was not possible. Clinicians who assume that patients are heterosexual until proven otherwise may come to erroneous conclusions and make insensitive remarks. Such heterocentrism can also lead to suboptimal health care.[12]

The following sections describe ways to create a safe clinical space so patients will feel more comfortable about disclosing their sexual attractions and behaviors.

Office Environment

Clinicians who do not have much control over the surroundings in which they deliver care can rest assured that simply engaging patients in a conversation about sexual attraction and behavior, without assuming heterosexuality, will likely lead to disclosure.[2] Reminding patients that what they say will remain confidential unless their or others' lives are in danger increases the likelihood of disclosure even further.[2,13] In a survey of 131 lesbian, gay, and bisexual adolescents, only 35% reported that their physician knew their sexual orientation, and only 21% of those whose physician knew reported that the physician had raised this topic. In addition, 66% of respondents thought that physician knowledge of their sexual orientation was an important prerequisite to providing the best health care possible. When asked what a physician could do to make disclosure more comfortable for them, 64% chose the response option "Just ask me."[2]

Sexual minority youths generally appreciate symbolic efforts by clinicians to enhance their comfort, but they do not consider such efforts as important as confidentiality and professionalism. Some have expressed concern that rainbow stickers and LGBT-oriented magazines might lead to greater stigma for patients in a clinician's office.[1] The author recommends posters and art that reflect all types of diversity—not just differences in sexual orientation, but also differences in culture, race, religion, and ability status—and displaying such items everywhere, including in reception, waiting, exam, and consultation rooms. Closeted youths will not likely look at LGBT-oriented education materials in a public place. Given an opportunity, patients are more likely to read them in the restroom or an exam room. All available literature should be screened for heterosexist content, and the language on office forms should never assume that patients are heterosexual. Ideally, bathrooms are private and unisex.[12]

Culture

Visual environmental messages fall flat if a facility is heterosexist. All health care professionals and administrative staff must routinely use nonheterocentric language and have a nonjudgmental attitude. As one focus group participant said, "Make it clear that [you] are not going to tolerate stereotypes, stigmas, derogatory comments.... Be an advocate and demand tolerance and respect for all diversities."[14] (p. 254). At least annually, all employees should participate in cultural competence training that includes sexual diversity issues.

It may be necessary to actively discourage heterosexist remarks or behaviors by heterosexual patients toward sexual minority patients. At Mount Sinai Adolescent Health Center in New York, patients, who span the entire spectrum of sexual identity, generally respect each other even though they often share very close quarters in the waiting areas. However, occasionally an adolescent—typically the male partner of a female patient—is disrespectful to a sexual minority patient. Trained staff must be on the look-out for these interactions because the victim rarely complains. If disrespect occurs, the first staff member who notices it quietly asks the offending party to step into a private room for an explanation of why such behavior is unacceptable and a quick review of the health center's policy. Then, the staff member invites the individual to wait in the registration area, away from patients. About equal numbers of teens accept the invitation or return to the waiting area. The author has yet to see an adolescent who did not respond to this respectful yet firm intervention.

Confidentiality

Confidentiality is the cornerstone of all adolescent care. According to feedback from youths in focus groups, patients should be reminded on each visit that no one will share their personal information except in life-threatening circumstances, and the office should prominently post its confidentiality policy.[2,15]

Inclusive Language

Sexual minority youths "tire of the assumption that they are heterosexual and report in focus groups that it is an assumption they often do not correct"[1] (p. 414). Clinicians or staff who offend a patient by using noninclusive language miss an opportunity to counsel her effectively and may not get a chance to correct this error. According to sexual minority adolescents in focus groups, language affects their satisfaction, willingness to disclose, and desire to return for follow-up.[1,2,7,13,14] Consistent use of nondiscriminatory language supports LGBT patients, educates heterosexual patients, and signals respect for sexual minorities. It also makes family and friends feel less isolated. In some communities, a doctor's office may be the only place that adheres to these practices.

Respect and Referral

In addition to being nonjudgmental, clinicians must refrain from commenting on patients' concerns, opinions, or activities. If a clinician feels uncomfortable discussing something, it is acceptable to admit inexperience and tell the patient that the topic nevertheless deserves full consideration by a more experienced professional colleague. The clinician should later explore his or her discomfort privately, as this may indicate a need for personal growth.[16] When an uncomfortable subject arises during a patient encounter, it is never appropriate to leave the patient abruptly or not provide an explanation. And clinicians should always explain the reason for a referral. Asking a patient if she has a referral preference might elicit a surprising response. For example, a lesbian teen may in fact prefer to see a heterosexual rather than lesbian clinician.

MEDICAL AND SOCIAL HISTORY

Comprehensive exploration of any teen's social history is time-consuming. However, in-depth coverage of all these topics at the initial visit is usually unnecessary and, in some cases, may be counterproductive. The most important task on the first visit is to communicate to the patient concern, respect, and an openness and understanding of lesbian and WSW health issues. Broaching sensitive issues tells the adolescent she has permission to discuss them. An endless battery of questions, no matter how well-phrased, does not give the patient time to talk. As Savin-Williams wrote:

> Pediatricians should avoid assuming that homosexuality is foremost about sex, that only one "gay lifestyle" exists, that same-sex relationships are not romantic, that bisexuality is a transitional state that will resolve in an eventual heterosexual identity, and that homosexuality is a psychological defense. Following these preliminary assessments and precautions, *physicians can create opportunities for non-heterosexual youth to share concerns and request advice by conducting a more detailed history* [italics added]. This history should incorporate the timing and subjective experience of sexual developmental milestones, social support, parental reactions, family discord, harassment/violence, psychosocial stressors, mental health concerns, and coping strategies such as alcohol and drug use, social withdrawal, and eating disorders. In many cases, these factors contribute more to negative health outcomes than does sexual orientation per se[7] (p. 369).

Clinicians need to address many issues during a patient visit: risk reduction, treatment of any pathology, screening, and the like. However, if an adolescent's presenting complaint is not addressed by the end of the clinical encounter, she will leave dissatisfied and be less likely to return. Addressing her chief concern, even if it cannot be resolved initially, will go a long way toward building trust and respect. This also sends the message that her concerns deserve the clinician's utmost attention.

In a pioneering focus group study by Ginsburg and colleagues that involved 94 sexual minority youths, participants rated concerns not directly related to sexual minority status as their highest priorities. Indeed, reducing an office visit to generalizations about the patient's sexual orientation was very off-putting for teens. Most youths said they had the same basic needs as all young people and that attending to those needs was a prerequisite for meeting any special needs.[1]

Medical History

For young lesbian patients, as for all adolescents, a complete medical history includes a review of systems plus surgical, gynecologic, and family-illness histories. The systems review aids the physical exam and guides referrals or future investigation, as most adolescents do not volunteer information about symptoms unless the clinician specifically asks. For instance, the question "How are your periods?" may elicit "Fine, I guess," when in fact the patient has significant dysmenorrhea, takes ibuprofen by the handful on an empty stomach, and typically skips school on the first day of menses. She considers her symptoms normal or has heard that they are "part of being a woman" and not worth mentioning.

For all female adolescents, the transition to an adult woman's body is some-times scary and usually emotionally charged. Sexual minority female adolescents—especially those who are more comfortable with a traditionally male appearance and those who are considering transitioning to male gender—may feel some loss about their progression away from the more unisex look of early adolescence. Any symptoms that remind them of this progression may be distressing. Therefore, along with routine questions about menses, dysmenorrhea symptoms, cyclical migraine, or cyclical gastrointestinal symptoms, clinicians should ask patients if they are experiencing bodily changes positively, negatively, or both, and seek elaboration. This is also a good time to inquire about eating habits. Like eating disorders, not eating breakfast, eating too few or no vegetables, and maintaining a diet that lacks sufficient calcium and vitamin D may have profound health consequences.

Because sexually active lesbian and WSW adolescents are just as prone to urinary tract infection as their heterosexual counterparts, clinicians should not overlook genitourinary aspects of the systems review. They can counsel the sexually active patient who has recurrent urinary tract infections to rinse after sexual activity by letting body-temperature water and a mild soap run from the anterior commissure to the posterior fourchette and over the perineum as she sits on the commode. Drinking a moderate quantity of water after sex, thereby flushing the urethra with outflowing urine, may prevent colonizing Gram-negative bacteria from ascending to the bladder. Many patients, concerned about nocturia, prefer not to do this before bedtime.

Health problems can interfere with or complicate some of the developmental tasks that adolescents face. These tasks include:

- Separating from family and making decisions;
- Learning to negotiate social relationships, which sets the stage for future friendships, partnerships, and professional relationships;
- Preparing for self-support and the world of adult work; and
- Developing personal values.[15]

Physical illness may interfere with preparing for self-support and the world of adult work, while mental illness can complicate learning how to negotiate social relationships and developing personal values. Illnesses that adolescents consider trivial, such as asthma and visual impairment, may in fact have a significant impact on school or work attendance and performance. (See box below.) Clinicians can obtain this important information by inquiring about health issues that are common among their patients. If a patient says such issues have not been a concern for her, further probing—by asking questions such as "Have you ever seen a doctor for anything other than a check-up or shots?" and then "Have you ever had to visit an emergency room?"—may elicit relevant details.

AN ENCOUNTER WORTH NOTING

An adolescent may dismiss a medical condition as an isolated occurrence in the distant past, when in fact it is currently relevant. The following exchange between the author and a patient illustrates this attitude:

Clinician: "Have you ever had an asthma attack?"

Patient: "That was a long time ago. I think I grew out of it."

Clinician: "When was the last time you had to visit the ER for asthma?"

Patient: "Last winter—almost a year ago."

Clinician: "And when was the last time you felt tight enough to use a pump?"

Patient: "Well, I felt a little tight a couple of weeks ago, but it wasn't all that serious, and I didn't have to use my inhaler."

Clinician: "Do you *have* an inhaler?"

Patient: "I haven't had one for awhile. I lost it and I didn't ask my mother to get another one because I don't really need it."

Social History

■ SEXUAL ATTRACTION AND BEHAVIOR

Clinicians signal their comfort with discussing same-sex attraction and behavior by using straightforward language that is inclusive and sensitive[15] (Table 2.2). Depending on whether the adolescent is in early, mid, or late development, it may help if questions refer to "girls" and "boys" or "women" and "men" rather than "partners" or "significant others," which might be too vague for young patients. Table 2.3 highlights differences between adolescents in the three developmental stages.

The clinician's most important task on the initial visit is to create a safe space in which a teen can explore developmental issues,[17] especially if she is distressed by her attraction to other females. She should be given enough time to respond uninterrupted to open-ended, nonjudgmental questions. Although clinicians are under pressure to keep discussions with patients brief, research indicates that giving patients free rein to air their concerns is a more efficient use of interview time.[18-21] Patients who are comfortable with their sexuality may need little more from clinicians than a physical exam and information about safe-sex practices, about reducing the risk of sexually transmitted infections, and about other health threats the interview and exam have revealed.

■ CONTRACEPTION

Assuming that a lesbian adolescent is not at risk for unintended pregnancy is a mistake that may have significant consequences for her. Large cross-sectional surveys clearly demonstrated that lesbian adolescents have penile-vaginal intercourse and that, compared with their heterosexual counterparts, intercourse is more likely to be unprotected.

Saewyc and colleagues surveyed more than 3,800 female high school students between 12 and 19 years old: 182 lesbian or bisexual females, 1,881 heterosexuals matched in terms of age and race, and 1,753 who were unsure of their sexuality. Thirty-three percent of the lesbians and bisexual females reported having had heterosexual sex compared with 29.3% of the heterosexuals and 21.6% of those in the unsure group. Among those who reported such experience, the unsure respondents were most likely not to have used contraception (43.5% vs. 29.8% of lesbian/bisexual respondents and 23.1% of heterosexual respondents). The frequency of heterosexual intercourse was greatest among lesbian/bisexual youths: 22% reported sex with a male two or more times per week compared with 14.8% of heterosexual teens and 17% in the unsure group. The riskiest activity mentioned in the survey was sex work: 9.7% of the lesbian/bisexual respondents, 3.4% of those in the unsure group, and 1.9% of the heterosexual respondents had engaged in this activity, likely reflecting the higher risk of survival sex among sexual minority adolescents. Although heterosexual teens were more likely to have undergone a pregnancy termination (38.2% vs. 29.4% of lesbian/bisexual youths and 31.2% in the unsure group), the lesbian/bisexual students had more repeat pregnancies, indicating more unprotected intercourse. Of the 172 ever-pregnant respondents, 23.5% of those in the lesbian/bisexual group reported two or more pregnancies compared with 9.8% of heterosexuals and 15.1% in the unsure group.[11] Smaller studies of high school students have obtained similar findings.[22]

Lesbian and WSW adolescents who answer affirmatively to inquiries about their need for contraception must receive extensive counseling regarding the options. They are just as likely as their heterosexual sisters to need contraceptive methods that others will not discover. For example, a parent who goes through her daughter's things might discover pills, patches, or rings; however, if the adolescent visits a clinic every 3 months for a contraceptive injection, her contraceptive use is more likely to remain confidential. Long-acting, reversible methods, such as subcutaneous delivery systems and intrauterine devices, are safe and very effective in teens, many of whom prefer these methods because they are less noticeable to parents and partners.[23] As always, the choice of a contraceptive is up to the patient after she receives counseling about the advantages, disadvantages, and side effects of each type. Teens often find it helpful if clinicians classify side effects as "probable" or "possible," thereby setting reasonable expectations. In addition, it may reassure patients to hear that a variety of methods are available and that switching to another contraceptive is an option if their first choice does not work out. The author recommends that 4 weeks after the initial prescription, all adolescents return for an assessment of the method's practicality and acceptability.

Giving lesbian and WSW adolescents advance information about, and a prescription for, the emergency contraceptive pill is prudent in light of available data on the sexual practices of young sexual minority women. Patients need to know that although they can take the pill up to 5 days after unprotected intercourse, it loses about 10% of its effectiveness each day. The pill can prevent 85% to 95% of potential pregnancies if taken within 24 hours—an effectiveness rate that falls to about 60% after 4 or 5 days.[24]

■ SAFER SEX

Counseling patients about the risk of sexually transmitted infection (STI) is now part of standard care regardless of age, marital status, or sexual orientation. About half of

---

WHAT TO SAY ABOUT EMERGENCY CONTRACEPTION

When clinicians recommend emergency contraceptive pills, they can avoid the perception that they are recommending heterosexual sex by initially telling the patient:

"Even girls who have sexual contact only with other girls may occasionally find that they have male sexual contact. Studies show that if this contact includes intercourse, it's more likely to be unplanned than when girls who usually have sexual contact with boys have intercourse. I'm not recommending sex without a condom, but if you have unplanned intercourse, I want you to know about emergency contraception and have it available."

TABLE 2.2. INCLUSIVE/SENSITIVE LANGUAGE

TOPIC	WHAT TO SAY
Confidentiality	▪ "I ask all my patients about personal subjects, and I want to let you know up front that I won't discuss this information with anyone unless your or someone else's life is in danger."
Body image	▪ "How do you view yourself?" ▪ "Do you consider yourself attractive?" ▪ "Do you feel that any part of your body needs improvement?" ▪ "Do you have any desire to modify or change any part of your body?"
Sexual attraction	▪ "Who do you find yourself attracted to? People who are tall, short, muscular, or skinny; who are of the same/different race or have the same/different religion; who are male or female?" ▪ "Are your sexual attractions a source of anxiety or distress?"
Sexual behavior	▪ "Have you become sexually active with a partner yet?" ▪ "Have you ever been sexually active with a boy, girl, or both?"
Sexual orientation	▪ "Do you see yourself as primarily having sexual interest in boys, girls, or both?" ▪ "I always ask my patients if they have any concerns about sexual orientation—that is, being gay, lesbian, or bisexual. Has that been a concern for you at all?"
Harassment	▪ "Is anyone making your life miserable right now?" ▪ "Do you ever avoid certain (situations, streets, parts of your school) because you think you might run into something unpleasant there?"
Partner violence	▪ "Have you ever felt afraid of your partner?" ▪ "Have you ever been slapped, punched, kicked, or hit by a partner?"
Risky sexual behavior	▪ "Have you ever had sex with someone who had a sexually transmitted infection before?" ▪ "What do you usually use for protection when you [give/receive oral sex, give anilingus (rim your partner), put your fingers in your partner's vagina, use toys, have vaginal or anal intercourse with a male partner]?"
Negotiating skills	▪ "How do you usually ask your partners about any sexually transmitted infections they may have had?" ▪ "How do you usually discuss having had any prior sexually transmitted infection with your partner?" ▪ "What do you usually say to a partner who says she doesn't like condoms on toys/dental dams/finger cots?" ▪ "What do you usually say to a partner who says he doesn't like condoms?"
Nonconsensual sex	▪ "A lot of my patients feel pressured to have sex. Has that ever happened to you?" ▪ "Has anyone ever forced sexual contact on you, even if it wasn't penetration?"
Sex work	▪ "Do you ever have sex when you really don't want to because you feel you need to for whatever reason?" ▪ "Have you ever had to have sex with someone to survive—for money, or a place to stay when you needed those things?"

(cont.)

TABLE 2.2. INCLUSIVE/SENSITIVE LANGUAGE *(cont.)*

TOPIC	WHAT TO SAY
Depression	■ "What are some things you enjoy doing? Have you been enjoying those things lately?" ■ "Do you ever wish you wouldn't wake up?" ■ "Do you ever wish you were dead?"
Academic performance	■ "What's your favorite class this year? Why?" ■ "Do you ever have problems learning?" ■ "Is there anything that you know you're interested in doing after all of your schooling is done?" ■ "Did you ever not do as well in school as you had hoped? What do you think got in your way?"
Family involvement	■ "Have you discussed any of your concerns with your family?" ■ "Which concerns, if any, have you felt like you couldn't discuss?" ■ "Would you like any help talking to your family?" ■ "What are your family's attitudes about lesbians?" ■ "Do you have a family member who identifies as lesbian, gay, bisexual, or transgender? How is he or she treated?"
Substance abuse	■ "How often would you say you smoke cigarettes?" ■ "How often would you say you use [name the drug]?" ■ "How often would you say you took someone else's prescription medicine, even if that person gave it to you for a good reason?" ■ "Have you ever taken a prescription medicine to feel high?"
Contraception	■ "Do you ever have any need for something to help you avoid pregnancy?" ■ "There is no perfect method, but you and I will work together to figure out which one is best for you. Sometimes my patients have to try different methods before they find the one they like best."
Unintended pregnancy	■ Always refer to the "pregnancy," not the "baby" or the "fetus." ■ Warn patients who decide to terminate a pregnancy that they may feel emotional, even though this was the right decision for them, and that this is natural.
Assessment of patient's understanding	■ "Is there anything you'd like me to go over again?"

Sources:

(1) Ensign, J. (2000). Reproductive health of homeless adolescent women in Seattle, Washington, U.S.A. *Women & Health, 31,* 133–151.

(2) Nucci-Sack, A., Rojas, M., Alpert, I. L., Lorde-Rollins, E., Minguez, M., & Diaz, A. (2009). Approach to and evaluation of the female. In A. Altchek & L. Deligdisch (Eds.), *Pediatric, adolescent, & young adult gynecology* (pp. 134–140). Oxford: Blackwell.

(3) Alexander, B., & Schrauben, S. (2006). Outside the margins: Youth who are different and their special health care needs. *Primary Care, 33,* 285–303.

(4) Perrin, E. C., Cohen, K. M., Gold, M., Ryan, C., Savin-Williams, R. C., & Schorzman, C. M. (2004). Gay and lesbian issues in pediatric health care. *Current Problems in Pediatric and Adolescent Health Care, 34,* 355–398.

(5) Sison, A. C., & Greydanus, D. E. (2007). Deconstructing adolescent same-sex attraction and sexual behavior in the twenty-first century: Perspectives for the clinician. *Primary Care, 34,* 293–304.

TABLE 2.3. ADOLESCENT DIFFERENCES ACROSS DEVELOPMENTAL STAGES

DEVELOPMENTAL AREA	EARLY DEVELOPMENT ISSUES (11–13 YEARS OLD)	MID DEVELOPMENT ISSUES (14–16 YEARS OLD)	LATE DEVELOPMENT ISSUES (17–20 YEARS OLD)
Physical	Body changes: beginning of menstruation, growth of breasts and public hair, acne	Nearly completed physical development: filling in, hips widen, vaginal discharge, body odor	Physical development completed
Cognitive	Concrete	Concrete with increased capacity for abstraction	Abstraction
Body image	Concern about body changes	■ Becoming comfortable with "new body" ■ Concerns about "looking good": clothing, hair, make-up, piercings, tattoos, etc.	Usually comfortable with body image
Emotional	■ Mood swings ■ Concern about peer acceptance ■ Wants to fit in	■ Feelings contribute to behavior but do not control it ■ Sense of vulnerability	■ Greater understanding of behavioral consequences ■ Greater awareness of self relative to others
Social relationships	■ Friend-based peer groups ■ Some romantic attractions	Peer groups based on friends and romantic interest	Individual relationships more important than peer groups
Values	Begins testing the parental value system	■ Self-centered ■ Conflict with parents regarding beliefs and values	■ Self-centered idealism ■ Right and wrong thinking ■ Becomes more other-oriented
Independence	■ Begins separating from parents ■ Rejects childhood things ■ Prefers peers to family	■ Ambivalence about separating from parents ■ Challenges rules and tests limits	■ Begins integrating independence issues ■ Assumes adult roles

Source: Nucci-Sack, A., Rojas, M., Alpert, I. L., Lorde-Rollins, E., Minguez, M., & Diaz, A. (2009). Approach to and evaluation of the female. In A. Altchek & L. Deligdisch (Eds.), *Pediatric, adolescent, & young adult gynecology* (pp. 134–140). Oxford: Blackwell.

new HIV diagnoses in the United States are among people ≤ 21 years old; therefore, HIV risk counseling is necessary during every clinical encounter with adolescents. Research has revealed woman-to-woman STI transmission, including HIV, despite early reports to the contrary.

The literature is rife with anecdotes from lesbians and WSW who said a clinician told them they were at low risk of STI transmission. Studies have reported female-to-female transmission of HIV, gonorrhea, chlamydia, herpes simplex virus (HSV), human papillomavirus (HPV), and syphilis.[25-28] HSV and HPV are extremely prevalent, as their transmission requires only contact rather than body-fluid exchange. Investigations have found higher rates of bacterial vaginosis and lower concentrations of protective hydrogen-producing lactobacilli among adult lesbians and WSW.[28-30] The prevalence of bacterial vaginosis among lesbian adolescents may be especially significant. Current work on the vaginal microbiome indicates there is a higher risk of acquiring STIs in the presence of bacterial vaginosis. The vagina and cervix in adolescents are relatively immature, with a larger surface area of glandular epithelium on the ectocervix, less defensive mucous production in the endocervix, and smaller numbers of protective lactobacilli in the vaginal vault. Consequently, these tissues may be more vulnerable to viral and bacterial attack.

Unprotected anilingus may result in oropharyngeal carriage of gonorrhea and/or chlamydia. Reports probably underestimate the prevalence of such transmission, as many institutional laboratories cannot test oral cultures. Because anilingus can also transmit *Giardia lamblia*, *Entamoeba histolytica*, *Shigella*, *Salmonella*, *Campylobacter*, and hepatitis A, it always warrants barrier protection.

Lesbian and WSW adolescents deserve a frank, informative explanation of barrier protections and how to use them. Clinicians should not be reluctant to inquire about specific sexual activities; they need this knowledge to tailor meaningful discussions about risk reduction. Recommended protective measures include:

- Condoms on sex toys and penises, regardless of whether these are inserted vaginally, orally, or anally;
- Male or female condoms during every episode of sexual contact involving vaginal penetration by either a male or female partner;
- Dental dams for oral sex; and
- Latex or polyurethane gloves for digital contact with genitals or anal areas. If a partner finds these objectionable, finger cots are much less obtrusive and cover the most vulnerable cuticles and nail beds.*

---

* See www.lesbianstd.com for the latest evidence-based recommendations regarding STIs.

Many of the author's patients do not practice safer sex at this level. Indeed, a survey by Pinto and colleagues found that adult lesbians used barrier methods for penile/vaginal sex 40% to 65% of the time and for oral-genital sex with female partners less than 5% of the time.[31] Lesbians and WSW use condoms for shared toys 54% to 80% of the time, most surveys show. These patients may mistakenly believe that partnerships with women are inherently safer than partnerships with men. In Pinto and colleagues' survey, 42.2% of 145 women said they "didn't see a need" for barrier methods with their female partners, 17.3% said they did not use barriers because they "trusted the partner," and 16.5% said they "didn't know they should" use them. Significantly, 38.6% of the respondents had a history of STIs.[31]

■ SUBSTANCE USE

The use of club and prescription drugs in the general U.S. adolescent population has increased in recent years.[32,33] Despite time constraints and clinicians' fears of being too "preachy," all teens on all visits should receive substance use counseling and screening. Sexual minority patients warrant special vigilance: according to a recent meta-analysis, lesbian and bisexual youths are four times more likely than their heterosexual counterparts to be taking substances. The prevalence of cocaine and injection drug use is even higher.[34]

In a study of 400 young adults who patronized clubs, women were more likely than men to misuse prescription drugs, and 98% of the lesbian/bisexual women reported misuse of any prescription drug compared with 90% of the heterosexual women.[†][35] Results from earlier surveys, which did provide separate data for lesbian teens, suggested that sexual minority youths were nine times more likely than their heterosexual counterparts to use injectable drugs.[36]

These figures are sobering. Certainly, there are sexual minority populations, such as LGBT youth, that are more likely than other club-goers to use substances. Limited evidence suggests that the use of drugs, especially club and prescription drugs, by lesbian and WSW adolescents has been underestimated.[34]

■ HOBBIES AND INTERESTS

Learning about a patient's hobbies, participation in sports, and other after-school activities on every visit manifests her strengths and counters negative messages in society at large about sexual minorities. Such pursuits can be potent antidotes for poisonous misconceptions, such as media portrayals of illicit drugs as glamorous and fun.

---

† *The researchers grouped lesbians and bisexual women together for statistical power.*

■ ACADEMIC LIFE

More than 95% of sexual minority youths feel separated and emotionally isolated from their peers because they feel different. Nearly 50% of gay adolescents and 20% of lesbians are victims of verbal or physical assault in secondary school.[36] LGBT youths are four times more likely than their heterosexual counterparts to be threatened on school property.[37] For many, the end result is poor academic performance. One study reported that 25% of gay high school males dropped out before graduation and that 53% of those who stayed in school saw their grades deteriorate.[38] Parallel data regarding young sexual minority women are unavailable, but some lesbian and adolescent WSW probably feel "under fire" at school. In studies of adult lesbian and bisexual women, the vast majority—regardless of whether they had disclosed their sexual orientation—said they felt alienated in middle and high school.[22,37,38] Research in Massachusetts, after state legislation in 1993 mandating institutional support for sexual minority youths, found fewer risks for and better attendance among adolescents whose schools had complied with the law.[22]

■ SUICIDE AND DEPRESSION

Lesbian and bisexual female adolescents are twice as likely as their heterosexual counterparts to attempt suicide.[39] Statistics on completed suicides are difficult to obtain, as authorities rarely investigate or document a deceased youth's sexual orientation, but the figures regarding attempts suggest that lesbian and WSW adolescents are indeed at risk. In the Minnesota Student Survey, 52.4% of lesbian and WSW students ($n = 803$) compared with 24.8% of heterosexual female students ($n = 10,452$) reported they had attempted suicide. Family connectedness, other adult caring, and school safety emerged as significant protective factors in regression models. Consistent with other studies, family connectedness had a much greater impact than any other protective factor on suicidality than did sexual orientation.[40] Thus, clinicians must screen teens for suicidality and engage their families—*protective factors can considerably reduce the risk*. Introducing one or more protective factors into the lives of lesbian and WSW adolescents might prevent 12,000 suicide attempts among young nonheterosexual women each year.[40]

Ryan and colleagues recently found that family acceptance can save the lives of young LGB adults. In their study of 224 such adults between 21 and 25 years old, 19.7% of those who experienced low levels of family rejection as teens had ever attempted suicide compared with 67.6% of those who had experienced high levels of family rejection. These findings, which reflect results from earlier research on disparities between LGB and heterosexual youths who attempt suicide, are especially significant because they did not rely on self-reports and are especially provocative because they suggest that the greater likelihood of suicidality in this population compared with young heterosexual adults is not inevitable.[‡4]

■ HOME/LIVING ENVIRONMENT

Inquiring about a teen's living situation is an essential part of the social history. Adolescents will likely be relieved to discover that in a clinical setting they can discuss general family discord or difficulties with one or more family members. The second most frequently reported problem among sexual minority adolescents, after a general sense of social isolation, is distress regarding family acceptance.[38,41] Few perceive their family's response as supportive.[42] Feeling uncomfortable in one's own home, incessant fear that others will find out about their sexual orientation, and a profound lack of social support sensed by many youths in ambivalent families probably have far-reaching health consequences. The study by Ryan and colleagues also reported large differences between nonheterosexual youths with family support and those without such support regarding the incidence of depression (22.4% vs. 63.5%), substance-related problems (48% vs. 68.9%), and unprotected sex with a casual partner in the last 6 months (23.7% vs. 45.9%).[4] Data indicate a high frequency of penile/vaginal intercourse among lesbian and WSW adolescents, and studies confirm that unprotected sex with a casual partner in the last 6 months is associated with negative health outcomes.

Consequences for sexual minority youths are even more severe when their families completely reject them. Evidence demonstrates that family acceptance is the most important determinant of whether or not a young lesbian or WSW will progress through adolescence without major health risks.[15] Sadly, many sexual minority youths find it necessary to leave home due to family stressors and/or abuse, or they are thrown out by parents. Homophobia prompts many foster homes to reject openly LGBT youths, fearing they will sexually prey on other children in the home.[14] Six percent of all runaway teens in the United States identify as gay or lesbian, but the percentage of homeless sexual minority adolescents in some urban areas is much higher—for example, 40% in Seattle and 30% in Los Angeles.[36]

Once a lesbian teen is homeless, her risk of comorbidities increases exponentially. Homeless young women, including young lesbians, are more likely to engage in survival sex, become sexual victims, take substances, and suffer depression. Risky sexual behavior, in turn, places them at risk of acquiring HIV and other STIs. In

---

‡ *The study by Ryan and colleagues was an outgrowth of the Family Acceptance Project (familyproject. sfsu.edu), a research, intervention, and education initiative that focuses on the impact of family acceptance on LGBT youth. The Trevor Project (www.thetrevorproject.org/home1.aspx) offers a toll-free, 24-hour suicide prevention hotline for nonheterosexual youth: (866) 488-7386. It has fielded more than 96,000 phone calls since 1998.*

addition, unintended pregnancy is far more common among homeless lesbian youths than among those who are sheltered.[43-46]

Taking a thorough home-environment history lays the foundation for engaging the family, which is possible without compromising the patient's confidentiality. Families are responsive to intervention: most parents, like most clinicians, are committed to the care and positive development of their adolescent child.

The author encourages clinicians to proceed as they would with families of other patients. For example, just as a clinician would not shame the family of an asthmatic whose caregivers are heavy smokers, the family of a sexual minority patient needs to know that the clinician does not consider them to be bad people. The clinician should take these consecutive steps:

1. Clarify that he or she values the family's strengths;
2. Communicate the gravity of the situation and how instrumental the family's actions will be in avoiding negative outcomes;
3. Give family members credit for handling this difficult situation and allow them to talk about it; and
4. Suggest strategies to limit the adolescent's exposure to family rejection.

Table 2.4 lists family actions that lesbian and WSW adolescents may experience at home.

In working with families, Ryan found that it was therapeutic for them to be able to discuss their experiences and that talking about having LGBT adolescents changed their behavior. For the first time, families could see the effect their words and actions had on their children.[47] Clinicians also must be sensitive to family culture and culture of origin,[48] and take the family's unique experiences into account. What does having an LGBT child mean to them? What are their feelings, fears, and expectations? To develop coping strategies, this information is essential.

Educating families about the negative effects of rejection behaviors is key because many of them believe that by rejecting sexually nonconformist choices and LGBT contacts, they are helping their children adapt to a homophobic world. Ryan found that many family members who came to realize the impact of such actions were eager to change them.[47,48] When counseling families, it is OK to ask about specific rejection behaviors and encourage positive ones.

PHYSICAL EXAMINATION

Regardless of sexual orientation, all patients deserve a comprehensive, head-to-toe physical exam and investigation of anything significant the medical history or review of systems has revealed. However, some lesbian or WSW adolescents need special

TABLE 2.4. FAMILY ACTIONS

ACCEPTANCE/SUPPORT	REJECTION
■ Allowing a teen to post LBGT-friendly decorations in her room	■ Banning or removing LGBT-friendly decorations
■ Allowing disclosure of same-sex attraction ■ Allowing expression of affection after adolescent discloses her sexual orientation	■ Denying that disclosure was ever made ■ Telling a teen that her attraction is not real or that she "will grow out of it"
■ Supporting a teen in her efforts to fight LGBT discrimination ■ Advocating for a teen when she is mistreated because of sexual orientation	■ Blaming a teen when she is discriminated against because of sexual orientation
■ Supporting a teen's sexual identity even if the parent feels uncomfortable about it	■ Asking a teen to keep her sexual identity a secret ■ Not letting a teen talk about her sexual identity
■ Welcoming a teen's LGBT friends and partners into the home	■ Banning a teen's LGBT friends and partners from the home
■ Connecting a teen with an LGBT adult role model to illustrate options for the future	■ Telling an LGB youth she is bad or doomed ("you're going to hell")
■ Including the teen in family functions and events, and requiring that other family members respect the adolescent	■ Excluding the teen from family functions and events

care during a gynecologic exam, especially if it includes use of a speculum; the related difficulties, especially for survivors of sexual assault, are well-documented. As one lesbian adolescent told Ginsburg and colleagues:

> When I go to an ob/gyn, she needs to understand that I'm a lesbian and I do not like anything penetrating my body. And as a female, that's what you are going to an ob/gyn for. So she would need to understand or be sensitive to that aspect of me. Because the only way she's going to get me on the table is to calm me down…. But if she's a straight woman who enjoys penetration, she might be like, child, girl….[1] (p. 412)

This comment raises important considerations for clinicians. First, a clinician's understanding of LGBT patients and ability to care for them outweighs the clinician's gender or sexual orientation.[1] This may not be true for all patients, but broaching the topic directly and respectfully tells a patient that the clinician's foremost concern is her comfort and health care. A male clinician who has female patients, or a heterosexual clinician whose practice includes sexual minority patients, may consider asking the adolescent after taking a medical history or while discussing sexual orientation, and before physically examining her, if she is comfortable with him or her as the provider. The clinician could say: "I feel very comfortable being your provider, but it's your comfort that is important here, so I wanted to ask if you'd prefer to be examined by a [female, lesbian, nonheterosexual male, etc.] provider." Second, clinicians must dispel the common perception that doctors are insensitive to patients' concerns. The adolescent quoted above perceives or fears that the clinician will trivialize her concerns about the speculum exam and that the provider thinks all females should be able to deal with an intravaginal speculum. Some clinicians tell sexually active patients before a gynecologic exam: "It's not going to be that bad—the speculum is much smaller than a penis." Drawing this parallel may be problematic for any female patient, regardless of sexual orientation, because a clinical exam has virtually nothing in common with sex except tactile contact.

Clinicians can increase patient comfort in numerous ways:

- With the patient still dressed, introduce the gynecologic exam, even if she has been examined before. Discuss what tests will be performed and why they are valuable. If the patient identifies as butch or as a transgender male, acknowledge that some transgender patients are uncomfortable with a gynecologic exam and explain that it is an important part of maintaining good health. Give the patient an opportunity to discuss how he feels and to disclose his limits or preferences. For example, some lesbians or transgender patients may initially prefer not to have their breasts examined;
- Have a variety of speculums available. A Pederson speculum is adequate in most cases (medium size = 7/8 of an inch wide and 4 inches long). An extra-narrow Pederson speculum (typically 5/8 of an inch wide and 4 inches long) should be available for patients who prefer it. However, this speculum is painful for some patients because its small footprint feels sharper on the posterior fornix. Let the patient handle a speculum and select one she prefers;
- Make a hand mirror available so the patient can observe the exam if she wants to;
- Reassure the patient that the exam is under her control. Tell her the exam will stop immediately upon her request;
- Before each step, tell the patient everything about it;

- Consider examining the vault with a single digit before inserting the speculum to ascertain the vaginal trajectory and location of the cervix. This will preclude unnecessary movement of the speculum in the vault; and
- Note the speculum size and vault trajectory for future exams.

AFTER THE EXAM

In the doctor's office, most people feel more comfortable dressed. This may be particularly true for lesbian or WSW adolescents who prefer traditional male clothing and for young transgender men. Clinicians should resist the urge to hastily conclude an exam, reassure the patient everything is fine, and move on to the next appointment. All adolescent patients must be debriefed after a visit. In general, the more time a clinician spends reviewing a consultation, the more likely patients are to comply with instructions, medications, and/or referrals. Patients should receive a written summary of the consultation.

Instructions should be geared to the patient's developmental stage (see Table 2.3). The author suggests assessing her full understanding by means of a quick role reversal: she instructs the clinician about what to do after the visit—schedule a follow-up appointment, keep a food journal, take an antibiotic twice daily, or comply with other directives. Many patients find this to be empowering rather than patronizing, and it rapidly exposes any unclear or forgotten instructions.

Verbalized encouragement or suggestions during the debriefing may be helpful, as teens often crave praise, acceptance, and advice from adults they trust. This is even more likely if a patient has experienced stigmatization or outright rejection at home, school, or in peer groups. Clinicians can promote a positive identity and counterbalance negative messages a patient may have received by:

- Individualizing the patient. Reaffirm her unique and positive traits so she further internalizes them;
- Searching for and highlighting her strengths. The clinician may be able to build on these strengths by, for example, referring the patient for academic counseling, suggesting she work as a volunteer for the American Society for the Prevention of Cruelty to Animals if she has veterinary interests, or connecting her with a social worker to find classes that will lead to a general equivalency diploma;
- Affirming her experiences and struggles; and
- Normalizing her feelings, concerns, and desires—communicating that these are normal and natural even if others disagree. Referring sexual minority

youths to books, movies, and other resources with positive messages may be especially helpful.[14]

This may seem daunting. But, as in dealing with most cultural competence issues, clinicians need not be experts on sexual minority youths to provide quality care. Remaining open and honest, offering encouragement, and asking questions fosters comfort and trust, as patients can clarify for themselves and the clinician what they mean and feel. One youth told Ragg and colleagues:

> [Clinicians] have to be like true to you because a kid can tell if a person is just bullshitting you…. You can give the best million dollar speech in the world, I ain't gonna buy it…. Their actions…the way they talk to you and treat you…simple little things mean so much to a kid…especially to a queer kid…."[14] (p. 261)

SCREENING AND IMMUNIZATION

Development and Behavior

Although an extensive battery of screening tests is not necessary during every patient encounter, a checklist of general topics that warrant attention ensures comprehensive adolescent care. HEADSS, which stands for home, education, activities, drugs, sexuality, and suicide/depression, is a medical interview checklist for development and behavior (Table 2.5). Clinicians can adapt the list on each visit. Adolescents with special needs or medical conditions that could impact their physical or mental health may require more routine screening. The author recommends the Pediatric Symptom Checklist—Youth Report (Y-PSC) for clinicians who want a systematic developmental screening tool.§ They can refer to this checklist during the interview or have the patient complete it.

Dental Health

Inspecting the patient's mouth during an annual exam can be very informative, as evidence of poor dentition may indicate a need for nutrition and substance-use screening. Such inspection often can detect tobacco and/or marijuana use. The author recommends that clinicians look for gingival inflammation in all teens and teach them how to floss or reinforce their flossing skill. At their age, education by a concerned professional about future cosmetic appearance may have a big impact, even though the primary goal is to promote oral health.

---

§ *Available at www.brightfutures.org/mentalhealth/pdf/professionals/ped_sympton_chklst.pdf, p. 18.*

TABLE 2.5. THE HEADSS MEDICAL INTERVIEW

GENERAL TOPIC	DETAILS
Home	■ Family dynamics ■ Living arrangements
Education	■ School attendance ■ Failures ■ Goals ■ Strengths
Activities	■ Exercise ■ Hobbies ■ Fighting, violence, gang activities
Drugs	■ Alcohol and tobacco ■ Frequency and duration of use ■ Attempts to quit ■ Unhealthy eating habits
Sexuality	■ Attractions ■ Behaviors ■ Identity ■ Risk assessment
Suicide/depression	■ Feelings about self ■ History of mental problems ■ Suicidal ideation and/or suicide attempts ■ Cutting

Adapted from Goldenring, J., & Cohen, E. (1988). Getting into adolescent heads. *Contemporary Pediatrics, 200,* 75–90.

Sexually Transmitted Infection

Sexually active teens should be screened annually for syphilis using the rapid plasma reagin test. This includes teens in geographic areas where syphilis prevalence is low. The author advises clinicians never to omit the test when patients are lesbian adolescents, as they have more sexual contact with MSM youths than adolescent heterosexual females do and the incidence of syphilis in the United States is highest among MSM.[49] Sexually active teens should have annual screening for chlamydia and gonorrhea. Pap smears are not indicated until age 21.

Although bacterial vaginosis (BV) is not officially a STI, evidence suggests it can pass from one female partner to another via vaginal fluid.[29] When an exam reveals that a lesbian and WSW patient has BV, the author recommends that she and her partner take 500 mg of metronidazole twice daily for 7 days. According to guidelines from the Centers for Disease Control and Prevention, clinicians can treat BV with 2 gm of metronidazole upon diagnosis, but in the author's experience, rapid recurrence is more frequent with the single-dose regimen.

Immunization

Immunization recommendations are the same for all adolescents.[¶] However, vaccination against HPV is especially warranted for lesbian adolescents because clinicians traditionally have not considered lesbians to be at risk for cervical cancer and other HPV-related health consequences.

■ ■ ■

In the scenario at the beginning of this chapter, Stevie was triaged and found to have normal vital signs, with only slight discomfort but decreased range of motion at her right elbow. After calling Stevie and her mother, Ms. G, into the exam room, the physician introduced herself and asked the patient and Ms. G how they preferred to be addressed, and noted this on the chart. She welcomed them to the urgent care center and explained that she always meets with families and patients. She also explained that she customarily spends some time speaking with patients alone, for confidentiality reasons, and that she only discusses their care with loved ones if the teen gives permission, unless patients are in danger of hurting themselves or someone else.

In a supportive, friendly way, the physician asked Ms. G: "Is there anything you would like me to know, do you have any special concerns, or is there any information you're afraid Stevie will forget to mention?"

"Not really," Ms. G replied. "I just wanted to make sure she's all right. But it wouldn't kill her to stay off roofs and out from under cars!" Turning to her daughter, she said in an exasperated voice: "Honestly, Stevie, you don't have to do everything Vincent does. It was cute when you were 5 and he was 10, but you're becoming a young lady now and those things are too dangerous for girls."

Stevie, looking down at her sneakers, protested: "He was the one who asked me to help him, Mom." The physician gently interrupted this exchange, reassuring Ms. G that the x-rays did not show a fracture. She told Ms. G she would summon her back in after the exam.

The interview began with the physician asking Stevie how her arm was and about the time and nature of her fall. Stevie's big concern was that she might not be able to pitch in her next softball game in three days. The physician said they would discuss that more after the exam. She also said Stevie could choose to be examined alone or with her mother present. Stevie said she preferred to be examined alone.

¶ *An immunization schedule is available at www.aap.org/immunization/IZSchedule7-18.pdf.*

The physician informed Stevie that she always asks patients about their medical history as part of the initial exam, about their last full physical, if they have received a doctor's care (excluding check-ups) for anything, and if they have any other symptoms or concerns. Stevie's history was negative.

When asked if she had begun to menstruate, Stevie rolled her eyes and said: "Have I ever! Three years ago. It's been downhill ever since." When asked to explain, she expressed some discomfort with her body's changing contours—that her breasts were too large, that she was a faster runner without them. "I'm getting fat," she added, indicating her hips.

According to the triage notes, Stevie was 5 feet 7 inches tall and weighed 145 pounds. She denied dieting, purging, or excessive exercise, but she said she started wearing two sports bras a couple of years ago and then found "something better."

"Female boxers wrap up, so that's what I do, and it's much better than those bras," she said.

In discussing family, school, and hobbies, the physician learned that Stevie is the oldest of three. Her brother Joe, 11, "is a great kid, a fantastic athlete" and her sister Cynthia, 9, "is the sweetest, but we don't hang out or anything—she's only in fourth grade." Stevie said she wants to be a forensic scientist when she grows up— "Dead people don't scare me at all. I think that stuff is mad interesting"—and is doing well in school. She denied being teased or bullied. "Sure, in junior high somebody always had something to say," she said, "but people have chilled about my appearance, saying stupid stuff like 'Are you a boy or a girl? We can't figure it out!'—shit like that. No one has time for that now. Besides, I don't hang out with those people—most of my friends are on the team."

Stevie said her preference for male garb and jewelry bothers her mother: "What she wouldn't give if I was like Cindy! That girl hasn't met a pink she didn't wanna wear!" Stevie denied having interest in or experience with drugs and alcohol: "Are you kidding? That stuff will mess you up bad. Believe me, I've seen it." When asked if there is someone special in her life, she replied: "I'd have to say my cousin Vincent. He's my idol. There's nothing he can't do. I can tell him anything and he's completely cool with it." When asked if there's anyone in her life she is sexually attracted to or has a romantic or sexual relationship with, Stevie said: "Well, I have two best friends, Jessica and Peter. Peter and I have messed around, made out, stuff like that, but we never went all the way or anything. I kind of think about Jessica in a romantic way— like, when sappy songs come on the radio. But we're really just friends."

The physician said she supported Stevie waiting to have sex until she really feels ready, reiterated the practice's confidentiality policy, and made it clear she was a source of information. In addition, she talked about contraceptives and said the clinic has emergency contraceptive pills, which Stevie had never heard of, and some contraceptive methods available to teens free of charge. Stevie declined an advance prescription for emergency contraception, grinned, and said: "My Mom wants me to go out with Peter, but she'd kill me if I slept with him! I really can't have that stuff in my room."

The physician asked if Stevie had ever heard of gonorrhea, chlamydia, and herpes, then dispelled a few misconceptions. She briefly explained the pelvic exam and recommended that Stevie get an exam if any problems arise or after her first sexual contact, regardless of whether her partner is male or female.

The exam revealed that Stevie had strained some tendons at her right elbow in the fall. The physician also noted that Stevie binds her breasts with an extra-wide ACE bandage, but that this had not caused constriction or chafing of the skin and that the wrap does not constrict her breathing. The discussion with Stevie took 40 minutes and the exam 5 minutes.

After Stevie got dressed, the physician discussed her findings and recommendations with Stevie. She recommended nonsteroidal anti-inflammatories and periodic icing of the elbow to keep the swelling down, and said she would prescribe a sling for Stevie to wear at all times, except while sleeping. She emphasized that Stevie not play softball until her evaluation by the orthopedist in two days. She also warned that she might prescribe a course of physical therapy and explained that, while recognizing Stevie's eagerness to return to full activity, complete healing now would reap large rewards later.

The physician acknowledged Stevie's discomfort with her physical maturation and preference for male garb, saying she thought they were normal. But, she noted, some parents may feel uncomfortable about their children's nontraditional choices of clothing and accessories. She told Stevie that her attraction to Jessica is normal and that she was glad Stevie did not feel distressed about her feelings. Many lesbian and bisexual adolescents, she explained, have sexual contact with male partners, and said it is important to protect against pregnancy and STIs.

Then the physician asked for Stevie's permission to talk with her mother, reviewing in advance the topics to be discussed: the injured arm and treatment recommendations for the following week. They agreed that discussing Stevie's nontraditional, gender-related choices with her mother, and discussing support for any discomfort Ms. G may feel regarding her daughter's choices, will wait for another encounter, as the doctor/family relationship evolves. Stevie told her mother she would like to have the physician as her primary provider, which was arranged.

CONCLUSION

The adolescent transition is filled with hazards and pitfalls for young lesbians, WSW, and young heterosexual women but also with excitement and growth. Clinicians can help manage some of the physical, mental, social, and developmental challenges these adolescents face and also acknowledge and foster patients' strengths. Ideally, clinical interventions engage both patients and their families. Given research showing that sexual identity is fluid for many women, clinicians must approach every patient in a nonheterosexist, nonjudgmental manner. Only then will they be able to tailor therapy to individuals rather than a demographic group. Truly listening to adolescent patients, regardless of their sexual orientation, reveals that they can often teach clinicians much more than clinicians could ever teach them.

ADDITIONAL RESOURCES

- Asian & Pacific Islander Family Pride: ✎ www.apifamilypride.org
- Family Acceptance Project: ✎ familyproject.sfsu.edu
- Gender Spectrum Education & Training: ✎ www.genderspectrum.org
- Parents, Families and Friends of Lesbians and Gays: ✎ www.pflag.org

REFERENCES

1. Ginsburg, K. R., Winn, R. J., Rudy, B. J., Crawford, J., Zhao, H., & Schwarz, D. F. (2002). How to reach sexual minority youth in the health care setting: The teens offer guidance. *Journal of Adolescent Health, 31,* 407–416.

2. Meckler, G. D., Elliott, M. N., Kanouse, D. E., Beals, K. P., & Schuster, M. A. (2006). Nondisclosure of sexual orientation to a physician among a sample of gay, lesbian, and bisexual youth. *Archives of Pediatrics & Adolescent Medicine, 160,* 1248–1254.

3. Marrazzo, J. M. (2000). Sexually transmitted infections in women who have sex with women: Who cares? *Sexually Transmitted Infections, 76,* 330–332.

4. Ryan, C., Huebner, D., Diaz, R. M., & Sanchez, J. (2009). Family rejection as a predictor of negative health outcomes in White and Latino lesbian, gay, and bisexual young adults. *Pediatrics, 123,* 346–352.

5. Diamond, L. M. (2008). Female bisexuality from adolescence to adulthood: Results from a 10-year longitudinal study. *Developmental Psychology, 44,* 5–14. Available at www.apa.org/journals/releases/dev4415.pdf.

6. Savin-Williams, R. C. (2001). A critique of research on sexual-minority youths. *Journal of Adolescence, 24,* 5–13.

7. Perrin, E. C., Cohen, K. M., Gold, M., Ryan, C., Savin-Williams, R. C., & Schorzman, C. M. (2004). Gay and lesbian issues in pediatric health care. *Current Problems in Pediatric and Adolescent Health Care, 34,* 355–398.

8. Drummond, K. D., Bradley, S. J., Peterson-Badali, M., & Zucker, K. J. (2008). A follow-up study of girls with gender identity disorder. *Developmental Psychology, 44,* 34–45.

9. Diamond, L. M. (1998). Development of sexual orientation among adolescent and young adult women. *Developmental Psychology, 34,* 1085–1095.

10. Savin-Williams, R. C., & Ream, G. L. (2007). Prevalence and stability of sexual orientation components during adolescence and young adulthood. *Archives of Sexual Behavior, 36,* 385–394.

11. Saewyc, E. M., Bearinger, L. H., Blum, R. W., & Resnick, M. D. (1999). Sexual intercourse, abuse and pregnancy among adolescent women: Does sexual orientation make a difference? *Family Planning Perspectives, 31,* 127–131.

12. Savin-Williams, R. C. (2008). Then and now: Recruitment, definition, diversity, and positive attributes of same-sex populations. *Developmental Psychology, 44,* 135–138.

13. Allen, L. B., Glicken, A. D., Beach, R. K., & Naylor, K. E. (1998). Adolescent health care experience of gay, lesbian, and bisexual young adults. *Journal of Adolescent Health, 23,* 212–220.

14. Ragg, D. M., Patrick, D., & Ziefert, M. (2006). Slamming the closet door: Working with gay and lesbian youth in care. *Child Welfare, 85,* 243–265.

15. Alexander, B., & Schrauben, S. (2006). Outside the margins: Youth who are different and their special health care needs. *Primary Care, 33,* 285–303.

16. Sison, A. C., & Greydanus, D. E. (2007). Deconstructing adolescent same-sex attraction and sexual behavior in the twenty-first century: Perspectives for the clinician. *Primary Care, 34,* 293–304.

17. Blythe, M. J., & Rosenthal, S. L. (2000). Female adolescent sexuality. Promoting healthy sexual development. *Obstetrics and Gynecology Clinics of North America, 27,* 125–141.

18. Teutsch, C. (2003). Patient-doctor communication. *Medical Clinics of North America, 87,* 1115–1145.

19. Haidet, P., & Paterniti, D. A. (2003). "Building" a history rather than "taking" one: A perspective on information sharing during the medical interview. *Archives of Internal Medicine, 163,* 1134–1140.

20. Swenson, S. L., Zettler, P., & Lo, B. (2006). "She gave it her best shot right away": Patient experiences of biomedical and patient-centered communication. *Patient Education and Counseling, 61,* 200–211.

21. Mast, M. S. (2007). On the importance of nonverbal communication in the physician-patient interaction. *Patient Education and Counseling, 67,* 315–318.

22. Blake, S. M., Ledsky, R., Lehman, T., Goodenow, C., Sawyer, R., & Hack, T. (2001). Preventing sexual risk behaviors among gay, lesbian, and bisexual adolescents: The benefits of gay-sensitive HIV instruction in schools. *American Journal of Public Health, 91,* 940–946.

23. Deans, E. I., & Grimes, D. A. (2009). Intrauterine devices for adolescents: A systemic review. *Contraception, 79,* 418–423.

24. Cheng, L., Gülmezoglu, A. M., Piaggio, G., Ezcurra, E., and Van Look, P. F. (2008). Interventions for emergency contraception. *Cochrane Database of Systemic Reviews, Apr 16,* CD001324.

25. Fethers, K., Marks, C., Mindel, A., & Estcourt, C. S. (2000). Sexually transmitted infections and risk behaviours in women who have sex with women. *Sexually Transmitted Infections, 76,* 345–349.

26. Bauer, G. R., & Welles, S. L. (2001). Beyond assumptions of negligible risk: Sexually transmitted diseases and women who have sex with women. *American Journal of Public Health, 91,* 1282–1286.

27. Benson, P. A., & Hergenroeder, A. C. (2005). Bacterial sexually transmitted infections in gay, lesbian, and bisexual adolescents: Medical and public health perspectives. *Seminars in Pediatric Infectious Diseases, 16,* 181–191.

28. Marrazzo, J. M. (2004). Barriers to infectious disease care among lesbians. *Emerging Infectious Diseases, 10,* 1974–1978.

29. Bailey, J. V., Farquhar, C., & Owen, C. (2004). Bacterial vaginosis in lesbians and bisexual women. *Sexually Transmitted Diseases, 31,* 691–694.

30. Evans, A. L., Scally, A. J., Wellard, S. J., & Wilson, J. D. (2007). Prevalence of bacterial vaginosis in lesbians and heterosexual women in a community setting. *Sexually Transmitted Infections, 83,* 470–475.

31. Pinto, V. M., Tancredi, M. V., Tancredi Neto, A., & Buchalla, C. M. (2005). Sexually transmitted disease/HIV risk behaviour among women who have sex with women. *AIDS, 19*(Suppl. 4), S64–69.

32. Wu, L.-T., Schlenger, W. E., & Galvin, D. M. (2006). Concurrent use of methamphetamine, MDMA, LSD, ketamine, GHB, and flunitrazepam among American youths. *Drug and Alcohol Dependence, 84,* 102–113.

33. Brief Addiction Science Information Source. (2009, July 29). Self-treatment versus recreation as motivations for prescription drug misuse [Forum article]. Available at www.basisonline.org/2009/07/stash-vol-56-selftreatment-versus-recreation-as-motivations-for-prescription-drug-misuse.html.

34. Marshal, M. P., Friedman, M. S., Stall, R., King, K. M., Miles, J., Gold, M. A., et al. (2008). Sexual orientation and adolescent substance use: A meta-analysis and methodological review. *Addiction, 103,* 546–556.

35. Kelly, B. C., & Parsons, J. T. (2007). Prescription drug misuse among club drug-using young adults. *American Journal of Drug and Alcohol Abuse, 33,* 875–884.

36. Lee, R. (2000). Health care problems of lesbian, gay, bisexual, and transgender patients. *Western Journal of Medicine, 172,* 403–408.

37. Garofalo, R., & Katz, E. (2001). Health care issues of gay and lesbian youth. *Current Opinion in Pediatrics, 13,* 298–302.

38. Hart, T. A., & Heimberg, R. G. (2001). Presenting problems among treatment-seeking gay, lesbian, and bisexual youth. *Journal of Clinical Psychology, 57,* 615–627.

39. King, M., Semlyen, J., Tai, S. S., Killaspy, H., Osborn, D., Popelyuk, D., et al. (2008). A systematic review of mental disorder, suicide, and deliberate self harm in lesbian, gay and bisexual people. *BMC Psychiatry, 8,* 70.

40. Eisenberg, M. E., & Resnick, M. D. (2006). Suicidality among gay, lesbian and bisexual youth: The role of protective factors. *Journal of Adolescent Health, 39,* 662–668.

41. Martin, A. D., & Hetrick, E. S. (1988). The stigmatization of the gay and lesbian adolescent. *Journal of Homosexuality, 15,* 163–183.

42. D'Augelli, A. R., Hershberger, S. L., & Pilkington, N. W. (1998). Lesbian, gay, and bisexual youth and their families: Disclosure of sexual orientation and its consequences. *American Journal of Orthopsychiatry, 68,* 361–371.

43. Ensign, J. (2000). Reproductive health of homeless adolescent women in Seattle, Washington, U.S.A. *Women & Health, 31,* 133–151.

44. Cochran, B. N., Stewart, A. J., Ginzler, J. A., & Cauce, A. M. (2002). Challenges faced by homeless sexual minorities: Comparison of gay, lesbian, bisexual, and transgender homeless adolescents with their heterosexual counterparts. *American Journal of Public Health, 92,* 773–777.

45. Rew, L., Whittaker, T. A., Taylor-Seehafer, M. A., & Smith, L. R. (2005). Sexual health risks and protective resources in gay, lesbian, bisexual, and heterosexual homeless youth. *Journal for Specialists in Pediatric Nursing, 10,* 11–19.

46. Van Leeuwen, J. M., Boyle, S., Salomonsen-Sautel, S., Baker, D. N., Garcia, J. T., Hoffman, A., et al. (2006). Lesbian, gay, and bisexual homeless youth: An eight-city public health perspective. *Child Welfare, 85,* 151–170.

47. Rudolph, D. (2009, January 8). Treating families as allies, not enemies. *365 Gay.* Available at www.365gay.com/living/treating-families-as-allies-not-enemies.

48. Ryan, C. (2009). *Supportive families, healthy children: Helping families with lesbian, gay, bisexual & transgender children.* San Francisco: San Francisco State University.

49. Centers for Disease Control and Prevention. (2008, March 12). New data reveal 7th consecutive syphilis increase in the U.S. and opportunities to improve STD screening and prevention for gay and bisexual men [Press release]. Available at www.cdc.gov/stdconference/2008/press/release-12march2008.htm.

ABOUT THE AUTHOR

Elizabeth Lorde-Rollins, MD, MSc is Assistant Professor in Pediatrics and Obstetrics, Gynecology and Reproductive Science at Mt. Sinai, School of Medicine in New York City. She concentrates her clinical time in adolescent gynecology. She is on the Board of the Callen-Lorde Community Health Center which provides health care primarily to New York's lesbian, gay, bisexual, and transgender communities.

CHAPTER 3

"Can I Get Herpes From My Girlfriend?"

LESBIANS' SEXUAL HEALTH

JEANNE M. MARRAZZO, MD, MPH

DANA *is a 19-year-old woman who recently made an appointment with a new health care provider so she could get a Pap smear. She has a new girlfriend with whom she started having sex about 4 months ago.*

When she told the provider that she had only had sex with women in her lifetime, the provider said Dana probably did not need a Pap smear because the human papillomavirus (HPV) that causes most cervical cancer is sexually transmitted and "that doesn't really happen with women." Dana thought she had read online that HPV could be transmitted from one woman to another during sex, but she could not remember the details and, in any case, felt too intimidated to correct the provider. Instead, she said she really would rather have a Pap smear "just to be sure." The provider relented and, a week later, called to tell Dana that the results indicated low-grade, precancerous changes and that she needed to have a repeat test in several months. The provider then asked, "Have you really not had sex with men?"

Dana is concerned that she might transmit HPV to her current partner. Her provider tells her that genital HPV is such a common sexually transmitted infection, most people who have sex are infected relatively soon after they start having sex.

■　■　■

Sexually transmitted infection (STI) is among the most commonly reported infections worldwide. In a striking 2008 report, the U.S. Centers for Disease Control and Prevention (CDC) estimated that a quarter of adolescents are infected with one of the major STIs at any given time.[1] These infections have extremely important implications for women's sexual and reproductive health. For example, *Chlamydia trachomatis* is thought to be the major infectious cause of tubal infertility, and genital infection with certain types of HPV is responsible for up to 90% of cervical cancers. Worldwide, genital herpes significantly increases women's risk of HIV infection, which is devastating women's health in many countries, especially the health of those in sub-Saharan Africa.[2]

Despite these statistics and the fact that about 4% of women in the United States are sexually active with other women,[3] relatively few data are available to inform estimates of the risk of woman-to-woman sexual transmission of STI. This is problematic. The absence of solid data makes it very difficult to provide comprehensive information to lesbians that can empower them to protect themselves and their partners from infection or from experiencing the associated consequences. Such empowerment constitutes the foundation of attaining and maintaining good sexual health.

Moreover, numerous studies have demonstrated that lesbians face significant barriers to accessing health care generally. The barriers include, but are not limited to, a lack of patient education materials aimed specifically at lesbians' risks and circumstances, health care providers' lack of context-specific knowledge, low socioeconomic status, an absence of spousal insurance benefits, and the impact of lesbians' prior negative experiences in the health care system. When the challenge of discussing sex is added to this mix, the barriers can become even greater, as Dana's case illustrates. Even providers who are comfortable assessing STI-related risks may not be knowledgeable about lesbians' sexual practices or the limited, disease-specific information in the literature.

Available data on STI transmission between women come primarily from four sources:

- Records at clinics that provide care to lesbians;
- Studies of women typically recruited through advertisements, community network approaches, or peer referral who report having had sex with other women;
- Population-based surveys that enroll a more representative sample of women but often rely on self-reported STI history; and
- Case reports of STI transmission between women that provide the only available documented evidence for some types of infection.

Although these sources yield helpful data on lesbians' risk of STI acquisition and transmission, they all have considerable limitations. Further research is critically necessary.

SEXUAL HISTORY AND RISK ASSESSMENT

There are comprehensive resources for learning how to take a sexual history, but the critical lesson is this: clinicians should not assume anything! Assumptions can arise from perceptions based on physical appearance, statements that may not tell the whole story, or information the patient herself provides. For example, "I am a lesbian" may mean different things to different people and does not necessarily exclude current—and especially past—sexual activity with men. Whatever the information source, assumptions can lead the clinician/patient exchange in the wrong direction and preclude complete health care.

The assumption that a self-identified lesbian is not currently, or has not been, sexually active with men is usually incorrect. In one study, 74% of self-identified lesbians had male partners in the past and 98% of self-identified bisexual women currently or previously had male partners.[4] Of lesbians recruited for studies in Seattle, 80% to 86% reported prior sex with men, 23% to 28% had sex with a man in the previous year, and the median number of male and female lifetime partners was the same.[5-7] In a sample of women who visited a London clinic for STIs, 69% of those identifying as lesbian had prior male partners.[8] At another London clinic specializing in the sexual health of lesbians, 91% had prior male partners.[9] Of course, heterosexual intercourse can result in transmission of chronic viral STI, including HPV, genital herpes, hepatitis B, and HIV, any of which may be undetected for years.

Important components of the sexual history include the number of recent and lifetime sexual partners, both male and female. Asking about the number of sexual partners in the previous 2 months provides an index of recent risk behaviors, while asking about the number in the previous year gives a more comprehensive view, so both of these timeframes should be assessed. Other key components include types of sexual practices (discussed below) that could pose a STI transmission risk. Practices involving digital-vaginal or digital-anal contact, particularly with shared penetrative sex toys, are plausible means of transmission of infectious secretions arising from the cervix or vagina.

Women who have sex with both women and men appear to have more sexual partners over their lifetime than do women who have sex exclusively with either women or men. In a population-based survey of 2,547 young women in low-income neighborhoods, Scheer and colleagues found that those who had sex with men only (88%) reported a mean of 16 lifetime partners, whereas women who had sex with both women and men (7%) reported a mean of 307 lifetime partners.[10] Similarly, among clients attending a STI clinic in Seattle, women with only female partners in the prior 2 months had 3.4 partners in the previous year compared with the 5.3 for women with only male partners and the 16.5 for women with female and male partners.[11] Women who report sex with both women and men are likely to be at highest risk for STIs.

SEXUAL PRACTICES: WHAT DO LESBIANS DO?

Common sexual practices between female partners include oral-genital sex; vaginal or anal sex using hands, fingers, or penetrative sex toys; and oral-anal sex.[6,12,13] Oral sex, in particular, appears to be extremely common, probably more common than among heterosexual women. Other sexual practices include digital-vaginal or digital-anal contact, particularly with shared penetrative sex toys. These sexual practices are plausible means of transmission of infected cervicovaginal secretions, although the frequency of transmission associated with these practices is not well documented. Table 3.1 lists sexual practices that lesbians may engage in, along with the estimated STI risk of each and possible ways to reduce STI transmission between women.

TABLE 3.1. SEXUAL PRACTICES AMONG LESBIANS: FREQUENCY AND ASSOCIATED STI RISK

PRACTICE	DESCRIPTION AND VERNACULAR TERMS	ESTIMATED FREQUENCY	FACTORS MODIFYING RISK OF STI*
Oral-vulvovaginal contact (cunnilingus)	• "Going down" • Top = performing partner • Bottom = receiving partner	Very common (> 95%)	• Presence of oral lesions in top partner (herpes, syphilis, possibly gonorrhea)(+) • Use of barriers (plastic wrap, dental dams, condoms)(–)
Digital-vaginal contact	Range of penetration, from "finger fucking" to "fisting"	Very common (> 85%)	• Sharing infected cervicovaginal secretions (trichomoniasis ["trich"], chlamydia, gonorrhea, HPV, herpes)(+)
Digital-anal contact	Range of penetration, from "finger fucking" to "fisting"	Common (25%)	• Sharing infected anorectal secretions (hepatitis A, enteric pathogens, gonorrhea, HPV, herpes)(+) • Use of gloves(–)
Insertive sex objects (vagina or anus)	Toys, dildos	• Very common vaginally (60%) • Common anally (25%)	• Sharing infected cervicovaginal or anal fluid (trichomoniasis ["trich"], chlamydia, gonorrhea, HPV, herpes)(+) • Use of condoms with sex toys(–) • Sharing insertive toys without prior cleaning(+)
Oral-anal contact	"Rimming"	Common (35%)	• Presence of oral infection in performing partner (syphilis, genital herpes)(+) • Presence of anorectal infection in receiving partner (hepatitis A, enteric pathogens)(+) • Use of barriers(–)
Direct genital-to-genital contact	Tribadism	Very common (> 95%)	• Direct contact of susceptible skin/mucosa (HPV, herpes, syphilis)(+) • May involve use of interposed devices such as vibrators, which can cause mechanical vulvar irritation(+)
Sadomasochism	Bondage; bondage/discipline, dominance/submission, sadism/masochism	Unknown, but probably uncommon (< 2%)	Sharing blood (hepatitis B, hepatitis C, HIV)(+)

* (+) = factor likely to enhance risk of STI transmission or acquisition; (–) = factor with probable protective effect.

Source: Author.

EDUCATING LESBIANS ABOUT SEXUAL HEALTH AND STI PREVENTION

As noted above, relatively little data are available to inform health messages for maintaining sexual health through STI prevention in lesbians. No studies have directly addressed the acceptability or efficacy of STI risk-reduction measures. However, measures that reduce the potential for transmission of cervicovaginal secretions are likely to be effective. As is the case when counseling anyone about modifying the risk of STI acquisition, the particular measure depends on the activity, a woman's sexual network, and the STI in question. This highlights the need for individual risk assessment and targeted risk-reduction counseling based on a complete sexual history.

For women who practice digital-vaginal or digital-anal sex, the risk is probably low unless secretions are transferred from the infected partner to the other. Avoiding the behavior or using gloves will likely interrupt such transfer. Regarding insertive sex toys, preventive measures may include not sharing them, cleaning the toys between use in one or the other partner, using condoms on the toys, and not using them anally and vaginally in succession. Regarding oral sex and STI, lesbians may be at greater risk of genital herpes as a result of infection by herpes simplex virus type-1 (HSV-1), due to the relatively higher frequency of orogenital sex. Serologic screening for HSV-1 is not useful because most adults are infected orally and serology does not reveal where the infection was established. However, women should be counseled to avoid having oral and/or genital sex when, consistent with a herpes outbreak, a lesion is present—for example, a cold sore or a recurrent ulcer or vesicle in the genital area—and when there is a recognizable prodrome such as ear pain or local lymphadenopathy.

Data are relatively unequivocal about sexual transmission of genital HPV between women (discussed in greater detail below), which likely occurs with some efficiency. Lesbians should have Pap smears and receive the HPV vaccine according to current guidelines.

SEXUALLY TRANSMITTED ETIOLOGIC AGENTS AND CONDITIONS

Chlamydia trachomatis

No data are available for estimating the risk of transmission of *Chlamydia trachomatis* between women, but in surveys lesbians have reported chlamydial infection and pelvic inflammatory disease.[4] A recent analysis of a large database of women screened at family planning clinics in the Pacific Northwest from 1995 to 2002 found that chlamydial infection was surprisingly common among women who reported sex with other women. Prevalence of *C. trachomatis* among 5,714 women who reported sex only with other women in the prior 60 days was 7.1%, and 5.3% among 3,644 women who reported sex with both men and women in that timeframe.[14]

Equally important, lesbians may engage in sexual networks that involve men and not be aware of their female partners' exposure to men. In the absence of contradictory data, lesbians should be screened for *C. trachomatis* according to current screening guidelines—annually up to age 25 or older, depending on risk.

Gonorrhea

There are no documented cases of gonorrhea transmission between women. Given the relatively low prevalence of this STI in many clinical settings, routine screening of asymptomatic lesbians who are sexually active only with women and do not have the relevant clinical syndromes is not indicated.

Bacterial Vaginosis

Health care providers should consider other STIs—if, for example, a woman complains of abnormal vaginal discharge or genital ulcers. Bacterial vaginosis (BV), a highly prevalent infection among lesbians, has been the most common diagnosis in lesbians evaluated at STI clinics. In 2007, researchers reported BV prevalence among women in the National Health and Nutrition Survey, which uses a complex, stratified, multistage probability sample design with unequal probabilities of selection to obtain a nationally representative sample of the U.S. civilian, noninstitutionalized population. Of more than 12,000 women who supplied a self-collected swab of vaginal secretions for Gram stain analysis by Nugent score, BV prevalence was 45.2% (95% *CI*: 35.5–57.4) among women who reported having had a female sexual partner compared with an overall prevalence of 29.2% (95% *CI*: 27.2–31.3) ($p = 0.003$).[15] Risks for BV among lesbians who participated in the Seattle study included a greater number of lifetime female sexual partners; having a female sexual partner with BV; use of a shared, vaginally inserted sex toy; and receptive oral-anal sex.[13] BV is characterized by a loss of vaginal lactobacilli, but its cause is unknown.

These data suggest that a factor that promotes or causes the condition may be transmissible between women during sex. Whether female partners of women diagnosed with BV should be routinely tested and treated is unknown. One reasonable approach is to test a woman's partner for BV if she is symptomatic or if BV in the index case is recurrent, as treatment of the partner might theoretically help to cure BV in the index case. However, this approach has not been studied.

Trichomonas vaginalis

Other etiologies of abnormal vaginal discharge include infection with *Trichomonas vaginalis,* which women who have not had prior sex with men have self-reported in surveys. The infection has also been reported as metronidazole-resistant trichomoniasis in both members of a monogamous lesbian couple.[4,14,16] These data and the plausibility of transmitting vaginal fluid through lesbian sexual practices strongly support the notion that such practices can transmit *T. vaginalis.*

Human Papillomavirus

HPV, a group of viruses that causes anogenital warts and cervical cancer, may be transmissible between women by skin-to-skin contact, digital-genital contact, and the use of sex toys. In some studies, women who said they did not have sexual contact with men reported vulvar warts, cervical neoplasia associated with HPV, and high-risk HPV DNA (i.e., associated with oncogenic risk) determined by polymerase chain reaction, a genetic probe.[5,6,17] In one study, among women who had not had prior sexual contact with men, 14% tested positive for cervical dysplasia and genetic probes detected HPV DNA in 19%.[6] In other studies, women who had not had prior sexual contact with men self-reported anogenital warts and/or abnormal Pap smears.[4,18] In studies using genetic probes to detect HPV, women who had sex with both women and men in the previous year were more than twice as likely to be infected with HPV than were women who had sex only with women in the same time period.[5,6]

The finding that HPV is present in women whose sexual contact with men is remote or nonexistent has important implications regarding Pap screening. Such women may believe they are at low risk for cervical cancer, and their health care providers may assume this is true.[19] For example, in the study that Marrazzo and colleagues did in Seattle from 1998 to 2000, 36% of 248 women who had sex with women had not gotten a Pap smear in the previous two years and 9% said they were told by a physician they did not need such screening.[5] Thus, routine screening for cervical dysplasia in these women may be neglected.[20] Women who have sex with women should undergo Pap screening for cervical dysplasia according to the same guidelines that apply to other sexually active women.

■   ■   ■

In the scenario at the beginning of this chapter, Dana expressed concern that she might transmit HPV to her partner. In fact, most people infected with genital HPV never develop genital warts or cancerous changes at the cervix. Therefore, screening for genital HPV—checking for its presence in the absence of these conditions—is not recommended unless screening takes place in conjunction with a Pap smear in two particular groups: women with certain types of abnormal Pap smears and those older than 30 who are getting routine smears. Nor is screening recommended for partners of persons diagnosed with HPV or related complications, such as genital warts, cervical cancer, or precancer.

Researchers have not studied prevention of genital HPV transmission in lesbians, but male condoms do help protect young heterosexual women. Barrier methods such as female condoms, male condoms on sex toys, or gloves might reduce a woman's risk of getting HPV from her female partner. However, Dana should keep in mind that the likelihood of her partner already being infected with genital HPV is fairly high, depending on the partner's sexual history and on what their sexual practices have been. The most important prevention message for Dana and her partner is that routine Pap smears can detect potentially cancerous changes at the cervix before they are likely to become a problem.

Human Immunodeficiency Virus

There are published case reports of sexual HIV transmission between women. One found an identical genotype of the HIV isolates from both women and a plausible clinical history.[21] Oral-genital contact, mucosa-to-mucosa genital contact, sharing of blood or menstrual fluid, and contact with genital herpes lesions could facilitate transmission. Because the CDC now recommends universal HIV screening in all primary care settings, lesbians should be tested for HIV at least once and, depending on sexual risk assessment, possibly again. Decisions to rescreen for HIV should be based on risk factors such as unprotected sex with men, particularly gay or bisexual men; the number of recent female sexual partners; and intravenous drug use.

Genital Herpes

Herpes simplex virus-2 (HSV-2) usually causes genital herpes, but occasionally herpes simplex virus-1 (HSV-1) can be transmitted by mucous membrane to mucous membrane contact or vulnerable skin. Therefore, transmission between women is theoretically possible. Genital herpes has been reported in women who have not had prior sexual contact with men.[14,18] In a study of nearly 400 women who reported sex with at least one other woman in the prior year, 2.6% of those who reported no male partners had HSV-2 antibodies. The likelihood of having such antibodies increased with the increasing lifetime number of male sexual partners. The authors concluded that HSV-2 can be transmitted between women, though less efficiently than between men and women.[7]

Thus, routine screening for HSV-2 infection using type-specific serology is not recommended for lesbians unless individual risk assessment indicates it should be performed—for example, when there is a history of unexplained genital lesions or the woman has recently had multiple sexual partners, especially men. In the Seattle study, the likelihood of participants having antibodies to HSV-1, which typically causes oral herpes, increased with the increasing number of lifetime female partners, suggesting that orogenital sex plays a role in facilitating transmission in this population.[7] However, serologic screening for HSV-1 is not indicated, as infection is widely prevalent, the test does not distinguish between established oral and genital infection, and HSV-1 genital infection is associated with minimal recurrences and subclinical shedding.

Treponema pallidum

Although *Treponema pallidum*, which causes syphilis, is relatively uncommon compared with the viral STIs discussed above, sexual transmission between female partners has been reported.[22] Because some lesbians who choose to have sex with men may be more likely to choose bisexual men as partners, health care providers should keep in mind that in the last several years, the incidence of early syphilis and fluoroquinolone-resistant *N. gonorrhoeae* has markedly increased among men who have sex with men, and should screen lesbians appropriately based on STI risk assessment.

PREGNANCY

Routine STI screening of pregnant lesbians is as important as routine screening of all pregnant women. Many lesbians use frozen sperm from sperm banks, which reduces the risk of STI if the donor was screened at the time of donation and 6 months later when the sperm sample was quarantined. In this situation, a STI would not likely occur, although it is not impossible.

Many other lesbians use fresh-sperm donors—perhaps an unknown person or friend. In these cases, appropriate screening often does not occur.

CONCLUSION

Available data strongly suggest that HPV—and probably other STIs, especially herpes simplex virus—are sexually transmitted between women. For these reasons, Pap smear recommendations, *C. trachomatis* screening, and HPV vaccination should not differ for lesbians. Bacterial vaginosis may eventually be defined as a STI between women, but the exact etiology of the condition remains unknown. Nevertheless, BV is very common in lesbians and should be a main consideration for health care providers when they evaluate those who complain of abnormal (increased or malodorous) vaginal discharge.

STI screens should be individualized for lesbians, as lesbian self-identification may include high-risk sexual practices with women as well as current or recent past sexual activity with men. Taking a sexual history and inquiring about specific, risky sexual behaviors can provide more complete information for the purpose of assessing patients, counseling them, and helping lesbians maintain excellent sexual health.

REFERENCES

1. Centers for Disease Control and Prevention. (2008, March). Prevalence of STD among U.S. adolescents. Presentation at the National STD Prevention Conference, Chicago.

2. Wald, A. (2004). Synergistic interactions between herpes simplex virus type-2 and human immunodeficiency virus epidemics. *Herpes, 11,* 70–76.

3. Mosher, W. D., Chandra, A., & Jones, J. (2005). Sexual behavior and selected health measures: Men and women 15–44 years of age, United States, 2002. *Advance Data, Sep 15,* 1–55.

4. Bauer, G. R., & Welles, S. L. (2001). Beyond assumptions of negligible risk: Sexually transmitted diseases and women who have sex with women. *American Journal of Public Health, 91,* 1282–1286.

5. Marrazzo, J. M., Koutsky, L. A., Kiviat, N. B., Kuypers, J. M., & Stine, K. (2001). Papanicolaou test screening and prevalence of genital human papillomavirus among women who have sex with women. *American Journal of Public Health, 91,* 947–952.

6. Marrazzo, J. M., Koutsky, L. A., Stine, K. L., Kuypers, J. M., Grubert, T. A., Galloway, D. A., et al. (1998). Genital human papillomavirus infection in women who have sex with women. *Journal of Infectious Diseases, 178,* 1604–1609.

7. Marrazzo, J. M., Stine, K., & Wald, A. (2003). Prevalence and risk factors for infection with herpes simplex virus type-1 and -2 among lesbians. *Sexually Transmitted Diseases, 30,* 890–895.

8. Evans, B. A., Kell, P. D., Bond, R. A., & MacRae, K. D. (1998). Racial origin, sexual lifestyle, and genital infection among women attending a genitourinary medicine clinic in London (1992). *Sexually Transmitted Infections, 74,* 45–49.

9. Skinner, C. J., Stokes, J., Kirlew, Y., Kavanagh, J., & Forster, G. E. (1996). A case-controlled study of the sexual health needs of lesbians. *Genitourinary Medicine, 72,* 277–280.

10. Scheer, S., Peterson, I., Page-Shafer, K., Delgado, V., Gleghorn, A., Ruiz, J., et al. (2002). Sexual and drug use behavior among women who have sex with both women and men: Results of a population-based survey. *American Journal of Public Health, 92,* 1110–1112.

11. Marrazzo, J. M., Koutsky, L. A., & Handsfield, H. H. (2001). Characteristics of female sexually transmitted disease clinic clients who report same-sex behaviour. *International Journal of STD & AIDS, 12,* 41–46.

12. Fethers, K., Marks, C., Mindel, A., & Estcourt, C. S. (2000). Sexually transmitted infections and risk behaviours in women who have sex with women. *Sexually Transmitted Infections, 76,* 345–349.

13. Marrazzo, J., Koutsky, L. A., Eschenbach, D. A., Agnew, K., Stine, K., & Hillier, S. L. (2002). Characterization of vaginal flora and bacterial vaginosis in women who have sex with women. *Journal of Infectious Diseases, 185,* 1307–1313.

14. Singh, D., Fine, D., & Marrazzo, J. M. (n.d.). *Chlamydia trachomatis infection among women reporting same sex behavior screened in family planning clinics in the Pacific Northwest, 1997–2005.* Manuscript submitted for publication.

15. Koumans, E. H., Sternberg, M., Bruce, C., McQuillan, G., Kendrick, J., Sutton, M., et al. (2007). The prevalence of bacterial vaginosis in the United States, 2001–2004; associations with symptoms, sexual behaviors, and reproductive health. *Sexually Transmitted Diseases, 34,* 864–869.

16. Kellock, D., & O'Mahony, C. P. (1996). Sexually acquired metronidazole-resistant trichomoniasis in a lesbian couple. *Genitourinary Medicine, 72,* 60–61.

17. Edwards, A., & Thin, R. N. (1990). Sexually transmitted diseases in lesbians. *International Journal of STD & AIDS, 1,* 178–181.

18. Carroll, N., Goldstein, R. S., Lo, W., & Mayer, K. H. (1997). Gynecological infections and sexual practices of Massachusetts lesbian and bisexual women. *Journal of the Gay and Lesbian Medical Association, 1,* 15–23.

19. Marrazzo, J. M., Stine, K., & Koutsky, L. A. (2000). Genital human papillomavirus infection in women who have sex with women: A review. *American Journal of Obstetrics & Gynecology, 183,* 770–774.

20. Ferris, D. G., Batish, S., Wright, T. C., & Cushing, C. (1996). A neglected lesbian health concern: Cervical neoplasia. *Journal of Family Practice, 43,* 581–584.

21. Kwakwa, H. A., & Ghobrial, M. W. (2003). Female-to-female transmission of human immunodeficiency virus. *Clinical Infectious Diseases, 36,* e40–e41.

22. Campos-Outcalt, D., & Hurwitz, S. (2002). Female-to-female transmission of syphilis: A case report. *Sexually Transmitted Diseases, 29,* 119–120.

ABOUT THE AUTHOR

JEANNE M. MARRAZZO, MD, MPH is Associate Professor in the Division of Infectious Diseases at the University of Washington, Seattle as well as Medical Director of the Seattle STD/HIV Prevention and Training Center. Her research interests include the molecular epidemiology, pathogenesis, and management of bacterial vaginosis; diagnosis and screening of chlamydial infection; and the epidemiology and management of cervicitis.

CHAPTER 4

"Will the Real Lesbian Couple Please Stand Up?"

LESBIAN RELATIONSHIPS

ESTHER D. ROTHBLUM, PhD

SAMANTHA *and Josie met at a women's college, fell in love, and moved to Northampton, Massachusetts, to become part of a vibrant lesbian community. Samantha is a counselor in a lesbian therapy collective; Josie works for the local women's bookstore. Their social life consists of gatherings with lesbian friends, and Samantha plays on the local lesbian softball team. They are "out" to everyone. Indeed, they would have difficulty hiding their lesbianism, given their jobs, their matching tattoos with interlocking women's symbols, and the extensive amount of women's erotic art in their home.*

ELEANOR *is single and lives alone. Her best friend is Bianca, who has been married to Ed for 31 years and has three children. The two women spend part of every day together and travel together several times a year. What Eleanor and Bianca have never told anyone else is that they have had a sexual relationship for several decades.*

DOROTHY *and Susan met Diana at a gay bar and were both sexually attracted to her. They got to know Diana and soon Diana was staying over at their house on weekends. They asked Diana to move in with them and all three agreed to be monogamous—that is, to have sex just as a threesome and not with anyone outside the relationship. There was only one problem: Diana had just accepted a job 2,000 miles away. So Dorothy and Susan found jobs in the same city and all three moved so they could continue living together.*

TANYA *has multiple sclerosis and uses a wheelchair. She employs a former high school classmate, Starr, as her helper/companion. Starr accompanies Tanya to church, college classes, and medical appointments. Tanya's family is delighted that she has found such a friendly and competent assistant, especially given that her health is failing. Several years later, Tanya dies due to complications of multiple sclerosis. Only then does Starr confide in a few friends that the two of them were lovers.*

LATOYA, *a young lesbian, moved to San Francisco and became attracted to Violet, her heterosexual roommate. Violet seemed to encourage the relationship in multiple ways, such as having heart-shaped tattoos made that included each other's name and telling Latoya it was OK that people mistook*

them for lovers. Latoya suggested they become lovers, but Violet declined.
Latoya was devastated.

YI SUN *and Marianne have been in a 10-year lesbian relationship. Recently,*
however, Marianne has wanted to be known as Mark, asks people to use the
pronoun "he" when referring to her, and has begun taking testosterone. Mark's
appearance has changed markedly; people assume that Mark is a man. Others
now view Yi Sun as a heterosexual woman involved with a man.

AMY *and Debra met in high school and became sexually involved. Amy*
immediately identified herself as a lesbian. Debra, meanwhile, continued to see
herself as a heterosexual girl who happened to find Amy sexually attractive.
This led to some arguments. Amy did not consider Debra to be a "real" lesbian
and worried that Debra would leave her for a man. The couple stayed involved
for 17 years. Then, ironically, Amy left Debra for a man and now identifies
herself as bisexual/queer.

■   ■   ■

As these scenarios illustrate, there are many ways to be a lesbian and multiple kinds of lesbian relationships. For readers who know little about lesbians, the Samantha and Josie scenario might best fit their perception of such relationships. They may picture lesbians as women who have a masculine appearance (short hair, deep voices, male clothing), live in "gay ghettos" like Northampton or San Francisco, participate in lesbian organizations or gay pride marches, and are open about their sexual orientation. Yet components of relationships, such as sexual orientation, gender identity, sexual behavior, level of outness, and participation in lesbian organizations and events, do not always correspond. Many people would define a lesbian as a woman who has sex with women, but who qualifies as a lesbian, who qualifies as a woman, and what qualifies as sex are multifaceted and complex issues.

This chapter explores a variety of factors in lesbian relationships.

WHO IS A LESBIAN?

When researchers recruit lesbian participants for studies via announcements on lesbian Internet sites, fliers distributed at gay pride marches, or questionnaires mailed to subscribers of lesbian magazines, they may overlook the fact that such women are multidimensional. Using a lesbian wellness survey, Morris and Rothblum examined the degree to which 2,393 women, a quarter of them women of color, were distributed in five dimensions of lesbian sexuality and the coming-out process: sexual orientation (whether they identified as lesbian, bisexual, or something else), how many years they had been out, level of disclosure of sexual orientation to others, proportion of sexual relationships with women versus men, and extent of participation in lesbian community events. These dimensions did not overlap much, which suggests that being lesbian is not a homogeneous experience. A closer look at demographic factors such as race/ethnicity and age revealed a diversity of experiences. African American, Native American, and Latina respondents showed moderate correlations among the dimensions of lesbian experience, while the correlations for European American and Asian American respondents tended to be weak or insignificant.[1] These results indicate that if researchers are recruiting subjects via one dimension, such as participation in gay pride marches, they should not assume that the subjects necessarily fit into one or more other dimensions—that, for example, they are having sex only with other women. Rust found that a significant subgroup of women in a lesbian bar who self-identified as lesbian were having sex with men.[2]

The dynamics are particularly complex when two women have a same-sex relationship. How do the five dimensions affect the way they meet? What attracts them to each other? What makes them decide to enter into a relationship? Do women who have only had same-sex relationships seek partners with similar experiences or women who have been heterosexually married? Do bisexuals partner with other bisexuals? What if, as in Amy's case, one partner self-identifies as lesbian and the other does not? Do the five dimensions change over time, perhaps causing conflict within couples? How do similarities and differences between partners affect satisfaction in a relationship? Such questions highlight the need for research, which could reveal potentially complex and interesting interactions.

WHAT IS A RELATIONSHIP?

There are very few countries and only six states—Connecticut, Iowa, Maine, Massachusetts, New Hampshire, and Vermont—where women can legally marry each other. Consequently, lesbians are legally single in most of the world. More than 25 years ago, Gartrell described the unique situation of partnered lesbians being considered socially single, at least when they are not out. Family members, coworkers, and the general public often view lesbians, unlike their heterosexual married siblings, as being single even when they are in coupled relationships.[3]

The relatively recent media focus on lesbians and gay men influences the way health professionals view lesbian issues in the clinical setting. Certain cues, such as two women who want to rear a child together or the woman who wears a T-shirt advertising the local gay bar, may lead a practitioner to presume that the patient is lesbian. However, a practitioner may not be aware that Eleanor, the single woman involved with her married friend Bianca, or Tanya, the woman involved with her paid companion, are lesbians.

What about lesbians who are not in coupled relationships? "Single" is a poor description of them, given that many belong to a community of women. Because women in general are socialized to be relational, lesbians may have a large network of friends and acquaintances. The "women's community" in Alison Bechdel's cartoon strip "Dykes to Watch Out For" and the television drama "The L Word" depict an interlocking neighborhood of lesbian lovers, ex-lovers, friends, softball partners, women's bookstore staff, and sisters in political activism, among other types of relationships. In this Internet age, lesbian communities cross state and national borders (see Sablove and Rothblum[4] for a review); they are no longer limited to physical space.

Research has shown that lesbians:

- Come out to their parents later, if at all, than they do to their friends[5];
- Perceive that they receive more social support from friends than their family of origin, the opposite perception of heterosexual women[6,7];
- Live farther away from their parents than their heterosexual sisters do[8]; and
- Have less contact with their family of origin than heterosexual women do.[7]

For all of these reasons, lesbians gravitate toward a "family of friends" that replaces family of origin in importance, especially if they are European American. In contrast, lesbians of color often do stay close to their family of origin.[9] Surrounded by a community of lesbian friends and acquaintances, lesbians are hardly "single" in the sense of being isolated or alone. In fact, lesbians may find it easier than heterosexual women do to find community, whether they are moving to San Francisco or Jackson, Mississippi. Many lesbians check out lesbian activities on the Internet before they relocate, finding everything from the lesbian realtor to the weekly calendar of lesbian events at their destination.

CHARACTERISTICS OF LESBIAN COUPLES

How many lesbians are in partnered relationships? Convenience samples yield a wide range of percentages. Bell and Weinberg found that 72% of white lesbians and 70% of black lesbians were in partnered relationships,[10] but other studies have reported figures closer to 40%. (See Peplau and colleagues[11] for a review.) According to the U.S. Census in 2000, which for the first time asked people about adults living with a same-sex partner, around 25% to 30% of lesbians live with such a partner.[12] These data do not include lesbians in partnered relationships who do not live with their partner or lesbians who do not want the federal government to know about their sexual orientation.

Researchers prefer national probability data such as those generated by the U.S. Census, but lesbians are more likely to self-disclose relationship status when they know the researchers or the researchers also are lesbian. Few of the women in the scenarios at the beginning of this chapter would fit well into the U.S. Census category of two women living together and partnered.

Relationship Satisfaction

Are lesbian couples just like heterosexual couples except for common gender? Not really. Research has focused on a number of factors as predictors of happiness over time. (For specific citations, see Rothblum.[13]) A large body of research on married heterosexual couples indicates that demographic similarity, or "assortative mating," is a predictor of relationship satisfaction. Laumann and colleagues describe how assortative mating among heterosexuals is the norm because heterosexual couples meet in schools, colleges, neighborhoods, and the military, which are often stratified by age, social class, race, ethnicity, religion, or other factors. They speculate that lesbians, gay men, and bisexuals (LGBs) meet partners in settings, such as gay bars and LGB pride marches, that are less demographically stratified.[14] Rosenfeld and Kim argue that interracial couples and same-sex couples are more geographically mobile, which frees them from parental control, and more likely to live in urban settings, which increases the likelihood they will meet others similar to them.[15]

Peplau and colleagues found that African American lesbians were generally similar to their partners in age, educational level, and employment status. Thirty percent were in inter-racial relationships. This contrasts sharply with data on heterosexuals: only 2.1% of African American women and 4.6% of African American men marry spouses of a different race.[16] Compared with heterosexual couples, same-sex couples are more likely to be interracial.[15]

In another study, relationship satisfaction in lesbian couples was not significantly related to partners being similar in terms of age, the number of previous lesbian relationships, education, and/or the degree of religiousness.[17] Todosijevic and colleagues, in examining partner similarity in 199 lesbian couples in Vermont who had civil unions, found that couple similarity in terms of age, income, and education was unrelated to relationship satisfaction.[18]

Level of Outness

Given these mixed results, it is possible that a lesbian couple's similarity in terms of the extent to which each has disclosed her sexual orientation to others may be more important than demographic likeness for relationship satisfaction. Couples who are discrepant on outness may have conflict regarding issues such as where to live (in an obviously gay neighborhood vs. another neighborhood, for example), whether to bring a partner to work-related social events, and how to introduce a partner to family members.

Jordan and Deluty investigated the correlation between outness and relationship satisfaction among 305 lesbians who were in committed relationships. Their results indicated that the degree of openness about sexual orientation was positively correlated with satisfaction and that discrepant outness between partners was negatively correlated with it.[19] Caron and Ulin surveyed 124 lesbians in coupled relationships via convenience sampling in Maine. There was a significant correlation between self and partner's degree of outness: if one of them was out to others, her partner was more likely to be out as well.[20]

In contrast, using data from 784 lesbian couples whom researchers surveyed in 1979 for the American Couples Study,[21] Beals and Peplau found that discrepant outness was not predictive of relationship satisfaction.[22] Todosijevic and colleagues assessed similarity in the level of outness among 199 lesbian couples who had civil unions in Vermont. There was no significant correlation between outness level and relationship satisfaction.[18]

Frequency of Sex

Gay men have sex more frequently, and lesbians less frequently, than heterosexual married couples.[11,21] Solomon and colleagues found that lesbian couples had sex less frequently than did married heterosexual women.[7] Couples consisting of two women lack someone socialized to be the sexual initiator[11,21,23] and a significant amount of testosterone, the hormone that stimulates sexual desire. Lesbian couples, being female, may spend more time on romance than they do on having genital sex, but in Western societies researchers think of "real" sex as genital activity.[23,24] This is a domain where an absence of traditional roles may reduce relationship satisfaction among lesbians.

Housework and Finances

As Green and colleagues pointed out, the general public often believes that lesbians and gay men play male and female roles in relationships. They stated: "Yet this same public remains largely unconscious…about its own problematic conformity to the socially constructed 'butch/femme' roles in heterosexual relationships"[25] (p. 219).

Kurdek studied the allocation of household tasks in lesbian, gay male, and heterosexual married couples. Lesbian couples tended to share tasks, but married heterosexual women did most of them.[26] Another study examined the division of household tasks and finances among same-sex couples in Vermont who were in civil unions, their coupled same-sex friends who were not in civil unions, and married heterosexual siblings and spouses. Compared with lesbian couples (whether or not they were in civil unions), married heterosexuals had a more traditional, gendered division of household tasks and finances; women did the housework and men paid for more items.[7]

Money and housework are not unrelated concepts. Blumstein and Schwartz noted the relationship between money and power: people who earn a higher income (men) do less housework than those who earn a lower income (women).[21] In this regard, lesbian couples provide a model for ways to equalize the division of housework.

RELATIONSHIPS AND THE LAW

Same-sex marriage is not a new concept. As far back as the fourth century, marriage-related words were used in India to describe sexual relationships between two women or two men.[27]

Lewin interviewed couples about their same-sex commitment ceremonies, which range from traditional weddings to new rituals that reflect lesbian identity and culture. Long before same-sex marriage legislation or similar legislation was enacted anywhere in the world, same-sex couples were creating rituals and ceremonies to celebrate their relationships. These partly reflected traditional weddings and partly consisted of novel, counterculture, and creative aspects that mirrored LGB communities. Couples debated whether to include their families of origin and how to combine or exclude various religious traditions.[28,29] Lewin concluded:

> In short, our ceremony turned out to have the classic attributes—socially standardized, dramatic action wrapped in a web of symbolism that links the present, past, and future, and that generates powerful emotional reactions among participants—that have long made ritual a key area of concern for anthropologists[28] (p. xix).

Same-sex marriage has suddenly become a focus of the mainstream media. A Google search using those keywords generates more than 3 million links. More than

60 books have been published in the United States, mostly since 2000, that focus affirmatively on same-sex marriage. Nations in Europe, Africa, Asia, and the Americas are debating legal rights for same-sex couples. (See Wintemute and Andenaes[30] for an international review.)

There are few places in the world where same-sex couples can legalize their relationship. In 1989, Denmark became the first nation to legalize gay and lesbian registered partnerships.*[31] Only Belgium, Canada, the Netherlands, Norway, South Africa, Spain, and Sweden have legalized marriage for same-sex couples at the federal level. A number of countries recognize registered, same-sex cohabitants or civil unions. (See Wintemute and Anderaes[30] for a review and www.ilga.org.) Other countries, including the United States, have legalized same-sex relationships in some cities or counties, but not nationwide. As mentioned earlier, only six states permit same-sex marriage. New Jersey allows civil unions, and California, Colorado, the District of Columbia, Hawaii, Nevada, Oregon, Washington, and Wisconsin allow domestic partnerships. Some states, such as New York, recognize same-sex marriages legally performed outside their jurisdiction, even though the state itself does not permit them.

The list of countries and regions where same-sex relationships are legal can be misleading. For example, same-sex couples in Belgium may legally marry, but such relationships do not include legal coparenting status. Although Denmark has had registered partnerships for 20 years, partners could not adopt each other's children until 1999.[32] In contrast, a number of American states and the District of Columbia permit two legal mothers or fathers of a child.[33]

In the United States, only states legalize relationships. Thus, in contrast to Europe and Canada, legal same-sex relationships are primarily symbolic. Most benefits of marriage, such as inheritance, pensions, Social Security, sponsorship of an immigrant partner, and joint income tax returns are at the federal level.[34] A majority of states have introduced legislation prohibiting recognition of same-sex marriages from other states. Even though the U.S. Constitution stipulates that states must recognize each other's laws, including those regarding marriage, under the Defense of Marriage Act of 1996 no state is required to honor same-sex, out-of-state marriages. Furthermore, opponents of same-sex marriage are advocating a constitutional amendment that would ban such marriage nationally.

The media focus on same-sex marriage might lead to the conclusion that all same-sex couples would marry given the chance. This topic is somewhat controversial in LGB communities. (See Rothblum[35] for a review.) Yep and colleagues presented a model of two different sexual ideologies in the United States. The assimilationist

---

* *"Registered partnerships" is one of many different terms that nations and states use to describe legal same-sex relationships.*

ideology argues that all people have a right to marry and that marriage results in stable relationships. The radical ideology asserts that marriage of any type is an oppressive institution and that same-sex relationships should be unique and freely chosen, not mimic heterosexual norms.[36] Books such as *That's Revolting! Queer Strategies for Resisting Assimilation,*[37] *I Do, I Don't: Queers on Marriage,*[38] and *Same-Sex Marriage Pro and Con: A Reader*[39] argue that marriage and other mainstream issues have drained LGBT communities of power and cultural identity. As Canadian gay magazine editor Mitchel Raphael said of gay marriage in that country:

> I'd be for marriage if I thought gay people would challenge and change the institution and not buy into the traditional meaning of 'till death do us part' and monogamy forever. We should be Oscar Wildes and not like everyone else watching the play[40] (pp. 1, 6).

Lesbians did not grow up in societies where same-sex marriage was a possibility. Now that some couples can legally marry or partner, conflict may arise in a relationship when one partner wants legal sanction and the other does not. There has been very little research anywhere on same-sex couples in legalized relationships, including comparisons between same-sex couples who do or do not choose legalization.

LESBIANS PREVIOUSLY IN HETEROSEXUAL MARRIAGES

The general heterosexual public may not know much about lesbian couples, but lesbians know a great deal about heterosexual marriage. Fairy tales end with couples getting married and living "happily ever after." Most official documents ask about marital status. There are other constant reminders about the importance of marriage, and popular songs, television shows, magazines, books, and advertisements focus on marital themes.

Moreover, many lesbians have been heterosexually married. A survey by Bell and Weinberg in the 1970s found that 47% of African American lesbians and 35% of European American lesbians had been married.[10] In a study of same-sex registered partnerships in Norway and Sweden, one-quarter of both lesbians and heterosexual women had been heterosexually married.[41]

Wyers interviewed 74 lesbians and gay men who were separated or divorced from heterosexual spouses. The lesbians' former marriages lasted 8.6 years on average, compared with 11 years for the gay men. Additionally, gay men were about twice as likely as lesbians to rate their former marriage as satisfying. Only 26.5% of female participants were aware of their lesbianism when they got married, compared with 68.8% of men who were aware of their gayness. Few participants had disclosed their sexual orientation to their former spouse before marriage. Among the gay men, 81%

indicated that the coming-out process during marriage was difficult, compared with 53% of the lesbians.[42]

HETEROSEXUALLY MARRIED LESBIANS

Very little is known about the differences between self-identified lesbians and women in heterosexual marriages who covertly have sexual relationships with women. In many cases, the spouse, children, and/or society are unaware of the same-sex relationship. Two books on this phenomenon are *And Then I Met This Woman: Previously Married Women's Journeys Into Lesbian Relationships*[43] and *Married Women Who Love Women.*[44] However, systematic research on such relationships is lacking.

Closeted couples surely differ from out lesbian couples in myriad ways, but finding samples for research would be challenging. For example, Wyers set out to study lesbian and gay male parents who were heterosexually married, separated, or divorced. Before the study began, it was widely publicized in the area around Portland, Oregon, yet only 2 of the 74 people who agreed to participate were married.[42] Nevertheless, women who are heterosexually married but also partnered with other women may be a very large subgroup.

OLDER LESBIANS

Most research on lesbians has focused on young women in their twenties and thirties, although studies conducted 30 years ago involved lesbians now entering midlife. Women who were attracted to women before the modern LGB rights movement, which dates to the Stonewall Riots of 1969, lived through different historical and political times than did lesbians who are coming out today. Back then, gay bars were regularly raided, homosexuality was listed as a mental illness until 1973, and lesbian mothers lost 80% of all custody battles in lower courts. (See Rothblum[45] for a review.)

In the 1940s and '50s, many lesbians in relationships played butch and femme gender roles that paralleled those of their heterosexual counterparts. Faderman noted:

> Perhaps the tyranny of "appropriate" butch and femme dress in working-class bars can be explained in part by patrons' fears: A Columbus, Ohio, woman recalls walking into a lesbian bar in the 1950s and finding that no one would speak to her. After some hours the waitress told her it was because of the way she was dressed—no one could tell what her sexual identity was, butch or femme, and they were afraid that if she did not know enough to dress right it was because she was a policewoman[46] (pp. 164–165).

Middle-class and wealthy lesbians tended to avoid butch and femme appearance and were more likely to pass as heterosexual. Consequently, poor and working-class lesbians were the ones who communicated through their appearance to the dominant culture that lesbians existed, who were portrayed in the media, and who paid for such exposure by frequent arrests and police raids of bars.

CHANGES IN SAME-SEX RELATIONSHIPS OVER TIME

Are lesbian relationships today similar to those 30 years ago? The late 1970s marked the beginning of research on same-sex couples, most notably by Peplau and colleagues[47] and by Blumstein and Schwartz.[21] This was the height of the second wave of the feminist movement, when feminism played a role in lesbians' lives. In the 1960s, many lesbians identified with feminism and began to look down on butch/femme roles.[48] Peplau and colleagues asked lesbians to rate the importance of various statements about romantic/sexual relationships; about half of the sample belonged to feminist organizations. Feminism was positively associated with personal autonomy (having an independent and equal relationship) and negatively associated with dyadic attachment (having a close, monogamous, and permanent relationship that included shared activities).[47] Feminism is probably less important to younger lesbians today.

YOUNGER LESBIANS TODAY

Diamond[49] and Savin-Williams[50] conducted longitudinal research on sexual minority youth. Although their studies did not focus on couples, they showed that concepts of sexual orientation have changed dramatically in the last decade. Sexual orientation and self-identity are more fluid and flexible, more resistant to easy categorization, and may be independent of sexual behavior. Over a 10-year period, Diamond followed 80 nonheterosexual women who initially were 18 to 25 years old. Within the first 5 years of follow-up interviews, one-quarter of the women relinquished their identity as lesbian or bisexual, half identified as heterosexual, and half gave up all labels.[49] Amy and Debra in one of the scenarios at the beginning of this chapter are quite typical of young lesbians and self-identity today. As this youthful cohort enters long-term, partnered, same-sex relationships, they may appear to be markedly different from older generations. Much of the previously cited research may not apply to them as they enter adulthood.

Young lesbians are also more likely than older lesbians to have more fluid concepts of gender identity. For example, they may reclaim butch and femme roles. However, unlike lesbians in the 1940s and '50s who were expected to maintain rigid gender roles, young lesbians today may "play" with gender roles—that is, be butch one day and femme the next. Butches no longer need to find femme partners. In "gender blending," clothing may combine stereotypically masculine and feminine aspects.

In addition, the LGB and transgender movements have intersected, such that people's sense of themselves as male or female is also more fluid and flexible. Women who once may have identified as butch lesbians may now view themselves as transgendered. Women who do not think they fit into traditional norms may use a large array of words to describe their personal gender: gender blender, transman, FTM (female-to-male), sex radical, two-spirit, and omnigendered, to name just a few.[51] Regarding the Marianne scenario, many young LGBTs today would readily accept her decision to be known as Mark.

LESBIAN POLYAMORY

In the 1960s, lesbian circles frowned upon monogamy, as did many heterosexuals during the sexual revolution. Lesbian feminists criticized marriage and romantic love as oppressive to women. The slogan "Freedom to Marry," which is also the name of a coalition currently promoting same-sex marriage, would have seemed like an oxymoron. In "Denny's Tune," lesbian musician Alix Dobkin sang: "I'm not monogamous anymore/But Denny you're so adorable/A one-woman woman I'm not but.../It's not what I expected, I stand/Politically corrected"[52] (p. 186).

As lesbians have become more accepted by mainstream society, they have adopted some mainstream conventions, including long-term monogamous relationships and relationship commitment ceremonies. In addition, the term "polyamory," which means "many loves,"[53] has replaced "nonmonogamy" to describe lesbian relationships with more than two lovers. In the Dorothy, Susan, and Diana scenario, all are monogamous in the sense that they agreed not to have lovers outside their threesome. Books such as *The Lesbian Polyamory Reader*[53] and *Lesbian Polyfidelity*[54] describe some of the issues that arise when lesbians do not fit the traditional couple model. In a world in which people are expected to have only one lover, polyamorous lovers struggle to negotiate living spaces, office parties, hotel rooms, family reunions, and the many other circumstances that are not arranged to accommodate them.

CONCLUSION

Same-sex relationships among lesbians take many forms. Depending on a woman's age and geographic location, she may keep her same-sex attractions and behavior a secret to everyone. One might suspect that an unmarried aunt was involved with her best friend or that the two older women who live together down the street and claim to be sisters are not actually related. And several of the scenarios described at the outset of this chapter may change over time. If Eleanor and Bianca break up, Eleanor may become more active in the lesbian community; meanwhile, Bianca may suffer in silence because there are few if any resources for married women who break up with female lovers. Dorothy, Susan, and Diana may struggle to be accepted in a world that frowns on threesomes. Yi Sun and Mark may attempt to get married heterosexually if Mark can prove that he is now male. On the other hand, most of the women described in these scenarios might live happily ever after with their current partners.

A great deal has changed in lesbian communities in the last 40 years. Issues such as lesbians losing jobs and custody of children have given way to media debates about same-sex marriage and increasing acceptance of LGBs in many institutions. Women now question their identities and roles in society. Much of the material in this chapter may be dated in a few years as women create new words and ideas to describe lesbianism, relationships, and community. In any case, perhaps lesbians will never become so assimilated into mainstream society that they lose their unique ways of relating to each other.

REFERENCES

1. Morris, J. F., & Rothblum, E. D. (1999). Who fills out a "lesbian" questionnaire? The interrelationship of sexual orientation, years out, disclosure of sexual orientation, sexual experience with women, and participation in the lesbian community. *Psychology of Women Quarterly, 33,* 537–557.

2. Rust, P. (1995). *Bisexuality and the challenge to lesbian politics: Sex, loyalty, and revolution.* New York: New York University Press.

3. Gartrell, N. (1981). The lesbian as a "single" woman. *American Journal of Psychotherapy, 35,* 502–516.

4. Sablove, P., & Rothblum, E. D. (2005). *Lesbian communities.* New York: Harrington Park Press.

5. Morris, J. F., Waldo, C., & Rothblum, E. D. (2001). A model of predictors and outcomes of outness among lesbian and bisexual women. *American Journal of Orthopsychiatry, 71,* 61–71.

6. Kurdek, L. A., & Schmitt, J. P. (1987). Perceived emotional support from family and friends in members of homosexual, married, and heterosexual cohabiting couples. *Journal of Homosexuality, 14,* 57–68.

7. Solomon, S. E., Rothblum, E. D., & Balsam, K. F. (2004). Pioneers in partnership: Lesbian and gay male couples in civil unions compared with those not in civil unions, and heterosexual married siblings. *Journal of Family Psychology, 18,* 275–286.

8. Rothblum, E. D., & Factor, R. J. (2001). Lesbians and their sisters as a control group: Demographic and mental health factors. *Psychological Science, 12,* 63–69.

9. Greene, B. (1994). Lesbian women of color: Triple jeopardy. In L. Comas-Diaz & B. Greene (Eds.), *Women of color: Integrating ethnic and gender identities in psychotherapy* (pp. 389–427). New York: Guilford Press.

10. Bell, A. P., & Weinberg, M. S. (1978). *Homosexualities: A study of diversities among men and women.* New York: Simon & Schuster.

11. Peplau, L. A., Fingerhut, A., & Beals, K. P. (2004). Sexuality in the relationships of lesbians and gay men. In J. Harvey, A. Wenzel, & S. Sprecher (Eds.), *Handbook of sexuality in close relationships* (pp. 349–369). Mahwah, NJ: Erlbaum.

12. Gates, G. J., & Ost, J. (2004). *The gay & lesbian atlas.* Washington, DC: Urban Institute Press.

13. Rothblum, E. D. (2008). An overview of same-sex couples in relationships: A research area still at sea. In D. A. Hope (Ed.), *Contemporary perspectives on lesbian, gay and bisexual identities* (Vol. 54, pp. 113–140). New York: Springer.

14. Laumann, E. O, Gagnon, J. H, Michael, R. T, & Michaels, S. (1994). *The social organization of sexuality: Sexual practices in the United States.* Chicago: University of Chicago Press.

15. Rosenfeld, M. J., & Kim, B. (2005). The independence of young adults and the rise of interracial and same-sex unions. *American Sociological Review, 70,* 541–562.

16. Peplau, L. A., Cochran, S. D., & Mays, V. M. (1997). A national survey of the intimate relationships of African American lesbians and gay men: A look at commitment, satisfaction, sexual behavior, and HIV disease. In B. Greene & G. Herek (Eds.), *Psychological perspectives on lesbian and gay issues: Ethnic and cultural diversity among lesbians and gay men* (pp. 11–38). Newbury Park, CA: Sage Publications.

17. Peplau, L., Padesky, C., & Hamilton, M. (1982). Satisfaction in lesbian relationships. *Journal of Homosexuality, 8,* 23–35.

18. Todosijevic, J., Rothblum, E. D., & Solomon, S. E. (2005). Relationship satisfaction, affectivity, and gay-specific stressors in same-sex couples joined in civil unions. *Psychology of Women Quarterly, 29,* 158–166.

19. Jordan, K. M., & Deluty, R. H. (2000). Social support, coming out, and relationship satisfaction in lesbian couples. *Journal of Lesbian Studies, 4,* 145–164.

20. Caron, S. L., & Ulin, B. M. (1997). Closeting and the quality of lesbian relationships. *Families in Society: The Journal of Contemporary Human Services, 78,* 413–419.

21. Blumstein, P., & Schwartz, P. (1983). *American couples: Money, work, sex.* New York: William Morrow.

22. Beals, K., & Peplau, L. A. (2001). Social involvement, disclosure of sexual orientation, and the quality of lesbian relationships. *Psychology of Women Quarterly, 25,* 10–19.

23. Rothblum, E. D., & Brehony, K. A. (1993). *Boston marriages: Romantic but asexual relationships among contemporary lesbians.* Amherst, MA: University of Massachusetts Press.

24. McCormick, N. B. (1994). *Sexual salvation: Affirming women's sexual rights and pleasures.* Westport, CT: Praeger.

25. Green, R. J., Bettinger, M., & Zacks, E. (1996). Are lesbian couples fused and gay male couples disengaged? Questioning gender straightjackets. In J. Laird & R. J. Green (Eds.),

Lesbians and gays in couples and families: A handbook for therapists (pp. 185–230). New York: Jossey-Bass.

26. Kurdek, L. (1993). The allocation of household labor in gay, lesbian, and heterosexual married couples. *Journal of Social Issues, 49,* 127–130.

27. Vanita, R. (2005). *Love's rite: Same-sex marriage in India and the West.* New York: Palgrave-Macmillan.

28. Lewin, E. (1998). *Recognizing ourselves: Ceremonies of lesbian and gay commitment.* New York: Columbia University Press.

29. Lewin, E. (2001). Weddings without marriage: Making sense of lesbian and gay commitment rituals. In M. Bernstein & R. Reimann (Eds.), *Queer families, queer politics: Challenging culture and the state* (pp. 44–52). New York: Columbia University Press.

30. Wintemute, R., & Andenaes, M. (2001). *Legal recognition of same-sex partnerships: A study of national, European and international law.* Oxford: Hart Publishing.

31. Soland, B. (1998). A queer nation? The passage of the gay and lesbian partnership legislation in Denmark, 1989. *Social Politics, 5,* 48–69.

32. Lund-Andersen, I. (2001). The Danish Registered Partnership Act, 1989: Has the act meant a change in attitudes? In R. Wintemute & M. Andenaes (Eds.), *Legal recognition of same-sex partnerships: A study of national, European and international law* (pp. 417–426). Oxford: Hart Publishing.

33. Eskridge, W. N. (2001). *Equality practice: Civil unions and the future of gay rights.* New York: Routledge.

34. Cahill, S., Ellen, M., & Tobias, S. (2002). *Family policy: Issues affecting gay, lesbian, bisexual and transgender families.* National Gay and Lesbian Task Force Policy Institute.

35. Rothblum, E. D. (2004). Same-sex marriage and legalized relationships: I do, or do I? *Journal of GLBT Family Studies, 1,* 21–31.

36. Yep, G. A., Lovaas, K. E., & Elia, J. P. (2003). A critical appraisal of assimilationist and radical ideologies underlying same-sex marriage in LGBT communities in the United States. *Journal of Homosexuality, 45,* 45–64.

37. Mattilda, a.k.a. Matt Bernstein Sycamore. (2004). *That's revolting! Queer strategies for resisting assimilation.* Berkeley, CA: Soft Skull Press.

38. Wharton, G., & Philips, I. (Eds.). (2004). *I do, I don't: Queers on marriage.* San Francisco: Suspect Thoughts Press.

39. Sullivan, A. (2004). *Same-sex marriage: Pro and con: A reader.* New York: Vintage Books.

40. Kraus, C. (August 31, 2003). Now free to marry, Canada's gays say, 'Do I?' *New York Times,* pp. 1, 6.

41. Andersson, G., Noack, T., Seierstad, A., & Weedon-Fekjaer, H. (2004, April). Divorce-risk patterns in same-sex "marriages" in Norway and Sweden. Paper presented at the annual convention of the Population Association of America, Boston.

42. Wyers, N. L. (1987). Homosexuality in the family: Lesbian and gay spouses. *Social Work, 32,* 143–148.

43. Cassingham, B. J., & O'Neil, S. M. (1993). *And then I met this woman: Previously married women's journeys into lesbian relationships.* Racine, WI: Mother Courage Press.

44. Strock, C. (2000). *Married women who love women.* New York: Alyson Publications.

45. Rothblum, E. D. (1989). Introduction: Lesbianism as a model of a positive lifestyle for women. *Women & Therapy, 8,* 1–12.

46. Faderman, L. (1991). *Odd girls and twilight lovers: A history of lesbian life in twentieth-century America.* New York: Columbia University Press.

47. Peplau, L. A., Cochran, S., Rook, K., & Padesky, C. (1978). Loving women: Attachment and autonomy in lesbian relationships. *Journal of Social Issues, 34,* 7–27.

48. Loulan, J. A. (1990). *The lesbian erotic dance: Butch, femme, androgyny and other rhythms.* San Francisco: Spinster Book Company.

49. Diamond, L. M. (2005). A new view of lesbian subtypes: Stable versus fluid identity trajectories over an 8-year period. *Psychology of Women Quarterly, 29,* 119–128.

50. Savin-Williams, R. C. (2005). *The new gay teenager.* Cambridge, MA: Harvard University Press.

51. Factor, R., & Rothblum, E. D. (2008). A study of transgender adults and their non-transgender siblings on demographic characteristics, social support, and experiences of violence. *Journal of LGBT Health Research, 3,* 11–30.

52. Dobkin, A. (1999). ("Denny's Tune"). I'm not monogamous anymore, but.... In M. Munson & J. Stelboum (Eds.), *The lesbian polyamory lover: Open relationships, non-monogamy, and casual sex.* Binghamton, NY: Haworth Press.

53. Munson, M., & Stelboum, J. (Eds.). (1999). *The lesbian polyamory reader: Open relationships, non-monogamy, and casual sex.* Binghamton, NY: Haworth Press.

54. West, C. (1996). *Lesbian polyfidelity.* San Francisco: Booklegger Publishing.

ABOUT THE AUTHOR

ESTHER D. ROTHBLUM, PhD is Professor of Women's Studies at San Diego State University and editor of the *Journal of Lesbian Studies.* She has studied same-sex couples in legal relationships in Massachusetts, California, and Vermont. She has edited over 20 books, including *Lesbian Friendships* (New York University Press), *Lesbian Ex-Lovers* (Haworth Press) and *Preventing Heterosexism and Homophobia* (Sage Publications).

CHAPTER 5

"Can Two Eggs Make a Baby?"
FERTILITY OPTIONS FOR LESBIANS

PAULA AMATO, MD

MARY CASEY JACOB, PhD

DONNA *is a 38-year-old lesbian who comes in for an annual exam. Just as the clinician is about to send her off to the lab for lipid screening and a thyroid stimulating hormone (TSH) test, Donna says: "My partner and I are planning to get pregnant this year with sperm from my partner's brother. Are there any other lab tests we need?"*

■ ■ ■

Even though lesbians are less likely than heterosexual women to report having biological children, many are parents.[1] In 2000, according to the U.S. Census, 34% of cohabitating female couples were raising children younger than 18.[2] There were nearly 381,000 same-sex female couples in 2005, so if the 34% figure is still accurate, more than 129,000 same-sex female couples are raising children under age 18,[3] which does not include single lesbians who are parents. An estimated 50% to 70% of lesbians of child-bearing age plan to become parents.[4,5]

This chapter focuses on the donor insemination options available to lesbians and the unique clinical, legal, and other issues that arise.

BACKGROUND

In the past, lesbians usually became parents through heterosexual contact or adoption. Today, there are more fertility options, including donor insemination and assisted reproductive technologies (ART). Sometimes lesbians need ART because of fertility difficulties, but these technologies also enable a partner to undergo ovarian stimulation and egg retrieval, fertilization of the eggs with donor sperm, and transfer of one or more embryos to the other partner's uterus. There has been little research on intra-partner in vitro fertilization: One small study demonstrated that it reduced jealousy between comothers who were then both biological partners in the pregnancy.[6]

Another way for both women to establish a biological link is to have the brother of the biological mother's partner be the sperm donor; thus, the nonbiological mother becomes the child's aunt. Some lesbian couples take turns getting pregnant through donor insemination, perhaps using the same sperm donor multiple times so the children will be biological half-siblings. Or different couples may use the same donor to create an extended, biologically related family. Other lesbians may choose to adopt, step parent, or raise foster children—alternatives that are beyond the scope of this chapter.

As of 2001, 74% of assisted reproductive technology clinics in the United States offered fertility services for lesbian couples, and 79% served single women, some of whom were lesbian.[7] Leading medical, psychiatric, psychological, child welfare, and children's health organizations, among others, have policy or position statements declaring that a parent's sexual orientation is irrelevant to his or her abilities as a parent.* Many of them also condemn sexual orientation-based discrimination in adoption, custody, and other parenting situations, and have called for equal rights for all parents and children. Nevertheless, some health care professionals oppose helping les-

---

* *These organizations include the American Academy of Pediatrics, American Academy of Family Physicians, American Society for Reproductive Medicine, American Psychiatric Association, American Psychoanalytic Association, American Psychological Association, Child Welfare League of America, North American Council on Adoptable Children, National Association of Social Workers, and American Bar Association.[8]*

bians who want to become mothers, perhaps out of concern for the children's welfare. A California court found in favor of a lesbian who sued after she was denied fertility treatment because of her sexual orientation.[9]

Empirical studies on lesbian and gay parenting show that children of lesbian parented families do not experience any unique disadvantages.[10,11] According to a meta-analysis, the psychosocial development of children and the quality of parenting in lesbian parented families are not significantly different from those in heterosexual parented families.[12]

Given the current scientific evidence and the opinions of child development experts, there are no *a priori* reasons to exclude lesbian couples from fertility programs. The ethics committee of the American Society for Reproductive Medicine believes that fertility programs have an ethical duty to offer treatment to gay, lesbian, and single persons consistent with treatment offered to heterosexual married couples.[8]

CLINICAL ISSUES

Who Will Become Pregnant?

When lesbian couples choose donor insemination, they must decide who will carry the baby. Some of the relevant factors, such as the impact of age on fertility and risk of chromosomal abnormalities, and the partners' medical and gynecological histories, are within the physician's domain of advice. Women need to know that aging reduces fertility and increases the likelihood of miscarriage and chromosomal defects. Other factors are outside that domain. For example, lesbian couples themselves need to consider each partner's desire to be or not be pregnant, the availability of health insurance to cover donor insemination and/or pregnancy, the attitudes of extended family members toward lesbian parenthood, and how existing children will fit into the plan.

Known Versus Anonymous Sperm Donor

Lesbian couples also must decide if they prefer a known sperm donor—maybe a family member of the nonbiological mother, thus ensuring her biological connection to the child—or an anonymous donor. Commercial sperm banks screen and test anonymous donors, whose medical and family history, physical characteristics, education, occupation, and other personal information are available to help women select one. Such donors may or may not agree to be identified after their offspring become legal adults, an issue that stems primarily from the desire of some donor-conceived persons, like some adoptees, to know their genealogy. In addition, clinicians may need more medical information about the donor in the future so they can treat his offspring or request his bone marrow for a transplant.

One vial of sperm costs $300 to $600 at most sperm banks. Patients may have to pay for insemination, in vitro fertilization, or another type of treatment, the cost of which varies.

Although working with a known altruistic donor can reduce treatment expenses, as sperm need not be purchased, the cost of having the donor screened and counseled generally counterbalances those savings. (Commercial sperm banks can spread screening and counseling costs among multiple recipients.) Nevertheless, some women prefer a known donor because it enables the child to know the identity of the donor and perhaps have a relationship with him. This can be legally risky in some states if all participants initially agree that the donor will not have any legal rights or responsibilities and then he changes his mind and requests them.

Typically, a known donor helps make some important decisions, such as whether or not to disclose his identity to the child. Fertility programs may also allow him to help decide what to do with excess gametes and embryos after in vitro fertilization. However, not everyone favors shared decision-making.

Identification of the Donor

Nearly all lesbian parents are open with their donor-conceived children about the conception circumstances.[13,14] Some known donors and most anonymous donors who agree to be identified do not expect or want an ongoing relationship with the offspring, yet they accept the possibility that the child may want more information about them or want to meet them. Even in these cases, though, few donors think of themselves as a parent. An important task for the mother(s) is to help their child understand that the donor is not a "dad," which for children means having a social relationship. Ideally, sperm banks counsel all donors to carefully consider their willingness to be identified, whether or not they should donate, why they would be comfortable doing so, and other issues.

Frozen Sperm and Testing of Donors

Using fresh sperm is not advisable, even when the donor is known, because of the risk of sexually transmitted infections. The American Society for Reproductive Medicine (ASRM)[15] and the U.S. Food and Drug Administration[16] recommend that all sperm donors be tested for such infections, including HIV; provide a medical history; and undergo a semen analysis, physical exam, and genetic evaluation. Sperm should then be frozen and quarantined for 6 months, and the donor retested after that interval and before insemination.

Counseling of Recipients

ASRM recommends that fertility doctors offer psychological counseling to all recipients of donated sperm.[15] Such counseling is generally part of the informed consent process. A physician must speak with patients about the medical aspects of donor-assisted conception. An infertility counselor can educate them about the many genetic variables to consider in donor selection; how to help children understand, in an age-appropriate manner, their mode of conception; and how to help families of origin understand the decision to become pregnant and ways they can support them during the process. In addition, the counselor can ensure that both members of a lesbian couple agree which one will try to conceive and, if applicable, discuss issues regarding coming out to family and friends.[†]

Testing of Recipients

ASRM also recommends that recipients provide a medical and reproductive history, and undergo a physical exam, standard preconception screening, and testing. Tests should include those for blood type, Rh factor, rubella, varicella, and HIV and other sexually transmitted infections, including hepatitis B and C, cytomegalovirus, and syphilis. In addition, the clinician might suggest cervical cultures or polymerase chain reaction testing for gonorrhea and chlamydia.

Physicians should explain the test for cystic fibrosis and other genetic evaluations, and order them when appropriate. Possible ethnicity-related tests include hemoglobin electrophoresis for sickle cell disease in African American recipients; an enzyme or DNA test for Tay-Sachs and other genetic diseases in Jewish recipients, particularly those of Eastern European heritage; and hemoglobin electrophoresis for thalassemias in women of South Asian or Mediterranean descent. Three months before conception, all women should take daily vitamins containing at least 400 mcg of folic acid to reduce the risk of birth defects.

Reproductive abnormalities that turn up in the recipient's medical history or physical exam may warrant more-detailed evaluation and treatment before insemination. A study of women undergoing intrauterine insemination found that the prevalence of polycystic ovary syndrome was significantly higher among lesbian women than among heterosexual women (42% vs. 14%).[17] However, results from a more recent study showed no difference in prevalence.[18]

---

† *ASRM's qualification guidelines for infertility counselors are available at www.asrm.org/Professionals/ PG-SIG-Affiliated_Soc/MHPG/MHPG_Guidelines.pdf.*

Insemination and Infertility

Intrauterine insemination is more effective than intracervical insemination in achieving pregnancy.[19,20] The cumulative pregnancy success rate after 12 cycles of donor intrauterine insemination in 2,193 nulliparous women with azoospermic partners—men who do not have any measurable level of sperm in their semen—was 73%, 61%, and 54% for those younger than 31, between 31 and 35 years old, and older than 35, respectively.[21] If a lesbian fails to conceive within three to six cycles of well-timed inseminations, a hysterosalpingogram to document tubal patency is warranted. It also may be warranted before inseminations, particularly if the history or physical exam reveals risk factors for tubal or uterine pathology.

Many women who seek donor insemination because they lack a male partner have unrealistic expectations of how soon they may conceive, a topic that counseling should address. Although some conceive quickly, many do not. Longer time to conception does not necessarily indicate a problem. Infertility is defined as a year of well-timed conception attempts that are unsuccessful, but the definition usually refers to conception as a result of intercourse or insemination with fresh sperm rather than frozen sperm, which may be less potent and thus reduce the likelihood of success.

Patients older than 35 who have not conceived after three well-timed cycles of donor insemination, and those younger than 35 who have not succeeded after six well-timed cycles, may be referred to an infertility specialist. These patients should contact their health insurer regarding eligibility requirements for donor insemination cycles because unsuccessful attempts may need to be documented before additional treatment qualifies for coverage.

Ovarian hyperstimulation with the fertility drugs clomiphene citrate or gonado-tropins is an option for patients who are diagnosed as infertile. However, patients need to know beforehand that these drugs increase the risk of twins and more than two fetuses, and can cause ovarian hyperstimulation syndrome—an excess accumula-tion of fluid in different body compartments that may require hospitalization.

Accommodating Lesbian Patients

Physicians can better accommodate lesbians who seek their infertility services by:
- Educating the entire medical and office staff about lesbian parenting and pregnancy, addressing any discomfort or concerns they may have;
- Revising educational materials and consent forms to reflect "partner" and "civil union"/"domestic partnership" in addition to "spouse" and "marriage";
- Making sure lesbian patients understand that the practice may refer *any* recipient of donated sperm, regardless of sexual orientation, for psychological counseling; and
- Enlarging the office's resource list to include lesbian-specific materials.

LEGAL ISSUES

State laws vary regarding adoption, custody, visitation, and surrogacy. One state need not honor parental rights granted in another. Lesbian couples and individuals who plan to conceive should consult a lawyer who is an expert in a variety of family structures, especially if they intend to use a known donor. The lawyer can prepare documents stating their coparenting‡ intentions and the arrangements they have made in the event of death or separation.

Patients should be aware of options in their state regarding second-parent adoption (also called coparent adoption)—that is, when a same-sex partner legally becomes a child's second parent. This protects everyone's best interests: the relationships among both parents and the child are legally recognized and have all the attendant rights and responsibilities. Second-parent adoption also fosters the child's emotional well-being and sense of safety, provides a cushion if the biological or original adoptive parent dies or becomes incapacitated, and protects the child's and nonbiological parent's relationship if the couple's relationship ends. In states that allow it, same-sex marriage is another way to protect these interests.§ Because partners in same-sex relationships, including civil unions, do not automatically qualify for child custody, wrongful death benefits, or visitation rights, they must obtain legal advice on these issues.

■　■　■

In the scenario at the beginning of this chapter, Donna surprised the clinician when she mentioned almost as an afterthought that she planned to get pregnant. The clinician should be supportive of Donna, refer her for prepregnancy tests as well as the lipid screening and TSH test, and mention that the office has served other lesbian patients who wanted to conceive. The clinician should also advise Donna to schedule a preconception appointment two weeks out for both her and her partner to discuss pregnancy issues, including Donna's advanced maternal age. Meanwhile, Donna should immediately begin taking a daily multivitamin.

CONCLUSION

More options than in the past are available to lesbians who want to become parents, including donor insemination and shared conception with the aid of reproductive

---

‡ *"Coparenting" in this context means two intended parents of the same gender, each of whom assumes parental rights and responsibilities for the same child or children.*

§ *Information about which states permit gay marriage, civil unions, and coparent adoption is available at www.lambdalegal.org/states-regions.*

technologies such as intrapartner in vitro fertilization. Although some physicians are reluctant to provide fertility services to lesbians, there is no evidence-based reason to withhold them.

Lesbians considering pregnancy have unique clinical and legal issues in addition to those that all prospective mothers encounter, such as age. These issues include whether the sperm donor should be known or anonymous and the child-rearing implications; insurance coverage of fertility procedures; the role of the nonbiological mother, if applicable; the extent to which the doctor's office accommodates lesbian patients; and state laws regarding adoption, custody, visitation, and surrogacy. Lesbian patients should receive thorough counseling about insemination and other fertility options, and, like all women, undergo prepregnancy testing to rule out potential medical or genetic problems before conception.

ADDITIONAL RESOURCES

- American Fertility Association: ✍ www.theafa.org
- American Society for Reproductive Medicine: ✍ www.asrm.org
- Brill, S., & Sacks, P. (2006). *The new essential guide to lesbian conception, pregnancy, and birth*. New York: Alyson Books.
- Gay & Lesbian Medical Association: ✍ www.glma.org
- Human Rights Campaign: ✍ www.hrc.org
- National Center for Lesbian Rights: ✍ www.nclrights.org/site/PageServer
- Pacific Reproductive Services: ✍ www.pacrepro.com/index.php
- Pepper, R. (1995). *The ultimate guide to pregnancy for lesbians: How to stay sane and care for yourself from pre-conception through birth* (2nd ed.). San Francisco: Cleis Press.
- Rainbow Flag Health Services: ✍ www.gayspermbank.com
- Society for Assisted Reproductive Technology: ✍ www.sart.org

REFERENCES

1. Marrazo, J. M., & Stine K. (2004). Reproductive health history of lesbians: Implications for care. *American Journal of Obstetrics & Gynecology, 190*, 1298–1304.

2. Grossman, G. (2007). *Review of research relevant to same-sex marriage*. American Psychoanalytic Association. Available at www.apsa.org/portals/1/docs/about%20apsaa/positionpapergaymarriage.pdf.

3. Romero, A. P., Baumle, A. K., Lee Badgett, M. V., & Gates, G. J. (2007). *Census snapshot. United States.* Williams Institute, UCLA School of Law. Available at www.law.ucla.edu/williamsinstitute/publications/USCensusSnapshot.pdf.

4. Johnson, S. R., Guenther, S. M., Laube, D. W., & Keettel, W. C. (1981). Factors influencing lesbian gynecologic care: A preliminary study. *American Journal of Obstetrics & Gynecology, 140,* 20–28.

5. Zeidenstrein, L. (1990). Gynecological and childbearing needs of lesbians. *Journal of Nurse-Midwifery, 35,* 10–18.

6. Pelka, S. (2009). Sharing motherhood: Maternal jealousy among lesbian co-mothers. *Journal of Homosexuality, 56,* 195–217.

7. Stern, J. E., Cramer, C. P., Garrod, A., & Green, R. M. (2001). Access to services at assisted reproductive technology clinics: A survey of policies and practices. *American Journal of Obstetrics & Gynecology, 184,* 591–597.

8. Ethics Committee, American Society for Reproductive Medicine. (2009). Access to fertility treatment by gays, lesbians, and unmarried persons. *Fertility and Sterility, 92,* 1190–1193.

9. Benitez v. North Coast Women's Care Medical Group, No. S147999 (California Supreme Court, August 18, 2008). Available at data.lambdalegal.org/in-court/downloads/benitez_ca_20080818_supreme-court-decision.pdf.

10. Committee on Lesbian, Gay, and Bisexual Concerns; Committee on Children, Youth, and Families; & Committee on Women in Psychology. (2005). *Lesbian & gay parenting.* Washington, DC: American Psychological Association. Available at www.apa.org/pi/lgbc/publications/lgparenting.pdf and www.apa.org/pi/parent.html.

11. Gartrell, N., Deck, A., Rodas, C., Peyser, H., & Banks, A. (2005). The National Lesbian Family Study: 4. Interviews with the 10-year-old children. *American Journal of Orthopsychiatry, 75,* 518–524.

12. Hunfeld, J. A., Fauser, B. C., de Beaufort, I. D., & Passchier, J. P. (2002). Child development and quality of parenting in lesbian families: No psychosocial indications for a-priori withholding of infertility treatment. A systematic review. *Human Reproduction Update, 8,* 579–590.

13. Wendland, C. L., Burn, F., & Hill, C. (1996). Donor insemination: A comparison of lesbian couples, heterosexual couples and single women. *Fertility and Sterility, 65,* 764–770.

14. Leiblum, S. R., Palmer, M. G., & Spector, I. P. (1995). Non-traditional mothers: Single heterosexual/lesbian women and lesbian couples electing motherhood via donor insemination. *Journal of Psychosomatic Obstetrics & Gynaecology, 16,* 11–20.

15. Practice Committee, American Society for Reproductive Medicine, & Practice Committee, Society for Assisted Reproductive Technology. (2008). 2008 guidelines for gamete and embryo donation: A practice committee report. *Fertility and Sterility, 90(Suppl. 5),* S30–44.

16. U.S. Food and Drug Administration. (2007, June 19). Human cells, tissue, and cellular and tissue-based products; donor screening and testing, and related labeling (21 CFR Part 1271). *Federal Register, 72,* 33667–33669. Available at frwebgate.access.gpo.gov/cgi-bin/getdoc.cgi?dbname=2007_register&docid=fr19jn07-11.pdf.

17. Agrawal, R., Sharma, S., Bekir, J., Conway, G., Bailey, J., Balen, A. H., et al. (2004). Prevalence of polycystic ovaries and polycystic ovary syndrome in lesbian women compared with heterosexual women. *Fertility and Sterility, 82,* 1352–1357.

18. De Sutter, P., Dutré, T., Vanden Meerschaut, F., Stuyver, I., Van Maele, G., & Dhont, M. (2008). PCOS in lesbian and heterosexual women treated with artificial donor insemination. *Reproductive BioMedicine Online, 17,* 398–402.

19. Besselink, D. E., Farquhar, C., Kremer, J. A., Marjoribanks, J., & O'Brien, P. (2008). Cervical insemination versus intra-uterine insemination of donor sperm for subfertility. *Cochrane Database of Systematic Reviews, 16,* CD000317.

20. Carroll, N., & Palmer, J. R. (2001). A comparison of intrauterine versus intracervical insemination in fertile single women. *Fertility and Sterility, 75,* 656–660.

21. Schwartz, D., & Mayaux, M. J. (1982). Female fecundity as a function of age: Results of artificial insemination in 2,193 nulliparous women with azoospermic husbands. Federation CECOS. *New England Journal of Medicine, 306,* 404–406.

ABOUT THE AUTHORS

PAULA AMATO, MD is a reproductive endocrinologist and Associate Professor at Oregon Health & Science University. Her areas of clinical/research interest include patients with infertility, menopause, polycystic ovary syndrome and endometriosis. She serves on the Advisory Board of the Lesbian Health Fund and on the Board of Directors of the Gay & Lesbian Medical Association.

MARY CASEY JACOB, PhD is Professor of Psychiatry and Obstetrics and Gynecology; she is also the Associate Dean for Faculty Affairs at the University of Connecticut, School of Medicine. She is a health psychologist who counsels lesbian couples about their family-building options and has conducted research on donor conception in lesbians and others.

CHAPTER 6

"Which One of Us Should Get Pregnant?"
LESBIANS AND PREGNANCY

CHRISTY M. ISLER, MD

LESLIE M. CRAGIN, PhD, CNM

MARY, 32, *comes to the office for prenatal care. Twenty-four weeks pregnant, she conceived by donor insemination with sperm from the same donor for her son, age 2. She came to this practice when her nurse-midwife began working with a new obstetrician.*

According to Mary's prenatal questionnaire, she is single and lives with two children and a friend, Donna. The obstetrician is seeing her today about managing her gestational diabetes, which also developed during her previous pregnancy. Although Mary gave birth two years ago to a healthy, 9-pound boy at term; the delivery was complicated by a moderate shoulder dystocia without newborn sequelae. Mary's nurse-midwife has assured her that the obstetrician has previously cared for lesbian-parented families, but the idea of disclosing her same-sex orientation, especially in the written record, makes Mary feel nervous and vulnerable.

■ ■ ■

"A bun in the oven," "in trouble," and "in confinement" (from "estimated date of confinement") are among the many euphemisms people use to denote pregnancy. "In a family way" aptly describes pregnancy's ultimate goal and applies to lesbians no less than it does to heterosexual women. However, today's families often extend beyond biological relationships, and legal issues as well as cultural and social norms, can complicate matters.

This chapter discusses the care of lesbians who are "in a family way" and the many issues they encounter.

BACKGROUND

Research on lesbians and pregnancy, like research on lesbian health generally, is inadequate. Most studies rely on descriptive or qualitative methods to explore and refine researchers' understanding of the related health and social issues. These methods, which investigators use because recruiting subjects from sensitive and vulnerable populations is so difficult, limit the generalizability of findings. Lesbians of color, financially disadvantaged lesbians, and those living in rural areas are particularly underrepresented in studies.

Fertility rates for lesbians are difficult to calculate. The Nurses Health Study II reported that 34% of 694 lesbians had given birth.[1] In a Women's Health Initiative sample that included 264 lifetime lesbians (sex with women only, mean age = 59.4 years) and 309 adult lesbians (sex with women only after age 45, mean age = 56.7 years), 35% of lifetime lesbians and 63% of adult lesbians had been pregnant.[2] In both reports, it is unclear how many of the pregnancies occurred in prior heterosexual relationships or in lesbian relationships. More recently, researchers in New Zealand determined that of 603 lesbians who had children, the fertility rate was 2.04 before they came out as lesbian and 1.74 afterward,[3,4] compared to a national fertility rate of 2.11 in New Zealand[5] and 2.0 in the United States.[6]

GETTING PREGNANT

For lesbians, conceiving usually requires more detailed planning than it does for heterosexual women. The two main options for getting pregnant are intercourse with a man and donor insemination. Compared to the 1980s, when many lesbians conceived through sexual relations, a larger percentage now conceive through donor insemination.[7] Either way, before and early in pregnancy, health care providers should raise issues such as whether or not the parents and/or child will know the donor, and whether or not the donor will participate in parenting and share custody of the child.[7] Importantly, clinicians need to understand that for lesbians, the "normal" experience of getting pregnant is much more like the complex and stressful experience that infertile heterosexual women go through when they try to conceive, and less like typical heterosexual conception.[8]

If a lesbian patient is not legally married, the clinician must find out whom she has designated as her health care agent if an emergency arises and she cannot make decisions. Legal rights and responsibilities differ among states. Same-sex marriages, civil unions, and domestic partnerships are increasingly common nationwide and may confer similar rights and responsibilities as heterosexual marriage.*

In order to provide safe and effective services, clinicians must understand the legal implications of caring for lesbian clients. For example, if a pregnant mother is unable to consent to treatment, can her life partner legally consent to nonemergency care for the mother or newborn? Health care power of attorney enables others to make such decisions if necessary.† Lesbian couples may want advice on this matter before the birth, and on other issues, from a lawyer who has experience with nontraditional families.

HOW HOMOPHOBIA IN HEALTH CARE AFFECTS LESBIANS AND THEIR PREGNANCIES

A major issue for lesbians contemplating pregnancy is homophobia (the irrational fear, dislike, and hatred of lesbians and/or gay men) and heterosexism (the assumption of heterosexuality) on the part of medical professionals and related institutions.[9] A common fear among lesbians is that, because of their sexual orientation, health professionals will treat them suboptimally. Consequently, many are reluctant to dis-

---

* At www.hrc.org/issues/parenting/adoption.asp, the Human Rights Campaign offers valuable information about parenting by lesbian couples and the rapidly changing legal environment. The National Center for Lesbian Rights (www.nclrights.org) offers information for lesbians who are planning a pregnancy.

† A generic medical power of attorney form is available at www.expertlaw.com/library/estate_planning/medical_power_of_attorney.html. Most hospitals also have these forms available.

close their same-sex orientation to providers.[7,10] Historically, 53% to 72% of homosexual patients did not report their sexual orientation to their health care provider during general medical care.[11] As one lesbian told Renaud: "My insurance will pay, which is why I am the one having the baby. I heard it is best to say you are single, or they might deny you.... They cover fertility for single mothers but not lesbians, so we lied"[12] (p. 193).

Some studies show that more sexual minorities are disclosing their sexual orientation to providers and experiencing less homophobia and homophobic attitudes on the part of physicians.[13,14] Practitioners may express homophobia and heterosexism in subtle or overt ways, such as nonverbal behavior and outright negative stereotyping.[15] Two qualitative studies cite examples of lesbian parents' positive and negative experiences with health care providers. Some of the parents were delighted that providers offered information about breast- and infant-feeding to both mothers, without assuming only the birth mother would be interested. On the negative side, some providers verbally and nonverbally expressed overt discomfort with lesbian mothers. Clients who perceive homophobic attitudes are unlikely to continue seeking care from that provider or institution unless no other alternative is available.[12,16]

Lesbians generally prefer a female—and, if possible, a lesbian—health care provider.[17] In addition, they report positive experiences with nonphysician practitioners. In one study, for example, 46% said in interviews that they preferred a certified nurse-midwife and/or a doula‡ during pregnancy or birth because these practitioners did a better job than physicians of advocating on lesbian couples' behalf with other providers.[18] In another study, based on focus groups, lesbians said they were very pleased with the care they received from certified nurse-midwives, doulas, and public health nurses but dissatisfied with physician care.[19] Regardless of provider type, important qualities of excellent pregnancy care include sensitive, nonjudgmental, accepting, and competent care; knowledge about lesbian health; and use of inclusive gender language without heterosexual assumptions.

THE OFFICE VISIT

Although it is patients' choice whether or not to disclose their sexual orientation to health care providers, physician offices can create an atmosphere in which lesbians feel comfortable doing so.§ A good place to start is to post a nondiscrimination policy

---

‡ *A layperson educated to provide nonpharmacological pain relief and other nonmedical care to a woman or couple during birth and postpartum.*

§ *Information about how to create a welcoming environment for lesbians in health care offices is available from the Gay and Lesbian Medical Association at www.glma.org/_data/n_0001/resources/live/ Welcoming%20Environment.pdf.*

that addresses sexual orientation, post photographs of same-sex parents, including some with their children, and print such photographs in brochures.

Many participants in qualitative research on this topic cited examples of language or communication that contributed to their positive experiences. For instance, instead of asking patients about their "marital status," it is better if clinicians caring for pregnant women ask about their "relationship status," a more inclusive term that includes the options "married," "single," "domestic partnership," and "committed partnership." If requesting more specific information, they can ask if the patient lives with her legal spouse (male or female), life/domestic partner (male or female), friends (male or female), children (biological, step, or foster children, and so on). Hallmarks of good communication are a lack of heterosexist assumptions or expressions, openness, and respectful curiosity.

Clinicians should inquire about and respect patients' choice of terminology for family roles. Given the diversity of family structures in the lesbian, gay, bisexual, and transgender community, Neville and Henrickson state that it is "inadvisable and ethically questionable...to make any assumptions about how LGB persons construct their identities and relationships.... It is important to ask each person who the important people are in their households and lives, and be open to hearing the answers"[4] (p. 6).

The nonpregnant partner in a couple may prefer to be called "partner," "nonbiological mother," "coparent," "comother," or "social mother." After the birth, many lesbian couples designate one partner as "mommy" and the other as "momma." Occasionally, lesbians coparent with the sperm donor, who may participate in office visits or the birth.

Clinicians and staff should learn about culturally appropriate care and inclusive language. A patient's cultural identity is often complex—lesbian Scottish-American Buddhist, for example—and can never be assumed based on appearance, education level, or language. Studies describe this outlook as "cultural humility,"[20] which involves developing skills for exploring the diversity of beliefs, assumptions, expectations, and goals that providers and patients bring to all clinical interactions. Achieving cultural humility is a life-long process that requires introspection and nonjudgmental curiosity.

One of the most important aspects of pregnancy-related health care for lesbians is including the patient's family of choice, if she so desires. Most often, the family of choice includes a committed partner. In these cases, clinicians should interact with the partners simply as a couple having a baby.[16] Office staff need to include the nonbiological mother in visits, as they would in scheduling a visit for a heterosexual couple. Inclusiveness is particularly important if a complication such as a miscarriage or stillbirth occurs. The biological mother's friends and family will acknowledge her loss, but the nonbiological mother often is unrecognized and may not receive support for her grief.

Clinicians should facilitate participation of the biological mother's partner and/or family members of choice in prenatal visits, ultrasound examinations, hospitalizations, labor, delivery, and the postpartum period. They can suggest during the prenatal period that family members discuss their individual roles and responsibilities and note them in a birth plan. Some lesbians use sperm from a male relative of the nonbiological mother to conceive, which, depending on state statutes, may mean he has a stronger legal right than the nonbiological mother does regarding treatment consent. In couples that acknowledge butch/femme roles, the butch may be the biological mother—if, for example, the femme cannot conceive or is uninsured—yet the femme may assume the major parenting role. If such roles are not noted in the birth plan, clinical staff may unnecessarily fear that the biological mother is rejecting or unable to bond with her baby.

Codified roles make it easier for staff to negotiate care in a respectful and legally accurate manner. If, in the scenario at the beginning of this chapter, Donna were Mary's registered domestic partner and Donna's brother, John, were the sperm donor, a health care power of attorney for Mary, the biological mother, could grant authority to Donna to make decisions on Mary's behalf if Mary were unable to make them. This document could also certify that John is the infant's biological father and that he grants to Donna the right and responsibility for making decisions regarding the newborn's health care if Mary cannot make them.

PRECONCEPTION COUNSELING

All women who are planning a pregnancy, including those who have disclosed their sexual minority status, should undergo preconception counseling during well-woman visits. As nearly all lesbian pregnancies are planned and, during well-woman visits, patients may or may not mention their intent to become pregnant, clinicians must ask all female patients about plans for children. Preconception counseling should include the partner and sperm donor (or at least knowledge of his medical history) if the patient identifies a donor because information about him could affect which partner intends to carry the pregnancy.¶ Table 6.1 lists the clinical steps necessary to provide quality care before, during, and after pregnancy.

¶ *The Childbirth Connection (www.childbirthconnection.org) has a wealth of information for women and clinicians about maternity care, including what to discuss in preconception counseling. This and similar resources clarify for patients the importance of such counseling.*

TABLE 6.1. PREGNANCY AND CHILDBIRTH CARE FOR LESBIANS

PHASE	CONSIDERATIONS
Preconception care	▪ Counsel regarding pregnancy risk ▪ Determine which partner will carry the pregnancy if partnered ▪ Prepare health care power of attorney
Antenatal care	▪ Provide a lesbian-friendly office ▪ Include nonbiological mother/family of choice in care ▪ Provide routine prenatal care ▪ Recommend lesbian-sensitive prenatal classes ▪ Screen for lesbian-associated risks: alcohol, tobacco, obesity, depression, cardiovascular disease, history of physical/sexual abuse, intimate partner violence, homophobia experiences
Preparation for delivery	▪ Complete hospital registration ▪ Prepare a birth plan ▪ Complete paperwork for nonbiological mother's employment leave (e.g., adoption leave) if partnered ▪ Refer to a lesbian-sensitive pediatrician/family physician ▪ Provide breast-feeding information to patient and partner, if appropriate ▪ Assess labor and delivery staff's ability to provide culturally appropriate care ▪ Confirm visitation policies in labor and delivery, well-baby nursery, and neonatal intensive care unit for partner/family of choice
Labor and delivery	▪ Facilitate culturally appropriate care
Postpartum care	▪ Review risk factors requiring postpartum follow-up: obesity, risk of postpartum depression, intimate partner violence, substance use ▪ Assess social support for immediate postpartum period

Source: Authors

ANTENATAL CARE

Antenatal care for lesbian and heterosexual mothers-to-be is similar. However, clinicians should pay special attention to certain risk factors and psychosocial issues that are more prevalent among lesbians. If a patient does not participate in preconception counseling or comes to a nurse practitioner, midwife, or doctor visit after she is pregnant, the risk assessment/reduction considerations cited in the box below apply to early obstetrical care.

RISK ASSESSMENT/REDUCTION CONSIDERATIONS IN PRECONCEPTION COUNSELING

▪ Folic acid supplementation	▪ Alcohol/illegal substance use
▪ Rubella (German measles)	▪ Obesity
▪ Diabetes	▪ Sexually transmitted infections
▪ Hypothyroidism	▪ Hepatitis B
▪ HIV/AIDS	▪ Blood pressure management
▪ Phenylketonuria	▪ Chronic disease management
▪ Oral anticoagulants	▪ Exposure to unsafe chemicals
▪ Accutane and other retinoids	▪ Stress reduction
▪ Antiepileptic medications	▪ Interpregnancy interval
▪ Other medications or supplements	▪ Intimate partner violence
▪ Smoking	

Source: March of Dimes. (2009). Preconception risk reduction. Available at www.marchofdimes.com/professionals/19695.asp.

Medical Risks

Taking a detailed sexual and obstetric history is routine for any new patient; the history should be updated periodically. Lesbian patients, like heterosexual patients, need to be screened for sexually transmitted infections, including HIV. Lesbian and single women are more likely not to have received cancer screenings according to the recommended schedule, especially when providers do not assess patients' intimate relationships and sexual history.[21] Human papillomavirus can be transmitted by any type of vaginal penetration, including sex toys, so all patients should receive Pap smears according to the most recent guidelines.[22]

Lesbians are at higher risk for medical conditions associated with behavioral risk factors, including obesity and tobacco, alcohol, and drug use.[1,2,13,23-25] Clinicians should assess lesbian patients for all these factors on the first prenatal visit. The greater incidence of obesity and overweight among lesbians may place pregnant lesbians at higher risk of gestational diabetes and pregnancy-induced hypertension. Women with a body mass index > 25 are candidates for early diabetes screening. Parental obesity increases children's risk of obesity.[26] Therefore, exercise and avoidance of excessive weight gain are important topics to be emphasized during pregnancy.

All women should be carefully screened for use of substances, including alcohol and tobacco. Although lesbians are more likely than women in general to smoke,[27] it is unknown if this also applies to lesbians who choose pregnancy. One study found high smoking rates among African American lesbians.[24] The links between smoking and low birth weight, preterm birth, and stillbirth are well-documented. Patients who smoke and their housemates should receive smoking-cessation resources.

There is a great deal of information on lesbians' use of alcohol and illegal substances. More heterosexual women than lesbians abstain from alcohol, but at comparable drinking levels, lesbians report more alcohol-related problems.[28] One descriptive study found that the rate of alcohol use among lesbians declined from 7% when they were trying to get pregnant to 5% at 2 years postpartum.[18] Clinicians should inform patients that researchers have not documented any safe level of alcohol consumption during pregnancy or breast-feeding.

Psychosocial Risks

Lesbians are also at greater risk of depression.[1] In a study of lesbian, heterosexual, and bisexual women, Koh and Ross found strong associations between "being out" and mental health status. Lesbians who were not out were 2 to 2.5 times more likely than heterosexual women to have experienced suicidal ideation in the previous 12 months and to have a history of suicide attempt. Additionally, compared with heterosexual women, lesbians used psychotherapy more commonly than antidepressants for depression.[29] It is unknown how the prevalence of depression among lesbians who become pregnant compares with that among lesbians in general and heterosexual women. Screening for a history of depression and current symptoms is an important part of antenatal care for lesbians. Clinicians need to be particularly vigilant regarding depression in pregnant lesbians, especially those who are uncomfortable being out.

Physical or Sexual Abuse and Intimate Partner Violence

According to Austin and colleagues, the link between a history of childhood abuse and intimate partner violence is stronger in the lesbian community than in the general population.[30] Because intimate partner violence tends to increase during pregnancy and is associated with poor pregnancy outcomes and infant/child health problems,[31] universal screening is imperative.**

PREPARATION FOR DELIVERY

The list below summarizes clinical and other considerations regarding pregnant lesbian patients in their third trimester. These include:

- Hospital registration forms. Some hospitals require that patients cite a legal or blood relative as next of kin if certain legal forms have not already been filed;
- Employment leave. If the biological and nonbiological mothers are a couple, they need to know their options. The nonbiological mother may qualify for adoption leave;
- Prenatal classes. When clinicians recommend these, they should also acknowledge that the classes may be heterosexist and may not recognize a nonbiological mother as a parent. Many lesbian couples experience heterosexism in prenatal classes, particularly in the form of exclusive language such as "husband."[32] If lesbian-inclusive classes are not available locally, individual sessions can be arranged with a sensitive childbirth educator;
- Pediatrician/family physician. The clinician should recommend a pediatrician or family physician who has experience with lesbian mothers. This is especially important for recognition of a nonbiological mother as a parent;
- Breast-feeding. Clinicians should discuss this before the birth. They can refer a couple to a lactation specialist if the nonbiological mother wants to breast-feed (lactation can be hormonally induced). Many lesbians choose to breast-feed; their median length of breast-feeding is 12 months.[18] A lesbian mother told Renaud: "One thing you need to tell nurses is that both the birth mother and the co-mother might want to breastfeed.... Nobody asked us, and we tried it on our own at home, but it would have been a lot easier if they [had] asked in the hospital"[12] (p. 197);
- Anticipatory preparation of the hospital staff. Clinicians should ensure that the labor and delivery unit, birth center, and pediatric nurseries provide culturally appropriate care for lesbians and their families. Such care includes nonjudgmental attitudes and behaviors on the part of nurses and other personnel, who need to be able to accept expressions of support and intimacy during labor and delivery and in the postpartum period; and

---

** *A compendium of tools for assessing intimate partner violence is available from the Centers for Disease Control and Prevention at www.cdc.gov/ncipc/dvp/Compendium/IPV%20Compendium.pdf.*

- Legal issues. The family must be legally prepared for the unexpected—if, for example, the biological mother were to become incapacitated and unable to make medical decisions for herself or the baby.

LABOR AND DELIVERY

Finding the right environment for birth is important to lesbian mothers. Although hospital delivery is most common, they may prefer to deliver at home or in a birth center.[18] Mothers and their families consider all aspects of care when they weigh the options: how other lesbians felt about their experience, if lactation support is available, if rooming-in is permissible, and overall quality of care. A vitally important aspect of quality of care is inclusion of the nonbiological mother (if applicable) and/or family of choice in the labor and delivery process. In this regard, hospitals and birth centers should have policies in place that address partner involvement and same-sex relationships.

For a patient and her partner/family, the most helpful part of a birth plan is its preparation. The process can clarify preferences, such as intermittent versus continuous fetal monitoring, and serve as a guide for discussions with the clinician. During labor and delivery, staff can consult the birth plan if they are uncertain about the patient's preferences and her particular family structure, which may be complex. The plan should also address the health care power of attorney issue.

POSTPARTUM CARE

In the postpartum period, clinicians must assess mothers and counsel them about the transition to parenthood. Many of the same postpartum themes apply to both heterosexual and lesbian mothers, but there are some differences.[33] For example, frequent factors in same-sex parenting, such as a planned pregnancy, preparation that gives mothers more time to assess their readiness for motherhood, and a more likely equal division of labor, might counter the risks for postpartum depression.

On the other hand, a small qualitative study by Ross and colleagues revealed that while having a female partner who shared the mother role was positive, negotiating equality in that role created a different kind of stress. As a study participant told these researchers:

> Realizing that I wanted to be as active a mother as [my partner] has...caused some tension between us.... It was just something again that we had to negotiate that I didn't see with any of our straight couples at all because the guy just backed right out of it[34] (p. e67).

Sometimes the family(ies) of origin do not support the biological or nonbiological mother(s) and the lesbian mother(s) may unrealistically think they do not need help with their parenting venture. However, friends and family of choice frequently provide physical and emotional support. Children often improve the relationship between lesbian mothers and their families of origin, but occasionally they cause additional strain.

A patient and her family of origin also may be anxious about whether the bond between the nonbiological mother and child will be as close as that between the biological mother and child. Gartrell and colleagues, in their longitudinal study of lesbian-parented families, concluded that in mother-child bonding, time spent with the child is more important than the biological relationship.[18]

Nonbiological mothers may feel unsupported at work, in the pediatrician's office, or at a day care facility if they have not disclosed their status. Invisibly transitioning to motherhood without social support can be stressful for them.

Postpartum Depression

The prevalence of postpartum depression among lesbians is not known. In one small study based on a convenience sample, the incidence of perinatal clinical depression in lesbian and bisexual women was 8.2%, which is less than the estimated 10% to 15% of women in the general population who experience postpartum depression.[19]

Because lesbians are at higher risk of depression,[1] and women with a history of depression are more likely to experience it again postpartum, the postpartum risk for lesbians may be greater. Male partners of women who give birth also can experience postpartum depression, so it is safe to assume that the partners of lesbian mothers are at risk for this illness too. Ross and colleagues studied risk factors for postpartum depression to see if they are similar in lesbian and heterosexual mothers. In the late third trimester, there was no significant difference in mean scores on the Edinburgh Postnatal Depression Scale between pregnant lesbians and heterosexual women. At 4 months postpartum, lesbians had slightly higher, statistically significant mean scores on the scale than heterosexual women did. The study did not find a correlation between depression scores and social support or marital satisfaction in the lesbian population.[19] Given the contradictory study results regarding risk of depression in gravid and postpartum lesbians, further investigation is warranted. Certainly, all parents are at risk for postpartum depression.

Social pressure on lesbian parents to succeed may deter new mothers from seeking medical care for postpartum depression. Clinicians should look for signs and symptoms of "baby blues," which are normal and temporary in the first 2 weeks of motherhood, and differentiate them from postpartum depression. A verbal or written postpartum depression screen consisting of two questions is effective: "Since your new baby was born, how often have you felt down, depressed, or hopeless?" and

"Since your new baby was born, how often have you had little interest or pleasure in doing things?" The response choices are "always," "often," "sometimes," "rarely," and "never." Women who respond "often" or "always" to either or both questions have postpartum depressive symptoms. Because the questions have a high sensitivity (96%), health professionals recommend them as a first screen for postpartum depression.[35,36]

■ ■ ■

On Mary's first visit, the obstetrician discusses her last pregnancy and her gestational diabetes (she has been following the recommended diet—her blood sugars are generally within normal range), and gives her exercise and nutrition advice. The nurse-midwife has provided comprehensive care up to this point; the obstetrician suggests that Mary and Donna continue her care by the midwife and return for a follow-up visit at 36 weeks. Mary says she will fax her weekly blood glucose readings to the office. If she needs insulin, the obstetrician will request that Mary schedule an additional appointment before 36 weeks.

By way of reassuring Mary that the office welcomes pregnant lesbians and their partners, the obstetrician suggests that both she and Donna participate in visits as a couple. The obstetrician acknowledges the additional stress that homophobia places on pregnancy. Mary senses the clinician's acceptance of her particular circumstances and realizes she is free to discuss any of her concerns.

During the weekly case conference with staff, the obstetrician discusses Mary's diabetes and reviews the care plan with the nurse-midwife. The plan includes:

■ A health care power of attorney document that, if needed, grants decision-making authority to Donna;
■ Mary's and Donna's employment leave options. If Donna is "out," she will ask her employer about parental/paternity/adoption leave;
■ The name of the pediatrician or family physician they have selected;
■ Events in the previous pregnancy that made Donna feel excluded from the birth process, and alternative approaches this time that will maximize her participation in obstetric care;
■ Breast-feeding options and prenatal classes;
■ Choice of birthing places: at home, a birth center, or a hospital;
■ The hospital's labor/delivery and nursery policies regarding lesbian partners;
■ An assessment of the postpartum support that will be available to Mary and Donna, as well as a review of postpartum depression signs and symptoms; and
■ A talk by the nurse-midwife to the office and hospital staff and the local health care community about lesbian health care.

CONCLUSION

Pregnancies in lesbians have become more common. Clinicians should recommend preconception counseling for those who are contemplating pregnancy. Advanced maternal age may place lesbian patients at risk for obstetric complications. Once a patient is pregnant, routine prenatal care should be lesbian-sensitive and, if applicable, involve her partner. In the third trimester, extra preparation for delivery includes discussion about choosing a pediatrician or family physician who is comfortable with lesbian parents, obtaining health care power of attorney, and preparing the labor and delivery staff to provide culturally appropriate care. Before the postpartum period, discussions about postpartum depression and social support are warranted.

REFERENCES

1. Case, P., Austin, S. B., Hunter, D. J., Manson, J. E., Malspeis, S., Willett, W. C., et al. (2004). Sexual orientation, health risk factors, and physical functioning in the Nurses' Health Study II. *Journal of Women's Health, 13,* 1033–1047.

2. Valanis, B. G., Bowen, D. J., Bassford, T., Whitlock, E., Charney, P., & Carter, R. A. (2000). Sexual orientation and health: Comparisons in the Women's Health Initiative sample. *Archives of Family Medicine, 9,* 843–853.

3. Lev, A. I. (2008). More than surface tension: Femmes in families. *Journal of Lesbian Studies, 12,* 127–144.

4. Neville, S., & Henrickson, M. (2008). The constitution of 'lavender families': A LGB perspective. *Journal of Clinical Nursing, 18,* 849–856.

5. Agency, C. I. (Ed.). (2008). *The world fact book.* Washington, DC: Central Intelligence Agency.

6. Martin, J. A., Hamilton, B. E., Sutton, P. D., Ventura, S. J., Menacker, F., & Munson, M. L. (2005). *Births: Final data for 2003.* Hyattsville, MD: National Center for Health Statistics.

7. McManus, A. J., Hunter, L. P., & Renn, H. (2006). Lesbian experiences and needs during childbirth: Guidance for health care providers. *Journal of Obstetric, Gynecologic, and Neonatal Nursing, 35,* 13–23.

8. Wojnar, D. (2007). Miscarriage experiences of lesbian couples. *Journal of Midwifery & Women's Health, 52,* 479–485.

9. Zeidenstein, L. (1990). Gynecological and childbearing needs of lesbians. *Journal of Nurse-Midwifery, 35,* 10–18.

10. Roberts, S. J., & Sorenson, L. (1995). Lesbian health care: A review and recommendations for health promotion in primary care settings. *Nursing Practice, 20,* 42–47.

11. Smith, E., Johnson, S. R., & Guenther, S. M. (1985). Health care attitudes and experiences during gynecologic care among lesbians and bisexuals. *American Journal of Public Health, 75,* 1086–1087.

12. Renaud, M. T. (2007). We are mothers too: Childbearing experiences of lesbian families. *Journal of Obstetric, Gynecologic, and Neonatal Nursing, 36,* 190–199.

13. Roberts, S. J., Patsdaughter, C. A., Grindel, C. G., & Tarmina, M. S. (2004). Health related behaviors and cancer screening of lesbians: Results of the Boston Lesbian Health Project II. *Women & Health, 39,* 41–55.

14. Smith, D. M., & Mathews, W. C. (2007). Physicians' attitudes toward homosexuality and HIV: Survey of a California Medical Society—revisited (PATHH-II). *Journal of Homosexuality, 52,* 1–9.

15. Trippet, S. E., & Bain, J. (1993). Physical health problems and concerns of lesbians. *Health Care of Women International, 20,* 59–70.

16. Spidsberg, B. D. (2007). Vulnerable and strong—lesbian women encountering maternity care. *Journal of Advanced Nursing, 60,* 478–486.

17. Tash, D. T., & Kenney, J. W. (1993). The lesbian childbearing couple: A case report. *Birth, 20,* 36–40.

18. Gartrell, N., Banks, A., Hamilton, J., Reed, N., Bishop, H., & Rodas, C. (1999). The National Lesbian Family Study: 2. Interviews with mothers of toddlers. *American Journal of Orthopsychiatry, 69,* 362–369.

19. Ross, L. E., Steele, L., Goldfinger, C., & Strike, C. (2007). Perinatal depressive symptomatology among lesbian and bisexual women. *Archives of Women's Mental Health, 10,* 53–59.

20. Tervalon, M., & Murray-Garcia, J. (1998). Cultural humility versus cultural competence: A critical distinction in defining physician training outcomes in multicultural education. *Journal of Health Care for the Poor and Underserved, 9,* 117–125.

21. Politi, M. C., Clark, M. A., Rogers, M. L., McGarry, K., & Sciamanna, C. N. (2008). Patient-provider communication and cancer screening among unmarried women. *Patient Education and Counseling, 73,* 251–255.

22. ACOG Committee on Practice Bulletins – Gynecologic (2009). ACOG Practice Bulletin No. 109: Cervical cytology screening. *Obstetrics & Gynecology, 114,* 1409–1420.

23. Dibble, S. L., Roberts, S. A., & Nussey, B. (2004). Comparing breast cancer risk between lesbians and their heterosexual sisters. *Women's Health Issues, 14,* 60–68.

24. Hughes, T. L., Johnson, T. P., & Matthews, A. K. (2008). Sexual orientation and smoking: Results from a multisite women's health study. *Substance Use & Misuse, 43,* 1218–1239.

25. Wilsnack, S. C., Hughes, T. L., Johnson, T. P., Bostwick, W. B., Szalacha, L. A., Benson, P., et al. (2008). Drinking and drinking-related problems among heterosexual and sexual minority women. *Journal of Studies on Alcohol and Drugs, 69,* 129–139.

26. Robinson, T. N. (2000). The epidemic of pediatric obesity. *Western Journal of Medicine, 173,* 220–221.

27. Cochran, S. D., Mays, V. M., Bowen, D, Gage, S., Bybee, D., Roberts, S. J., et al. (2001). Cancer-related risk indicators and preventive screening behaviors among lesbians and bisexual women. *American Journal of Public Health, 91,* 591–597.

28. National Institute on Alcohol Abuse and Alcoholism. (2005). *Module 10G: Sexual orientation and alcohol use disorders*. Available at pubs.niaaa.nih.gov/publications/Social/Module10GSexualOrientation/Module10G.html.

29. Koh, A. S., & Ross, L. K. (2006). Mental health issues: A comparison of lesbian, bisexual and heterosexual women. *Journal of Homosexuality, 51,* 33–57.

30. Austin, S. B., Jun, H. J., Jackson, B., Spiegelman, D., Rich-Edwards, J., Corliss, H. L., et al. (2008). Disparities in child abuse victimization in lesbian, bisexual, and heterosexual women in the Nurses' Health Study II. *Journal of Women's Health, 17,* 597–606.

31. Burke, J. G., Lee, L. C., & O'Campo, P. (2008). An exploration of maternal intimate partner violence experiences and infant general health and temperament. *Maternal and Child Health Journal, 12,* 172–179.

32. Ross, L. E., Steele, L. S., & Epstein, M. A. (2006). Service use and gaps in services for lesbian and bisexual women during donor insemination, pregnancy, and the postpartum period. *Journal of Obstetrics and Gynaecology Canada, 28,* 505–511.

33. Ross, L. E. (2005). Perinatal mental health in lesbian mothers: A review of potential risk and protective factors. *Women's Health, 41,* 113–128.

34. Ross, L. E., Steele, L., & Sapiro, B. (2005). Perceptions of predisposing and protective factors for perinatal depression in same-sex parents. *Journal of Midwifery & Women's Health, 50,* e65–70.

35. Berg, A. O. (2002). Screening for depression: Recommendations and rationale. *American Journal of Nursing, 102,* 77–80.

36. Whooley, M. A., Avins, A. L., Miranda, J., & Browner, W. S. (1997). Case-finding instruments for depression. Two questions are as good as many. *Journal of General Internal Medicine, 12,* 439–445.

ABOUT THE AUTHORS

CHRISTY M. ISLER, MD is Associate Professor in the Division of Maternal-Fetal Medicine, Department of Obstetrics and Gynecology at East Carolina University in North Carolina. Her areas of clinical/research interest are diabetes, hypertensive disease, and cardiomyopathy in pregnant women. She serves on the Board for Women in Medicine, an association for lesbian physicians.

LESLIE M. CRAGIN, PhD, CNM is Professor Emerita in the Department of Obstetrics, Gynecology and Reproductive Sciences at the University of California, San Francisco. She was Director of the Clinical Midwifery Practice at San Francisco General Hospital where she taught midwifery students, medical students, and residents. Her research has focused on outcomes of midwifery care for women in vulnerable populations.

CHAPTER 7

"Yup, I Have Two Moms."

CHILDREN OF LESBIAN PARENTS

MARY ANN A. VAN DAM,
PhD, RN, PNP

DANIEL, *a 12-year-old son of lesbian mothers, has historically been a good student. Today, his mothers received a call from the middle-school principal saying Daniel is complaining of a severe headache and nausea. The principal also told them Daniel's teachers have relayed concerns about his diminished academic performance and withdrawn behavior in the last few weeks.*

His mothers pick him up from school and bring him to a health care provider, who diagnoses a migraine headache. In discussing possible headache triggers, Daniel says the kids at school were teasing him about his lesbian mothers, which made him frustrated and angry. He also discloses that the teasing has gone on for many weeks and that kids have called him a "faggot" and other names. When his mothers ask him why he had not told them, Daniel says he did not want to hurt their feelings or for them to "make a big deal out of it at school."

■   ■   ■

Excellent health encompasses well-being in many dimensions—physical, emotional, spiritual, and social. In these dimensions, families create a complex web of interactions that are the essence of its integrated whole: any issue that affects the health and well-being of one member often affects all. If a family member experiences social discrimination as a result of the mothers' sexual orientation, how the mothers and children respond can impact the family positively, negatively, or both. Clinical assessments of patients' health and well-being should not overlook the potential effects of discrimination.

CONSEQUENCES OF DISCLOSURE AND NONDISCLOSURE

For lesbian mothers, parenthood carries an especially heavy social burden. One component of that burden is disclosure—the degree to which they are open or secretive about their sexual identity and to what extent, if any, they camouflage characteristics that others may interpret as signs of lesbianism. The degree of disclosure is often related to lesbians' perception of heterosexism and/or homophobia in their environment.[1-5]

Children growing up in lesbian-parented families learn they are different. They also learn how to read the environment as friendly or unfriendly and to decide if they should or should not disclose their family constellation. Researchers have found that potential health hazards for lesbians are associated with nondisclosure,[6-12] an association that may also apply to children. When children of lesbians do not disclose their parents' sexual orientation, they participate in maintaining a family façade which puts them in a dissonant position between the family and society at large.[13] The consequences of nondisclosure and the threats of social visibility may make children anxious and prompt them and/or their parents to create protective boundaries around the family,[14-19] perhaps isolating the children from available or potential support. These consequences are a product of the cross-cultural assumption that heterosexuality is a prerequisite for adequate parenting.[20] A secondary consequence may be lesbian parents' decision to isolate themselves socially to protect their family from harm by the surrounding hostile environment.

Stigmatization and the consequences of disclosure or nondisclosure may create burdens for lesbian-parented families at many levels in society[5] and affect the daily lives of family members individually and collectively, which in turn can interfere with the well-being of the integrated whole.

Lesbian mothers are concerned about raising their children in a heterosexist and homophobic world.[11,19,21] They must make decisions about disclosing their family constellation to teachers, principals, day care providers, health care providers, coaches, and the parents of their children's friends. They fear that their children will experience ridicule and discrimination because of the parents' sexual identity, a finding related to how tolerant they think other state residents are of lesbian identities.[11,22–24] A common reason for not disclosing their identity is to protect their children from criticism.[11,16,17,25] However, most lesbian-parented families thrive despite the burdens of stigmatization and they receive support from many sources.[11]

TYPES OF LESBIAN FAMILIES

The origins and constellations of lesbian families are as varied and creative as those of heterosexual families. The three most common types are original lesbian-parented families, lesbian-parented step families, and lesbian-parented single families.

Original Lesbian-Parented Families

This type of family consists of two lesbian mothers who decided to become parents after they acknowledged their sexual identity and began an intimate relationship. Either or both partners may have become pregnant with the help of male friends, sperm banks, or reproductive technology, or they may have chosen to adopt. In original lesbian-parented families, child care is egalitarian for 50% of mothers. For the other 50%, child care is not necessarily relegated to the birth mother.[11]

Some lesbian mothers in this arrangement coparent with either a man or gay male couple, creating a binuclear family. The men may provide the sperm for conception and the children may have three or four active parents who cooperatively raise them. Often the parents live in close proximity to facilitate fluid family function. Until they attend school and meet peers who come from heterosexual families, the children may not realize that society considers their family constellation unusual or unacceptable. This realization and the need to adapt to it can be stressful, especially if other children think their mothers' sexuality is unacceptable or their family constellation is ludicrous.

One concern of both biological and nonbiological mothers in original lesbian-parented families is the lack of social recognition for the nonbiological parent, regardless of how active she is in her child's life.[26] Even though, typically, both mothers have helped plan and conceive the child, and have more egalitarian parenting roles than many birth fathers in heterosexual families do,[27] a nonbiological mother may feel like she is not a "real" parent because she is not biologically connected to the child or socially recognized as a mom. Some lesbian parents address this issue through therapy, peer counseling, or a mothers' group. In other cases, both women become pregnant, sometimes simultaneously. Another approach is comaternity: one partner donates an egg and, after fertilization with sperm, an embryo is implanted in the uterus of the other, such that both women are biologically linked to the child. Comaternity is very expensive and beyond the financial means of most lesbians.

Lesbian-Parented Step Families

Many women have become mothers heterosexually and later unveiled their lesbian identity. If they subsequently partner with a lesbian, they create a lesbian-parented step family. In this constellation, the two partners started their intimate relationship after one or both women had children as single mothers or after a heterosexual or lesbian relationship ended.

As in heterosexual step families, blending in the second partner or step brothers and sisters is a complex challenge, one that involves realigning boundaries, power, and roles in the new constellation.[19] For lesbian-parented step families, adaptation to change may be even more complex, depending on the children's age and experience.[18] In addition to the typical adaptations that newly formed heterosexual step families must make, lesbian-parented step families have to contend with the disclosure issue. Adaptation and disclosure often occur simultaneously, such that parents may need to disclose their sexual identity to the children for the first time.[18] Lesbian-parented step families in which both partners bring children to the family may double the adaptation and disclosure burden and concerns.

Depending on their age and whether their social and relational environments tolerate lesbian identities, children may accept or reject the parents' identities and intimate relationship to varying degrees. The parents may have custody-related fears if one or both were previously married heterosexually and a legal ex-spouse threatens the family.[28] Lesbian-parented step families are more likely to reside in less-tolerant states that have few if any family protection laws.[11,24] Thus, for lesbian parents in these states, nondisclosure could be a pragmatic and wise choice.

Lesbian-Parented Single Families

Lesbians can become single mothers by adopting, getting pregnant outside of a relationship, or as a result of divorce after they have had children with a male or female partner. They may not reveal their sexual orientation to the children until they become intimate with a new partner.

A single lesbian mother may be able to pass as heterosexual because she is not paired with another woman in her daily life. This is especially possible if she does not fit the "butch" stereotype; very few lesbian mothers do.[11] In the absence of another parent (except in cases where a female coparent and ex-partner is involved), most people assume that the single lesbian is heterosexual, a misperception she may feel little need to correct. Issues related to disclosure and nondisclosure may be different for her than they are for partnered lesbian coparents. For example, a child who is aware of her sexual identity may disclose this fact to friends and others.

CHILDREN OF LESBIANS

The assumption for many years was that lesbians make poor mothers and that their children will grow up to be homosexual. Some individuals or groups consider that children who grow up to be homosexual or who differ from customary gender and sex roles have inherent problems and are deviant, thus posing concerns about the gender and sex roles of children raised in lesbian families.

Researchers have conducted many quantitative studies—classic psychiatric evaluations—in response to these concerns.[29-32] Studies in the late 1970s found these assumptions to be erroneous, but they had methodological limitations.[33,34] In the 1990s, researchers focused on the behavior and relationship characteristics of children whose parents were lesbian.[35-38] No studies in the '70s and '90s revealed any significant differences between children raised in heterosexual families and those raised in lesbian-parented families.[21,29-32,35-44] A meta-analysis of the studies also did not find any differences.[45]

However, after reviewing of 21 studies published since 1980, Stacey and Biblarz reported in 2001 that children raised by lesbians were more likely to depart from traditional gender roles and were more open to same-sex relationships compared with children raised by heterosexual parents. These two characteristics, the authors contended, may be neutral, may be secondary effects of social stigma, and/or may benefit the children of lesbian parents.[46] Whether the departures from usual social and role expectations are positive or negative may depend on the interpreter's value system along a liberal-traditional continuum. More and larger studies in the United States, Great Britain, and New Zealand found no significant differences between children raised by lesbian parents vs. heterosexual parents.[42,43,47,48] The researchers in these studies argued that Stacey and Biblarz overemphasized the differences they found.[42]

Although studies have not demonstrated any long-term harmful effects on children due to their mothers' sexual identity, such children do face additional challenges. The degree of these challenges may be related to the social hostility they and their mothers experience. For children, the hostility may be expressed by coaches, health care providers, religious persons, government officials, and others.[5] As the scenario at the beginning of this chapter illustrates, some of the biggest challenges for children arise in their relationships with peers.

BURDENS AND SUPPORTS

Research has shed light on the experiences of children with lesbian mothers and on the families' burdens and supports.[11,44,47-50] In one study, 16% of mothers delayed health care for themselves because they feared discrimination, but only 1.4% delayed health care for their children. About 85% of children in lesbian-parented families had grandparents in their lives, which may have been a source of family support or stigma. The vast majority of children (91%) in lesbian-parented families also had at least one man in their lives—usually a grandfather, friend, and/or uncle—who knew the children very well. Many of the children also knew their biological father. Fifty percent of lesbian-parented families belonged to a gay and/or lesbian-parent family support group where children could associate with other similar children. Another 25% of lesbian-parented families wanted to participate in such a group.[11] Children acknowledged that participating in a support group benefited them and that frequent contact with other children whose mothers were lesbian protected them from the negative effect stigmatization had on their self-esteem.[47]

In a study of 360 lesbian mothers, nearly 78% were concerned about verbal harassment their children might experience. Sixteen percent of participants' children had experienced harassment fairly often and 17% had experienced it once or twice. Thirty-two percent were concerned fairly often or always about physical harm to their children, but only 1.8% of the children had admitted to their mothers that they had been physically harmed. Twenty-eight percent of the mothers said their children were too young to have experienced such harm.[11] Importantly, studies that rely on reports from mothers about their children's experiences may not accurately reflect the children's true experiences, as Daniel's case illustrates. Many children are protective of their mothers and the gay community,[51] and they often develop a sophisticated understanding of diversity and tolerance at a young age.[44] Some may struggle with the stigma associated with their mothers' sexual identity.

Gershon and colleagues studied adolescents' perception of stigma and the degree to which they disclosed and coped with their mother's sexual identity. Greater perception of stigma was related to lower self-esteem scores. When adolescents perceived high levels of stigma, their self-esteem was lower regardless of whether they had good or poor coping skills, and when they perceived lower levels of stigma, self-esteem was higher.[52]

In a Dutch study of children who generally experienced low levels of stigma, boys between 8 and 12 years old said they felt excluded by peers because of their mothers' sexual identity. Girls felt they were the topic of gossip among school peers because of their lesbian parents.[47] Another study analyzed the accounts of older children and young adults in the United States, Great Britain, and New Zealand which reflected on their experiences growing up. They said they had experienced homophobia expressed by members of their extended families, by peers, by other parents, and institutionally.[48] Homophobia in general has a negative impact on children; those who experience less of it demonstrate fewer emotional and behavioral issues on standardized measures.[49]

The author found that many lesbian mothers (53%) were concerned fairly often that any negative behaviors their children expressed or difficulties they demonstrated would be blamed on lesbian parenting. This concern may interfere with lesbian-parented families seeking health care providers' help for problems many of them experience.[11]

Duran-Aydintug and Causey found that child custody issues were of great concern to 54% of lesbian mothers and that these fears were based on real or perceived issues in their daily lives.[53] In another study, 50% of children had mothers who were both legal parents. When both mothers were not legal parents, 21% said this was because their state did not recognize lesbian parenthood. Their state did not sanction many lesbian-parented step families because the ex-husband or partner was the other legal parent.[11]

Shapiro and colleagues compared lesbian mothers in the United States with those in Canada who were legally able to marry. The American mothers reported more family worries about legal status and discrimination (but not more general family worries), and had more depressive symptoms, than their Canadian counterparts did.[54] These results indicate that legal and social contexts influence maternal mental health, which in turn may affect lesbian-parented children.

IMPLICATIONS FOR HEALTH CARE PROVIDERS

Current knowledge helps health care providers understand the issues that may be affecting patients' health and well-being, and compassion compels them to provide the best possible care without moral judgment. If providers feel they cannot care for people who identify as lesbian, they should refer them to other knowledgeable, nonjudgmental professionals who can. A list of such professionals facilitates this task.

Health care providers must encourage patients to disclose their sexual orientation and family constellation to them, thus enabling appropriate care. Lesbians may feel more comfortable about disclosure if they see a rainbow flag, triangle, magazines, or other symbols of gay and lesbian friendliness in the office. Inclusive terminology in history-taking also helps. For example, questions that use the word "married" usually denote a legal relationship between two heterosexual individuals but may overlook a life-long partnership. Instead, "partner" gives a lesbian patient an opportunity to disclose her relationship with another woman. Asking her to describe the "family constellation" may elicit the fact that the household consists of two women. If there are children, the clinician can ask if she is a "coparent," which acknowledges the often-ignored status of the other mother and may prompt a more specific description of the family. Age-appropriate questions for children, especially preschoolers, are likely to yield straightforward responses. Children may refer to either or both of their parents as "momma" or "mommy," regardless of which one is the biological mother.

Providers need to assess family support systems without implying that being lesbian or having children as a lesbian is problematic. Questions regarding the patient's experience with discrimination gives the impression that the provider is knowledgeable about lesbian issues. Inquiries about support systems, child custody issues, and fear of job and housing loss are especially pertinent in states where nondiscrimination laws do not address sexual identity.[11]

Lesbian mothers, particularly those in lesbian-parented step families, may ask if telling the children about their sexual identity is best done at a certain age. Because children understand the concept of gay/lesbian around age 5 and react to disclosure most positively before puberty,[14,18] clinicians and lesbian mothers should discuss the possibility of having the parents disclose their sexual identity as soon as possible.[11,55,56] Disclosure requires two preconditions: the custody arrangement must be as secure as possible, given that many lesbian parents have lost custody and visitation rights simply because of their sexual orientation,[56,57] and parents must feel positive about their sexual identity.[56] Otherwise, a therapist can help them counter the negative effects of nondisclosure and improve their self-esteem.[11,56]

The community's tolerance of, and the state's legal protections for lesbians are important considerations. Because parents must protect themselves and their children from harm, health care providers would be ill-advised to recommend unselective disclosure in an intolerant community. On the other hand, if parents are very uncomfortable about disclosure in a highly tolerant community, a therapist may be able to help them overcome the trauma of past stigma experiences.[11]

Parents may be worried about harassment or teasing of their children because of the mothers' sexual identity. Health care providers should inquire about and acknowledge such concerns. Wellness visits with children often give providers an opportunity to ask about their school and friends, sometimes in the parents' absence. Questions about teasing may open the door to discussion of homophobic attitudes and overt discrimination the child may be experiencing and his or her ability to cope with them. The child's need for support and/or referral to a therapist may become apparent.

RESOURCES FOR LESBIAN PARENTS
■ Parents, Families, and Friends of Lesbians and Gays: 🖐 www.pflag.org
■ Children of Lesbians and Gays Everywhere: 🖐 www.colage.org
■ Metropolitan Community Churches: 🖐 www.mcchurch.org
■ Other welcoming/inclusive churches*
■ Parenting groups
■ Community centers
■ Other supportive health care providers

* Lesbians may be skeptical of religious institutions, given that some churches are biased against same-sex relationships. Health care providers should remain neutral about religious preference when they recommend church-related resources.

A list of local lesbian and gay resources can be of great service to lesbian families, many of whom find support among similar families (see box above). Children who attend schools that offer lesbian/gay/bisexual/transgender curricula, and lesbian mothers who participate in the lesbian community, are factors that protect youth from the harmful influences of homophobia.[50] These are options that, if available, health care providers might also suggest.

■ ■ ■

To get all perspectives on Daniel's circumstances, the health care provider might find it helpful to first speak with him alone, then with his mothers alone, then with all three together.

The provider should acknowledge the peer pressure Daniel is enduring by saying: "This must be hard for you because you have a great family and you obviously care about your moms, but your friends are making fun of you because of them. That puts you in the middle of a hurtful situation." It opens the door for additional comments by Daniel and shows that the provider is supportive of him and his family constellation. Asking Daniel about events that sparked the ridicule from peers and how long it has been going on could yield important context. Soliciting suggestions from Daniel about how he might alleviate the ridicule may give the parents some worthwhile ideas to consider.

Empathizing with the mothers conveys support for them as lesbians and for their challenging situation. An opening statement such as "It must be difficult for both of you to hear that homophobic remarks are affecting your son" shows that the provider recognizes both women as Daniel's mothers and may prompt them to talk more about their concerns.

To better understand the issues in Daniel's life, it is important for the provider to know what type of lesbian-parented family he has. If the mothers are Daniel's original parents, they have raised him exclusively, which means he may only need help learning how to cope with ridicule from peers. If his family is a newly formed lesbian-parented step family, Daniel may also need help coping with his mothers' newly unveiled sexual identity and a new lesbian relationship at home.

If the family lives in a socially intolerant area, suggesting that the mothers discuss Daniel's situation with his teachers and principal might not be wise because it could threaten the family's integrity. In a socially tolerant area, such a discussion is warranted, as long it respects Daniel's request for confidentiality.

When speaking with the parents and Daniel together, the health care provider should encourage them to participate in a support group for gay/lesbian families, and encourage Daniel to join a group for children of gay/lesbian parents. There, Daniel may learn about ways to cope with ridicule and realize he is not alone.[*] If Daniel prefers not to participate, individual therapy is warranted, given his stress-related migraines and declining academic performance. The provider can facilitate a discussion between Daniel and his mothers about keeping them informed when there are problems at school, with the parents agreeing not to "make a big deal out of it" unless negative events are truly harmful. In addition, the provider should support Daniel's stated need for confidentiality. He and his parents may choose to discuss these parameters further on their own.

If there is little progress on resolving the issues Daniel faces, referring him and his mothers to a family therapist would be prudent. Within 2 months, the provider

---

[*] *COLAGE has a pen pal program that links children of lesbians. See www.colage.org/programs/penpals.*

should follow up on his migraines and treatment, his school performance, and his adherence to plans for social support.

CONCLUSION

Health care providers need to support patients and their families, recognize developmental challenges, and provide the best evidence-based care regardless of family constellation. Intrafamilial and social issues are more pressing when that constellation is marginalized and stigmatized.

Providers and researchers who ignore lesbian-parented families are overlooking the diversity of families in today's world, contributing to their harm, and fostering a climate of heterosexism and intolerance. Intolerance instigates violence and social negation, which place the health and well-being of lesbians and their children at risk. Providers should care for lesbians and their families as they would any other patients, and be knowledgeable about the unique issues these families often encounter.

REFERENCES

1. Anderson, M. K., & Mavis, B. (1996). Sources of coming out self-efficacy for lesbians. *Journal of Homosexuality, 32,* 37–52.

2. Gentry, S. (1992). Caring for lesbians in a homophobic society. *Health Care for Women International, 13,* 173–180.

3. Morris, J. (1997). Lesbian coming out as a multidimensional process. *Journal of Homosexuality, 33,* 1–22.

4. Rosario, M., Hunter, J., Maguen, S., Gwadz, M., & Smith, R. (2001). The coming-out process and its adaptational and health-related associations among gay, lesbian, and bisexual youths: Stipulation and exploration of a model. *American Journal of Community Psychology, 29,* 133–160.

5. Van Dam, M. A. (2003). Bronfenbrenner's ecological theory and lesbian families. *Clinical Excellence for Nurse Practitioners, 7,* 99–105.

6. Bradford, J., Ryan, C., & Rothblum, E. D. (1994). National lesbian health care survey: Implications for mental health. *Journal of Consulting and Clinical Psychology, 62,* 228–242.

7. Jordan, K. M., & Deluty, R. H. (1998). Coming out for lesbian women: Its relation to anxiety, positive affectivity, self-esteem, and social support. *Journal of Homosexuality, 35,* 41–63.

8. Jordan, K. M., & Deluty, R. H. (2000). Social support, coming out, and relationship satisfaction in lesbian couples. *Journal of Lesbian Studies, 4,* 145–164.

9. Morris, J., Balsam, K., & Rothblum, E. (2002). Lesbian and bisexual mothers and nonmothers: Demographics and the coming-out process. *Journal of Family Psychology, 16,* 144–156.

10. Morris, J., Waldo, C., & Rothblum, E. (2001). A model of predictors and outcomes of outness among lesbian and bisexual women. *American Journal of Orthopsychiatry, 71,* 61–71.

11. Van Dam, M. A. (2004). Mothers in two types of lesbian families: Stigma experiences, supports, and burdens. *Journal of Family Nursing, 10,* 450–484.

12. Van Dam, M. A., Koh, A., & Dibble, S. (2001). Lesbian disclosure to health care providers and delay of care. *Journal of the Gay and Lesbian Medical Association, 5,* 11–19.

13. Slater, S. (1995). *The lesbian family life cycle.* New York: Free Press.

14. Baptiste, D. (1987). The gay and lesbian stepparent family. In F. W. Bozett (Ed.), *Gay and lesbian parents* (pp. 112–137). New York: Praeger.

15. Crawford, S. (1987). Lesbian families: Psychosocial stress and the family building process. In Boston Lesbian Psychologies Collective (Ed.), *Lesbian psychologies: Explorations & challenges* (pp. 195–214). Chicago: University of Illinois Press.

16. Hare, J. (1994). Concerns and issues faced by families headed by a lesbian couple. *Families in Society: The Journal of Contemporary Human Services, 42,* 249–255.

17. Lott-Whitehead, L., & Tully, C. T. (1993). The family lives of lesbian mothers. *Smith College Studies in Social Work, 63,* 265–280.

18. Lynch, J. M., & Murray, K. (2000). For the love of the children: The coming out process for lesbian and gay parents and stepparents. *Journal of Homosexuality, 39,* 1–24.

19. Wright, J. M. (1998). *Lesbian step families: An ethnology of love.* Birmingham, NY: Harrington Park Press.

20. Crawford, I., & Solliday, E. (1996). The attitude of undergraduate college students toward gay parenting. *Journal of Homosexuality, 30,* 63–77.

21. Gartrell, N., Hamilton, J., Banks, A., Mosbacher, D., Reed, N., Sparks, C. H., et al. (1996). The national lesbian family study: 1. Interviews with prospective mothers. *American Journal of Orthopsychiatry, 66,* 272–281.

22. Kirkpatrick, M. (1987). Clinical implications of lesbian mother studies. *Journal of Homosexuality, 13,* 201–211.

23. Gibbs, E. (1989). Psychosocial development of children raised by lesbian mothers: A review of research. *Women & Therapy, 8,* 55–75.

24. Van Dam, M. A. (2006). *Lesbian mother disclosure: A geopolitical perspective.* Unpublished manuscript. San Francisco State University.

25. Lewin, E. (1993). *Lesbian mothers: Accounts of gender in American culture.* London: Cornell University Press.

26. Comeau, D. (1999). Lesbian nonbiological mothering: Negotiating an (un)familiar existence. *Journal of the Association for Research on Mothering, 1,* 44–57.

27. Tasker, F., & Golombok, S. (1998). The role of co-mothers in planned lesbian-led families. *Journal of Lesbian Studies, 2,* 49–68.

28. Hartman, A. (1996). *Social policy as a context for gay and lesbian families.* San Francisco: Jossey-Bass.

29. Hoeffer, B. (1981). Children's acquisition of sex-role behavior in lesbian-mother families. *American Journal of Orthopsychiatry, 51*, 536–543.

30. Kirkpatrick, M., Smith, C., & Roy, R. (1981). Lesbian mothers and their children: A comparative survey. *American Journal of Orthopsychiatry, 51*, 545–551.

31. Golombok, S., Spencer, A., & Rutter, M. (1983). Children in lesbian and single-parent households: Psychosexual and psychiatric appraisal. *Journal of Child Psychology and Psychiatry, 24*, 551–572.

32. Green, R., Mandel, J. B., Hotvedt, M. E., Gray, J., & Smith, L. (1986). Lesbian mothers and their children: A comparison with solo parent heterosexual mothers and their children. *Archives of Sexual Behavior, 15*, 167–184.

33. Patterson, C. J. (1992). Children of lesbian and gay parents. *Child Development, 63*, 1025–1042.

34. Belcastro, P. A., Gramlich, T., Nicholson, T., Price, J., & Wilson, R. (1993). A review of data-based studies addressing the affects of homosexual parenting on children's sexual and social functioning. *Journal of Divorce & Remarriage, 20*, 105–122.

35. Flaks, D. K., Ficher, I., Masterpasqua, F., & Joseph, G. (1995). Lesbian choosing motherhood: A comparative study of lesbian and heterosexual parents and their children. *Developmental Psychology, 31*, 105–114.

36. Patterson, C. J. (1995). Lesbian mothers, gay fathers, and their children. In A. R. D'Augelli & C. J. Patterson (Eds.), *Lesbian, gay, and bisexual identities over the lifespan: Psychological perspectives* (pp. 262–290). New York: Oxford University Press.

37. Brewaeys, A., Ponjaert, I., van Hall, E. V., & Golombok, S. (1997). Donor insemination: Child development and family functioning in lesbian mother families. *Human Reproduction, 12*, 1349–1359.

38. Patterson, C. J., Hurt, S., & Mason, C. D. (1998). Families of the lesbian baby boom: Children's contact with grandparents and other adults. *American Journal of Orthopsychiatry, 68*, 390–399.

39. Miller, J. A., Jacobson, R. B., & Bigner, J. J. (1981). The child's home environment for lesbian vs. heterosexual mothers: A neglected area of research. *Journal of Homosexuality, 7*, 49–56.

40. Huggins, S. L. (1989). A comparative study of self-esteem of adolescent children of divorced lesbian mothers and divorced heterosexual mothers. *Journal of Homosexuality, 18*, 123–135.

41. Hare, J., & Richards, L. (1993). Children raised by lesbian couples: Does the context of birth affect father and partner involvement? *Family Relations, 42*, 249–255.

42. Golombok, S., Perry, B., Burston, A., Murray, C., Mooney-Somers, J., Stevens, et al. (2003). Children with lesbian parents: A community study. *Developmental Psychology, 39*, 20–33.

43. Tasker, F. (2005) Lesbian mothers, gay fathers, and their children: A review. *Journal of Developmental & Behavioral Pediatrics, 26*, 224–240.

44. Gartrell, N., Deck, A., Rodas, C., Peyser, H., & Banks, A. (2005). The National Lesbian Family Study: 4. Interviews with the 10-year-old children. *American Journal of Orthopsychiatry, 75*, 518–524.

45. Allen, M., & Burrell, N. (1996). Comparing the impact of homosexual and heterosexual parents on children: Meta-analysis of existing research. *Journal of Homosexuality, 32,* 19–35.

46. Stacey, J., & Biblarz, T. (2001). (How) does the sexual orientation of parents matter? *American Sociological Review, 66,* 159–183.

47. Bos, H. M. W., & van Balen, F. (2008). Children in planned lesbian families: Stigmatisation, psychological adjustment and protective factors. *Culture, Health & Sexuality, 10,* 221–236.

48. Fairlough, A. (2008). Growing up with a lesbian or gay parent: Young people's perspective. *Health and Social Care in the Community, 16,* 521–528.

49. Bos, H. M. W., Gartrell, N. K., Peyser, H., & van Balen, F. (2008). The USA National Longitudinal Lesbian Family Study (NLLFS): Homophobia, psychological adjustment, and protective factors. *Journal of Lesbian Studies, 12,* 455–471. Available at www.nllfs.org/publications/pdf/Gartrell-J_Lesbian_Studies_article_PDF.pdf.

50. Bos, H. M. W., Gartrell, N. K., van Balen, F., Peyser, H., & Sandfort, T. G. M. (2008). Children in planned lesbian families: A cross-cultural comparison between the United States and the Netherlands. *American Journal of Orthopsychiatry, 78,* 211–219.

51. Goldberg, A. E. (2007). (How) does it make a difference? Perspectives of adults with lesbian, gay, and bisexual parents. *American Journal of Orthopsychiatry, 77,* 550–562.

52. Gershon, T., Tschann, J., & Jemerin, J. (1999). Stigmatization, self-esteem, and coping among the adolescent children of lesbian mothers. *Journal of Adolescent Health, 24,* 437–445.

53. Duran-Aydintug, C., & Causey, K. A. (1996). Child custody determination: Implications for lesbian mothers. *Journal of Divorce & Remarriage, 25,* 55–74.

54. Shapiro, D. N., Peterson, C., & Stewart, A. J. (2009). Legal and social contexts and mental health among lesbian and heterosexual mothers. *Journal of Family Psychology, 23,* 255–262.

55. Pennington, S. B. (1987). Children of lesbian mothers. In F. W. Bozett (Ed.), *Gay and lesbian parents* (pp. 58–74). New York: Praeger.

56. Martin, A. (1998). Clinical issues in psychotherapy with lesbian-, gay-, and bisexual-parented families. In C. J. Patterson & A. R. D'Augelli (Eds.), *Lesbian, gay and bisexual identities in families: Psychological perspectives* (pp. 270–291). New York: Oxford University Press.

57. Rivera, R. R. (1987). Legal issues in gay and lesbian parenting. In F. W. Bozett (Ed.), *Gay and lesbian parents* (pp. 199–227). New York: Praeger.

ABOUT THE AUTHOR

Mary Ann A. van Dam, PhD, RN, PNP is Associate Professor of Pediatric Nursing at San Francisco State University where she teaches pediatric pathophysiology and medical ethics. Her research emphasis is on stigma and health, particularly in lesbian family stigma and disclosure issues as well as the quantitative measurement of disclosure for lesbian mothers.

CHAPTER 8

"Got a Light?"

SMOKING AND LESBIANS

MICHELE J. ELIASON,
PhD

LAURIE DRABBLE,
PhD, MPH, MSW

JAN, *a 42-year-old lesbian, is a public health professional. She has smoked for 24 years and has tried unsuccessfully to quit several times in the previous 5 years. Life stressors include her job (she feels scrutinized by coworkers, who know she is a lesbian—some are highly judgmental), her family (which is not very accepting of her partner), and her partner (who smokes but does not want to quit). Jan has asthma and a chronic cough, and fears more serious health consequences in the near future. She wants a health care provider's help in developing a more effective smoking cessation plan. What would the provider's plan look like?*

There is a fairly large and methodologically sound body of research demonstrating that lesbians smoke at higher rates than heterosexual women do. Although researchers used different measures of smoking, different definitions of sexual identity, and a wide variety of sampling strategies in various geographic regions, the findings are strikingly similar. Much less is known about why smoking rates are higher among lesbians or how treatment and prevention might best address the problem. A growing body of evidence suggests that the frequency of risk behaviors may be equal to or even greater among bisexual women and women who have sex with women but label themselves as heterosexual.

This chapter summarizes the known risk of and protective factors for smoking among lesbians, discusses the clinical implications of smoking cessation efforts, and proposes some interventions.

BACKGROUND

Tobacco use is the leading known cause of preventable death in the United States.[1] Studies on the prevalence of smoking among sexual minority women—which began only about 10 years ago, reflecting the recency of lesbian, gay, bisexual, and transgender (LGBT) health research—confirm that tobacco use is an important risk factor for increased morbidity and mortality in the lesbian community. A few studies have reported higher rates of asthma among sexual minority women,[2,3] but they did not investigate smoking. The first studies to examine smoking in sexual minority populations were done by Aaron and colleagues,[4] Skinner,[5] Skinner and Otis,[6] Valanis and colleagues,[7] and others. More recent research specifically on lesbian health, including tobacco use and dependence, has provided insight into their particular health risks and needs.

Table 8.1 summarizes results from population-based studies of the prevalence of smoking among sexual minority women. Although these studies differ in a number of ways, the results are quite similar. In nearly every case, lesbians reported higher rates of lifetime and current smoking than did women in the general population or those in heterosexual comparison groups.

The studies in Table 8.1 are very important because they add to the body of research demonstrating health disparities and health risk factors for lesbians, and suggest a link between sexual minority status and adverse health risks. However, research to date has largely been descriptive or has focused on prevalence; it provides little insight into specific risk and protective factors that may underlie higher rates of tobacco use. Other studies, reviewed in the section below, have suggested hypothetical factors, but these await empirical testing.

Researchers have proposed potential correlates of smoking among lesbians, including demographic factors, targeted tobacco advertising, mental health disorders, minority stress, body image and weight, social networks and significant others, and alcohol and drug use. Hughes and Jacobson pointed out that understanding risk and protective factors among women in the general population, and how these might differentially impact sexual minority women, may provide some important direction for intervention and prevention.[20]

Demographics

Age is the most studied factor for health risks, including smoking. Smoking rates decline with age in the general population and among lesbians. For example, a survey of members in a large HMO reported that 33.3% of lesbians and bisexuals 20 to 34 years old smoked compared with 29.1% of those 35 to 49 years old and 12.1% of those 50 or older.[18] Similar findings were even more dramatic in a random digit dial survey of Californians: nearly 74% of lesbians 18 to 24 years old smoked compared with 29% of those who were 25 to 44 years old, 20% of those between 45 and 64, and less than 1% of those older than 65.[8] In another study, low educational attainment and low income were associated with higher smoking rates.[15] Sanchez and colleagues found very high smoking rates among poor lesbians of color living in the Bronx, New York.[21]

Targeted Tobacco Advertising

The tobacco industry engages in substantial targeted marketing to ethnic minorities[22] and LGBT communities.[23,24] Smith and colleagues, in examining 20 LGB press magazines and community newspapers published between 1990 and 2000, found 3,428 ads that addressed tobacco in some way, 689 for tobacco products, 1,067 for smoking cessation products or services, 99 with tobacco-related political messages, and 1,033 nontobacco ads that showed tobacco use. The many cessation ads were small and often text-only. They peaked in 1995 and had declined dramatically by 2000.[23] Brownworth reported in 1995 that lesbian periodicals published fewer tobacco ads than magazines oriented to gay males did, as lesbians were not yet considered a valuable market,[25] but the lesbian periodicals had the highest rate of nontobacco ads showing tobacco use. It is possible that lesbians are influenced by ads that target women in general or lesbian/bisexual women. For example, in subtly coded lesbian messages, the 1994 Virginia Slims campaign showed two or more women together.[24] In one study, 94% of LGB respondents indicated they would support companies that advertised in gay magazines and companies that contributed to gay organizations, which suggests the ads do influence lesbian communities and individuals.[26]

TABLE 8.1. POPULATION-BASED STUDIES OF SMOKING PREVALENCE AMONG SEXUAL MINORITY WOMEN*

AUTHORS	METHODS	DEFINITION OF SEXUALITY	FINDINGS
Gruskin et al.[8]	Random digit dial survey in California of lesbian, gay, and bisexual people, compared with California Tobacco Survey data for the general population	Identity and behavior	▪ Lesbians (n = 307): 22.0% daily smokers ▪ Bisexual (n = 263): 23.0% daily smokers ▪ Women who have sex with women (n = 328): 30.0% daily smokers versus 9.0% in the general population of women
Gruskin and Gordon[9]	Random-sample general health surveys (1999 and 2002) of adult HMO members. Combined lesbian/bisexual women for analysis.	Identity	After adjusting for age, race/ethnicity, education, and year, lesbians/bisexual women (n =210) were more likely to be current smokers than were heterosexual women (n = 12,188). Smoking differences were large in younger age groups for lesbians but not significantly different in older groups.
Burgard et al.[10]	1998–2000 California Women's Health Survey	Behavior	Higher smoking rates among women reporting same-sex partners (n = 350) versus women with only male partners (n = 10,854): 29.8% versus 17.0%
Dilley et al.[11]	Data from the Behavioral Risk Factor Surveillance System in Washington State and Oregon. Random digit dial survey.	Identity	Current women smokers: ▪ Heterosexual (n = 14,362): 18.3% ▪ Lesbian/bisexual (n = 350): 31.4% (odds ratio [OR] = 2.2)
Drabble and Trocki[12]	National Alcohol Survey of lesbians, bisexual women, heterosexual women with same-sex partners, and exclusively heterosexual women	Identity and behavior	OR for current smoking: ▪ No difference between exclusively heterosexual women (n = 3,723) and lesbians (n = 36) ▪ Bisexual (n = 50): 3.45 ▪ Heterosexual with same-sex partners (n = 71): 2.04
Bowen et al.[13]	Probability sampling for a women's health survey in Boston based on census tracts rich in sexual minority women	Behavior, attraction, and identity. Only identity used for analysis.	No significant differences in smoking rates between lesbian/bisexual women (n = 35, 20% current smokers) and heterosexual women (n = 170, 18.0% current smokers). Other demographic differences by neighborhood may have impacted the results.
Case et al.[14]	Nurses' Health Study, a longitudinal national survey of lesbians, bisexual women, and heterosexual women	Identity	Current smokers: ▪ Lesbians (n = 694): 19.0% ▪ Bisexual women (n = 317): 21.0% ▪ Heterosexual women (n = 90,823): 11.0%

(cont.)

TABLE 8.1. POPULATION-BASED STUDIES OF SMOKING PREVALENCE AMONG SEXUAL MINORITY WOMEN* *(cont.)*

AUTHORS	METHODS	DEFINITION OF SEXUALITY	FINDINGS
Diamant and Wold[16]	Los Angeles County Health Survey, 1999, random digit dial	Identity	Current smokers: ■ Lesbians ($n = 43$): 27.9% ■ Bisexual women ($n = 60$): 30.4% ■ Heterosexual women ($n = 4,023$):13.9%
Cochran et al.[17]	Pooled data from seven large studies (two national, five regional) of 3cancer-related risk factors among lesbians. Researchers compared results for nearly 12,000 lesbians with national estimates for women in general.	Each study used different measures. The common definition for pooled data was women who have sex with women (WSW).	Current smokers: ■ WSW: 21.0% ■ Heterosexual women:16.0%
Gruskin et al.[18]	General health survey of randomly selected HMO members, 1996	Identity	Lesbian/bisexual women ($n = 120$) compared with heterosexual women ($n = 7,993$). Lesbian/bisexual women < 50 years old were significantly more likely to be smokers than were heterosexual women of comparable age: ■ 20–34 years: 33.3% versus 12.6% ■ 35–49 years: 29.1% versus 13.2% ■ 50+ years: 12.1% versus 11.3% Overall: 25.4% of lesbian/bisexual women versus 12.6% of heterosexual women
Diamant et al.[19]	Los Angeles County Health Survey, 1997, random digit dial	Identity	Current smokers: ■ Lesbians ($n = 51$): 37.0% ■ Bisexual women ($n = 36$): 50.0% ■ Heterosexual women ($n = 4,610$): 14.0%. Lesbians/bisexual women were more likely to report both current and past tobacco use ($OR = 1.73$ for lesbians and bisexual women)

* These studies varied in terms of:

(1) Measures of smoking. Generally, there were only a few questions about lifetime and/or current smoking;

(2) Definitions of sexual identity. Some relied on behavioral measures, others on sexual identity categories. Still others used a combination of behavioral and identity measures;

(3) Categories of sexual orientation. Some combined "lesbian" and "bisexual women" categories, others separated them;

(4) Sampling. Many recent studies involved random sampling of the general population, unlike many earlier studies that relied on convenience sampling. This makes it difficult to compare older and newer studies. In addition, some population-based studies were limited to one state, county, or HMO, while others were national in scope.

(5) Designs. Not all studies had comparison groups;

(6) Regional study populations. Respondents represented diverse urban and rural areas and parts of the world.

Mental Health

Many studies of the general population have found an association between mental health disorders and smoking by both women and men.[27–29] Several studies have identified higher rates of depression and anxiety disorders among lesbians.[2,30,31]

Minority Stress

There is growing evidence that health disparities may be largely related to the effects of minority stress caused by perceived, threatened, and actual discrimination, and by harassment of and violence against people who adopt a lesbian or other minority identity.[32] Cochran and Mays found higher rates of physical health disorders among women with female partners than among women with only male partners, but the difference virtually disappeared when the researchers controlled for psychological stress.[2] In an earlier study, they had found that middle-age lesbians, compared with heterosexual women, reported substantially more experiences of work-related discrimination and harassment, and threats, name-calling, and other forms of harassment outside of work.[33] Health disparities may be even more dramatic when multiple sources of minority stress exist, as they do for poor lesbians of color who experience sexism, racism, classism, and heterosexism simultaneously. For example, in comparing ethnic minority heterosexual women with lesbians, Mays and colleagues found that current smoking rates were higher among lesbians of color than among heterosexual women in all three study groups: Hispanics (lesbians, 30%, vs. heterosexuals, 13%), African Americans (28% vs. 22%), and Asian Americans (20% vs. 13%).[34] (See also Sanchez and colleagues.[21])

Body Image and Weight

Many women in the general population smoke to control their weight and are reluctant to quit for fear of gaining weight.[35] Numerous studies have found that lesbians are more likely than heterosexual women to be overweight.[14] However, research suggests that lesbians have fewer problems related to body dissatisfaction and weight preoccupation than heterosexual women do.[36–38] If indeed lesbians are less vulnerable to societal messages for women about size and appearance, a key barrier to smoking cessation in the general population—fear of gaining weight—may be less formidable for them. To date, no study has examined body image in relation to smoking and smoking cessation among lesbians.

Social Networks and Significant Others

Lesbians and other sexual minority women are more likely than heterosexual women to go to bars and socialize in other drinking contexts.[39] In some communities, gay bars may still be among the few places where lesbians can completely be themselves and meet others for friendship and relationships. Drinking and smoking are the main activities in bars, and the exposure may prompt many lesbians to begin and continue smoking. In addition, if one makes friends and meets partners who smoke, quitting becomes much more difficult without support from the entire social network.[40] Hughes and Jacobson noted that lesbian smokers were more likely than heterosexual female smokers to have partners who smoked.[20]

Alcohol and Drug Use

Drinking and smoking, as well as other drug use, tend to go hand-in-hand. National population-based studies suggest a strong correlation between alcohol consumption, particularly heavy drinking, and tobacco use.[41–43] According to one study, 79% of LGBT people in treatment for substance abuse were current smokers compared with 73% of heterosexual people in treatment.[44] Similarly, Eliason and Worthington found that smoking rates were about 50% among lesbian/bisexual women in recovery from alcohol and drug problems compared with 26% among those without such problems.[45] Although risks for smoking are particularly high among individuals in recovery, research suggests that smoking cessation programs during substance abuse treatment are effective.[46,47]

For better treatment and prevention, more research is necessary on how interrelationships among these factors affect the onset and continuation of smoking by lesbians. Also unclear is how other psychological, social, or environmental factors related to smoking in the general population, such as childhood trauma and sensation seeking, may differ among sexual minority populations. Although many of the same factors predictive of smoking in heterosexual women may be relevant to lesbians as well, it is likely that heterosexism and minority stress create unique risk factors.

INTERVENTIONS FOR SMOKING CESSATION

What type of treatment plan might a clinician develop for Jan, the woman in the scenario at the beginning of this chapter? Little research has evaluated smoking cessation interventions for specific populations, including LGBT smokers.[48] Only one study has asked LGBT participants about tobacco treatments. In examining their use of cessation interventions and their attitudes, it found that 63% had attempted to quit in the previous year and that women were more likely than men to have tried. One-fourth of attempts involved a nicotine replacement therapy, a higher percentage than in the general population (16%), suggesting that lesbians might be more amenable to this approach. Notably, health care professionals had advised 57% of smokers in the general population, but only 40% of the lesbians, to quit.[49]

In the absence of empirical data to guide a discussion of treatment, a theoretical framework serves as a starting point. Table 8.2 shows an integral approach to tobacco treatment that takes into account the multiple factors impacting any individual's health behavior. This model suggests that changing any lifestyle behavioral pattern, be it smoking, drinking, or eating, is more likely to succeed if interventions are drawn from all four quadrants. Psychological/spiritual interventions address the individual's inner world of thoughts, feelings, identities, and beliefs. The quadrant includes spiritual practices because research suggests that spirituality is a major motivation for transformational change in people with drug and alcohol dependencies[50] and other life-threatening illnesses and experiences.[51] Although no one has studied spirituality in relation to smoking cessation, it may play a major role in treatment.

TABLE 8.2. INTERVENTIONS TO TREAT SMOKING

PSYCHOLOGICAL/SPIRITUAL	BIOLOGICAL
■ Therapy for symptoms of mental illness—depression, anxiety, stress ■ Smoking cessation counseling ■ Individual spiritual practice ■ Counseling about coping with a stigmatized identity	■ Nicotine replacement therapy ■ Medications for mental or physical disorders ■ Nutrition ■ Complementary therapies (acupuncture, meditation)

SOCIAL/CULTURAL	SOCIETAL/ENVIRONMENTAL
■ Support groups ■ Family and peer support ■ Changing community norms ■ Changing access to tobacco ■ Culturally sensitive treatment and prevention models (e.g., The Last Drag, Lesbian Kisses)	■ Policies: (1) regarding paid advertising and smoking images in mainstream and LGBT media, tobacco-tax laws, tobacco availability; (2) regarding payment for treatment ■ Stigma of sexual orientation ■ Messages from national and international LGBT and women's organizations about health behaviors and smoking cessation

Sources: Amodia, D. S., Cano, C., & Eliason, M. J. (2005). An integral approach to substance abuse treatment. *Journal of Psychoactive Drugs, 37,* 363–371; Eliason, M. J., & Amodia, D. S. (2007). Drug craving: An integral approach. *Addiction Research and Theory, 15,* 343–364.

Biological interventions comprise nicotine-replacement patches, gum, lozenges, and nasal sprays, and medications such as Chantix or Zyban to reduce craving. The support cited under social/cultural interventions includes that provided by educational groups and help from family members, friends, and partners. Studies have shown that lesbians are amenable to individual and group treatment as well as support groups,[52,53] so a smoking cessation group might be attractive. Perhaps other social institutions, such as LGBT community agencies, can help change community norms about the acceptability of smoking or offer lesbian- or LGBT-specific smoking cessation groups that address the role of sexual stigma and minority stress in tobacco use. An example is The Last Drag (www.lastdrag.org), a curriculum developed in California and available in several other locations that entails seven group sessions.

Finally, broader societal/environmental interventions address issues such as state and federal policies and laws, conservative religious dogmas that uphold the stigma of minority sexual identity, media and the tobacco industry roles in marketing cigarettes to LGBT communities, and the few LGBT health organizations that attempt to counter such efforts with meager resources.

■　■　■

Given these intervention options, Jan's clinician may be able to help by:
- Prescribing nicotine replacement therapy and/or other appropriate pharmaceuticals to ease her off nicotine addiction and avoid withdrawal;
- Suggesting strategies that would help her cope with homophobic coworkers;
- Enlisting the support of her partner, who, with a little motivational coaching, might also be willing to consider smoking cessation;
- Finding a lesbian- or LGBT-specific smoking cessation support group for her or, if she lives in a rural area, perhaps an online support group; and
- Suggesting meditation as a coping strategy or referring her to an acupuncturist.

SMOKING PREVENTION

What types of environmental changes are necessary in the community, media, and health care system to prevent smoking among lesbians like Jan, to intervene early when they begin, and to prevent relapse after they quit? Researchers who have documented smoking disparities in sexual minority populations point to the importance of adapting evidenced-based treatment and prevention models to LGBT communities[54]; developing partnerships between LGB communities and tobacco control efforts at the local, state, and national level[8]; and ensuring that health care environments for lesbians and bisexuals are safe, responsive, and unbiased.[14,17,20] As Gruskin and colleagues noted, greater risk of tobacco use is only one of multiple health-related risks that appear to be higher among LGB populations. The authors suggested that efforts to address other health and mental health problems, including depression, substance abuse, victimization, and childhood trauma, may help reduce the greater smoking risk.[8]

Although lesbians apparently are less likely than heterosexual women to access preventive health care,[17,19] interventions by health care providers remain an important evidence-based strategy for both primary and secondary prevention of smoking among sexual minority women. Research suggests that effective communication between providers and patients is critical to quality care and improved health status. For example, a review of 96 studies found that risk communication interventions, particularly those in which a provider assesses an individual patient's risk, positively affect health outcomes.[55] Providers' bias, discomfort, or lack of education and training in working with sexual minority health consumers may substantially impair communications between them and lesbian/bisexual women.[56–59] There is some evidence that practitioner attitude toward nonheterosexual identity may be particularly important in terms of the health care provider women choose[60] and whether or not they disclose their sexual orientation.[61] Health communications with sexual minority consumers may improve if providers do not assume that patients are heterosexual, use gender-neutral and sensitive language when asking about sexual orientation and relationship status, adopt and communicate nondiscrimination and confidentiality policies, and present a positive and inclusive attitude about family and significant relationships.[56]

Hughes and Jacobson pointed out that because most smokers begin smoking during adolescence, prevention efforts should target young lesbians and bisexual women.[20] There is a paucity of research on preventing tobacco use among LGBT youth, but Remafedi and Carol, citing qualitative research involving this population, wrote: "Prevention programs should involve young people in enjoyable and engaging activities, address the psychosocial and cultural underpinnings of tobacco use, support healthy psychosocial development, and consider offering pharmacological smoking cessation aids"[62] (p. 249).

Environmental strategies for preventing health problems are often effective in altering health behaviors and social norms. These strategies include policy changes, such as clean air laws and reducing youth access to tobacco; financial incentives or disincentives, such as lowering the cost of smoking cessation programs or increasing tobacco taxes; and controls on advertising and other communications.[63] Environmental prevention efforts in LGBT communities have evolved in recognition of the importance of LGBT organizations and alternative media as a nexus for creating and maintaining community.[64] The tobacco industry aggressively markets to the LGBT community through direct and indirect advertising, community outreach, and sponsorship.[23,24] This targeted marketing is generally conducted in the guise of philanthropy.[64,65] The tobacco industry also designs products to appeal to specific psychological and psychosocial needs.[66] In response, some LGBT organizations and media have adopted policies, such as prohibiting or limiting tobacco promotions, sponsorship, and advertisements, to affirm the value they place on LGBT health and ensure their independence from profit-making influences.[64]

LGBT health advocates have used other media strategies to advance health in LGBT communities, including counter-advertising and media advocacy.[67] Counter-ads focus attention on how the tobacco industry promotes misinformation and influences social norms.[68] An evaluation of antismoking campaigns found that counter-advertising strategies were successful and that messages focusing on industry manipulation and secondhand smoke most effectively reduced consumption and challenged cultural norms that enable smoking.[69] There have been efforts to develop LGBT-specific counter-advertising. For example, the Tobacco Education Clearinghouse of California (www.tecc.org) distributes a poster identifying tobacco as a killer in LGBT communities, with the message: "We've won so many battles over the years—now, let's beat tobacco." A campaign called "Delicious Lesbian Kisses" by the Mautner Project (www.mautnerproject.org), a lesbian-health advocacy organization, promoted clean breath by encouraging lesbians not to smoke. Capturing the attention of LGBT news media is important because it strategically applies pressure for policy changes in the LGBT community to abolish the various forms of cigarette advertising.[70]

CONCLUSION

There is sufficient research to state definitively that lesbians—particularly young, less educated, and lower-income lesbians—are more likely than comparable heterosexual women to smoke. However, some studies point to higher risk for bisexual women and women who have sex with women but do not adopt a lesbian or bisexual identity. Combining these groups with lesbians may inflate the risk specifically for lesbians. Very little is known about the relationships between sexual orientation and risk and protective factors. And studies have not determined if the risk and protection profiles of lesbians and bisexual women are similar or different. Such knowledge is critical for building effective treatment and prevention strategies.

Meanwhile, emerging research findings underscore the important role played by all health care providers and LGBT health advocates in adapting evidence-based interventions to sexual minority populations and ensuring that both individual and community-level interventions are inclusive and responsive to sexual minority needs and concerns.

REFERENCES

1. Mokdad, A. H., Marks, J. S., Stroup, D. F., & Gerberding, J. L. (2004). Actual causes of death in the United States, 2000. *Journal of the American Medical Association, 291,* 1238–1245.

2. Cochran, S. D., & Mays, V. (2007). Physical health complaints among lesbians, gay men, and bisexual and homosexually experienced heterosexual individuals: Results from the California Quality of Life Survey. *American Journal of Public Health, 97,* 1–8.

3. Heck, J. E., & Jacobsen, J. S. (2006). Asthma diagnosis among individuals in same-sex relationships. *Journal of Asthma, 43,* 579–584.

4. Aaron, D. J., Markovic, N., Danielson, M. E., Honnold, J. A., Janosky, J. E., & Schmidt, N. J. (2001). Behavioral risk factors for disease and preventive health practices among lesbians. *American Journal of Public Health, 91,* 972–975.

5. Skinner, W. F. (1994). The prevalence and demographic predictors of illicit and licit drug use among lesbians and gay men. *American Journal of Public Health, 84,* 1307–1310.

6. Skinner, W. F., & Otis, M. D. (1996). Drug and alcohol use among lesbian and gay people in a southern U.S. sample: Epidemiological, comparative, and methodological findings from the Trilogy Project. *Journal of Homosexuality, 30,* 59–92.

7. Valanis, B. G., Bowen, D. J., Bassford, T., Whitlock, E., Charney, P., & Carter, R. A. (2000). Sexual orientation and health: Comparisons in the Women's Health Initiative sample. *Archives of Family Medicine, 9,* 843–853.

8. Gruskin, E. P., Greenwood, G. L., Matevia, M., Pollack, L. M., & Bye, L. L. (2007). Disparities in smoking between the lesbian, gay, and bisexual population and the general population in California. *American Journal of Public Health, 97,* 1496–1502.

9. Gruskin, E. P., & Gordon, N. (2006). Gay/lesbian sexual orientation increases risk for cigarette smoking and heavy drinking among members of a large Northern California health plan. *BMC Public Health, 6,* 241.

10. Burgard, S. A., Cochran, S. D., & Mays, V. M. (2005). Alcohol and tobacco use patterns among heterosexually and homosexually experienced California women. *Drug and Alcohol Dependence, 77,* 61–70.

11. Dilley, J. A., Maher, J. E., Boysun, M. J., Pizacani, B. A., Mosbaek, C. H., Rohde, K., et al. (2005). Response letter to: Tang, H., Greenwodd, G. L., Cowling, D. W., Lloyd, J. C., Roeseler, A. G., & Bal, D. G. Cigarette smoking among lesbians, gays, and bisexuals: How serious a problem? *Cancer Causes and Control, 16,* 1133–1134.

12. Drabble, L., & Trocki, K. (2005). Alcohol consumption, alcohol-related problems, and other substance use among lesbian and bisexual women. *Journal of Lesbian Studies, 9,* 19–30.

13. Bowen, D. J., Bradford, J. B., Powers, D., McMorrow, P., Linde, R., Murphy, B. C., et al. (2004). Comparing women of differing sexual orientation using population-based sampling. *Women and Health, 40,* 19–34.

14. Case, P., Austin, S. B., Hunter, D. J., Manson, J. E., Malspeis, S., Willett, W. C., et al. (2004). Sexual orientation, health risk factors, and physical functioning in the Nurses' Health Study II. *Journal of Women's Health, 13,* 1033–1047.

15. Tang, H., Greenwood, G. L., Cowling, D. W., Lloyd, J. C., Roeseler, A. G., & Bal, D. G. (2004). Cigarette smoking among lesbians, gays, and bisexuals: How serious a problem? (United States). *Cancer Causes and Control, 15,* 797–803.

16. Diamant, A. L., & Wold, C. (2003). Sexual orientation and variation in physical and mental health status among women. *Journal of Women's Health, 12,* 41–49.

17. Cochran, S. D., Mays, V. M., Bowen, D., Gage, S., Bybee, D., Roberts, S. J., et al. (2001). Cancer-related risk indicators and preventive screening behaviors among lesbians and bisexual women. *American Journal of Public Health, 91,* 591–597.

18. Gruskin, E. P., Hart, S., Gordon, N., & Ackerson, L. (2001). Patterns of cigarette smoking and alcohol use among lesbians and bisexual women enrolled in a large health maintenance organization. *American Journal of Public Health, 91,* 976–979.

19. Diamant, A. L., Wold, C., Spritzer, K., & Gelberg, L. (2000). Health behaviors, health status, and access to and use of health care: A population-based study of lesbian, bisexual, and heterosexual women. *Archives of Family Medicine, 9,* 1043–1051.

20. Hughes, T. L., & Jacobson, K. M. (2003). Sexual orientation and women's smoking. *Current Women's Health Report, 3,* 254–261.

21. Sanchez, J. P., Meacher, P., & Beil, R. (2005). Cigarette smoking and lesbian and bisexual women in the Bronx. *Journal of Community Health, 30,* 23–37.

22. Moore, D., Williams, J. D., & Qualls, W. J. (1996). Target marketing of tobacco and alcohol-related products to ethnic minority groups in the United States. *Ethnicity & Disease, 6,* 83–98.

23. Smith, E. A., Offen, N., & Malone, R. E. (2005). What makes an ad a cigarette ad? Commercial tobacco imagery in the lesbian, gay, and bisexual press. *Journal of Epidemiology and Community Health, 59,* 1086–1091.

24. Stevens, P., Carlson, L. M., & Hinman, J. M. (2004). An analysis of tobacco industry marketing to lesbian, gay, bisexual, and transgender (LGBT) populations: Strategies for mainstream tobacco control and prevention. *Health Promotion Practice, 5*(Suppl. 3), 129S–134S.

25. Brownworth, V. (1995). The truth behind lesbians and advertising. *Lesbian News,* pp. 42–43.

26. Goebel, K. (1994). Lesbians and gays face tobacco targeting. *Tobacco Control, 3,* 65–67.

27. Goodwin, R. D., Keyes, K., & Simuro, N. (2007). Mental disorders and nicotine dependence among pregnant women in the United States. *Obstetrics & Gynecology, 109,* 875–883.

28. Jané-Llopis, E., & Matytsina, I. (2006). Mental health and alcohol, drugs, and tobacco: A review of the comorbidity between mental disorders and the use of alcohol, tobacco, and illicit drugs. *Drug & Alcohol Review, 25,* 515–536.

29. Lasser, K., Boyd, J. W., Woolhandler, S., Himmelstein, D. U., McCormick, D., & Bor, D. H. (2000). Smoking and mental illness: A population-based prevalence study. *Journal of the American Medical Association, 284,* 2606–2610.

30. Gilman, S. E., Cochran, S. D., & Mays, V. M. (2001). Risk of psychiatric disorders among individuals reporting same-sex sexual partners in the National Comorbidity Survey. *American Journal of Public Health, 91,* 933–939.

31. Warner, J., McKeown, E., Griffin, M., Johnson, K., Ramsay, A., Cort, C., et al. (2004). Rates and predictors of mental illness in gay men, lesbians, and bisexual men and women:

Results from a survey based in England and Wales. *British Journal of Psychiatry, 185,* 479–485.

32. Meyer, I. H. (2004). Prejudice, social stress, and mental health in lesbian, gay, and bisexual populations: Conceptual issues and research evidence. *Psychological Bulletin, 129,* 674–697.

33. Mays, V. M., & Cochran, S. D. (2001). Mental health correlates of perceived discrimination among lesbian, gay, and bisexual adults in the United States. *American Journal of Public Health, 91,* 1869–1876.

34. Mays, V. M., Yancey, A. K., Cochran, S. D., Weber, M., & Fielding, J. E. (2002). Heterogeneity of health disparities among African American, Hispanic, and Asian American women: Unrecognized influences of sexual orientation. *American Journal of Public Health, 92,* 632–639.

35. Pomerleau, C. S., Zucker, A. N., Namenck Brouwer, R. J., Pomerleau, O. F., & Stewart, A. J. (2001). Race differences in weight concerns among women smokers: Results from two independent samples. *Addictive Behaviors, 26,* 651–663.

36. Heffernan, K. (1996). Eating disorders and weight concern among lesbians. *International Journal of Eating Disorders, 19,* 127–138.

37. Owens, L. K., Hughes, T. L., & Owens-Nicholson, D. (2003). The effects of sexual orientation on body image and attitudes about eating and weight. *Journal of Lesbian Studies, 7,* 15–33.

38. Siever, M. D. (1994). Sexual orientation and gender as factors in socioculturally acquired vulnerability to body dissatisfaction and eating disorders. *Journal of Consulting and Clinical Psychology, 62,* 252–260.

39. Trocki, K. F., Drabble, L., & Midanik, L. (2005). Use of heavier drinking contexts among heterosexuals, homosexuals and bisexuals: Results from a national household probability survey. *Journal of Studies on Alcohol, 66,* 105–110.

40. Scout Miele, A. M., Bradford, J. B., & Perry, D. (2007). *Running an LGBT smoking treatment group.* Boston: Fenway Institute.

41. Anthony, J. C., & Echeagaray-Wagner, F. (2000). Epidemiologic analysis of alcohol and tobacco use. *Alcohol Research & Health, 24,* 201–208.

42. Grucza, R. A., & Bierut, L. J. (2006). Cigarette smoking and the risk for alcohol use disorders among adolescent drinkers. *Alcoholism: Clinical and Experimental Research, 30,* 2046–2054.

43. Office of Applied Studies. (2006). *Results from the 2005 National Survey on Drug Use and Health: National findings* (Publication No. 06-4194). Rockville, MD: Substance Abuse and Mental Health Services Administration. Available at www.oas.samhsa.gov/nsduh/2k5nsduh/2k5results.pdf.

44. Cochran, B. N., & Cauce, A. M. (2006). Characteristics of lesbian, gay, bisexual, and transgender individuals entering substance abuse treatment. *Journal of Substance Abuse Treatment, 30,* 135–146.

45. Eliason, M. J., & Worthington, L. (2003). Alcohol, tobacco, and drug use in LGBT participants of pride events. San Francisco: UCSF Institute of Health and Aging.

46. Prochaska, J. J., Delucchi, K., & Hall, S. M. (2004). A meta-analysis of smoking cessation interventions with individuals in substance abuse treatment or recovery. *Journal of Consulting and Clinical Psychology, 72,* 1144–1156.

47. Sussman, S. (2002). Smoking cessation among persons in recovery. *Substance Use & Misuse, 37,* 1275–1298.

48. Doolan, D. M., & Froelicher, E. S. (2006). Efficacy of smoking cessation intervention among special populations: Review of the literature from 2000 to 2005. *Nursing Research, 55,* S29–37.

49. Bye, L., Gruskin, E., Greenwood, G., Albright, V., & Krotki, K. (2005). *California lesbians, gays, bisexuals, and transgender tobacco use survey 2004.* Sacramento, CA: California Department of Health Services. Available at ww2.cdph.ca.gov/programs/tobacco/Documents/CTCP-LGBTTobaccoStudy.pdf.

50. Eliason, M. J., Amodia, D. S., & Cano, C. (2006). Spirituality and alcohol and other drug treatment: The intersection with culture. *Alcoholism Treatment Quarterly, 24,* 121–141.

51. Miller, W. R., & C'de Baca, J. (2001). *Quantum changes: When epiphanies and sudden insights transform ordinary lives.* New York: Guilford Press.

52. Cochran, S. D., Mays, V. M., & Sullivan J. G. (2003). Prevalence of mental disorders, psychological distress, and mental health services use among lesbian, gay, and bisexual adults in the United States. *Journal of Consulting and Clinical Psychology, 71,* 53–61.

53. Morgan, K. S., & Eliason, M. J. (1992). The role of psychotherapy in Caucasian lesbians' lives. *Women and Therapy, 13,* 27–52.

54. O'Hanlan, K. A. (2006). Health policy considerations for our sexual minority patients. *Obstetrics & Gynecology, 107,* 709–714.

55. Edwards, A., Hood, K., Matthews, E., Russell, D., Russell, I., Barker, J., et al. (2000). The effectiveness of one-to-one risk-communication interventions in health care. *Medical Decision Making, 20,* 290–297.

56. Bonvicini, K. A., & Perlin, M. J. (2003). The same but different: Clinician-patient communication with gay and lesbian patients. *Patient Education and Counseling, 51,* 115–122.

57. Eliason, M. J., & Schope, R. (2001). Does "don't ask, don't tell" apply to health care? Lesbian, gay, and bisexual people's disclosure to health care providers. *Journal of the Gay and Lesbian Medical Association, 5,* 125–134.

58. Hinchliff, S., Gott, M., & Galena, E. (2005). "I daresay I might find it embarrassing": General practitioners' perspectives on discussing sexual health issues with lesbian and gay patients. *Health & Social Care in the Community, 13,* 345–353.

59. Smith, D. M., & Mathews, W. C. (2007). Physicians' attitudes toward homosexuality and HIV: Survey of a California Medical Society—revisited (PATHH-II). *Journal of Homosexuality, 52,* 1–10.

60. Neville, S., & Henrickson, M. (2006). Perceptions of lesbian, gay and bisexual people of primary healthcare services. *Journal of Advanced Nursing, 55,* 407–415.

61. Klitzman, R. L., & Greenberg, J. D. (2002). Patterns of communication between gay and lesbian patients and their health providers. *Journal of Homosexuality, 42,* 65–75.

62. Remafedi, G., & Carol, H. (2005). Preventing tobacco use among lesbian, gay, bisexual, and transgender youths. *Nicotine & Tobacco Research, 7,* 249–256.

63. Brownson, R. C., Haire-Joshu, D., & Luke, D. A. (2006). Shaping the context of health: A review of environmental and policy approaches in the prevention of chronic diseases. *Annual Review of Public Health, 27,* 341–370.

64. Drabble, L. (2000). Alcohol, tobacco, and pharmaceutical industry funding: Considerations for organizations serving lesbian, gay, bisexual, and transgender communities. *Journal of Gay and Lesbian Social Services, 11,* 1–26.

65. Offen, N., Smith, E. A., & Malone, R. E. (2003). From adversary to target market: The ACT-UP boycott of Philip Morris. *Tobacco Control, 12,* 203–207.

66. Le Cook, B., Wayne, G. F., Keithly, L., & Connolly, G. (2003). One size does not fit all: How the tobacco industry has altered cigarette design to target consumer groups with specific psychological and psychosocial needs. *Addiction, 98,* 1547–1561.

67. Drabble, L., Keatley, J., & Marcelle, G. (2006). Media strategies for advancing health in lesbian, gay, bisexual, and transgender communities. In M. Shankle (Ed.), *Handbook of lesbian, gay, bisexual and transgender public health: A practitioner's guide to service* (pp. 335–352). Binghamton, NY: Harrington Park Press.

68. Dorfman, L., & Wallack, L. (1993). Advertising health: The case for counter-ads. *Public Health Reports, 108,* 716–726.

69. Goldman, L. K., & Glantz, S. A. (1998). Evaluation of antismoking advertising campaigns. *Journal of the American Medical Association, 279,* 772–777.

70. Wallack, L., & Dorfman, L. (1996). Media advocacy: A strategy for advancing policy and promoting health. *Health Education Quarterly, 23,* 293–317.

ABOUT THE AUTHORS

Michele J. Eliason, PhD is Assistant Professor in the Department of Health Education at San Francisco State University. She has written many articles on LGBT health issues and is co-author of the recent book *LGBTQ Cultures: What Health Care Professionals Need to Know about Sexual and Gender Diversity* (Lippincott Press).

Laurie Drabble, PhD, MPH, MSW is Associate Professor in the School of Social Work at San Jose State University in California. Her research and community practice center on addressing alcohol and other substance abuse problems among marginalized populations of women with a special emphasis on the relationships between alcohol consumption, health, and mental health in women, especially sexual minority women.

CHAPTER 9

"Meet Me at the Bar?"

PATTERNS OF ALCOHOL AND DRUG ABUSE AMONG LESBIANS

LAURIE DRABBLE,
PhD, MPH, MSW

MICHELE J. ELIASON,
PhD

MIGDALIA REYES,
EdD, MSW

CARMEN *is a 26-year-old Chicana from Los Angeles who has been sober for 6 years. While growing up as an only child, her parents actively hosted and participated in family parties that included lots of drinking. She characterizes her father and uncles as alcoholics who often got drunk and had violent outbursts during family gatherings. Carmen began to drink at age 11 during those gatherings and, at the time, considered it normal. She never saw or understood drinking in moderation.*

Carmen also reports being sexually abused by several family members at a young age, which she attributes to the "alcohol-saturated environment." In her judgment, this, along with her parents' divorce (partly a result of her father's alcoholism and drug addiction), issues such as not knowing how to speak for herself as a woman and Latina, and "being different" as a lesbian, contributed to her drinking.

By the time Carmen was 13, she began to experience depressive symptoms, isolate herself, and have suicidal ideation. She drank more as a way to self-medicate the symptoms. She attempted suicide once and was admitted numerous times to psychiatric hospitals over a period of about 18 months. During that period, Carmen says she alternated between heavy drinking and hospitalization.

Carmen came out as a lesbian at age 15. She discovered softball. This sport and the lesbian-oriented environment she joined gave her a reason for living, but it was another environment involving lots of drinking. She began to frequent bars because "it was the only place I could be out as a lesbian." Despite this new found social group, Carmen felt extremely lonely and isolated. She cites the sexual abuse, her developing political consciousness, her struggles with internalized homophobia, and her exposure to racism as primary reasons for the heavy drinking.

By her seventeenth birthday, Carmen was alcohol-dependent. She describes herself then as a "periodic alcoholic" who binged, stayed sober for a couple of weeks, and "went out again to drink alcoholically" for a few weeks. She says alcohol got in the way of everything. One time, she recalls, her friend received a DUI and shared with Carmen a questionnaire that had questions such as: "Does drinking get in the way of your work?" and "Does drinking get in the way of your life at home?" Carmen filled out the questionnaire, too, but refused to admit what the assessment showed: that she was an alcoholic.

She eventually admitted to herself and to her mother and stepfather that she was an alcoholic. Her mother suggested that she enter a recovery program. Although at first Carmen refused to do so, rationalizing that she could recover on her own, she ultimately relented and entered a 10-day, inpatient hospital program where she was treated and became sober. About 2 years into recovery, Carmen began to experience suicidal ideation again, attributing it to the unresolved sexual abuse. "Alcohol must have been the foundation for not dealing with the abuse," she says. "Once alcohol was gone, I began to feel the pain." She moved past this period, primarily with help from the 12-Step Program in Alcoholics Anonymous, and entered her sixth year of sobriety.

She cites a number of challenges to maintaining her recovery. Because she identifies as a feminist, one challenge is the 12-Step Program's patriarchal, primarily White-oriented, and heterosexual ideology. However, she also recognizes that 12-Step meetings contribute to people's recovery, including her own recovery and spiritual journey. Another challenge for her was coming out as a lesbian to her family—a very slow and difficult process.

Carmen says she can relate to how alcohol and drugs affect Latino communities in the United States. Members of these traditionally poor communities, she notes, often do not have access to formal education and employment opportunities, which places them at risk for targeting by the alcohol and tobacco industries. She also notes that the sober lesbian community, particularly its Latina members, is very small; it is extremely difficult to meet Latinas who do not drink; and there are not many places where lesbians can go for alcohol-free entertainment.

BACKGROUND

Based on opportunistic samples in bars and other social settings, early studies of alcohol and drug use in gay and lesbian communities suggested particularly high rates of alcoholism and drug addiction—about 30%.[1-3] Although these early studies represented an important first step in health research in sexual minority populations, methodological problems such as small and biased samples limited their usefulness in understanding the prevalence of alcohol and other drug abuse, and the attendant problems in gay, lesbian, and bisexual populations.[4,5] For example, if a study sample is drawn from a bar, one would expect higher rates of alcohol problems than if it were drawn from a community center or church group.

In more recent years, a number of studies with stronger methodologies have contributed to an emerging understanding of substance use and abuse among lesbians and other sexual minority women. However, the few population-based studies that examined sexual orientation and substance abuse varied in terms of how they defined sexual orientation (identity, behavior, or both) and how they measured alcohol and other drug abuse. Some of them, for example, included limited measures of alcohol-related problems.

Several studies based on the National Household Survey on Drug Abuse found that women who reported same-sex partners used alcohol and other drugs more frequently than did women with opposite-sex partners, were more likely to be dependent on alcohol and drugs, and were more likely to report having received treatment in the previous year.[6-8] Other national, population-based studies of mental health issues in the United States found elevated rates of substance use disorders among women reporting same-sex partners[9] and among women who identified as lesbian or bisexual (researchers aggregated the two groups for analysis).[10] Similarly, a study based on the National Latino and Asian American Survey, which combined same-sex behavior and lesbian/bisexual identity, found a greater likelihood of drug dependence among sexual minority women but little difference in alcohol dependence.[11]

Studies based on the National Alcohol Survey are among the few that disaggregated sexual minority groups by analyzing alcohol and drug problems among four groups: lesbians, bisexual women, heterosexual-identified women who report same sex partners, and exclusively heterosexual women.[12] They found that both lesbians and bisexual women were more likely to experience negative consequences from drinking, to report symptoms of alcohol dependence, and to have sought help in the past for alcohol problems.[12] All three sexual minority groups were more likely to use marijuana.[13] Lesbians were more likely to go to bars, but they did not always drink more heavily in those settings.[14]

A number of regional, population-based studies of women's health found higher rates of alcohol and other drug abuse among lesbian and bisexual women, but measures of alcohol- or drug-related problems were limited.[15-17] Bloomfield's research in the San Francisco Bay Area found few differences in alcohol consumption between lesbian and heterosexual women, but lesbians were more likely to report being in recovery from alcohol problems.[18] Studies that were not population-based but recruited a broad cross-section of lesbians and bisexual women also generally suggested elevated risks of illicit drug use[19] and risks for alcohol abuse among sexual minority women.[20-26] Similarly, several studies of lesbian health found heavier alcohol use among lesbians.[27-30]

Although few population-based studies examine lesbians' illicit drug choices, research suggests that marijuana use is significantly higher among lesbian and bisexual women than among heterosexual women.[6,13] Cochran and colleagues found a higher risk of cocaine use among women who reported same-sex partners, and higher rates of problems associated with both marijuana and cocaine use. They also found that recent hallucinogen use was more common among younger women (18 to 26 years old) who had same-sex partners.[6] There is some indication that both lesbians and bisexuals are more likely to be active users of club drugs such as ecstasy, cocaine, methamphetamine, and LSD.[31,32] In another study, the risk for abuse of prescription drugs by young adults who went to clubs was highest among lesbian and bisexual women.[33]

Findings vary depending on how researchers measured sexual orientation. In a study based on a random sample of students, for example, different sexual-orientation measures—identity, behavior, and attraction—produced substantial variation in alcohol and drug abuse, particularly among women.[34] Another study, which compared identity measures with behavior measures in assessing alcohol dependence and alcohol-related problems, found that behavior as a gauge obscured the risks among lesbians.[35] Some findings suggest that risks for heavier drinking, other drug abuse, and alcohol- and drug-related problems may be particularly high among bisexual women.[15,17,34,36-38] On the other hand, another study found that bisexual college women drank less than their heterosexual counterparts, and drinking-related problems were comparable.[39]

Studies of alcohol consumption in general populations of women have revealed heavier use and a greater number of related problems among White women compared with other ethnic groups. But the few studies that examined differences in alcohol use, related problems, or other drug abuse among diverse populations of lesbians have found few or no differences by ethnicity, and higher rates of use and abuse appeared to be consistent across subpopulations of sexual minority women.[11,40] In contrast to general population studies, rates of drinking among sexual minority women do not appear to decline with age.[40]

CORE ISSUES FOR SEXUAL MINORITY WOMEN WITH SUBSTANCE ABUSE PROBLEMS

Qualitative studies,[41–43] literature reviews,[44] and publications that guide treatment of lesbian/gay/bisexual/transgender (LGBT) populations[45,46] have identified key issues related to alcohol and drug problems among lesbians and other sexual minority women. These include openness about sexual orientation/confidentiality, coming out, societal homophobia, internalized homophobia, family and social support, and socializing in contexts where alcohol and drug abuse is normative. All of these issues intersect with cultural context[43,47–51] and provide a useful framework for examining the literature and considering implications for substance abuse assessment, treatment, and prevention in lesbians and other sexual minority women.

Feeling Safe Enough to Disclose Sexual Orientation

In general, feeling that it is safe to disclose one's sexual orientation may be positively related to satisfaction with substance abuse treatment and with health, mental-health, and other human services.[52] Qualitative studies of sexual minorities in treatment suggest that treatment was not as successful for clients in settings in which they were unable to disclose their sexual orientation.[41,42] As the scenario at the beginning of this chapter illustrated, Carmen's inability to disclose her sexual orientation affected her drinking, recovery, and attempt to remain sober by attending Alcoholics Anonymous sessions. Many sexual minority women have been pathologized or discriminated against while receiving health care or addiction services. Consequently, service providers need to make clear that a given program is inclusive and affirmative regarding sexual orientation.[41,42] A sense of safety is a fundamental component of treatment for all women; for sexual minority women, safety and an ability to be open and honest about their lives and experiences, including their sexuality, is critical to recovery.[42]

Coming Out

"Coming out" is the process of exploring sexual identity and acknowledging minority sexual identity to oneself and others.[46] Finnegan and McNally outlined five stages of developing a positive lesbian or gay identity, noting that treatment issues may vary accordingly:

- Pre-encounter/identity confusion: essentially, not knowing and/or being in denial;
- Encounter/identity comparison: becoming aware and coming to terms with sexual orientation;
- Immersion into lesbian social worlds and "emersion" from an "oversimplified, either/or view of the world";

- Internalization and acceptance of identity; and
- Synthesis or self-acceptance as lesbian or gay.[45]

Some authors suggest that among women, traumatic stress in the coming-out process may contribute to more problems like substance abuse and that the degree of trauma and associated problems may be mediated by a combination of contextual and individual factors, such as actual or anticipated reactions to coming out.[53] From this perspective, trauma is a useful framework for understanding how contextual issues, such as victimization, and how the experience of coming out may create stress that contributes to behavioral problems.

Oftentimes, disclosure of sexual orientation to family members is also an important consideration in counseling. Morrow offers the following guidelines to social workers whose clients are considering coming out to family members:

- Evaluate the client's social context, such as the likely response of family members and family support issues;
- Identify supportive relatives or family friends;
- Develop a social support system;
- Assess the client's level of secure and positive lesbian-identity development;
- Educate the client about gay and lesbian issues;
- Have the client come out to trusted individuals first as a way to prepare for coming out to other family members;
- Select a method for delivering the coming-out news—for example, in person, by phone, or in a letter;
- Select the timing for coming out; and
- Prepare the client for family upheaval.[54]

Smith observed that some common assumptions about the coming-out process—for example, that the degree of "outness" is related to self-esteem, and not coming out is a form of denial—may be more salient for White Americans than for other ethnic groups.[55] White lesbians in the National Lesbian Health Care Survey were more likely to be out to various people than were African American or Latina lesbians.[56] Researchers who studied African American lesbians and gay men observed that disclosure to family members poses certain risks, such as scorn and rejection. Respondents preferred to disclose their sexual identity to women (sister and mother), which, the researchers noted, may point to the importance of sympathetic family members who can mediate reactions to disclosure throughout the family network.[57] In Carmen's case, the process of identifying "safe" family members and strategizing about if and when to come out to additional families members were important themes in her recovery.

Homophobia, Heterosexism, and Minority Stress

Minority stress is a result of chronic, traumatic events stemming from prejudice related to sexual identity, race, class, gender, disability, or other distinguishing characteristics. Two types of prejudice fuel sexual minority stress: homophobia and heterosexism. Homophobia, the negative attitudes of some people toward others who have same-sex desires or identities, can result in direct acts of discrimination, harassment, social invalidation, and violence.[58] Heterosexism refers to the effects of institutionalized prejudice, such as laws that prohibit same-sex marriage and workplace policies that enable harassment of LGBT individuals.[59] An accumulation of such prejudices causes minority stress, which, according to one hypothesis, underlies the differential rates of physical and mental health problems among people in sexual minorities.[60] The amount of psychological distress that arises from minority stress can be enormous, but very little research has focused on the relationships between such distress and alcohol or drug abuse. In the general population, many distressed people self-medicate with alcohol and/or drugs.

A study of problems among African American women in the United States who reported having same-sex partners found that 18.1% used illicit drugs or alcohol to make themselves feel better and 7.2% considered such use to be their most upsetting problem. Although participants most often cited romantic-relationship and financial problems, among the most chronic difficulties they reported were those related to using alcohol and drugs for self-medication of stress.[61] The earlier one comes out, the more stress he or she may experience. Data from a large study of adolescents found that lesbian or bisexual girls were more likely than heterosexual girls to have begun drinking before age 12 (13% vs. 2%). Alcohol use patterns among "mostly heterosexual" girls were similar to those among lesbian/bisexual girls, and, compared with the heterosexual girls, the two sexual minority groups reported higher levels of alcohol use and binge drinking in the previous month.[62]

Internalized Homophobia and the Importance of Self-Acceptance

Internalized homophobia—the negative effect that homosexuality has on oneself and others as a result of prejudice in the dominant culture—is often cited as a reason for greater alcohol and other drug problems among sexual minorities.[45,46,63] The few studies that have explored this possible correlation yielded mixed results.[63–65] However, one of the stronger studies, which used research-based measures of internalized heterosexism and multiple measures of alcohol use and problems, found partial support for a positive relationship between internalized heterosexism and alcohol use among women.[66] Hughes and colleagues found that psychological distress greatly contributed to the higher risk of lifetime alcohol-dependence symptoms.[67]

Although the degree to which internalized homophobia contributes to substance abuse problems is unclear, there is stronger support for the premise that self-acceptance as a lesbian and recovering alcohol/addict is an important element of recovery from addiction.[68] According to researchers, lesbians must be connected with support systems that at any given time will affirm their most salient identities, which may include identity related to gender, sexual orientation, ethnicity, and recovery. Carmen's narrative reflects the journey toward developing a strong and positive sense of identity.

Trauma

Carmen, like many women who have alcohol and drug abuse problems or are recovering from them, described traumatic experiences. In the general population, such experiences are associated with risks for alcohol and other drug abuse, and there is growing evidence that lifetime victimization, including childhood psychological, sexual, and physical abuse, and adult victimization, may be greater among lesbians and bisexuals.[69] A study of a large, diverse national sample of lesbian and bisexual women in the United States found that most respondents (62.3%) experienced victimization because of bias related to sexual orientation, and that lifetime history of victimization was greater among Native American, Latina, and African American lesbians than among White or Asian American lesbians.[70] Hughes and colleagues conducted one of the few studies to comprehensively examine childhood abuse experiences relative to age at the onset of drinking and sexual activity, psychological distress, and negative consequences of alcohol use. Among the 31% of lesbians who had experienced sexual abuse, the researchers found a direct relationship to lifetime alcohol dependency symptoms. However, other factors contributed to a complex pathway of events. Lesbians reported higher rates of early heterosexual activity, which also was directly related to alcohol abuse symptoms. This activity may have been "heterosexual immersion"—that is, the lesbians sought to prove they were "normal" in response to their own confusion or concern about same-sex attractions—or it may have been due to the fact that lesbians are more likely to run away or be forced out of their homes, and therefore need to have sex to survive on the street.[67] Several studies have identified higher rates of reported childhood sexual abuse among lesbian/bisexual women, but the reason for this is still uncertain. As one research team noted:

> Unlike heterosexual women, lesbian and bisexual women who experience sexual abuse must contend with the cultural myths regarding the impact of abuse on sexual identity. In the current study, some participants expressed concern about their lesbian identity development being seen as a reaction to negative experiences with men, especially childhood sexual abuse"[70] (p. 81).

Others suggest that the rates are higher because of a response bias: once lesbians have processed sexual orientation issues and disclosed them to researchers, they are more willing than heterosexual women to also report traumatic events laden with shame and guilt, such as sexual abuse. Another possibility is that lesbians and bisexual women are more vulnerable to sexual abuse if they display gender-atypical behaviors or appearance, or if they come out in their youth.

Social and Family Support

Relationships and encouragement from family are often considered to be important factors in mediating alcohol and other drug problems and in providing support during treatment.[45] Lesbians may rely on different social support networks than heterosexual women do. For example, they may be more likely to turn to friends and some ex-lovers ("family of choice") rather than their family of origin.[57]

As LaSala noted, theoretical and therapy models regarding traditional families do not always reflect the experiences and needs of lesbian couples and families, and consequently may need to be adapted. The boundaries, distance, and level of disclosure and communication in family-of-origin relationships may vary considerably in lesbian families, depending on the level of parental acceptance or disapproval. This means a client's perception of and preferences for how "family" is constructed and navigated are critical.[71] Professionals need to consider multiple factors when they address lesbian family issues. Such factors include who a client considers to be a significant other, recognizing the diverse ways that lesbians may configure their families of choice, and the degree to which lesbians may be connected to or distanced from their family of origin. In addition, cultural context intersects with dynamics related to possible support from families of origin. For example, Latino culture values *familismo* (familial loyalty and closeness) and *marianismo* (traditional sex-role expectations for women). *Familismo* and *marianismo* are sources of both support and conflict for some Latina lesbians.[51,72]

Self-help programs for substance abuse problems can provide substantive support for lesbians in recovery. Carmen's description of both her ambivalence toward and positive impression of the social support offered by 12-Step programs reflect themes in the literature. One of the few studies to explore how lesbians perceive addiction and self-help groups found that they perceive Alcoholics Anonymous (AA) as potentially liberating but also as potentially oppressive.[73] In another study, most recovering lesbians (74%) relied on sources of support in addition to AA. Participants were ambivalent about AA's ideological underpinnings and torn between assimilating into the program and having a strong sense of autonomy.[74] Professionals should acknowledge such concerns when they help lesbians access an array of support resources.

Although lesbians' reliance on bars as one of the few "safe" places to socialize has long been considered a contributing factor to their higher rates of alcohol use and related problems, only a few studies have specifically examined this notion. Research generally suggests that drinking contexts such as bars and social events are entry points into the lesbian community and may facilitate the development of lesbian identity and the creation of social networks.[75-77] In one study, for example, reliance on bars as a primary social setting was predictive of problematic substance use; other factors, such as perceived stress and social resources, were not significant.[76] Another population-based study, in contrast, found that lesbians were more likely to patronize bars but did not necessarily drink more heavily there compared with heterosexuals.[14] Qualitative interviews with 31 self-identified lesbian social drinkers showed that alcohol-related problems tended to be higher earlier in the lesbian identity-development process but tended to decrease as lesbians developed a stronger social network and resolved their identity conflict.[77] Gruskin and colleagues reported that lesbians experienced many positive outcomes of bar-going, such as connecting to community, mediating stress, and developing social networks. However, there were also a number of negative health consequences, such as binge drinking or illicit drug use to cope with social discomfort.[75]

As Carmen's story illustrates, processes such as identity development may interact with environmental factors as the risk for alcohol and other drug abuse problems arises. For example, a study by Parks and Hughes of the relationship between milestones in lesbian identity development and alcohol problems found that such problems were associated with age and level of disclosure of sexual orientation. Disclosure of lesbian identity at a younger age was generally associated with subsequent reports of alcohol dependence symptoms, lending support to the theory that greater exposure to minority stress may contribute to risk of alcohol-related problems. In the oldest cohort (born before 1952), levels of disclosure to family members and people outside the family, and identity milestones—the ages at which participants wondered about and decided on their sexual orientation, for example—were not associated with more alcohol dependence symptoms. In contrast, among middle-age participants (born between 1952 and 1967), being out to family was associated with more symptoms, and, among those in the younger group (born in 1968 or later), so was wondering about sexual identity.[78]

Differences in stress and social context may have implications for treatment and prevention. Parks and Hughes noted:

> Among younger women, the potential for negative alcohol use outcomes appears to be greatest in the early phases of lesbian identity development,

indicating a need for accessible information, social support, and non-alcohol "safe havens" within which these women may safely explore this new identity[78] (p. 375).

IMPLICATIONS FOR TREATMENT

Screening and Assessment Considerations

Many health and human services entities recommend routine screening for alcohol and drug abuse, especially in populations, including lesbians, that are at higher risk for drinking-related problems. (See the sample alcohol screening test in Table 9.1.[*]) Like other patients or clients, lesbians who have alcohol or drug problems need to be assessed in terms of motivation to change their abuse or dependence and their current stage of change. Professionals who use standardized assessment tools must be aware of issues that may disproportionately impact lesbians. For example, in assessing lesbians' health, they should keep in mind that sexual minority women are more likely to be uninsured, to have had negative experiences with insensitive or judgmental health care providers, and to not visit providers because of concerns about revealing personal information.[79] In addition, as mentioned earlier, past experiences of violence may be particularly salient for lesbians.

It is also important to create a sense of safety and to integrate sexual orientation into the assessment process. Barbara and Chaim developed and tested a tool to help substance abuse treatment counselors facilitate self-disclosure during this process (Table 9.2). Both therapists and clients generally reacted positively to questions in the two-part test. Basic questions about relationships and identity make up the first part. Open-ended questions in the second part are targeted to clients who identify as lesbian, gay, or bisexual; have or have had relationships with same sex-partners; or express concerns or awkward feelings about sexual orientation. The researchers suggested that these questions be integrated into an assessment or be asked later during treatment, depending on the treatment context, client needs, and counselor competence.[80]

Treatment Considerations

Despite research showing more prevalent and more severe substance abuse problems among sexual minority women compared with heterosexuals, treatment programs may not be adequately prepared to meet this population's needs. One study found that even though the odds of reporting past treatment for alcohol and drug problems

---

[*] *Information about a drug abuse screening test is available from the National Institute on Drug Abuse at www.nida.nih.gov/Diagnosis-Treatment/DAST10.html.*

TABLE 9.1. SAMPLE ALCOHOL SCREENING TEST: TWEAK[†]

SCREENING QUESTIONS

1. How many drinks does it take to make you feel high?
2. Have close friends or relatives worried or complained about your drinking in the past year?
3. Do you sometimes take a drink in the morning when you first get up?
4. Has a friend or family member ever told you about things you said or did while you were drinking that you could not remember?
5. Do you sometimes feel the need to cut down on your drinking?

SCORING

- Questions 1–2: 2 points each. Questions 3–5: 1 point each. Maximum score: 7.
  A total score ≥ 2 = harmful drinking and warrants further evaluation of the respondent.
- Question 1: If the respondent replies "3 or more drinks," score 2 points; if "less than 3," score 0 points.

[†]"Tolerance," "Worried," "Eye opener," "Amnesia," and "K/cut down" on drinking.

Source: Russell, M. (1994). New assessment tools for drinking in pregnancy: T-ACE, TWEAK, and others. *Alcohol Health and Research World, 18,* 55–61. Available at pubs.niaaa.nih.gov/publications/Assesing%20Alcohol/InstrumentPDFs/74_TWEAK.pdf.

TABLE 9.2. SAMPLE QUESTIONNAIRE FOR LESBIANS SEEKING HELP FOR ALCOHOL OR DRUG PROBLEMS

CORE ASSESSMENT QUESTIONS

- Are you currently in a relationship? If yes, is your partner a man or a woman? How long have you been together? If you have had previous relationships, were they with men, women, or both?
- In terms of your sexual orientation, which group do you identify with: gay, lesbian, straight/heterosexual, bisexual, unsure, none of the above? Do you have concerns related to your sexual orientation/identity or do you ever feel awkward about your sexuality?

FOLLOW-UP QUESTIONS

- Can you tell me about any particular challenges you have faced because of homophobia?
- How open are you about your sexual orientation? How do you feel about being gay/lesbian/bisexual?
- Tell me a bit about where you are in your coming-out process?
- How has your sexual orientation affected your relationship with your family? Do you have support from your family?
- Tell me about your involvement in the lesbian, gay, bi, and trans communities?
- Do you have any concerns about your gender identity and what are they?
- Do you use substances to cope with any of the issues we mentioned above? If yes, in what ways?

Source: Barbara, A. M., & Chaim, G. (2004). Asking about sexual orientation during assessment for drug and alcohol concerns: A pilot study. *Journal of Social Work Practice in the Addictions, 4,* 89–109.

were about eight times greater among lesbians and five times greater among bisexual women, sexual minority women were less likely than heterosexual women (58% vs. 86%) to report feeling satisfied with their treatment.[13]

Counselor-level factors, such as affirmative beliefs and attitudes about lesbians, and organizational factors, such as a nonheterosexist organizational climate, affect the treatment experiences of sexual minority clients.[81,82] Substance abuse counselors often do not understand internalized homophobia and other particular issues that may be of concern to LGBT clients, and up to half have negative or ambivalent attitudes toward such clients.[83,84] Biases appear to be stronger among heterosexual counselors and counselors with few LGBT friends.[85] Furthermore, substance abuse treatment agencies may not pay sufficient attention to creating programs that are responsive to LGBT needs. Cochran and colleagues contacted all 911 treatment programs listed in the National Survey of Substance Abuse Treatment Services (NSSATS) and asked if they provided LGBT-specific services. About 71% did not and only about 7% could identify a service targeted to LGBT clients. About 2% indicated they had offered such services in the past, 4% characterized their agencies as accepting, and about 9% stated they did not have separate treatment groups and did not discriminate.[86] Another study, also based on the NSSATS, found that less than half of facilities offered key services designed for particular populations, such as LGBT individuals, women, adolescents, and people with HIV/AIDS. For-profit facilities were less likely than nonprofit and public facilities to provide specialized services. Most of the LGBT services this study examined were focused on HIV/AIDS and other sexually transmitted infections.[87]

Few studies have looked at LGBT populations in substance abuse treatment, and those that did generally targeted men.[5,88] A notable exception is one that compared LGBT and heterosexual clients based on data gathered from treatment providers in Washington State.[89] This study was stronger than others because it collected data from treatment providers throughout the state, compared sexual minorities with heterosexuals in the same sample, and, given the sufficiently large number of participants, explored differences in both gender and sexual orientation. It generally found that in key areas, sexual minority women and men entered treatment with more severe problems than their heterosexual counterparts did. For example, their substance abuse was more frequent and they had more indications of psychopathology, such as current or prior mental health treatment or use of psychiatric medications. Sexual minority men, but not women, reported higher rates of medical service utilization and more problems related to homelessness, legal issues, and past domestic violence.

Although little research has examined treatment outcomes among sexual minority clients, those with at least 1 year of recovery reported a positive association between treatment success and counselors and social service agencies that affirm clients' sexual orientation.[82] There is evidence that lesbian- and gay-affirmative practices may be enhanced when practitioners have personal contact with lesbian and gay family members, friends, and clients; attend workshops and training that focus specifically on gay and lesbian issues; and address their own attitudes and feelings about lesbians and gay men.[90]

Because institutions often provide alcohol and drug treatment and prevention services, their policies, staffing patterns, program designs, and training must be sensitive to lesbians' recovery needs. Administrative policies should explicitly affirm an institution's commitment to serving lesbians and prohibit discrimination based on sexual orientation, gender, and/or cultural background. Their publicity and communications should include lesbian-oriented material. Staff need to use gender-neutral and inclusive language when they assess and treat lesbian clients and when they refer to clients' current or past partners and significant others. In addition, institutions should recruit lesbian staff, develop lesbian-specific and inclusive programming, and educate and provide guidelines for heterosexual clients about appropriate language and behaviors when they interact with and support lesbian peers in recovery.[91] Ongoing staff training can address current research on lesbian issues, create opportunities for staff to explore their fears and prejudices in a safe environment, and orient them to community resources. Table 9.3 lists key policies, training, skills, and knowledge that are necessary for appropriate treatment of lesbians who have substance abuse problems.

Prevention Considerations

Carmen's story includes a discussion of risk factors that have implications for prevention—individual factors, such as isolation and a need to connect to community; environmental factors, such as cultural and community norms related to heavy drinking; and targeted marketing by the alcohol industry. The availability of safe gathering places to create community, find support, meet potential partners, and deal with the stress often associated with drinking environments[75] underscores the importance of alcohol- and drug-free alternatives for socialization. Public health approaches that show potential promise for reducing problems in drinking contexts include responsible beverage service, promotion of nonalcoholic drinks, and hosting entertainment not centered on drinking.[75,92] Alcohol and tobacco businesses have increasingly targeted LGBT communities with specialized forms of marketing, such as advertising, event sponsorships, and donations to organizations that seek to increase the visibility and consumption of products.[92] Some LGBT health organizations have launched effective counter-advertising campaigns to expose the profit motives of these industries and the health problems associated with heavy use of their products. Other LGBT organizations have adopted policies affirming the value they place on LGBT health and ensur-

TABLE 9.3. KEY CONSIDERATIONS IN TREATING LESBIANS' SUBSTANCE ABUSE

COUNSELOR / AGENCY COMPETENCY	APPLICATIONS
POSITIVE:	
Creates safety for clients.	■ Include sexual orientation in clients' rights or nondiscrimination policies and post them prominently. ■ Use inclusive language at all levels (advertising, assessments, brochures, treatment information). ■ Impose sanctions for harassment or discrimination by staff or clients. ■ Pay careful attention to confidentiality. How is sexual orientation recorded on forms? Is the client's permission necessary to record this information? Do staff informally talk or gossip about clients' sexual orientation?

Is familiar with the lesbian community and culture.	■ Train staff about LGBT topics (coming out, heterosexism, legal issues, family issues, the role that minority stress plays in substance use, etc).
	■ Know the local community:
	  (1) Are there lesbian bars? How many? Where? Do counselors have a relationship with the owners?
	  (2) Is there an LGBT religious organization, such as a Metropolitan Community Church, or an LGBT group within a mainstream church?
	  (3) Where do lesbians gather in the community?
	  (4) Are there newsletters, newspapers, or LGBT community agencies?
	  (5) Does the state or city include sexual orientation in nondiscrimination statements? Does the state permit same-sex marriages or civil unions?
	■ Form an LGBT community advisory group.

Acknowledges clients' significant others and encourages their participation in treatment.	■ Does the agency have an inclusive definition of family? ■ Assess clients with inclusive language to identity significant others and family. Lesbians often have nontraditional family structures that heterosexist standards may overlook.
Listens to clients and to what they say is comfortable for them.	Be open to learning from clients. Their perceptions are key.
Trains staff to be more knowledgeable and sensitive. (One resource: *A Provider's Introduction to Substance Abuse Treatment for Lesbian, Gay, Bisexual, and Transgender Individuals*. Available at ⟡ www.kap.samhsa. gov/products/manuals/pdfs/lgbt.pdf.)	Ongoing training keeps staff abreast of current lesbian issues, creates opportunities for them to explore their fears and prejudices, and orients them to community resources.

(cont.)

TABLE 9.3. KEY CONSIDERATIONS IN TREATING LESBIANS' SUBSTANCE ABUSE *(cont.)*

COUNSELOR / AGENCY COMPETENCY	APPLICATIONS
NEGATIVE:	
Labels clients.	Labels are for clothes, not people. Some clients do not label their sexual orientation; some use labels other than "lesbian." To be inclusive, use generic terms such as "sexual identity."
Pressures clients to come out.	Safety is the first priority. Support clients until (and if) they decide they are ready to come out, recognizing the power of rejection by family and community, discrimination in the workplace and elsewhere, the risk of losing their children, and violence.
Ignores significant others and family members.	For lesbians, "family" may include a broader community (ex-lovers, ex-spouses, former in-laws, etc.) than it does for heterosexual women.
Interprets on behalf of the client. For example: "It must be hard being a lesbian" or "You must be angry because your parents do not accept your being a person of transgender experience." Instead, follow the client's lead.	■ Assumption-free, client-centered assessment and treatment works best. ■ Do not assume that sexual orientation is the underlying cause or the major factor in substance abuse, although it may be in some cases.

Source: Adapted from Center for Substance Abuse Treatment. (2001). *A provider's introduction to substance abuse treatment for lesbian, gay, bisexual, and transgender individuals* (U.S. Department of Health and Human Services Publication No. [SMA] 01-3498). Rockville, MD: Substance Abuse and Mental Health Services Administration. Available at www.kap.samhsa.gov/products/manuals/pdfs/lgbt.pdf.

ing their independence from profit-making influences in the pursuit of their mission. They prohibit or limit donations from the alcohol industry or, if they accept funding, restrict the type or scope of promotions or advertising associated with it.[92]

Although researchers have paid great attention to the risks associated with club drug use in gay male communities, a disproportionate number of lesbian and bisexual women also may abuse prescription and illicit drugs. Public health agencies and LGBT organizations need to develop initiatives targeted to lesbians as well as gay men that aim to prevent and reduce the harm associated with high-risk behavior among club drug users. In addition, researchers should determine what types of messages and interventions for younger lesbians might be effective.

CONCLUSION

Alcohol and drug abuse and dependence are complex, chronic, relapsing conditions related to biological, social, psychological, and cultural factors. The same risk factors—sexual and physical abuse experiences, genetics and family history, and a tendency to self-medicate physical and psychological pain, among others—apply to both sexual minority and heterosexual women. However, sexual minority women also face unique risk factors, such as the stress associated with coming out or encountering personal and institutionalized forms of prejudice.

Heterosexism has made it difficult for many lesbian and bisexual women to access substance abuse treatment and other health care services. And if they do receive services, they often encounter the same hostile environment that created the conditions for substance abuse in the first place. Health care providers need to understand that sexual identity alone does not give rise to alcohol or drug problems. While all lesbians should be screened for such problems, those who present for treatment are often grappling with other issues that clinicians must address.

REFERENCES

1. Fifield, L. H. (1975). *On my way to nowhere: Alienated, isolated and drunk.* Los Angeles: Gay Community Services Center.

2. Lewis, C. E., Saghir, M. T., & Robins, E. (1982). Drinking patterns in homosexual and heterosexual women. *Journal of Clinical Psychiatry, 43,* 277–279.

3. Saghir, M. T., Robins, E., Walbran, B., & Gentry, K. (1970). Homosexuality: Psychiatric disorders and disability in the female homosexual. *American Journal of Psychiatry, 127,* 147–154.

4. Bux, D. (1996). The epidemiology of problem drinking in gay men and lesbians: A critical review. *Clinical Psychology Review, 16,* 227–298.

5. Paul, J. P., Barrett, D. C., Crosby, G. M., & Stall, R. D. (1996). Longitudinal changes in alcohol and drug use among men seen at a gay-specific substance abuse treatment agency. *Journal of Studies on Alcohol, 57,* 475–485.

6. Cochran, S. D., Ackerman, D., Mays, V. M., & Ross, M. W. (2004). Prevalence of non-medical drug use and dependence among homosexually active men and women in the U.S. population. *Addiction, 99,* 989–998.

7. Cochran, S. D., Keenan, C., Schober, C., & Mays, V. M. (2000). Estimates of alcohol use and clinical treatment needs among homosexually active men and women in the U.S. population. *Journal of Consulting and Clinical Psychology, 68,* 1062–1071.

8. Cochran, S. D., & Mays, V. M. (2000). Relation between psychiatric syndromes and behaviorally defined sexual orientation in a sample of the U.S. population. *American Journal of Epidemiology, 151,* 516–523.

9. Gilman, S. E., Cochran, S. D., Mays, V. M., Hughes, M., Ostrow, D., & Kessler, R. C. (2001). Risk of psychiatric disorders among individuals reporting same-sex sexual partners in the National Comorbidity Survey. *American Journal of Public Health, 91,* 933–939.

10. Cochran, S., Mays, V. M., & Sullivan, J. G. (2003). Prevalence of mental disorders, psychological distress, and mental health services use among lesbian, gay, and bisexual adults in the United States. *Journal of Consulting and Clinical Psychology, 71,* 53–61.

11. Cochran, S. D., Mays, V. M., Ortega, A. N., Alegria, M., & Takeuchi, D. (2007). Mental health and substance abuse disorders among Latino and Asian American lesbian, gay, and bisexual adults. *Journal of Consulting and Clinical Psychology, 75,* 785–794.

12. Drabble, L., Trocki, K. F., & Midanik, L. T. (2005). Reports of alcohol consumption and alcohol-related problems among homosexual, bisexual and heterosexual respondents: Results from the 2000 National Alcohol Survey. *Journal of Studies on Alcohol, 66,* 111–120.

13. Drabble, L., & Trocki, K. (2005). Alcohol consumption, alcohol-related problems, and other substance use among lesbian and bisexual women. *Journal of Lesbian Studies, 9,* 19–30.

14. Trocki, K., Drabble, L., & Midanik, L. T. (2005). Use of heavier drinking contexts among heterosexuals, homosexuals and bisexuals: Results from a national household probability survey. *Journal of Studies on Alcohol, 66,* 105–110.

15. Burgard, S. A., Cochran, S. D., & Mays, V. M. (2005). Alcohol and tobacco use patterns among heterosexually and homosexually experienced California women. *Drug and Alcohol Dependence, 77,* 61–70.

16. Diamant, A. L., Wold, C., Spritzer, K., & Gelberg, L. (2000). Health behaviors, health status, and access to and use of health care: A population-based study of lesbian, bisexual, and heterosexual women. *Archives of Family Medicine, 9,* 1043–1051.

17. Scheer, S., Parks, C. A., McFarland, W., Page-Shafer, K., Delgado, V., Ruiz, J. D., et al. (2003). Self-reported sexual identity, sexual behaviors and health risks: Examples from a population-based survey of young women. *Journal of Lesbian Studies, 7,* 69–83.

18. Bloomfield, K. (1993). A comparison of alcohol consumption between lesbians and heterosexual women in an urban population. *Drug and Alcohol Dependence, 33,* 257–269.

19. Corliss, H. L., Grella, C. E., Mays, V. M., & Cochran, S. D. (2006). Drug use, drug severity, and help-seeking behaviors of lesbian and bisexual women. *Journal of Women's Health, 15,* 556–568.

20. Bergmark, K. H. (1999). Drinking in the Swedish gay community. *Drug and Alcohol Dependence, 56,* 133–143.

21. Gruskin, E. P., Hart, S., Gordon, N., & Ackerson, L. (2001). Patterns of cigarette smoking and alcohol use among lesbians and bisexual women enrolled in a large health maintenance organization. *American Journal of Public Health, 91,* 976–979.

22. Hughes, T. L. (2003). Lesbians' drinking patterns: Beyond the data. *Substance Use & Misuse, 38,* 1739–1758.

23. King, M., McKeown, E., Warner, J., Ramsay, A., Johnson, K., Cort, C., et al. (2003). Mental health and quality of life of gay men and lesbians in England and Wales: Controlled, cross-sectional study. *British Journal of Psychiatry, 183,* 552–558.

24. McCabe, S. E., Boyd, C., Hughes, T., & d'Arcy, H. (2003). Sexual identity and substance use among undergraduate students. *Substance Abuse, 24,* 77–91.

25. Skinner, W. F., & Otis, M. D. (1996). Drug and alcohol use among lesbian and gay people in a southern U.S. sample: Epidemiological, comparative, and methodological findings from the Trilogy Project. *Journal of Homosexuality, 30,* 59–92.

26. Wilsnack, S. C., Hughes, T. L., Johnson, T. P., Bostwick, W. B., Szalacha, L. A., Benson, P., et al. (2008). Drinking and drinking-related problems among heterosexual and sexual minority women. *Journal of Studies on Alcohol and Drugs, 69,* 129–139.

27. Aaron, D. J., Markovic, N., Danielson, M. E., Honnold, J. A., Janoskey, J. E., & Schmidt, N. J. (2001). Behavioral risk factors for disease and preventive health practices among lesbians. *American Journal of Public Health, 91,* 972–975.

28. Brandenburg, D. L., Matthews, A. K., Johnson, T. P., & Hughes, T. L. (2007). Breast cancer risk and screening: A comparison of lesbian and heterosexual women. *Women & Health, 45,* 109–130.

29. Case, P., Austin, S. B., Hunter, D. J., Manson, J. E., Malspeis, S., Willett, W. C., et al. (2004). Sexual orientation, health risk factors, and physical functioning in the Nurses' Health Study. *Journal of Women's Health, 13,* 1033–1047.

30. Grindel, C. G., McGehee, L. A., Patsdaughter, C. A., & Roberts, S. J. (2006). Cancer prevention and screening behaviors in lesbians. *Women & Health, 44,* 15–39.

31. Degenhardt, L. (2005). Drug use and risk behaviour among regular ecstasy users: Does sexuality make a difference? *Culture, Health & Sexuality, 7,* 599–614.

32. Parsons, J. T., Kelly, B. C., & Wells, B. E. (2006). Differences in club drug use between heterosexual and lesbian/bisexual females. *Addictive Behaviors, 31,* 2344–2349.

33. Kelly, B. C., & Parsons, J. T. (2007). Prescription drug misuse among club drug-using young adults. *American Journal of Drug and Alcohol Abuse, 33,* 875–884.

34. McCabe, S. E., Hughes, T. L., & Bostwick, W. (2005). Assessment of difference in dimensions of sexual orientation: Implications for substance use research in a college-age population. *Journal of Studies on Alcohol, 66,* 620–629.

35. Midanik, L. T., Drabble, L., Trocki, K., & Sell, R. (2006). Sexual orientation and alcohol use: Identity versus behavior measures. *Journal of Lesbian, Gay, Bisexual, and Transgender Health Research, 3,* 25–35.

36. Eisenberg, M., & Wechsler, H. (2003). Substance use behaviors among college students with same-sex and opposite-sex experience: Results from a national survey. *Addictive Behaviors, 28,* 899–913.

37. Jorm, A. F., Karten, A. E., Rodgers, B., Jacomb, P. A., & Christensen, H. (2002). Sexual orientation and mental health: Results from a community survey of young and middle-aged adults. *British Journal of Psychiatry, 180,* 423–427.

38. McCabe, S. E., Hughes, T., & Boyd, C. (2004). Substance use and misuse: Are bisexual women at greater risk? *Journal of Psychoactive Drugs, 36,* 217–225.

39. Bostwick, W. B., Esteban, S., Horn, S., Hughes, T., Johnson, T., & Valles, J. R. (2007). Drinking patterns, problems, and motivations among collegiate bisexual women. *Journal of American College Health, 56,* 285–292.

40. Hughes, T. L., Wilsnack, S. C., Szalacha, L. A., Johnson, T., Bostwick, W. B., Seymour, R., et al. (2006). Age and racial/ethnic differences in drinking and drinking-related problems in a community sample of lesbians. *Journal of Studies on Alcohol, 67,* 579–590.

41. Barbara, A. (2002). Substance abuse treatment with lesbian, gay and bisexual people: A qualitative study of service providers. *Journal of Lesbian and Gay Social Services, 14,* 1–17.

42. Matthews, C. R., Lorah, P., & Fenton, J. (2006). Treatment experiences of gays and lesbians in recovery from addiction: A qualitative inquiry. *Journal of Mental Health Counseling, 28,* 110–132.

43. Reyes, M. (1998). Latina lesbians and alcohol and other drugs: Social work implications. *Alcoholism Treatment Quarterly, 16,* 179–192.

44. Cheng, Z. (2003). Issues and standards in counseling lesbians and gay men with substance abuse concerns. *Journal of Mental Health Counseling, 25,* 323–336.

45. Finnegan, D. G., & McNally, E. B. (2002). *Counseling lesbian, gay, bisexual, and transgender substance abusers: Dual identities.* Binghamton, NY: Haworth Press.

46. Center for Substance Abuse Treatment. (2001). *A provider's introduction to substance abuse treatment for lesbian, gay, bisexual, and transgender individuals* (U.S. Department of Health & Human Services Publication No. [SMA] 01-3498). Rockville, MD: Substance Abuse and Mental Health Services Administration. Available at www.kap.samhsa.gov/products/manuals/pdfs/lgbt.pdf.

47. Battle, J., & Crum, M. (2007). Black LGB health and well-being. In I. H. Meyer & M. Northridge (Eds.), *The health of sexual minorities: Public health perspectives on lesbian, gay, bisexual, and transgender populations* (pp. 320–352). New York: Springer.

48. Estrada, D. (2006). Using the multiple lenses of identity: Working with ethnic and sexual minority college students. *Journal of College Counseling, 9,* 158–166.

49. Fieland, K., Walters, K., & Simoni, J. (2007). Determinants of health among two-spirit American Indians and Alaska Natives. In I. H. Meyer & M. Northridge (Eds.), *The health of sexual minorities: Public health perspectives on lesbian, gay, bisexual, and transgender populations* (pp. 268–300). New York: Springer.

50. Mays, V. M., Yancey, A. K., Cochran, S. D., Weber, M., & Fielding, J. E. (2002). Heterogeneity of health disparities among African American, Hispanic, and Asian American women: Unrecognized influences of sexual orientation. *American Journal of Public Health, 92,* 632–639.

51. Wilson, P. A., & Yoshikawa, H. (2007). Improving access to health care among African-American, Asian and Pacific Islander, and Latino LGB populations. In I. H. Meyer & M. Northridge (Eds.), *The health of sexual minorities: Public health perspectives on lesbian, gay, bisexual, and transgender populations* (pp. 609–637). New York: Springer.

52. Maccio, E. M., & Doueck, H. J. (2002). Meeting the needs of the gay and lesbian community: Outcomes in the human services. *Journal of Gay & Lesbian Social Services, 14,* 55–73.

53. Swindell, M., & Pryce, J. (2003). Self-disclosure stress: Trauma as an example of an intervening variable in research with lesbian women. *Journal of Gay & Lesbian Social Services, 15*, 95–108.

54. Morrow, D. F. (2000). Coming out to families: Guidelines for intervention with gay and lesbian clients. *Journal of Family Social Work, 5*, 53–66.

55. Smith, A. (1997). Cultural diversity and the coming-out process: Implications for clinical practice. In B. Greene (Ed.), *Ethnic and cultural diversity among lesbians and gay men* (pp. 279–300). Thousand Oaks, CA: Sage Publications.

56. Bradford, J., Ryan, C., & Rothblum, E. D. (1994). National Lesbian Health Care Survey: Implications for mental health care. *Journal of Consulting and Clinical Psychology, 62*, 228–242.

57. Mays, V. M., Chatters, L. M., Cochran, S. D., & Mackness, J. (1998). African American families in diversity: Gay men and lesbians as participants in family networks. *Journal of Comparative Family Studies, 29*, 73–87.

58. Eliason, M. J., Dibble, S. D., DeJoseph, J., & Chinn, P. (in press). *LGBTQ cultures: What health care professionals need to know about sexual and gender diversity.* New York: Lippincott Williams & Wilkins.

59. Herek, G. M., & Garnets, L. D. (2007). Sexual orientation and mental health. *Annual Review of Clinical Psychology, 3*, 353–375.

60. Meyer, I. H. (2003). Prejudice, social stress, and mental health in lesbian, gay, and bisexual populations: Conceptual issues and research evidence. *Psychological Bulletin, 129*, 674–697.

61. Mays, V. M., Cochran, S. D., & Roeder, M. R. (2003). Depressive distress and prevalence and common problems among homosexually active women in the United States. *Journal of Psychology & Human Sexuality, 15*, 27–46.

62. Ziyadeh, N. J., Prokop, L. A., Fisher, L. B., Rosario, M., Field, A. E., Camargo, C. A., et al. (2007). Sexual orientation, gender, and alcohol use in a cohort study of U.S. adolescent girls and boys. *Drug and Alcohol Dependence, 87*, 119–130.

63. Amadio, D. M., & Chung, Y. B. (2004). Internalized homophobia and substance use among lesbian, gay and bisexual persons. *Journal of Gay & Lesbian Social Services, 17*, 83–101.

64. McKirnan, D. J., & Peterson, P. L. (1989). Psychosocial and cultural factors in alcohol and drug abuse: An analysis of a homosexual community. *Addictive Behaviors, 14*, 555–563.

65. Saghir, M. T., & Robins, E. (1973). *Male and female homosexuality: A comprehensive investigation.* Baltimore, MD: Williams & Wilkins.

66. Amadio, D. M. (2006). Internalized heterosexism, alcohol use, and alcohol-related problems among lesbians and gay men. *Addictive Behaviors, 31*, 1153–1162.

67. Hughes, T. L., Johnson, T. P., Wilsnack, S. C., & Szalacha, L. A. (2007). Childhood risk factors for alcohol abuse and psychological distress among adult lesbians. *Child Abuse & Neglect, 31*, 769–789.

68. McNally, E., & Finnegan, D. G. (1992). Lesbian recovering alcoholics: A qualitative study of identity transformation. A report on research and application to treatment. *Journal of Chemical Dependency Treatment, 5*, 93–103.

69. Balsam, K. F., Rothblum, E. D., & Beauchaine, T. P. (2005). Victimization over the life span: A comparison of lesbian, gay, bisexual, and heterosexual siblings. *Journal of Consulting and Clinical Psychology, 73,* 477–487.

70. Morris, J. F., & Balsam, K. F. (2003). Lesbian and bisexual women's experiences of victimization: Mental health, revictimization, and sexual identity development. *Journal of Lesbian Studies, 7,* 67–85.

71. LaSala, M. (2007). Old maps, new territory: Family therapy theory and gay and lesbian couples. *Journal of GLBT Family Studies, 3,* 1–14.

72. Marsiglia, F. F. (1998). Homosexuality and Latino/as: Towards an integration of identities. *Journal of Lesbian and Gay Social Services, 8,* 113–121.

73. Hall, J. M. (1993). Lesbians and alcohol: Patterns and paradoxes in medical notions and lesbians' beliefs. *Journal of Psychoactive Drugs, 25,* 109–117.

74. Hall, J. M. (1994). The experiences of lesbians in Alcoholics Anonymous. *Western Journal of Nursing Research, 16,* 556–576.

75. Gruskin, E., Byrne, K., Kools, S., & Altschuler, A. (2006). Consequences of frequenting the lesbian bar. *Women & Health, 44,* 103–120.

76. Heffernan, K. (1998). The nature and predictors of substance abuse among lesbians. *Addictive Behaviors, 23,* 517–528.

77. Parks, C. A. (1999). Lesbian social drinking: The role of alcohol in growing up and living as a lesbian. *Contemporary Drug Problems, 26,* 75–129.

78. Parks, C. A., & Hughes, T. L. (2007). Age differences in lesbian identity development and drinking. *Substance Use & Misuse, 42,* 361–380.

79. Bowen, D., Bradford, J. B., Powers, D., McMorrow, P., Linde, R., Murphy, B. C., et al. (2004). Comparing women of differing sexual orientations using population-based sampling. *Women & Health, 40,* 19–34.

80. Barbara, A. M., & Chaim, G. (2004). Asking about sexual orientation during assessment for drug and alcohol concerns: A pilot study. *Journal of Social Work Practice in the Addictions, 4,* 89–109.

81. Matthews, C. R., Lorah, P., & Fenton, J. (2005). Toward a grounded theory of lesbians' recovery from addiction. *Journal of Lesbian Studies, 9,* 57–68.

82. Matthews, C. R., & Selvidge, M. M. D. (2005). Lesbian, gay, and bisexual clients' experiences in treatment for addiction. *Journal of Lesbian Studies, 9,* 79–90.

83. Eliason, M. J. (2000). Substance abuse counselors' attitudes regarding lesbian, gay, bisexual, and transgendered clients. *Journal of Substance Abuse, 12,* 311–328.

84. Eliason, M. J., & Hughes, T. L. (2004). Treatment counselors' attitudes regarding lesbian, gay, bisexual, and transgendered clients: Urban vs. rural settings. *Substance Use & Misuse, 39,* 625–644.

85. Cochran, B. N., Peavy, K. M., & Cauce, A. M. (2007). Substance abuse treatment providers' explicit and implicit attitudes regarding sexual minorities. *Journal of Homosexuality, 53,* 181–207.

86. Cochran, B. N., Peavy, K. M., & Robohm, J. S. (2007). Do specialized services exist for LGBT individuals seeking treatment for substance misuse? A study of available treatment programs. *Substance Use & Misuse, 42,* 161–176.

87. Olmstead, T., & Sindelar, J. L. (2004). To what extent are key services offered in treatment programs for special populations? *Journal of Substance Abuse Treatment, 27,* 9–15.

88. Driscoll, R. (1982). A gay-identified alcohol treatment program: A follow-up study. *Journal of Homosexuality, 7,* 71–80.

89. Cochran, B. N., & Cauce, A. M. (2006). Characteristics of lesbian, gay, bisexual, and transgender individuals entering substance abuse treatment. *Journal of Substance Abuse Treatment, 30,* 135–146.

90. Crisp, C. (2006). Correlates of homophobia and use of gay affirmative practice among social workers. *Journal of Human Behavior in the Social Environment, 14,* 119–143.

91. Drabble, L., & Underhill, B. L. (2002). Effective interventions and treatment for lesbians. In S. L. Straussner & S. E. Brown (Eds.), *Handbook for addiction treatment for women: Theory and practice* (pp. 399–422). New York: Jossey-Bass.

92. Drabble, L. (2000). Alcohol, tobacco, and pharmaceutical industry funding: Considerations for organizations serving lesbian, gay, bisexual, and transgender communities. *Journal of Lesbian and Gay Social Services, 11,* 1–26.

ABOUT THE AUTHORS

Laurie Drabble, PhD, MPH, MSW is Associate Professor in the School of Social Work at San Jose State University in California. Her research and community practice center on addressing alcohol and other substance abuse problems among marginalized populations of women with a special emphasis on the relationships between alcohol consumption, health, and mental health in women, especially sexual minority women.

Michele J. Eliason, PhD is Assistant Professor in the Department of Health Education at San Francisco State University. She has written many articles on LGBT health issues and is co-author of the recent book *LGBTQ Cultures: What Health Care Professionals Need to Know about Sexual and Gender Diversity* (Lippincott Press).

Migdalia Reyes, EdD, MSW is Professor and former Associate Dean in the School of Social Work at San Jose State University in California. Previously, she was Director of the Puerto Rican Studies Program in the School of Social Work at the University of Connecticut. Her research focus is alcohol and drug abuse among those of Latin heritage and lesbians.

CHAPTER 10

"But I Have Big Bones!"
OBESITY IN THE LESBIAN COMMUNITY

SARAH C. FOGEL, PhD, RN

MARTI, *45, weighed 10.5 pounds when she was born. She likes to say that she got a good start on her current 360-pound body. She has always felt OK with her big bones, strong musculature, and large size; after all, she is 5 feet 11 inches tall. She admits that her size is an issue when she has to travel on a plane or go to a ballgame. The seats crowd her and everyone around her. Although Marti exercises regularly, she has started to have back pain that she knows would be alleviated if she lost some weight. Recently, the pain became so unbearable that she decided to seek medical help.*

Marti dreaded this appointment. She feared that the health care provider might ridicule her weight, as all previous providers had. Even if nothing was said, the chairs in the waiting room were built for size 6 people and there would be "that look" when the scale could not go beyond 350 pounds. She resisted seeking health care even when she needed it for her diabetes because providers always said: "If you would just lose weight, you probably wouldn't need most of this medication."

"If you would just lose weight"—Marti loved that expression. She had lost more than 50 pounds countless times, and nearly 100 pounds twice. It always came back! She had tried every diet and supplement on the market. Marti often considered gastric bypass surgery, but she realized this would not solve her problem and worried that she might regain weight after surgery. All this came to mind whenever she considered seeking any type of health care. When Marti set foot in the health care provider's office, she was in a panic. During appointments, her blood pressure was always high, her face was red, and she frequently cried.

It seemed that no provider could see her true self. Marti was a big, strong, beautiful lesbian and, regardless of her size, many people cared about her. She had lots of frustrating questions about providers' attitudes. "Why are they unable to recognize that I am more than a fat woman? Why must I feel like a criminal just because I need medicine to keep me as healthy as possible until I lose weight and keep it off? Why do I have to check 'single' on the patient form every time I see a provider and then try to explain that I receive wonderful support from someone named Teresa? Is it not possible to include options on forms that make all patients feel welcome? Why do I have to worry about finding a provider who will not re-act negatively to my sexual identity? And, anyway, why do chairs need arms?"

Obesity in the United States has reached epidemic proportions. In 2006, about two-thirds of Americans were overweight or obese.[1] Obesity, a complex health concern, is intertwined with genetics, culture, environmental influences, societal standards, and ideals of beauty that contribute to a vast array of opinions and conflict. Although research on obesity in the lesbian population is scant, four large comparison studies suggest that lesbians are at greater risk for obesity than are heterosexual women, that they are one-and-a-half to two times more likely than heterosexual women to be overweight or obese.[2-5] Marti's experience in the scenario above is compounded by her sexual identity.

Obesity rates are higher among many ethnic minority heterosexual women, particularly African Americans and Latinas, compared with White heterosexual women. And they are higher among African American and Latina lesbians than White lesbians,[6] though not among lesbians of Asian descent.[7] It is important to identify and explore the reasons for this elevated risk and address each in the context of health.

From the standpoint of health, obesity—a body mass index (BMI), or weight relative to height ratio, of > 27.3[8]—contributes to higher rates of hypertension, dyslipidemia, type 2 diabetes, coronary artery disease, stroke, gallbladder disease, osteoarthritis, sleep apnea, respiratory problems, and a number of cancers (for women: ovarian, endometrial, breast, anal, colon, and gastric cancer).[9,10] The National Heart, Lung, and Blood Institute defines overweight, obesity, and extreme obesity as a BMI of 25.0 to 29.9, 30.0 to 39.9, and > 40.0, respectively.[10] Therefore, Marti, who has a BMI of 50 to 51, is extremely obese and at risk for many health problems.*

FACTORS THAT CONTRIBUTE TO HIGHER RISK AMONG LESBIANS

Genetics

There are still more questions than answers about the role of genetics in obesity. What is known is that genetics may predispose some people to obesity. However, being predisposed to obesity does not mean it is preordained. A variety of factors are responsible.[11] Although everyone on both the maternal and paternal sides of Marti's family was obese, it is impossible to know for sure which genetic and/or other factors contributed to her condition.

Because the human genome comprises more than 20,000 genes, pinpointing those responsible for obesity is difficult. Researchers have identified six genes that lead to

---

* BMI calculators for adults and children/teens are available at www.cdc.gov/healthyweight/assessing/bmi/index.html.

rare forms of severe obesity, which account for less than 1% of all obesity and are caused by a mutation in just one gene. Common forms of obesity most likely result from an interaction between genes or between them and environmental influences. More than 430 genes have been loosely implicated, yet only 15 of them have produced the same results in multiple studies.[12]

The current state of science regarding genetic predisposition to obesity is very similar to that regarding genetic predisposition to addiction. In the latter case, researchers have identified several responsible genes: DRD2, Cnr1, and CYP2A6.[13] But there has not been any genetic research on addiction to food.

Cultural and Environmental Factors

It is difficult, if not impossible, to separate out culture and environment when examining nongenetic contributors to obesity. One environmental contributor is automobiles: they have eliminated much of the impetus for Americans to walk more than a few steps in most metropolitan and rural areas. This, along with television viewing and the growing use of computers, make for an extremely sedentary lifestyle. A telling fact is the relatively low rates of obesity among the Amish, an orthodox Christian sect that resists modern conveniences.[14] In some metropolitan areas in the United States and abroad where walking, cycling, and use of public transportation are more common, obesity rates have declined.[15,16] Most research regarding lesbian health is based on samples drawn from these areas; disparities there in the rate of obesity between lesbians and heterosexual women suggest that obesity among lesbians is more of a cultural than environmental phenomenon.

Researchers have yet to study sexual identity in relation to culture, an integral factor in lesbianism. Culture is a complex whole that includes knowledge, belief, art, morals, laws, customs, and habits acquired by virtue of belonging. This definition exemplifies the sense of community many lesbians feel: their attraction to other women extends beyond the sexual and it influences their tastes in art and music as well as customs for celebrating spirituality or religion, daily life, and even death. Although lesbian celebrations may be unique, the impetus for customs is not. Most humans gravitate to others who make them feel comfortable and with whom they share a commonality, which is how cultures and societies arise.

Eating Disorders and Culture

Environment outside the context of culture does not affect eating disorders; rather, these disorders are a mixture of culture and genetics. Until the 1990s, anorexia and bulimia were considered to be diseases of the White middle and upper classes. Since then, research has demonstrated that girls and women of all ethnicities are at risk. The one common factor among females with eating disorders, regardless of cultural affiliation, is low self-esteem.[17-20] There has been no definitive research on differences in the prevalence of eating disorders between lesbians and heterosexual women.

Societal Standards and Ideals of Beauty

How people conceive of beauty depends on when and where they live. Additional influences are culture and ethnicity. Although the concept of beauty in the United States shows signs of changing,[21] the prevailing standard throughout the twentieth century was a tall, extremely thin body type with white skin and, oftentimes, exaggerated characteristics, including large breasts and a tiny waist. Historically, related health issues have at times influenced body shape and size. For example, tuberculosis was so rampant in the nineteenth century that the associated emaciation became the standard of beauty for that era. In the twentieth century and with the advent of tuberculosis treatment, the norm shifted to a "healthier" body type. Nevertheless:

> Standards of female beauty have in fact become progressively more unrealistic during the 20th century. In 1917, the physically perfect woman was about 5ft 4in tall and weighed nearly 10 stone [140 pounds]. Even 25 years ago, top models and beauty queens weighed only 8% less than the average woman, now they weigh 23% less. The current media ideal for women is achievable by less than 5% of the female population—and that's just in terms of weight and size.[22]

Such standards contrast with those in the late Middle Ages. As works of art from the fourteenth and fifteenth centuries attest, Western cultures revered curvy women, who would be overweight by current standards.

Research has shown that ideals of beauty differ between Black and White women.[23,24] Black women are less concerned about weight, dieting, or thinness, and the African American culture is supportive of different female perceptions of body type and physical attractiveness.[25] African American and Hispanic women describe themselves as "looking beautiful" at a higher rate than Caucasian women do (61%, 57%, and 38%, respectively).[21]

Although there is little published research on lesbians' perceptions of beauty, a fair amount of theoretical literature addresses this subject. Schorb and Hammidi explored the concept of lesbian beauty through a discourse on hair and thoroughly described the elements, dynamic nature, "alienating nature," and evolution of such beauty. They maintained that this evolution has resulted in the creation of "exiles"—lesbians who are rejected or ridiculed by other lesbians.[26] A 2007 study highlights the conundrum many lesbians experience as a byproduct of this evolution. As all lesbians are female and live in a gender-based world, heterosexist stereotypes are instilled from birth. When a lesbian identity emerges, expectations based on the dominant culture's view of female beauty persist. Add to this the prevailing standard of lesbian expression, which sometimes includes an androgynous, if not butch, appearance, and many lesbians struggle with their own self-expression and with rejection by both heterosexual women and lesbians.[27]

TREATMENT

The medical options for treating obesity are very similar for heterosexual women and lesbians, but the latter have less access to therapy. For example, there are fewer support groups for lesbians. Although support groups such as Weight Watchers are typically open to all women and men, lesbians face barriers. Not unlike society at large, the groups are geared toward the majority, such that lesbians' weight loss difficulties go unaddressed in meetings. Lesbian members may not raise issues for fear of a homophobic response from the group or because they are unwilling to share feelings and experiences if other members' understanding or acceptance is not likely. An online Weight Watchers program may reduce the stress lesbians feel in face-to-face settings.

Marti's case illustrates the issue of access to health care in general. She delayed seeing a doctor out of fear that her weight and sexual identity would incite ridicule. Access to care for sexual minorities is limited mainly by their fear of mistreatment and frequently by lower economic status.[28] Furthermore, unlike heterosexual couples, lesbians may not be able to take advantage of their partner's health insurance benefits. Perhaps the biggest concern is that many lesbians seek care only after their obesity or some other health condition has advanced to a point where treatment options are more limited and invasive.

Pharmaceuticals

There are two main types of drugs for treating obesity: monoamine reuptake inhibitors (serotonin and norepinephrine) and lipase inhibitors. The former mimic the sympathetic nervous system and tend to cause elevated blood pressure and other side effects, such as nervousness and jitteriness, that are related to stimulation of the sympathetic nervous system. They can also reduce appetite and result in satiety by increasing the level of the neurotransmitters serotonin and norepinephrine at the synapse between nerve endings in the brain. Lipase inhibitors reduce intestinal absorption of fat by 30%.[29] These drugs do not affect brain chemistry; rather, their efficacy derives from the severe gastric upset they cause under certain conditions.

• Monoamine Reuptake Inhibitors

Sibutramine (Meridia) is the only drug in this class approved by the U.S. Food and Drug Administration (FDA) for long-term treatment of obesity, including maintaining weight loss. However, FDA guidelines stipulate that sibutramine is appropriate only for patients with a BMI ≥ 30 or for those with a BMI ≥ 27 who have comorbidities, such as hypertension or diabetes, that would improve if the patient were to lose weight. The agency also suggests that regular exercise and an appropriate diet accompany sibutramine use.[30]

Monoamine reuptake inhibitors approved for short-term treatment of obesity include phentermine (Adipex and Ionamin), diethylpropion (Tenuate), phendimetrazine (Bontril and Prelu-2), and benzphetamine (Didrex).

• Lipase Inhibitors

There is also only one FDA-approved lipase inhibitor for weight loss: orlistat (Xenical). In 11 studies between 1998 and 2002, pooled results indicated that orlistat contributed to a 2.7 kg (95% confidence interval [CI]: 2.3–3.1 kg), or 2.9% (95% CI: 2.3–3.4%), greater decrease in body weight than a placebo did. Furthermore, another 12% of the subjects (95% CI: 8–16%) achieved a minimum 10% weight loss with orlistat compared with those who received a placebo.[31] The most common side effects of orlistat are gastrointestinal: fatty or oily stool, liquid stool, fecal urgency, and flatulence. In a 2-year trial, the side effects diminished in the second year. Over the long term, however, fat absorption can result in a deficiency of fat-soluble vitamins, which means patients must take vitamin supplements daily. Advantages of orlistat include a reduction in low-density lipoprotein cholesterol independent of weight loss[32] and inhibition of dietary cholesterol absorption.[32] Over-the-counter orlistat (Alli) became available in 2007.

Nonprescription Diet Pills and Herbs

In addition to Alli, a number of dietary supplements for weight loss are available, but little or no scientific evidence supports the efficacy or safety of many of these products. They include chitosan, conjugated linoleic acid, coenzyme Q10, coral calcium, Herbalife, Hoodia, human growth hormone, Hydroxycut, Megadrine, Metabolife, and Vasopro. There are many other ephedrine or pseudoephedrine-type pills ("fat burners").

Naturalists have recommended herbs, including cascara sagrada, dandelion, ephedra (natural ephedrine), garcina cambogia, licorice root, psyllium, St. John's wort, senna, and others for weight loss.[34] But like over-the-counter (OTC) medications, herbs raise safety and efficacy concerns; the FDA does not regulate them. Efficacy data are not readily available. Health care practitioners must take a complete history of all medications and supplements, as some supplements can interfere with medications used to treat obesity and comorbid conditions. For example, ephedra may contribute to an increased pressor effect—a result of unopposed alpha-receptor stimulation—when patients take noncardioselective beta-blocking agents.[35]

TABLE 10.1. WEIGHT LOSS OPTIONS

PROGRAM/ PRODUCT/ PROCEDURE	TYPE	EFFICACY	WEB SITE
Atkins	High-protein, very-low-carbohydrate, low-calorie diet	▪ Rapid weight loss. No difference at 12 months compared with low-, moderate-, and high-carbohydrate diets. ▪ Participants in three of five studies in a meta-analysis were predominantly female.[37] ▪ Participants in one study were all women.[38]	⌐ www.atkins.com
Biliopancreatic diversion	Surgical	Most patients lost up to 75–80% of excess weight and most maintained weight loss after 5 years.[39]	
eDiets	Low calorie (online)	1.1–4.0% loss of initial weight at 1 year. Those who used a weight loss manual lost more weight. Participants were all female.[40]	⌐ www.ediets.com
Gastric banding	Surgical	▪ Results differ among studies about the amount of weight lost and maintained compared with more complicated surgical procedures. ▪ No long-term comparison studies. ▪ Initial weight loss is not as great as with gastric bypass.[41–43]	
Health Management Resources (HMR)	Low- to very-low-calorie meal replacement with prepackaged meals	27.3% loss of initial weight at 26 weeks, with 15.2% of the loss maintained at 2 years. 69% of participants were women.[44]	⌐ www.hmrprogram.com
Jenny Craig	Low-calorie, prepackaged meals	7.3 kg of weight lost at 12 months compared to 0.7 kg lost in the control group. All participants were female.[45]	⌐ www.jennycraig.com
Nutrisystem	Low-calorie, prepackaged meals	All efficacy studies were industry-sponsored. No reported data for ≥ 12 months.	⌐ www.nutrisystem.com

(cont.)

TABLE 10.1. WEIGHT LOSS OPTIONS *(cont.)*

PROGRAM/ PRODUCT/ PROCEDURE	TYPE	EFFICACY	WEB SITE
OPTIFAST	Low-calorie meal replacement	24.3% loss of initial weight among those who completed a 26-week program. Participants had maintained an average 4.7% loss of initial weight at 4-year follow-up.[46]	⟲ www.optifast.com
Ornish (Eat More, Weigh Less)	Low- to no-fat, high-complex-carbohydrate diet	Difficult for nonvegetarians to sustain. Average weight loss of 2.6 kg at 12 months. Participants were all women.[38]	⟲ www.ornishspectrum. com
Roux-en-Y gastric bypass	Surgical	▪ Hypertension, hyperlipidemia, diabetes mellitus, obstructive sleep apnea, gastroesophageal reflux, and asthma improved in 80–100% of patients. Arthritis, pain, and depression improved in 52–73%. Quality of life greatly improved in > 80% after 18 months. Male and female participants.[47] ▪ 55–70% of participants had maintained the expected weight loss at 5 years.[41–43]	
Slim-Fast	Low-calorie meal replacement	Weight loss in meal replacement group (4.57%, ± 0.81%) was significantly greater ($p < 0.05$) than in individualized diet plan group (2.25%, ± 0.72%). Male and female participants.[48]	⟲ www.slim-fast.com
South Beach	Low-calorie diet based on glycemic index and low carbohydrate intake	12-week studies showed an average weight loss of 13.6 lbs compared to 7.5 lbs lost on a low-fat diet. Equal numbers of male and female participants.[49]	⟲ www.southbeachdiet. com
Weight Watchers	Low-calorie diet based on exchange of food groups	In industry-supported trials, participants on average lost 5% of initial weight. At 2 years, according to one study, participants had maintained 60% of initial weight loss. 85–100% of subjects were female.[50–52]	⟲ www.weightwatchers. com

Weight Loss Programs

There are many weight loss programs nationwide. Several of them severely restrict calories and/or promote OTC weight loss medications that enhance metabolism. Some are based on sound nutritional standards and social support. Theoretically, weight loss programs are open to everyone, although, as mentioned earlier, lesbians may not feel comfortable attending meetings that do not openly address their personal needs. Typical weight loss support groups focus on the concerns of women with husbands and children, and offer support geared toward dieting or lifestyle changes in that environment. A lesbian, in contrast, may need to know about how to find a partner who will support her weight loss regimen or how to survive a night out with friends at a bar or coffee house. Because many lesbians feel compelled to adjust their vocabulary according to the immediate social environment, the attention and energy they should devote to getting their needs met in a weight loss group are focused instead on protecting themselves from potential harm.

The lesbian community increasingly recognizes the obesity problem. Consequently, lesbian support groups and weight loss groups targeted to lesbians are forming. Anecdotal reports suggest that such efforts may help, but there has not been any research to determine their effectiveness. These groups are few and far between, so most obese lesbians are on their own.

A government-sponsored conference in 1997 on information that consumers need to evaluate weight loss products and programs generated a call to "devise means by which value and performance data about weight loss options are readily available at an acceptable cost and in a format that does not discourage obese consumers from attempting to lose weight."[36] Information on the efficacy of products and programs is limited, even though several of them boast high rates of success. Furthermore, there is little, if any, published data on their efficacy in lesbians. Available data on general efficacy (Table 10.1) indicate a need for much more research. In considering the weight loss options, consumers need health care providers' help in sorting out the facts and determining which strategies would meet their specific needs.

Surgical Procedures

There are two basic types of surgical treatments for severe obesity (BMI > 40): restrictive and combined restrictive/malabsorptive. The former include adjustable gastric banding and vertical banded gastroplasty. Combined restrictive/malabsorptive surgeries include Roux-en-Y gastric bypass, biliopancreatic diversion, and gastric sleeve. Combined restrictive/malabsorptive surgeries are more complicated and entail more risks, but they produce quicker and more sustained weight loss. Ten years after combined restrictive/malabsorptive surgeries, many patients maintain 60% to 80% of their weight loss, depending on the type of surgery. Restrictive surgeries are considered safer but less effective in maintaining weight loss; 10 years after surgery, as few as 20% of patients had kept the weight off.[53] Criteria set by the National Institute of Diabetes and Digestive and Kidney Diseases for consideration of surgical intervention for severe obesity are a BMI ≥ 40.0 (about 100 pounds overweight for men and 80 pounds for women); a BMI of 35.0 to 39.9 and a serious obesity-related health problem, such as type 2 diabetes, heart disease, or severe sleep apnea; and the patient's understanding of the operation and of the lifestyle changes that must be made.[53]

Surgical options may be limited for lesbians if they do not have health insurance and they lack access to health care in general.[54] Importantly, surgical intervention is never a cure for obesity and, after surgery, many lifestyle changes are necessary to maintain any weight loss.

CONFLICTS IN THE COMMUNITY

Just as the concept of "lesbian community" is arguable, so are numerous topics regarding lesbian obesity. This section addresses the role of the feminist movement in lesbian history and fat acceptance, and explains some of the conflicts, different views of attractiveness, and the alienating nature of lesbian factions.

The Role of Feminism in Lesbian History and Fat Acceptance

Feminism in America consists of "three waves."[55] The first wave was rooted in the abolitionist movement of the mid- to late 1800s, which sought to eliminate inequality. The connection between feminism and lesbianism arose in the second wave, during the 1960s, when social activism was at its height. Most lesbians believed that male-dominated gay liberation groups perpetuated sexist attitudes. Consequently, many lesbians joined forces with mainstream feminists. However, these feminists did not welcome the lesbians in their ranks and expected them to take a back seat and stay out of public view.[55] In the early 1970s, the National Organization of Women, led by Gloria Steinem, voted to include oppression of lesbians as a concern of the women's movement, although mainstream feminists still considered such issues to be peripheral to women's issues in general. Lesbians and all types of minority women, including transgender women, were frequently excluded from mainstream feminist discourse. Frustration with this state of affairs prompted lesbian feminists to branch off from the mainstream feminist movement. They articulated their stance in *The Woman-Identified Woman*,[56] arguing that women were completely disengaged from male-dominated society. They discouraged use of the word "lesbian" because, in their view, society wielded it as a weapon against any woman who asserted herself, and they encouraged all women to exert their rights through personhood and self-actualization.

Since the 1980s, a third wave of feminism has evolved that strives to include women of color, lesbians, and transgender women. But controversy remains. "Second wavers" are critical of "third wavers," and many Black feminists decry the "wave system" generally, saying it drowns Black feminism.[57] The wave model, as it is portrayed in literature and history today, does not acknowledge the contributions of many minority or feminist lesbians.

To understand some of the health issues that women—especially lesbians and ethnic minority women—still face, it is important to understand the inextricable link between feminists and lesbians. In the early 1970s, the "fat liberation" movement arose within feminism. Because women were diligently challenging societal norms and male domination, this movement, which today is more commonly called "size acceptance," attacked the weight loss industry as harmful and partly responsible for the link between eating disorders and preoccupation with dieting[58]. Many feminists still believe that health and fitness are not inversely related to size. Feminists shifted the emphasis on "thin is beautiful" to a focus on health. Now there is a better under-standing of obesity-related health risks. Robinson delineates a positive approach to a healthier lifestyle for everyone, regardless of sexual orientation, that may result in a healthy weight. It includes acceptance of:

- The natural diversity in body shape and size;
- The ineffectiveness and dangers of dieting to lose weight;
- The importance of relaxed eating in response to internal body cues; and
- The critical contribution of social, emotional, spiritual, and physical factors to health and happiness.[59]

Despite the influence of feminism, women are still fighting for equality in terms of economic parity and political parity, both of which affect health access and outcomes.[60]

Different Views of Attractiveness: The Butch/Femme Phenomenon

In the 1960s and before the advent of feminist lesbians, the only public identification of lesbians was in the butch/femme setting of lesbian and gay bars.[61] The butch/femme phenomenon is likely a response to the need or desire to make oneself visible to other lesbians.[27] It also may be related to defying gender roles and exerting the right to em-phasize the characteristics of one's self that previously had been hidden.[62] Women who identify as butch have a more masculine appearance, which sometimes prompts a less positive appraisal by the dominant culture. The dominant culture tends to accept femme-identified lesbians more readily than it does lesbians who appear to be more masculine, but they are not as acceptable to other lesbians.[27] Many lesbians adhere to the butch/femme form of expression, while many others prefer a more androgynous appearance. The importance of butch/femme roles in the obesity issue relates to the larger, more muscular body type characterized by butch identification and attractiveness.

The Alienating Nature of Lesbian Factions

People naturally seek groups that will make them feel valued and safe. Group identification based on gender, ethnicity, body type, or sexual identity is inherently exclusionary, which creates factions among lesbians. In terms of obesity, there are two distinct factions in the very diverse lesbian community: "large" or "not large." For example, although many butch lesbians are extremely fit, others generally view those who are "large" as butch or androgynous regardless of how they identify themselves. As Myers and colleagues pointed out, "the beauty mandate of the dominant culture has apparently been reproduced to some extent within women's [lesbian and bisexual] communities"[63] (p. 24). So has the controversy and conflict surrounding obesity.

CONCLUSION

Alarmingly, the prevalence of obesity is higher among lesbians than among heterosexual women. Obesity's impact on lesbians is likely to remain disproportionate as well, given that many have less access to health care and are economically disadvantaged. Clinical trials should not only investigate effective treatments for and prevention of obesity among lesbians, but also seek better understanding of lesbian-specific issues to maximize favorable health outcomes.

REFERENCES

1. National Institute of Diabetes and Digestive and Kidney Diseases. (2006). *Statistics related to overweight and obesity.* Washington, DC: U.S. Department of Health & Human Services.

2. Aaron, D., Markovic, N., Danielson, M., Honnold, J., Janosky, J., & Schmidt, N. (2001). Behavioral risk factors for disease and preventive health practices among lesbians. *American Journal of Public Health, 91,* 972–975.

3. Boehmer, U., Bowen, D. J., & Bauer, G. R. (2007). Overweight and obesity in sexual-minority women: Evidence from population-based data. *American Journal of Public Health, 97,* 1134–1140.

4. Case, P., Austin, S. B., Hunter, D. J., Manson, J. E., Malspeis, S., Willett, W. C., et al. (2004). Sexual orientation, health risk factors, and physical functioning in the Nurses' Health Study II. *Journal of Women's Health, 13,* 1033–1047.

5. Valanis, B. G., Bowen, D. J., Bassford, T., Whitlock, E., Charney, P., & Carter, R. A. (2000). Sexual orientation and health: Comparisons in the Women's Health Initiative sample. *Archives of Family Medicine, 9,* 843–853.

6. Mays, V. M., Yancey, A. K., Cochran, S. D., Weber, M., & Fielding, J. E. (2002). Heterogeneity of health disparities among African American, Hispanic, and Asian American women: Unrecognized influences of sexual orientation. *American Journal of Public Health, 92,* 632–639.

7. Dibble, S. L., Sato, N., & Haller, E. (2007). Asians and native Hawaiian or other Pacific Islanders midlife lesbians' health: A pilot study. *Women & Therapy, 30,* 129–143.

8. Wilcosky, T., Hyde, J., Anderson, J. J., Bangdiwala, S., & Duncan, B. (1990). Obesity and mortality in the Lipid Research Clinics Program Follow-up Study. *Journal of Clinical Epidemiology, 43,* 743–752.

9. O'Hanlan, K. A., Dibble, S. L., Hagan, H. J., & Davids, R. (2004). Advocacy for women's health should include lesbian health. *Journal of Women's Health, 13,* 227–234.

10. National Heart, Lung, and Blood Institute. (1998). *Clinical guidelines on the identification, evaluation, and treatment of overweight and obesity in adults. The evidence report* (Publication No. 98-4083). Washington, DC: U.S. Government Printing Office. Available at www.nhlbi.nih.gov/guidelines/obesity/ob_gdlns.pdf.

11. Centers for Disease Control and Prevention. (2009). *Overweight and obesity: An overview.* Available at www.cdc.gov/nccdphp/dnpa/obesity/contributing_factors.htm.

12. Center for Genomics and Public Health, University of Washington. (2004). *Obesity. Current topics in genetics. Implications for public health practice* [Brochure]. Available at depts.washington.edu/cgph/pdf/Obesity_Brochure_Final.pdf.

13. Genetic Science Learning Center, University of Utah. (2008). *Genetics is an important factor in addiction.* Available at learn.genetics.utah.edu/content/addiction/genetics.

14. Bassett, D. R. Jr., Tremblay, M. S., Esliger, D. W., Copeland, J. L., Barnes, J. D., & Huntington, G. E. (2007). Physical activity and body mass index of children in an old order Amish community. *Medicine & Science in Sports & Exercise, 39,* 410–415.

15. Pucher, J., & Dijkstra, L. (2003). Promoting safe walking and cycling to improve public health: Lessons from the Netherlands and Germany. *American Journal of Public Health, 93,* 1509–1516.

16. Transportation Research Board. (2001). *Making transit work: Insight from Western Europe, Canada and the United States.* Washington, DC: National Academy of Sciences Press.

17. Claude-Pierre, P. (1997). *The secret language of eating disorders.* New York: Random House.

18. Lester, R., & Petrie, T. (1995). Personality and physical correlates of symptomatology among Mexican American female college students. *Journal of Counseling Psychology, 42,* 199–203.

19. Lester, R., & Petrie, T. (1998). Physical, psychological and societal correlates of bulimic symptomatology in African-American college women. *Journal of Counseling Psychology, 45,* 315–321.

20. Malson, H. (1998). *The thin woman: Feminism, post-structuralism and the social psychology of anorexia nervosa.* New York: Routledge.

21. Downing Street Group. (2004). *The Dove Report: Challenging beauty.* Greenwich, CN: Unilever. Available at www.campaignforrealbeauty.com/uploadedFiles/challenging_beauty.pdf.

22. Fox, K. (1997). *Mirror, mirror. A summary of research findings on body image.* Oxford, UK: Social Issues Research Center. Available at www.sirc.org/publik/mirror.html.

23. Frisby, C. (2004). Does race matter? Effects of idealized images on African American women's perceptions of body esteem. *Journal of Black Studies, 34,* 323–347.

24. Schooler, D., Ward, L., Merriwether, A., & Caruthers, A. (2004). Who's that girl: Television's role in the body image development of young white and black women. *Psychology of Women Quarterly, 28,* 38–47.

25. Rucker, C., & Cash, T. (1992). Body images, body-size perceptions, and eating behaviors among African-American and white college women. *International Journal of Eating Disorders, 12,* 291–299.

26. Schorb, J., & Hammidi, T. (2000). Sho-lo showdown: The do's and don'ts of lesbian chic. *Tulsa Studies in Women's Literature, 19,* 255–268.

27. Kelly, L. (2007). Lesbian body image perceptions: The context of body science. *Qualitative Health Research, 17,* 873–883.

28. Heck, J. E., Sell, R. L., & Gorin, S. S. (2006). Health care access among individuals in same-sex relationships. *American Journal of Public Health, 96,* 1111–1118.

29. Zhi, J., Melia, A. T., Guerciolini, R., Chung, J., Kinberg, J., Hauptman, J. B., et al. (1994). Retrospective population-based analysis of the dose-response (fecal fat excretion) relationship of orlistat in normal and obese volunteers. *Clinical Pharmacology & Therapeutics, 56,* 82–85.

30. U.S. Food and Drug Administration. (1997, November 24). *FDA approves sibutramine to treat obesity* [Press release].

31. Padwal, R., Li, S., & Lau, D. (2003). Long-term pharmacotherapy for overweight and obesity: A systematic review and meta-analysis of randomized controlled trials. *International Journal of Obesity, 27,* 1437–1446.

32. Erdman, J., Lippl, F., Klose, G., & Schusdziarra, V. (2004). Cholesterol lowering effect of dietary weight loss and orlistat treatment—efficacy and limitations. *Alimentary Pharmacology & Therapeutics, 19,* 1173–1179.

33. Mittendorfer, B., Ostlund, R., Patterson, B., & Klein, S. (2001). Orlistat inhibits dietary cholesterol absorption. *Obesity Research, 9,* 599–604.

34. Dworkin, N. (1999, January). 8 great weight-loss herbs. *Vegetarian Times.* Available at findarticles.com/p/articles/mi_m0820/is_1999_Jan/ai_53459050.

35. Gandy, W. (1989). Severe epinephrine-propranolol interaction. *Annals of Emergency Medicine, 18,* 98–99.

36. Gross, W. C, & Daynard, M. (1997, October). *Commercial weight loss products and programs. What consumers stand to gain and lose.* Proceedings of a public conference on the information consumers need to evaluate weight-loss products and programs. Federal Trade Commission, American Society for Clinical Nutrition, National Institute of Diabetes and Digestive and Kidney Diseases, and Centers for Disease Control and Prevention, Washington, DC. Available at www.ftc.gov/os/1998/03/weightlo.rpt.htm#C.%20 Information%20Revealing.

37. Nordmann, A. J., Nordmann, A., Briel, M., Keller, U., Yancy, W. S., Jr., Brehm, B. J., et al. (2006). Effects of low-carbohydrate vs. low-fat diets on weight loss and cardiovascular risk factors: A meta-analysis of randomized controlled trials. *Archives of Internal Medicine, 166,* 285–293.

38. Gardner, C. D., Kiazand, A., Alhassan, S., Kim, S., Stafford, R. S., Balise, R. R., et al. (2007) Comparison of the Atkins, Zone, Ornish, and LEARN diets for change in weight and related risk factors among overweight premenopausal women: The A TO Z Weight Loss Study: A randomized trial. *Journal of the American Medical Association, 297,* 969–977.

39. Brolin, R. E. (2002). Bariatric surgery and long-term control of morbid obesity. *Journal of the American Medical Association, 228,* 2793–2796.

40. Womble, L. G., Wadden, T. A., McGuckin, B. G., Sargent, S. L., Rothman, R. A., & Krauthamer-Ewing, E. S. (2004). A randomized controlled trial of a commercial Internet weight loss program. *Obesity Research, 4,* 1011–1018.

41. Angrisani L., Lorenzo M., & Borrelli, V. (2007) Laparoscopic adjustable gastric banding versus Roux-en-Y gastric bypass: 5-year results of a prospective randomized trial. *Surgery for Obesity and Related Diseases, 3,* 127–132.

42. Jan, J. C., Hong D., Bardaro, S. J., July, L. V., & Patterson, E. J. (2007). Comparative study between laparoscopic adjustable gastric banding and laparoscopic gastric bypass: Single-institution, 5-year experience in bariatric surgery. *Surgery for Obesity and Related Diseases, 3,* 42–50.

43. Mognol, P., Chosidow, D., & Marmuse, J. P. (2005). Laparoscopic gastric bypass versus laparoscopic adjustable gastric banding in the super-obese: A comparative study of 290 patients. *Obesity Surgery, 15,* 76–81.

44. Anderson, J. W., Brinkman-Kaplan, V. L., Lee, H., & Wood, C. L. (1994). Relationship of weight loss to cardiovascular risk factors in morbidly obese individuals. *Journal of the American College of Nutrition, 13,* 256–261.

45. Rock, C. L., Pakiz, B., Flatt, S. W., & Quintana, E. L. (2007). Randomized trial of a multifaceted commercial weight loss program. *Obesity, 7,* 939–949.

46. Walsh, M. F., & Flynn, T. J. (1995). A 54-month evaluation of a popular very low calorie diet program. *Journal of Family Practice, 41,* 231–236.

47. Peluso, L., & Vanek, V. W. (2007). Efficacy of gastric bypass in the treatment of obesity-related comorbidities. *Nutrition in Clinical Practice, 22,* 22–28.

48. Li, Z., Hong, K., Saltsman, P., DeShields, S., Bellman, M., Thames, G., et al. (2005). Long-term efficacy of soy-based meal replacements vs. an individualized diet plan in obese type II DM patients: Relative effects on weight loss, metabolic parameters, and C-reactive protein. *European Journal of Clinical Nutrition, 59,* 411–418.

49. Aude, Y. W., Agatston, A. S., Lopez-Jimenez, F., Lieberman, E. H., Almon, M., Hansen, M., et al. (2004). The National Cholesterol Education Program diet vs. a diet lower in carbohydrates and higher in protein and monounsaturated fat: A randomized trial. *Archives of Internal Medicine, 164,* 2141–2146.

50. Heshka, S., Anderson, J. W., Atkinson, R. L., Greenway, F. L., Hill, J. O., Phinney, S. D., et al. (2003). Weight loss with self-help compared with a structured commercial program: A randomized trial. *Journal of the American Medical Association, 289,* 1792–1798.

51. Djuric, Z., DiLaura, N. M., Jenkins, I., Darga, L., Jen, C. K., Mood, D., et al. (2002). Combining weight-loss counseling with the Weight Watchers plan for obese breast cancer survivors. *Obesity Research, 10,* 657–665.

52. Rippe, J. M., Price, J. M., Hess, S. A., Kline, G., DeMers, K. A., Damitz, S., et al. (1998). Improved psychological well-being, quality of life, and health practices in moderately overweight women participating in a 12-week structured weight loss program. *Obesity Research, 6,* 208–218.

53. National Institute of Diabetes and Digestive and Kidney Diseases. (2004). *Gastrointestinal surgery for severe obesity* (Publication No. 04-4006). Bethesda, MD: Author.

54. Heck, J., Sell, R., & Gorin, S. S. (2006). Health care access among individuals involved in same-sex relationships. *American Journal of Public Health, 96,* 1111–1118.

55. Chenier, E. (2004). *Lesbian feminism.* glbtq. Available at www.glbtq.com/social-sciences/lesbian_feminism.html.

56. Radicalesbians. (1970). *The woman identified woman.* Pittsburgh, PA: Know. Available at scriptorium.lib.duke.edu/wlm/womid.

57. Springer, K. (2002). Third wave Black feminism? *Signs: Journal of Women in Culture and Society, 27,* 1060–1082.

58. Rothblum, E., & Solovay, S. (Eds.). (2009). *The fat studies reader.* New York: New York University Press.

59. Robinson, J. (2005, July). Healthy weight at every size: Toward a new paradigm of weight and health. *Medscape.* Available at www.medscape.com/viewarticle/506299.

60. Office of Disease Prevention and Health Promotion. (2000). *Healthy people 2010.* Washington, DC: U.S. Department of Health & Human Services. Available at www.healthypeople.gov.

61. Theophano, T. (2004). *Butch-femme.* glbtq. Available at www.glbtq.com/social-sciences/butch_femme_ssh.html.

62. Smith, E. (1989). Butches, femmes and feminists: The politics of lesbian sexuality. *NWSA Journal, 1,* 398–421.

63. Myers, A., Taub, J., Morris, J., & Rosenbaum, E. (1999). Beauty mandates and the appearances obsession: Are lesbian and bisexual women better off? In J. Cogan & J. Erickson (Eds.), *Lesbians, Levis and lipstick: The meaning of beauty in our lives* (pp. 15–26). New York: Hayworth Press.

ABOUT THE AUTHOR

Sarah C. Fogel, PhD, RN is Associate Professor of Nursing at Vanderbilt University. Her research interests include the information needs of people living with HIV/AIDS, factors that facilitate or create barriers to disclosure of sexual identity to health care providers, health disparities, text messaging for smoking cessation in low-income women of child-bearing age, and obesity among lesbians.

"Who, Me? Exercise?"

PHYSICAL ACTIVITY AMONG LESBIANS

DANIELLE R. BRITTAIN, PhD

NANCY *is a 58-year-old lesbian whose job involves sitting in front of a computer for many hours. She considers herself a social person and loves the outdoors—the thought of getting back to the physically active lifestyle she once knew is very appealing. Over the years, Nancy has been bombarded by work, partner commitments, community functions, and several other demands that have slowly taken priority over the time she once reserved for evening walks and jogs, softball games, and canoeing down rivers. Nancy knows that physical activity confers many health benefits but says she does not know how to become active again.*

■ ■ ■

Since the post-World War II era, lesbians have been publicly associated with participation in physical activity, largely through sports.[1] While some probably did find refuge in sports, the association was essentially a result of the lesbian athlete stereotype—that is, all female athletes are lesbians.[1-3] This stereotype continues to be a means of socially controlling all women's participation in sports, regardless of sexual orientation. As Griffin wrote: "The underlying function of the lesbian label: to intimidate all women in sport, to warn us to watch our step. Women athletes are still trespassers on male turf and the lesbian label is used to mark the boundaries"[3] (p. 54).

The stereotype also bred the notion that all lesbians are athletic. Over time, its influence has caused many people, including some lesbians, to assume that all lesbians are indeed athletic and, therefore, they regularly participate in physical activity, including sports.[4,5] Can this be true? Are all or most lesbians physically active?

PHYSICAL ACTIVITY AMONG ADULT LESBIANS

Participation in regular, moderate physical activity for at least 30 minutes a day on 5 or more days per week, or regular, vigorous physical activity for at least 20 minutes a day on 3 or more days per week, is recommended to combat obesity and reduce the risk of chronic conditions, such as cardiovascular disease, diabetes, certain cancers, and osteoporosis.[6] (See Appendix A for information regarding types of moderate and vigorous physical activities.) Many studies have examined the extent of women's physical activity. Generally, these studies have found that most women are not regularly active at sufficient levels to achieve health benefits. The Centers for Disease Control and Prevention estimates that up to 53% of women are not regularly active.[7] Published research on women's participation in physical activity has rarely included an assessment of sexual orientation, so it is difficult to ascertain lesbians' participation rates.[8] Furthermore, health behavior research on topics such as smoking, alcohol and drug use, and depression among adult lesbians has largely excluded physical activity assessments.[8]

Findings from three landmark studies that addressed these research shortcomings suggest that, although lesbians tend to be more physically active than heterosexual women, most adult lesbians still are not active enough to achieve health benefits.

Valanis and colleagues studied the prevalence of moderate to strenuous physical activity among more than 93,000 postmenopausal women who were 50 to 79 years old and participated in the Women's Health Initiative (Figure 11.1). Their research included mostly White, college-educated women. They divided participants into four groups according to sexual orientation: women who had never had sex in their adult lives, heterosexuals, bisexuals, and lesbians. The researchers assessed sexual orientation by asking participants about their lifetime biological sex and recent sexual partners. Based on this assessment, they then assigned lesbians to one of two groups: lifetime lesbians (women who had ever had sex only with women) and adult lesbians (women who had had sex only with women after age 45). On a questionnaire, the participants reported how many times per week they engaged in moderate to strenuous physical activity lasting at least 20 minutes. Only 30.3% of lifetime lesbians and only 21.6% of adult lesbians engaged in four or more weekly episodes of physical activity compared with 33.1% of bisexual women, 26.9% of heterosexual women, and 19.4% of those in the no-adult-sex group.[9]

FIGURE 11.1. MODERATE TO STRENUOUS PHYSICAL ACTIVITY

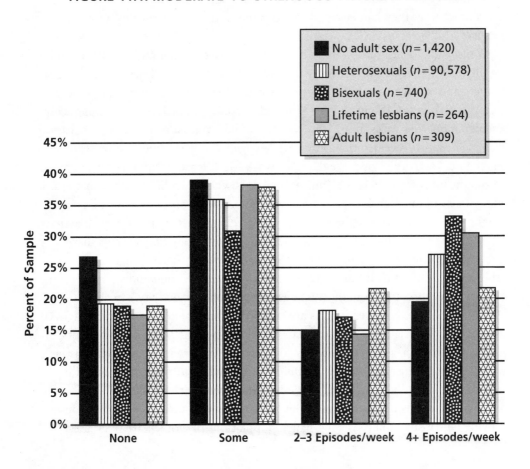

Source: Adapted from Valanis, B. G., Bowen, D. J., Bassford, T., Whitlock, E., Charney, P., & Carter, R. A. (2000). Sexual orientation and health: Comparisons in the Women's Health Initiative sample. *Archives of Family Medicine, 9,* 843–853.

In the Epidemiologic Study of Health Risk in Lesbians, Aaron and colleagues compared the physical activity levels of 1,010 mostly White, college-educated, self-identified lesbians 18 years old or older around Pittsburgh, Pennsylvania, with the general population of 88,191 women who participated in the 1998 Behavioral Risk Factor Surveillance System (BRFSS) study. The researchers assessed physical activity by asking participants to answer two questions that required a yes or no response: "Did you participate in any physical activities in the past month?" and "Did you participate in regular vigorous physical activities at least 3 days a week that caused the body to sweat or the heart to beat fast?" More than one-third of the lesbian sample (34.2%) and nearly one-third of the BRFSS sample (31.4%) had not engaged in any physical activities in the previous month, an insignificant difference. However, there was a significant difference between the lesbian group and BRFSS group in terms of whether they had engaged in recommended regular, vigorous physical activity: 63.2% versus 86.3%, respectively.[10]

Yancey and colleagues examined correlates of overweight and obesity, including physical activity, among racially diverse, self-identified adult lesbians, bisexual women, and women who self-identified as neither lesbian nor bisexual but were homosexually active (Figure 11.2). Although the more than 1,100 participants represented numerous races, most were White and had at least some college education. Their self-reports revealed that only 45.1% engaged in recommended levels of vigorous physical activity (3 or more days per week for at least 20 minutes). There were no significant racial differences, but participants who had a limiting health condition, who perceived themselves as much heavier than desired, or who qualified as overweight or obese were more likely to report infrequent participation in such activity.[11]

Despite the paucity of research examining lesbians' physical activity, these three studies illustrate that most adult lesbians are not sufficiently active to achieve health benefits. Future studies should use reliable and valid self-report and objective measures for more thorough assessment of such activity.[*] In addition, because national recommendations are clear regarding the frequency and length of moderate and/or vigorous physical activity necessary to achieve health benefits,[6] physical activity measures should provide outcome data that enable comparisons with these recommendations. This would bring the data for lesbians more in line with data collected nationally, as in the BRFSS study, which would enable more direct comparisons between lesbians and other women. Such information would provide better direction regarding which populations of women are in greatest

---

[*] For a review of self-report and objective measures of physical activity, see Welk, G. J., Corbin, C. B., & Dale, D. (2000). Measurement issues in the assessment of physical activity in children. Research Quarterly for Exercise and Sport, 71, S59–73.

need of interventions to promote health through physical activity. Finally, future research should include a diverse range of lesbians in terms of age, education level, socioeconomic status, race, and geographic location, which would yield a better understanding of the generalizabilty of data.

BARRIERS TO PHYSICAL ACTIVITY

There is also a need to identify barriers that may prevent or limit lesbians' participation in regular physical activity. Brittain and colleagues were the first to use an ecological approach to examine barriers cited by lesbians (Table 11.1). The 21 subjects in

FIGURE 11.2. RATES OF AGE-ADJUSTED, VIGOROUS PHYSICAL ACTIVITY BY RACE OF LESBIAN/BISEXUAL WOMEN

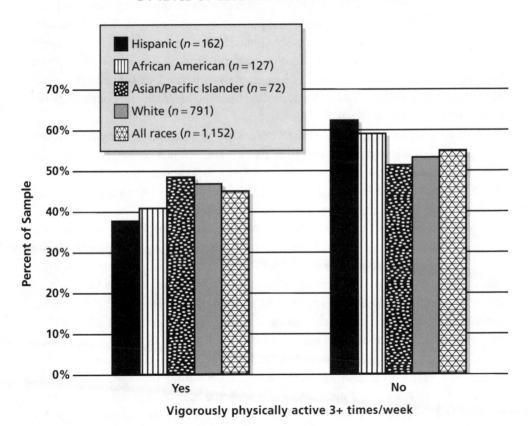

Source: Adapted from Yancey, A. K., Cochran, S. D., Corliss, H. L., & Mays, V. M. (2003). Correlates of overweight and obesity among lesbian and bisexual women. *Preventive Medicine, 36,* 676–683.

their study were self-identified lesbians 22 to 61 years old who participated in focus groups. Most were White and had at least some college education. They cited barriers unique to lesbians and general barriers unrelated to sexual orientation. Among the former were *intra*personal barriers related to the expectation that one must be "out" to join lesbian sports teams, concerns about being seen exercising with a lesbian partner, and no motivation to exercise. *Inter*personal barriers included discomfort with participating on sports teams consisting primarily of lesbians, feeling that heterosexual women would be uncomfortable sharing a locker room with a lesbian, and a lack of social support. The lack of same-sex-partner family memberships at exercise facilities, an institutional barrier, also curtailed participation in physical activity.[5]

Bowen and colleagues also used a focus group methodology to identify personal and situational barriers, both general and lesbian-specific, in a sample of 42 self-identified lesbian and bisexual women 22 to 71 years old. Among general intrapersonal barriers were a lack of time, confusion about physical activity goals, and no motivation. Inclement weather was a general community barrier, and family responsibilities were a general interpersonal barrier. Lesbian-specific barriers included the expectation that "real lesbians" do not like sports and do not like participating in them, and less desire to participate in physical activity because of the perception that the lesbian community may be more accepting than the heterosexual community of women with a larger body type.[4]

A Web-based, cross-sectional study[12] examined the relationship between the barriers that adult lesbians perceive and their participation in physical activity. Subjects in the Barriers to Engaging in Physical Activity Among Lesbians Study (BE-PALS) were 516 self-identified lesbians 21 to 75 years old. The first objective was to assess perceived barriers using a measure developed in previous research on adult lesbian women[5] to determine if the presence of general and lesbian-specific barriers and the degree to which barriers limited physical activity differed among insufficiently active and sufficiently active adult lesbians. "Insufficiently active" and "sufficiently active" were defined as less than 150 minutes of moderate activity per week, in line with national recommendations, and at least 150 minutes of moderate activity per week, respectively. Subjects indicated whether each of the listed barriers "was a barrier" (present) or "was not a barrier" (not present) to participation in physical activity in a typical week. For each present barrier, the researchers assessed the related limitation using a 0-to-9 interval scale (0 = "doesn't limit me," 9 = "fully limits me"). The second objective was to identify the most frequently reported barriers and determine if the presence and limitation if each one differed between the two physical activity groups.

The insufficiently active participants in this study reported the presence of more general barriers than the sufficiently active participants did. They also reported a higher degree of limitation for general and lesbian-specific barriers. Four general

TABLE 11.1. ECOLOGICAL BARRIERS TO PHYSICAL ACTIVITY

INTRAPERSONAL

General:
- No time
- Caregiving responsibilities
- Laziness or lack of motivation
- Physical body limitations
- Distractions at home
- Cost or lack of financial resources
- No opportunity for women (only among those ≥ 50 years old)

Lesbian-specific:
- Level of public disclosure of sexual orientation
- Acceptance by lesbian subculture of larger body type

INTERPERSONAL

General:
- No exercise partner
- No social support
- Uncomfortable exercising around other people

Lesbian-specific:
- No acceptance by others of lesbian sexual orientation
- No "out" lesbians in certain physical activities
- No desire to join sports teams consisting primarily of lesbians

INSTITUTIONAL

General:
- Work-related issues
- No role models in the family

Lesbian-specific:
- No acceptance by religious institutions of lesbian sexual orientation
- Fitness facilities do not allow family memberships for lesbians
- No acceptance by the military of lesbian sexual orientation (only among those 31–40 years old)

COMMUNITY/PUBLIC POLICY

General:
- Safety issues (e.g., violence, physical environment)
- Too many stoplights on street intersections (only among those 21–30 years old)

Lesbian-specific:
- No lesbian sports teams or physical activity opportunities in community
- No fitness facility membership coverage by the domestic partner's workplace benefits (only among those age 21–30 years, 41–55 years, and ≥ 56 years)

Source: Adapted from Brittain, D. R., Baillargeon, T., McElroy, M., Aaron, D. J., & Gyurcsik, N. C. (2006). Barriers to moderate physical activity in adult lesbians. *Women & Health, 43,* 75–92.

barriers and one lesbian-specific barrier among all 40 obstacles were the most frequently cited. As in previous research on other populations,[13] the most frequently reported barriers were those cited by at least 30% of each group. Among these, one was intrapersonal ("I can't find a time to exercise that fits with my schedule"), two were interpersonal ("When I go to a place to exercise, I'm worried about how my body looks" and "I don't feel like I am athletic enough to be part of a lesbian sport/exercise group"), one was institutional ("I don't have time to exercise because I spend so much time at work"), and one was community-related ("The temperature outside keeps me from exercising"). The insufficiently active group reported a significantly higher barrier limitation than the sufficiently active group did for three of the five barriers: "The temperature outside keeps me from exercising," "When I go to a place to exercise, I'm worried about how my body looks," and "I don't have time to exercise because I spend so much time at work."

The BE-PALS methodology addressed two key limitations of prior research on barriers in other populations.[14] First, it did not borrow measures from previous studies of other populations, as investigators often do and which runs the risk of forcing subjects to respond to irrelevant barriers. Rather, the BE-PALS investigators developed a measure based on previous focus group research targeted to lesbians.[8] Second, unlike most previous barriers research, the BE-PALS measure assessed both barrier presence and limitation, which more accurately gauges the salience of barriers. (See Brawley and colleagues[14] for a detailed review.) This is important because some individuals may experience a greater number and frequency of barriers throughout the course of a day or week that impede participation in physical activity. Furthermore, although a barrier such as lack of time may always be present in a person's life, the extent to which it limits participation in physical activity may vary as a function of if and when she can cope with the barrier.[14] For example, on some days she may be able to cope with a lack of time by rearranging her work schedule to fit physical activity into the lunch hour. On other days, a lunch meeting might preclude this adjustment and, therefore, she would have to forego physical activity. Assessing both barrier presence and limitation captures the variable influence that a barrier may have on activity over the period of assessment.[14]

Identifying salient, perceived barriers is imperative when designing population-specific and appropriate interventions. In studies, adult lesbians, like other populations of women, have reported many general personal and situational barriers unrelated to sexual orientation, such as being too tired to engage in physical activity and not having a partner for this purpose. Research has identified a number of personal and situational barriers unique to lesbians, such as a lack of lesbian-focused, physically active groups and of same-sex partner memberships at fitness facilities. In addition, for adult lesbians who are insufficiently active, both general and lesbian-specific personal and situational barriers are more limiting than they are for those who engage in moderate physical activity.

While recent research provides a sound basis for understanding perceived barriers as a potentially important correlate of adult lesbians' regular participation in physical activity, future research must improve on and expand current knowledge. Structural barriers, such as a lack of green space for sports and other physical activities, also warrant investigation. An intervention in this case might be to require green space in new housing subdivisions. According to Bandura, structural barriers prevent people from even beginning to participate in physical activity.[15] Delineating which barriers are perceived and which are actual is important because interventions for either type would be different.

For frequent, highly limiting perceived barriers to physical activity, interventions that help individuals self-regulate and cope with or overcome them will likely prove effective. According to social cognitive theory,[16] participation in motivated behaviors requires successful self-regulation—that is, altering one's responses and behaviors to achieve a desired outcome, such as regular physical activity.[17] Self-regulation includes goal-setting (in this case, physical activity goals), self-monitoring (tracking physical activity, assessing whether goals have been met, and readjusting them if necessary), and preventing relapse (coping with salient perceived barriers).[18] These types of self-regulatory behaviors tend to persist only when people have confidence in their skills and in their ability to perform them, which is called self-regulatory efficacy.[16,19,20]

Individuals who can self-regulate expend considerable effort coping with or overcoming barriers to physical activity.[15] They diagnose the task at hand and adopt appropriate strategies and courses of action. Individuals less adept at self-regulation might easily be deterred when barriers arise and therefore not engage in physical activity. Future research should focus on improving lesbians' self-regulatory efficacy in not only overcoming perceived barriers, but also in performing other self-regulatory behaviors that play an important role in regular physical activity.

Group-mediated cognitive behavioral (GMCB) interventions may be one way to improve such efficacy. They typically combine principles from group dynamics and social cognitive theory[16] in a multiweek, center-based program. An interventionist leads the group initially, then there is a weaning-off and/or no-contact period during which participants are expected to have learned the self-regulatory behaviors they need to maintain regular physical activity.[21-23] During the interventionist-led sessions, participants learn, practice, and become confident in their self-regulatory skills, and also learn and practice physical activity. During the weaning-off period, the interventionist and participants typically stay in touch with each other through meetings and/or phone calls. They discuss and try to resolve any issues the participants are encountering. GMCB interventions have increased self-regulation efficacy and activity during the center-based aspect of the intervention as well as maintenance of activity during the no-contact phase. This is particularly impressive given that people often reduce their physical activity when interventions cease. GMCB interventions have been conducted with older adults in general; older adults at risk for, or with a history of, cardiovascular disease; and postnatal mothers,[21-23] and thus provide promising direction for additional research on lesbians.

Future research should also broaden the focus of theory-based correlates of physical activity—from perceived barriers to other correlates that studies have identified consistently across other populations.[24] Although some distinct correlates of activity may exist in the lesbian population, findings from studies in other populations should be a starting point. Such investigation would do well to examine two types of correlates: personal (related to individuals) and situational (related to social environments). Recent research on physical activity illustrates an understanding that the responsibility for being physically active rests with society as well as the individual. Social environmental factors that could impact physical activity include the extent to which a person receives support from a partner for such activity, unsafe neighborhoods, the distance to free physical activity resources, and discrimination, like the lack of same-sex partner memberships at fitness facilities. Simply blaming the individual and placing all responsibility on her to be active is not a solution. Only by recognizing, understanding, and taking action on both the individual and social environmental factors can there be hope for a positive, long-lasting impact on participation in physical activity and on health.

Clinicians can significantly influence patients in this regard by simply asking them on each visit about the frequency, intensity, and duration of their physical activity. (See the clinician's guide to physical activity in Appendix B.) A controlled trial demonstrated the effectiveness of clinician counseling. The intervention group consisted of sedentary patients who received 3 to 5 minutes of structured counseling from a physician or nurse practitioner and a 10-minute booster phone call that gave them an opportunity to ask questions and discuss their progress. Participants in the intervention group ($n=98$) reported a greater increase in the number of minutes they walked each week (37 minutes) than did those in the nonintervention control group ($n=114$) (7 minutes). The former also demonstrated a greater increase than control subjects in readiness to adopt physical activity. Eighty-four percent of patients in the study were women.[25]

Ortega-Sanchez and colleagues reported similar results among adolescents: the proportion of active adolescents, and the duration, frequency, and intensity of leisure-time physical activity and/or sports, were significantly greater among those who had received physician advice.[26]

■ ■ ■

In the scenario at the beginning of this chapter, Nancy needs guidance on how to return to a regular regimen of physical activity. Her clinician could:

- Discuss with Nancy the physical, psychological, and social benefits of routine moderate or vigorous activity. This highlights the importance the clinician places on physical activity as a way to achieve a healthy lifestyle;

- Ask Nancy to monitor her current level of physical activity;

- Based on the self-monitoring results, have Nancy set short- and long-term goals that are realistic and achievable. She should adjust the short-term goals as her activity level increases, and progress to a recommended program of regular activity;

- Discuss with Nancy the barriers that prevent regular activity, and strategies for overcoming them;

- Request that she bring documentation of her self-monitoring and goal-setting to subsequent appointments, which may prompt her to continue performing self-regulatory behaviors;

- Continuously encourage and support Nancy's progress toward an active lifestyle by calling her or sending her e-mail or a postcard; and

- Encourage Nancy to join a group-mediated cognitive behavioral program if one is available in her area.

CONCLUSION

Stereotypes have contributed to the notion that all lesbians are athletes and therefore physically active. But the truth is that most adult lesbians do not meet national, physical-activity recommendations for achieving the related health benefits. For this reason, clinicians need to assess lesbian patients' current level of physical activity, encourage them to set activity goals that will foster overall health, and refer them to a group-mediated cognitive behavioral program, if one is available. Future research should include a diverse range of lesbians and employ a mix of rigorous methodologies that include valid and reliable measures of physical activity. It should also examine other theory-based, physical-activity correlates, building on previous studies of barriers. With more knowledge in hand, researchers could design and implement interventions that, through social and cognitive behavioral change, may effectively promote more physical activity among lesbians.

APPENDIX A. PHYSICAL ACTIVITIES DEFINED BY INTENSITY LEVEL*

MODERATE ACTIVITY	VIGOROUS ACTIVITY
■ Walking at a moderate or brisk pace of 3–4 mph on a level surface inside or outside Examples: Walking to class, work, or the store; walking for pleasure or as a break from work; walking the dog.	■ Race walking and aerobic walking (≥ 5 mph)
	■ Jogging or running
	■ Wheeling a wheelchair
■ Walking down stairs or down a hill	■ Walking briskly up a hill
■ Race walking (< 5 mph)	■ Backpacking
■ Using crutches	■ Mountain climbing, rock climbing, and repelling
■ Hiking	
■ Roller skating or in-line skating at a leisurely pace	■ Roller skating or in-line skating at a brisk pace
■ Bicycling 5–9 mph on level terrain or a terrain with few hills	■ Bicycling > 10 mph or on steep uphill terrain
■ Stationary bicycling (moderate effort)	■ Stationary bicycling (vigorous effort)
■ Aerobic dancing (low impact)	■ Aerobic dancing (high impact)
■ Water aerobics	■ Step aerobics
	■ Water jogging
	■ Teaching an aerobic dance class
■ Calisthenics (light)	■ Calisthenics (vigorous effort), such as push-ups or pull-ups
■ Yoga	■ Karate, judo, tae kwon do, jujitsu
■ Gymnastics	■ Jumping rope
■ General home exercises (light or moderate effort), such as getting down on and rising up from the floor	■ Jumping jacks
	■ Using a stair-climbing machine (fast pace)
■ Jumping on a trampoline	■ Using a rowing machine (vigorous effort)
■ Using a stair-climbing machine (light to moderate pace)	■ Using an arm-cycling machine (vigorous effort)
■ Using a rowing machine (moderate effort)	

(cont.)

APPENDIX A. PHYSICAL ACTIVITIES DEFINED
BY INTENSITY LEVEL* *(cont.)*

MODERATE ACTIVITY	VIGOROUS ACTIVITY
■ Weight training and body building with free weights	■ Circuit weight training
■ Boxing a punching bag ■ Ballroom, line, square, folk, or modern dancing/disco ■ Ballet	■ Professional-ballroom, square, or folk dancing (energetically) ■ Clogging
■ Table tennis (competitive) ■ Tennis (doubles)	■ Tennis (singles) ■ Wheelchair tennis
■ Golf (wheeling or carrying clubs)	
■ Softball (fast or slow pitch) ■ Shooting baskets ■ Coaching youth or adult sports	■ Most competitive sports ■ Football or basketball ■ Wheelchair basketball ■ Soccer ■ Rugby ■ Kickball ■ Field or rollerblade hockey ■ Lacrosse

Source: Adapted from Brittain, D. R., Baillargeon, T., McElroy, M., Aaron, D. J., & Gyurcsik, N. C. (2006). Barriers to moderate physical activity in adult lesbians. *Women & Health, 43,* 75–92.

APPENDIX B. PHYSICAL ACTIVITY GUIDE FOR CLINICIANS

Review the patient's history.
Examine the patient for health conditions that may impact physical activity.

Ask the patient: Are you currently participating in one of the following?

1. Moderate physical activity on 5 or more days each week for 30 minutes?
2. Vigorous physical activity on 3 or more days each week for 20 minutes?
3. A combination of moderate (at least 30 minutes) and vigorous (at least 20 minutes) physical activity?

A patient who is moderately active should be able to carry on a conversation comfortably while performing a moderately intense activity. If the patient becomes winded or too out of breath to carry on a conversation, that activity can be considered vigorous.

YES

Congratulate the patient for maintaining a healthy program of physical activity.

Remind the patient of self-regulatory behaviors that help maintain regular participation in recommended levels of physical activity.

NO

To get an estimate of current participation in physical activity, ask the patient:

1. In a usual week, how many days per week do you participate in moderate activities for at least 10 minutes at a time? _____

   On days when you do moderate activities for at least 10 minutes at a time, how much total time per day do you spend on these activities? _____

2. In a usual week, how many days per week do you participate in vigorous activities for at least 10 minutes at a time? _____

   On days when you do vigorous activities for at least 10 minutes at a time, how much total time per day do you spend on these activities? _____

Ask the patient: Do you want to be more physically active?

YES

Ask the patient: In the past, what types of activities did you participate in?

What types of activities would you like to participate in?

(See Appendix A for a list of moderate and vigorous physical activities.)

Encourage patients to perform self-regulatory behaviors:

1. Patients should monitor and document their participation in physical activity. On a calendar, they can record the frequency, intensity, time, and type of activities. Emphasize the importance of honesty in record-keeping.

2. Encourage patients to write down short- and long-term, realistic, and achievable goals based on the extent of their current activity. Self-monitoring helps them set goals; therefore, it should be done before goal-setting. For example, if a patient is now moderately active for one, 10-minute bout 3 days a week, have her set a slightly higher short-term goal, such as two, 10-minute bouts 3 days a week. Patients should set short-term goals weekly and adjust them to match their current level of participation in physical activity.

3. Ask patients about barriers that prevent or make it difficult for them to participate in moderate and vigorous physical activity.

4. Solicit ideas from patients about how they can cope with or overcome physical activity barriers. Have them focus on barriers that they believe

NO

Educate the patient about the physical, psychological, and social benefits of regular participation in moderate and vigorous physical activity.

During subsequent appointments, continue to stress the importance of physical activity until the patient decides to participate.

they can overcome rather than on those that seem insurmountable. For example, a patient should not focus on advocating for bike paths in her town if she believes this is unachievable, but rather on altering her time management skills or motivation.

5. Remind patients that a lapse in attempting to achieve a goal is a learning experience and that they should continue to strive to meet their goals.

6. Remind patients to bring their self-monitoring calendar and goal-setting logs to the next appointment. This will prompt them to maintain physical activity.

7. After the initial visit, call or e-mail patients, or send them a postcard, encouraging them to use self-regulatory behaviors to improve or maintain their current level of participation in physical activity.

8. Encourage patients to become involved in a group-mediated cognitive behavioral program if one is available locally.

Remember, the goal is to improve patients' health by encouraging regular participation in recommended levels of physical activity.

Sources:
(1) Brawley, L. R., Rejeski, W. J., & Lutes, L. (2000). A group-mediated cognitive behavioral intervention for increasing adherence to physical activity in older adults. *Journal of Applied Biobehavioral Research, 5,* 47–65.
(2) Centers for Disease Control and Prevention. (2007). *Behavioral risk factor surveillance system questionnaire.* Available at www.cdc.gov/brfss/questionnaires/pdf-ques/2007brfss.pdf.
(3) Centers for Disease Control and Prevention. (2008). *Measuring physical activity intensity.* Available at www.cdc.gov/nccdphp/dnpa/physical/everyone/measuring/index.htm.
(4) Meichenbaum, D., & Turk, D. C. (1987). *Facilitating treatment adherence: A practitioner's guidebook.* New York: Plenum Press.

REFERENCES

1. Cahn, S. K. (1994). *Coming on strong: Gender and sexuality in twentieth-century women's sport.* New York: Free Press.

2. Griffin, P. (1998). *Strong women, deep closets.* Champaign, IL: Human Kinetics.

3. Griffin, P. (1999). Lesbians and bisexual women in sport. *Journal of Physical Education, Recreation & Dance, 70,* 53–62.

4. Bowen, D. J., Balsam, K. F., Diergaarde, B., Russo, M., & Escamilla, G. M. (2006). Healthy eating, exercise, and weight: Impressions of sexual minority women. *Women & Health, 44,* 79–93.

5. Brittain, D. R., Baillargeon, T., McElroy, M., Aaron, D. J., & Gyurcsik, N. C. (2006). Barriers to moderate physical activity in adult lesbians. *Women & Health, 43,* 75–92.

6. Haskell, W. L., Lee, I. M., Pate, R. R., Powell, K. E., Blair, S. N., Franklin, B. A., et al. (2007). Physical activity and public health: Updated recommendation for adults from the American College of Sports Medicine and the American Heart Association. *Medicine and Science in Sports and Exercise, 39,* 1423–1434.

7. Centers for Disease Control and Prevention. (2008). *Physical activity statistics.* Available at http://www.cdc.gov/nccdphp/dnpa/physical/stats/index.htm.

8. Brittain, D. R., McElroy, M., Gyurcsik, N. C., Allen, C., & Aaron, D. J. (2004). Do lesbians face unique barriers to physical activity? An ecological examination. *Journal of Sport & Exercise Psychology, 26,* S41.

9. Valanis, B. G., Bowen, D. J., Bassford, T., Whitlock, E., Charney, P., & Carter, R. A. (2000). Sexual orientation and health: Comparisons in the Women's Health Initiative sample. *Archives of Family Medicine, 9,* 843–853.

10. Aaron, D. J., Markovic, N., Danielson, M. E., Honnold, J. A., Janosky, J. E., & Schmidt, N. J. (2001). Behavioral risk factors for disease and preventive health practices among lesbians. *American Journal of Public Health, 91,* 972–975.

11. Yancey, A. K., Cochran, S. D., Corliss, H. L., & Mays, V. M. (2003). Correlates of overweight and obesity among lesbian and bisexual women. *Preventive Medicine, 36,* 676–683.

12. Brittain, D. R., Gyurcsik, N. C., & McElroy, M. (2008). Perceived barriers to physical activity among adult lesbians. *Women in Sport and Physical Activity Journal, 17,* 68–79.

13. Spink, K. S., Shields, C. A., Chad, K., Odnokon, P., Muhajarine, N., & Humbert, L. (2006). Correlates of structured and unstructured activity among sufficiently active youth: A new approach to understanding youth and adolescents' level of physical activity. *Pediatric Exercise Science, 26,* 203–215.

14. Brawley, L. R., Martin, K. A., & Gyurcsik, N. C. (1998). Problems in assessing perceived barriers to exercise: Confusing obstacles with attributions and excuses. In J. L. Duda (Ed.), *Advances in sport and exercise psychology measurement* (pp. 337–350). Morgantown, WV: Fitness Information Technology.

15. Bandura, A. (1997). *Self-efficacy. The exercise of control.* New York: W. H. Freeman and Company.

16. Bandura, A. (1986). *Social foundations of thought and action.* New York: Prentice-Hall.

17. Baumeister, R. F., & Vohs, K. D. (2003). Self-regulation and the executive function of the self. In M. R. Leary & J. P. Tangney (Eds.), *Handbook of self and identity* (pp. 197–217). New York: Guilford Press.

18. Meichenbaum, D., & Turk, D. C. (1987). *Facilitating treatment adherence: A practitioner's guidebook.* New York: Plenum Press.

19. Maddux, J. E., & Gosselin, J. T. (2003). Self-efficacy. In M. R. Leary & J. P. Tangney (Eds.), *Handbook of self and identity* (pp. 218–238). New York: Guilford Press.

20. Woodgate, J., Brawley, L. R., & Weston, Z. (2005). Maintenance cardiac rehabilitation exercise adherence: Effects of task and self-regulatory self-efficacy. *Journal of Applied Social Psychology, 35,* 183–197.

21. Brawley, L. R., Rejeski, W. J., & Lutes, L. (2000). A group-mediated cognitive behavioral intervention for increasing adherence to physical activity in older adults. *Journal of Applied Biobehavioral Research, 5,* 47–65.

22. Cramp, A. G., & Brawley, L. R. (2006). Moms in motion: A group-mediated cognitive-behavioral physical activity intervention. *International Journal of Behavioral Nutrition and Physical Activity, 3,* 23.

23. Rejeski, W. J., Brawley, L. R., Ambrosius, W. T., Brubaker, P. H., Focht, B. C., Foy, C. G., et al. (2003). Older adults with chronic disease: Benefits of group-mediated counseling in the promotion of physically active lifestyles. *Health Psychology, 22,* 414–423.

24. Sallis, J. F., & Owen, N. (1999). *Physical activity and behavioral medicine.* Thousand Oaks, CA: Sage Publications.

25. Calfas, K. J., Long, B. J., Sallis, J. F., Wooten, W. J., Pratt, M., & Patrick, K. (1996). A controlled trial of physician counseling to promote the adoption of physical activity. *Preventive Medicine, 25,* 225–233.

26. Ortega-Sanchez, R., Jimenez-Mena, C., Cordoba-Garcia, R., Muñoz-Lopez, J., Garcia-Machado, M. L., & Vilaseca-Canals, J. (2004). The effect of office-based physician's advice on adolescent exercise behavior. *Preventive Medicine, 38,* 219–226.

ABOUT THE AUTHOR

Danielle R. Brittain, PhD is Assistant Professor in the Department of Health and Exercise Science at the University of Oklahoma, Norman. Her research interests are identifying perceived personal and situational barriers to physical activity among adult lesbians and developing theory-driven social and behavioral interventions that will help people self-manage and maintain physical activity.

CHAPTER 12

"I Have a Bad Back!"

BACK PAIN: THE BASICS

HEATHER RACHEL DAVIDS, MD

LATISHA *is a 42-year-old lesbian who presents with complaints of chronic low-back pain and acute-onset pain radiating down her left leg. She is a nurse and works in an intensive care unit. Latisha rarely has an opportunity to exercise regularly and often avoids vigorous activity out of fear that it will exacerbate the back pain. However, this new pain makes even her daily routine more difficult.*

Her medical history is fairly unremarkable, except for depression, moderate overweight, and smoking about one-half pack of cigarettes a day. Latisha says she has had low-back pain for years. There was not an inciting event or injury.

When the pain flares, her upper back and shoulders also ache. The acute-onset pain radiating down her leg came on suddenly after she helped move a patient up in bed. The physical exam is significant for trigger points in the bilateral trapezius region, and tenderness to palpation over the paraspinal muscles and spinous processes in the lower lumbar region. She denies new numbness, tingling, weakness, or any new bowel or bladder issues. Bilateral lower-extremity strength, reflexes, and sensation are normal. A straight-leg raise of the left lower extremity reproduces her pain. She also reports that coughing and sneezing exacerbate the pain. Her pain level today is a 6/10 on a visual analog scale.

On this visit, Latisha says she not only wants to address the acute pain but also to learn what she can do to reduce or eliminate the chronic back pain. Her physical exam is consistent with a lumbar herniated disc. Magnetic resonance imaging (MRI) is unnecessary because there are no neurological deficits. Her clinician concludes that conservative treatment is appropriate and prescribes a nonsteroidal anti-inflammatory to help control the pain and inflammation. Some clinicians would also prescribe muscle relaxants, narcotics, or a steroid pack (tapering dose).

Regarding Latisha's upper-back pain, the exam is consistent with myofascial pain and trigger points, so trigger point injections are a possibility. The clinician refers her for physical therapy for the holding patterns, such as poor posture, that exacerbate the myofascial pain, for core strengthening, and for education about ways that Latisha can protect her back while performing daily activities at work and home. The clinician asks her to schedule an appointment in 2 weeks to see how she is progressing and decide if other strategies are necessary to manage her pain.

■ ■ ■

EPIDEMIOLOGY

Back pain is one of the most prevalent medical conditions in industrialized countries. More than 70% of people will complain of back pain at some point in their lives.[1,2] Most cases resolve over time without intervention, but when back pain is persistent or severely acute, the impact on every aspect of a person's life can be profound. The repercussions for the U.S. economy and health care system are immense: lost work time due to chronic back pain costs an estimated $50 billion a year.[3,4] According to other estimates, acute low-back pain is the fifth most common reason that people visit their physicians[4] and a major cause of absence from work.[5]

Although acute episodes often resolve spontaneously, back pain frequently recurs. For people like Latisha in the scenario above, the pain may become chronic. There is disagreement among experts about the definition of chronic back pain: some use a cut-off of more than 3 months, others a cut-off of more than 6 months. Identifying the cause of pain or when it began may not be possible, further complicating the issue. Regardless, if pain persists for more than 3 months, the chances of spontaneous resolution or return to work decrease dramatically.[6,7] If the pain is severe enough to result in absence from work for 6 months, the odds of still being off work 1 year later are greater than 50%.[8] Back pain's impact on quality of life is tremendous: in the United States, it is the most common cause of activity limitation in people younger than 45.[5] Ongoing pain can interfere with daily functions such as walking, dressing, work, leisure, and quality of sleep.

CAUSES AND POTENTIAL RISK FACTORS

There are multiple physiological causes of back pain (Table 12.1). The following section discusses some of the many factors that may or may not put people at greater risk of developing it.

Manual Labor

Workers who regularly move heavy material, lift repetitively, are exposed to vibration, sit or stand for long periods, or bend or twist have a higher incidence of back pain.[9,10] Back pain is prevalent among nurses whose work involves many of these activities.[11,12]

Depression

The fact that chronic pain may lead to depression is well-documented. In addition, nearly all of the numerous studies that have investigated or summarized research findings on depression as a risk factor for the development of chronic pain found a positive association, the strength of which varied.[13–15]

TABLE 12.1. CAUSAL FACTORS IN BACK PAIN

TYPE OF PAIN	FACTORS
Musculoskeletal	Muscle strain, myofascial pain, fibromyalgia, mechanical back pain (including pain secondary to pregnancy)
Degenerative	Degenerative joint disease, osteoarthritis, facet joint disease, lumbar spondylosis, spinal stenosis (may cause radicular symptoms)
Traumatic	Fractures (including compression fractures secondary to osteoporosis and spondylosis), dislocations
Related to disc pathology	Degenerative disc disease, herniated disc. Disc pathology may cause local and/or radicular pain, sciatica.
Infection-related and inflammatory	Discitis, rheumatism, spondyloarthropathies, sacroiliitis, osteomyelitis
Neoplasm	Benign or malignant, spinal or intraspinal
Developmental	Scoliosis, Scheuermann's kyphosis

Source: Author

Gender

Findings on whether gender affects the risk of developing back pain are mixed. Some researchers believe that this risk is the same for women and men until they reach age 60; thereafter, the risk for women is higher due to osteoporosis.[16] A study in Finland found that men are at greater risk of developing sciatica,[17] and other studies reported on women's back pain during pregnancy.[18,19] Some research suggests that gender does not play a role in the risk of developing back pain.[9]

Ethnicity/Race

Although ethnic and racial minorities face issues regarding access to health care, treatment decision-making, and secondary effects if in a marginalized group, there is no evidence of factors that would put them at higher risk of developing back pain.

Age

Research generally suggests that the likelihood of developing low-back pain increases up until the mid- to late fifties and sixties.[8,16] However, there are many potential contributors, including osteoporosis, osteoarthritis, spinal stenosis, and disc degeneration, all of which become more severe as people age. According to some studies, the incidence of severe back pain and disability does increase with age.[8,20]

Genetics

To investigate the potential role of genetics in back pain, some studies have evaluated twins.[21-23] The general conclusion is that genetics influence some aspects of back pain. But it is difficult to predict if, based on genetic history, an individual will develop such pain.

Obesity

Most people erroneously assume that obesity is a strong risk factor for higher incidence of back pain. At most, it is a weak risk factor, primarily due to a lack of strong evidence indicating otherwise.[24,25] Physical activity seems to help alleviate back pain[26-30]; thus, such activity or the lack of it is a confounding factor in studies of the relationship between obesity and back pain.

Smoking

Although many studies assert that smoking is a risk factor for back pain,[31-33] a review of 47 studies revealed only a weak correlation.[34] Results from a study of twins suggested that while there does seem to be a link between smoking and back pain, smoking probably is not causal.[35] Research in 2008 found no direct link between smoking and back pain, but it did show that smoking combined with hard physical work—repetitive micro- or macrotrauma—caused a vertebral inflammatory process associated with back pain.[36] A review of smoking and the effects on the spinal column concluded that smokers are more likely to suffer from bony degradation and spinal column degenerative disease.[37] Although the relationship between smoking and back pain might not be direct, smokers may very likely experience secondary consequences or effects that put them at greater risk of such pain.

Alcohol

Few studies have looked at whether or not alcohol increases back pain risk. According to a review article, no studies reported a positive link between alcohol and low-back pain.[38]

Education/Social Class

In a review of research on education and social class relative to back pain, Waddell concluded that education level seems to be associated with the severity and duration of disability secondary to back pain, more education is associated with better rehabilitation outcomes, and lower social class may be a weak risk factor for developing such pain.[8]

Exercise

Obese people may be less inclined to participate in regular physical activity, which, as mentioned earlier, can help alleviate back pain. A study by Yancey and colleagues confirmed the relationship between higher body mass index and lower fitness level and exercise frequency.[39] Better fitness may enable faster recovery from acute episodes of back pain and prevent chronic back pain from developing.[8]

■ ■ ■

There is no evidence that sexual orientation has any effect on the risk of developing back pain. But when clinicians treat patients like Latisha, they must address other issues prevalent in the lesbian community that could have an impact. These include depression, obesity, smoking, and the higher stress that can result from being in a marginalized population.

BACK PAIN EVALUATION

Clinicians should take a thorough history and examine the patient to determine the nature of the back pain—whether, for example, it is musculoskeletal or stems from nerve root pain or serious pathology. They can begin by inspecting the patient for anatomical deformity, hypertrophy, muscle wasting, or asymmetry, and by palpating soft tissues, vertebral bodies, piriformis muscles, and sacroiliac joints. The exam should include lumbar flexion and extension, rotation and extension (if facet loading is painful, the facet [zygapophyseal] may be generating back pain), and evaluation of strength, sensation, and reflexes. Strength can be assessed by having the patient do 10, single-foot toe raises, testing great toe dorsiflexion or having her walk on her heels, and testing the quadriceps by having her squat and rise. Provocative maneuvers may include a straight-leg raise (seated or supine) to look for dural tension signs. The clinician should also evaluate and rule out referred pain from lower-extremity joints.

Imaging options include x-ray, MRI, or computed tomography (CT). Imaging is unnecessary if there are no neurological deficits or if the clinical exam prompts a diagnosis. Suspected spondylolisthesis (forward slippage of vertebra over the vertebra below), anatomical deformities such as scoliosis, or an associated trauma that has initiated the pain, especially in patients at risk for osteoporosis, warrants x-ray. Generally, x-ray and CT scans are of limited utility and not deemed appropriate for back pain.[40] MRI is much more appropriate because it shows vertebral bodies, discs, and surrounding soft tissue. However, MRI findings do not always correspond with patient presentation; for example, there may be a bulging disc without correlative pain complaints.

TREATMENT

Treatment should include educating the patient about risk factors. In Latisha's case, the clinician can counsel her to stop smoking, become more physically active, and seek immediate treatment for depression. Treating chronic pain requires treating depression if it is present. Even though patients may have difficulty increasing their physical activity out of fear it will exacerbate the pain, all options, including walking and water therapy, should be exhausted.

Studies suggest that it is more difficult for lesbians than heterosexual women to access health care,[41,42] perhaps because they have experienced discrimination, are afraid of discrimination, or lack adequate health insurance. Yet access to care is essential for treating recurrent and acute episodes of pain, managing debilitating and chronic back pain, and preventing pain.

Before clinicians consider treatment options, they must perform a thorough physical exam and rule out neurologic compromise, myelopathy, cauda equina syndrome, and neoplasm. The type of treatment will depend on the etiology of the back pain. For instance, effective therapy for myofascial pain may be medication, massage, and trigger point injections. Back pain secondary to facet joint pain, on the other hand, may require medial branch blocks, and back pain originating from postthoracotomy pain that is resistant to all forms of conservative management may ultimately require implantation of a nerve stimulator. In any case, initial therapy should be conservative.

A multidisciplinary treatment approach often is most effective. For example, after medication or trigger point injections have brought pain of myofascial origin under control, the patient should be referred to physical therapy to address holding patterns that exacerbate development of the pain. One holding pattern is poor posture—rounded shoulders and neck bent forward. A patient who presents with a bulging disc and radicular symptoms also can benefit from physical therapy after her pain is under control. A physical therapist will teach her how to protect her back and thereby help prevent the pain from recurring.

Multiple concurrent treatments may be effective. For instance, prescribing an oral pain medication, transcutaneous electrical nerve stimulation, and a lidoderm patch to a patient who has postlaminectomy syndrome would not be unreasonable.

Although pinpointing the etiology of chronic pain is virtually impossible, clinicians should nevertheless treat the pain. They should also set realistic pain-relief expectations for patients. If, for example, a patient consistently rates the intensity of her pain as 8 on a 10-point visual analog scale, reducing the pain by 50%, to 4 on the scale, is a more realistic goal than eliminating it.

One way to assess the effectiveness of a treatment is to measure the patient's function and her ability to participate in daily activities. For example, if her pain intensity continues to rate 6 on a 10-point visual analog scale but she can return to work and, unlike previously, play with her children, do housework, and engage in leisure activities, the treatment may have succeeded.

If conservative therapy fails, referral to a pain medicine specialist is appropriate. Many primary care physicians refer patients with back pain to orthopedic surgeons or neurosurgeons, but these specialists typically evaluate such patients only to determine if they are surgical candidates. A pain medicine specialist, in contrast, may be a physiatrist, neurologist, psychiatrist, or anesthesiologist who has completed a pain medicine fellowship. Preferably, the specialist will be adept at both medication management and procedural intervention.

Medications

▇ NONSTEROIDAL ANTI-INFLAMMATORY DRUGS

Nonsteroidal anti-inflammatory drugs (NSAIDs) are reasonable, first-line agents for treating back pain. Although this may seem obvious, many patients report that low-dose NSAIDs taken as needed do not work. Before assuming that this approach has failed, the clinician, having ruled out gastrointestinal or renal issues, should try a high-dose, scheduled medication for at least 2 weeks. Moreover, individual patients may respond differently to various NSAIDS, so it is worth trying at least two agents serially. A fairly new product available in the United States delivers diclofenac via a topical patch.

▇ TRAMADOL

Tramadol is both a weak mu opioid receptor activator and a norepinephrine and serotonin reuptake inhibitor. Although the drug is not officially an opioid, some practitioners consider it to be a narcotic. Prescribing tramadol before opioids on a trial basis is not unreasonable.

▇ CALCITONIN

Calcitonin, a thyroid hormone involved in calcium regulation, relieves pain. It may work both peripherally and centrally, but the mechanism of action is unknown. Clinicians often use calcitonin, which typically is administered nasally or via injection, when they treat acute, osteoporosis-related vertebral compression fractures.[43,44]

Evidence suggests it may also be beneficial in treating chronic back pain secondary to other etiologies.[45,46]

■ MUSCLE RELAXANTS

Muscle relaxants include benzodiazepines, carisoprodol, and baclofen, which are typically indicated for short-term use only. Evidence is mixed regarding their effectiveness in alleviating chronic back pain. Sedation is a prevalent side effect because meprobamate, a tranquilizer, is an active metabolite in carisoprodol. Consequently, carisoprodol has fallen out of favor with many pain medicine specialists. Clinicians should be cautious about prescribing baclofen for diabetic patients, as the drug may make it challenging for these patients to manage their blood sugar.

■ ANTICONVULSANTS

Gabapentin and pregabalin are anticonvulsants often used to treat chronic back pain, especially if there are accompanying radicular symptoms.

■ ANTIDEPRESSANTS

Antidepressants are particularly useful because many of them also treat chronic pain, which causes depression. The four classes of antidepressants are selective serotonin reuptake inhibitors, tricyclics, serotonin and norepinephrine reuptake inhibitors, and combined reuptake inhibitors and receptor blockers, such as trazodone and mirtazapine.

■ OPIOIDS

When chronic pain does not respond to other medications, opioids may be appropriate, although many clinicians are hesitant to prescribe them. Opioids can be very effective, but regular use causes significant side effects, especially constipation. Clinicians prefer short-acting opioids for treating breakthrough pain, and long-acting opioids for steadily controlling pain, ultimately reducing it, and improving function. The fentanyl patch is an option for patients with persistent, moderate-to-severe chronic pain who have proved to be opioid-tolerant.

■ LIDOCAINE AND CAPSAICIN

Lidocaine is available as a patch applied to the focal area of pain for 12 hours, then removed for 12 hours, and as a cream. Another cream contains capsaicin—the active ingredient in chili peppers—that may deplete substance P, a neuropeptide involved in transmitting pain. Patients must apply the capsaicin cream regularly over several weeks to achieve pain relief.

■ INJECTIONS

Interventional pain specialists use a variety of different injections, usually under fluoroscopic guidance, to treat back pain. Trigger point injections of a local anesthetic alone or in combination with a steroid, and chemodenervation using botulinum toxin, can effectively treat pain of myofascial origin. Typically, patients should receive physical therapy after injection because they must correct the holding patterns that contributed to the pain; otherwise, it inevitably returns. Repetitive injections may be necessary to manage the pain if it is secondary to other factors, such as scoliosis or other anatomical conditions. Treatment with botulinum toxin may become less effective over time if antibodies form. Another approach is neurolytic injections of alcohol or phenol, which can destroy the pain-causing nerve.

■ EPIDURAL STEROIDS

The goal of interlaminar and transforaminal injections of epidural steroids is to target the inflamed, pain-causing nerve. This approach is especially useful in treating radicular pain.

■ FACET INJECTIONS/MEDIAL BRANCH BLOCKS

Spondylosis (spinal degeneration and deformity) may cause the facet joints to generate pain and refer the pain in typical patterns. Injecting a local anesthetic and/or steroids into the joint or around the medial nerves innervating it can block the associated pattern. If successful, the next step may be radiofrequency ablation, in which heat transmitted through a needle destroys the problematic nerve.

■ SYMPATHETIC NERVE BLOCKS

Chronic pain can alter regulation of the autonomic nervous system. Injecting a local anesthetic around sympathetic nerve bundles can "reset" these nerves and thereby reduce or shut off the pain.

■ SACROILIAC JOINT INJECTIONS

The sacroiliac joint, located in the buttock region, often refers pain to the lower back. Injecting a local anesthetic and steroid into the joint can alleviate this pain. If successful, some practitioners also perform radiofrequency ablation in the joint.

Stimulation by Implants

■ SPINAL CORD STIMULATION

An interventional pain specialist or surgeon can place one or more electrodes in the epidural space, or outermost part of the spinal canal, and attach them to an implantable pulse generator. Electric pulses delivered to the spinal cord generate a paresthesia that alters the patient's sensation of pain. The mechanism of action may be activation of nerves that, although not involved in transmitting pain, can interfere with signals from pain fibers and thus alter the perception of pain.

PERIPHERAL NERVE STIMULATION

This technique is similar to spinal cord stimulation, except electrode placement is subcutaneous, in the area of pain, and the stimulation target is peripheral nerves.

INTRATHECAL PUMP

Intrathecal pump implants deliver concentrated pain medication through a catheter into the spinal cord area. Some physicians reserve this treatment only for patients with the most severe pain, including cancer pain.

Surgery

Surgery is the treatment of last resort; few patients with back pain need it. Typically, back surgery only seeks to correct a pinched nerve, spinal cord compromise, or bony instability. Pain relief is not the only goal of back surgery and should not be the expected outcome.

Other Modalities

An earlier section explained the importance of physical therapy in precluding further back pain. Other noninvasive treatments are hot or cold packs, water therapy, transcutaneous electrical nerve stimulation, and occupational therapy if poor ergonomics may be exacerbating the pain. An occupational therapist can assess the patient's workplace and recommend appropriate equipment or environmental changes.

Lesbians increasingly are turning to complementary and alternative medicine.[47,48] Options include acupuncture, acupressure, massage, chiropractic, osteopathic manipulation, and herbal remedies.

ACUPUNCTURE

Relieving pain with acupuncture remains controversial because the mechanism of action is unknown. However, some evidence, including a review of clinical trials by the World Health Organization,[49] supports acupuncture's effectiveness in treating back pain. After evaluating 33 randomized controlled trials, Manheimer and colleagues concluded that acupuncture can effectively relieve chronic low-back pain, but they could not conclude that it was more effective than any other therapy.[50] Most likely, effectiveness depends on back-pain etiology.

■ ACUPRESSURE

Acupressure and acupuncture stem from the same general philosophy, but acupressure relies on fingers instead of needles to stimulate pressure points. It may be a stand-alone treatment or incorporated into massage.

■ MASSAGE

Massage is particularly effective in treating pain of myofascial origin, although patients experiencing other types of pain often achieve relief as well. The benefits of massage are usually transient, necessitating follow-up treatments.

■ CHIROPRACTIC

Chiropractic, or manipulation of the spine and other body structures, is a reasonable option for treating back pain. As with massage, the transient effects of chiropractic necessitate multiple treatments. Patients who have osteoporosis or signs of nerve compromise, such as weakness or changes in sensation, are not appropriate candidates for chiropractic, and those with a history of back surgery should obtain a doctor's permission before they undergo any manipulation.

■ OSTEOPATHIC MANIPULATION

Osteopaths have completed 4 years of medical school and usually at least 3 years of residency training. They believe that structural problems in the spine affect physiological function and therefore cause disease, unlike chiropractors, who focus on alignment of joints. Regarding low-back pain, the guidelines for chiropractic also apply to osteopathic manipulation.

■ HERBAL REMEDIES

There are many claims that herbal remedies can relieve pain. Some remedies may be similar to better-known traditional treatments. For example, white willow bark contains the anti-inflammatory agent salicin, which is derived from salicylic acid, an ingredient in aspirin. Some people think of capsaicin cream as an herbal remedy. Because herbs may interact with drugs, the clinician should include all products on the patient's medication list.

■ COGNITIVE THERAPY AND BIOFEEDBACK

These enable patients to develop coping skills and tools to manage chronic pain more effectively. Cognitive therapy and biofeedback may be reasonable adjuncts to other types of treatment.[51]

■ BED REST

Patients experiencing an episode of acute back pain may rest in bed for a maximum of 1 to 2 days. No bed rest is probably better: studies have shown that maintaining the highest level of activity possible leads to more rapid recovery from low-back pain than does strict adherence to bed rest.[52,53] Prolonged immobilization also puts the patient at greater risk of deconditioning and blood clots.

■ EXERCISE

Exercise not only relieves chronic pain; it also helps prevent it.[29,30] Regular exercise maintains strength and flexibility, enabling the body to compensate for back pain.

PREVENTION

Preventing back pain and its recurrence is the best strategy, although this can be difficult because many risk factors are only weakly associated with the development of back pain and such pain has multiple components. Starting points for prevention include regular exercise, physical fitness, no tobacco use, and proper ergonomics and body mechanics when lifting. In a study of a secondary prevention program for nurses with low-back pain, those who modified their lifestyles showed a significant reduction in pain intensity and improvement in physical activity and mood.[54] Prevention is especially important for people whose occupations demand hard physical labor, exposure to whole-body vibration, or repetitive bending, twisting, or lifting. Clinicians can play an important role in educating patients about back pain, especially when risks are evident.

CONCLUSION

A large majority of people experience acute or chronic back pain in their lifetime. Back-pain etiology varies and is difficult to ascertain, given the myriad factors involved in its development. The good news is that most cases of back pain resolve over time. However, recurrence is common, and once the pain becomes chronic, the odds that it can be resolved fall dramatically. Most clinicians appropriately start with conservative treatment. If that fails, they can refer the patient to a pain specialist who will consider more aggressive pharmaceutical management or other interventions. Clinicians should continue to emphasize prevention.

Lesbians are probably at the same risk as the general population to develop back pain. Some risk factors for back pain, such as smoking, depression, and inadequate physical activity, are more prevalent among lesbians. Furthermore, lesbians may have less access to health care or choose not to seek it if real or perceived discrimination is an issue. Clinicians need to be aware of and address these factors.

REFERENCES

1. Damkot, D. K., Pope, M. H., Lord, J., & Frymoyer, J. W. (1984). The relationship between work history, work environment and low-back pain in men. *Spine, 9*, 395–399.

2. Frymoyer, J. W. (1988). Back pain and sciatica. *New England Journal of Medicine, 318*, 291–300.

3. Frymoyer, J. W., & Cats-Baril, W. L. (1991). An overview of the incidences and costs of low back pain. *Orthopedic Clinics of North America, 22*, 263–271.

4. Hart, L. G., Deyo, R. A., & Cherkin, D. C. (1995). Physician office visits for low back pain. Frequency, clinical evaluation, and treatment patterns from a U.S. national survey. *Spine, 20*, 11–19.

5. Andersson, G. B. (1999). Epidemiological features of chronic low-back pain. *Lancet, 354*, 581–585.

6. Frymoyer, J. W. (Ed.). (1997). *The adult spine: Principles and practice* (2nd ed., Vol. 1). Philadelphia: Lippincott-Raven.

7. Frank, J. W., Brooker, A. S., DeMaio, S. E., Kerr, M. S., Maetzel, A., Shannon, H. S., et al. (1996). Disability resulting from occupational low back pain. Part II: What do we know about secondary prevention? A review of the scientific evidence on prevention after disability begins. *Spine, 21*, 2918–2929.

8. Waddell, G. (Ed.). (2004). *The back pain revolution* (2nd ed.). Edinburgh: Churchill Livingstone.

9. Burdorf, A., & Sorock, G. (1997). Positive and negative evidence of risk factors for back disorders. *Scandinavian Journal of Work, Environment & Health, 23*, 243–256.

10. Frymoyer, J. W., Pope, M. H., Clements, J. H., Wilder, D. G., MacPherson, B., & Ashikaga, T. (1983). Risk factors in low-back pain. An epidemiological survey. *Journal of Bone and Joint Surgery (American Volume), 65*, 213–218.

11. Smedley, J., Egger, P., Cooper, C., & Coggon, D. (1995). Manual handling activities and risk of low back pain in nurses. *Occupational and Environmental Medicine, 52*, 160–163.

12. Coggan, C., Norton, R., Roberts, I., & Hope, V. (1994). Prevalence of back pain among nurses. *New Zealand Medical Journal, 107*, 306–308.

13. Croft, P. R., Papageorgiou, A. C., Ferry, S., Thomas, E., Jayson, M. I., & Silman, A. J. (1995). Psychologic distress and low back pain. Evidence from a prospective study in the general population. *Spine, 20*, 2731–2737.

14. Linton, S. J. (2000). A review of psychological risk factors in back and neck pain. *Spine, 25*, 1148–1156.

15. Carroll, L. J., Cassidy, J. D., & Cote, P. (2004). Depression as a risk factor for onset of an episode of troublesome neck and low back pain. *Pain, 107*, 134–139.

16. Braddom, R. (Ed.). (2000). *Physical medicine and rehabilitation* (2nd ed.). Philadelphia: W. B. Saunders.

17. Heliövaara, M., Impivaara, O., Sievers, K., Melkas, T., Knekt, P., Korpi, J., et al. (1987). Lumbar disc syndrome in Finland. *Journal of Epidemiology and Community Health, 41*, 251–258.

18. Ostgaard, H. C., Andersson, G. B., & Karlsson, K. (1991). Prevalence of back pain in pregnancy. *Spine, 16,* 549–552.

19. Greenwood, C. J., & Stainton, M. C. (2001). Back pain/discomfort in pregnancy: Invisible and forgotten. *Journal of Perinatal Education, 10,* 1–12.

20. Dionne, C. E., Dunn, K. M., & Croft, P. R. (2006). Does back pain prevalence really decrease with increasing age? A systematic review. *Age and Ageing, 35,* 229–234.

21. MacGregor, A. J., Andrew, T., Sambrook, P. N., & Spector, T. D. (2004). Structural, psychological, and genetic influences on low back and neck pain: A study of adult female twins. *Arthritis & Rheumatism, 51,* 160–167.

22. Leboeuf-Yde, C. (2004). Back pain—individual and genetic factors. *Journal of Electromyography and Kinesiology, 14,* 129–133.

23. Videman, T., Battié, M. C., Gibbons, L. E., Maravilla, K., Manninen, H., & Kaprio, J. (2003). Associations between back pain history and lumbar MRI findings. *Spine, 28,* 582–588.

24. Leboeuf-Yde, C. (2000). Body weight and low back pain. A systematic literature review of 56 journal articles reporting on 65 epidemiologic studies. *Spine, 25,* 226–237.

25. Leboeuf-Yde, C., Kyvik, K. O., & Bruun, N. H. (1999). Low back pain and lifestyle. Part II—Obesity. Information from a population-based sample of 29,424 twin subjects. *Spine, 24,* 779–783.

26. Frost, H., Klaber Moffett, J. A., Moser, J. S., & Fairbank, J. C. (1995). Randomised controlled trial for evaluation of fitness programme for patients with chronic low back pain. *BMJ, 310,* 151–154.

27. Moffett, J. K., Torgerson, D., Bell-Syer, S., Jackson, D., Llewlyn-Phillips, H., Farrin, A., et al. (1999). Randomised controlled trial of exercise for low back pain: Clinical outcomes, costs, and preferences. *BMJ, 319,* 279–283.

28. Taimela, S., Diederich, C., Hubsch, M., & Heinricy, M. (2000). The role of physical exercise and inactivity in pain recurrence and absenteeism from work after active outpatient rehabilitation for recurrent or chronic low back pain: A follow-up study. *Spine, 25,* 1809–1816.

29. Kuukkanen, T., Mälkiä, E., Kautiainen, H., & Pohjolainen, T. (2007). Effectiveness of a home exercise programme in low back pain: A randomized five-year follow-up study. *Physiotherapy Research International, 12,* 213–224.

30. Hayden, J. A., van Tulder, M. W., Malmivaara, A. V., & Koes, B. W. (2005). Meta-analysis: Exercise therapy for nonspecific low back pain. *Annals of Internal Medicine, 142,* 765–775.

31. Deyo, R. A., & Bass, J. E. (1989). Lifestyle and low-back pain. The influence of smoking and obesity. *Spine, 14,* 501–506.

32. Goldberg, M. S., Scott, S. C., & Mayo, N. E. (2000). A review of the association between cigarette smoking and the development of nonspecific back pain and related outcomes. *Spine, 25,* 995–1014.

33. Wright, D., Barrow, S., Fisher, A. D., Horsley, S. D., & Jayson, M. I. (1995). Influence of physical, psychological and behavioural factors on consultations for back pain. *British Journal of Rheumatology, 34,* 156–161.

34. Leboeuf-Yde, C. (1999). Smoking and low back pain. A systematic literature review of 41 journal articles reporting 47 epidemiologic studies. *Spine, 24,* 1463–1470.

35. Leboeuf-Yde, C., Kyvik, K. O., & Bruun, N. H. (1998). Low back pain and lifestyle. Part I: Smoking. Information from a population-based sample of 29,424 twins. *Spine, 23,* 2207–2213.

36. Leboeuf-Yde, C., Kjaer, P., Bendix, T., & Manniche, C. (2008). Self-reported hard physical work combined with heavy smoking or overweight may result in so-called Modic changes. *BMC Musculoskeletal Disorders, 9,* 5.

37. Hadley, M. N., & Reddy, S. V. (1997). Smoking and the human vertebral column: A review of the impact of cigarette use on vertebral bone metabolism and spinal fusion. *Neurosurgery, 41,* 116–124.

38. Leboeuf-Yde, C. (2000). Alcohol and low-back pain: A systematic literature review. *Journal of Manipulative and Physiological Therapeutics, 23,* 343–346.

39. Yancey, A. K., Cochran, S. D., Corliss, H. L., & Mays, V. M. (2003). Correlates of overweight and obesity among lesbian and bisexual women. *Preventive Medicine, 36,* 676–683.

40. Bogduck, N., & McGuirk, B. (Eds.). (2002). *Medical management of acute and chronic low back pain. An evidence-based approach* (Vol. 13). New York: Elsevier.

41. Diamant, A. L., Wold, C., Spritzer, K., & Gelberg, L. (2000). Health behaviors, health status, and access to and use of health care: A population-based study of lesbian, bisexual, and heterosexual women. *Archives of Family Medicine, 9,* 1043–1051.

42. White, J. C., & Dull, V. T. (1997). Health risk factors and health-seeking behavior in lesbians. *Journal of Women's Health, 6,* 103–112.

43. Blau, L. A., & and Hoehns, J. D. (2003). Analgesic efficacy of calcitonin for vertebral fracture pain. *Annals of Pharmacotherapy, 37,* 564–570.

44. Knopp, J. A., Diner, B. M., Blitz, M., Lyritis, G. P., & Rowe, B. H. (2005). Calcitonin for treating acute pain of osteoporotic vertebral compression fractures: A systematic review of randomized, controlled trials. *Osteoporosis International, 16,* 1281–1290.

45. Eskola, A., Pohjolainen, T., Alaranta, H., Soini, J., Tallroth, K., & Slätis, P. (1992). Calcitonin treatment in lumbar spinal stenosis: A randomized, placebo-controlled, double-blind, cross-over study with one-year follow-up. *Calcified Tissue International, 50,* 400–403.

46. Onel, D., Sari, H., & Donmez, C. (1993). Lumbar spinal stenosis: Clinical/radiologic therapeutic evaluation in 145 patients. Conservative treatment or surgical intervention? *Spine, 18,* 291–298.

47. Matthews, A. K., Hughes, T. L., Osterman, G. P., & Kodl, M. M. (2005). Complementary medicine practices in a community-based sample of lesbian and heterosexual women. *Health Care for Women International, 26,* 430–447.

48. Johnson, S. R., Guenther, S. M., Laube, D. W., & Keettel, W. C. (1981). Factors influencing lesbian gynecologic care: A preliminary study. *American Journal of Obstetrics & Gynecology, 140,* 20–28.

49. World Health Organization. (2003). *Acupuncture: Review and analysis of reports on controlled clinical trials.* Available at who.int/medicinedocs/collect/medicinedocs/pdf/s4926e/s4926e.pdf.

50. Manheimer, E., White, A., Berman, B., Forys, K., & Ernst, E. (2005). Meta-analysis: Acupuncture for low back pain. *Annals of Internal Medicine, 142,* 651–663.

51. Kröner-Herwig, B. (2009). Chronic pain syndromes and their treatment by psychological interventions. *Current Opinion in Psychiatry, 22,* 200–204.

52. Malmivaara, A., Häkkinen, U., Aro, T., Heinrichs, M.-L., Koskenniemi, L., Kuosma, E., et al. (1995). The treatment of acute low back pain—bed rest, exercises, or ordinary activity? *New England Journal of Medicine, 332,* 351–355.

53. Hagen, K. B., Hilde, G., Jamtvedt, G., & Winnem, M. (2004). Bed rest for acute low-back pain and sciatica. *Cochrane Database of Systematic Reviews, Oct. 18,* CD001254.

54. Linton, S. J., Bradley, L. A., Jensen, I., Spangfort, E., & Sundell, L. (1989). The secondary prevention of low back pain: A controlled study with follow-up. *Pain, 36,* 197–207.

ABOUT THE AUTHOR

Heather Rachel Davids, MD is a Physical Medicine and Rehabilitation physician and is Division Head of Pain Medicine for Mercy Medical Group, Sacramento, California. She has received additional fellowship training in the field of pain medicine and medical acupuncture, and has a special interest in the role of nutrition and fitness in pain and its management.

CHAPTER 13

"I Ruined My Knees Playing Softball."

ORTHOPEDIC ISSUES FOR LESBIANS

LESLEY J. ANDERSON, MD   LYNN M. FORSEY, PhD, RN

SUSIE *is a 52-year-old gardener who comes to the office complaining of a painful right knee. She says she injured her knee in college in 1971 while playing softball and was told she had "torn cartilage and ligament damage." Her knee was locking and unstable. Surgery removed the torn cartilage, but the orthopedic surgeon told her he did not fix the ligament "because women don't put the same stresses on the knee as men do and fixing the ligament was not necessary. You shouldn't play sports anyway."*

Susie, who is overweight, cannot walk more than three blocks without pain; her only activities are occasional bicycle riding and swimming. Her exam shows a severely degenerated and arthritic knee with bone on bone in the medial compartment where her meniscus had been removed. The only surgical option is total knee replacement, but she is considered to be too young for this operation. Could her knee problem have been prevented?

She tells the nurse taking her history that she suspects that the old, untreated sports injury may have led to her current condition. Evaluating Susie for osteoarthritis, the nurse empathizes with the obvious effects the pain and dysfunction have had on her life and wishes she had come in sooner.

■ ■ ■

There are no studies highlighting lesbians' orthopedic problems, including sports injuries. Not long ago, the general public assumed that women "jocks" were lesbians by nature. Tennis icon Billie Jean King paved the way for lesbian jocks everywhere and, more importantly, for all women in many different sports. Her defeat of Bobby Riggs in the 1973 "Battle of the Sexes" tennis tournament proved that women could compete with men on the same playing field. Her courage and leadership resulted in equivalent tournament payouts for men and women professional tennis players.

Most orthopedic issues are similar for lesbians and heterosexual women. Of all the factors that impact bone health, obesity most urgently needs intervention.[1] It affects the hip,[2] spine,[3] and knee.[4] This chapter focuses on knee, shoulder, and foot problems; osteoarthritis; and hip fractures secondary to osteoporosis.

KNEE PROBLEMS

A number of knee problems with multiple etiologies and involving ligaments, menisci, and tendons are common in women. The prevalence of knee injuries has increased as more women and girls play sports.

ACL Injuries

The anterior cruciate ligament (ACL) runs through the center of the knee joint, providing stability for cutting, pivoting, and twisting motions that are typical in sports. An ACL injury occurs when the short, stout ligament is stretched or torn due to twisting.[5] Injury incidence varies depending on gender and, for women, ethnicity. ACL tears occur four to six times more commonly among women than men,[6,7] and, among female soccer and basketball players, three times more commonly compared with men who play these two sports.[8] In professional basketball, White European American players are more than six times as likely as all other ethnic groups to experience an ACL injury.[9] The incidence of such injuries is 3.51 per 100 collegiate athletes.[10] Given that about 145,000 college women compete in sports and 80,000 ACL injuries occur annually (nearly half of them in women), female injuries have become epidemic.[6,11,12] This is particularly true in high school, where the level of competition is more intense than in the past.

Someone who tears an ACL usually hears a pop, is immediately disabled, and cannot continue the activity. Such tears most commonly occur in recreational skiing, soccer, and basketball.[8] Oftentimes, there are other associated injuries, including damage to the collateral ligaments (on the side), meniscus cartilages (the shock absorbers between the femur and tibia), or the articular cartilage itself. The most common theories about why women and girls are more prone to ACL injury include anatomical differences (pelvis-to-knee angle, small intercondylar notch), muscular imbalances between the quadriceps and hamstrings, and movement patterns, as women tend to hyperextend the leg.[13–16]

Treatment consists of rest, ice, compression, and elevation (RICE), and crutches are usually necessary. Evaluation by an orthopedic surgeon is critical for determining the extent of injury. Magnetic resonance imaging is not necessary for diagnosis, but orthopedists often order a MRI to look for other intra-articular injuries, such as damage to the meniscus and chondral surfaces. Nor is immediate surgery absolutely necessary. The most important remedial action is to control swelling and enable the knee to regain range of motion and muscle control. Surgery, which involves reconstructing a new ligament, is usually recommended for women who want to remain physically active, given the unreliability of repair; the rate at which ACLs tear again is quite high.[17] In reconstruction, surgeons use tendon from the patient or a cadaver—either the patellar tendon or two hamstrings, which make for a strong allograft that develops its own blood supply over time.

Four percent to 5% of ACL reconstructions fail, but most patients who undergo the procedure can resume active lifestyles. While one study found no gender differences in surgical outcomes related to knee function, donor-site pain, patellofemoral crepitus, or stair climbing,[18] the evidence is mixed. The use of allografts for ACL reconstruction has increased dramatically in the last several years, yet concerns remain about the very small risk of transmitting infectious disease.[19,20] The surgeon must know which tissue bank is providing the graft and that the American Association of Tissue Banks has certified the bank. For ACL reconstruction to succeed, the patient's commitment to rehabilitation is critical. Rehabilitation takes 3 to 6 months. Patients can usually return to full activity in 6 to 9 months and about 80% of them can participate in high-level sports again as long as there are no other significant ligament or cartilage injuries.

Preventing ACL tears is key. A number of preseason, sport-specific programs seek to reduce their incidence in athletes.*[21-23] For recreational athletes during a sport season, prevention includes routine warm-ups, regular stretching and weight-bearing exercises, avoidance of sudden changes in exercise intensity, and a slow increase in the force and duration of activities.[5]

Meniscus Tears

The meniscus is fibrocartilage between the tibia and femur consisting of two, horse-shoe-shaped gaskets (menisci)—one on the inside (medial) and one on the outside (lateral) of the tibia. The menisci move with the tibia: when the leg is extended, they promote a snug fit between the tibia and femur.[24] They absorb shock to the joint and provide lubrication and stability. As people age, the meniscus can degenerate and tear; in younger, physically active persons, a sudden twist, pivot, or squat can cause an acute tear and immediate disability. Tears in the medial meniscus are more common than tears in the lateral meniscus. However, tear and removal of the lateral meniscus is associated with earlier onset of degenerative changes in the lateral compartment of the knee, usually within 8 to 10 years of removal and especially in persons older than 40. Meniscal injuries occur more commonly in men than women, by a ratio of 2.5:1. Women at risk of meniscal injury include athletes and those older than 40 who have a history of smoking and obesity.[25]

A better understanding of the role of the meniscus in knee biomechanics has prompted a shift from automatic meniscectomy to attempts to preserve and repair the torn cartilage. If the knee is stable and not locked after initial RICE treatment, blood vessels feeding the outer meniscus may be able to heal a small outer tear.[26] About 15% to 20% of such injuries can be sutured when the tear is near the periphery, and they heal fairly quickly. Most meniscus injuries require surgery because the torn and loose fragment must be removed; it will not heal. After arthroscopic surgery to remove a fragment, rehabilitation and a return to full activity is fairly rapid. Surgical repair requires 3 to 4 months of recovery before the patient can resume full activity. For these patients, maintaining an intact and functioning meniscus is a major factor in reducing the development of arthritis,[27] which arises in those with an unstable knee.

Meniscus transplants, in which the surgeon takes a meniscus from a cadaver donor, have been performed for more than 20 years on young patients with knees that

* An example is the Prevent Injury, Enhance Performance Program, developed by the Santa Monica ACL Prevention Project, that focuses on female soccer players. See www.aclprevent.com/pepprogram.htm.

do not show evidence of arthritic wear. A transplant can salvage a knee that otherwise would degenerate over the years. There do not appear to be any gender differences in long-term outcomes of meniscal repair surgery. Rather, the type of initial tear determines the outcome.[28]

Chondromalacia

Women have more laxity in their joints than men do. In addition, the wider pelvis in women makes for different alignment patterns in the lower extremities. The knees are often in a slightly more valgus position (knock-kneed), which causes the kneecap to track off to the lateral side and become unstable and dislocate or, in subtler cases, causes wear and softening of the cartilage underneath the kneecap, a condition called chondromalacia.[14] The condition is much more common in women than men. It often occurs in women in their early twenties who begin to get back into shape by participating in an aerobics or weight lifting program involving significant flexing or bending activities, which place additional pressure on the back of the kneecap and can cause pain. Weakness of the inner (medial) quadricep muscles increases the risk of anterior knee pain.[29]

Adequate physical therapy and strengthening programs can treat chondromalacia; surgery is usually unnecessary. When the kneecap is off-center or tilted, surgery often helps, but the patient must rigidly adhere to a rehabilitation regimen.

Chondromalacia is very common in runners who have anterior knee pain syndrome. The syndrome is not associated with any thinning of the cartilage; it is primarily related to biomechanical stressors extending across the anterior part of the knee joint and causing pain. Proper footwear, orthotics, adequate stretching and strengthening, and anti-inflammatory medication and ice often are extremely beneficial and can help control the symptoms. Avoiding prolonged downhill activities will prevent knee pain from developing, as any activities that involve full flexing or bending of the knee increase pressure across the kneecap.[30]

New Repair Procedures

New surgical procedures to repair knee injuries include resurfacing of articular cartilage defects, meniscus transplantation after meniscus removal, advanced ligament reconstruction techniques, and, in very select patients, cloning of cartilage and using it to resurface joint defects.[31,32] They are generally performed when the indications are very specific, not in patients who have osteoarthritis or a significantly worn knee. The procedures require special training, and surgeons must do them often to become proficient. A number of these innovations show exciting promise in delaying the onset of osteoarthritis and disability in patients who have knee pain.

SHOULDER PROBLEMS

While shoulder pain is the third most common musculoskeletal complaint,[33] only a few shoulder problems occur specifically in women. Problems that arise in women are often related to shoulder instability resulting from ligamentous laxity (loose joints), frozen shoulder, or rotator cuff disease.

Instability

Shoulder instability is the most common cause of shoulder pain in athletes younger than 30.[32] Loose-jointed women who can hyperextend their elbows, thumbs, and knees often also have ligamentous laxity in their shoulders. These ligaments otherwise constrain the shoulder joint and keep it located. The inherently unstable joint has a very flat socket (glenoid). Ligaments in the front connect to the collar- or gasket-shaped labrum around the socket and help contain the sliding of the humeral head in and out of the glenoid cavity.

Patients with loose joints are more at risk of complete or partial dislocation of the shoulder when, for example, they throw a ball, cock an arm backward, make an overhead tennis stroke, or swim repetitively. This repetitive motion, which is also common in throwing sports, can cause progressive stretching of ligaments in the shoulder joint, leading to instability. Patients often present with tendonitis symptoms rather than complain of a shoulder that "pops out." The symptoms include a lateral ache radiating down from the shoulder to mid-arm that becomes worse during overhead activities , when reaching, or when putting on a coat.

Clinicians should determine if the tendonitis is due to underlying instability or extrinsic factors, such as a bone spur causing a partial tear of the rotator cuff tendon. Patients with instability need to undergo a strengthening program, particularly of the rotator cuff muscles and scapular stabilizers—the trapezius, rhomboids, and serratus anterior. This is best accomplished if the patient initially lifts weights under the watchful eye of a trainer to ensure she maintains proper form. Strengthening the muscles around the shoulder joint enables many patients to participate in sports without recurrent symptoms. Such exercises generally are not effective in those who have a history of trauma causing shoulder dislocation. But in patients with congenitally loose joints, strengthening the scapular stabilizers or upper back muscles is critical. Surgery should be delayed in this subgroup until consistent rehabilitation fails.

Surgery is occasionally necessary to correct the instability of, and to tighten ligaments around, the shoulder joint. Recovery takes several months. Surgical correction involves reconstructing the ligaments and/or repairing the labrum back to the bone. After reconstruction, the normal bumper effect of the labrum and ligament complex restricts the excursion of the humeral head out of the socket when a motion such as throwing puts the shoulder at risk. The procedure is generally quite successful, with a failure rate of 4% to 6%.[34] Arthroscopic techniques have improved over the years to the point that, in skilled hands, the results are comparable to those obtained using larger incisions.[35] A small subgroup of patients should not be treated arthroscopically.[36]

Adhesive Capsulitis

Adhesive capsulitis, or "frozen shoulder," is more common than the above conditions. It is seven times more prevalent in women than men, more prevalent in women 35 to 55 years old, and more common in diabetics and those with thyroid conditions.[33,37] A characteristic of adhesive capsulitis, the cause of which is unknown, is onset of significant pain after minor trauma. The pain is more severe at night and worse with movement. Subsequently, patients experience a progressive loss of movement and stiffness in the shoulder.

There are three consecutive phases in classic adhesive capsulitis: the freezing phase, the adhesive phase, and the thawing phase, or resolution. Freezing, the most painful, involves significant inflammation in the shoulder joint and, frequently, severe night pain and severe limitation of activities. Treatment focuses on pain management with oral anti-inflammatories and often an intra-articular steroid injection, which can reverse progression to a more severe phase. Maintaining mobility and range of motion during freezing is important, but physical therapy often does not help and can make the patient's shoulder even worse when it is acutely inflamed and irritable.

The adhesive phase occurs sometime between 6 weeks and 4 months after the onset of pain. It is marked by progressive stiffness in the shoulder; disappearance of constant, daily pain; improvement in night pain; and pain that still occurs when the individual reaches or assumes a position exceeding the shoulder joint's limitation. The shoulder capsule or lining of the shoulder joint becomes tight and fibrotic. Oftentimes, physical therapy to progressively stretch the shoulder out is very helpful, but recovery is slow and gradual. A more rapid way to regain range of motion is shoulder manipulation under anesthesia, which acutely releases the adhesions. If the adhesions are quite firm, a common procedure is arthroscopic release of scar tissue during manipulation.

Thawing, the third phase, can last 12 to 42 months. The tissue starts to stretch out and is characterized by slowly improving range of motion, less pain, and greater function. There is a 10% risk that adhesive capsulitis will also occur in the opposite shoulder.[38]

Rotator Cuff Tears and Disease

Rotator cuff disease and tears are becoming more common as baby boomers age and maintain an active lifestyle.[39] Overhead sports such as tennis, throwing sports, and work involving overhead positions can cause degeneration of the rotator cuff, a group of four muscles attached to the lateral part of the shoulder that motor it through a range of motions. Degeneration and subsequent fraying, followed by a partial or complete tear, may occur gradually or acutely after a fall.

Rotator cuff disease often begins in people in their thirties, when the tendons start to lose their ability to heal and repair themselves after minor trauma. A concomitant spur in the undersurface of the acromion, a bony arch above the rotator cuff, can speed the disease process. In the earliest phases, the disease is called rotator cuff tendonitis or impingement syndrome. The best treatment is to strengthen the scapular and rotator cuff muscles, and sometimes to cease the offending activity. Judicious cortisone injections may ease acute flares or severe night pain. However, repetitive use of steroids is not indicated because they can cause some thinning and degeneration of the tendon.

Patients with rotator cuff disease that has progressed to a complete tear may present with weakness, night pain, and a limited range of motion. Interestingly, such tears are asymptomatic in up to 80% of patients older than 60,[40] not all of whom need treatment. Active treatment of rotator cuff tears is indicated for weakness, for pain, or in a young person whose future lifestyle needs will require normal strength. Tears can be repaired arthroscopically or, through a very small incision, by placing anchors in the bone and reattaching the tendon to them. Rehabilitation may take as long as 4 to 6 months. Most patients can return to full activity, but those whose work involves heavy physical demands may need much more time to regain their full strength.

FOOT PROBLEMS

In the movie "Good Morning, Vietnam," disc jockey Adrian Cronauer (Robin Williams) was asked how an observer could spot lesbians in a crowd. "By the ones with the comfortable shoes," he replied.[41] There is some wisdom in this, given the foot problems that women experience.

One of the most common problems is hallux valgus, an abnormal deviation of the big toe away from the midline of the body or toward the other toes. This can lead to a bunion—an inflamed swelling of the small, fluid-filled sac on the outside of the first joint of the big toe—that makes the second toe cock up, causing painful calluses, difficulty wearing shoes, and pain while walking. Bunions, which most often occur in the fourth to sixth decade of life, stem from congenital alignment problems in the foot, when the space between the first and second toe is widened and the great toes curve inward. Years of wearing shoes that cramp the toes together also can cause bunions.

Thirty years ago, the stereotypical lesbian would not have been caught dead wearing pointy shoes or high heels. Today, many "lipstick lesbians" and lesbians working in the corporate world must wear types of shoes that may not be good for long-term foot health. The American Foot and Ankle Society has tried unsuccessfully for years to educate manufacturers about the health hazards of shoes that force the toes together. The large majority of surgical forefoot repairs are performed on women.[42]

Correcting bunion deformity is indicated when the main complaint is pain, the patient has difficulty wearing "practical" shoes, or a young woman has a congenital malalignment between the first and second metatarsals. The most common complication is recurrence followed by overcorrection. A poor surgical outcome may make the foot very painful and walking very difficult. A surgeon who is tempted to remove an unsightly bump for cosmetic reasons must fully understand what caused it to form. Orthopedic surgeons see far too many patients with poor surgical outcomes, as reconstructive surgery is technically challenging.

OSTEOARTHRITIS

Osteoarthritis (OA) is the gradual degeneration or wearing down of articular joint cartilage, causing progressive pain, disability, deformity, and loss of function. The disease can affect any joint, but in women it most often occurs in the knees, hands, and hips, especially the knees and fingers—particularly in the basal joint of the thumb, which is necessary for pinching. An estimated 20 million Americans have difficulty walking, lifting, or kneeling due to knee OA, a leading cause of physical disability.[43–45] Women are almost twice as likely as men to develop OA.[46,47]

The disease has multiple causes, including age, previous injury or surgery, genetics, obesity, and inflammatory conditions.[48] Obesity is a very strong predictor of knee OA.[4] Heberden's nodes, a manifestation of OA in the fingers that often is genetic, occur more commonly in women as they age.[49] The nodes can become painful and cause deformed fingers, making pinching, grasping, and other activities difficult. When arthritis affects the base of the thumb (carpo-metacarpal joint), pinching—opening jars and bottles, for example—is not easy. This type of arthritis affects 1 in 4 women compared with 1 in 12 men.[50]

Initial treatment involves supportive splints for the fingers. Treatment of the thumb consists of a splint followed by cortisone injections and ultimately surgery if the arthritis causes deformity and the patient has difficulty performing daily tasks. Surgery generally produces excellent results, although recovery takes several months. Evidence-based outcomes have yet to demonstrate that one surgical method is superior to another.[51]

Since 1972, when Title IX opened up sports to girls and college-age women, a population now in their forties and fifties has become very committed to continuing an active lifestyle despite OA caused by previous sports injuries. Treating these women is challenging because they want to remain physically active at an intense level and have high expectations of surgery. An injured meniscus in the knee or an old ligament injury from earlier sporting days increases the rate at which OA in the knee develops. Greater wear on one or the other side of the knee joint, which occurs as a result of lost cartilage and subsequent settling, can cause bow-legged or knock-kneed deformity and pain. The rate of OA progression depends on activity level, genetics, and weight.[52]

Obesity plays a major role in the onset of OA.[1] Because lesbians are more likely than heterosexual women to be obese, the disease is probably more common in lesbians. Chistensen and colleagues found that an 11% weight loss in older adults with knee OA over a 6-week period resulted in a threefold improvement in self-reported function compared with a control group.[53] Patients who lose as few as 15 pounds often see a significant reduction in pain. Clinicians are responsible for encouraging patients to shed weight—not by shaming them, but by bringing forthrightness and professionalism to the task, as they would when treating patients who have diabetes or hypertension. Offering specific suggestions, directions, and resources is helpful.

Weight loss is the first and foremost treatment for OA if, based on body mass index, a patient is overweight or obese. Other treatments include a general fitness program, local ice or heat, and physical therapy to maintain or regain joint motion and muscle strength. Protecting joints from overuse is also beneficial. To manage pain and inflammation, medications such as acetaminophen and prescription or over-the-counter nonsteroidal anti-inflammatory drugs are appropriate.[49] Nutraceuticals like glucosamine, chondroitin sulfate, and fish oil may help relieve pain and inflammation.[54] The U.S. Food and Drug Administration does not regulate these supplements, and their efficacy varies. However, according to one literature review, they are a good first-line treatment for OA and, compared with standard anti-inflammatories, have fewer side effects. Patients on warfarin and those with renal disease should not take nutraceuticals, and people with high cholesterol and/or diabetes should use them cautiously.[54]

Oral anti-inflammatories can be very beneficial in maintaining a moderate level of function and reducing swelling and pain, which may help the patient continue her exercise and weight loss regimens. Because there is a potential risk of stroke and heart attack in those who take some anti-inflammatories over the long term, patients should first consult their primary care physician.

Importantly, OA patients must not stop moving. They need to engage in some type of activity or exercise that will keep their joints mobile and their muscles strong, and optimize their balance. Stretching, swimming, and water aerobics are good, low-impact activities for this purpose.[†]

---

† The American Academy of Orthopaedic Surgeons offers useful information on healthy aging at orthoinfo.aaos.org/topic.cfm?topic=A00191.

For patients who cannot tolerate anti-inflammatories, options include injecting cortisone or viscosupplements—hyaluronic acid preparations such as Synvisc, Supartz, Orthovisc, or Euflexxa—into the joint. Although any injection into the joint carries a low risk of infection, these preparations can be effective in up to 80% of patients for about 6 to 9 months.[55] Most viscosupplements are contraindicated in patients with egg allergies, as all but Euflexxa are derived from rooster combs. A trial not sponsored by industry found no difference in outcomes between steroid injections and viscosupplements at 6 months.[56]

Patients with mechanical symptoms or recurrent swelling can gain short-term relief from surgical procedures such as arthroscopy. An option for select patients who meet strict screening criteria is biologic joint replacement using meniscal or cartilage-restoring procedures. The ultimate treatment for disabling OA of the knee is partial or total knee replacement. Outcomes are excellent—more than 90% of replacements still function after 15 years. The ideal patient is not significantly overweight, older than 60, and medically cleared for surgery. Complications such as infection and wound-healing problems are more common in patients with diabetes or vascular disease and in smokers. Because of the higher risk of fatal blood clots in patients who undergo hip or knee replacement, prophylactic anticoagulation is usually indicated.[57]

Total joint replacements will increase an estimated 673% by 2030 due to aging baby boomers and rising obesity in the United States.[58] According to the American Academy of Orthopaedic Surgeons, this could create access-to-care issues because the number of new orthopedic surgeons has not kept pace with the anticipated workload.[59] Preventing the progression of conditions that lead to OA, such as meniscus repair in the knee, ligament stabilization after injuries, reduction of obesity, and proper exercise as people age, is very important.

OSTEOPOROSIS AND HIP FRACTURES

In 2006, 71% of the 307,336 persons hospitalized in the United States for hip fracture were women and 86% were at least 65 years old.[60] In 2005, osteoporosis, or weakening of bone due to structural deterioration, was the leading cause of an estimated 297,000 hip fractures, which are two to three times more likely to occur in women than in men. Half of women older than 50 are likely to have an osteoporosis-related fracture during their remaining lifetime.[61] Thus, older lesbians may well experience this debilitating problem.

Treatment of hip fracture is predominantly surgical and depends on the type of fracture and its specific location. The goal of intervention is to stabilize the fracture to achieve better pain control and facilitate early ambulation. Despite technical advances, high morbidity and mortality rates are associated with hip repair surgery. About 24%

of patients older than 50 who fracture their hip die within a year and, 6 months after fracture, only about 15% of patients can walk across a room unaided. Many older adults cannot return to their presurgery level of function.[61,62] Among the leading, patient-related factors predictive of outcomes are age, cognitive function, comorbidities, and gender. Pain, fatigue, and balance are the most amenable to treatment.[62]

TABLE 13.1. OTHER RISK FACTORS ASSOCIATED WITH HIP FRACTURE

In addition to osteoporosis, female gender, and older age, risk factors include:

- Race (Caucasian and Asian)
- Chronic medical conditions (e.g., endocrine, gastrointestinal, or rheumatoid disorders; Parkinson's disease; multiple sclerosis; dementia; depression)
- Limited physical activity
- Poor nutrition (e.g., calcium or vitamin D deficiency)
- Tobacco/alcohol use that interferes with bone metabolism
- Certain medications (e.g., corticosteroids, anticonvulsants, anticoagulants, thyroid drugs, some diuretics)

Source: Busconi, B., & Harder, A. (2008). Hip fracture. In F. J. Domino (Ed.), *The 5-minute clinical consult 2008* [Online database].

Given the serious consequences, preventing hip fracture is an important aspect of primary care and orthopedic practice. Key strategies include preventing falls, strengthening bones to preclude osteoporosis, and protecting bones.[63] The U.S. Preventive Services Task Force recommends routine osteoporosis screening of women ≥ 65 years old and women ≥ 60 years old who are at high risk for fracture.[64] New medications rebuild bone density.[65] People can optimize their bone health and help prevent osteoporosis by:

- Getting the daily recommended amounts of calcium and vitamin D3;
- Engaging in regular weight-bearing and muscle-strengthening exercise;
- Not smoking and not drinking excessively;
- Talking to their health care provider about bone health; and
- Undergoing a bone density test and taking medication when appropriate.[61]

■ ■ ■

If Susie, the woman in the scenario at the beginning of this chapter, were a young woman and presented to the authors' clinic, treatment would consist of reconstructing her ACL and repairing her meniscus. She would be a candidate for a meniscal transplant if the repair failed. The treatment Susie received decades earlier doomed her to arthritis by the time she reached her current age. Today, orthopedic surgeons recognize that sports are important to women and that gender is not a relevant factor in reconstructive procedures. Significant technical advances in surgically treating Susie's type of injury are such that, compared to the early 1970s, her outcome would be much better.

Regarding Susie's arthritis, the clinician should recommend that she start a weight reduction program such as Weight Watchers (the online program, if she is uncomfortable about participating in face-to-face, traditionally "straight" sessions), increase her bicycling or swimming frequency to 30 minutes per day, use anti-inflammatory medications, supplement her diet with chondroitin sulfate and glucosamine, and take the daily recommended amounts of calcium and vitamin D. Susie should return in 6 months for reassessment.

CONCLUSION

This chapter reviewed orthopedic conditions that affect women in general, as clinical orthopedics research has not focused specifically on lesbians. But most orthopedic issues are probably similar for lesbians and heterosexual women. There is growing evidence that gender-related factors predispose women to knee injuries, a few shoulder injuries, and foot problems. Conditions that place women at risk for orthopedic injuries include osteoarthritis and osteoporosis. Better understanding of factors that predispose women to such injuries is leading to better preventive measures. The last several decades have seen significant advances in treating sports injuries in both women and men.

ADDITIONAL RESOURCES

- American Academy of Orthopaedic Surgeons:
  www.orthoinfo.aaos.org

- American Orthopaedic Society for Sports Medicine:
  www.aossm.org

- Arthroscopy Association of North America:
  www.aana.org

- Knee Injuries and Disorders (Medline Plus):
  www.nlm.nih.gov/medlineplus/kneeinjuriesanddisorders.html

REFERENCES

1. Rodts, M. F. (2007). The impact of obesity on bone health. *Orthopaedic Nursing, 26,* 269.

2. Gelber, A. C. (2003). Obesity and hip osteoarthritis: The weight of the evidence is increasing. *American Journal of Medicine, 114,* 158–159.

3. Fanuele, J. C., Abdu, W. A., Hanscom, B., & Weinstein, J. N. (2002). Association between obesity and functional status in patients with spine disease. *Spine, 27,* 306–312.

4. Pearson-Ceol, J. (2007). Literature review on the effects of obesity on knee osteoarthritis. *Orthopaedic Nursing, 26,* 289–292.

5. National Institute of Arthritis and Musculoskeletal and Skin Diseases. (2006). *Questions & answers about knee problems* (NIH Publication No. 06-4912). Bethesda, MD: National Institutes of Health. Available at www.niams.nih.gov/Health_Info/Knee_Problems/knee_problems_qa.pdf.

6. Griffin, L. Y., Agel, J., Albohm, M. J., Arendt, E. A., Dick, R. W., Garrett W. E., et al. (2000). Noncontact anterior cruciate ligament injuries: Risk factors and prevention strategies. *Journal of the American Academy of Orthopaedic Surgeons, 8,* 141–150.

7. Agel J., Arendt E. A., & Bershadsky B. (2005). Anterior cruciate ligament injury in National Collegiate Athletic Association basketball and soccer: A 13-year review. *American Journal of Sports Medicine, 33,* 524–530.

8. Prodromos, C. C., Han, Y., Rogowski, J., Joyce, B., & Shi, K. (2007). A meta-analysis of the incidence of anterior cruciate ligament tears as a function of gender, sport, and a knee injury- reduction regimen. *Arthroscopy, 23,* 1320–1325.

9. Trojian, T. H., & Collins, S. (2006). The anterior cruciate ligament tear rate varies by race in professional women's basketball. *American Journal of Sports Medicine, 34,* 893–894.

10. Mountcastle, S. B., Posner, M., Kragh., J. F. Jr., & Taylor, D. C. (2007). Gender differences in anterior cruciate ligament injury vary with activity: Epidemiology of anterior cruciate ligament injuries in a young, athletic population. *American Journal of Sports Medicine, 35,* 1635–1642.

11. Pallarito, K. (2008, April 24). Women risk bone loss after knee surgery. *HealthDay.* Available at abcnews.go.com/Health/Healthday/Story?id=4721141&page=1.

12. Smith, I. K. (2000, November). On bended knee: More girls are tearing ligaments in their knees. Here's what they can do to prevent it. *Time.* Available at www.time.com/time/magazine/article/0,9171,59782,00.html.

13. Boden, B. P., Griffin, L. Y., & Garrett, W. E. (2000). Etiology and prevention of noncontact ACL injury. *The Physician and Sportsmedicine, 28,* 53–60.

14. Harmon, K. G., & Ireland, M. L. (2000). Gender differences in noncontact anterior cruciate ligament injuries. *Clinics in Sports Medicine, 19,* 287–302.

15. Vlach, S. (n.d.). ACL and the female athlete: Theoretical causes and prevention. *LifeFitness.* Available at us.commercial.lifefitness.com/Content.cfm/aclandthefemaleathletetheoreticalcausesandprevention.

16. Griffin, L. Y., Albohm, M. J., Arendt, E. A., Bahr, R., Beynnon, B. D., Demaio, M., et al. (2006). Understanding and preventing noncontact anterior cruciate ligament injuries: A

review of the Hunt Valley II meeting, January 2005. *American Journal of Sports Medicine, 34,* 1512–1532.

17. Kaplan, N., Wickiewicz, T. L., & Warren, R. F. (1990). Primary surgical treatment of anterior cruciate ligament ruptures: A long-term follow-up study. *American Journal of Sports Medicine, 18,* 354–358.

18. Ferrari, J. D., Bach, B. R. Jr., Bush-Joseph, C. A., Wang, T., & Bojchuk., J. (2001). Anterior cruciate ligament reconstruction in men and women: An outcome analysis comparing gender. *Arthroscopy, 17,* 588–596.

19. Centers for Disease Control and Prevention. (2002). Update: Allograft-associated bacterial infections—United States, 2002. *Morbidity and Mortality Weekly Report, 51,* 207–210.

20. Wheeless, C. R. (2008). *Allografts: Wheeless' textbook of orthopaedics.* Available at www.wheelessonline.com/ortho/allografts.

21. Heidt, R. S. Jr., Sweeterman, L. M., Carlonas, R. L., Traub, J. A., & Tekulve, F. X. (2000). Avoidance of soccer injuries with preseason conditioning. *American Journal of Sports Medicine, 28,* 659–662.

22. Hart, L. E., Silvers, H. J., & Mandelbaum, B. R. (2001). Preseason conditioning to prevent soccer injuries in young women. *Clinical Journal of Sport Medicine, 11,* 206.

23. Hewitt, T. E., Lindenfeld, T. N., Riccobena, J. V., & Noyes, F. R. (1999). The effect of neuromuscular training on the incidence of knee injuries in female athletes. A prospective study. *American Journal of Sports Medicine, 27,* 699–706.

24. Schoen, D. C. (2000). The knee and lower leg. In *Adult orthopaedic nursing* (pp. 317–355). Philadelphia: Lippincott Williams & Wilkins.

25. Saluti, C., & Stevenson, J. (2008). Meniscal injury. In F. J. Domino (Ed.), *The 5-minute clinical consult 2009* [Online database].

26. American Academy of Orthopaedic Surgeons. (2007). Meniscal tear. *Your Orthopaedic Connection.* Available at horthoinfo.aaos.org/topic.cfm?topic=A00358.

27. Schoen, D. C. (2007). Meniscal knee pathologies. *Orthopaedic Nursing, 26,* 388–391.

28. Endlund, M., Roos, E. M., Roos, H. P., & Lohmander, L. S. (2001). Patient-relevant outcomes fourteen years after meniscectomy: Influence of type of meniscal tear and size of resection. *Rheumatology, 40,* 631–639.

29. Witvrouw, E., Lysens, R., Bellemans, J., Cambier, D., & Vanderstraeten, G. (2000). Intrinsic risk factors for the development of anterior knee pain in an athletic population. *American Journal of Sports Medicine, 28,* 480–489.

30. American Academy of Orthopaedic Surgeons. (2007). Knee osteoarthritis statistics. *Your Orthopaedic Connection.* Available at orthoinfo.aaos.org/topic.cfm?topic=A00399.

31. Brittberg, M., Lindahl, A., Nilsson, A., Ohlsson, C., Isaksson, O., & Peterson, L. (1994). Treatment of deep cartilage defects in the knee with autologous chondrocyte transplantation. *New England Journal of Medicine, 331,* 889–895.

32. Safran, M. R., Kim, H., & Zaffagnini, S. (2008). The use of scaffolds in the management of articular cartilage injury. *Journal of the American Academy of Orthopaedic Surgeons, 16,* 306–311.

33. Stevenson, J., & Mancini, L. (2008). Shoulder pain. In F. J. Domino (Ed.), *The 5-minute clinical consult 2009* [Online database].

34. Vaccaro, A. R. (Ed.). (2005). *Orthopaedic knowledge update 8: Home study syllabus.* Rosemont, IL: American Academy of Orthopaedic Surgeons.

35. Kim, S. H., Ha, K. I, & Kim, S. H. (2002). Bankart repair in traumatic anterior shoulder instability: Open versus arthroscopic technique. *Arthroscopy, 18,* 755–763.

36. Cole, B. J., & Warner, J. J. (2000). Arthroscopic versus open Bankart repair for traumatic anterior shoulder instability. *Clinics in Sports Medicine, 19,* 19–48.

37. Harryman, D. T. II. (1993). Shoulders: Frozen and stiff. *Instructional Course Lectures, 42,* 247–257.

38. Dias, R., Cutts, S., & Massoud, S. (2005). Frozen shoulder. *BMJ, 331,* 1453–1456.

39. Buckwalter, J. A., Heckman, J. D., & Petric, D. P. (2003). An AOA critical issue: Aging of the North American population: New challenges for orthopaedics. *Journal of Bone and Joint Surgery (American Volume), 85,* 748–758.

40. Wheeless, C. R. (2008). Rotator cuff tears: Frequency of tears. In *Wheeless' textbook of orthopaedics.* Available at wheelessonline.com/ortho/rotator_cuff_tears_frequency_of_tears.

41. Brezner, L., & Johnson, M. (Producers); Levinson, B. (Director). (1987). *Good morning, Vietnam* [Motion picture]. United States: Touchstone Pictures.

42. Coughlin, M. J. (1995). Women's shoe wear and foot disorders. *Western Journal of Medicine, 163,* 569(2).

43. American Academy of Orthopaedic Surgeons. (2007). Care of the aging or post-traumatic knee. *Your Orthopedic Connection.* Available at wheelessonline.comhttp://orthoinfo.aaos.org/topic.cfm?topic=A00344.

44. Cicuttini, F. M., Teichtahl, A. J., Wluka, A. E., Davis, S., Strauss, B. J., & Ebeling, P. R. (2005). The relationship between body composition and knee cartilage volume in healthy, middle-aged subjects. *Arthritis & Rheumatism, 52,* 461–467.

45. Lawrence, R. C., Helmick, C. G., Arnett, F. C., Deyo, R. A., Felson, D. T., Giannini, E. H., et al. (1998). Estimates of the prevalence of arthritis and selected musculoskeletal disorders in the United States. *Arthritis & Rheumatism, 43,* 778–799.

46. Felson, D. T., Zhang, Y., Hannan, M. T., Naimark, A., Weissman, B. N., Aliabadi, P., et al. (1995). The incidence and natural history of knee osteoarthritis in the elderly. The Framingham Osteoarthritis Study. *Arthritis & Rheumatism, 38,* 1500–1505.

47. Lacey, R. J., Thomas, E., Duncan, R. C., & Peat, G. (2008). Gender difference in symptomatic radiographic knee osteoarthritis in the Knee Clinical Assessment—CAS(K): A prospective study in the general population. *BMC Musculoskeletal Disorders, 9,* 82. Available at www.biomedcentral.com/1471-2472/9/82.

48. Kalunian, K. C. (2007). Risk factors for and possible causes of osteoarthritis. *UpToDate.* Available at www.uptodate.com/patients/content/topic.do?topicKey=~MoRo6jZJ3hjA3E.

49. Gilliland, B. (2008). Arthritis, osteo. In F. J. Domino (Ed.), *The 5-minute clinical consult 2008* [Online database].

50. Barron O. A., Glickel, S. Z., & Eaton, R. G. (2000). Basal joint arthritis of the thumb. *Journal of the American Academy of Orthopaedic Surgeons, 8,* 314–323.

51. Shuler, M. S., Luria, S., & Trumble, T. E. (2008). Basal joint arthritis of the thumb. *Journal of the American Academy of Orthopaedic Surgeons, 16,* 418–423.

52. Kalunian, K. C. (2007). Pathogenesis of osteoarthritis. *UpToDate.* Available at www. uptodate.com/patients/content/topic.do?topicKey=osteoart/4607&title=Osteoarthritis.

53. Christensen, R., Astrup, A., & Bliddal, H. (2005). Weight loss: The treatment of choice for knee osteoarthritis? A randomized trial. *Osteoarthritis and Cartilage, 13,* 20–27.

54. Watterson, J. R., & Esdaile, J. M. (2000). Viscosupplemention: Therapeutic mechanisms and clinical potential in osteoarthritis of the knee. *Journal of the American Academy of Orthopaedic Surgeons, 8,* 277–284.

55. Petrella, R. J. (2005). Hyaluronic acid for the treatment of knee osteoarthritis: Long-term outcomes from a naturalistic primary care experience. *American Journal of Physical Medicine & Rehabilitation, 84,* 278–283.

56. Leopold, S. S., Redd, B. B., Warme, W. J., Wehrle, P. A., Pettis, P. D., & Shott, S. (2003). Corticosteroid compared with hyaluronic acid injections for the treatment of osteoarthritis of the knee. A prospective, randomized trial. *Journal of Bone and Joint Surgery (American Volume), 85,* 1197–1203.

57. White, R., & Henderson, M. (2002). Risk factors for venous thromboembolism after total hip and knee replacement surgery. *Pulmonary Medicine, 8,* 365–371.

58. Kurtz, S. M., Lau, E., Ong, K., Zhao, K., Kelly, M., & Bozic, K. J. (2009). Future young patient demand for primary and revision joint replacement: National projections from 2010 to 2030. *Clinical Orthopaedics and Related Research, Apr 10* [Epub ahead of print].

59. Salsberg, E. S., Grover, A., Simon, M. A., Frick, S. L., Kuremsky, M. A., & Goodman, D. C. (2008). An AOA critical issue. Future physician workforce requirements: Implications for orthopaedic surgery education. *Journal of Bone and Joint Surgery (American Volume), 90,* 1143–1159.

60. Agency for Health Research and Quality. (2008). *2006 national statistics.* Available at hcupnet.ahrq.gov/HCUPnet.jsp.

61. National Osteoporosis Foundation. (2008). *Fast facts on osteoporosis.* Available at www.nof.org/osteoporosis/diseasefacts.htm.

62. Folden, S., & Tappen, R. (2007). Factors influencing function and recovery following hip repair surgery. *Orthopaedic Nursing, 26,* 234–241.

63. Schoen, D. C. (2008). Preventing hip fractures. *Orthopaedic Nursing, 27,* 148–152.

64. Nelson, H. D., Helfand, M., Woolf, S. H., & Allan, J. D. (2002). Screening for postmenopausal osteoporosis: A review of the evidence for the U.S. Preventive Services Task Force. *Annals of Internal Medicine, 137,* 529–541.

65. Licata, A. A. (2007). Update on therapy for osteoporosis. *Orthopaedic Nursing, 26,* 162–166.

ABOUT THE AUTHORS

Lesley J. Anderson, MD is an orthopedic surgeon in private practice in San Francisco. She was the first woman to complete an orthopedic surgery residency at the University of California, Los Angeles. She also completed a fellowship in sports medicine. She specializes in knee and shoulder surgery and reconstruction.

Lynn M. Forsey, PhD, RN is a Nurse Scientist at Stanford Hospital and Clinics in Palo Alto, California. She is responsible for advancing the nursing research and evidenced-based practice programs, and supporting the development of professional nursing. Prior to obtaining her doctorate, she worked in many adult medical/surgical specialties including orthopedics.

CHAPTER 14

"What's That Bump Down There?"

UNIQUE ASPECTS OF BENIGN GYNECOLOGY FOR LESBIANS

CLAIRE HERRICK, MD

ALISON F. JACOBY, MD

STACEY, *a 26-year-old nulliparous lesbian, comes in for a visit at the insistence of her partner, Jean, who felt a bump near Stacey's vagina when they were having sex. Jean is also concerned that Stacey has not had a Pap smear for 5 years—the last one was when she was in college. Stacey says she does not need another Pap smear because, for the previous 3 years, she has been sexually active only with her female partner. Before then, she had had three female and three male partners.*

The clinician tells Stacey that even though her current partner is female, she is still at risk for cervical dysplasia and should receive Pap smears every 2 years until she is 29 years old. After that point, the smears can be every 2—3 years if the previous three have been normal, although Stacey will still need to come in for a physical exam annually for other reasons. After completing Stacey's medical history, the clinician realizes this is a good opportunity to address other health issues: Each day, Stacey consumes alcohol and smokes half a pack of cigarettes.

■ ■ ■

Best practices in women's health care offer guidance on appropriate treatment for patients like Stacey. However, there have been few studies on benign gynecologic conditions in lesbians specifically, although research shows that lesbian sexual identity may affect such conditions.[1] This chapter provides background information on, and treatment options for, benign gynecologic conditions, taking into account the potential influence that sexual identity might have on them.

GYNECOLOGIC HISTORY

Many lesbians have also had male partners, sexually transmitted infections, and abortions; in these respects, they are similar to heterosexual women. But important differences highlight the need for an inclusive and thorough history. The form patients fill out when they arrive for a visit must be one that sexual minority patients feel comfortable completing. In addition to providing a range of options describing their current relationship—choices such as "domestic partner" and "significantly involved" as well as "married" and "single"—the form should explore history of sexual abuse, physical abuse, substance use, intimate partner violence, and current sexual orientation, all of which are especially relevant to lesbian health. Because self-identity may not reflect sexual behavior, clinicians need to determine either on the form or verbally if a patient is currently having sex with men, women, both, or neither. A gynecologic history interview should be done in private, even if the patient's partner accompanies her to the visit.

PELVIC EXAMS

Although most lesbian patients tolerate pelvic exams as well as heterosexual women do, many lesbians experience severe pain when a speculum is inserted, especially if there has not been recent vaginal penetration. Furthermore, because the incidence of childhood sexual abuse is higher among lesbians than among heterosexual women,[2] pelvic exams may add to lesbian patients' discomfort. A supply of pediatric speculums in each exam room for those who cannot tolerate a Graves or Pederson speculum is advisable. In rare cases, lesbians need sedation or general anesthesia for pelvic exams. Cervical cytology screening guidelines should be the same for lesbians and heterosexual women.[3]

Endometrial Biopsy and Ultrasound

If a pelvic exam indicates that an endometrial biopsy or other evaluative procedure is warranted, clinicians should determine if the patient will be able to tolerate it in the office or will need sedation in an ambulatory surgery center. Regarding ultrasound, some lesbians may not be able to tolerate the vaginal probe. In these cases, one option is to perform only an abdominal sonogram.

GYNECOLOGIC CONDITIONS

Abnormal Uterine Bleeding

Abnormal uterine bleeding (AUB) means the frequency and/or quantity of menstrual bleeding is unusual. It includes:

- Oligomenorrhea—menstrual cycles lasting longer than 35 days;
- Polymenorrhea—cycles lasting fewer than 21 days;
- Menorrhagia—an increase in the amount of menstrual blood loss during regular cycles;
- Metrorrhagia—irregular cycles; and
- Menometrorrhagia—greater menstrual bleeding at irregular intervals.

Very little is known about how AUB affects lesbians. Whether incidence differs between lesbians and heterosexual women can only be inferred from associated comorbidities and other causes. For example, average body mass index is higher in lesbians, so they are at greater risk of insulin resistance and polycystic ovarian syndrome, which can be associated with AUB. Prolonged, unopposed estrogen exposure puts all women at higher risk of endometrial hyperplasia and cancer. Because lesbians are less likely to use hormonal contraception than heterosexual women are, they may experience more heavy bleeding and irregular cycles.

The most common causes of AUB are anatomic abnormalities of the uterus, such as fibroids, endometrial cancer, endometrial hyperplasia, adenomyosis, and hormonal abnormalities related to infrequent or absent ovulation. Oligo-ovulatory or anovulatory bleeding results from a build-up of the endometrial lining under persistent exposure to estrogen. Without ovulation, the corpus luteum cyst in the ovary never forms and therefore no progesterone is produced. In ovulatory cycles, a decrease in progesterone levels after involution of the corpus luteum triggers menstruation. In the absence of ovulation, bleeding can be delayed for months; it eventually occurs as the unstable endometrial lining breaks down.

Polycystic ovarian syndrome most commonly causes anovulatory bleeding in women of reproductive age. Other causes are hypothalamic dysfunction as a result of high stress, eating disorders, extreme exercise, pituitary adenomas that produce excess prolactin, and thyroid abnormalities. Hormonal changes leading to anovulatory cycles and AUB often affect adolescents and perimenopausal women. Clinicians frequently overlook thrombophilias and platelet disorders, particularly von Willebrand disease, in work-ups of women with AUB. Ectopic pregnancies or miscarriages may present with heavy or irregular vaginal bleeding. Endometrial polyps also can cause bleeding.

■ ASSESSMENT

Initial assessment of vaginal bleeding in women of reproductive age usually includes a pregnancy test. A common saying among gynecologists is: "Every woman is pregnant until proven otherwise." However, a pregnancy test for patients who self-identify as lesbian presents a special challenge. Clinicians should pose the possibility of pregnancy, when no one else is present, by asking a standard question about sexual behavior: "Are you sexually active with women, men, or both, or have you not been sexually active in the last few months?" A pregnancy test is indicated if there has been sexual activity with men. If the completed medical history form includes a question about sexual orientation, the clinician might ask: "I see you circled lesbian as your sexual orientation. I know that most lesbians are sexually active with women only but that some lesbians also have sex with men. Because I am going to order tests to evaluate your abnormal bleeding, I would also like to order a pregnancy test if you have been sexually active with men in the last few months to be sure that an unrecognized pregnancy is not causing it." A possibility to keep in mind is that sexual assault also can result in pregnancy.

Once pregnancy has been ruled out, evaluation focuses on identifying the anatomic, hormonal, or hematologic causes of AUB. Common diagnostic tests are pelvic ultrasound, endometrial biopsy, complete blood count, and clotting studies for von Willebrand disease.

■ TREATMENT

Treatment for AUB depends on the underlying etiology. Initial treatment usually involves therapies such as contraceptives containing estrogen and progesterone, oral or intramuscular progestins, and the levonorgestrel-releasing intrauterine device.[4] Other options are endometrial ablation, uterine artery embolization, myomectomy, and hysterectomy. A discussion about pregnancy impacts the choice of treatment, as lesbians might want to conceive ultimately. If endometrial biopsy rules out endometrial hyperplasia or cancer, perimenopausal women may benefit from close surveillance and supportive care until menopause, precluding any need for surgery.

Dysmenorrhea

Dysmenorrhea means extremely painful menses. Primary dysmenorrhea refers to painful periods without evidence of an anatomic abnormality; secondary dysmenorrhea is painful periods associated with an anatomic etiology such as fibroids, adenomyosis, or endometriosis. A study of the prevalence of dysmenorrhea among lesbians versus a control group of heterosexual women reported a rate of nearly 50%, but this finding was not statistically significant.[5]

■ ASSESSMENT

Clinicians should ask lesbian patients about dysmenorrhea, as there are many effective treatments.

■ TREATMENT

Most women with dysmenorrhea benefit from nonsteroidal anti-inflammatory drugs. Hormonal menstrual suppression with continuous oral contraceptive pills or progestins are extremely effective. Inadequate response to therapies warrants a diagnostic laparoscopy to rule out endometriosis or pelvic adhesions.

Sexual Dysfunction

Sexual dysfunction may occur less frequently in lesbians than it does in heterosexual women.[6] In one survey, the incidence among lesbians was 23%, and of these, only 3% sought help from a physician.[6] The National Health and Social Life Survey found that 43% of all women ages 18 to 59 experienced a sexual problem.[7] A common topic of discussion in the lesbian community is "lesbian bed death" at the 2-year mark in monogamous, long-term relationships. Tracey and Junginger analyzed correlates of lesbian sexual function in 350 self-identified lesbians. Older age was associated with less sexual desire, greater difficulty with lubrication during sex, and lower scores for overall sexual function. Psychological symptoms were associated with less arousal, pleasure, satisfaction, and overall sexual function, and greater difficulty with lubrication during sex. Higher relationship satisfaction was associated with more arousal during sex, less difficulty with lubrication, greater pleasure/orgasm, more sexual satisfaction, and better overall sexual function.[8]

■ ASSESSMENT

Sexual dysfunction in lesbians may be due to discordant sexual desires in a couple, a common complaint. Discordance can occur if one of the partners is taking an antidepressant that interferes with libido, especially a selective serotonin reuptake inhibitor. Clinicians need to be sensitive when they assess these cases, and consider providing appropriate therapy or referral to a nonjudgmental counselor. A study of sexual function in lesbians after a cancer diagnosis found differences between them and heterosexual women. Lesbians experienced less disruption in their sexual relationships; fewer sexual problems, such as insufficient lubrication and difficulty achieving orgasm; better body image; and more support from their partners.[9]

■ TREATMENT

Treatment varies depending on the particular problem. However, clinicians generally can resolve many problems by listening to the patient, gauging the amount of distress an issue is causing, and asking sensitive questions regarding intimacy, arousal, and other factors. Educating patients about female physiology and sexual response also is important. Pain at the introitus or deep in the pelvis during penetration of the vagina warrants a thorough gynecologic exam. A trial of testosterone patches may help postmenopausal lesbians whose sexual desire has declined. If this problem seems to be related to an antidepressant, switching to an alternative medication or treatment is an option. If past sexual trauma seems to be contributing to sexual dysfunction, referral to a therapist is appropriate.

Polycystic Ovarian Syndrome

Polycystic ovarian syndrome (PCOS) is characterized by infrequent or absent ovulation, resulting in irregular menstrual cycles, long intervals between menses, and heavy, prolonged periods. The classic PCOS phenotype is an obese woman with hirsutism and acne, but many women with PCOS do not have this appearance. Because such women have ovulation abnormalities, they often find it difficult to get pregnant.

■ ASSESSMENT

PCOS is a clinical diagnosis. As such, characteristic menstrual irregularities, rather than abnormal lab or radiographic findings, suggest its presence. If lab tests are performed, an increased luteinizing-hormone/follicle-stimulating hormone ratio is common, estrone levels are higher than estradiol levels, and androstenedione and testosterone levels are normal or above the upper limits of normal. Another common finding, though a PCOS diagnosis does not require it, is multiple small cysts lined up just below the thickened ovarian capsule on ultrasound.

One study reported that 38% of lesbians seeking treatment at a fertility clinic had PCOS compared with 14% of heterosexual women.[10] However, a more recent study of women presenting for donor insemination found that 8% of both lesbians and heterosexual women had PCOS.[11]

Treatment options include hormonal methods, such as oral contraceptives, to regulate menstruation; hirsutism medications, such as spironolactone, that target androgen's effect on hair follicles; and fertility drugs, such as clomiphene citrate, to stimulate ovulation.

Chronic Pelvic Pain

Chronic pelvic pain refers to pain of at least 6 months duration that is severe enough to cause functional disability or require treatment. Although the differential diagnosis is long, the most common conditions are endometriosis, chronic pelvic inflammatory disease, interstitial cystitis, irritable bladder, pelvic floor myalgias, myofascial pain, and neuralgias of the pelvic nerves. Johnson and colleagues found that 28% of lesbians had a history of pelvic pain and that 17% had sought a physician's help.[6]

■ ASSESSMENT

Initial evaluation involves a detailed medical history, including questions about depression and past or current sexual or physical abuse. Then, a thorough pelvic exam pays special attention to the tone/tenderness of the abdominal wall and pelvic floor muscles, and whether or not there is localized or diffuse pain. Depending on the exam findings, a pelvic sonogram may aid the diagnosis. A diagnostic laparoscopy or referral to a pain clinic is indicated in some circumstances.

■ TREATMENT

The pain's etiology determines the type of treatment. Options include nonsteroidal anti-inflammatories, combined oral contraceptives, low-dose tricyclic antidepressants, gabapentin, and trigger point injections. Referral to gastrointestinal and genitourinary specialists is appropriate in the treatment of irritable bowel syndrome and interstitial cystitis, respectively.

Endometriosis

Endometriosis is the presence of endometrial tissue in extrauterine sites, such as the pelvic peritoneum, ovarian capsule, or uterine serosa. This hormonally sensitive tissue triggers an inflammatory response that causes adhesions and scarring. The condition usually affects women of reproductive age. Symptoms in postmenopausal women are rare, but endometriosis can recur in those on hormone replacement therapy. Dysmenorrhea or noncyclic pelvic pain are characteristic symptoms, which may include dyspareunia and dyschezia. The severity of symptoms varies considerably and is not directly related to the extent of visible disease. Although biopsy of the characteristic lesions during laparoscopy or laparotomy is the only definitive way to diagnose endo-metriosis, the diagnosis is often presumed if classic symptoms are present.

There are many theories about the etiology of endometriosis, such as retrograde flow of endometrial tissue through the fallopian tubes, lymphovascular spread, coelomic metaplasia, reduced cellular immunity, and genetic predisposition. But no single theory fully accounts for all of its manifestations.

Endometriosis, a leading cause of infertility, has a prevalence of 0.5% to 5% in fertile women and 25% to 40% in infertile women.[12] In advanced stages, scarring and adhesions can lead to obstruction of the fallopian tubes. Because subfertility is a potential consequence for lesbians as well as heterosexual women, clinicians should not assume lesbian patients are uninterested in future fertility and therefore omit this issue when counseling them about endometriosis.

There is little theoretical reason to suspect a difference in the incidence or presentation of endometriosis in lesbians versus heterosexual women. Studies have found comparable prevalence rates (3% to 4%) in both populations.[5,6] Among all women who undergo laparoscopy, 5% to 15% show signs of endometriosis, and at least a third of those who undergo diagnostic laparoscopy for pelvic pain are diagnosed with endometriosis.[13]

■ ASSESSMENT

Common findings on physical exam include a firmly fixed and retroflexed uterus, nod-ularity on the uterosacral ligaments, and adnexal tenderness. Women with endometrio-sis may have elevated levels of the ovarian tumor marker CA-125, but the lab test for CA-125 is nonspecific and should not be ordered routinely. Microscopic examination of laparoscopically biopsied lesions is the gold standard for definitive diagnosis.

■ TREATMENT

Treatment options include suppression of extra-uterine endometrial tissue with cyclic or continuous oral contraceptives, progestins such as depot medroxyprogesterone ace-tate (Depo-Provera), androgens such as Danazol, and gonadotropin-releasing hormone agonists. Laparoscopic removal of ovarian endometriomas, laser ablation of lesions, and lysis of adhesions may relieve symptoms, although relief might be temporary. For recalcitrant pelvic pain caused by endometriosis, a hysterectomy and bilateral salpingo-oophorectomy may be indicated in women who have completed child-bearing.

Fibroids

Fibroids are benign tumors of the uterine smooth muscle that occur in 25% to 50% of women in their thirties and forties,[14] and more commonly in African Americans.[15] Researchers have not studied the incidence of fibroids in lesbians, but epidemiologic evidence suggests that parity is associated with a lower incidence.[16] Given the lower pregnancy rates among lesbians, they might be more likely than heterosexual women to have fibroids.

Fibroids vary in size—from as small as a pea to as large as a melon—and may be solitary or multiple. Although the etiology is unknown, the inciting event seems to be a genetic alteration in a single uterine muscle cell, proliferation of which is stimulated by estrogen and progesterone. When women with fibroids enter menopause and their hormone levels drop, the fibroids stop growing and gradually become smaller.

The most common fibroid-related symptoms are heavy and prolonged menstrual bleeding, pelvic pressure, heaviness, and discomfort; and frequent urination and nocturia. Urinary retention, urinary incontinence, dyspareunia, and pelvic pain are less frequent complaints. At least half of all women with fibroids do not experience symptoms.[17]

Only 3 in 1,000 presumed fibroids are malignant.[18] Leiomyosarcomas, which can be difficult to distinguish from fibroids radiographically, are more likely to occur in postmenopausal women and are associated with frequent and irregular vaginal bleeding, pelvic pain, and severe bloating. One myth is that rapidly growing fibroids are more likely to be malignant.

■ ASSESSMENT

A routine pelvic exam or palpation of a firm mass in the lower abdomen can usually detect fibroids. Pelvic ultrasound is the best way to confirm a clinical suspicion of fibroid. Pelvic magnetic resonance imaging (MRI) is rarely indicated, but, for treatment purposes, it may help determine the exact number, size, and location of fibroids. Routine ultrasound surveillance is unwarranted. However, follow-up ultrasounds are warranted if symptoms worsen and treatment becomes necessary. Saline sonohysterography and office diagnostic hysteroscopy can determine if submucosal fibroids are present.

■ TREATMENT

Treatment is necessary only when symptoms are severe enough that they impact a woman's quality of life. The clinician should encourage a patient to undergo treatment if, for example, she wakes up multiple times at night to urinate, cannot attend an event because her bladder capacity is so limited, avoids sex due to discomfort, or misses work due to unmanageable heavy bleeding. Other candidates for treatment are women with menorrhagia that causes significant anemia, especially if blood transfusions have been necessary.

Clinicians typically try to reduce heavy bleeding through hormonal management—contraceptive pills, progestins, or intrauterine devices—before they recommend surgery. Uterine artery embolization, myomectomy, and hysterectomy are treatments for symptoms caused by the bulkiness of fibroids. Myomectomy is the treatment of choice for women who want to remain fertile or keep their uterus. Depending on the number, size, and location of fibroids, the procedure can be hysteroscopic, laparoscopic, or abdominal. Similarly, hysterectomy can be vaginal, laparoscopic, or abdominal. Physicians must thoroughly explain the treatment options to patients because each alternative has different implications. Clinicians also must respect a woman's possible desire to keep her uterus even if she does not plan to bear children.

Adnexal Masses

Adnexal masses include a variety of physiologic, inflammatory, and neoplastic growths on the fallopian tubes and ovaries. There are no published data on the prevalence of adnexal masses in lesbians versus heterosexual women.[*]

■ ASSESSMENT

Symptoms of adnexal masses include dysmenorrhea, pelvic pain or pressure, dyspareunia, and, rarely, gastrointestinal symptoms. Endometriomas, dermoids, and cystadenomas are common benign cysts. Simple cysts are unilocular and thin-walled, and either follicular cysts or benign cystadenomas. Complex cysts contain multiple septations and/or solid components. A cyst containing blood products is a hemorrhagic corpus luteum or an endometrioma. Follicular and corpus luteum cysts regress over 6 to 12 weeks; cystadenomas and endometriomas, in contrast, persist or enlarge over that time period.

Detecting adnexal masses in women who have a high body mass index can be challenging. The primary diagnostic modality for all women is pelvic ultrasound, with MRI reserved for cases in which ultrasound does not lead to a diagnosis.

Another relatively common type of adnexal mass is a tubo-ovarian abscess (TOA), which can present as a persistent cystic remnant of previously treated pelvic inflammatory disease (PID). Women who have acute PID with a TOA present with an adnexal mass and fever, lower abdominal pain, and cervical motion tenderness. Although unusual in lesbians, TOA and acute PID are worth considering, especially in lesbians who are sexually active with both women and men. Sexually transmitted bacteria as well as gastrointestinal bacteria, like those in a polymicrobial infection such as diverticulitis, cause PID. Lesbians who engage in penetrative sexual contact with fingers or sex toys may inadvertently introduce gastrointestinal bacteria into the vagina and cervix. Therefore, clinicians should not rule out acute PID in the differential diagnosis based on assumptions about lesbian sexual practices.

---

[*] *The discussion here focuses on benign, rather than malignant, adnexal masses.*

■ TREATMENT

Initial treatment for TOA and PID is intravenous antibiotics.[†] A patient with a TOA who does not respond to antibiotics may need a hysterectomy and bilateral salpingo-oophorectomy.

General principles of cyst management dictate that clinicians consider surgical removal if a simple cyst is larger than 8 cm on initial presentation or larger than 5 cm on serial ultrasounds over several cycles, or if a cyst is complex. Delaying cystectomy carries the risk of ovarian torsion, failure to detect a borderline or malignant neoplasm in a timely manner, and more difficult surgery as the mass grows.

The usual treatment for cystadenomas, dermoids, and endometriomas is laparoscopic ovarian cystectomy. Because complex masses raise greater concern about malignancy, they warrant a salpingo-oophorectomy. Surgeons should carefully avoid spilling the contents of a complex cyst, as doing so affects cancer staging if the mass is malignant.

Vaginitis

Vaginitis, specifically bacterial vaginosis (BV), is one of the most common topics in the limited literature on lesbian health. A persistent question over the decades has been whether women can sexually transmit BV to other women.

BACTERIAL VAGINOSIS

■ ASSESSMENT

BV results from a shift in normal vaginal flora from acid-producing strains of lactobacilli to other species, most commonly *Gardnerella vaginalis*, anaerobes, and mycoplasmas. The most characteristic symptoms are vulvo-vaginal irritation and a grayish, watery, foul-smelling vaginal discharge. Sometimes BV is asymptomatic. A BV diagnosis is warranted when investigation reveals three of these four conditions:

1. A vaginal discharge;
2. A strong fishy odor emanating from a vaginal discharge sample mixed with potassium chloride;
3. An elevated pH, measured by touching a vaginal discharge sample to nitrazine paper; and
4. Detection on light microscopy of "clue cells"—epithelial cells whose edges are obscured by bacteria.

[†] *See Workowski, K. A., & Berman, S. M. (2006). Sexually transmitted diseases treatment guidelines, 2006. Morbidity and Mortality Weekly Report, 55, 1–94. Available at www.cdc.gov/mmwr/preview/ mmwrhtml/rr5511a1.htm.*

Several studies have reported higher rates of BV in lesbians than in heterosexual women, although others have reported similar rates. Among 363 women having sex with women, Marrazzo found a significantly greater prevalence than expected. Risk factors for BV included more lifetime female sexual partners, failure to always clean an insertive sex toy before use, and oral-anal sex with a female partner. Neither recent douching nor sexual practices with male partners were associated with BV. These data support the hypothesis that sexual exchange of vaginal secretions is a possible way to contract the disease.[19]

■ TREATMENT

Metronidazole, administered either orally or vaginally, is a treatment option. In the past, clinicians informed heterosexual women that BV is not a sexually transmitted infection and that their male partners do not need therapy. However, given the evidence for BV transmission between female sexual partners, it is reasonable to encourage both partners in a female couple to be evaluated for BV and to simultaneously undergo treatment if the results are positive.

VAGINAL CANDIDIASIS

Vaginal candidiasis is an overgrowth of yeast, usually of *Candida albicans*. The infection may be slightly more prevalent among lesbians as a result of woman-to-woman transmission.[20]

■ ASSESSMENT

The typical diagnostic sign of vaginal yeast infection is a cottage cheese-like vaginal discharge amid vulvar and vaginal pruritus, usually in the presence of budding yeast on a saline or KOH wet prep. In some cases of culture-proven yeast candidiasis, the slide may not reveal budding yeast.

■ TREATMENT

First-round treatment of lesbians with symptomatic candidiasis is an over-the-counter, topical antifungal such as clotrimazole (Gyne-Lotrimin or MONISTAT, for example) or one oral dose of the prescription medication fluconazole (Diflucan) if there is no liver impairment. Initially, only the infected woman needs treatment. But if infections recur, also treating her partner, taking cultures for unusual strains of candida, and screening for diabetes are warranted.

TRICHOMONAS VAGINITIS

Infection with *Trichomonas vaginalis*, a parasitic protozoan, often presents as vaginal irritation and pruritus with a greenish vaginal discharge.

■ ASSESSMENT

Microscopic examination of the vaginal discharge mixed with normal saline confirms the diagnosis if *T. vaginalis* is visible.

■ TREATMENT

An oral antiprotozoal medication (Flagyl)—typically one, 2.0 gm dose—is the most effective treatment. Due to the highly infectious nature of *T. vaginalis* and its ability to survive on fomites such as towels or bathtubs, also treating the patient's female or male partner is advisable.

ATROPHIC VAGINITIS

Atrophic vaginitis is an inflammation of the vagina due to thinning of the endothelium when the body produces less estrogen. Postmenopausal women frequently complain of vaginal atrophy.

■ ASSESSMENT

Symptoms that usually confirm the diagnosis are atrophy, vaginal dryness, pruritus, discomfort, and pain on penetration. One measure of atrophy is the percentage of superficial cells in the vaginal maturation index.

■ TREATMENT

Effective treatments are hormone-containing creams, pessaries, tablets, and vaginal rings.[21] However, patients must not use them excessively because systemic absorption of the hormones can cause the endometrial lining and breast tissue to proliferate.

CONTRACEPTION

Globally, contraception management remains one of the major entry points to medical care for women of reproductive age. Women often link their need for a refill of birth control pills to their annual preventive health visit. Many lesbians do not receive routine screening because there is no impetus for them to obtain contraceptives and they anticipate or have had negative interaction with the health care system due to their sexual orientation. Gynecologic visits that include questions about sexual activity and birth control can be very stressful for lesbians in an environment they perceive as unsafe. This may prompt them to avoid or delay seeking medical attention or getting screened.

While birth control questions from a health care provider can be off-putting for lesbian patients, studies show that around 77% to 80% of self-identified lesbians have had sex with men at some point in their lives.[22,23] Fifty-three percent have used birth control pills at some point[22] and 5.7% have had intercourse with men within the last year.[23] Therefore, clinicians should not assume that a woman who has sex with women does not need birth control or education about safer sex. In one study, only 69% of lesbians who reported having sex with men indicated they had ever used a condom for vaginal intercourse, and 15.8% had had anal intercourse without using a condom.[23]

About 25% of lesbians report they were previously pregnant, and of these pregnancies, 26% occurred during adolescence.[22] Unintended pregnancies are more prevalent among lesbian female youth than they are among heterosexual female youth, according to national survey data.[24]

Contraceptive options for lesbians are the same as those for heterosexual women, although certain circumstances warrant consideration. If a lesbian patient is having sporadic sexual intercourse with a man, it might be more appropriate to counsel her to use condoms and spermicide, and to educate her about Plan B, the "morning-after pill," in case the condom breaks. If a lesbian patient has frequent sex with a male partner, the best option is reliable daily contraception—birth control pills or an intrauterine device and, if appropriate, condoms for protection from sexually transmitted infection. Patients who prefer not to be seen in the local pharmacy purchasing contraceptives should know that they can order items by mail.

■ ■ ■

In the scenario at the beginning of this chapter, Stacey underwent a pelvic exam as her partner held her hand. Stacey's high body mass index made the exam difficult. Nevertheless, despite some discomfort, she was able to tolerate the speculum long enough for purposes of a Pap smear and screening cultures for chlamydia and gonorrhea. The exam did not reveal any masses or tenderness. A sebaceous cyst on the right vulva accounted for the bump Stacey's partner had felt. The clinician reassured Stacey that the cyst was benign and could be excised if it bothered her, and ordered a rapid plasma reagin test, a complete blood count, and tests for fasting blood glucose and HIV antibodies.

Stacey received the phone number of a smoking cessation program and chose a quit date. She planned to return for a follow-up visit the week after that target date. She promised to start an exercise program and reduce her alcohol consumption. Stacey said she is not interested in attending Alcoholics Anonymous because she thinks she can drink less without help, which the clinician will confirm on the follow-up visit to review the lab results. The clinician told Stacey that lesbians are among the practice's patients and expressed an eagerness to help her manage her health.

CONCLUSION

Clinicians can improve lesbians' gynecologic health in numerous ways. One is to encourage them to disclose their sexual orientation/behavior, then screen for sexually transmitted infection if appropriate, and assess the need for birth control. Another is to follow standard Pap smear recommendations even if patients have never been sexually active with men. In addition, clinicians should be aware that bacterial vaginosis is probably more prevalent among lesbians than it is among heterosexual women, and that lesbians may be at higher risk of endometrial and ovarian cancer due to a greater likelihood of nulliparity and other risk factors. Finally, because lesbians, like heterosexual women, can experience sexual dysfunction, treatment and sensitive referrals may be necessary.

REFERENCES

1. Hiestand, K. R., Horne, S. G., & Levitt, H. M. (2007). Effects of gender identity on experiences of healthcare for sexual minority women. *Journal of LGBT Health Research, 3,* 15–27.

2. Stoddard, J., Dibble, S. L., & Fineman, N. (2009). Sexual and physical abuse: A comparison between lesbians and their heterosexual sisters. *Journal of Homosexuality, 56,* 407–420.

3. ACOG Committee on Practice Bulletins – Gynecologic (2009). ACOG Practice Bulletin No. 109: Cervical cytology screening. *Obstetrics & Gynecology, 114,* 1409–1420.

4. Mansour, D. (2007). Modern management of abnormal uterine bleeding: The levonorgestrel intra-uterine system. *Best Practice & Research. Clinical Obstetrics & Gynaecology, 21,* 1007–1021.

5. Johnson, S., Smith, E., & Guenther, S. (1987). Comparison of gynecologic health problems between lesbians and bisexual women. *Journal of Reproductive Medicine, 32,* 805–810.

6. Johnson, S., Guenther, S., Laube, D., & Keettel, W. (1981). Factors influencing lesbian gynecologic care: A preliminary study. *American Journal of Obstetrics & Gynaecology, 140,* 20–25.

7. Lauman, E. O., Paik, A., & Rosen, R. C. (1999). Sexual dysfunction in the United States: Prevalence and predictors. *Journal of the American Medical Association, 281,* 537–544.

8. Tracey, J. K., & Junginger, J. (2007). Correlates of lesbian sexual functioning. *Journal of Women's Health, 16,* 499–509.

9. Boehmer, U., Potter, J., & Bowen, D. J. (2009). Sexual functioning after cancer in sexual minority women. *Cancer Journal, 15,* 65–69.

10. Agrawal, R., Sharma, S., Bekir, J., Conway, G., Bailey, J., Balen, A. H., et al. (2004). Prevalence of polycystic ovaries and polycystic ovary syndrome in lesbian women compared with heterosexual women. *Fertility and Sterility, 82,* 1352–1357.

11. De Sutter, P., Dutré, T., Vanden Meerschaut, F., Stuyver, I., Van Maele, G., & Dhont, M. (2008). PCOS in lesbian and heterosexual women treated with artificial donor insemination. *Reproductive BioMedicine Online, 17,* 398–402.

12. Ozkan, S., Murk, W., & Arici, A. (2008). Endometriosis and infertility: Epidemiology and evidence-based treatments. *Annals of the New York Academy of Sciences, 1127,* 92–100.

13. Howard, F. M. (2000). The role of laparoscopy as a diagnostic tool in chronic pelvic pain. *Best Practice & Research. Clinical Obstetrics & Gynaecology, 14,* 467–494.

14. Buttram, V. C. Jr., & Reiter, R. C. (1981). Uterine leiomyomata: Etiology, symptomatology, and management. *Fertility and Sterility, 36,* 433–445.

15. Marshall, L. M., Spiegelman, D., Barbieri, R. L., Goldman, M. B., Manson, J. E., Colditz, G. A., et al. (1997). Variation in the incidence of uterine leiomyoma among premenopausal women by age and race. *Obstetrics & Gynecology, 90,* 967–973.

16. Parazzini, F., Negri, E., La Vecchia, C., Chatenoud, L., Ricci, E., & Guarnerio, P. (1996). Reproductive factors and risk of uterine fibroids. *Epidemiology, 7,* 440–442.

17. Stovall, D. W. (2001). Clinical symptomatology of uterine leiomyomas. *Clinical Obstetrics and Gynecology, 44,* 364–371.

18. Parker, W. H., Fu, Y. S., & Berek, J. S. (1994). Uterine sarcoma in patients operated on for presumed leiomyoma and rapidly growing leiomyoma. *Obstetrics & Gynecology, 83,* 414–418.

19. Marrazzo, J. M., Koutsky, L. A., Eschenbach, D. A., Agnew, K., Stine, K., & Hillier, S. L. (2002). Characterization of vaginal flora and bacterial vaginosis in women who have sex with women. *Journal of Infectious Diseases, 185,* 1307–1313.

20. Bailey, J. V., Benato, R., Owen, C., & Kavanagh, J. (2008). Vulvovaginal candidiasis in women who have sex with women. *Sexually Transmitted Diseases, 35,* 533–536.

21. Suckling, J., Lethaby, A., & Kennedy, R. (2006). Local oestrogen for vaginal atrophy in postmenopausal women. *Cochrane Database of Systematic Reviews,* Oct 18, CD001500.

22. Marrazzo, J., & Stine, K. (2004). Reproductive health history of lesbians: Implications for care. *American Journal of Obstetrics & Gynaecology, 190,* 1298–1304.

23. Diamant, A. L., Schuster, M. A., McGuigan, K., & Lever, J. (1999). Lesbians' sexual history with men: Implications for taking a sexual history. *Archives of Internal Medicine, 159,* 2730–2736.

24. Saewyc, E. M., Bearinger, L. H., Blum, R. W., & Resnick, M. D. (1999). Sexual intercourse, abuse and pregnancy among adolescent women: Does sexual orientation make a difference? *Family Planning Perspectives, 31,* 127–131.

ABOUT THE AUTHORS

Claire Herrick, MD is a senior resident in obstetrics and gynecology in the Department of Obstetrics, Gynecology and Reproductive Sciences at the University of California, San Francisco. Her clinical interests include global women's health, reproductive health of the women in East Africa, and history of science. She hopes to return to Tanzania to continue her work on repairing obstetric fistulas.

Alison F. Jacoby, MD is Professor in the Department of Obstetrics, Gynecology & Reproductive Sciences at the University of California, San Francisco. She is also the founder and Director of the Comprehensive Fibroid Center there. Her research focuses on new treatments for fibroids and understanding factors that contribute to decisions by women about fibroid therapy.

CHAPTER 15

"Is It Hot in Here or Is It Just Me?"

MENOPAUSE AND LESBIANS

SUSAN R. JOHNSON, MD, MS

JANE, 42, *is a partnered woman who had regular menstrual periods, without any problems, until the last 6 months. She has noticed that her periods are a bit closer together. In addition, her menstrual flow is considerably heavier, she is experiencing increasingly frequent episodes of intense heat, and she has felt more fatigued in recent weeks. Her general health is good and there are no significant illnesses in her family history.*

When Jane's gynecologist suggests that she might be entering menopause, Jane responds: "This can't possibly be menopause—I'm too young! And how could I be having hot flashes if I'm still having periods? What's that about? Isn't there a blood test that can tell me if I am in menopause? I'm also a little worried about the increased menstrual flow. I wonder if I have cancer. Will I need a hysterectomy? If this is menopause, should I take hormones, like my mother did? My partner says they're too dangerous. Everything I read on the Web is different. What's the truth? Are there any other treatments for hot flashes?"

■ ■ ■

Findings over the last decade from randomized trials of hormone treatment have dramatically altered the medical profession's understanding of menopause. Research has included the Women's Health Initiative[1] and longitudinal studies of the menopause transition, the largest being the Study of Women Across the Nation.[2] Clinicians need to educate middle-age women about the menopause transition and postmenopause stage, sort out which presenting symptoms are attributable to menopause, offer evidence-based treatment options for the related symptoms, and recommend screening and interventions for the age-related chronic diseases that begin to emerge during this phase of life.[*]

This chapter summarizes current thinking and controversies regarding the menopause experience, and discusses management of and treatment for bothersome symptoms.

LESBIANS AND MENOPAUSE

Very little research has focused on health issues related to lesbians in middle age, and none on their menopause experience. The consequences of obesity and excessive alcohol and tobacco use, which are more common among lesbians, accelerate in midlife. The fact that lesbians are less likely to have health insurance, seek health care, or undergo screening magnifies these risks.[3,4] The postmenopause and the transition to it are normal phases of life. Because lesbians almost certainly experience the same range of symptoms and encounter the same issues as heterosexual women do, clinicians who treat middle-age lesbians must be knowledgeable about the medical aspects of menopause.

The experience of and attitudes toward menopause are complex and affected by race, ethnicity, socioeconomic status, education, and "marital status." Thus, lesbians may report experiences that differ from those of heterosexual women. For example,

---

[*] *See the North American Menopause Society's position statements regarding management of menopausal symptoms and problems at www.menopause.org/aboutmeno/consensus.aspx.*

Galavotti and Richter compared attitudes about hysterectomy, oophorectomy, and hormone treatment among multicultural, multiethnic focus groups of women in midlife. One of the study centers included a group of partnered lesbians. The main differences between this group and heterosexual women who had male partners was that female partners were more likely to be supportive and there was no concern that a hysterectomy might disrupt the lesbian relationship.[5] To the extent that lesbians may be less concerned about menopause-related infertility or the "loss of femininity" associated with loss of periods, they may have a more positive outlook on this phase than heterosexual women do.

Finally, evidence suggests that lesbians are more likely to use complementary and alternative medicine (CAM), such as herbs, to treat menopause-related symptoms.[6] Clinicians must be prepared to describe the evidence for the potential risks and benefits of these treatments, and to ask patients if they are using CAM, as some women do not automatically disclose this information. A large randomized trial showed that black cohosh, a frequently recommended treatment for hot flashes, has no proven benefit and may pose a low risk of liver toxicity.[7]

THE BIOLOGY OF MENOPAUSE

The underlying biology of menopause is not fully understood. The prevailing theory is that the loss of ovarian follicles below a critical mass, which begins before a female is born, dictates the timing of menopause. Newer evidence suggests that the hypothalamus may influence the timing—that the hypothalamus and pituitary gland become insensitive to estrogen.[8] The primary hormonal changes associated with postmenopausal status, in contrast to premenopause, are a marked decrease in estradiol, the disappearance of progesterone, and a marked increase in follicle-stimulating hormone (FSH) and luteinizing hormone (LH).

The defining event of menopause is the final menstrual period (FMP), which can only be determined after 12 months of amenorrhea. The average age at menopause for White women is 51 years.[9] However, the normal age range is wide—40 to 60 years. A variety of factors affect the age at which the FMP occurs. Smoking has toxic effects on the ovaries and is associated with an earlier-than-expected FMP. In addition, a family history of very early or very late menopause is associated with the same outcome in daughters. Thus, it may be possible in the future to calculate with some precision the expected FMP date in women who have entered the transition.

In pursuit of this idea, Santoro and colleagues found that a woman's current age, menstrual cycle pattern, current smoking status, and selected hormone measurements were predictive of the FMP. A profile of older age, current smoking, more menstrual irregularity, and higher FSH was associated with a shorter time to the FMP. One counter-intuitive finding was that an estradiol value above the normal range (> 100 pg/mL) predicted a shorter interval compared to a value in the normal premenopausal range. This effect was inexplicably different in African American versus White women.[10]

DIAGNOSIS AND EVALUATION

Determining if a woman is postmenopausal or nearly so is usually straightforward. For women 47 years old or older who have missed several periods and are experiencing vasomotor symptoms, there is almost no other explanation; hormone testing is unnecessary. Women younger than 40 who present with these conditions need further evaluation for possible premature, spontaneous menopause. Women between these two age groups who have prolonged amenorrhea should be evaluated based on the clinical presentation, and an FSH level should be obtained. If the level is above 40 miu/L in a woman who has had amenorrhea for a number of months, ovarian insufficiency is likely and menopause might be the cause.[11]

Premature Spontaneous Menopause

About 1% of women experience spontaneous loss of ovarian function before age 40. Premature menopause can occur earlier as a statistical phenomenon—that is, at the tail end of the normal range that falls below the arbitrary definition of normal—or as a result of pathologic conditions. It is referred to as "premature ovarian failure" or, more recently, "ovarian insufficiency." The latter term is probably better because spontaneous resumption of ovarian activity is not uncommon. Indeed, about 5% to 10% of women with ovarian insufficiency become pregnant. Thus, women with this condition who are sexually active with men should be advised to use contraception if they want to avoid pregnancy. Because oral contraceptives are not as effective in women who have a high FSH level, barrier methods or an intrauterine device are preferable.[12]

Girls with primary amenorrhea and all women younger than 40 who present with secondary amenorrhea should be evaluated for ovarian insufficiency by measuring their FSH level, even if other menopausal symptoms are absent. In most cases, confirming this level with a repeat test and measuring the levels of LH (which should be elevated) and estradiol (which should be low) are a good idea.

Nonspecialists should consider referring women with a suspected diagnosis of primary or secondary amenorrhea, after pregnancy has been ruled out, to a reproductive endocrinologist, as the recommendations for further diagnostic testing, treatment, and follow-up are constantly evolving. Further testing will usually be performed to determine the etiology of the ovarian insufficiency, although testing does not yield a pathologic cause in 90% of cases. The specific battery of recommended tests depends on the patient's age and other signs and symptoms.[13]

Regardless of the etiology, clinicians should offer hormone treatment to women who are experiencing early menopause, unless such treatment is clearly contraindicated, to protect against bone loss and to prevent or treat vasomotor symptoms and vaginal atrophy. A diagnosis of early menopause can have devastating emotional consequences, especially for the very young and for patients who postponed child-bearing. Although diagnosis and clinical management are fairly straightforward, the clinician must be prepared to provide support and referrals for the difficult emotional issues that often arise.

The Menopause Transition

The simple definition of the menopause transition is the time from the beginning of changes in ovarian function to the final menstrual period—that is, the transition from pre- to postmenopausal status.[14] Currently, clinicians can only give rough advice to women about the possible timing of their FMP, but an understanding of the menopause transition will enhance that advice. On average, the transition lasts about 4 years, although duration varies considerably. Because the lower boundary of a normal, final menstrual period is age 40, clinical signs of the transition may first appear in the late thirties in some women. Thus, women in this age group who experience changes in menses and/or have hot flashes should be assessed for menopause transition. There are "early" and "late" parts in the transition, which is defined by clinical features rather than hormone levels.

Subtle changes in the menstrual cycle characterize the early transition. The first change is a shortening of the intermenstrual interval by 6 or more days—for example, from 30 to 24 days.[15] About half of women experience hot flashes. The FSH level may be in the premenopausal range or slightly elevated. Estradiol levels are usually in the normal premenopausal range and may be higher than average.[16] The variability of estradiol levels might explain the hot flashes despite normal estrogen levels.

Increasingly irregular menstrual periods (the hallmark is ≥ 60 days of amenorrhea) and a sharp increase in the prevalence of hot flashes characterize the late transition.[17] FSH levels rise and estradiol levels fall toward the postmenopausal range. Again, menstrual patterns vary considerably among women.

CLINICAL ISSUES IN THE MENOPAUSE TRANSITION

■ ABNORMAL BLEEDING

A minority of women in the menopause transition present with bleeding problems. The majority have a bleeding pattern that is not usually problematic; most of them experience more time between periods and a lightening of flow until the final period, defined as a period followed by at least 12 months of amenorrhea. A few go from an early transition pattern to the final menstrual period without a discernable late phase.

For the minority of women with bleeding at irregular intervals, the cause is probably "hormone changes" (anovulatory cycles) associated with the transition. Among the causes of heavy bleeding that occurs at regular intervals are underlying uterine pathology (endometrial hyperplasia/neoplasia, submucous leiomyomas, or endometrial polyps) and systemic pathology (hypothyroidism or Von Willebrand disease). If there is no underlying condition, the term "idiopathic menorrhagia" applies. Women with heavy vaginal bleeding and regular or irregular cycles must be evaluated for possible underlying causes before treatment proceeds. A basic evaluation of abnormal uterine bleeding should include an assessment for anemia and thyroid function, and a transvaginal ultrasound, the findings of which determine the need for further endometrial evaluation, including endometrial biopsy.[18]

Most abnormal bleeding can be managed without resorting to hysterectomy. Effective treatments for idiopathic menorrhagia are prostaglandin synthetase inhibitors, such as mefenamic acid[19]; oral contraceptives; tranexamic acid, an antifibrinolytic[20]; the levonorgestrel intrauterine device[21]; or endometrial ablation.[22] Irregular, anovulatory bleeding can be managed with combined oral contraceptives or continuous progestin—either a progestin-only contraceptive or medroxyprogesterone (Depo-Provera).

■ VASOMOTOR SYMPTOMS

The prevalence of vasomotor symptoms—hot flashes, cold flashes, and night sweats—peaks in the late menopause transition and in early postmenopause. More than three-quarters of women experience these symptoms at some level. Five years after their FMP, most women see a marked reduction in symptoms, but 10% to 15% have vasomotor symptoms that persist indefinitely.[23]

The pathophysiology of symptoms is complex and not completely understood. The body's "thermostat" apparently resets during the menopause transition, such that smaller changes in core body temperature lead to vasodilatation and sweating (when the temperature exceeds the upper threshold) or shivering (when the temperature falls below the lower threshold).[24]

Vasomotor symptoms can adversely affect quality of life, as they are associated with sleep disturbance and disturbed mood. Risk factors include smoking, anxiety, and alcohol and caffeine consumption. The prevailing notion is that overweight women should have fewer vasomotor symptoms because of higher endogenous estrone, which fat cells produce. In fact, the opposite is true. Women with a high body mass index and, specifically, high abdominal adiposity are at greater risk of hot flashes.[25] Cultural and racial/ethnic differences in reporting hot flashes suggest that other factors also play a role.

Most women do not seek treatment, either because they prefer to "wait it out" or symptoms are not particularly bothersome. Common strategies that may minimize symptom severity include reducing the room temperature, using a fan, and wearing layered clothing so items can be quickly removed or added as needed. If alcohol or caffeine triggers symptoms, eliminating or moderating consumption may help. Other potential remedies are management of anxiety, which is associated with both the onset and severity of vasomotor symptoms,[26] and regular moderate exercise.[27]

Efficacy varies among the many different treatments for symptoms. The most common treatments are hormonal and nonhormonal medications and botanicals. Estrogen remains the gold standard.[28,29] The prevailing notion before the Women's Health Initiative was that effective treatment required a threshold dose of estrogen. Studies since then have found that estrogen's effect is dose-dependent and that even very low doses can be beneficial.[30] The addition of progestin improves its effectiveness.[31] Estrogen doses can be administered orally, vaginally, or transdermally via a patch, gel, or cream. For women in early menopause transition, combined oral contraceptives, unless contraindicated, are best.[32]

Some women cannot safely take estrogen or they prefer not to. Several drugs are superior to placebo for treating hot flashes, including two classes of antidepressants (selective serotonin reuptake inhibitors and serotonin-norepinephrine reuptake inhibitors), gabapentin, and clonidine.[33–35] None are as effective as estrogen. The choice of drug depends on cost and the woman's preferences regarding side effects. Gabapentin is administered as 900 mg daily in a divided dose. Side effects include dizziness, somnolence, and nausea. Clonidine is usually administered in a dose of 0.05 mg to 0.15 mg per day. The results of clinical trials on clonidine's efficacy are mixed, with about half showing a benefit and the other half showing no benefit.[35]

Among the most common botanicals for treating vasomotor symptoms are isoflavones, a class of phytoestrogens in certain plants, including soy and legumes. However, well-designed studies have not demonstrated their effectiveness.[35] The idea that isoflavones might reduce vasomotor symptoms is based on observations of women in the Pacific Rim whose diets are high in soy-based foods and who report a low rate of hot flashes. Red clover, products with isoflavone extracts, and foods such as soy milk, tofu, and soy protein contain significant amounts of isoflavones. A study that rigorously assessed well-designed, randomized, placebo-controlled clinical trials of isoflavone-containing therapies concluded that such therapies are not effective.[35] Nor has research shown that evening primrose oil, dong quai, ginseng, and wild yam are effective.[29]

Findings from clinical trials of black cohosh for treating menopausal symptoms have been mixed. Black cohosh is the most widely used herb for treating vasomotor symptoms. One large, well-designed trial found no benefit during 1 year of use.[7] Black cohosh is usually portrayed as a safe alternative, even if it is not necessarily effective, but it has never undergone rigorous safety testing. Furthermore, clinical studies lasted a year or less and comprised too few participants to assess the risk of uncommon adverse events. Several case reports have cited fulminate liver failure leading to death or requiring liver transplantation.[36] Although a cause-and-effect relationship has not been conclusively established, clinicians should be aware of possible severe side effects.

■ VAGINAL DRYNESS

Vaginal dryness usually presents as a problem related to sexual function; discomfort is associated with vaginal penetration by fingers, sex toys, or a penis. Estrogen deficiency is not the only cause of dryness, and dryness is not strongly associated with the menopause transition.[37] Other common causes are oral contraceptive pills and various medications, such as aromatase inhibitors.[38] Perhaps the most common cause of dryness associated with sexual function is inadequate arousal. Clinicians should consider these other causes before they prescribe estrogen therapy.

When a loss of estrogen is the cause of dryness related to sexual function, most women benefit from estrogen treatment—largely to improve sexual function and satisfaction—and clinicians should encourage them to consider local therapy. Low-dose estrogen cream (≤ 0.5 g), the low-dose vaginal ring (Estring), and vaginal estrogen tablets (Vagifem) are highly effective. Each is associated with some systemic absorption, but the amount absorbed is quite small. Long-term safety is not guaranteed, but any risks are likely to be much less than those associated with systemic therapy. Alternatives to estrogen are water-soluble lubricants for use before vaginal penetration during sex and vaginal moisturizers for use on a regular schedule.

OTHER COMMON ISSUES

During the menopause transition, the risk of conceiving markedly declines. However, pregnancies do occur. The risk of unintended pregnancy may not be a concern for most lesbians, but lesbians and bisexual women who engage in even occasional heterosexual sex need to be aware that irregular periods are not protective. Contraceptive options include the pill,[32] intrauterine devices,[39] and barrier methods.

Although sexual dysfunction is common in all age groups, sexual desire (libido) decreases with age, sometimes due to untreated, menopause-related vaginal symptoms. The role of the menopause transition in this decline, independent of aging, is unclear. Clinicians should become familiar with the new model of female sexual function that Basson describes.[40] The U.S. Food and Drug Administration (FDA) has not approved testosterone treatment for women, so it is warranted only in carefully selected cases due to a theoretical risk of long-term side effects.[41] Women who have undergone premenopausal oophorectomy are most likely to benefit.

Urinary incontinence increases with age and is more common in women who are parous, obese, diabetic, and in generally poor health.[42] The menopause transition does not appear to affect the occurrence of incontinence.[43] Hormone therapy increases the incidence of incontinence as well as the severity of incontinence that is present when estrogen treatment begins.[44]

The menopause transition increases the risk of obesity, metabolic syndrome, and hypertension, all of which are major risk factors for cardiovascular disease.[45] Hormone treatment does not cause weight gain.

Irritability and depressive mood symptoms appear to be associated with the menopause transition,[46,47] but clinicians should always consider other explanations. Major depressive disorder, in particular, may occur for the first time during the transition. The effect of hormone treatment on minor, transition-associated mood symptoms may be positive, but it is not an appropriate therapy for major depression.

Women in the transition are also at higher risk of sleep problems.[48] The traditional view has been that vasomotor symptoms at night ("night sweats") are the primary cause of sleep disturbance in the menopause transition and after menopause. However, better sleep-disorder evaluation methods reveal that for up to half of perimenopausal women who present with a sleep problem, there is a different explanation, such as restless leg syndrome or sleep apnea.[49] If a short trial of hormone therapy does not effectively relieve the problem, further diagnostic evaluation is warranted.

Finally, women in the menopause transition commonly report memory problems and difficulty concentrating. Some of these difficulties are age-related—they also occur in men of the same age. The transition may have an independent but transitory adverse effect on memory and concentration. In women who also have significant hot flashes, hormone treatment may help. Postmenopausal women with these complaints but no hot flashes do not benefit from such treatment, and women older than 65 who start hormones are at greater risk of mild cognitive impairment and dementia.[50,51]

RISKS AND BENEFITS OF HORMONE THERAPY

In July 2002, researchers in the Women's Health Initiative (WHI) first announced the primary endpoints of the estrogen/progestin, placebo-controlled, randomized clinical trial.[52] Prescriptions for estrogen and progestin dropped by 30% almost immediately, including among women who took only estrogen or who did not otherwise fit the profile of the WHI participants. Since then, many other studies have followed up on the WHI's findings.[53]

The major conclusion of the WHI hormone therapy research still holds: older women generally should not start taking long-term, standard-dose, combined estrogen/progestin nor undergo estrogen-only therapy to prevent chronic disease. Estrogen with progestin increases the risk of breast cancer, stroke, heart attack, and thromboembolic events. In a randomized trial that assigned women treated for breast cancer to hormone therapy or placebo, those who received such therapy had a higher risk of cancer recurrence.[54] Estrogen alone increases the risk of stroke and probably thromboembolic events but not the risk of breast cancer, based on the original WHI results and a 10-year follow-up of the cohort.[55] Both types of hormone therapy increase the risk of mild cognitive impairment—a strong risk factor for dementia—in women older than 65,[50] and the risk of urinary incontinence.[56]

The question of whether the timing of estrogen therapy matters in terms of cardiovascular disease risk or prevention is still open; researchers are investigating this possibility. A reanalysis of the WHI data found that participants between 50 and 60 years old did not experience more heart disease events during the trials.[57]

Until relatively recently, hormone therapy was the only effective way to treat and prevent osteoporosis. Clinicians should consult the 2008 revised guidelines from the National Osteoporosis Foundation for up-to-date screening, diagnosis, and treatment recommendations.[58] Adequate calcium and vitamin D are necessary for optimal bone health, and supplementation with either or both reduces the risk of fracture, although not to the same extent as pharmacologic therapy.[59]

Both estrogen and estrogen/progestin have demonstrated they prevent vertebral and hip fractures.[53] However, bone loss resumes when hormone therapy is discontinued, even after 10 years of use.[60] Because the overall risk/benefit ratio of such therapy is negative in older women, using estrogen to treat osteoporosis indications should generally be limited to women younger than 50, women older than 50 with menopausal symptoms, and women who do not tolerate the other options. A possible exception is transdermally administered, ultralow-dose estradiol, which the FDA has approved for the prevention of osteoporosis.[61] The dose of estradiol is such that serum levels do not exceed the normal postmenopausal range and there is almost no endometrial effect.[62]

Several pharmacologic options for osteoporosis prevention and treatment are available. Raloxifene, a selective estrogen receptor modulator, reduces the risk of vertebral (but not hip) fractures, and reduces by 50% the risk of invasive, estrogen receptor-positive breast cancer in high- and low-risk women.[63] The drug carries an increased risk of thromboembolic disease equivalent to the risk of estrogen and it causes side effects such as hot flashes and leg cramps. Several bisphosphonates available in the United States have dosage schedules that vary from once a day to once a year. Bisphosphonates effectively reduce the risk of all types of fractures and cause relatively few adverse effects.

Common questions and answers regarding hormone therapy include these:

- Is it safe for women younger than 50 to undergo such therapy? Those who are healthy have such a low baseline risk of stroke, myocardial infarction, and thromboembolic events that estrogen or estrogen/progestin therapy is relatively safe and may be administered long-term up to the age of natural menopause;
- How long should women undergo this therapy for vasomotor symptoms? Although the duration of vasomotor symptoms in any individual is unpredictable, most women see a marked decrease in symptoms within 1 to 2 years of the FMP. A trial-and-error approach—either stopping hormone therapy or trying a reduced dose periodically—is the only option;
- What is the best way to discontinue hormone therapy? The common-sense, frequently recommended approach is to taper off, but evidence does not show that tapering off is superior to stopping "cold turkey." The best rationale for tapering, if therapy cannot be stopped altogether, is to find out if a lower dose suppresses symptoms;
- Should hormone levels be measured before or during therapy? Hormone levels are of no benefit in selecting an initial dose or monitoring therapy;
- Are bioidentical hormones advantageous? Claims that these preparations, marketed as drug compounds, are safer or more effective than other forms of hormone therapy are unfounded.[†] Women who choose compounded estrogen preparations should be aware that the risks are most likely the same as risks for commercially available estrogen preparations.

■ ■ ■

After evaluating Jane's menstrual symptoms, her gynecologist concluded that it was very likely she had entered the menopause transition. Jane had not missed any periods, and her pattern of shortened intermenstrual intervals—25 days versus the previous 29—and occasional hot flashes were consistent with this phase. The gynecologist assured Jane that her age was within the age range of women who experience these normal transitional changes. A FSH test probably would not help because the results would likely be in the premenopausal range. Jane's heavier-than-usual periods prompted a test for baseline hematocrit, which was normal (40%); a transvaginal ultrasound, which was normal (endometrial thickness < 5 mm), and a TSH, also normal. She could have taken birth control pills to control the bleeding and hot

---

[†] *See the North American Menopause Society's views on this issue at www.menopause.org/ bioidentical.aspx.*

flashes; instead, she decided to wait and see how things progressed over the next several months. Jane and her physician discussed the pros and cons of hormone therapy, including the most recent data from the Women's Health Initiative and other recent studies. They also briefly discussed her current risks for osteoporosis and heart disease.

Later, Jane told her partner: "I found out that I'm normal!" She said she would wait and see what happened to her symptoms as her periods begin to abate. Based on the discussion with her doctor, Jane also said she would feel comfortable using low-dose estrogen for a few months if she could not sleep and experienced severe mood problems. "But I'll check in with her again to learn about the latest research before making a decision."

Finally, Jane said she learned that several of the herbal supplements for hot flashes she had read about either do not work or may have side effects. In any case, she would consult her gynecologist before considering any new treatments. Jane also vowed to start paying more attention to the amount of calcium in her diet and begin an exercise program.

CONCLUSION

Lesbians most likely experience the same range of menopause-related symptoms and encounter the same issues as heterosexual women do, although research to date has not focused specifically on this population. Because factors such as race, ethnicity, socioeconomic status, education, and "marital status" affect attitudes toward menopause, lesbians may report experiences that differ from those of their heterosexual counterparts. Furthermore, lesbians are more likely to use complementary and alternative medicine, even though most research has not demonstrated the efficacy of nontraditional treatments for vasomotor symptoms. Clinicians must be familiar with such issues so they can provide the best possible care to lesbians. Other considerations include premature spontaneous menopause, the menopause transition, pregnancy during menopause, sexual dysfunction, incontinence, and the higher risk of obesity, metabolic syndrome, hypertension, irritability and depressive moods, and sleep and memory problems during the menopause transition. Current knowledge about hormone therapy applies regardless of sexual orientation.

REFERENCES

1. Women's Health Initiative Study Group. (1998). Design of the Women's Health Initiative clinical trial and observational study. *Controlled Clinical Trials, 19,* 61–109.

2. Sowers, M. F., Crawford, S. L., & Sternfeld, B. (2000). SWAN: A multicenter, multiethnic, community-based cohort study of women and the menopausal transition. In R. A. Lobo,

R. Marcus, & J. Kelsey (Eds.), *Menopause: Biology and Pathobiology* (pp. 175–188). New York: Academic Press.

3. Heck, J. E., Sell, R. L., & Gorin, S. S. (2006). Health care access among individuals involved in same-sex relationships. *American Journal of Public Health, 96,* 1111–1118.

4. Valanis, B. G., Bowen, D. J., Bassford, T., Whitlock, E., Charney, P., & Carter, R. A. (2000). Sexual orientation and health: Comparisons in the Women's Health Initiative sample. *Archives of Family Medicine, 9,* 843–853.

5. Galavotti, C., & Richter, D. L. (2000). Talking about hysterectomy: The experiences of women from four cultural groups. *Journal of Women's Health & Gender-Based Medicine, 9,* S63–67.

6. Matthews, A. K., Hughes, T. L., Osterman, G. P., & Kodl, M. M. (2005). Complementary medicine practices in a community-based sample of lesbian and heterosexual women. *Health Care for Women International, 26,* 430–447.

7. Newton, K. M., Reed, S. D., LaCroix, A. Z., Grothaus, L. C., Ehrlich, K., & Guiltinan, J. (2006). Treatment of vasomotor symptoms of menopause with black cohosh, multibotanicals, soy, hormone therapy, or placebo: A randomized trial. *Annals of Internal Medicine, 145,* 869–879.

8. Weiss, G., Skurnick, J. H., Goldsmith, L. T., Santoro, N. F., & Park, S. J. (2004). Menopause and hypothalamic-pituitary sensitivity to estrogen. *Journal of the American Medical Association, 292,* 2991–2996.

9. McKinlay, S., Jeffreys, M., & Thompson, B. (1972). An investigation of the age at menopause. *Journal of Biosocial Science, 4,* 161–173.

10. Santoro, N., Brockwell, S., Johnston, J., Crawford, S. L., Gold, E. B., Harlow, S. D., et al. (2007). Helping midlife women predict the onset of the final menses: SWAN, the Study of Women's Health Across the Nation. *Menopause, 14,* 415–424.

11. Randolph, J. F. Jr., Crawford, S., Dennerstein, L., Cain, K., Harlow, S. D., Little, R., et al. (2006). The value of follicle-stimulating hormone concentration and clinical findings as markers of the late menopause transition. *Journal of Clinical Endocrinology & Metabolism, 91,* 3034–3040.

12. Nelson, L. M., Covington, S. N., & Rebar, R. W. (2005). An update: Spontaneous premature ovarian failure is not an early menopause. *Fertility and Sterility, 83,* 1327–1332.

13. Rebar, R. W. (2009). Premature ovarian failure. *Obstetrics & Gynecology, 113,* 1355–1363.

14. Soules, M. R., Sherman, S., Parrott, E., Rebar, R., Santoro, N., Utian, W., et al. (2001). Executive summary: Stages of Reproductive Aging Workshop (STRAW). *Fertility and Sterility, 76,* 874–878.

15. Harlow, S. D., Mitchell, E. S., Crawford, S., Nan, B., Little, R., Taffe, J., et al. (2008). The ReSTAGE Collaboration: Defining optimal bleeding criteria for onset of early menopausal transition. *Fertility and Sterility, 89,* 129–140.

16. Santoro, N., Brown, J. R., Adel, T., & Skurnick, J. H. (1996). Characterization of reproductive hormonal dynamics in the perimenopause. *Journal of Clinical Endocrinology & Metabolism, 81,* 1495–1501.

17. Harlow, S. D., Crawford, S., Dennerstein, L., Burger, H. G., Mitchell, E. S., Sowers, M. F., et al. (2007). Recommendations from a multi-study evaluation of proposed criteria for staging reproductive aging. *Climacteric, 10,* 112–119.

18. Goldstein, S. R. (2004). Menorrhagia and abnormal bleeding before the menopause. *Best Practice & Research. Clinical Obstetrics & Gynaecology, 18,* 59–69.

19. Van Eijkeren, M. A., Christiaens, G. C., Geuze, H. J., Haspels, A. A., & Sixma, J. J. (1992). Effects of mefenamic acid on menstrual hemostasis in essential menorrhagia. *American Journal of Obstetrics & Gynecology, 166,* 1419–1428.

20. Wellington, K., & Wagstaff, A. J. (2003). Tranexamic acid: A review of its use in the management of menorrhagia. *Drugs, 63,* 1417–1433.

21. American College of Obstetricians and Gynecologists Committee on Gynecologic Practice. (2006). ACOG committee opinion. No. 337: Noncontraceptive uses of the levonorgestrel intrauterine system. *Obstetrics & Gynecology, 107,* 1479–1482.

22. Shaw, R. W., Symonds, I. M., Tamizian, O., Chaplain, J., & Mukhopadhyay, S. (2007). Randomised comparative trial of thermal balloon ablation and levonorgestrel intrauterine system in patients with idiopathic menorrhagia. *Australian & New Zealand Journal of Obstetrics & Gynaecology, 47,* 335–340.

23. Barnabei, V. M., Grady, D., Stovall, D. W., Cauley, J. A., Lin, F., Stuenkel, C. A., et al. (2002). Menopausal symptoms in older women and the effects of treatment with hormone therapy. *Obstetrics & Gynecology, 100,* 1209–1218.

24. Shanafelt, T. D., Barton, D. L., Adjei, A. A., & Loprinzi, C. L. (2002). Pathophysiology and treatment of hot flashes. *Mayo Clinic Proceedings, 77,* 1207–1218.

25. Thurston, R. C., Sowers, M. R., Chang, Y., Sternfeld, B., Gold, E. B., Johnston, J. M., et al. (2008). Adiposity and reporting of vasomotor symptoms among midlife women: The Study of Women's Health Across the Nation. *American Journal of Epidemiology, 167,* 78–85.

26. Freeman, E. W., Sammel, M. D., Lin, H., Gracia, C. R., Kapoor, S., & Ferdousi, T. (2005). The role of anxiety and hormonal changes in menopausal hot flashes. *Menopause, 12,* 258–266.

27. Daley, A. J., Stokes-Lampard, H., & MacArthur, C. (2007). "Feeling hot, hot, hot": Is there a role for exercise in the management of vasomotor and other menopausal symptoms? *Journal of Family Planning and Reproductive Health Care, 33,* 143–145.

28. Nelson, H. D. (2004). Commonly used types of postmenopausal estrogen for treatment of hot flashes: Scientific review. *Journal of the American Medical Association, 291,* 1610–1620.

29. North American Menopause Society. (2004). Treatment of menopause-associated vasomotor symptoms: Position statement of the North American Menopause Society. *Menopause, 11,* 11–33.

30. Bachmann, G. A., Schaefers, M., Uddin, A., & Utian, W. H. (2007). Lowest effective transdermal 17beta-estradiol dose for relief of hot flushes in postmenopausal women: A randomized controlled trial. *Obstetrics & Gynecology, 110,* 771–779.

31. Utian, W. H., Shoupe, D., Bachmann, G., Pinkerton, J. V., & Pickard, J. H. (2001). Relief of vasomotor symptoms and vaginal atrophy with lower doses of conjugated equine estrogens and medroxyprogesterone acetate. *Fertility and Sterility, 75,* 1065–1079.

32. Kaunitz, A. M. (2008). Clinical practice. Hormonal contraception in women of older reproductive age. *New England Journal of Medicine, 358,* 1262–1270.

33. Hickey, M., Saunders, C., Partridge, A., Santoro, N., Joffe, H., & Stearns, V. (2008). Practical clinical guidelines for assessing and managing menopausal symptoms after breast cancer. *Annals of Oncology, 19,* 1669–1680.

34. Tice, J. A., & Grady, D. (2006). Alternatives to estrogen for treatment of hot flashes: Are they effective and safe? *Journal of the American Medical Association, 295,* 2076–2078.

35. Nelson, H. D., Vesco, K. K., Haney, E., Fu, R., Nedrow, A., Miller, J., et al. (2006). Non-hormonal therapies for menopausal hot flashes: Systematic review and meta-analysis. *Journal of the American Medical Association, 295,* 2057–2071.

36. Dunbar, K., & Solga, S. F. (2007). Black cohosh, safety, and public awareness. *Liver International, 27,* 1017–1018.

37. Freeman, E. W., Sammel, M. D., Lin, H., Gracia, C. R., Pien, G. W., Nelson, D. B., et al. (2007). Symptoms associated with menopausal transition and reproductive hormones in midlife women. *Obstetrics & Gynecology, 110,* 230–240.

38. Mok, K., Juraskova, I., & Friedlander, M. (in press). The impact of aromatase inhibitors on sexual functioning: Current knowledge and future research directions. *The Breast.*

39. Peterson, H. B., & Curtis, K. M. (2005). Long-acting methods of contraception. *New England Journal of Medicine, 353,* 2169–2175.

40. Basson, R. (2006). Clinical practice. Sexual desire and arousal disorders in women. *New England Journal of Medicine, 354,* 1497–1506.

41. Wierman, M. E., Basson, R., Davis, S. R., Khosla, S., Miller, K. K., Rosner, W., et al. (2006). Androgen therapy in women: An Endocrine Society clinical practice guideline. *Journal of Clinical Endocrinology & Metabolism, 91,* 3697–3710.

42. Waetjen, L. E., Liao, S., Johnson, W. O., Sampselle, C. M., Sternfield, B., Harlow, S. D., et al. (2007). Factors associated with prevalent and incident urinary incontinence in a cohort of midlife women: A longitudinal analysis of data: Study of Women's Health Across the Nation. *American Journal of Epidemiology, 165,* 309–318.

43. Waetjen, L. E., Feng, W. Y., Ye, J., Johnson, W. O., Greendale, G. A., Sampselle, C. M., et al. (2008). Factors associated with worsening and improving urinary incontinence across the menopausal transition. *Obstetrics & Gynecology, 111,* 667–677.

44. Steinauer, J. E., Waetjen, L. E., Vittinghoff, E., Subak, L. L., Hulley, S. B., Grady, D., et al. (2005). Postmenopausal hormone therapy: Does it cause incontinence? *Obstetrics & Gynecology, 106,* 940–945.

45. Carr, M. C. (2003). The emergence of the metabolic syndrome with menopause. *Journal of Clinical Endocrinology & Metabolism, 88,* 2404–2411.

46. Freeman, E. W., Sammel, M. D., Lin, H., Gracia, C. R., & Kapoor, S. (2008). Symptoms in the menopausal transition: Hormone and behavioral correlates. *Obstetrics & Gynecology, 111,* 127–136.

47. Bromberger, J. T., Matthews, K. A., Schott, L. L., Brockwell, S., Avis, N. E., Kravitz, H. M., et al. (2007). Depressive symptoms during the menopausal transition: The Study of Women's Health Across the Nation (SWAN). *Journal of Affective Disorders, 103,* 267–272.

48. Kravitz, H. M., Ganz, P. A., Bromberger, J., Powell, L. H., Sutton-Tyrrell, K., & Meyer, P. M. (2003). Sleep difficulty in women at midlife: A community survey of sleep and the menopausal transition. *Menopause, 10,* 19–28.

49. Freedman, R. R., & Roehrs, T. A. (2007). Sleep disturbance in menopause. *Menopause, 14,* 826–829.

50. Shumaker, S. A., Legault, C., Kuller, L., Rapp, S. R., Thal, L., Lane, D. S., et al. (2004). Conjugated equine estrogens and incidence of probable dementia and mild cognitive impairment in postmenopausal women: Women's Health Initiative Memory Study. *Journal of the American Medical Association, 291,* 2947–2958.

51. Shumaker, S. A., Legault, C., Rapp, S. R., Thal, L., Wallace, R. B., Ockene, J. K., et al. (2003). Estrogen plus progestin and the incidence of dementia and mild cognitive impairment in postmenopausal women: The Women's Health Initiative Memory Study: A randomized controlled trial. *Journal of the American Medical Association, 289,* 2651–2662.

52. Rossouw, J. E., Anderson, G. L., Prentice, R. L., LaCroix, A. Z., Kooperberg, C., Stefanick, M. L., et al. (2002). Risks and benefits of estrogen plus progestin in healthy postmenopausal women: Principal results from the Women's Health Initiative randomized controlled trial. *Journal of the American Medical Association, 288,* 321–333.

53. Anderson, G. L., Limacher, M., Assaf, A. R., Bassford, T., Beresford, S. A., Black, H., et al. (2004). Effects of conjugated equine estrogen in postmenopausal women with hysterectomy: The Women's Health Initiative randomized controlled trial. *Journal of the American Medical Association, 291,* 1701–1712.

54. Holmberg, L., Iversen, O. E., Rudenstam, C. M., Hammar, M., Kumpulainen, E., Jaskiewicz, J., et al. (2008). Increased risk of recurrence after hormone replacement therapy in breast cancer survivors. *Journal of the National Cancer Institute, 100,* 475–482.

55. Prentice, R. L., Chlebowski, R. T., Stefanick, M. L., Manson, J. E., Langer, R. D., Pettinger, M., et al. (2008). Conjugated equine estrogens and breast cancer risk in the Women's Health Initiative clinical trial and observational study. *American Journal of Epidemiology, 167,* 1407–1415.

56. Hendrix, S. L., Cochrane, B. B., Nygaard, I. E., Handa, V. L., Barnabei, V. M., Iglesia, C., et al. (2005). Effects of estrogen with and without progestin on urinary incontinence. *Journal of the American Medical Association, 293,* 935–948.

57. Rossouw, J. E., Prentice, R. L., Manson, J. E., Wu, L., Barad, D., Barnabei, V. M., et al. (2007). Postmenopausal hormone therapy and risk of cardiovascular disease by age and years since menopause. *Journal of the American Medical Association, 297,* 1465–1477.

58. Dawson-Hughes, B., Tosteson, A. N., Melton, L. J. III, Baim, S., Favus, M. J., Khosla, S., et al. (2008). Implications of absolute fracture risk assessment for osteoporosis practice guidelines in the U.S.A. *Osteoporosis International, 19,* 449–458.

59. Dawson-Hughes, B., & Bischoff-Ferrari, H. A. (2007). Therapy of osteoporosis with calcium and vitamin D. *Journal of Bone and Mineral Research, 22,* V59–63.

60. Heikkinen, J., Vaheri, R., Haapalahti, J., & Timonen, U. (2008). A 10-year follow-up of the effect of continuous-combined hormone replacement therapy and its discontinuation on bone in postmenopausal women. *Menopause International, 14,* 70–77.

61. Ettinger, B., Ensrud, K. E., Wallace, R., Johnson, K. C., Cummings, S. R., Yankov, V., et al. (2004). Effects of ultralow-dose transdermal estradiol on bone mineral density: A randomized clinical trial. *Obstetrics & Gynecology, 104,* 443–451.

62. Johnson, S. R., Ettinger, B., Macer, J. L., Ensrud, K. E., Quan, J., & Grady, D. (2005). Uterine and vaginal effects of unopposed ultralow-dose transdermal estradiol. *Obstetrics & Gynecology, 105,* 779–787.

63. Grady, D., Cauley, J. A., Geiger, M. J., Kornitzer, M., Mosca, L., Collins, P., et al. (2008). Reduced incidence of invasive breast cancer with raloxifene among women at increased coronary risk. *Journal of the National Cancer Institute, 100,* 854–861.

ABOUT THE AUTHOR

Susan R. Johnson, MD, MS is Professor of Obstetrics/Gynecology and Epidemiology at the University of Iowa in Iowa City. She was an investigator in several large menopause-related clinical trials, including the Women's Health Initiative. She is chairing the Study of Women Across the Nation (SWAN), a study of the transition into menopause.

CHAPTER 16

"I'm So Sad, Just Let Me Be."
LESBIANS AND DEPRESSION

CYNTHIA L. BENTON, MD

ELLEN HALLER, MD

BY THE TIME *she reached her late forties, Kay had achieved more in life than she ever dreamed possible. She had a successful career in a rewarding field and a long-term relationship with a woman she loved.*

Despite all this, Kay noticed that her mood was spiraling downward. She had trouble sleeping, less energy, poor concentration, and crying spells. She forced herself to function at work but found herself withdrawing at home. She spent her evenings watching the History Channel and eating junk food instead of participating in activities she had previously enjoyed, like coaching women's sports teams. Her symptoms got worse over many months before she finally acknowledged to herself that she needed help and sought a psychiatric referral.

On psychiatric assessment, Kay met all the diagnostic criteria for major depression. She did not meet criteria for dysthymia or an adjustment disorder with depressed mood, and results from a work-up to rule out a general medical condition such as anemia or thyroid dysfunction were completely normal. She had chronic pain from several old sports-related injuries, which, the psychiatrist concluded, contributed to but did not cause her depression.

The initial interview clearly revealed that Kay had experienced many stressors that can contribute to depression. Particularly in lesbians, these stressors include childhood sexual abuse, internalized homophobia, heavy alcohol use, and discrimination. As a child, Kay had always felt "different"— people thought she was a tomboy—and had difficulty finding friends who would accept her. Once, a male babysitter sexually molested Kay.

As she moved into adulthood, Kay acknowledged her sexual attraction to other women—a distressing fact, given that she taught at college campuses where lesbianism was literally forbidden. For a brief time, she turned to alcohol to manage this distress and the isolation she felt. Kay failed to hide and deny her sexuality: she lost two teaching jobs and her career was essentially ruined as a result of accusations and fears related to her sexual orientation.

Kay reported one previous course of psychotherapy that focused on helping her cope with the discrimination she had encountered in her career. She resolved during this therapy to return to school and enter a new profession that would be more accepting of her sexual orientation. By her mid-forties, Kay was very successful professionally, "out" as a lesbian, and in a committed, long-term relationship with a woman. At that point, she exhibited several common lesbian

strengths: a high level of education, professional achievement, and membership
in social networks that provide the kind of support available to heterosexual
women.

After ruling out other possible causes of Kay's symptoms, the
psychiatrist prescribed an antidepressant, which was partially effective. Initially,
Kay was not interested in more psychotherapy. But lingering symptoms of
depression eventually prompted her to seek additional weekly therapy, over the
course of which she came to understand how multiple past stressors currently
affected her self-esteem, ability to trust, and comfort with intimate relationships.
Ultimately, her depression completely resolved. Today, she is still in remission.
Kay still takes maintenance antidepressants but no longer needs psychotherapy.

■ ■ ■

The lifetime prevalence of major depression in the general U.S. population is about
15%; among women, it may be as high as 25%.[1] There is some concern that
prevalence may be even higher among lesbians, given the stresses they encounter in
today's culture. This chapter defines depression, examines whether or not it is more
prevalent among lesbians than heterosexual women, considers possibly predisposing
and contributing factors in lesbians, and discusses treatment options.

DEFINITION AND DIAGNOSIS

The *Diagnostic and Statistical Manual of Mental Disorders* (DSM) provides diagnostic
criteria for major depression, dysthymia, and adjustment disorder with depressed
mood. An episode of major depression is characterized by a depressed mood or "loss
of interest or pleasure in nearly all activities" that lasts at least 2 weeks and is accompanied by at least four other symptoms, including increased or decreased appetite, too
much or too little sleep, fatigue, feelings of worthlessness or guilt, trouble concentrating,
and contemplation of or an attempt at suicide. To meet these criteria, symptoms of
major depression cannot be due to substance abuse, medication, or a general medical
condition.[2] One or more major depressive episodes do not include manic, mixed, or
hypomanic episodes. Mental health professionals commonly add "specifiers" to the
diagnosis of major depression to further describe its course—the severity of depression,

if there has been more than one episode, if there is a seasonal pattern, and if the depression is accompanied by hallucinations or delusions. The specifier "postpartum onset" means depressive symptoms occurred within 4 weeks of childbirth.[2] Many clinicians, however, issue a diagnosis of postpartum depression when any major depressive episode occurs within the first 6 months of delivery.

Dysthymia is more chronic and less acute than major depression. To be diagnosed with dysthymia, a person must be depressed on most days for at least 2 years. In addition, the depressed mood in dysthymia must be accompanied by some of the same symptoms in major depression—changes in sleep or appetite, poor energy, or poor concentration, for example—but cannot include suicidal feelings. An individual could have dysthymia with a superimposed major depressive episode (a condition sometimes referred to as "double depression") or have either dysthymia or major depression separately.[2]

Adjustment disorder with depressed mood probably comes closest to describing what most people mean when they say, "I feel down." Diagnostic criteria include symptoms such as depressed mood, tearfulness, or feelings of hopelessness that arise within 3 months of exposure to an "identifiable stressor."[2] Identifiable stressors could be events such as breaking up with a girlfriend or coming out as a lesbian to a family member or friend who subsequently is not supportive.

In 2002, the U.S. Preventive Services Task Force recommended that primary care physicians routinely screen all adults for depression. It concluded that many formal tools are available for this purpose, among them the Zung Self-Assessment Depression Scale, the Beck Depression Inventory, the General Health Questionnaire, and the Center for Epidemiologic Study Depression Scale.[3] However, asking two simple questions about mood and lack of interest or pleasure in activities may be just as illuminating: "Over the past 2 weeks, have you felt down, depressed, or hopeless?" and "Over the past 2 weeks, have you felt little interest or pleasure in doing things?" Because there is little evidence to recommend one screening method over another, clinicians can choose the technique that best fits into their practice.[4-6] Patients who screen positive for depression should undergo a full diagnostic interview based on the DSM diagnostic criteria. The clinician should specifically ask about suicidality and assess the severity of depression.

EPIDEMIOLOGY

The notion that depression is more common among lesbians than heterosexual women may offend some people, who might ask: "Why would this population be any more susceptible than others?"

As a minority group, lesbians do not have the same legal and social protections other women have; consequently, they face unique daily stresses. More research on lesbians and stress is warranted, given that current models of depression view stress as a contributing factor. Table 16.1 summarizes three surveys in the United States that examined this topic.

TABLE 16.1. U.S. STUDIES ON LESBIANS AND DEPRESSION

AUTHORS	METHOD	DEFINITION OF SEXUALITY	MAJOR DEPRESSION IN THE PREVIOUS YEAR
Cochran et al.[7]	National survey by the MacArthur Foundation (population-based): midlife development in English-speaking adults 25–74 years old. Random-digit dial plus follow-up by mail.	Identity	Lesbian/bisexual women ($n = 37$): 33.5%* Heterosexual women ($n = 1,604$): 16.8%*
Gilman et al.[8]	National Comorbidity Survey (representative households): people 15–54 years old. Face-to-face interviews, 1990–92.	Behavior in the preceding 5 years	Women with same-sex partners only and women with same-sex and opposite-sex partners ($n = 51$): 34.5%† Women with opposite-sex partners only ($n = 2,475$): 12.9%†
Cochran and Mays[9]	National Household Survey of Drug Abuse (population-based): people ≥ 12 years old. Yearly, face-to-face interviews.	Behavior in preceding 1 year	Women with same-sex partners only and women with same-sex and opposite-sex partners ($n = 96$): 15.0%* Women with opposite-sex partners only ($n = 5,792$): 8.4%*

* The difference between the two groups was not statistically significant.
† The difference was statistically significant.

All three surveys found a higher prevalence of major depression in the previous year among lesbian and bisexual women compared with heterosexual women, although the findings were not statistically significant in two of the studies. The survey by Gilman and colleagues highlights some of the common dilemmas in lesbian research. In the group of 51 women who were not strictly heterosexual, 15 had only same-sex partners and 36 had both same-sex and opposite-sex partners. The researchers combined these subgroups, presumably to increase statistical power. One might conclude from these results that depression is more prevalent in lesbians. But is it really? After all, 36 of the 51 homosexually active women (71%) had sex with both men and women. Some may have identified as bisexual and others may have been heterosexuals who had had just one episode of sex with a woman in the previous 5 years for whatever reason, such as impulsivity or intoxication. It is difficult to say how these findings—as well as those in the Cochran and Mays survey, which had a similar design—might apply to women with a stable lesbian identity.

The MacArthur Foundation survey also combined lesbian and bisexual women in one group, explicitly to increase statistical power. Interestingly, it found that 18.4% of both lesbian/bisexual women and heterosexual women were currently experiencing a high level of distress, measured by symptoms such as feeling nervous, hopeless, or worthless.

Researchers often cite such studies as evidence of a higher prevalence of mental disorders among lesbians.[10,11] But this assertion is questionable. To date, no studies have randomly sampled the adult U.S. population to compare lesbians defined by behavior or self-identity with bisexual and heterosexual women in terms of depression or any other mental disorder. The dearth of research is due mostly to a lack of research funding, which often obliges investigators either to conduct small studies or to reanalyze data from larger studies that focused on another issue, such as the prevalence of homosexual behavior as a risk factor for HIV.

EPIDEMIOLOGY IN PARTICULAR POPULATIONS

Researchers have also studied the prevalence of depression in certain lesbian populations, including adolescents, women in the postpartum period, postmenopausal women, and ethnic minorities. Most of these studies, excluding research on adolescents, used convenience sampling; they recruited participants via fliers and advertisements at lesbian and gay events and in lesbian and gay periodicals. Such samples are problematic because they may not represent lesbians as a whole and have the potential for selection bias. The results may not be generalizable. Furthermore, convenience sampling typically lacks an adequate control group.

Adolescents

A common belief is that lesbian and gay adolescents are more likely than their heterosexual counterparts to be depressed and to attempt or commit suicide. But some of the methodological problems that plague studies of adult lesbians also plague studies of adolescents. For instance, in a survey of high school students in an upper-middle-class district, Lock and Steiner found that lesbian, gay, and bisexual teenagers were more likely to have mental health problems and to be uncomfortable with their sexual orientation.[12] Because the researchers grouped all sexual minority teenagers together, it is difficult to know if this result applies specifically to lesbian teenagers. Indeed, a much larger study that differentiated between lesbian, gay, and bisexual teenagers produced very different results. Udry and Chantala analyzed data from the National Longitudinal Study of Adolescent Health, which conducted home interviews of adolescents in grades 7 through 12 during the 1994–95 school year. Teenage girls who reported only same-sex partners did not have a significantly higher level of depression or suicidal thoughts than did teenage girls who reported only opposite-sex partners. However, those with both same- and opposite-sex partners were about twice as likely as girls with only opposite-sex partners to be depressed or to have suicidal thoughts.[13]

Lesbians in the Postpartum Period

Several authors have hypothesized that risk factors for postpartum depression are different in lesbians and heterosexual women. Factors that might increase lesbian mothers' vulnerability to depression include the legal discrimination they may encounter in forming a family and potentially less pregnancy support from their family of origin.[14] Conversely, compared with heterosexual couples, more equal sharing of child-rearing and housework by lesbian couples might protect them from postpartum depression.[15] Ross and colleagues looked at rates of postpartum depression among lesbians in Canada. Comparing a convenience sample with a heterosexual sample from a previously published study, they found that lesbian/bisexual biological mothers and heterosexual mothers had similar amounts of depressive symptoms in the late third trimester of pregnancy, but the former had significantly more depressive symptoms at 16 weeks postpartum. The lesbian and bisexual biological mothers were combined in this study for statistical analysis; however, the bisexual women (biological and nonbiological mothers) actually had significantly more depressive symptoms than the lesbian women did.[16] This highlights yet again the perils of combining lesbian and bisexual women together in one study group.

Postmenopausal Women

There has been little research on older women in general or older lesbians in particular. Based on a convenience sample in the Women's Health Initiative, Valanis and colleagues found that the overall incidence of depression was 16.5% among lifetime lesbians (sex only with women ever), 15.4% among bisexual women, 15.0% among adult lesbians (sex only with women after age 45), and 11.1% among heterosexual women. Sexual minority women were more likely to be depressed and, interestingly, also more likely to have a graduate education and a managerial/professional job.[17]

Ethnic Minorities

Ethnic minority lesbians may encounter three types of discrimination simultaneously: homophobia, racism, and sexism. They also may have less family or community support after they "come out"—some ethnic groups are less accepting of lesbians and gay men—and therefore may be more vulnerable to depression.

A few studies have investigated depression in African American, Asian American, and Latina lesbians. In a convenience sample of homosexually active African American men and women, Cochran and Mays found that 38% of the women scored within the range for depression, higher than the 26% that previous, community-based studies of Black women reported. The researchers defined "homosexually active" as at least one homosexual experience in the individual's lifetime regardless of how she identified herself.[18] Cochran and colleagues investigated depression in Latino and Asian American sexual minorities using a national household survey. Lesbian/bisexual Latina and Asian American women—those who self-identified as lesbian or bisexual, grouped with those who had had any same-sex experiences in the previous year— were significantly more likely than their heterosexual counterparts to have a recent or lifetime history of depression.[19]

COMORBID DISORDERS

People with depression often suffer from other psychiatric disorders as well. Successful treatment of the depression requires concomitant assessment and treatment of these illnesses. Some evidence suggests that lesbians may be at higher risk of psychiatric comorbidity. In the MacArthur National Survey of Midlife Development, 54% of lesbians and bisexual women who met the criteria for one psychiatric disorder also met the criteria for at least another, compared with 30% of the heterosexual women. And lesbian and bisexual women were more likely than heterosexual women to meet criteria for generalized anxiety disorder.[7] Similarly, homosexually active women in the National Comorbidity Survey were more likely than heterosexual women to be diagnosed with anxiety, mood, or substance-use disorders.[8]

Among women in general, depression is strongly associated with alcohol consumption.[20] Early research reported that 33% of lesbians had alcohol-related problems,[20] but more recent research challenges this finding. In a 2003 study, for example, most lesbian and heterosexual women who drank alcohol indicated they had fewer than two drinks per day.[21] In another study, 27.9% of lesbians abstained from alcohol, 72.1% had 1 to 60 drinks per month, and none drank more than that.[22] Other findings suggest that lesbians are more likely than heterosexual women to abstain from alcohol or to be in recovery[21,23] and are more likely to report alcohol-related problems.[21,24]

Alcohol use and problems among heterosexual women decline with age, but it is unclear if this also occurs among lesbians. Studies that examined a cross-section of the lesbian population at a specific point in time have found more alcohol use than expected among older lesbians.[24,25] Conversely, among a sample of lesbians and bisexual women drawn from a large health maintenance organization, 23.3% of those between 20 and 34 years old met the criteria for heavy drinking compared to 7.1% of those between 35 and 39, and there were no heavy drinkers in the oldest group. In addition, abstinence rates were 0%, 24.5%, and 29.4% in the 20-to-34, 35-to-49, and oldest age groups, respectively.[26]

Based on more recent findings, some researchers have suggested that alcohol use may be declining among lesbians overall. Postulated reasons for this include a decline in the social stigma of lesbianism, less reliance on bars for socialization, and greater awareness of alcohol problems in the lesbian community.[20,21] However, as with other studies of lesbian behavior, research methods to assess alcohol use may limit the generalizability of findings. Hughes,[21] Heffernan,[22] McKirnan and Peterson,[24] and Skinner[25] relied on convenience samples; Bloomfield[23] did not adequately define categories of alcohol use for study participants; and McKirnan and Peterson[24] combined lesbians and gay men into one group for comparison with heterosexuals. Gruskin and colleagues[26] determined the sexual orientation of participants based only on self-identity, not behavior.

SUICIDE

A potentially devastating consequence of major depression is suicide, although not all depressed people want to kill themselves. Suicidal ideation and suicide attempts may occur as a result of major depression or other psychiatric illnesses or circumstances. Several studies cite a higher incidence of suicidal ideation and suicide attempts among lesbians compared with heterosexual women; participants in their teens or twenties made most of the attempts.[21,27] These age ranges most likely coincide with coming out, which often is associated with high stress and psychological turmoil.[21]

Such findings contrast with those from the National Comorbidity Survey: the incidence of thinking about or planning suicide was not significantly higher among women who had any same-sex partners than it was among women who had only opposite-sex partners, and the former were not more likely to have attempted suicide in the preceding year.[8] Because the mean age of participants in the survey was about 33, these results may more accurately reflect suicidality in adult women who have sex with women than do studies that assess for a lifetime history of suicidal ideation or attempts.

SOCIAL INFLUENCES ON LESBIAN DEPRESSION

Lesbians face additional challenges that possibly make them more vulnerable than heterosexual women to depression. For example, they are likely to have experienced discrimination or even hate crimes, and may struggle with internalized homophobia as a result of being exposed to many negative messages about homosexuality. Some research suggests that there may be a higher incidence of psychopathology, including mental-health and substance-use disorders, in lesbians' families of origin, and many studies have documented a greater likelihood of childhood sexual abuse among lesbians.[10,27,28] Lesbians also may be at higher risk of physical abuse in childhood.[29,30] Yet another possible risk factor is a predisposition for depression due to a lack of social support, although most lesbians seem to perceive that they have a high level of support.[17,22] Regardless, whenever clinicians evaluate or treat lesbians who are depressed, they must be aware of potentially related factors.

Discrimination and Victimization

The legal system and heterosexuals often discriminate against lesbians, a stigmatized sexual minority. In one study, sexual minority men and women were significantly more likely than heterosexuals to report a lifetime experience of discrimination, such as getting fired from a job or receiving inferior medical care. They were also significantly more likely to report day-to-day discrimination; for example, others gave them less respect or poorer service, and insulted, threatened, or harassed them. In addition, sexual minority participants were significantly more likely to report discrimination based on sexual orientation. Finally, the study found that experiencing discrimination, regardless of sexual orientation, increased the odds of a psychiatric disorder and a self-ranking of current mental health as "fair" or "poor."[31] A convenience sample in the National Lesbian Health Care Survey revealed that, based on self-reports, 52% of lesbians had been verbally attacked because of their sexual orientation, 8% had lost their jobs, 6% had been physically attacked, and 1% had been discharged from the military.[29]

Herek and colleagues used a convenience sample of homosexual and bisexual men and women in Sacramento, California, to further explore the deleterious effects of hate crimes on mental health. They compared the psychological impact of hate crimes with crimes for which the motivation was unknown. Twenty percent of lesbian/bisexual women reported they had been victims of at least one hate crime. Lesbians and gay men who had experienced at least one hate crime in the previous 5 years were more likely than victims of nonhate crimes or persons who had not been a victim of any crime to have symptoms of depression, traumatic stress, and anger. They were also more likely to "regard the world as unsafe, to view people as malevolent, to exhibit a relatively low sense of personal mastery, and to attribute their personal setbacks to sexual prejudice"[32] (p. 949).

Internalized Homophobia

Because heterosexism is so prevalent in American society, all children are exposed to and may internalize prejudicial beliefs.[33] Therefore, when nascent lesbians first recognize their attraction to persons of the same sex, they often have some degree of negative feeling about themselves that they must confront as their new identity develops. If this process goes awry, a lesbian may prefer heterosexuality and decide not to act on her same-sex attraction, to conceal her behaviors, or to seek a "cure" and try to change her sexual orientation. According to a theory that has yet to be thoroughly studied, higher levels of internalized homophobia contribute to a higher prevalence of depression. Is a greater degree of "outness" linked with lower rates of depression? Findings from at least two studies suggest it is not.[29,34]

Psychopathology in the Family of Origin

Studies have found that lesbians are more likely than heterosexual women to report psychopathology in their family of origin. For example, in a sample of women from an outpatient psychiatric clinic, lesbians were significantly more likely to report substance abuse and maternal psychopathology.[35] In another study, lesbian physicians were more likely than heterosexual female physicians to report a family history of alcoholism.[10] However, it is difficult to know in these studies whether the psychopathology differences were real or the comparison groups reported their experiences differently.

Several factors may increase lesbians' awareness of and willingness to discuss psychopathology issues. Compared with heterosexual women, lesbians may be more emotionally separated from their family of origin, and, as a section later in this chapter explains, are more likely to have been in therapy.

Childhood Sexual Abuse

Numerous studies have cited a higher prevalence of childhood sexual abuse among lesbians than heterosexual women.[10,27,28] In one study, 23% of lesbians perceived themselves as victims of childhood sexual abuse, and 42% reported experiences that qualified as abuse according to the research criteria. These percentages were significantly higher than those for heterosexual women (11% and 27%, respectively). Furthermore, 16% of lesbians versus 9% of heterosexual women reported childhood sexual abuse by a family member.[28] This type of abuse could theoretically increase the risk of depression because the victim may have to choose between continuing to communicate with the perpetrator in the family context or discontinuing communication, which could prompt family members to raise questions or express disapproval. Another study, based on a convenience sample of lesbians, found that childhood sexual abuse was significantly correlated with at least one lifetime occurrence of depression and/or alcohol dependence.[30]

Why lesbians are at greater risk of childhood sexual abuse is unclear. Among the unsubstantiated theories: that such abuse may "cause" a lesbian sexual orientation; that lesbian youth, isolated and lonely because they differ from their peers, may be more vulnerable to pedophiles; and that adults may be more likely to sexually abuse girls who do not conform with their gender.[36]

Childhood Physical Abuse

Hitting children is, to some degree, a cultural norm in the United States. This makes it difficult to define childhood physical abuse for research purposes and may hinder victims' ability to recognize abuse.

Some studies have explored the incidence of childhood physical abuse specifically among lesbians. Twenty-four percent of lesbians in the National Lesbian Health Care Survey reported they had been physically abused as children—70% of them by a male relative and 45% by a female relative.[29] Hughes and colleagues found that among the 22% of lesbians in their study who perceived childhood physical abuse, 71.9% experienced depression at some point in their lifetime compared with the 52.3% who had not been physically abused.[30]

Lack of Social Support

Some researchers speculate that potential alienation from society and family of origin puts lesbians at higher risk of depression because they have less social support. In one study, lesbians who perceived social support from family and friends were less likely to be depressed.[34] However, most lesbians believe that the social support they receive is no less than that for heterosexual women. Lesbians and heterosexual women in a Women's Health Initiative sample scored almost identically on a social-support scale.[17] In Heffernan's study, lesbians scored slightly above published norms for social resources such as number of friends and membership in social groups.[22]

BIOLOGICAL TREATMENTS

Treatment with antidepressants, one of the most common therapies, consists of three phases: acute, continuation, and maintenance. Typically, the acute phase (to relieve symptoms) lasts 4 to 8 weeks, the continuation phase (to protect against relapse) lasts 9 to 12 months, and the maintenance phase (to protect against relapse in cases where there have been two or more episodes of major depression) continues indefinitely. The first two phases are critically important for all patients with major depression because the treatments help achieve and maintain remission.

Although different antidepressants have similar efficacy, their effectiveness in individual patients varies. The choice of medication is often guided by potential side effects, overdose safety, cost, and, if available, a patient's history of response. At one time, only tricyclic antidepressants and monoamine oxidase inhibitors were available, but their poor tolerability and lethality in overdose inhibited widespread use, despite their effectiveness. Subsequently, selective serotonin reuptake inhibitors (SSRIs) revolutionized biological treatment of depression because they cause fewer side effects and are safer in overdose. Generic forms of several SSRIs—fluoxetine, paroxetine, and citalopram—are less costly, which greatly increases their accessibility.

Nevertheless, the side effects associated with SSRIs, the most commonly prescribed class of antidepressants, can be significant. They include weight gain, an inability to achieve orgasm, and low libido, which, for lesbian and other couples, may lead to discordant sex drives. Sexual side effects are commonly managed by switching to an antidepressant in a different class, such as bupropion, buspirone, or mirtazapine, or by lowering or skipping antidepressant doses. Research has not shown any single approach to be consistently effective.[37] Skipping doses is not generally recommended because doing so may cause withdrawal side effects and lead to inconsistent medication levels. Anecdotally, some women appear to respond to sildenafil (Viagra) before sexual activity.

Clinicians commonly prescribe venlafaxine and duloxetine, which are serotonin and norepinephrine reuptake inhibitors, as alternatives to SSRIs. They inhibit both the serotonin and norepinephrine/dopamine neural pathways, and thus may help patients who do not respond to SSRIs, which only inhibit serotonin. Although venlafaxine and duloxetine are less likely to cause weight gain and sexual side effects, they are much more expensive than generic SSRIs. Furthermore, venlafaxine can increase blood pressure.

Another alternative is bupropion, a norepinephrine/dopamine inhibitor. Bupropion does not cause weight gain or sexual side effects, but it is ineffective for treating anxiety, which often accompanies depression, and increases the risk of seizures. Effective but less commonly used antidepressants are mirtazapine and nefazodone. However, mirtazapine is associated with significant weight gain and sedation, and nefazodone may disrupt liver function.

To treat refractory depression, clinicians may initially combine antidepressants in different classes or augment them with lithium, thyroid supplementation, anticonvulsants, or atypical antipsychotics. If this approach fails, electroconvulsive therapy (ECT) is a safe and effective option. The general public has a negative view of ECT, due to reports of posttreatment amnesia and cognitive difficulties, yet it remains one of the most helpful therapies for patients who do not respond to multiple antidepressants. A more recent alternative for refractory depression is vagal nerve stimulation via a device implanted in the left side of the chest. Researchers are still investigating transcranial magnetic stimulation of neurons in the brain as a potential treatment for refractory depression.

PSYCHOTHERAPY

Although lesbians may have more difficulty than heterosexual women accessing health care and may be afraid to disclose their sexual orientation, they are more likely than their heterosexual counterparts to use mental health services, studies suggest. In the MacArthur Foundation survey of midlife development, 94% of lesbian/bisexual women with a high level of current distress or a psychiatric disorder, versus 54% of heterosexual women, received some sort of psychiatric therapy.[7] Seventy-five percent of lesbians in the National Lesbian Health Care Survey reported they had received counseling.[29]

Psychodynamic and Gay Affirmative Psychotherapy

Psychodynamic psychotherapy, a common type of treatment rooted in psychoanalysis, employs techniques that range from more expressive to more supportive.[38] Interventions on the expressive end include interpretation (linking a patient's current behavior to unconscious motives), confrontation (pointing out a behavior), and clarification (looking for and noting a common theme in a patient's stories). Interventions on the supportive end include empathy and direct advice.

Gay affirmative psychotherapy involves adapting psychodynamic psychotherapy to the treatment of lesbian and gay patients, without attempting to change their sexual orientation. The technique is somewhat nebulous because no manual exists to provide strict therapy guidance. Two books that describe this approach are *Affirmative Psychotherapy and Counseling for Lesbians and Gay Men*[39] and *Handbook of Affirmative Psychotherapy with Lesbians and Gay Men.*[40] They discuss theories about the stages of identity development in lesbians and gay men, mental health problems that may arise as people progress through these stages, and the related therapeutic considerations. For instance, lesbians first confront the possibility that they are lesbian in the identity confusion stage, which often is accompanied by depression and anxiety. The books also address heterosexist bias in many psychological assessment tools, under- or overdiagnosis of psychiatric illness in sexual minorities, legal and social discrimination against lesbians and gay men, whether or not lesbian and gay therapists are more suitable, and whether or not such therapists should disclose their sexual orientation to patients.

Some lesbians prefer to work with an "out" therapist, who may be more familiar with and have a better understanding of the challenges they face as lesbians. However, there are no empirical data to support the hypothesis that this positively or negatively affects outcomes. Cabaj cautioned that an openly lesbian or gay therapist may over-identify with lesbian or gay patients and thus insufficiently explore their experiences, or patients may feel uncomfortable discussing their negative feelings about being gay with the therapist.[41]

Cognitive Behavioral Therapy

Cognitive behavioral therapy (CBT) effectively treats depression.[11] The underlying theory is that cognition and behavior directly affect mood, and that by recognizing and changing them, patients can alter their mood. For example, a depressed lesbian might illogically think, "Everyone hates me," and maladaptively avoid all social contexts. Both the negative thoughts and the avoidant behavior reinforce her depression. A CBT therapist would help such a patient learn how to think more logically and to develop adaptive behaviors that could alleviate her depression. CBT typically consists of 12 to 20 individual or group sessions. The therapist actively participates in these structured sessions and assigns homework.

Researchers have written about CBT relative to sexual minority clients. Martell and colleagues discuss how, for lesbians, gays, and bisexuals, being raised in a heterosexist culture can lead to negative core beliefs, such as "I am bad because I am different," which in turn can lead to psychological stress and depression. They also discuss the importance of thoroughly evaluating patients' statements and symptoms for clues to the source of their distress. If, for example, a patient says she avoids the lesbian community, internalized homophobia or social anxiety may be driving her avoidance behavior.[11]

The self-help, CBT-oriented *Queer Blues: The Lesbian and Gay Guide to Overcoming Depression*[36] describes common distorted thinking patterns and suggests exercises for correcting them. It also discusses how readers can apply those exercises to their internalized homophobia, how internalized and external homophobia can contribute to depression, and how individuals can deal with external homophobia through positive self-affirmation, protesting, and self-nurturing.

Reparative Therapy

Before 1973, when the DSM stopped listing homosexuality as a psychiatric disorder, clinicians attributed depression and other symptoms to homosexuality itself. Repara-tive therapy seeks to "cure" lesbians and gay men of homosexuality by changing their sexual orientation. Even though professional organizations such as the American Psychiatric Association, the American Psychological Association, and the American Medical Association have widely denounced this approach, some therapists still practice it.

In a study of reparative therapy, Spitzer recruited a convenience sample of 143 men and 57 women from ex-gay religious ministries, reparative therapy practices, and other sources who reported at least a minimal change from homosexual to heterosexual orientation that lasted 5 or more years. Fifty-four percent of the women said that after therapy, they were only attracted to the opposite sex; among the 47% of women before therapy who were depressed, only 4% reported depression afterward. However, this study had numerous methodological flaws. For example, a more accurate description of the "homosexual" women in Spitzer's study might have been "bisexual," as only 42% reported they had "never" or "only rarely" been attracted to the opposite sex before reparative therapy began. Moreover, the study relied on participants' self-reports of conversion to heterosexuality. This is problematic because they were highly motivated to report successful treatment: before reparative therapy, 78% had publicly favored the technique and 19% were mental health professionals or directors of ex-gay ministries.[42]

In addition, reparative therapy raises serious ethical concerns. According to Drescher, reparative therapists do not always obtain informed consent, sometimes misinform patients (telling them, for example, that homosexuality is a disorder or is definitely not biologically determined), and may coerce patients by threatening to disclose their homosexuality to others. Reparative therapy, Drescher writes, is not unlike faith healing: practitioners focus on a small number of successes and blame the failures on patients.[43]

CONCLUSION

Whether or not lesbians are more likely than heterosexual women to suffer from depression is debatable. However, depression is a significant health issue for lesbians. The prevalence of depression may vary among subgroups, including lesbians who are in adolescence, in the postpartum period, or in the postmenopausal period, and in those who belong to an ethnic minority.

After a depression diagnosis, clinicians should screen for comorbid psychiatric disorders—particularly those that may be more common in lesbians, such as anxiety disorders and alcohol abuse or dependence—and for suicidality, as suicidal patients need to be hospitalized for their own safety. In thorough assessments, clinicians should pose questions to patients about the unique stresses of being in a sexual minority that may increase their vulnerability to depression. Stresses include discrimination or victimization, internalized homophobia, psychopathology in the family of origin, and childhood sexual or physical abuse.

Treating depression involves first ruling out a medical condition or substance use, then diagnosing the type—major depression, dysthymia, or adjustment disorder with depressed mood. The most common treatments are antidepressant medications and psychotherapy, a combination of which leads to the best outcomes. Among the current options for treating refractory depression are electroconvulsive therapy and vagal nerve stimulation.

REFERENCES

1. Sadock, B. J., & Sadock, V. A. (2003). *Synopsis of psychiatry: Behavioral sciences/clinical psychiatry* (9th ed.). Philadelphia: Lippincott Williams & Wilkins.

2. American Psychiatric Association. (2000). *Diagnostic and statistical manual of mental disorders* (4th ed., Text Revision). Arlington, VA: American Psychiatric Publishing.

3. Sharp, L. K., & Lipsky, M. S. (2002). Screening for depression across the lifespan: A review of measures for use in primary care settings. *American Family Physician, 66,* 1001–1008.

4. U.S. Preventive Services Task Force. (2002). Screening for depression: Recommendations and rationale. *Annals of Internal Medicine, 136,* 760–764.

5. Williams, J. W., Hitchcock, N. P., Cordes, J. A., Ramirez, G., & Pignone, M. (2002). Rational clinical examination. Is this patient clinically depressed? *Journal of the American Medical Association, 287,* 1160–1167.

6. Whooley, M. A., Avins, A. L., Miranda, J., & Browner, W. S. (1997). Case-finding instruments for depression. Two questions are as good as many. *Journal of General Internal Medicine, 12,* 439–445.

7. Cochran, S. D., Sullivan, J. G., & Mays, V. M. (2003). Prevalence of mental disorders, psychological distress, and mental health services use among lesbian, gay, and bisexual adults in the United States. *Journal of Consulting and Clinical Psychology, 71,* 53–61. Available at www.stat.ucla.edu/~cochran/PDF/PrevalenceDisordersLGBinUS.pdf.

8. Gilman, S. E., Cochran, S. D., Mays, V. M., Hughes, M., Ostrow, D., & Kessler, R. C. (2001). Risk of psychiatric disorders among individuals reporting same-sex sexual partners in the National Comorbidity Survey. *American Journal of Public Health, 91,* 933–939. Available at www.ajph.org/cgi/reprint/91/6/933.pdf.

9. Cochran, S. D., & Mays, V. M. (2000). Relation between psychiatric symptoms and behaviorally defined sexual orientation in a sample of the U.S. population. *American Journal of Epidemiology, 151,* 516–523.

10. Brogan, D. J., O'Hanlan, K. A., & Elon, L. (2003). Health and professional characteristics of lesbian and heterosexual women physicians. *Journal of the American Medical Women's Association, 58,* 10–19.

11. Martell, C. R., Safren, S. A., & Prince, S. E. (2004). *Cognitive-behavioral therapies with lesbian, gay and bisexual clients.* New York: Guilford Press.

12. Lock, J., & Steiner, H. (1999). Gay, lesbian, and bisexual youth risks for emotional, physical, and social problems: Results from a community-based survey. *Journal of the American Academy of Child & Adolescent Psychiatry, 38,* 297–304.

13. Udry, J. R., & Chantala, K. (2002). Risk assessment of adolescents with same-sex relationships. *Journal of Adolescent Health, 31*, 84–92.

14. Ross, L. E., Steele, L., & Sapiro, B. (2005). Perceptions of predisposing and protective factors for perinatal depression in same-sex parents. *Journal of Midwifery & Women's Health, 50*, 65–70.

15. Trettin, S., Moses-Kolko, E. L., & Wisner, K. L. (2006). Lesbian perinatal depression and the heterosexism that affects knowledge about this minority population. *Archives of Women's Mental Health, 9*, 67–73.

16. Ross, L. E., Steele L., Goldfinger, C., & Strike, C. (2007). Perinatal depressive symptomatology among lesbian and bisexual women. *Archives of Women's Mental Health, 10*, 53–59.

17. Valanis, B. G., Bowen, D. J., Bassford, T., Whitlock, E., Charney, P., & Carter, R. A. (2000). Sexual orientation and health: Comparisons in the Women's Health Initiative sample. *Archives of Family Medicine, 9*, 843–853.

18. Cochran, S. D., & Mays, V. M. (1994). Depressive distress among homosexually active African American men and women. *American Journal of Psychiatry, 151*, 524–529.

19. Cochran, S. D., Mays, V. M., Alegria, M., Ortega A. N., & Takeuchi, D. (2007). Mental health and substance abuse disorders among Latino and Asian American lesbian, gay, and bisexual adults. *Journal of Consulting and Clinical Psychology, 75*, 785–794.

20. Hughes, T. L., & Wilsnack, S. C. (1997). Use of alcohol among lesbians: Research and clinical implications. *American Journal of Orthopsychiatry, 6*, 20–36.

21. Hughes, T. L. (2003). Lesbians' drinking patterns: Beyond the data. *Substance Use & Misuse, 38*, 1739–1758.

22. Heffernan, K. (1998). The nature and predictors of substance abuse among lesbians. *Addictive Behaviors, 23*, 517–528.

23. Bloomfield, K. A. (1993). A comparison of alcohol consumption between lesbians and heterosexual women in an urban population. *Drug and Alcohol Dependence, 33*, 257–269.

24. McKirnan, D. J., & Peterson, P. L. (1989). Alcohol and drug use among homosexual men and women: Epidemiology and population characteristics. *Addictive Behaviors, 14*, 545–553.

25. Skinner, W. F. (1994). The prevalence and demographic predictors of illicit and licit drug use among lesbians and gay men. *American Journal of Public Health, 84*, 1307–1310.

26. Gruskin, E. P., Hart, S., Gordon, N., & Ackerson, L. (2001). Patterns of cigarette smoking and alcohol use among lesbians and bisexual women enrolled in a large health maintenance organization. *American Journal of Public Health, 91*, 976–979.

27. Matthews, A. K., Hughes, T. L., Johnson, T., Razzano, L. A., & Cassidy, R. (2002). Prediction of depressive distress in a community sample of women: The role of sexual orientation. *American Journal of Public Health, 92*, 1131–1139.

28. Hughes, T. L., Johnson, T., & Wilsnack, S. C. (2001). Sexual assault and alcohol abuse: A comparison of lesbians and heterosexual women. *Journal of Substance Abuse, 13*, 515–532.

29. Bradford, J., Caitlin, R., & Rothblum, E. D. (1994). National Lesbian Health Care Survey: Implications for mental health care. *Journal of Consulting and Clinical Psychology, 62,* 228–242.

30. Hughes, T. L., Johnson, T. P., Wilsnack, S. C., & Szalacha, L. A. (2007). Childhood risk factors for alcohol abuse and psychological distress among adult lesbians. *Child Abuse & Neglect, 31,* 769–789.

31. Mays, V. M., & Cochran, S. D. (2001). Mental health correlates of perceived discrimination among lesbian, gay, and bisexual adults in the United States. *American Journal of Public Health, 91,* 1869–1876.

32. Herek, G. M., Gillis, R. J., & Cogan, J. C. (1999). Psychological sequelae of hate-crime victimization among lesbian, gay, and bisexual adults. *Journal of Consulting and Clinical Psychology, 67,* 945–951.

33. Herek, G. M. (1996). Heterosexism and homophobia. In R. P. Cabaj & T. S. Stein, (Eds.), *Textbook of homosexuality and mental health.* Washington, DC: American Psychiatric Publishing.

34. Oetjen, H., & Rothblum, E. D. (2000). When lesbians aren't gay: Factors affecting depression among lesbians. *Journal of Homosexuality, 39,* 49–73.

35. Crothers, L., Haller, E., Benton, C., & Haag, S. (2008). A clinical comparison of lesbian and heterosexual women in a psychiatric outpatient clinic. *Journal of Homosexuality, 54,* 280–292.

36. Hardin, K., & Hall, M. (2001). *Queer blues: The lesbian and gay guide to overcoming depression.* Oakland, CA: New Harbinger Publications.

37. Balon, R. (2006). SSRI-associated sexual side effects. *American Journal of Psychiatry, 163,* 1504–1509.

38. Gabbard, G. O. (2000). Psychotherapies. In B. J. Sadock & V. M. Sadock (Eds.), *Comprehensive textbook of psychiatry* (7th ed.). Philadelphia: Lippincott Williams & Wilkins.

39. Chernin, J. N., & Johnson, M. R. (2003). *Affirmative psychotherapy and counseling for lesbians and gay men.* Thousand Oaks, CA: Sage Publications.

40. Ritter, K. Y., & Terndrup, A. I. (2002). *Handbook of affirmative psychotherapy with lesbians and gay men.* New York: Guilford Press.

41. Cabaj, R. P. (1996). Sexual orientation of the therapist. In R. P. Cabaj & T. S. Stein (Eds.), *Textbook of homosexuality and mental health.* Washington, DC: American Psychiatric Publishing.

42. Spitzer, R. L. (2003). Can some gay men and lesbians change their sexual orientation? 200 participants reporting a change from homosexual to heterosexual orientation. *Archives of Sexual Behavior, 32,* 403–417.

43. Drescher, J. (2002). Ethical issues in treating gay and lesbian patients. *Psychiatric Clinics of North America, 25,* 605–621.

ABOUT THE AUTHORS

Cynthia L. Benton, MD is a psychiatrist who provides psychopharmacology and/or psychotherapy services for adult patients in her private practice. Prior to moving to Austin, Texas; she was a psychiatrist at a community clinic in San Francisco that serves the gay, lesbian, and bisexual population.

Ellen Haller, MD is Professor and Director of the Residency Training Program in the Department of Psychiatry at the University of California, San Francisco. She serves as Co-Director of the Lesbian Health & Research Center there. Her primary interest is women's mental health including mental health in the lesbian, gay, bisexual, and transgendered communities.

CHAPTER 17

"Where Are These Voices Coming From?"

SERIOUS MENTAL ILLNESS AMONG LESBIANS

MARY E. BARBER, MD

MARTHA, *70, lives in a trailer in a rural area and supports herself on Social Security and her teacher's pension. She never had mental health problems until 5 years ago, when her female partner of 30 years died. They did not have any connections with the lesbian community, were never open at work or with family about their relationship, and did not have close friends who knew them as a couple.*

Since her partner's death, Martha has had a paralyzing depression and continues to find daily activities a struggle. She gets therapy and medications from the local community mental health center, where she is open about her sexuality with her social worker and psychiatrist but not with her women's therapy group. She also is not "out" to her primary care physician. Martha has been diagnosed with major depressive disorder and complicated bereavement.

ABBY, a 43-year-old lesbian, is a survivor of childhood sexual abuse and the foster care system. She has had contact with the mental health system since she was a child; for many years, she was in and out of psychiatric hospitals for cutting herself, alcohol abuse, and suicide attempts. She has been a recovering alcoholic for 4 years, attends social work therapy and psychiatric sessions monthly at the local university hospital clinic, and goes to Alcoholics Anonymous once a week.

Abby lives with her partner, who is also in recovery from alcoholism. Both women support themselves with government-provided Supplemental Security Income. Abby volunteers as a peer advocate in the university hospital's psychiatric emergency room and is considering transitioning to part-time paid work as a step toward getting off government aid. Over the years, she has been diagnosed with borderline personality disorder, posttraumatic stress disorder, bipolar disorder, and alcohol dependence.

KATE, 25, has struggled with intense mood swings, hallucinations, and paranoia since her teens. Around then, she began using crack cocaine. It is not clear whether her psychotic symptoms followed or preceded her drug use. What is clear now is that Kate often hallucinates when she is not using crack. Although her sexual partners are mostly female, she has sex with men sometimes and considers herself "queer." She attends a day program for

*mentally ill chemical abusers run by the state hospital but frequently misses
appointments. She goes to local emergency rooms when her symptoms are
bothersome. Kate has not followed through with Social Security applications
and mostly lives off friends and family. She has been diagnosed with
schizoaffective disorder and cocaine dependence.*

■ ■ ■

Very little has been written about lesbians with serious mental illness (SMI). Although
lesbians generally have the same mental health care needs as their heterosexual
counterparts, health care practitioners may lack a basic understanding of lesbians and
may be uncomfortable with them. Furthermore, while there are specialized services
for lesbian, gay, bisexual, and transgendered (LGBT) people with SMI in some large
metropolitan areas, more of these and other services need to be accessible, safe,
and welcoming to lesbians. Practitioners can help lesbian SMI patients by taking
a thorough sexual history, being aware of local, lesbian-affirmative mental health
services, and advocating for services where none exist.

DEFINITION AND PATIENT CHARACTERISTICS

Other terms for serious mental illness are "severe and persistent mental illness"
and "chronic mental illness." (See the glossary of mental illness terms at the end
of this chapter.) The differences between these definitions are operational,[1-3] but
they generally refer to someone who has a diagnosed psychiatric disorder that
over a period of time—not just acutely or as one episode of illness—causes serious
functional difficulties in one or more areas, such as work and relationships.[4] An
estimated 6% of the American population has a SMI.[5]

Definitions of SMI are not diagnosis-specific; rather, they reflect a lower level
of function or more serious illness across diagnostic categories. Thus, a person
diagnosed with major depression who cannot work and has had several recent
hospitalizations would be categorized as having SMI, while a person diagnosed with
schizophrenia who is on medication, is partnered and working, and has minimal
symptoms would not. "Schizophrenia" generally includes more people with SMI than
do "personality disorder" and "major depression," but there are wide ranges of illness
severity and level of function across most psychiatric diagnoses. A person in the SMI
category is likely to at least have major depression, bipolar disorder, schizophrenia

or schizoaffective disorder, obsessive-compulsive disorder, borderline personality disorder, or posttraumatic stress disorder.[4]

Although people with SMI are diagnostically heterogeneous, they share some common characteristics. Many cannot work regularly and therefore rely on support from long-term government assistance programs such as Social Security Disability (SSD) or Supplemental Security Income (SSI). People on SSD have accrued enough federal work credits before they became disabled; Medicare is their health insurer. People on SSI who did not have substantial work histories before they became disabled are covered under Medicaid. Both groups and the large number of uninsured and working poor with SMI typically receive help through the public mental health system.

The system—a patchwork of mental health agencies operated by state and local governments, and of voluntary, nonprofit organizations—serves people who have SMI and low-income people who have less severe mental health care needs. All or some of the funding and revenue these entities receive is state and federal. Public mental health care includes hospital and outpatient clinic treatment, intensive day programs, partial hospital programs, case management, housing, and vocational services for the mentally ill. Much has been written about the system's shortcomings and limited resources[6]; nevertheless, it is where most lesbians with SMI get treatment.

EPIDEMIOLOGY

A weakness of early studies on psychiatric disorders in lesbians was a lack of representative samples. In more recent and more scientifically rigorous studies of large representative samples, women who reported having female sexual partners showed higher incidences of depression, phobias, posttraumatic stress disorder, substance use, and suicidal behavior.[7-10] However, this research was limited by the fact that women who had sex with women may have identified as lesbian, bisexual, or heterosexual. The studies either did not ask about sexual orientation/identity or combined women who identified as lesbian together with women who reported sex with women.[7] One study using a national representative sample that did ask subjects about sexual orientation found higher rates of generalized anxiety among lesbians and bisexual women compared with heterosexual women but no differences in major depression, panic disorder, or substance abuse.[11] There is some support for the widely held belief that any higher incidence rates are attributable to the stress of being a sexual minority and to the discrimination LGBT people encounter.[12]

Research on the incidence of psychiatric illnesses in lesbian populations either has not included diagnoses such as bipolar disorder and schizophrenia or has not found those diagnoses in large enough numbers to warrant any conclusions. In general, it is unknown if more lesbians than heterosexual women have SMI; the assumption is that they do not.

By some estimates, as many as two-thirds of people with SMI have a co-occurring substance disorder, either abuse or dependence. Because substance abuse rates are higher among LGBT populations,[9,10] it is safe to infer that the percentage of lesbians with SMI who have a co-occurring substance disorder may be even higher.

SPECIAL CONSIDERATIONS REGARDING LESBIANS

The fact that little has been written about the sexual lives and activities of lesbians with SMI reflects a larger reality: little has been written about the sexual lives and activities of all people with SMI. The mental health system often views such people as children, reflecting traditional institutionalization practices. A frequent assumption is that individuals with SMI are asexual. Moreover, bipolar disorder and schizophrenia often begin in adolescence or early adulthood, the very time when people define their sexual identities and become sexually active. For many lesbian and heterosexual women with SMI, severe illness and hospitalizations in early adulthood have derailed the process of becoming sexual persons.

Mentally ill people rarely get all of their care in inpatient institutions, unlike in the past. Still, the system frequently treats them paternalistically, not as thinking adults. This approach arose as a beneficent alternative to previous harsher approaches. Although mental health clinicians and institutions now play a more directive care-giving role, some mental health providers and consumers are increasingly questioning the care paradigm and pushing to make the system more recovery-focused and person-centered.[13,14] Their efforts follow advocacy efforts in medicine, notably in obstetrics and oncology, that have prompted greater patient involvement and shared decision-making in treatment. In psychiatry, an important aspect of this shift is thinking of patients with SMI as whole persons in terms of their work, daily life, and relationships, including their sexuality.

Clinicians who encounter women with SMI must be mindful of a few important points. First, they should not assume that these patients are heterosexual or asexual. As with all patients, the clinician needs to take a sexual history and consider sexuality to be an important part of overall being, regardless of whether an individual is currently in a relationship. Second, it is vitally important to make contraception available to reproductive-age women with SMI and to remember that about 30% of lesbians are also sexually active with men on occasion. Third, one should not confuse a patient's sexuality with her psychiatric illness. For example, a clinician whose lesbian patient has posttraumatic stress disorder and a history of childhood sexual abuse may erroneously attribute her lesbian identity to her abuse history. While there is some data from unrepresentative samples suggesting that childhood sexual abuse is more prevalent among lesbians than heterosexual women,[15,16] concluding that the abuse is a causal factor in a woman's lesbian identity would be incorrect. Indeed, causality might flow in the opposite direction. Balsam and colleagues found higher rates of abuse among lesbians than their heterosexual siblings. The lesbian siblings were possibly at higher risk of abuse due to their lesbian identity, behaviors atypical of female gender, or childhood appearance.[15] Another study that supports this conclusion revealed higher rates of sexual and physical assault among lesbian, gay, and bisexual youth in general but even higher rates in the subset of youth who displayed gender-atypical behavior.[17]

According to past clinical teaching, physicians who saw patients with SMI and co-occurring substance-use disorders were supposed to identify the "primary" disorder, which led to delays in treating psychiatric disorders and prompted stern warnings by physicians not to mix recreational drugs and medications. Consequently, many people stopped taking their psychiatric medications and dropped out of treatment. Current thinking stresses the importance of treating both disorders simultaneously, preferably in the same program. Clinicians also know now that starting psychiatric medication early, regardless of whether or not a disorder is substance-induced, can lead to better retention in treatment and a greater likelihood the patient will stop using a substance. This approach is equally valid for lesbians with co-occurring disorders.

Research suggests that chronic health factors such as smoking, obesity, physical inactivity, and less access to care may reduce the life expectancy of adults with SMI by 25 years.[18] Presumably, lesbians with SMI bear the same illness burden. Therefore, clinicians can improve the lives of lesbian patients with SMI by attending to their basic health needs as they would in attending to the basic health needs of any other patients, which includes helping them to quit smoking and lose weight.

SERVICES

There is a growing body of literature on lesbian and gay-affirmative psychotherapy and mental health services.[19-24] The major principles underlying these therapies and services include viewing lesbian, gay, or bisexual identities as normal, being willing to examine antilesbian or antigay feelings in both the patient and therapist, and having at least some knowledge about issues specific to lesbians and gay men, such as coming out. While the literature focuses almost entirely on treatment of patients who do not have SMI, it also applies to those who do. Mental health practitioners in the public system are not always familiar with this body of knowledge. LGBT people receiving public mental health services continue to report discrimination and insensitive care.[25,26] At least one study has shown that, compared with a sample of patients in the general population, they are less satisfied with their care.[27]

Most large and many smaller urban areas have community centers that provide support and social services to LGBT people, yet the centers are primarily targeted to the general LGBT community, not specifically to those with SMI. Thus, lesbians with SMI may not feel welcome at these centers or, because of their illness, may feel alienated from other LGBT people there.[28,29] Some local Alcoholics Anonymous and Narcotics Anonymous chapters have established special groups for LGBT people in recovery. But lesbians with SMI may feel more comfortable in Double Trouble Recovery groups for people with co-occurring mental health and substance abuse problems, as the groups acknowledge members' mental illness and accept the fact that they are taking psychiatric medication. A few, peer-run psychosocial clubs and services within larger mental health programs or specialized health centers are available specifically to LGBT people with SMI,[29,30] providing a place where it is acceptable to be open about and address all aspects of one's identity. However, many areas of the country still lack social support services for lesbians with SMI.

Clinicians who want to provide the best care for lesbians with SMI must become advocates. They can:

- Call the local mental health center and ask if it offers lesbian-affirmative treatment;
- Determine if the local LGBT community center (if one exists) welcomes people who have SMI;
- Encourage the patient's mental health care provider to consult with LGBT-specific mental health services in other geographic areas;
- Enroll in courses or take advantage of other educational opportunities to learn about how best to treat LGBT patients; and
- Encourage state and local governments and community leaders to create more sensitive and welcoming services for this population.

CONCLUSION

Little is known about the sexual lives and activities of lesbians who have serious mental illness, as lesbian-specific research has not included diagnoses such as bipolar disorder and schizophrenia or has not found those diagnoses in large enough numbers to warrant any conclusions. However, lesbians with serious mental health illness presumably bear the same burden as heterosexual women. Lesbian patients can benefit from clinicians who attend to their basic health needs and refer them to lesbian-affirmative psychotherapy and mental health services. Clinicians should champion better services targeted to this population and become knowledgeable about lesbians' special mental health needs and the resources available to them.

ADDITIONAL RESOURCES

- Association of Gay and Lesbian Psychiatrists: ✍ www.aglp.org

- Callen-Lorde Community Health Center, New York City: ✍ www.callen-lorde.org

- Fenway Health, Boston: ✍ www.fenwayhealth.org/site/PageServer?pagename= FCHC_srv_services_home

- The Lesbian, Gay, Bisexual, & Transgender Community Center, New York City: ✍ www.gaycenter.org/?gclid=CNHq6ans65oCFQ6jagodq2oYBQ

- LGBT Affirmative Program
  South Beach Psychiatric Center
  25 Flatbush Ave., 3rd Floor
  Brooklyn, New York 11217

- Rainbow Heights Club, Brooklyn, NY: ✍ www.rainbowheights.org

GLOSSARY OF MENTAL ILLNESSES*

- **Bipolar disorder:** characterized by at least one episode of mania involving an extremely elevated or irritable mood. Other symptoms are less need for sleep, grandiosity, pressured speech, and an increase in risky activities. Most women with bipolar disorder have both depressive and manic episodes.

- **Borderline personality disorder:** the most commonly diagnosed personality disorder. It involves unstable emotions, relationships, and self-image; impulsive behaviors; and frantic attempts to avoid abandonment, either real or imagined. Borderline personality disorder is often comorbid with major depression or bipolar disorder and posttraumatic stress disorder. It is more common in women than men.

- **Major depressive disorder:** characterized by one or more episodes of major depression involving depressed mood and/or lack of interest or pleasure in activities. Additional symptoms are poor sleep and appetite, feelings of guilt or worthlessness, hopelessness, and suicidal thoughts or behaviors.

Source: American Psychiatric Association. (2004). Diagnostic and statistical manual of mental disorders (4th ed.). Washington, DC: American Psychiatric Publishing.

- **Obsessive-compulsive disorder:** includes recurrent, intrusive thoughts (obsessions) and/or an overwhelming pull toward repetitive, sometimes meaningless behaviors (compulsions). People with obsessive-compulsive disorder, unlike those with delusions, are aware that the thoughts or behaviors are illogical, but they cannot stop them. Obsessive-compulsive disorder is less common in women than men.

- **Posttraumatic stress disorder:** occurs after a major traumatic event. Posttraumatic stress disorder is characterized by re-experiencing the event (flashbacks, intrusive memories), attempts to avoid situations that trigger memories of the event, and hypervigilance (heightened startle response, a general feeling of danger). First identified in combat veterans, posttraumatic stress disorder also occurs in survivors of childhood sexual abuse. It is more common in women than men.

- **Schizoaffective disorder:** includes mood episodes, either depressive only or bipolar, and psychotic symptoms as in schizophrenia. The psychotic symptoms must occur at times when the individual is not having a mood episode.

- **Schizophrenia:** symptoms include delusions and/or hallucinations, paranoia, incoherent speech and thoughts, and negative symptoms (avolition, amotivation). Schizophrenia is likely to have a more severe and chronic course than other illnesses listed above.

REFERENCES

1. Parabiaghi, A., Bonetto, C., Ruggeri, M., Lasalvia, A., & Leese, M. (2006). Severe and persistent mental illness: A useful definition for prioritizing community-based mental health service interventions. *Social Psychiatry and Psychiatric Epidemiology, 41,* 457–463.

2. Ruggeri, M., Leese, M., Thornicroft, G., Bisoffi, G., & Tansella, M. (2000). Definition and prevalence of severe and persistent mental illness. *British Journal of Psychiatry, 177,* 149–155.

3. Schinnar, A. P., Rothbard, A. B., Kanter, R., & Jung, Y. S. (1990). An empirical literature review of definitions of severe and persistent mental illness. *American Journal of Psychiatry, 147,* 1602–1608.

4. American Psychiatric Association. (2004). *Diagnostic and statistical manual of mental disorders* (4th ed.). Washington, DC: American Psychiatric Publishing.

5. Kessler, R. C., Chiu, W. T., Demler, O., Merikangas, K. R., & Walters, E. E. (2005). Prevalence, severity, and comorbidity of twelve-month DSM-IV disorders in the National Comorbidity Survey Replication. *Archives of General Psychiatry, 62,* 617–627.

6. President's New Freedom Commission on Mental Health, Substance Abuse and Mental Health Services Administration. (2003). *Achieving the promise: Transforming mental health care in America* (Publication No. 03-3832). Washington, DC: U.S. Department of Health & Human Services. Available at www.mentalhealthcommission.gov/reports/FinalReport/downloads/downloads.html.

7. Cochran, S. D., Mays, V. M., Alegria, M., Ortega, A. N., & Takeuchi, D. (2007). Mental health and substance use disorders among Latino and Asian American lesbian, gay, and bisexual adults. *Journal of Consulting and Clinical Psychology, 75*, 785–794.

8. De Graaf, R., Sandfort, T. G., & ten Have, M. (2006). Suicidality and sexual orientation: Differences between men and women in a general population-based sample from the Netherlands. *Archives of Sexual Behavior, 35*, 253–262.

9. Gilman, S. E., Cochran, S. D., Mays, V. M., Hughes, M., Ostrow, D., & Kessler, R. C. (2001). Risk of psychiatric disorders among individuals reporting same-sex sexual partners in the National Comorbidity Survey. *American Journal of Public Health, 91*, 933–939.

10. Sandfort, T. G., de Graaf, R., Bijl, R. V., & Schnabel, P. (2001). Same-sex sexual behavior and psychiatric disorders: Findings from the Netherlands Mental Health Survey and Incidence Study (NEMESIS). *Archives of General Psychiatry, 58*, 85–91.

11. Cochran, S. D., Mays, V. M., & Sullivan, J. G. (2003). Prevalence of mental disorders, psychological distress, and mental health services use among lesbian, gay, and bisexual adults in the United States. *Journal of Consulting and Clinical Psychology, 71*, 53–61.

12. Mays, V. M., & Cochran, S. D. (2001). Mental health correlates of perceived discrimination among lesbian, gay, and bisexual adults in the United States. *American Journal of Public Health, 91*, 1869–1876.

13. Adams, N., & Grieder, D. M. (2005). *Treatment planning for person-centered care.* Burlington, MA: Elsevier Academic Press.

14. Davidson, L., Harding, C., & Spaniol, L. (Eds.). (2005). *Recovery from severe mental illness: Research evidence and implications for practice.* Boston: Center for Psychiatric Rehabilitation.

15. Balsam, K. F., Rothblum, E. D., & Beauchaine, T. P. (2005). Victimization over the life span: A comparison of lesbian, gay, bisexual, and heterosexual siblings. *Journal of Consulting and Clinical Psychology, 73*, 477–487.

16. Hughes, T. L., Johnson, T., & Wilsnack, S. C. (2001). Sexual assault and alcohol abuse: A comparison of lesbians and heterosexual women. *Journal of Substance Abuse, 13*, 515–532.

17. D'Augelli, A. R., Grossman, A. H., & Starks, M. T. (2006). Childhood gender atypicality, victimization, and PTSD among lesbian, gay, and bisexual youth. *Journal of Interpersonal Violence, 21*, 1462–1482.

18. Parks, J., Svendsen, D., Singer, P., & Foti, M. E. (2006). *Morbidity and mortality in people with serious mental illness.* Alexandria, VA: National Association of State Mental Health Program Directors. Available at www.nasmhpd.org/general_files/publications/med_ directors_pubs/Mortality%20and%20Morbidity%20Final%20Report%208.18.08.pdf.

19. Group for the Advancement of Psychiatry. (2007). *LGBT mental health syllabus.* Available at www.aglp.org/gap.

20. Drescher, J. (1998). *Psychoanalytic therapy and the gay man.* Hillsdale, NJ: Analytic Press.

21. Magee, M., & Miller, D. C. (1997). *Lesbian lives: Psychoanalytic narratives old & new.* Hillsdale, NJ: Analytic Press.

22. Cabaj, R. P., & Stein, T. S. (Eds.). (1996). *Textbook of homosexuality and mental health.* Washington, DC: American Psychiatric Publishing.

23. Domenici, T., & Lesser, R. C. (Eds.). (1995). *Disorienting sexuality.* New York: Routledge.

24. Isay, R. A. (1987). *Being homosexual.* New York: Farrar, Straus and Giroux.

25. Willging, C. E., Salvador, M., & Kano, M. (2006). Unequal treatment: Mental health care for sexual and gender minority groups in a rural state. *Psychiatric Services, 57,* 867–870.

26. Willging, C. E., Salvador, M., & Kano, M. (2006). Pragmatic help seeking: How sexual and gender minority groups access mental health care in a rural state. *Psychiatric Services, 57,* 871–874.

27. Avery, A. M., Hellman, R. E., & Sudderth, L. K. (2001). Satisfaction with mental health services among sexual minorities with major mental illness. *American Journal of Public Health, 91,* 990–991.

28. Hellman, R. E. (1996). Issues in the treatment of lesbian women and gay men with chronic mental illness. *Psychiatric Services, 47,* 1093–1098.

29. Hellman, R. E., & Drescher, J. (Eds.). (2004). *Handbook of LGBT issues in community mental health.* New York: Haworth Press.

30. Huygen, C. (2006). Understanding the needs of lesbian, gay, bisexual, and transgender people living with mental illness. *Medscape General Medicine, 8, 29.*

ACKNOWLEDGMENT: Portions of this chapter were included in Barber, Mary E. (2009), "Lesbian, gay, and bisexual people with severe mental illness," *Journal of Gay & Lesbian Mental Health* 13 (2): 133–142. Reprinted by permission of the publisher (Taylor & Francis, www.informaworld.com).

ABOUT THE AUTHOR

Mary E. Barber, MD is Clinical Director of Rockland Psychiatric Center in Orangeburg, New York and Clinical Assistant Professor of Psychiatry at Columbia College. She is a past President of the Association of Gay and Lesbian Psychiatrists, and currently serves as Co-Editor of the *Journal of Gay and Lesbian Mental Health.*

CHAPTER 18

"She Didn't Mean to Hit Me."
LESBIAN INTIMATE PARTNER VIOLENCE

KELLY A. BLASKO, PhD

MARY, *a 30-year-old woman of average build, arrives for a doctor visit the day after a physical fight with her partner, Linda, who hit her during an argument. She is visibly upset and has facial abrasions. Mary becomes tearful as she recalls the latest incident and talks about her relationship with Linda. She is concerned about continuing their 5-year relationship, given this latest incident.*

Mary and Linda have lived together for 4 of those 5 years. According to Mary, the fight was typical of arguments with Linda: although they do not argue frequently, the fights end in physical confrontation. In addition, Linda has always made it difficult for Mary to keep in touch with family and friends and to hold a job. Mary rarely goes out socially, as Linda becomes very jealous if Mary talks to anyone but her. Mary says Linda often puts her down and makes her feel unimportant.

The most recent fight began after Mary arrived home from work later than she usually does. Soon Linda arrived and became angry because Mary was on the phone with a friend. Linda yelled that Mary had housework to do and that she should get off the phone. Mary then went into the kitchen to prepare dinner. Linda followed her, grabbed her arm, and slapped her. Mary pushed Linda, then Linda knocked her to the floor and kicked her. Mary got up and left the house, even though Linda tried to stop her.

What should the clinician do to help Mary in her current situation?

■ ■ ■

Lesbian intimate partner violence is a significant social and medical concern in the lesbian community.[1-3] In a review of research on this topic, West reported that 30% to 40% of lesbians have been involved in at least one physically abusive relationship.[3] Table 18.1 summarizes the few prevalence studies of lesbian intimate partner violence published since 1986.

DEFINITIONS OF INTIMATE VIOLENCE

Until the mid-1980s, empirical researchers did not recognize lesbian intimate partner violence; they focused almost exclusively on husbands battering wives.[*] Studies since then have specifically investigated lesbian intimate partner violence. This type of violence and heterosexual domestic violence are similar in some respects, but lesbian intimate partner violence has unique characteristics, the focus of this chapter. As research has broadened, terminology regarding lesbian intimate partner violence has changed and new terms have entered the lexicon to better define it.

---

[*] For purposes of this chapter, "intimate partner violence," "domestic violence," and "battering" are synonymous.

TABLE 18.1. RESEARCH ON PREVALENCE OF INTIMATE PARTNER VIOLENCE AMONG LESBIANS

AUTHORS	METHOD	DEFINITION OF SEXUALITY	FINDINGS
Turell[4]	Survey. Restricted to lesbian/gay/bisexual/transgender community groups in the Houston area.	Identity	Among lesbians (n = 193), 55% reported past or present physical abuse, 61% reported coercion, and 84% reported emotional abuse.
Tjaden et al.[5]	Nationally representative telephone survey	Behavior	Among female, same-sex cohabitants (n = 79), 11.4% reported they had been physically assaulted by a partner.
Scherzer[6]	Nonrandom survey, including snowball sampling to distribute survey in the San Francisco Bay Area	Identity	Among lesbians (n = 256), 17% reported physical abuse at some time during their current or most recent relationship; 31% reported emotional abuse.
Lockhart et al.[7]	Nonrandom survey at a women's music festival in the Southeast	Identity	Among lesbians (n = 284), 31% reported physical abuse in the previous year or in a current relationship.
Coleman[8]	Nonrandom survey of lesbian couples	Identity	Among lesbian couples (n = 90), 40% reported acts of violence in their relationships.
Lie & Gentlewarrier[9]	Nonrandom survey of women at the Michigan Womyn's Music Festival	Identity	Among lesbians (n = 1,099), 52% reported physical or verbal abuse and/or sexual aggression by a former female lover.
Loulan[10]	Nonrandom survey of lesbians at lesbian-specific organizations, workshops, etc., in the United States and Canada, 1985–87	Identity	Among lesbians (n = 1,566), 17% reported they had been involved in violent relationships.
Brand & Kidd[11]	Nonrandom survey of heterosexual and lesbian women in the greater San Francisco Bay Area	Identity	Among lesbians (n = 55), 25% reported they had been physically abused by a partner in a past relationship.

In 1986, Hart defined lesbian battering as a "pattern of violence [or] coercive behaviors whereby a lesbian seeks to control the thoughts, beliefs, or conduct of her intimate partner or to punish the intimate partner for resisting the perpetrator's control"[12] (p. 173). Studies of domestic violence have traditionally defined "perpetrators" and "victims" in patriarchal terms: men are perpetrators, women are victims. Here, "perpetrator" refers to the abusive person in a relationship and "victim" to the one being abused. These terms have different meanings in abusive lesbian relationships than they do in abusive heterosexual relationships.

LESBIAN INTIMATE PARTNER VIOLENCE

Understanding lesbian intimate partner violence requires an understanding of the context in which it happens, the risk factors that contribute to it, and the dynamics of lesbian relationships, including control tactics and power imbalance.[1,2,13] Such violence occurs in a society that is heterosexist and homophobic,[14,15] and that offers limited services to women who seek help.[16,17] No demographic group in the lesbian community is immune from the potential for intimate partner violence; minorities such as lesbians of color often experience further oppression that makes it even more difficult for them to seek services.[18]

Miller and colleagues investigated four factors in lesbian relationships that might pose a greater risk of violence: control, fusion, dependency, and self-esteem. Their findings suggested that:

- Lesbians who felt they had less control were more likely to use violent tactics in conflicts with partners. The context for this finding is the community in which lesbians live: they may feel both internal and external oppression, and be unable to openly disclose their sexual orientation;
- Greater fusion in lesbian relationships—the degree to which partners balance their need for attachment and intimacy with their need for autonomy—was related to more frequent use of control tactics. Fusion may not give each partner enough room to differentiate herself and, therefore, could cause outbursts of rage;
- Lesbians with independent personalities are more likely to resort to violence, which may seem counterintuitive; and
- Lower self-esteem resulted in more abuse.[19]

Power and control dynamics are an integral part of assessing intimate partner violence.[1,13,20,21] Pence and Paymar developed the Power and Control Wheel, which highlights the control tactics that could be present in a heterosexual abusive relationship to varying degrees.[22] The types of tactics that cut across lines of gender identity and sexual orientation include intimidation; sexual and physical abuse; isolation; minimizing, denying, and blaming the abused; economic abuse; and coercion and threats.[13] The National Coalition of Anti-Violence Programs modified this model to include psychological and emotional abuse, and homophobia[23] (Figure 18.1). One control tactic based on homophobia, for example, is threatening to "out" the abused partner to friends, family, and employers.[2,13]

In a survey of 100 victims of lesbian battering, Renzetti found that psychological abuse occurred frequently. Such abuse included verbal threats; demeaning comments in front of friends, relatives, or strangers; interrupted eating or sleeping habits; and damage or destruction of property. Respondents also reported physical abuse that sometimes or frequently included pushing or shoving; hitting with open hands or a fist; scratching or hitting the face, breast, or genitals; and/or throwing objects.[24]

Scherzer reported findings similar to Renzetti's. A nonrandom survey of 256 lesbians revealed that emotional abuse occurred more frequently than physical abuse. The top three emotional-abuse control tactics in order of frequency were insults and swearing; throwing, smashing, hitting, or kicking something; and verbally putting down the other in front of friends or relatives. The top three physical-abuse control tactics in order of frequency were disrupting or impeding the other's eating or sleeping habits; pushing, grabbing, or shoving; and driving recklessly to punish or scare.[6]

HELP-SEEKING BEHAVIORS

Pervasive heterosexism and homophobia may make it difficult for lesbians to find help for violence in their intimate relationship.[6,14,15,24] Many third-party resources, such as mental health care providers, friends, and family, are unaware that intimate partner violence is a concern in the lesbian community. Some of them may also deny that intimate partner violence is an issue for lesbian couples.[16] Many of these resources—and lesbians themselves—think such violence is strictly a heterosexual issue. Lesbians who encounter this traditionally patriarchal phenomenon may believe it could not possibly occur in a lesbian relationship.[16] Homophobia can negatively influence help-seeking behaviors because lesbians already feel stigmatized by society as a consequence of their sexual orientation.[14,15] As a sexual minority, they may not want to fuel negative stereotypes, fearing there will be a backlash against the lesbian community.[16] Lesbians who seek help from a third-party resource may have to admit not only the seriousness of intimate partner violence, but also their sexual orientation.

Three survey-based studies investigated the third-party resources that lesbians who had experienced relationship violence would most likely seek or had sought for help. In all three, researchers had difficulty obtaining a representative sample of battered lesbians; nevertheless, the results were consistent.

FIGURE 18.1. TYPES OF ABUSE IN

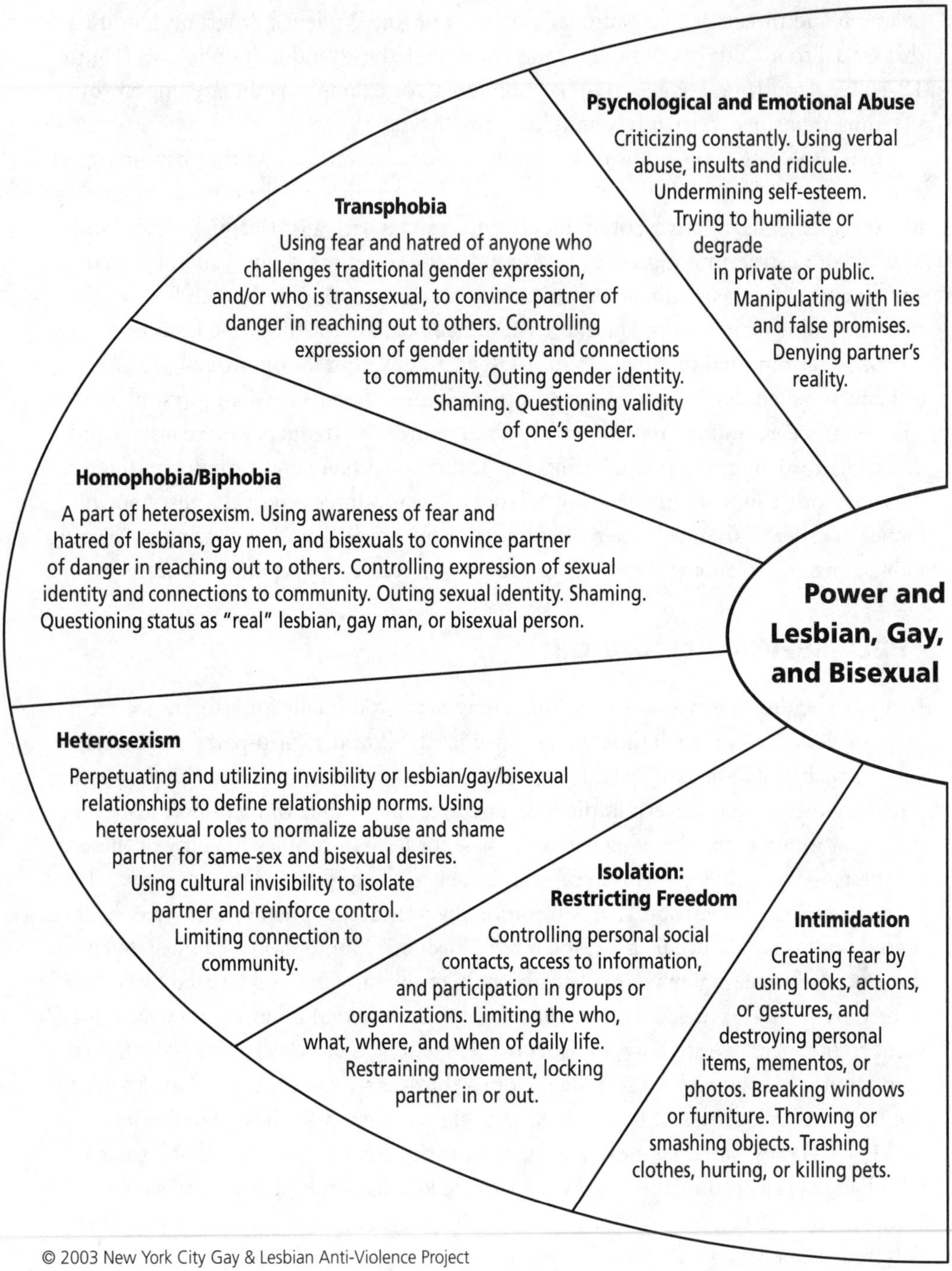

Psychological and Emotional Abuse

Criticizing constantly. Using verbal abuse, insults and ridicule. Undermining self-esteem. Trying to humiliate or degrade in private or public. Manipulating with lies and false promises. Denying partner's reality.

Transphobia

Using fear and hatred of anyone who challenges traditional gender expression, and/or who is transsexual, to convince partner of danger in reaching out to others. Controlling expression of gender identity and connections to community. Outing gender identity. Shaming. Questioning validity of one's gender.

Homophobia/Biphobia

A part of heterosexism. Using awareness of fear and hatred of lesbians, gay men, and bisexuals to convince partner of danger in reaching out to others. Controlling expression of sexual identity and connections to community. Outing sexual identity. Shaming. Questioning status as "real" lesbian, gay man, or bisexual person.

Power and Lesbian, Gay, and Bisexual

Heterosexism

Perpetuating and utilizing invisibility or lesbian/gay/bisexual relationships to define relationship norms. Using heterosexual roles to normalize abuse and shame partner for same-sex and bisexual desires. Using cultural invisibility to isolate partner and reinforce control. Limiting connection to community.

Isolation: Restricting Freedom

Controlling personal social contacts, access to information, and participation in groups or organizations. Limiting the who, what, where, and when of daily life. Restraining movement, locking partner in or out.

Intimidation

Creating fear by using looks, actions, or gestures, and destroying personal items, mementos, or photos. Breaking windows or furniture. Throwing or smashing objects. Trashing clothes, hurting, or killing pets.

© 2003 New York City Gay & Lesbian Anti-Violence Project

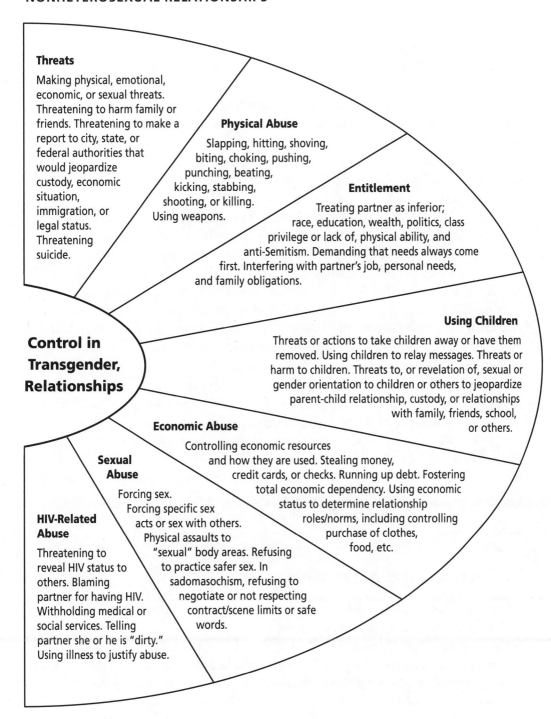

Threats

Making physical, emotional, economic, or sexual threats. Threatening to harm family or friends. Threatening to make a report to city, state, or federal authorities that would jeopardize custody, economic situation, immigration, or legal status. Threatening suicide.

Physical Abuse

Slapping, hitting, shoving, biting, choking, pushing, punching, beating, kicking, stabbing, shooting, or killing. Using weapons.

Entitlement

Treating partner as inferior; race, education, wealth, politics, class privilege or lack of, physical ability, and anti-Semitism. Demanding that needs always come first. Interfering with partner's job, personal needs, and family obligations.

Control in Transgender, Relationships

Using Children

Threats or actions to take children away or have them removed. Using children to relay messages. Threats or harm to children. Threats to, or revelation of, sexual or gender orientation to children or others to jeopardize parent-child relationship, custody, or relationships with family, friends, school, or others.

Economic Abuse

Controlling economic resources and how they are used. Stealing money, credit cards, or checks. Running up debt. Fostering total economic dependency. Using economic status to determine relationship roles/norms, including controlling purchase of clothes, food, etc.

Sexual Abuse

Forcing sex. Forcing specific sex acts or sex with others. Physical assaults to "sexual" body areas. Refusing to practice safer sex. In sadomasochism, refusing to negotiate or not respecting contract/scene limits or safe words.

HIV-Related Abuse

Threatening to reveal HIV status to others. Blaming partner for having HIV. Withholding medical or social services. Telling partner she or he is "dirty." Using illness to justify abuse.

Among 100 respondents who were victims of lesbian battering, Renzetti found that the top three sources of help were friends, counselors, and relatives; the resources they turned to least often were neighbors, attorneys, and physicians, including psychiatrists.[24] Lie and Gentlewarrier asked victims and perpetrators which resources they would most likely use after an abusive episode, assuming such resources were available. Victims cited support groups, self-help groups, private therapy/counseling, and battered women's shelters most frequently, while perpetrators cited private therapy/counseling, self-help groups, and support groups.[9] In a study by Scherzer, respondents had most frequently asked counselors, friends, and family for help; the least-sought resources were doctors, religious counselors, legal assistance services, and crisis lines. Significantly, more than half of these respondents had sought help from two or more resources.[6]

The victims of lesbian battering in Renzetti's survey said friends and counselors were somewhat helpful to very helpful.[24] According to qualitative evidence in Scherzer's survey, a few lesbians found that counselors were sometimes threatening to their relationships.[6] In all three studies, lesbians generally did not think that formal agencies (such as those for domestic violence), women's shelters, and crisis lines were helpful. Barriers that prevent lesbians from seeking help from formal domestic violence agencies are systemic (heterosexism), institutional (ambiguous policies that exclude lesbians), and individual (attitudes and discrimination).[16]

Health professionals play a critical role in serving lesbians who present with signs of intimate partner violence. They may be the front-line providers of care and/or the ones who identify a relationship as abusive.[1] Distressed victims and perpetrators may disclose this highly personal and serious concern to clinicians but nobody else.

How professionals choose to interact with lesbian patients or clients could affect their standard of care. They need to ask themselves these questions: Would I recognize the signs of lesbian intimate partner violence? Could my attitudes about intimate partner violence and lesbianism create assumptions that negatively affect my ability to provide the best care to lesbians? How competent am I to assess and treat lesbian victims and perpetrators?

SCREENING AND ASSESSMENT

Many psychologists do not routinely screen for intimate partner violence. In a study by Samuelson and Campbell, psychologists' top concerns about screening female patients for such violence were, in order: (1) the client might be unwilling to disclose information, (2) the psychologist lacked training in intimate partner violence issues, (3) screening might be overwhelming for the client, and (4) there is too little time during the intake process to screen.[25] A barrier to assessment for lesbian intimate partner violence is the assumption that a lesbian most likely is not being abused or is not abusive, or that lesbian abuse is mutual abuse.[16,24]

A number of researchers have proposed strategies for assessing intimate partner violence generally[25-29] and between lesbians.[30-32] However, there is no empirically validated method for assessing lesbian intimate partner violence.

The therapist's assessment may be prompted by an immediate crisis, like the physical confrontation between Mary and Linda in the scenario at the beginning of this chapter, or take place over time as a client reveals abuse. Abuse may not be the primary issue for a lesbian or lesbian couple that presents for help. The clinician must determine if there is intimate partner violence, who is perpetrating it, and if all individuals involved are safe.

In the assessment process proposed by McCloskey and Grigsby (Figure 18.2), the first step involves interviewing each presenting client separately.[26] If a client reports intimate partner violence, the next steps are history-taking, identifying the primary perpetrator and the victim, and assessing the lethality of the abuse. Skilled clinical interviewing rather than pencil-and-paper instruments is key to an accurate and complete evaluation.[33]

Whether a lesbian calls in for help or presents with her partner, the clinician must assess the relationship in terms of safety,[30] which is of utmost importance for both partners. The risk of further abuse may increase during the time of disclosure and lead to severe danger and consequences, especially for the abuse victim. Separating partners during the initial assessment can help the clinician make better decisions[34] and enable each of them to talk more freely.

To disclose abuse, the presenting client also must come out to the clinician as a lesbian.[16] This double disclosure may be difficult for the client and put her in a vulnerable position. For example, the abuser may have used threats as a control tactic to out her lesbian partner, which could cause the victim to lose family, friends, custody of children, or employment. The presenting client may fear these potential repercussions if she outs herself, especially if she is unsure whether she has been abused or is abusive.

The clinician must make the lesbian client feel safe about revealing what is happening in her relationship. Istar suggests focusing first on her current circumstances and listening carefully as she describes her experiences.[31] Ensuring confidentiality, which can be difficult in states that have mandatory reporting laws for adult abuse, is key to creating rapport and establishing safety in the therapeutic relationship.[30] Clinicians need to know if their state has such a law and, if it does, be familiar with the statute so they can explain the reporting process and potential consequences to clients.[35]

Clinicians can ask the lesbian client direct, formal questions, such as "Are you a victim of intimate partner violence?" or "Are you in an abusive relationship?"

FIGURE 18.2. AN ASSESSMENT FRAMEWORK

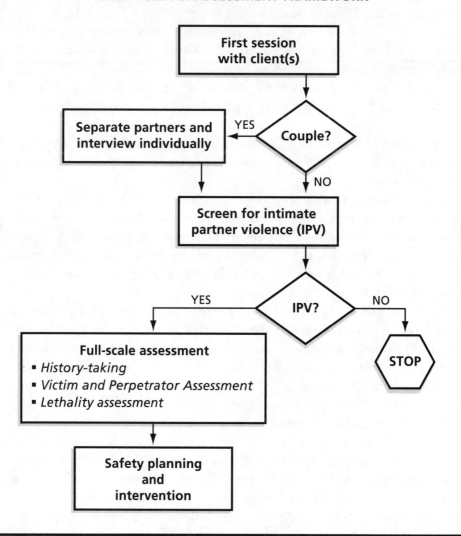

Source: Adapted from McCloskey, K., & Grigsby, N. (2005). The ubiquitous clinical problem of adult intimate partner violence: The need for routine assessment. *Preventive Medicine, 36,* 264–275.

However, lesbians who are experiencing abuse in their relationships may not be able to identify it as "abuse," "intimate partner violence," or "battering." Another strategy is to ask less-threatening questions first so the client can describe the relationship dynamics from her perspective. McCloskey and Grigsby suggest: "How do arguments usually begin?" "During your last argument, where were you?" "How long did the incident last?" "What happened when it was over?" Subsequent questions—such as

"During your arguments, did you or your partner ever slap, punch, threaten to hit?"—are narrower; they seek to elicit more details about the abuse, including the control tactics[20] (p. 271). To gain the most accurate picture of what is happening in the relationship, questions should be as specific as possible.

History-Taking

History-taking includes gathering information about intimate partner violence over time (e.g., current and past status of the relationship, abuse in the family of origin, abuse in past relationships), intervention by third parties (e.g., therapists, women's shelters, police), and any mental health and substance abuse issues (e.g., personality traits, diagnosis). This is an important step because accurately assessing the presence of lesbian intimate partner violence depends on understanding the context and patterns of the relationship.[1,30]

Studies have found a high incidence of physical and/or sexual abuse histories among lesbian perpetrators.[36,37] Lesbians who reported using alcohol and drugs were more likely to engage in battering behaviors.[2,36,37] In Farley's research, lesbian batterers exhibited personality traits that rate poorly in terms of boundaries, impulse control, problem-solving, regulation of emotion, and reality-testing. The batterers were likely to have low self-esteem, to fear abandonment, to be jealous, and to have an inflated sense of entitlement.[36]

Ristock found that lesbian abuse often happened in a first relationship when a lesbian was just coming out. Serial abusers in these cases often preyed on women who were just coming out or were new to the community. The abused partner may have accepted the abuse out of desperation rather than self-loathing because the relationship provided an outlet to be a "real live lesbian"[1] (p. 335).

History-taking enables the clinician to determine if the same power imbalance or abuse dynamic exists over time. Assessing power and control dynamics is necessary in order to discern who in a relationship is the primary victim and who is the perpetrator.[1]

Identifying the Perpetrator and Primary Victim

Identifying the perpetrator and primary victim enables the clinician to develop safety and treatment plans. This can be difficult because, as mentioned earlier, clinicians often assume that lesbians are more likely than heterosexuals to engage in mutual abuse and that both partners are responsible.[31,32,38] Given the influence of sexism and male dominance in heterosexual relationships, it can be easier in those relationships to identify the perpetrator (often the man) and the victim (often the woman) based on gender.[31] Gender differences are irrelevant in lesbian relationships, so the clinician must consider other cues. There has been limited research on how "butch" and "femme" stereotypes affect assessments of perpetrators and victims. However, according to qualitative data collected by Hassouneh and Glass, clinicians often assume that the butch partner is the perpetrator, even when this may not be true.[39]

Self-reports by clients who claim to be the perpetrator or victim may not accurately reflect the actual dynamics in a lesbian relationship. Victims often take more responsibility for the abuse, believing that their behavior provoked the abuse and, therefore, that they are the perpetrators.[1,30,31] Lesbian perpetrators of abuse have been known to show up at shelters and identify as victims because they feel like victims.[1,31] In one study, more than half of respondents who had been victimized by a lover/partner indicated they also had perpetrated abuse.[9]

Ristock's research suggests that power imbalances in lesbian relationships help define perpetrator and victim in any given abusive incident or in the relationship over time.[1] In the cycle of violence model that commonly applies to heterosexual intimate partner violence, relationships pass from the honeymoon stage to the tension-building stage to the blow-up.[21] The model assumes a constant imbalance between perpetrator and victim. According to Ristock, health providers whose lesbian patients were experiencing intimate partner violence noticed that power relations often shifted and power dynamics often fluctuated in lesbian relationships. Ristock suggested that because women lack privilege in society, neither partner in a lesbian relationship is always privileged and power can frequently change depending on the situation.[1] Submission and domination, for example, may alternate between partners. Such complexity can make it difficult for clinicians to identify perpetrators and victims. To understand what is happening in abusive relationships, they may need to consider nondichotomous paradigms, like the one Marrujo and Kreger proposed. Their paradigm defines roles based on who primarily perpetrates or initiates the intimate partner violence, who is victimized, and who fights back but rarely initiates the violence.[40]

Lethality Assessment

A lethality assessment is imperative because it helps clinicians plan initially for the safety of both partners.[26] It does not enable accurate predictions of future lethal outcomes; rather, it detects indicators of danger in a relationship. Importantly, however, relying exclusively on danger measures such as Campbell's Danger Assessment Instrument[41] is not sufficient. Thorough clinicians corroborate the information they obtain from these measures with other information regarding client history, personality traits, and dynamics in the relationship.[42] According to Campbell's instrument, risk factors to consider include access to or ownership of guns, use of a weapon in prior abusive incidents, threats with weapons, serious injury in prior abusive incidents, threats of suicide or homicide, and drug or alcohol abuse.[41]

■ ■ ■

In the Mary and Linda scenario, only Mary presents in crisis and seeks help, so the focus of assessment should be on her experience with intimate partner violence. Screening for such violence is relatively easy in this case because Mary reports the abuse. Although she talks about Linda, it is unclear if they are lesbian partners—information that would provide useful context for a full assessment and intervention. In history-taking, information about past relationship dynamics is important because it may reveal patterns of intimate partner violence that relate to the present. Mary cites the many tactics Linda uses to gain power and control, which suggests that Mary was the victim in their latest physical confrontation, even though she fought back. Given the incident's lethality, a safety plan is warranted. Gauging Mary's support network would help the clinician develop such a plan.

INTERVENTION AND TREATMENT

After assessment, clinicians should have enough information to move on to intervention and treatment planning. Fewer than 30 agencies in the United States exclusively address battering in gay and lesbian relationships, so lesbians seeking safety services must often turn to domestic violence agencies that primarily help heterosexual women.[43]

The initial intervention always focuses on safety planning.[26] Because few services are available to lesbians experiencing intimate partner violence, this can be challenging.[17,31] Each safety plan is unique: it depends on available services.[26] Both partners may or may not participate in safety planning, depending on whether one or both present for help. Such planning sends a message to them that the clinician takes the risk of harm very seriously.

There are many strategies for treating lesbian perpetrators and victims,[30,31,44–46] but none have been empirically validated in terms of their efficacy or impact on lesbian clients. The most effective strategy for eliminating abuse as rapidly as possible depends on the needs and characteristics of the client(s), the relationship dynamics, and the available services.[33] Treatment options include individual, couples, and group therapy. Clinicians who work with lesbians need to be knowledgeable about lesbian issues—for example, how family of origin, family of choice, and the extended friendship network are interconnected—and about gay/lesbian affirmative treatment practices and theories, such as lesbian identity development and the impact of homophobia and heterosexism.[45]

The types of therapy discussed below are not necessarily mutually exclusive. Margolies and Leeder tried a three-phased approach involving individual, couple, and family therapy[46] but did not report on its effectiveness.

Individual Therapy

Individual therapy is indicated when lesbians involved in an abusive relationship must change their personality in order to recover from or stop abuse.[45] Research on individual therapy for lesbian batterers suggests that the focus should be on personal history, self-image issues, fear of abandonment, loss, intimacy, and awareness of what triggers violence.[45,46] Perpetrators tend to resist this approach.

Couples Therapy

Couples therapy may or may not be contraindicated for lesbian intimate partner violence, a subject of considerable debate.[30,46] It depends on whether or not the abused partner will be safe from further violence during therapy. Victims are more likely to initiate couples therapy, which is also a way to initially engage the perpetrator in treatment and improve compliance with treatment recommendations, but it requires careful safety planning. This approach reveals communication patterns, power dynamics, lethality potential, and other characteristics of the relationship.[46] Clinicians who cannot discern the degree of violence should terminate couples therapy and recommend individual therapy.

Both partners must be committed to stopping all violence while they are undergoing treatment. The clinician can suggest "time outs" in confrontational circumstances[33,40,45] and should make it clear that couples therapy will cease if violence continues.

Group Therapy

The feasibility of group therapy depends mostly on whether such services are available locally.[45] More research has focused on group therapy for lesbian batterers than on group therapy for abuse victims.[44,45] Treatment seeks to counteract the social isolation that is common in abusive relationships, confront batterers' pride in violence, set new norms for recognizing and expressing anger, and teach conflict resolution behaviors.[40,45]

■ ■ ■

Treatment for Mary should include a safety plan that enables her to get assistance when she encounters a threat of violence. The plan could help Mary arrange to live with family or friends and make decisions about reporting abuse to the police. If state law requires that adult domestic violence with physical injury be reported, the clinician must inform Mary and file a report. Some communities only keep these reports as evidence in the event a restraining order is requested; elsewhere, the reports trigger judicial action that could require input from persons, like Mary, who were involved in the domestic violence.

Given Mary's facial abrasions, the clinician should recommend medical treatment. Individual therapy may be best for Mary, as it would give her an opportunity to explore the nature of—and, if she desires, to change—her relationship with Linda.

CONCLUSION

Clinicians and lesbians often ignore or do not recognize instances of lesbian intimate partner violence. When it occurs, few formal services are available to help perpetrators and victims, creating challenges for clinicians who treat them. Lesbian intimate partner violence is similar to heterosexual domestic violence, but there are important differences, among them the control tactics and power imbalance that characterize lesbian relationships. Assessment and intervention must take these differences, as well as the sensitivities of lesbian perpetrators and victims living in a predominantly heterosexist and homophobic society, into account.

REFERENCES

1. Ristock, J. L. (2003). Exploring dynamics of abusive lesbian relationships: Preliminary analysis of a multisite, qualitative study. *American Journal of Community Psychology, 31,* 329–341.

2. Speziale, B., & Ring, C. (2006). Intimate violence among lesbian couples: Emerging data and critical needs. *Journal of Feminist Family Therapy, 18,* 85–96.

3. West, C. M. (2002). Lesbian intimate partner violence: Prevalence and dynamics. *Journal of Lesbian Studies, 6,* 121–127.

4. Turell, S. C. (2000). A descriptive analysis of same-sex relationship violence for a diverse sample. *Journal of Family Violence, 15,* 281–293.

5. Tjaden, P., Thoennes, N., & Allison, C. J. (1999). Comparing violence over the life span in samples of same-sex and opposite-sex cohabitants. *Violence and Victims, 14,* 413–425.

6. Scherzer, T. (1998). Domestic violence in lesbian relationships: Findings of the lesbian relationships research project. *Journal of Lesbian Studies, 2,* 29–47.

7. Lockhart, L., White B., Causby, V., & Isaac, A. (1994). Letting out the secret: Violence in lesbian relationships. *Journal of Interpersonal Violence, 9,* 469–493.

8. Coleman, V. E. (1994). Lesbian battering: The relationship between personality and the perpetration of violence. *Violence and Victims, 9,* 139–152.

9. Lie, G., & Gentlewarrier, S. (1991). Intimate violence in lesbian relationships: Discussion of survey findings and practice implications. *Journal of Social Service Research, 15,* 41–59.

10. Loulan, J. (1987). *Lesbian passion: Loving ourselves and each other.* San Francisco: Spinsters/Aunt Lute.

11. Brand, P. A., & Kidd, A. H. (1986). Frequency of physical aggression in heterosexual and female homosexual dyads. *Psychological Reports, 59,* 1307–1313.

12. Hart, B. (1986). Lesbian battering: An examination. In K. Lobel (Ed.), *Naming the violence: Speaking out about lesbian battering* (pp. 173–189). Seattle, WA: Seal.

13. Allen, C., & Leventhal, B. (1999). History, culture, and identity: What makes GLBT battering different. In B. Leventhal & S. E. Lundy (Eds.), *Same-sex domestic violence* (pp. 73–81). Thousand Oaks, CA: Sage Publications.

14. Balsam, K. F. (2001). Nowhere to hide: Lesbian battering, homophobia, and minority stress. *Women & Therapy, 23,* 25–37.

15. Tigert, L. M. (2001). The power of shame: Lesbian battering as a manifestation of homophobia. *Women & Therapy, 23,* 73–85.

16. Simpson, E. K., & Helfrich, C. A. (2007). Lesbian survivors of intimate partner violence: Provider perspectives on barriers to accessing services. *Journal of Gay & Lesbian Social Services, 18,* 39–59.

17. Renzetti, C. M. (1996). The poverty of services for battered lesbians. *Journal of Gay & Lesbian Social Services, 4,* 61–68.

18. Waldron, C. M. (1996). Lesbians of color and the domestic violence movement. *Journal of Gay & Lesbian Social Services, 4,* 43–51.

19. Miller, D. H., Greene, K., Causby, V., White, B. W., & Lockhart, L. L. (2001). Domestic violence in lesbian relationships. *Women & Therapy, 23,* 107–127.

20. Johnson, M. P. (1995). Patriarchal terrorism and common couple violence: Two forms of violence against women. *Journal of Marriage and the Family, 57,* 283–295.

21. Pitt, E., & Dolan-Soto, D. (2001). Clinical considerations in working with victims of same-sex domestic violence. *Journal of the Gay and Lesbian Medical Association, 5,* 163–169.

22. Pence, E., & Paymar, M. (1993). *Education groups for men who batter: The Duluth model.* New York: Springer.

23. National Coalition of Anti-Violence Programs. (2007). *Lesbian, gay, bisexual and transgender domestic violence in the United States in 2006.* New York: Author. Available at www.ncavp.org/common/document_files/Reports/2006NationalDVReport(Final).pdf.

24. Renzetti, C. M. (1989). Building a second closet: Third party responses to victims of lesbian partner abuse. *Family Relations, 38,* 157–163.

25. Samuelson, S. L., & Campbell, C. D. (2005). Screening for domestic violence: Recommendations based on a practice survey. *Professional Psychology: Research and Practice, 36,* 276–282.

26. McCloskey, K., & Grigsby, N. (2005). The ubiquitous clinical problem of adult intimate partner violence: The need for routine assessment. *Professional Psychology: Research and Practice, 36,* 264–275.

27. Stayton, C. D., & Duncan, M. M. (2005). Mutable influences on intimate partner abuse screening in health care settings. *Trauma, Violence, & Abuse, 6,* 271–285.

28. Waalen, J., Goodwin, M. M., Spitz, A. M., Petersen, R., & Saltzman, L. E. (2000). Screening for intimate partner violence by health care providers: Barriers and interventions. *American Journal of Preventive Medicine, 19,* 230–237.

29. Witting, M. D., Furuno, J. P., Hirshon, J. M., Krugman, S. D., Perisse, A. R. S., & Limcangco, R. (2006). Support for emergency department screening for intimate partner violence depends on perceived risk. *Journal of Interpersonal Violence, 21*, 585–596.

30. Goddard, A. B., & Hardy, T. (1999). Assessing the lesbian victim. In B. Leventhal & S. E. Lundy (Eds.), *Same-sex domestic violence* (pp. 193–200). Thousand Oaks, CA: Sage Publications.

31. Istar, A. (1996). Couple assessment: Identifying and intervening in domestic violence in lesbian relationships. *Journal of Gay & Lesbian Social Services, 4*, 93–106.

32. Peterman, L. M., & Dixon, C. G. (2003). Domestic violence between same-sex partners: Implications for counseling. *Journal of Counseling and Development, 81*, 40–47.

33. Stuart, R. B. (2005). Treatment for partner abuse: Time for a paradigm shift. *Professional Psychology: Research and Practice, 36*, 254–263.

34. Rathus, J. H., & Feindler, E. L. (2004). *Assessment of partner violence.* Washington, DC: American Psychological Association.

35. Phelan, M. B. (2007). Screening for intimate partner violence in medical settings. *Trauma, Violence, & Abuse, 8*, 199–213.

36. Farley, N. (1996). A survey of factors contributing to gay and lesbian domestic violence. *Journal of Gay & Lesbian Social Services, 4*, 35–42.

37. Fortunata, B., & Kohn, C. S. (2003). Demographic, psychosocial, and personality characteristics of lesbian batterers. *Violence and Victims, 18*, 557–568.

38. Blasko, K. A., Winek, J. L., & Bieschke, K. J. (2007). Prototypical assessment by therapists of domestic violence situations. *Journal of Marital and Family Therapy, 33*, 258–269.

39. Hassouneh, D., & Glass, N. (2008) The influence of gender role stereotyping on women's experiences of female same-sex intimate partner violence. *Violence Against Women, 14*, 310–325.

40. Marrujo, B., & Kreger, M. (1996). Definition of roles in abusive lesbian relationships. *Journal of Gay & Lesbian Social Services, 4*, 22–32.

41. Campbell, J. C. (Ed.) (1995). *Assessing dangerousness: Violence by sexual offenders, batterers, and child abusers.* Thousand Oaks, CA: Sage Publications.

42. Websdale, N. (2000). *Lethality assessment tools: A critical analysis.* Violence Against Women Net Applied Research Forum. Available at new.vawnet.org/Assoc_Files_VAWnet/AR_lethality.pdf.

43. Helfrich, C. A., & Simpson, E. K. (2006). Improving services for lesbian clients: What do domestic violence agencies need to do? *Health Care for Women International, 27*, 344–361.

44. Cayouette, S. (1999). Running batterer groups for lesbians. In B. Leventhal & S. E. Lundy (Eds.), *Same-sex domestic violence* (pp. 233–242). Thousand Oaks, CA: Sage Publications.

45. Coleman, V. E. (2003). Treating the lesbian batterer: Theoretical and clinical considerations—a contemporary psychoanalytic perspective. *Journal of Aggression, Maltreatment & Trauma, 7*, 159–205.

46. Margolies, L., & Leeder, E. (1995). Violence at the door: Treatment of lesbian batterers. *Violence Against Women, 1*, 139–157.

ABOUT THE AUTHOR

Kelly A. Blasko, PhD has worked extensively as a psychotherapist in college counseling centers, especially with LGBT clients, and has trained students in university LGBT centers to be peer mentors to other students who are coming out. Dr. Blasko's research focus is same-sex intimate partner violence (IPV) and psychologists' biases in its assessment.

CHAPTER 19

"Hey, You Dyke!"

LESBIANS, VIOLENCE, AND HEALTH

KIMBERLY F. BALSAM, PhD   KEREN LEHAVOT, MS

ELENA, *a 28-year-old Latina lesbian, comes to the student health center at the university where she is a first-year graduate student. She arrives with her long-term partner, who urged Elena to get checked for the pelvic pain she has been feeling recently. Elena has never had a Pap smear or gynecologic exam and generally avoids seeking any medical care. During the pelvic exam, she begins to sweat, tremble, and cry, and then demands that the clinician stop. She curls up into a ball on the exam table, refusing to talk. Her partner explains that Elena's uncle sexually molested her as a child and suggests that the exam reminds Elena* *of this incident. Elena has been depressed for a long time but only recently revealed this experience—after her partner repeatedly inquired about Elena's avoidance of sexual intimacy.*

CATH, *42, is a European American lesbian who works as a police officer. She presents seeking treatment for recurrent headaches so severe that she has missed several days of work. She says the headaches began about 2 years ago when she was involved in an investigation and prolonged trial of a serial rapist. When asked why this case had been particularly significant for her, Cath reluctantly reveals that she herself was raped as a young woman in the military. The rapist, a fellow enlistee who had targeted Cath because of her suspected lesbianism, harassed her and called her "bull dyke" for weeks before the assault. Cath reported the rape to her commanding officer, who advised her not to pursue criminal charges because doing so might call attention to her sexual orientation and lead to an investigation of her homosexual conduct. Cath left the military after her tour of duty. Until now, she had successfully blocked the incident from her consciousness.*

ROXIE, *52, an African American lesbian, presents with sleeping difficulties, which have been problematic since the funeral of her 72-year-old father 3 months earlier. When the physician asks about the death's impact on her life, Roxie reports that, as a child, her father often beat her with a leather strap because she preferred to climb trees rather than stay in the house and play dolls with her sisters, who never suffered any beatings. "You dyke, I'll show you!" the father had yelled in the presence of her sisters. She left home at age 14 after a particularly severe beating. Roxie has had intermittent contact with her* *mother since then, but she never saw her father again. At the funeral, which she attended to ease her mother's loss, she started having flashbacks and nightmares about the physical and verbal abuse she suffered in childhood.*

■ ■ ■

The violence and abuse in these three scenarios are not uncommon. A U.S. Department of Justice analysis of survey data concluded in 2000 that two-thirds of women had been "physically assaulted as a child by an adult caretaker and/or as an adult by any type of attacker"[1] (p. iii). Researchers and health professionals increasingly recognize that violence and abuse are important determinants of physical and mental health.[1,2]

Until recently, however, researchers have paid relatively little attention to the role of sexual orientation in the experiences of violence and abuse victims. The vast majority of victimization studies, particularly those that relied on probability sampling, did not assess sexual orientation. Conversely, studies of lesbians did not probe victimization or they did so using inadequate questions or assessment tools. Furthermore, theoretical and clinical writings historically have examined violence against women from the perspective of heterosexual women, making lesbians' unique experiences and needs all but invisible.

This chapter provides an overview of theories about and research on victimization of lesbian women, who, studies suggest, are at higher risk compared with their heterosexual counterparts. It also examines the immediate and long-term health consequences of such victimization, the violence-related risk and impact of heterosexism, and the implications for health care providers who work with lesbian patients.

VIOLENCE AGAINST LESBIANS: A SOCIAL CONTEXT

Discussions of violence against women often take place in the context of their position in society, not simply as trauma perpetrated by one person against another. This sociocultural context encompasses the oppression of women, including their subordinate political and economic status, and society's expectations of male and female behavior.[3,4] Women's vulnerability is at least partly related to demographic and social factors that influence their access to resources and their power in society. For example, low socioeconomic status and living in a low-income neighborhood are associated with elevated victimization risk.[2]

Researchers have considered the role of other contextual factors, such as ethnicity and immigrant status, that increase women's vulnerability to violence.[5,6] Feminist models of violence against women examine how sexism in society can shape their psychological response to victimization experiences. Root coined the term "insidious trauma" to mean the ongoing traumatic impact of living with sexism or other oppressions.[7] Thus, a woman may already be experiencing insidious trauma symptoms that physical or sexual violence can compound.

In addition to sexism and other oppression that women in general experience, lesbians must contend with heterosexism. Day-to-day heterosexism is like the trauma of physical and sexual abuse, according to Neisen, who describes it as a type of "cultural victimization." Neisen notes that both heterosexism and physical and sexual abuse can lead to shame, a negative self-image, self-destructive behaviors, and a "victim mentality."[8]

A heterosexism-related concept is "minority stress,"[9,10] which refers to the multidimensional stresses associated with being in a sexual minority. In both cultural victimization and minority stress, heterosexism exerts its influence on three levels— individual, interpersonal, and institutional—just as sexism does. For lesbians of color, this effect is magnified: they experience the "triple jeopardy" of racism, sexism, and heterosexism.[11]

Cultural heterosexism can have a wide-ranging traumatic effect on family of origin, cultural or ethnic group, and religion or spiritual beliefs/affiliations, and lead to loss of privilege, an absence of legal protections, and laws of exclusion.[12] Therefore, it is important to consider the influence that cultural heterosexism has on the prevalence and health impact of violence against lesbians.

RESEARCH CHALLENGES

A methodological challenge for researchers is studying people who, as both lesbians and survivors of abuse, are doubly stigmatized. The common stereotype that abuse by men causes a girl or woman to become a lesbian may make some lesbians reluctant to reveal their abuse experience to researchers lest their revelations foster this stereotype. Indeed, in two large surveys,[13,14] several lesbians who reported a history of childhood sexual abuse clarified that they were not lesbians because of such abuse. Researchers may avoid examining this topic out of fear that they will perpetuate stereotypes or give more ammunition to homophobic groups.[15]

Another difficulty in victimization research is comparing results across studies. For example, one study might ask about particular behaviors (such as, "Were you slapped or punched?") while another might ask questions (such as, "Were you physically abused?") that may elicit more subjective responses. Subjective questions, the type posed by most studies of lesbians until recently, tend to yield lower prevalence rates because some victims do not view their experience as abuse or victimization.[16]

In addition, behavioral definitions vary. Common behaviors in physical abuse and assault are pushing, slapping, hitting, punching, choking, throwing objects, biting, kicking, and using a lethal weapon, all of which may incur injury.[17] Behaviors in sexual abuse and sexual assault range from unwanted touching to forced penetration or rape, and may vary depending on a victim's age.[18] For example, while most adult women view force or coercion as a necessary component of sexual assault, children under a certain age presumably cannot consent to sex; therefore, force or coercion need not be present if a sexual abuser is an adult or significantly older than the victim.

PREVALENCE OF VIOLENCE AGAINST LESBIANS

A limited but growing body of research on lesbian-specific violence and abuse suggests that lesbians are indeed at higher risk of victimization over the lifespan. The following sections discuss victimization in childhood, revictimization, sexual assault in adulthood, and pathways to victimization.

Childhood Victimization

Lesbians report more physical assaults in childhood than heterosexual women do. Based on data from the National Violence Against Women Survey, Tjaden and colleagues found that 59.5% of those who had ever lived with a same-sex partner versus 35.7% of those who had only lived with an opposite-sex partner reported a history of physical assault in childhood.[19] Many studies of childhood victimization focus on experiences at school. They suggest that victimization against sexual minority youth is sanctioned and normative in secondary schools.[20] According to findings based on state-level representative samples, sexual minority students were victimized at school more often than their heterosexual peers.[21–23] For example, gay and lesbian students more often reported that they missed school because of safety fears, that other students had threatened them with weapons, and that their personal property had been damaged or stolen. In addition, compared with heterosexual students, they were in more fights on school grounds.[22]

Lesbians are also at higher risk for childhood physical abuse at home. In examining data from the National Survey of Midlife Development in the United States, Corliss and colleagues found that 33.6% of lesbian/bisexual women reported a history of major physical maltreatment by a parent compared with 10.3% of heterosexual women.[24] A survey of lesbian, gay, and bisexual (LGB) adolescents, and of young adults, revealed that 22% of female participants had been verbally assaulted and 18% physically assaulted by a family member because of their sexual orientation.[25] Balsam and colleagues, in examining a national sample of LGB adults and their heterosexual siblings, found that lesbians reported more childhood psychological and physical abuse and were more likely to have been injured in childhood by an adult caretaker.[26] In other words, girls perceived as being lesbian or "different" are targets of the very people who supposedly protect and care for them, not just of schoolyard bullies.

Similarly, research has consistently shown higher rates of childhood sexual abuse among lesbians, although prevalence rates vary widely depending on the type of assessment questions. In one study, 16.5% of same-sex cohabiting women reported they had been "forcibly raped" (a subjective definition) before age 18 compared with 8.7% of opposite-sex cohabiting women.[19] In another study, 68% of lesbians had experienced childhood sexual abuse (a behavioral definition) versus 47% of heterosexual women. This study included a subjective question that asked participants if they thought they had been sexually abused before age 18. Even though, as expected, the subjective interpretation yielded lower rates for both lesbians and heterosexual women, the prevalence of sexual abuse among lesbians was still significantly higher (37% vs. 19%).[27] Balsam and colleagues used a cut-off age of 14 rather than 18 in assessing history of sexual abuse (a behavioral definition); prevalence was 18% among lesbians versus 11% among heterosexual women.[26]

Most of these studies relied on the recollections of adult lesbian women, yet findings from other studies based on the current experiences of adolescent lesbians are similar. A secondary analysis of seven, population-based high school health surveys found that while the proportion of teenagers reporting sexual abuse varied, adolescent lesbians in all of the surveys were significantly more likely than heterosexual girls of the same age to report it.[28] Investigators typically do not assess the gender of sexual abuse perpetrators. Balsam and colleagues are an exception: among the lesbians in their study who had a history of childhood sexual abuse, 94% reported at least one male perpetrator and 20% reported at least one female perpetrator.[26]

Revictimization

Robust findings from studies of women in the general population indicate that childhood sexual abuse is a significant risk factor for sexual assault in adulthood.[6,29] But only a handful of studies have examined revictimization among lesbians, gay men, and bisexuals.[30,31] In the Lesbian Wellness Survey, women who had been sexually or physically victimized in childhood were four times more likely than women who had not been victimized in childhood to experience the same type of victimization as an adult and about twice as likely to experience the other type of victimization (sexual or physical).[31] A study of lesbians, gay men, bisexuals, and their heterosexual siblings found that among women, sexual minority status was associated with greater risk of sexual revictimization, even in the same family.[32]

Sexual Assault in Adulthood

Sexual assault includes physical force or threats that result in sexual intercourse, and other sexual acts, such as vaginal, anal, or oral penetration.[33] Studies comparing lesbians with heterosexual women consistently found higher rates of sexual assault among the lesbians.[19,26,34–36] An assessment of a range of sexual assault experiences in adulthood using behavioral definitions revealed that more than twice as many lesbians as heterosexual women reported a rape experience in adulthood (15.5% vs. 7.5%).[26] Tjaden and colleagues got similar results when they assessed forcible rape using a subjective definition.[19] In a national, population-based sample of women older than 18, more lesbians and bisexual women than heterosexual women reported sexual assault by strangers (22.2% vs. 4.7%,) and more reported sexual assault by known assailants (47.1% vs. 13.1%).[37]

Findings from the relatively few studies in which investigators looked at the gender of persons who sexually assaulted lesbians suggest that, consistent with broader research on sexual assault, most perpetrators are male. In a study by Moore and Waterman, for example, lesbians with a sexual assault history most often reported that the perpetrator was a male date.[36] Thus, at least some of the risk may arise before lesbians come out, while they are dating men. But that may not always be the case: 7% of lesbians in another study said they had experienced a sexual assault by a female partner.[38] In the study by Balsam and colleagues, among women who reported sexual abuse, more lesbians than heterosexual women said other females coerced them into sexual experiences (41% vs. 0%). Still, lesbians said most rapes and attempted rapes were perpetrated by men; in this respect, they did not differ significantly from their heterosexual counterparts.[26] It is possible that females perpetrate less severe forms of sexual assault and men perpetrate most cases of more severe forms.

PATHWAYS TO VICTIMIZATION

Bias-Related Pathways

According to surveys of victims, at least some violent experiences are a direct result of the perpetrator knowing or perceiving that the victim is lesbian.[14,25] Bias-related victimization can occur in childhood or adulthood and by a stranger or a person the victim knows. In a sample of lesbian, gay, and bisexual adults, 19% of lesbians indicated they had experienced at least one incident of physical victimization that they believed was related to homophobic bias.[39] Survey responses from a national probability sample of these same types of adults revealed that 12.5% of lesbians had experienced a personal or property crime and that 54.5% had experienced verbal harassment or abuse due to their sexual orientation.[40]

Victimization related to sexual orientation bias may differ in substantive ways from other types of victimization. In reviewing more than 1,500 hate crimes committed in Los Angeles County, Dunbar found that 36% were classified as offenses motivated by sexual orientation bias. Sexual orientation hate crimes were more violent and had a greater impact on victims' level of functioning than did racial/ethnic and religious hate crimes. In particular, assault, sexual assault, sexual harassment, and stalking were more common in sexual orientation hate crimes. The more violent a hate crime, the less likely gay and lesbian victims were to report it to law enforcement authorities. Not only were sexual orientation hate crimes less likely than racial/ethnic and religious bias crimes to be reported, but lesbians were less likely than gay men to report them (66% vs. 74%). This was especially true among lesbians of color (52%).[41] Compared with heterosexual victims of hate crimes, gay and lesbian victims are held more accountable for their actions and elicit less sympathy,[42] which may partially explain why they do not report such crimes as often. Research also shows that fear of victimization and level of perceived risk are higher among lesbians than gay men.[43]

Other Pathways

Appearance, behavior, rejection by family and peers, and substance use and abuse are other pathways that can increase the risk of victimization.

Compared with their heterosexual counterparts, lesbian girls and women may have a more gender-nonconforming appearance and engage in more gender-atypical behaviors, which can increase their visibility to perpetrators and thus their vulnerability to abuse, as one qualitative study suggested.[44] This may be particularly true in childhood, when girls have less control over their immediate environment and people with whom they associate.[45] Indeed, D'Augelli and colleagues found that gender-atypical youth experienced more physical attacks during their lifetime and that the first attacks occurred at younger ages among lesbian youth who were called tomboys and whose parents discouraged their gender atypicality.[46]

Rejection by family and peers[47,48] may lead to other behaviors—running away from home, for example—that increase girls' risk of victimization in adolescence[49,50] and the likelihood of sexual activity with both boys and girls.[21] Finally, studies have consistently reported higher rates of substance use and abuse among adolescent lesbians[31] and adult lesbians.[51-53] Adolescent and adult women in general who have such problems may be more vulnerable to assault than those who do not as a result of greater exposure to, and/or impaired ability to detect, assailants. A 2-year longitudinal study of more than 3,000 women found that drug use increased women's risk of subsequent assault.[54]

VIOLENCE AGAINST LESBIANS OF COLOR

As mentioned earlier, lesbians of color face "triple jeopardy" because of their gender, sexual orientation, and race/ethnicity.[11] They experience multiple types of oppression that, in addition to the stigma associated with their sexual orientation, may include rejection by their cultural or ethnic community, and racial prejudice in both the general and lesbian communities.[55,56]

Limited data also suggest that they may be at greater risk of violence than White lesbians are. In Comstock's study, lesbians and gay men of color were more likely than White lesbians and gay men to report having been chased or followed (43% vs. 29%), pelted with objects (31% vs. 17%), or physically assaulted (21% vs. 18%).[57] Among 400 lesbians in another study, those of color were more likely than White lesbians to report physical violence, threats, vandalism, or rape.[58] Morris and Balsam found significant race/ethnicity-related differences in history of victimization, including physical and sexual abuse in childhood and adulthood. American Indian women reported the highest composite, lifetime number of victimizations (an average of 2.14 different types) followed by Latinas (1.67), African American women (1.42), Asian American women (1.17), and White women (1.16).[31]

THE HEALTH CONSEQUENCES OF VIOLENCE

Sharps and Campbell described violence against women as "a major health problem that is at an epidemic level"[59] (p. 163). A great deal of evidence indicates that victimization can have serious short- and long-term physical and mental health consequences.

Acute health consequences include bruises, cuts, broken bones, and head injuries immediately after a physical or sexual abuse incident.[60] Findings from the National Violence Against Women Survey reveal that about one-third of victims of a physical or sexual assault needed medical care.[2] Unique risks in sexual victimization can lead to unwanted pregnancy, sexually transmitted or urinary tract infections, vaginal bleeding, and other gynecologic problems.[1,61-65]

In a study of sexual assault victims, 24% met criteria for acute stress disorder (ASD) and 21% reported symptoms consistent with subclinical ASD.[66] Kawsar and colleagues assessed girls within 6 months after they had been sexually assaulted. About 81% reported they were having psychological difficulties; mood change and sleep disturbance were the most frequent symptoms. Fifteen percent of the girls tried to harm themselves.[67]

Physical and sexual abuse can also have a variety of long-term health consequences. Problems associated with childhood abuse may manifest in middle or late adulthood. A study of more than 1,000 randomly selected women who subscribed to a large HMO showed that adult women with a documented history of childhood sexual and nonsexual abuse had more medically documented, nonpsychiatric diagnoses than did women who had not reported such abuse.[68]

Logan and colleagues classify long-term health problems associated with victimization as either chronic or stress-related.[2] Chronic problems in physically or sexually abused women include headaches and gastrointestinal and gynecologic difficulties, such as pelvic pain and genital irritation. Arthritis, diabetes, hypertension, and other chronic medical conditions may be exacerbated in the aftermath of violence.[69] Additionally, head injuries from an assault can cause longer-term hearing-, vision-, and concentration-related problems. Stress-related problems as a result of victimization include chest and back pain, choking sensations, fatigue, eating and sleeping difficulties, diarrhea, and constipation. Many of these physical symptoms are nonspecific and not related to a particular illness. Indeed, when McNutt and colleagues interviewed ethnically diverse primary care patients, they found that women with victimization histories were more than twice as likely to report multiple nonspecific problems such as headaches and gastrointestinal distress.[70]

Women with victimization histories are at much greater risk for mental health distress and disorders than are women without such histories.[2] Research has linked physical and sexual abuse experiences in both childhood and adulthood with elevated rates of anxiety and depressive disorders as well as suicide attempts.[54,60,71-77] The mental health disorder most closely associated with victimization experiences is posttraumatic stress disorder (PTSD), the symptoms of which include re-experiencing the trauma, avoidance, or numbing of feelings, and hyperarousal or hypervigilance. Women may be particularly vulnerable to PTSD; epidemiologic studies indicate that they are twice as likely as men to experience PTSD and that this result cannot be simply explained by differential exposure to violence.[78] Women with victimization histories also experience higher rates of eating disorders[79] and other health risk behaviors such as smoking,[68] alcohol use,[54,68] drug use,[80] and sexual risk behaviors.[81] Overall, victimized women view themselves as being less healthy than nonvictimized women, and report lower levels of both physical and mental well-being than do women who have not been victimized.[61,64]

Very few studies have examined the health impact of violence on lesbians specifically. Most of these studies focused on childhood victimization, the results of which paralleled the findings in studies of heterosexual populations. Hughes and colleagues linked childhood sexual abuse with higher rates of lifetime alcohol abuse, and childhood physical abuse with greater adult psychological distress.[27,82] In another study, lesbian victims of childhood sexual abuse reported higher rates of eating disorders, anxiety disorders, and suicidality,[83] and Aaron and Hughes found that such abuse was an important risk factor for obesity.[84] According to other researchers, childhood sexual abuse and bias-related victimization are associated with depression, daily stress, and alcohol use.[85]

While most of these studies suggest that the sequelae of victimization do not differ relative to sexual orientation, the social context of heterosexism may exert influence in ways researchers have not adequately assessed. For example, perhaps the stress of living with homophobia interacts with the stress of a traumatic event in a manner similar to revictimization.[10] Women who have had multiple victimization experiences are at much greater risk of poor psychological outcome than are those who have had only one victimization experience.[86,87] For lesbians, physical or sexual abuse may occur in the context of the "insidious trauma"[7] of day-to-day discrimination, harassment, and stigmatization; thus, the impact of violence could be similar to revictimization. Furthermore, lesbians face the ongoing threat of bias-related victimization, before it takes place. Researchers have linked a woman's *perception* that her assault was related to sexual orientation, whether or not the perpetrator made this explicit, with particularly negative effects on mental health and well-being.[39] For a lesbian of color, there is the additional issue of racism and racially motivated bias events that can influence how she experiences and comprehends a violent attack. All of these factors may create a higher risk of victimization-related physical and mental health problems.

On the other hand, by weathering the daily challenges of oppression and coming to terms with an identity that runs counter to societal expectations, maybe lesbians develop unique strengths and resiliencies. Lock and Steiner found that lesbian and gay adolescents used a wide variety of coping strategies more often than heterosexual adolescents did.[88] A repertoire of strategies might be useful for coping with and recovering from the effects of victimization. In a study by Balsam and Rothblum, the lifetime victimization experiences of lesbian adults were less strongly linked to current psychological distress than such experiences were in their heterosexual siblings.[89] Oftentimes, lesbians with families of origin that do not understand them or that reject them create a "family of choice" or close support networks of friends to help alleviate the stress of living in a marginalized group. These networks may be particularly valuable in helping lesbians overcome the effects of violence. Studies have shown that social support is an important buffer against the impact of traumatic experiences in adulthood and childhood generally,[90] and against the impact of homophobic bias crimes specifically.[91]

VIOLENCE AND SEXUAL IDENTITY DEVELOPMENT

According to widespread cultural myths and stereotypes, abuse might "cause" homosexuality in women.[92] No scientific data support this notion. To the contrary, abundant evidence indicates that many sexually abused girls grow up to identify as heterosexual and that most lesbians are not sexually abused. Nevertheless, stereotypes may have implications for how lesbians come to understand their abuse experiences. In a study by Pantalone and Balsam, 41% of lesbians with a history of childhood sexual abuse reported that at some point they had wondered if the abuse "made them LGB." Forty-eight percent reported that at least one other person had posed this possibility.[93]

Childhood sexual abuse, which may be a girl's first encounter with sexuality, might impact sexuality-related psychological processes. Studies of heterosexual women have suggested a number of sexuality-related sequelae after such abuse, including earlier age of first intercourse,[94,95] more sexual partners,[96] and an increase in HIV-risk behaviors.[97] A meta-analysis concluded that childhood sexual abuse of women was associated with unprotected sex, multiple partners, and sex trading.[98]

Although researchers have not yet examined these issues relative to lesbians, the possibility that early negative experiences may impact sexuality later in life is an important consideration. A unique challenge for lesbians is coming to terms with same-sex attractions that run counter to the mainstream, sexuality-related messages and scripts presented by society, family, friends, and the media. If childhood sexual abuse heightens sexual awareness prematurely, perhaps it also calls attention to emerging same-sex sexuality. Data from the Pantalone and Balsam study suggest that lesbians with a history of childhood sexual abuse become aware of same-sex attractions, LGB identification, and first same-sex sexual experiences at younger ages than do lesbians with no such history.[93]

As awareness of same-sex attractions emerges, adolescent and adult lesbians face the challenge of developing a healthy identity and disclosing it to others. How they experience the coming out process may vary a great deal and be dynamic and nonlinear, research suggests.[99] More disclosure of and comfort with one's lesbian identity appear to be adaptive and associated with better mental health and well-being.[100,101] For some lesbians, victimization may complicate this process. For example, an adolescent girl in a violent home might delay coming out because she fears it will provoke further violence by family members.[102] In adulthood, the shame and self-doubt associated with a victimization history might make a woman less likely to trust her own feelings, and she may question whether her feelings of attraction to women are real or valid.[44] Surrounded by the stereotypical belief that sexual abuse causes women to become lesbians, a woman might believe that her same-sex attractions are merely a symptom of male-perpetrated abuse she has experienced.

CLINICAL IMPLICATIONS AND INTERVENTIONS

Given the greater prevalence of lifetime victimization among lesbians, and the various physical and mental health implications, health care providers who work with lesbians must be aware of the related issues and be prepared to address them with patients. In the scenarios at the beginning of this chapter, Elena's case illustrates how an abuse history may suddenly emerge, unsolicited, in the doctor's office relative to a pelvic exam. Cath's and Roxie's abuse histories, on the other hand, emerged as a result of direct questioning by their clinicians. In all three cases, nonspecific symptoms signaled the possibility of a victimization history.

Clinicians should assess all new lesbian patients—especially those they will care for over the long term—for victimization and avoid making assumptions based on stereotypes related to gender, race/ethnicity, social class, or age. Such stereotypes include the notions that only men are perpetrators and only poor lesbians are victimized. A clue to recent victimization is unexplained injuries, while clues to past victimization are chronic pain and PTSD symptoms. Even if there are no obvious signs, clinicians who look for victimization and understand its implications will provide better quality care, including any necessary referrals.

Intake forms can include behaviorally specific questions about emotional, physical, and sexual victimization. Although a woman may not consider herself a victim of childhood sexual abuse, a question that asks, "Did an adult ever touch you in an unwanted sexual way while you were growing up?" may prompt her to disclose that she is still troubled by nightmares stemming from the time a relative fondled her. Clinicians can also pose such questions during a patient interview and/or follow up with questions if the intake form reveals victimization experiences. Importantly, they must be empathic and nonjudgmental when broaching this subject.

Numerous screening tools and interview guides can help identify victimization histories in clinical settings. The National Center for Posttraumatic Stress Disorder has links to a number of trauma-exposure and symptom-screening instruments.* The Universal Violence Prevention Screening Protocol, which emergency rooms have used, assesses a range of victimization experiences in the previous year.[103] Thombs and colleagues suggest a two-item screener for childhood physical and sexual abuse history.[104]

In cases of current or recent victimization, clinicians must follow up with patients to determine if they are safe. Elena, Cath, and Roxie were victimized in the distant past and the perpetrators do not pose a present danger. But some patients disclose ongoing victimization or contact with the perpetrator, perhaps a family member, coworker, or acquaintance. In these cases, establishing safety is of utmost importance; the clinician and patient can work collaboratively on steps to prevent future victimization. An important consideration is whether emotional, practical, and financial barriers make the patient reluctant or unwilling to consider changing her relationship with the perpetrator (if, for example, the perpetrator is a partner or

---

* See www.ptsd.va.gov/professional/pages/assessments/list-screening-instruments.asp.

family member) or make it impossible for her to avoid known risks (if, for example, she must walk through an unsafe neighborhood). Identifying such barriers enables the clinician and patient to develop a plan for overcoming them, which may involve the criminal justice, social service, and mental health systems.

Laws in some states require that child and elder abuse—and, when there is physical evidence, abuse of one adult by another—be reported. Familiarity with these laws is important when a clinician and patient discuss victimization by a known perpetrator. If a report must be filed, the patient needs to know and should participate in the process. If the patient lives with or depends on the perpetrator, she and the clinician should explore housing and financial-support alternatives in the course of developing a safety plan.

With a comprehensive list of local resources in hand, clinicians can readily refer victims to sources of help. Among these resources are battered women's shelters, antiviolence projects, and entities in the justice, mental health, and social service systems. Support groups and services specifically for lesbian victims of violence may be available as a component of antiviolence projects—particularly in larger cities with visible sexual-minority communities—and at community centers and counseling or health clinics for lesbian/gay/bisexual/transgender (LGBT) persons. The National Coalition of Anti-Violence Programs lists local, lesbian-friendly resources, including hotlines, on its Web site,[†] and CENTERLINK keeps a national directory of LGBT centers.[‡] Additional resources are psychologists, psychiatrists, and counselors who have treated trauma victims. Lesbian-friendly resources are those that have had lesbian clients, are comfortable serving them, and offer services that address their particular needs. Clinicians might ask colleagues if they know of lesbian-friendly organizations and professionals within those organizations. Even if none are available, a resource list enables the clinician to help patients make informed choices.

■ ■ ■

Mental health treatment for Elena, Cath, and Roxie could address the psychological impact of their past victimization. This might also alleviate their physical symptoms and complaints. Lesbians undergo psychotherapy at higher rates than heterosexual women do, perhaps because there is relatively greater acceptance of such treatment in the lesbian community.[105] However, the approach and training of mental health professionals vary widely. Referrals should be made to those who are lesbian-friendly and can skillfully provide evidence-based treatments for trauma-related problems.

[†] See *www.ncavp.org*.

[‡] See *www.lgbtcenters.org*.

Ideally, Elena's clinician would refer her to a lesbian-friendly mental health professional who effectively works with Latina clients. Perhaps Elena has a personal preference. If the Latino community in her town is very small, she might be more comfortable with a therapist elsewhere who has experience in multicultural care. Or maybe she would prefer someone with the same cultural background whose familiarity or lack of familiarity with lesbian issues is irrelevant. Therapy could address her depressive symptoms, self-care, and ability to cope with memories of abuse. Perhaps relaxation skills would ultimately enable Elena to tolerate a gynecologic exam and Pap smear. The therapist should explore her internalized negative messages about her sexuality, especially relative to her current sexual life. Depending on the severity of Elena's depression, she may benefit from antidepressant medication. Finally, at some point during treatment, couples therapy with her partner and a support group for survivors of childhood sexual abuse could be helpful.

Cath's clinician should refer her to a psychotherapist who has experience treating survivors of rape. Learning stress-reduction techniques may alleviate the headaches. A diagnosis of PTSD warrants cognitive behavioral therapy from a trained professional, as evidence strongly supports the efficacy of such therapy, particularly if it addresses the components of exposure to posttraumatic stress.[106,107] In addition, the clinician could assess the impact of Cath's current physical and mental health on her work performance and, if necessary, help her take the necessary steps to remedy the impact and/or apply for medical disability or a temporary leave of absence, while working with Cath to alleviate her headache pain with medications or other alternative therapies.

Referral to psychotherapy is also appropriate for Roxie. The ideal therapist would have experience treating the long-term impact of childhood abuse and be culturally sensitive to the unique issues Roxie faces as an African American lesbian. Her insomnia may warrant cognitive behavioral therapy and, if it persists, evaluation in a sleep laboratory.

CONCLUSION

Health care providers must be aware of and knowledgeable about violence against lesbians and its impact on health. This type of violence typically occurs in the context of multiple, intersecting oppressions related to sexual orientation and factors such as race/ethnicity, age, and socioeconomic, disability, and immigration status. Providers should not make any assumptions about lesbian patients; rather, they need to understand that every individual has unique experiences and problems. Clinicians whose patients include lesbians will inevitably encounter women like Elena, Cath, and Roxie. Therefore, familiarity with assessment questions, treatments, and resources for lesbian victims of violence is essential.

REFERENCES

1. Tjaden, P., & Thoennes, N. (2000). *Full report of the prevalence, incidence, and consequences of violence against women. Findings from the National Violence Against Women Survey.* Washington, DC: U.S. Department of Justice. Available at www.ncjrs.org/pdffiles1/nij/183781.pdf.

2. Logan, T. K., Walker, R., Jordan, C. E., & Leukefeld, C. G. (2006). *Women and victimization: Contributing factors, interventions, and implications.* Washington, DC: American Psychological Association.

3. Koss, M. P., Goodman, L. A., Browne, A., Fitzgerald, L. F., Keita, G. P., & Russo, N. F. (1994). *No safe haven: Male violence against women at home, at work, and in the community.* Washington, DC: American Psychological Association.

4. Walker, L.E.A. (1994). *Abused women and survival therapy: A practical guide for the psychotherapist.* Washington, DC: American Psychological Association.

5. Root, M. P. P. (1996). Women of color and traumatic stress in "domestic captivity": Gender and race as disempowering statuses. In A. J. Marsella, M. J. Friedman, E. T. Gerrity, & R. M. Scurfield (Eds.), *Ethnocultural aspects of posttraumatic stress disorder* (pp. 363–388). Washington, DC: American Psychological Association.

6. Wyatt, G. E., Guthrie, D., & Notgrass, C. M. (1992). Differential effects of women's child sexual abuse and subsequent sexual revictimization. *Journal of Consulting and Clinical Psychology, 60,* 167–173.

7. Root, M. P. P. (1992). Reconstructing the impact of trauma on personality. In L. S. Brown & M. Ballou (Eds.), *Personality and psychopathology: Feminist reappraisals* (pp. 229–265). New York: Guilford Press.

8. Neisen, J. H. (1993). Healing from cultural victimization: Recovery from shame due to heterosexism. *Journal of Gay & Lesbian Psychotherapy, 2,* 49–63.

9. DiPlacido, J. (1998). Minority stress among lesbians, gay men, and bisexuals: A consequence of heterosexism, homophobia, and stigmatization. In G. M. Herek (Ed.), *Stigma and sexual orientation: Understanding prejudice against lesbians, gay men, and bisexuals* (pp. 138–159). Thousand Oaks, CA: Sage Publications.

10. Meyer, I. H. (2003). Prejudice, social stress, and mental health in lesbian, gay, and bisexual populations: Conceptual issues and research evidence. *Psychological Bulletin, 129,* 674–697.

11. Greene, B. (1994). Lesbian women of color: Triple jeopardy. In L. Comas-Diaz & B. Greene (Eds.), *Women of color: Integrating ethnic and gender identities in psychotherapy* (pp. 389–427). New York: Guilford Press.

12. Brown, L. S. (2008). *Cultural competence in trauma therapy: Beyond the flashback.* Washington, DC: American Psychological Association.

13. Morris, J. F. (1997). Set free: Lesbian mental health and the coming out process (Doctoral dissertation, University of Vermont, 1997).

14. Balsam, K. F. (2002). Traumatic victimization: A comparison of lesbian, gay, and bisexual adults and their heterosexual siblings (Doctoral dissertation, University of Vermont, 2002).

15. Balsam, K. F. (2003). Traumatic victimization in the lives of lesbian and bisexual women: A contextual approach. *Journal of Lesbian Studies, 7,* 1–14.

16. Silvern, L., Waelde, L. C., Baughan, B. M., Karyl, J., & Kaersvang, L. L. (2000). Two formats for eliciting retrospective reports of child sexual and physical abuse: Effects on apparent prevalence and relationships to adjustment. *Child Maltreatment, 5,* 236–250.

17. Straus, M. A., Hamby, S. L., Boney-McCoy, S., & Sugarman, D. B. (1996). The revised Conflict Tactics Scales (CTS2): Development and preliminary psychometric data. *Journal of Family Issues, 17,* 283–316.

18. Briere, J. N. (1992). *Child abuse trauma: Theory and treatment of the lasting effects.* Newbury Park, CA: Sage Publications.

19. Tjaden, P., Thoennes, N., & Allison, C. J. (1999). Comparing violence over the life span in samples of same-sex and opposite-sex cohabitants. *Violence and Victims, 14,* 413–425.

20. Rivers, I., & D'Augelli, A. R. (2001). The victimization of lesbians, gay, and bisexual youths. In A. R. D'Augelli & C. J. Patterson (Eds.), *Lesbian, gay, and bisexual identities and youth: Psychological perspectives* (pp. 199–223). New York: Oxford University Press.

21. Bontempo, D. E., & D'Augelli, A. R. (2002). Effect of at-school victimization and sexual orientation on lesbian, gay, or bisexual youths' health risk behavior. *Journal of Adolescent Health, 30,* 364–374.

22. Faulkner, A. H., & Cranston, K. (1998). Correlates of same-sex sexual behavior in a random sample of Massachusetts high school students. *American Journal of Public Health, 88,* 262–266.

23. Garofalo, R., Wolf, R. C., Kessel, S., Palfrey, J., & DuRant, R. H. (1998). The association between health risk behaviors and sexual orientation among a school-based sample of adolescents. *Pediatrics, 101,* 895–902.

24. Corliss, H. L., Cochran, S. D., & Mays, V. M. (2002). Reports of parental maltreatment during childhood in a United States population-based survey of homosexual, bisexual, and heterosexual adults. *Child Abuse & Neglect, 26,* 1165–1178.

25. Pilkington, N. W., & D'Augelli, A. R. (1995). Victimization of lesbian, gay, and bisexual youth in community settings. *Journal of Community Psychology, 23,* 34–56.

26. Balsam, K. F., Rothblum, E. D., & Beauchaine, T. P. (2005). Victimization over the life span: A comparison of lesbian, gay, bisexual, and heterosexual siblings. *Journal of Consulting and Clinical Psychology, 73,* 477–487.

27. Hughes, T. L., Johnson, T., & Wilsnack, S. C. (2001). Sexual assault and alcohol abuse: A comparison of lesbians and heterosexual women. *Journal of Substance Abuse, 13,* 515–532.

28. Saewyc, E. M., Skay, C. L., Pettingell, S. L., Reis, E. A., Bearinger, L., Resnick, M., et al. (2006). The sexual and physical abuse of gay, lesbian, and bisexual adolescents in the United States and Canada. *Child Welfare Journal, 85,* 195–214.

29. Cloitre, M., Tardiff, K., Marzuk, P. M., Leon, A. C., & Portera, L. (1996). Childhood abuse and subsequent sexual assault among female inpatients. *Journal of Traumatic Stress, 9,* 473–482.

30. Heidt, J. M., Marx, B. P., & Gold, S. D. (2005). Sexual revictimization among sexual minorities: A preliminary study. *Journal of Traumatic Stress, 18,* 533–540.

31. Morris, J. F., & Balsam, K. F. (2003). Lesbian and bisexual women's self-reported experiences of victimization: Mental health and sexual identity development. *Journal of Lesbian Studies, 7,* 67–85.

32. Balsam, K. F., & Lehavot, K. (2006, August). Sexual orientation and sexual revictimization: Results from a national study. Poster presented at the annual meeting of the American Psychological Association, New Orleans, LA.

33. Bachman, R., & Saltzman, L. E. (1995). *Violence against women: Estimates from the redesigned survey* (Report No. NCJ-154348). Washington, DC: U.S. Department of Justice.

34. Balsam, K. F., Beauchaine, T. P., Mickey, R. M., & Rothblum, E. D. (2005). Mental health of lesbian, gay, bisexual, and heterosexual siblings: Effects of gender, sexual orientation, and family. *Journal of Abnormal Psychology, 114,* 471–476. Available at tbeauchaine. psych.washington.edu/papers/Balsam,%20Beauchaine%20et%20al%202005.pdf.

35. Duncan, D. (1990). Prevalence of sexual assault victimization among heterosexual and gay/lesbian university students. *Psychological Reports, 59,* 1307–1313.

36. Moore, C. D., & Waterman, C. K. (1999). Predicting self-protection against sexual assault in dating relationships among heterosexual men and women, gay men, lesbians, and bisexuals. *Journal of College Student Development, 40,* 132–140.

37. Moracco, K. E., Runyan, C. W., Bowling, J. M., & Earp, J. A. (2007). Women's experiences with violence: A national study. *Women's Health Issues, 17,* 3–12.

38. Brand, P. A., & Kidd, A. H. (1986). Frequency of physical aggression in heterosexual and female homosexual dyads. *Psychological Reports, 59,* 1307–1313.

39. Herek, G. M., Gillis, J. R., & Cogan, J. C. (1999). Psychological sequelae of hate-crime victimization among lesbian, gay, and bisexual adults. *Journal of Consulting and Clinical Psychology, 67,* 945–951.

40. Herek, G. M. (2009). Hate crimes and stigma-related experiences among sexual minority adults in the United States: Prevalence estimates from a national probability sample. *Journal of Interpersonal Violence, 24,* 54–74. Available at psychology.ucdavis.edu/ rainbow/HTML/Herek_2007_JIV_preprint.pdf.

41. Dunbar, E. (2006). Race, gender, and sexual orientation in hate crime victimization: Identity politics or identity risk? *Violence and Victims, 21,* 323–337.

42. Lyons, C. J. (2006). Stigma or sympathy? Attributions of fault to hate crime victims and offenders. *Social Psychology Quarterly, 69,* 39–59.

43. Otis, M. D. (2007). Perceptions of victimization risk and fear of crime among lesbians and gay men. *Journal of Interpersonal Violence, 22,* 198–217.

44. Hall, J. M. (1998). Lesbians surviving childhood sexual abuse: Pivotal experiences related to sexual orientation, gender, and race. In C. M. Ponticelli (Ed.), *Gateways to improving lesbian health and health care: Opening doors* (pp. 7–28). Binghamton, NY: Haworth Press.

45. Horn, S. S. (2007). Adolescents' acceptance of same-sex peers based on sexual orientation and gender expression. *Journal of Youth and Adolescence, 36,* 363–371.

46. D'Augelli, A. R., Grossman, A. H., & Starks, M. T. (2006). Childhood gender atypicality, victimization, and PTSD among lesbian, gay, and bisexual youth. *Journal of Interpersonal Violence, 21,* 1462–1482.

47. D'Augelli, A. R., Hershberger, S. L., & Pilkington, N. W. (1998). Lesbian, gay, and bisexual youth and their families: Disclosure of sexual orientation and its consequences. *American Journal of Orthopsychiatry, 68,* 361–371.

48. Waldo, C. R., Hesson-McInnis, M. S., & D'Augelli, A. R. (1998). Antecedents and consequences of victimization of lesbian, gay, and bisexual young people: A structural model comparing rural university and urban samples. *American Journal of Community Psychology, 26,* 307–334.

49. Kruks, G. (1991). Gay and lesbian homeless/street youth: Special issues and concerns. *Journal of Adolescent Health, 12,* 515–518.

50. Savin-Williams, R. C. (1994). Verbal and physical abuse as stressors in the lives of lesbian, gay male, and bisexual youths: Associations with school problems, running away, substance abuse, prostitution, and suicide. *Journal of Consulting and Clinical Psychology, 62,* 261–269.

51. Cochran, S. D. (2001). Emerging issues in research on lesbians' and gay men's mental health: Does sexual orientation really matter? *American Psychologist, 56,* 931–947.

52. Gilman, S. E., Cochran, S. D., Mays, V. M., Hughes, M., Ostrow, D., & Kessler, R. C. (2001). Risk of psychiatric disorders among individuals reporting same-sex sexual partners in the National Comorbidity Survey. *American Journal of Public Health, 91,* 933–939.

53. Hughes, T. L., & Eliason, M. (2002). Substance use and abuse in lesbian, gay, bisexual, and transgender populations. *Journal of Primary Prevention, 22,* 263–298.

54. Kilpatrick, D. G., Acierno, R., Resnick, H. S., Saunders, B. E., & Best, C. L. (1997). A 2-year longitudinal analysis of the relationships between violent assault and substance use in women. *Journal of Consulting and Clinical Psychology, 65,* 834–847.

55. Greene, B. (1997). Ethnic minority lesbians and gay men: Mental health and treatment issues. In B. Greene (Ed.), *Ethnic and cultural diversity among lesbians and gay men* (pp. 216–239). Thousand Oaks, CA: Sage Publications.

56. Balsam, K. F., Plummer, M. D., Fieland, K. C., Gutierrez, B., & Yoshimoto, D. (2005, August). *Minority stress among LGBT people of color: A qualitative investigation.* Symposium held at the annual meeting of the American Psychological Association, Washington, DC.

57. Comstock, G. D. (1989). Victims of anti-gay/lesbian violence. *Journal of Interpersonal Violence, 4,* 101–106.

58. Von Schulthess, B. (1991). Violence in the streets: Anti-lesbian assault and harassment in San Francisco. In G. M. Herek & K. T. Berrill (Eds.), *Hate crimes: Confronting violence against lesbian and gay men* (pp. 65–75). Thousand Oaks, CA: Sage Publications.

59. Sharps, P., & Campbell, J. (1999). Health consequences for victims of violence in intimate relationships. In X. Arriaga & S. Oskamp (Eds.), *Violence in intimate partner relationships* (pp. 163–180). Thousand Oaks, CA: Sage Publications.

60. Kilpatrick, D. G., Resnick, H. S., & Acierno, R. (1997). Health impact of interpersonal violence: Implications for clinical practice and public policy. *Behavioral Medicine, 23,* 79–85.

61. Brokaw, J., Fullerton-Gleason, L., Olson, L., Crandall, C., McLaughlin, S., & Sklar, D. (2002). Health status and intimate partner violence: A cross-sectional study. *Annals of Emergency Medicine, 39,* 31–38.

62. Coker, A. L., Davis, K. E., Arias, I., Desai, S., Sanderson, M., Brandt, H. M., et al. (2002). Physical and mental health effects of intimate partner violence for men and women. *American Journal of Preventive Medicine, 23,* 260–268.

63. Greenfeld, L. A., Rand, M. R., Craven, D., Klaus, P. A., Perkins, C. A., Ringel, C., et al. (1998). *Violence by intimates: Analysis of data on crimes by current or former spouses, boyfriends, and girlfriends* (Report No. NCJ-167237). Washington, DC: U.S. Department of Justice. Available at www.ojp.usdoj.gov/bjs/pub/pdf/vi.pdf.

64. Hathaway, J. E., Mucci, L. A., Silverman, J. G., Brooks, D. R., Mathews, R., & Pavlos, C. A. (2000). Health status and health care use of Massachusetts women reporting partner abuse. *American Journal of Preventive Medicine, 19,* 302–307.

65. Letourneau, E., Holmes, M. M., & Chasendunn-Roark, J. (1999). Gynecologic health consequences to victims of interpersonal violence. *Women's Health Issues, 9,* 115–120.

66. Elklit, A., & Brink, O. (2004). Acute stress disorder as a predictor of post-traumatic stress disorder in physical assault victims. *Journal of Interpersonal Violence, 19,* 709–726.

67. Kawsar, M., Anfield, A., Walters, E., McCabe, S., & Forster, G. E. (2004). Prevalence of sexually transmitted infections and mental health needs of female child and adolescent survivors of rape and sexual assault attending a specialist clinic. *Sexually Transmitted Infections, 80,* 138–141.

68. Walker, E. A., Gelfand, A., Katon, W. J., Koss, M. P., von Korff, M., Bernstein, D., et al. (1999). Adult health status of women with histories of childhood abuse and neglect. *American Journal of Medicine, 107,* 332–339.

69. Stein, M., & Barrett-Connor, E. (2000). Sexual assault and physical health: Findings from a population-based study of older adults. *Psychosomatic Medicine, 62,* 838–843.

70. McNutt, L. A., Carlson, B. E., Persaud, M., & Postmus, J. (2002). Cumulative abuse experiences, physical health and health behaviors. *Annals of Epidemiology, 12,* 123–130.

71. Bergman, B., & Brismar, B. (1991). A 5-year follow-up study of 117 battered women. *American Journal of Public Health, 81,* 1486–1489.

72. Caetano, R., Cunradi, C. B., Schafer, J., & Clark, C. L. (2000). Intimate partner violence and drinking patterns among White, Black, and Hispanic couples in the U.S. *Journal of Substance Abuse, 11,* 123–138.

73. Drossman, D. A., Talley, N. J., Leserman, J., Olden, K. W., & Barreiro, M. A. (1995). Sexual and physical abuse and gastrointestinal illness: Review and recommendations. *Annals of Internal Medicine, 123,* 782–794.

74. Holmes, M. M., Resnick, H. S., & Frampton, D. (1998). Follow-up of sexual assault victims. *American Journal of Obstetrics & Gynecology, 179,* 336–342.

75. Humphreys, J., Lee, K., Neylan, T., & Marmar, C. (2001). Psychological and physical distress of sheltered battered women. *Health Care for Women International, 22,* 401–414.

76. Wyshak, G., & Modest, G. A. (1996). Violence, mental health, and substance abuse in patients who are seen in primary care settings. *Archives of Family Medicine, 5,* 441–447.

77. Simpson, T. L., & Miller, W. R. (2002). Concomitance between childhood sexual and physical abuse and substance use problems: A review. *Clinical Psychology Review, 22,* 27–77.

78. Norris, F. H., Foster, J. D., & Weisshaar, D. L. (2002). The epidemiology of sex differences in PTSD across developmental, societal, and research contexts. In R. Kimerling, P. Ouimette, & J. Wolfe (Eds.), *Gender and PTSD* (pp. 3–42). New York: Guilford Press.

79. Dansky, B., Brewerton, T., Kilpatrick, D., & O'Neill, P. (1997). The National Women's Study: Relationship of victimization and posttraumatic stress disorder to bulimia nervosa. *International Journal of Eating Disorders, 21,* 213–228.

80. Kendler, K. S., Buik, C. M., Silberg, J., Hettema, J. M., Myers, J., & Prescott, C. A. (2000). Childhood sexual abuse and adult psychiatric and substance use disorders in women. *Archives of General Psychiatry, 52,* 1048–1060.

81. Resnick, H. S., Acierno, R., & Kilpatrick, D. G. (1997). Health impact of interpersonal violence. 2: Medical and mental health outcomes. *Behavioral Medicine, 23,* 65–78.

82. Hughes T. L., Johnson, T. P., Wilsnack, S. C., & Szalacha, L. A. (2007). Childhood risk factors for alcohol abuse and psychological distress among adult lesbians. *Child Abuse & Neglect, 31,* 769–789.

83. Roberts, S. J., & Sorensen, L. (1999). Health related behaviors and cancer screening of lesbians: Results from the Boston Lesbian Health Project. *Women & Health, 28,* 1–12.

84. Aaron, D. J., & Hughes, T. L. (2007). Association of childhood sexual abuse with obesity in a community sample of lesbians. *Obesity, 15,* 1023–1028.

85. Descamps, M. J., Rothblum, E., Bradford, J., & Ryan, C. (2000). Mental health impact of child sexual abuse, rape, intimate partner violence, and hate crimes in the National Lesbian Health Care Survey. *Journal of Gay & Lesbian Social Services, 11,* 27–55.

86. Gidycz, C. A., Coble, C. N., Latham, L., & Layman, M. J. (1993). Sexual assault experience in adulthood and prior victimization experiences: A prospective analysis. *Psychology of Women Quarterly, 17,* 151–168.

87. Messman-Moore, T. L., Long, P. J., & Siegfried, N. J. (2000). The revictimization of child sexual abuse survivors: An examination of the adjustment of college women with child sexual abuse, adult sexual assault, and adult physical abuse. *Child Maltreatment, 5,* 18–27.

88. Lock, J., & Steiner, H. (1999). Gay, lesbian, and bisexual youth risks for emotional, physical, and social problems: Results from a community-based survey. *Journal of the American Academy of Child & Adolescent Psychiatry, 38,* 297–304.

89. Balsam, K. F., & Rothblum, E. D. (2003, August). Sexual orientation, victimization, and mental health. Poster presented at the annual meeting of the American Psychological Association, Toronto, Canada.

90. Carlson, E. B., & Dalenberg, C. J. (2000). A conceptual framework for the impact of traumatic experiences. *Trauma, Violence, & Abuse, 1,* 4–28.

91. Otis, M. D., & Skinner, W. F. (1996). The prevalence of victimization and its effect on mental well-being among lesbian and gay people. *Journal of Homosexuality, 30,* 93–121.

92. Butke, M. (1995). Lesbians and sexual child abuse. In L. A. Fuentes (Ed.), *Sexual abuse in nine North American cultures* (pp. 236–258). Thousand Oaks, CA: Sage Publications.

93. Pantalone, D. W., & Balsam, K. F. (2005, November). *Childhood abuse and beliefs about sexual identity development in a national sample of lesbian, gay, and bisexual adults.*

Paper presented at the annual meeting of the Association for Behavioral and Cognitive Therapies, Washington, DC.

94. Miller, B. C., Monson, B. H., & Norton, M. C. (1995). The effects of forced sexual intercourse on white female adolescents. *Child Abuse & Neglect, 19*, 1289–1301.

95. Wilsnack, S. C., Vogeltanz, N. D., Klassen, A. D., & Harris, T. R. (1997). Childhood sexual abuse and women's substance abuse: National survey findings. *Journal of Studies on Alcohol, 58*, 264–271.

96. Browning, C. R., & Laumann, E. O. (1997). Sexual contact between children and adults: A life course perspective. *American Sociological Review, 62*, 540–560.

97. Bensley, L. S., van Eenwyk, J., & Simmons, K. W. (2000). Self-reported childhood sexual and physical abuse and adult HIV-risk behaviors and heavy drinking. *American Journal of Preventive Medicine, 18*, 151–158.

98. Arriola, K. R. J., Louden, T., Doldren, M. A., & Fortenberry, R. M. (2005). A meta-analysis of the relationship of child-sexual abuse to HIV risk-behavior among women. *Child Abuse & Neglect, 29*, 725–746.

99. Diamond, L. M. (2007). A dynamical systems approach to the development and expression of female same-sex sexuality. *Perspectives on Psychological Science, 2*, 142–161.

100. Morris, J. F., Waldo, C. R., & Rothblum, E. D. (2001). A model of predictors and outcomes of outness among lesbian and bisexual women. *American Journal of Orthopsychiatry, 71*, 61–71.

101. Balsam, K. F., & Mohr, J. (2007). Adaptation to sexual orientation stigma: A comparison of bisexual and lesbian/gay adults. *Journal of Counseling Psychology, 54*, 306–319.

102. Hunter, J. (1990). Violence against lesbian and gay male youths. *Journal of Interpersonal Violence, 5*, 295–300.

103. Dutton, M. A., Mitchell, B., & Haywood, Y. (1995). The emergency department as a violence prevention center. *Journal of the American Medical Women's Association, 51*, 92–96.

104. Thombs, B. D., Bernstein, D. P., Ziegelstein, R. C., Bennett, W., & Walker, E. A. (2007). A brief two-item screener for detecting a history of physical or sexual abuse in childhood. *General Hospital Psychiatry, 29*, 8–13.

105. Rothblum, E. D., & Factor, R. (2001). Lesbians and their sisters as a control group: Demographic and mental health factors. *Psychological Science, 12*, 63–69.

106. Foa, E., Cascardi, M., Zoellner, L., & Feeny, N. (2000). Psychological and environmental factors associated with partner violence. *Trauma, Violence, & Abuse, 1*, 67–91.

107. Resick, P. A., & Schnicke, M. K. (1993). *Cognitive processing therapy for rape victims: A treatment manual*. Thousand Oaks, CA: Sage Publications.

ABOUT THE AUTHORS

Kimberly F. Balsam, PhD is Research Assistant Professor in the School of Social Work at the University of Washington, Seattle. Her research interests are the social, cultural, and individual factors that impact the health and well-being of stigmatized populations, with an emphasis on lesbian, gay, bisexual, and transgender adults. She also has a private practice in psychotherapy.

Keren Lehavot, MS is a doctoral student in Clinical Psychology at the University of Washington, Seattle. Her research interests are feminist psychology and lesbian gay bisexual and transgender psychology. Her dissertation project examines gender expression, minority stress and coping on health outcomes among lesbian and bisexual women.

CHAPTER 20

"I Feel So Vulnerable."

LESBIANS WITH DISABILITIES

DAWN MARIE WADLE, MD

CORBETT JOAN O'TOOLE, BSE

AS A CHILD *growing up in a family of boys, Anna, a 43-year-old lesbian, was expected to "push through" the pain of injuries, including knee and shoulder injuries she suffered while playing high school sports. She rarely saw a doctor, a pattern that continued into adulthood even when she had medical insurance. Three years ago, after she showed up at the emergency room with extreme abdominal pain, Anna underwent laparotomy for removal of her necrotic gall bladder. She pushed through the pain of recovery and soon resumed her busy life. However, Anna did not realize she had developed multiple hernias. Her* *continued activity exacerbated them to the point that she began feeling constant severe pain. Anna's partner finally convinced her to see a physician.*

During the doctor visit, Anna insisted she was not disabled, just temporarily sick. This attitude had created numerous and progressive health problems. Each time she became stable on pain medication, she increased her activities, which caused further injuries. Routine testing revealed she had diabetes, high blood pressure, and high cholesterol.

Anna is on high-dose pain medication. Her shoulder and knee are permanently injured, significantly restricting her activities, and she is depressed. She refuses to limit her activity or communicate with others who are dealing with chronic pain. She continues to "go it alone," much to the frustration of her physician and her partner. At each visit, Anna asks: "When will I get all better?"

__JESSICA,__ a 55-year-old lesbian, had polio as a child. Back then, her contact with other people with disabilities was limited. Now, as an informed medical consumer, she seeks their support and any information they may have to offer. She comes to doctor appointments with a checklist of questions and writes down the answers. Jessica understands that her health problems are permanent and require daily management. To minimize her pain, she balances rest and activity. However, in her view, medical care is only one aspect of the attention she needs; she also relies on support and information from the community of people with disabilities.

Jessica is frustrated by physicians' attitude toward her. "Just once in my life," she confides to a friend, "I would like a health care provider who sees me as a whole human being—to acknowledge my lesbian self, my disabled self, my mother self, my woman self, my middle-age and getting-close- to-60 self.

Occasionally, a doctor or nurse greets more than one part of my self, and I latch on to that person with gratitude. I willingly ignore the other parts and pretend they aren't important."

■ ■ ■

Given that one in five American women has a congenital or acquired disability, most adult medical practices have female patients with physical or mental disabilities.[1] Like Anna and Jessica, many of these women are dealing with health problems that impair their daily activities.

Disability poses numerous challenges not only for lesbians and women in general, but also for researchers who study them and their health care providers. It is unclear, for example, exactly how many lesbians are disabled.[2] Furthermore, most researchers focus on single health conditions, such as diabetes in women; they typically do not examine broader conditions, such as multiple disabilities among lesbians, which makes it difficult for clinicians to learn about these women. Finally, many clinicians have not been trained to address the barriers that prevent lesbians with disabilities from accessing health care.[3]

Access to good health care and services requires more than wheelchair ramps. Clinicians must be well-informed about the full range of health needs of women with disabilities and not focus exclusively on the disability. In addition, equipment and facilities must be able to accommodate these women, preserving their dignity and independence, and policies and programs must be in place to help overcome attitudes and prejudices that reinforce the stigma still associated with disability.[1]

Facing daily discrimination, lesbians with disabilities often establish supportive communities and provide valuable resources to each other. Many such women are flexible and creative, and have well-honed problem-solving skills—characteristics that they and their clinicians, as a team, can apply to maximizing health.

This chapter summarizes research on women and lesbians with disabilities, their health risks and concerns, and protective factors, such as social support and connecting with others who have similar medical conditions. It also addresses challenges they encounter in seeking care (Table 20.1).

WHO ARE LESBIANS WITH DISABILITIES?

Disabilities are characteristics of the mind, body, or senses that affect one's ability to deal with aspects of day-to-day life. They are present at birth or arise later in life, and may or may not be visible to others.[5] Although disabilities often result from medical

TABLE 20.1. SELECTED HEALTH CARE CHALLENGES AND POSSIBLE SOLUTIONS FOR LESBIANS WITH DISABILITIES

PROBLEM	SOLUTION
"I don't expect my clinicians to know everything. But I do expect them to find out the important stuff if they want to keep me as a patient. In addition, they should communicate with each other when appropriate."	Many lesbians with disabilities receive fragmented health care. When indicated, clinicians must communicate with each other regarding key issues.
"I hate it that my neurologist won't let me put up a poster about a support group for lesbians with multiple sclerosis. He says it might upset some people. Well, what does he think he's doing to me?"	Posted materials that specifically welcome lesbians and/or others who are disabled can help lesbians feel more comfortable with the office and clinician. This often results in more communication between the patient and health care provider.
"My doctor had me on blood pressure medicine for more than a year. But the blood pressure reading was wrong because blood pressure cuffs do not yield accurate readings in people with arms as small as mine. Luckily, I talked with my Little People of America friends and they told me what to do."	Medical equipment is calibrated based on "normal" people—usually White, nondisabled men. Lesbians with atypical bodies often test in abnormal ranges on standard equipment. Health care providers must be aware that normal ranges can be different in certain populations.
"I hate when doctors say, 'Just get a Pap smear.' Don't they have any idea how difficult it is to find an ob/gyn who has a wheelchair-accessible exam table?"	Clinicians must carefully evaluate medical offices to which they refer disabled lesbians in terms of sensitivity, access, and the availability of equipment designed for people with disabilities. Does the office have a high-low exam table, a sign language interpreter, a ban on scented cleaning products, extended appointment times, forms in a format for the visually impaired, and public transportation nearby? Given an opportunity, patients will cite items that are important to them and can confirm a checklist of items before they visit a specialist.
"I made an appointment with the biggest hospital clinic I could find for a Pap smear because I needed the lift team to get me on and off the table. Twice before the appointment, I confirmed that help would be available. But when I showed up, the receptionist acted like I made all this up on the spot. The nurse went down to the mail room and got two guys to lift me."	Getting cancer screening is complicated for women with disabilities. There are numerous physical and attitudinal barriers. Clinicians can train staff to provide care that is culturally appropriate for patients with disabilities and, in particular, for lesbians with disabilities.

(cont.)

TABLE 20.1. SELECTED HEALTH CARE CHALLENGES AND POSSIBLE SOLUTIONS FOR LESBIANS WITH DISABILITIES *(cont.)*

PROBLEM	SOLUTION
"I used drugs for years and not a single health care provider ever asked me about them. I guess being a blind woman meant I couldn't be a drug user."	Patients with disabilities are much more likely than others to abuse alcohol and both prescription and nonprescription drugs. Clinicians should ask all patients about their alcohol and drug use.
"My girlfriend was also my attendant. When she was angry or drunk, she would not help me out of bed and I got sores. I couldn't tell the doctors because they asked her to come to appointments to 'help' me."	Compared with heterosexual women, lesbians with disabilities are at higher risk of abuse and violence. All patients, including those with disabilities, should be interviewed alone and screened for abuse.
"Medical people expect us to have helpers, so just introduce your lover as such. You can both laugh about it later when you're home in bed."	Clinicians should talk openly with lesbians who are disabled about their support systems, and encourage them to bring others to appointments. These support persons can be introduced to medical personnel as friends, lovers, or note-takers.
"Doctors hate being wrong. So ask them: 'Is there another approach to problem X?' That way, they feel smart and you get the information you need."	Lesbians with disabilities often receive fragmented care; one doctor focuses on impairment, another on general care. After a lesbian lives with a disability for awhile, she realizes that important medical information is spread among different medical offices and that she is the only constant. Clinicians who encourage these patients to keep a record of their medical visits, medications, and treatments, and who treat them like experts regarding their health, will foster patients' trust and provide better care.
"Always contact the doctor's office before an appointment to make sure the office has arranged for an interpreter, then bring your best friend in case an interpreter isn't there. That way, you won't waste a doctor visit. Later, you can buy your friend lunch as compensation."	Far too often, health care providers tell lesbians with disabilities, in so many words, that they are too much trouble and too expensive. Yet, by law, nearly all health care facilities must provide basic access, such as wheelchair access and sign language interpreters. Office budgets should include funds to pay for the services and access that people with disabilities need.

Source: Authors

conditions, most are not illnesses. Disabilities can increase the risk of other health conditions and/or impact health-related behaviors. About 22% of Americans are living with disabilities,[6] a proportion that is expected to increase as the population ages. Poverty and unemployment place people at high risk of disability, as does being a minority person in poor health.[7] This disparity persists even among people receiving Medicare.[8] With aging come higher poverty and more impairments, further increasing the number of people with disabilities.[6,9]

Many of the conditions that cause disability affect women more frequently than they do men. More than half of all women older than 65 have a disability. Chronic conditions associated with the most common disabilities include back disorders, arthritis, heart disease, respiratory problems, and high blood pressure. Of course, injuries and birth defects also cause disabilities.[10]

Lesbians with disabilities often bear additional burdens that are unlike those borne by heterosexual women and men with disabilities, although all people with a disability experience ableism (discrimination or prejudice against individuals with disabilities) and must manage their disability-related symptoms.[11] Among these additional burdens are sexism[12] and homophobia,[13] which cause stress that can jeopardize health. An example is the Asian American lesbian with chronic fatigue syndrome who tries to navigate environments that are at times hostile to her as an Asian woman, a lesbian, and a person with a poorly understood impairment. Does she hide her lesbianism in order to fit in better with a chronic fatigue support group whose leader assumes everyone is heterosexual? How does she find health professionals who can explain chronic fatigue syndrome to her and her family of origin in a culturally sensitive way? How does she filter and balance the information she gets from the various communities to which she belongs? These are just a few of the many challenges she faces daily.

BARRIERS TO HEALTH CARE

Lesbians with disabilities, like people with disabilities in general, encounter myriad barriers to health care. The barriers may be physical, financial, and/or attitudinal. For example, clinics rarely provide ways for the deaf to communicate.[14] Height-adjustable examination tables are rare.[15] Sometimes blind patients are asked to sign printed consent forms unavailable on audiotape or in Braille or large print.

Health care affordability can be an especially difficult barrier for people with disabilities. An acquired disability often causes downward economic mobility.[11] Many of those with a congenital or childhood-onset condition never have an opportunity to become gainfully employed. To qualify for public health insurance, applicants must be extremely poor. Consequently, some people with disabilities who could work do not; they cannot risk losing their insurance coverage. Lesbians may choose not to enter a legal same-sex civil union or marriage out of fear that this will make them ineligible for public health care benefits. Private insurers generally do not cover people with disabilities and others who have pre-existing conditions. Medicare and Medicaid typically do not cover all health care costs, such as copayments, medications not on a formulary, and expenses related to equipment or an attendant, interpreter, or reader.[2,16] In recent years, finding health care providers willing to accept Medicare or Medicaid has become increasingly difficult, further compromising health care for people with disabilities.[16] For lesbians with disabilities, an additional concern may be revelation of their sexual orientation. Might "coming out" risk the clinician's scorn or result in poorer health care? The decision about whether or not to come out is a difficult one for many lesbians, even if they do not have a disability.

Some health researchers and providers ascribe to the "medical model of disability." They view people who have disabilities as incomplete and in need of being "fixed," and seek solutions only within the confines of the medical profession. This approach addresses the human body's systemic challenges, but it does little to help patients function in their everyday lives. In contrast, the "social model of disability" assumes that patients are whole individuals with medical issues. An impairment's existence and severity neither diminishes nor negates patients' normalcy; rather, it merely informs and shapes their lives in much the same way that sexuality, race/ethnicity, and age do.[17] From the social model perspective, lesbians with disabilities have the same needs as any other lesbian, and the presence or absence of a significant impairment is additive, not definitive. All aspects of health care for lesbians in general also apply to lesbians with disabilities. The social model of disability also acknowledges that the community, including relatives, friends, acquaintances, and members of support groups, affects health behaviors. For example, many people who have chronic disabilities talk with others like them to get information about treatments, strategies for living with the impairment, and health care providers. They may consider such information to be more reliable than what clinicians tell them or may use it to initiate discussions with clinicians about treatment options. In any case, information exchange is a significant source of support for the emotional and logistical challenges of living with a chronic impairment.[18]

People with disabilities may erect their own attitudinal barriers. They may view disability through the lens of the medical model, such that many lesbians with disabilities see themselves as "broken" or "impaired" and definitely not "normal."[19,20] The feeling of brokenness often is broader than the disability itself and encouraged by experiences common in medical settings and society: the individual overly focuses on what she cannot do rather than on what she can and/or talks with family members or caregivers instead of other people with disabilities.[21] This is an especially harmful attitude among those with a newly diagnosed impairment. In contrast, people with disabilities who connect with the disability rights movement and adopt the social model of disability see their impaired bodies as normal and realize that many of the problems they face are mostly due to discrimination. Disability activists believe that society is ableist and that "normal" should be defined more broadly. One such activist, Harriet McBryde Johnson, describes society's general attitude this way:

> I used to try to explain that in fact I enjoy my life, that it's a great sensual pleasure to zoom by power chair on these delicious muggy streets, that I have no more reason to kill myself than most people…. But they don't want to know. They think they know everything there is to know, just by looking at me. That's how stereotypes work. They don't know that they're confused, that they're really expressing the discombobulation that comes in my wake.[22]

Feeling "broken" definitely affects self-esteem and alters medical, social, and sexual encounters.[11,13,19] For lesbians with disabilities, establishing and maintaining an effective social support network to counterbalance this feeling is challenging. They need environments that see their families of choice as normal[19] and that help them fight homophobia and challenge ableism.[4] Such environments are not always easy to find. Nearly all support groups for people with disabilities do not even acknowledge homophobia, and few lesbian support systems, including gay centers, lesbian Web sites, and formal or informal networks, understand the insidious effects of ableism. Consequently, lesbians with disabilities often must seek support in one place for dealing with homophobia and in another for dealing with ableism. Compartmentalizing one's identity in this manner may partly explain how and why the impact of social bias on health is negative.[23,24]

Being lesbian and having a disability compounds numerous barriers to health care. Such women must find not only medical offices that are physically accessible, but also clinicians who are knowledgeable about their particular disability, lesbian-friendly, and trustworthy. They also may have to overcome their reluctance to seek health care.

HEALTH RISKS FOR LESBIANS WITH DISABILITIES

Few studies have focused specifically on lesbians with disabilities. However, the limited evidence from this research and findings from broader studies on women with disabilities illuminates the health risks and other issues faced by lesbians who are disabled.

Women with disabilities have greater primary care needs.[15] Among Medicaid recipients, they and nondisabled women are equally likely to have primary care physicians, but women with disabilities are 50% less likely to be satisfied with their care, which correlates with a higher likelihood of delaying recommended medical care (three times greater) and/or medications (two times greater).[16] The rate of obesity among women with physical disabilities is twice that among nondisabled women.[21] Many physician offices do not have scales for people who cannot stand, and oftentimes weight loss suggestions for people with disabilities are not articulated or are poorly adapted to their circumstances.[21]

Cancer Screening and Therapy

Women with disabilities are less likely than nondisabled women to receive Pap smears and mammograms, even when they have equivalent insurance coverage.[7,25-27] In a study of women with physical disabilities, participants said transportation, heavy doors, inaccessible exam tables, and inaccessible or partially accessible bathrooms were barriers to cancer screening and other health care. Many also said they felt that clinicians devalued them when they expressed a desire to be partners in their care.[25] Another study found that few gynecologic clinicians were comfortable doing even routine screening of adolescents with disabilities. The reasons they cited were time constraints, poor reimbursement, inadequate knowledge, no physical access for people with disabilities, and a preference not to serve this population.[28] Women with disabilities often sense a provider's discomfort and allow it to affect their self-care and health-care-seeking behaviors.

Women with cancer and disabilities do not always receive the same treatment as other women. McCarthy and colleagues found that those with breast cancer and disabilities were less likely to receive breast-conserving surgery, and if they did receive it, they were less likely to also undergo standard radiation therapy and lymph node dissection.[29] In another study, breast cancer mortality was higher among women with disabilities even when researchers adjusted the data for treatment differences. A greater likelihood of treatment complications arising from the disabling conditions may explain this discrepancy.[29,30] Physicians may be less likely to offer women with disabilities the less invasive option of breast-conserving surgery on the assumption that physical appearance is not important to them, which would account for the higher rates of mastectomy versus breast-conserving surgery among these women. Logistical issues also may play a role. For example, perhaps women with disabilities cannot arrange for transportation to and from radiation therapy or, in the case of patients with movement disorders, their conditions might make it physically difficult for them to undergo such therapy.[30,31] Other research indicates that women with mental and neurological disorders had less of both breast conserving surgery and radiation therapy.[2]

Substance Abuse

Cigarette smoking is more common among women with disabilities. Younger women with physical disabilities are twice as likely as their age-related peers to smoke; they cite depression and stress as reasons for smoking.[16] In a Canadian study, women with disabilities said they smoke because of low self-esteem, issues of independence, and stress, particularly the stress of discrimination based on disability.[31] Despite the higher likelihood of smoking, doctors are less likely to ask women with disabilities if they smoke than to ask other women.[16] This is especially disturbing regarding women with mobility limitations, as they are already at higher risk of poor circulation, osteoporosis, and skin problems. Smoking increases the risks of these conditions.

Alcohol and other drug addiction are problems for lesbians[32] and people with disabilities.[33,34] Addiction itself may be a disability[35]; it also complicates the lives and care of people with other disabilities. According to the U.S. Department of Health & Human Services, rates of addiction are higher among people with disabilities than in the general population, although this seems to depend partly on the type of disability. The rates are lower among people with developmental delays but as much as 50% higher among those with spinal cord injuries, traumatic brain injuries, or mental illness. Forty percent to 50% of people with spinal cord injuries, orthopedic disabilities, vision impairment, and amputations are heavy drinkers,[36] and evidence suggests that more people with disabilities abuse prescription drugs.[34] There has been little research on substance abuse among women with disabilities and even less on lesbians with disabilities.[34,37]

Treatment facilities are not keeping pace with the increase in substance abuse rates among people with disabilities.[37] Not only are ramps and electric doors in short supply, but insight-oriented talk therapy in individual and group sessions, the most popular addiction treatment model, is especially challenging for people who have difficulty hearing or verbalizing, and for those with brain injuries or other communication and cognitive impairments.[34]

Violence

Disability increases one's risk of being a victim of violence.[38] As many as 90% of people with developmental disabilities will be physically or sexually assaulted at some point in their lives, and half of them will experience repeated assaults.[39] Rape, assault, and abuse rates for women with disabilities are more than two times higher than those for nondisabled women, and the violence in abuse cases is likely to be more severe and prolonged, resulting in more serious chronic effects.[40] In one study, women with disabilities were significantly more likely than nondisabled women to report having experienced some form of intimate partner violence in their lifetime (37.3% vs. 20.6%); having ever been threatened with violence (28.5% vs. 15.4%) or having been hit, slapped, pushed, kicked, or physically hurt (30.6% vs. 15.7%); and having a history of unwanted sex with an intimate partner (19.7% vs. 8.2%).[41] Lesbians with disabilities are at least as vulnerable as the larger population of girls and women with disabilities, perhaps more so.

Women with disabilities who need physical assistance from attendants have vulnerabilities that able-bodied women may not. Physical needs create opportunities for neglect, roughness in dealing with those needs, and dangerous inattention to detail, all of which can be forms of abuse.[38] A lesbian's need for assistance with shopping, paying bills, or using an ATM creates opportunities for financial abuse. Emotional abuse can occur when family members or friends help, as this requires a balancing of roles that is challenging at best.[42] Whenever a volunteer or paid attendant or interpreter is tired and frustrated, the possibility of abuse increases. For lesbians with disabilities, sharing personal information with others who come into the home and who may be homophobic can create additional vulnerabilities. Women with disabilities are also vulnerable to abuse by partners and others in the home, yet resources that might help them counter such abuse are extremely limited or nonexistent.[16] Shelter and support for lesbians in violent relationships also are extremely limited.[42]

PROTECTIVE FACTORS

Although lesbians with disabilities are often invisible to nondisabled people, they may benefit from socially connecting with them.[33] Patients who think of themselves as "sick" and removed from society experience negative health consequences. Just as many lesbians believe that connecting with other lesbians is an important way to battle homophobia, many lesbians with disabilities believe that connecting with other lesbians like them helps them fight homophobia and ableism.[43]

Research on highly networked lesbians and women with disabilities shows that they are less depressed, have higher self-esteem, face fewer health risks, and manage their health better.[19] Lesbians with disabilities who are isolated by homophobia and ableism have a greater need for support from networks of others like them.[19,20] Such networks provide valuable information about how to manage impairments, deal with medical specialists' homophobia, navigate the community of lesbians with disabilities, communicate with sexual partners about impairment, and engage lesbian support when dealing with possibly unfriendly health care personnel.[13]

■ ■ ■

In the scenario at the beginning of this chapter, Jessica bemoaned the problems she encountered finding culturally appropriate health care. She eventually learned to incorporate disability education and advocacy into her health care appointments, to be her own health advocate, and to both learn from and teach clinicians. Today, her lesbian-friendly primary care physician understands the many health issues lesbians face and is willing to consult the resources Jessica suggests regarding polio as well as post-polio syndrome and how it might affect her multiple medical problems. Most importantly, the doctor truly listens to Jessica, which in turn increases her attention to the doctor's advice.

Anna, on the other hand, still has not reframed her self-image to include her physical challenges. With her partner's and health care provider's support, Anna began individual therapy for help in dealing with all of her concerns, including chronic pain.

CONCLUSION

Lesbians with disabilities want what all patients want: respectful and competent health care. But they encounter numerous physical, financial, and attitudinal barriers that may prevent them from getting the care they need. These barriers include inaccessible facilities, medical equipment not designed for people with disabilities, the cost of care, homophobia and ableism among health care providers, and their own negative feelings about disability or impairment. Factors that increase health risks for women with disabilities—obesity, inadequate cancer screening and therapy, smoking, substance abuse, and abuse and violence—may be even greater for lesbians with disabilities. Lesbian-friendly clinicians who accommodate these patients, plus strong social support and networking, can help lesbians with disabilities overcome the special challenges they face.

ADDITIONAL RESOURCES

- Access to Health Care by Women With Disabilities:
  www.bcm.edu/crowd/access_health_care/access_health_care.html
- Breast Health Access for Women With Disabilities:
  www.bhawd.org
- Centers for Disease Control and Prevention. (2006). *Women with disabilities. Access to health.* Available at www.cdc.gov/ncbddd/women/access.htm.
- Kaiser Permanente. (2004). *A provider's handbook on culturally competent care: Individuals with disabilities.* Oakland, CA: Author. Discusses disability-related research and offers practical information and tools that can help providers become more aware of and knowledgeable about the health care needs of people with disabilities. To order, call (510) 271-6663.
- Mace, R. L. (n.d.). *Removing barriers to health care: A guide for health professionals.* Raleigh, NC: Center for Universal Design and North Carolina Office on Disability and Health. Available at www.fpg.unc.edu/~ncodh/rbar.
- Mösdeux Productions. (2005). *Till domestic violence do us part* [DVD]. Oakland, CA. Available for purchase at www.deaf-hope.org/information/dvd.php.

A 20-minute film about the life of a deaf woman who is abused by her deaf husband, and the range of abusive tactics he uses to gain power and control.

- NSW Cervical Screening Program. (2003). *Preventive women's health care for women with disabilities.* Eveleigh, New South Wales, Australia: Author. Available at ⚓ www.csp.nsw.gov.au/downloads/Prev_Women_HC_Disabilities.pdf.

- Smeltzer, S. C., & Sharts-Hopko, N. C. (2005). *A provider's guide for the care of women with physical disabilities and chronic health conditions.* Raleigh, NC: North Carolina Office on Disability and Health. Available at ⚓ www.fpg.unc.edu/~ncodh/htmls/providersguide.htm.

- Special Olympics. (2005). *Changing attitudes, changing the world: The health and health care of people with intellectual disabilities.* Available at ⚓ northamerica.specialolympics.org/research/documents/CACW_Health.pdf.

- Welner, S. L., & Haseltine, F. (Eds.). (2003). *Welner's guide to the care of women with disabilities.* Lippincott Williams & Wilkins.

- World Institute on Disability. (n.d.). *Recognizing and interrupting abuse of adults with disabilities.* Available at ⚓ www.wid.org/programs/health-access-and-long-term-services/curriculum-on-abuse-prevention-and-empowerment-cape/recognizing-and-interrupting-abuse-of-adults-with-disabilities.

REFERENCES

1. Office on Women's Health. (2004). *Breaking down barriers to health care for women with disabilities: A white paper from a national summit.* Washington, DC: U.S. Department of Health and Human Services. Available at www.hhs.gov/od/summit/whitepaper.doc.

2. Iezzoni, L. I., Ngo, L. H., Li, D., Roetzheim, R. G., Drews, R. E., & McCarthy, E. P. (2008). Early stage breast cancer treatments for younger Medicare beneficiaries with different disabilities. *Health Services Research, 43,* 1752–1767.

3. Turk, M. A. (2004, December). *Barriers to health care for women with disabilities: Education of health care providers.* Presentation at a U.S. Department of Health & Human Services national summit, Washington, DC. Available at www.hhs.gov/od/120604meeting.html.

4. Clare, E. (2002, June). *Sex, celebration, and justice: A keynote for QD2002.* Presentation at the Queer Disability conference, San Francisco, CA. Available at www.disabilityhistory.org/dwa/queer/paper_clare.html.

5. Office of the Surgeon General. (2005). *The 2005 Surgeon General's call to action to improve the health and wellness of persons with disabilities.* Washington, DC: U.S. Department of Health & Human Services. Available at www.surgeongeneral.gov/library/disabilities/calltoaction/whatitmeanstoyou.pdf.

6. McNeil, J. M., & Binette, J. (2001). Prevalence of disabilities and associated health conditions among adults—United States 1999. *Morbidity and Mortality Weekly Report, 50,* 120–125.

7. National Council on Disability. (1993). *Meeting the unique needs of minorities with disabilities: A report to the President and the Congress.* Washington, DC: Author. Available at www.ncd.gov/newsroom/publications/1993/minority.htm.

8. Ciol, M. A., Shumway-Cook, A., Hoffman, J. A., Yorkston, K. M., Dudgeon, B. J., & Chan, L. (2008). Minority disparities in disability between Medicare beneficiaries. *Journal of the American Geriatrics Society, 56,* 444–453.

9. Administration on Aging, U.S. Department of Health & Human Services. (2008). *A profile of older Americans: 2008.* Available at www.aoa.gov/AoARoot/Aging_Statistics/Profile/2008/docs/2008profile.pdf.

10. Centers for Disease Control and Prevention. (2006). *Women with disabilities.* Available at www.cdc.gov/ncbddd/women/default.htm.

11. Chevarley, F. M., Thierry, J. M., Gill, C. J., Ryerson, A. B., & Nosek, M. A. (2006). Health, preventive health care, and health care access among women with disabilities in the 1994–1995 National Health Interview Survey, Supplement on Disability. *Women's Health Issues, 16,* 297–312.

12. Shakespeare, T., Gillespie-Sells, K., & Davies, D. (1996). *The sexual politics of disability: Untold desires.* London: Cassell.

13. Tremain, S. (Ed.). (1996). *Pushing the limits: Disabled dykes produce culture.* Ontario, Canada: Women's Press.

14. Steinberg, A. G., Wiggins, E. A., Barmada, C. H., & Sullivan, V. J. (2002). Deaf women: Experiences and perceptions of healthcare system access. *Journal of Women's Health, 11,* 729–741.

15. Reis, J. P., Breslin, M. L., Iezzoni, L. I., & Kirschner, K. (2004). *It takes more than ramps to solve the crisis of healthcare for people with disabilities.* Rehabilitation Institute of Chicago. Available at dredf.org/healthcare/RIC_whitepaperfinal.pdf.

16. Parish, S. L., & Ellison-Martin, M. J. (2007). Health-care access of women Medicaid recipients: Evidence of disability-based disparities. *Journal of Disability Policy Studies, 18,* 109–116.

17. Oliver, M. (1995). *Understanding disability: From theory to practice.* New York: St. Martin's Press.

18. O'Toole, C. J. (2002). Sex, disability and motherhood: Access to sexuality for disabled mothers. *Disability Studies Quarterly, 22,* 81–101.

19. Axtell, S. (1999). Disability and chronic illness identity: Interviews with lesbians and bisexual women and their partners. *Journal of Gay, Lesbian, and Bisexual Identity, 4,* 53–72.

20. Clare, E. (1999). *Exile & pride: Disability, queerness, and liberation.* Cambridge, MA: South End Press.

21. Center for Research on Women with Disabilities. (2005). *Removing disability disparities in women's health, 2005, 1:2.* Available at www.bcm.edu/crowd/?pmid=3851.

22. Johnson, H. M. (2003, February 16). Unspeakable conversations. *New York Times.* Available at query.nytimes.com/gst/fullpage.html?sec=health&res=9401EFDC113BF935A25751C0A9659C8B63.

23. Richman, L. S., Bennett, G. G., Pek, J., Siegler, I., & Williams, R. B. Jr. (2007). Discrimination, dispositions, and cardiovascular responses to stress. *Health Psychology, 26,* 675–683. Available at news.duke.edu/mmedia/pdf/richman.pdf.

24. Kirschner, K. L., Breslin, M. L., & Iezzoni, L. I. (2007). Structural impairments that limit access to health care for patients with disabilities. *Journal of the American Medical Association, 297,* 1121–1125.

25. Mele, N., Archer, J., & Pusch, B. D. (2005). Access to breast cancer screening services for women with disabilities. *Journal of Obstetric, Gynecologic, and Neonatal Nursing, 34,* 453–464.

26. Chan, L., Doctor, J. N., MacLehose, R. F., Lawson, H., Rosenblatt, R. A., Baldwin, L. M., & Jha, A. (1999). Do Medicare patients with disabilities receive screening and preventive care services? *Archives of Physical Medicine and Rehabilitation, 80,* 642–646.

27. Iezzoni, L. I., McCarthy, E. P., Davis, R. B., & Siebens, H. (2000). Mobility impairments and use of screening and preventive services. *American Journal of Public Health, 90,* 955–961.

28. Panko-Reis, J., Breslin, M. L., Iezzoni, L. I., & Kirschner, K. (2004). *It takes more than ramps to solve the crisis in healthcare for people with disabilities.* Chicago: Rehabilitation Institute of Chicago LIFE Center.

29. McCarthy, E. P., Ngo, L. H., Roetzheim, R. G., Chirikos, T. N., Li, D., Drews, R. E., & Iezzoni, L. I. (2006). Disparities in breast cancer treatment and survival for women with disabilities. *Annals of Internal Medicine, 145,* 637–645.

30. Beth Israel Deaconess Medical Center. (2006, November 6). *Disparities in breast cancer treatment for women with disabilities.* Available at www.bidmc.org/News/InResearch/2006/November/DisparitiesinBreastCancerTreatmentforWomenwithDisabilities.aspx.

31. Health Canada. (1997). *A way out: Women with disabilities and smoking.* Available at www.hc-sc.gc.ca/hc-ps/pubs/tobac-tabac/awayout-sortie/index-eng.php.

32. Hughes, T. L. (2005). Alcohol use and alcohol-related problems among lesbians and gay men. *Annual Review of Nursing Research, 23,* 283–325.

33. Brownworth, V. A., & Raffo, S. (1999). *Restricted access: Lesbians on disability.* Seattle: Seal Press.

34. Rehabilitation Research and Training Center on Drugs and Disability. (2004). *Final report for RRTC on drugs and disability.* Dayton, OH: Wright State University School of Medicine. Available at www.med.wright.edu/citar/sardi/files/pdf_technicalfinalreport.pdf.

35. Nosek, M. A. (1996). *National study of women with physical disabilities. Final report 1992–1996.* Houston, TX: Center for Research on Women With Disabilities. Available at www.bcm.edu/crowd/?pmid=1408.

36. Office on Disability, U.S. Department of Health & Human Services. (n.d.). *Substance abuse and disability.* Available at www.hhs.gov/od/about/fact_sheets/substanceabuse.html.

37. Ford, J. A., Glenn, M. K., Li, L., & Moore, D. (2004). Substance abuse and women with disabilities. In S.L. Welner & F. Haseltine (Eds.), *Welner's guide to the care of women with disabilities* (pp. 315–332). Philadelphia: Lippincott Williams & Wilkins.

38. World Institute on Disability. (n.d.). *Recognizing and interrupting abuse of adults with disabilities.* Available at www.wid.org/programs/health-access-and-long-term-services/

curriculum-on-abuse-prevention-and-empowerment-cape/recognizing-and-interrupting-abuse-of-adults-with-disabilities.

39. Valenti-Hein, D., & Schwartz, L. (1995). *The sexual abuse interview for those with developmental disabilities.* Santa Barbara, CA: James Stanfield Company.

40. Sobsey, D. (1994). *Violence and abuse in the lives of people with disabilities: The end of silent acceptance?* Baltimore, MD: Paul H. Brookes Publishing.

41. Rauscher, M. (2008, October 27). Women with disabilities at risk for partner abuse. Reuters. Available at www.reuters.com/article/healthNews/idUSTRE49Q5LJ20081027.

42. Rems-Smario, J. (2007, March–April). Domestic violence: We can't ignore it anymore. *National Association of the Deaf Magazine,* 16–18. Available at www.deaf-hope.org/information/DeafHope%20NAD%20article.pdf.

43. Shakespeare, T. (1999). Coming out and coming home. *International Journal of Sexuality and Gender Studies, 4,* 39–51.

ABOUT THE AUTHORS

Dawn Marie Wadle, MD is a family physician in a clinic that serves an ethnically diverse, multilingual, and economically disadvantaged urban population in Northern California and is Medical Director of a women's alcohol and drug recovery program. She experienced a disabling injury in 1995. Her special areas of clinical interest include post-traumatic stress disorder, chronic pain, and substance abuse.

Corbett Joan O'Toole, BSE is a health care advocate for women with disabilities. She is a founding mother of the national and international disabled women's movement. In addition to authoring numerous articles, she has contributed to many books, including *Deaf Meets Disability*, the *Encyclopedia of Americans With Disabilities*, and *Mental Health Issues for Sexual Minority Women*.

CHAPTER 21

"How Do I Live with Cancer?"

THE IMPACT OF A CANCER DIAGNOSIS ON LESBIANS

ALICIA K. MATTHEWS, PhD

BARB, *53, is a lesbian who has just been diagnosed with stage 3 breast cancer and must undergo extensive surgery, radiation, and chemotherapy. She is uninsured and receives medical care in a publicly funded hospital. Concerned about discrimination because of her sexual orientation, Barb does not want to include her partner in her medical care, so she attends most medical appointments alone. She is extremely apprehensive about her health, the quality of care she will receive, and her ability to manage her finances if she cannot work. She was referred to, but declined to participate in, a hospital-based* *breast cancer support group and has not yet found a support group for lesbians in her community.*

When Barb presented at her first medical appointment after the diagnosis, she seemed overwhelmed by it and the lengthy treatments ahead. Sensing her level of distress, the physician asked if she was married and wanted her husband to come to future appointments. Barb responded in a quiet voice that she was not married. The physician hesitated briefly but, without further inquiry, went on to explain what Barb should expect in the coming months.

During cancer treatment, Barb's partner and friends were instrumental in giving her the emotional and day-to-day support she needed to manage her illness. She never disclosed her sexual orientation to her doctor, but eventually she began to incorporate her partner and daughter into her medical care. She attended a general cancer support group led by a gay male facilitator and learned skills for managing emotional distress. Although Barb gets tired easily, her quality of life is improving steadily and she looks forward to completing therapy.

■ ■ ■

Cancer, a life-changing illness, often challenges how patients view the world, themselves, and the future.[1] Facing a cancer diagnosis, many of them experience significant emotional distress and uncertainty about the future.[2] For women who are socially and medically marginalized, the challenges associated with a life-threatening illness such as cancer may be exacerbated.[3]

This chapter describes factors that affect the quality of life and the psychosocial adjustment of cancer patients and survivors. It highlights the unique needs and concerns of lesbians, aiming to improve the culturally appropriate care that sexual minority women receive. Because breast cancer is one of the most common carcinomas in women and the focus of most behavioral research regarding cancer in women, many of the examples in the chapter relate specifically to this disease.

CANCER RATES

More than half of all the approximately 1.4 million cases of cancer diagnosed in the United States in 2007 were cancers of the prostate (219,000), lung (213,000), female breast (178,000), and colon/rectum (154,000).[4] Deaths from these cancers and all cancers combined are declining.[5] Nevertheless, there are stark disparities in terms of income, race/ethnicity, culture, geography (urban/rural), age, sex, sexual orientation, and literacy.[6] For example, the highest rates of new cancers and cancer deaths are among African Americans and people with low socioeconomic status.[4]

Reducing such disparities has become a primary goal on the nation's health care agenda.[7] Although precise data on cancer rates among lesbians are lacking, evidence suggests that sexual minority status may contribute to excess risk for the development of certain types of cancers, including breast and ovarian cancers.[8-10] The causes of these disparities are complex and likely influenced by poor continuity of care[11]; socioeconomic factors, such as lack of adequate insurance coverage[12]; medical mistrust[13]; cultural and emotional factors[14]; and providers' unintentional bias and inadequate cultural competency.[15]

While more studies are necessary to determine if the frequency of cancer among lesbian and heterosexual women is similar, sexual minority women report numerous factors that may increase their risk. Cochran and colleagues reviewed data from five survey sets on lesbian health, an aggregate sample of nearly 12,000 women. Their meta-analysis found that, compared with heterosexual women, the prevalence of behavioral and lifestyle risk factors for breast and gynecologic cancers, such as obesity and alcohol and tobacco use, was higher; parity and use of birth control pills were lower; and lesbians were less likely to have had a recent pelvic or breast exam.[16]

Studies have identified other factors that may increase the risk of cancer-related health disparities among sexual minority women. These include clinicians' limited knowledge about the health needs of lesbian and bisexual women[17,18]; poor access to culturally competent, preventive, and ongoing health care services[19]; clinicians' homophobia and heteronormative focus[20]; discrimination in health care settings[21]; less participation in preventive cancer health screenings[22-24]; less access to care[25]; and mistrust of the medical establishment.[26] More epidemiological and behavioral research is necessary to understand the associations between sexual minority status and breast cancer disparities in areas such as quality of life and psychosocial outcomes.[27]

CANCER AND QUALITY OF LIFE

Cancer profoundly affects the lives of women.[28] Health-related quality of life (QOL) is the most common means of assessing the impact of an illness on an individual.

QOL encompasses physical, functional, psychological, social, spiritual, and sexual well-being related to a major illness.[27]

Research suggests there is a relationship between demographics, medical and psychosocial risk factors that affect QOL, and adjustment to a cancer diagnosis. Demographic risk factors for low cancer-related QOL and psychosocial distress include lower socioeconomic status,[29,30] younger age,[31] single marital status,[32] female gender,[32] and lower levels of formal education.[33] Medical variables that affect QOL and related adjustments include more advanced stage of illness,[34] the presence of a serious comorbidity,[35] and a poor patient-provider relationship.[36] Finally, psychosocial correlates of lower QOL and poorer adjustment include a history of depression or psychological distress,[37] inadequate social support,[32] less-adaptive coping responses,[38] and lower levels of spirituality.[39]

Despite the well-known demographic differences, cancer's effect on the QOL of lesbians specifically is largely unexplored. Sexual orientation may interact with some or all of the above risk factors and influence how lesbians adjust to a cancer diagnosis.

QUALITY OF LIFE DOMAINS

Physical Well-Being

Physical well-being refers to how cancer and/or related treatments may impact the body. For example, satisfaction with medical treatments and the quality of the patient-provider relationship are important determinants of health outcomes, including QOL.[40] Other data suggest that lesbians are less likely to have access to health care,[16] are subjected to more bias and discrimination in medical settings,[41] receive substandard or inadequate medical treatment,[42] and, due to their perceptions of bias, underutilize the medical services they need.[43] Fobair and colleagues reported that lesbians had a significantly more negative perception of their medical care than did heterosexual women. For example, lesbians were less satisfied with their physicians' care and the inclusion of their partner in medical treatment discussions than were heterosexual patients. The two groups did not differ in terms of how they perceived their communication with physicians or their sense of control over treatment.[44] Determining how these findings apply specifically to lesbian cancer patients is critical to improving their adjustment to cancer and treatment, and to improving patient and clinician education.

Functional Well-Being

Functional well-being refers to satisfaction with one's overall physical functioning and ability to perform important routine activities.[45] The quality of patient-provider interaction is a key part of a patient's health care experience and has implications for a variety of patient outcomes.[46–48] Problems in the patient-provider relationship contribute to patients' less-positive perceptions of the quality of health services they receive,[49] lower treatment satisfaction,[50] higher levels of emotional distress and poorer emotional adjustment to illness,[51] fewer preventive health screenings,[52] less use of health care services,[47] and less adherence to clinical advice.[53]

Problems in the doctor-patient relationship are common.[51] Research suggests a relationship between such problems and demographic variables.[54–56] For example, in a study of the association between patient race/ethnicity and patient-physician communication during medical visits, physicians were more verbally dominant and had less patient-centered communication with African American patients than they did with Caucasian patients. Moreover, African American patients and their Caucasian physicians exhibited lower levels of positive affect than did Caucasian patients and their Caucasian physicians.[55] Other demographic variables that negatively impact the dynamics of doctor-patient communication are age,[57] socioeconomic status,[58] and sexual orientation.[59]

Such communication is a critical component of health care delivery and patients' subsequent physical and mental health.[60] Barriers to positive interactions for lesbian, gay, and bisexual patients include clinicians' presumption of heterosexuality,[61] the insensitivity of and negative social judgments by health care personnel,[62] denial of care following disclosure of sexual orientation,[63] not understanding health care issues unique to sexual minorities,[64] and providers' failure to consider or acknowledge a patient's same-sex partner.[65]

Disclosure to clinicians of sexual orientation is a unique decision and concern for lesbian patients in general and lesbian cancer patients in particular. Disclosure by lesbians and gay men outside of the health care setting has been associated with better mental health adjustment.[66,67]

Boehmer and Case found that few clinicians inquire about breast cancer patients' sexual orientation. A number of lesbian respondents disclosed their sexual orientation to health professionals they saw regularly, such as primary care physicians, but did not disclose it to medical personnel they saw infrequently. Before a cancer diagnosis, questions for patients during gynecologic exams about the possibility of pregnancy, use of birth control, and history of sexual activity typically prompted discussions, if any, with a clinician regarding sexual identity. Lesbians who disclosed their sexual orientation to medical personnel during treatment did not notice a discernable change in their physician's attitude toward them or any decline in treatment quality. Although most lesbian respondents in this study said they considered sexual identity of little or no importance in the health care environment, many found reason to disclose their sexual orientation in the course of cancer treatment. They typically introduced their partner to medical staff early on so she would receive the same recognition a heterosexual spouse would. One respondent said doctors needed to know that her ordeal dramatically affected her partner as well. In almost all cases, according to respondents, medical staff extended the same respect and professional courtesy to their partners as a heterosexual spouse would likely receive. Some respondents who before their illness were ambivalent about identifying themselves as lesbians, or were disinclined to do so, said the cancer diagnosis was a catalyst for disclosure. Others continued to hide their sexual orientation and their partners from family members, friends, and coworkers during treatment and recovery.[68] Matthews found that lesbians who did not disclose their sexual orientation while they were ill bore an additional burden of secrecy.[69]

Additional research is necessary to understand the associations between disclosure of sexual minority status to providers of cancer treatment and physical and emotional health outcomes.[70]

Psychological Well-Being

Cancer-related distress is "an unpleasant emotional experience that may be psychological, social, or spiritual in nature."[1] (p. 2). Other research has shown elevated levels of distress among cancer patients.[71] For example, in a study of women with breast and gynecologic cancers, a significant proportion met the criteria for major depressive disorder.[72] Hinnen and colleagues identified a higher risk of acute distress after a cancer diagnosis, but psychological functioning returned to baseline levels within 6 months.[73] Overall, researchers have paid little attention to the psychosocial health needs of cancer patients.[1]

There is scant empirical data on differences between lesbian and heterosexual women in terms of psychological adjustment to cancer.[70,74,75] One notable exception is the study by Fobair and colleagues, which explored differences between these two groups of women in response to a recent breast cancer diagnosis. Lesbian and heterosexual patients with a history of breast cancer were similar in terms of overall emotional adjustment, distress, and sexual satisfaction. But there were important differences in factors that may have influenced emotional adjustment: the lesbian patients reported fewer body image problems, were more likely to obtain social support from partners and friends, and had less trust in the health care system. Differences also emerged in terms of how lesbian and heterosexual patients coped with the emotional difficulties of a cancer diagnosis. However, the authors noted that the small number of lesbian participants limited their study's generalizability and called for further research to clarify its findings.[44]

Social Well-Being

Social well-being refers to one's ability to engage in desired social roles and tasks. Because heterosexuality is the social convention, lesbians may experience higher stress levels and receive less support from their family of origin.[76] Research has documented the positive relationship between social support and adjustment to chronic illness.[77,78] Social support is vital for improving adjustment to, and reducing the psychological stresses of, a cancer diagnosis and subsequent treatment.[79,80] Furthermore, cancer patients with adequate social support are more likely to engage in healthy behavior and to exhibit enhanced coping skills, higher self-esteem, and fewer symptoms of anxiety and depression.[81]

The availability of social support may differ depending on sexual orientation. For example, lesbians who are open about their orientation often receive less social support, feel stigmatized by family and friends, lose financial and occupational resources, and experience prejudice.[82] Family members and clinicians may withhold emotional support from partners of lesbian cancer patients.[69] Consequently, lesbians may be more vulnerable to the adverse psychosocial effects of cancer and experience a lower QOL.

In a qualitative study, Matthews and colleagues compared the availability of cancer-related support services to lesbian and heterosexual breast cancer survivors. Lesbians had a more difficult time finding a cancer support group that they believed would meet their needs and concerns. Among those who had previously participated in support groups comprising mostly heterosexual women, dissatisfaction was associated with the groups' emphasis on the importance of breasts to sexually attract men. Lesbians who had participated in support groups of mixed sexual orientations did not think the groups were open and accepting enough that they could disclose their own orientation. Thus, the support group setting did not meet many of the emotional needs associated with the impact that cancer had on their relationships or partners. In contrast, lesbians who had participated in lesbian-specific cancer support groups emphasized the level of safety they felt. But they also cited insufficient resources for these groups compared with the resources available in hospitals or other mainstream settings for heterosexual women who have breast cancer.[74]

Spiritual Well-Being

One of the definitions of spirituality is "the way in which people interpret and live their lives in light of their ultimate meaning and values"[83] (p. 346). Spirituality differs from religiosity, which is adherence to the beliefs and practices of an organized church or religious institution.[84] Research has established that spiritual and religious faith plays a role in patients' adjustment to cancer.[85] Spirituality or religion promotes adjustment by giving meaning and hope and by providing an explanation for illness and suffering.[86] In a study of older women recently diagnosed with breast cancer, religious and spiritual beliefs helped by providing emotional support, social support, and meaning.[87] In a study of women with gynecologic cancer, 50% of respondents said they had become more religious after their diagnosis, and those with strong religious beliefs remained more hopeful than did women without such belief systems.[88] Furthermore, strong religious beliefs among cancer patients have been linked to less pain,[89] lower levels of anxiety,[90] and higher quality of life despite cancer symptoms.[85] While these studies support the notion that religion and spirituality help patients in general adjust to cancer,[91] little is known about if or how they help sexual minority patients adjust, a subject that warrants more research.

Sexual Well-Being

Sexual well-being refers to overall satisfaction with the various aspects of sexuality. Sexual dysfunction is an important sequela of cancer diagnosis and treatment.[92,93] Sexual difficulties, including reduced libido and sexual satisfaction, are distressing problems that affect about 50% of cancer survivors.[94,95] Unlike other side effects of cancer and treatment for it, sexual problems tend not to resolve after 1 or 2 disease-free years. Depending on which sexual function is measured (desire, arousal, orgasm, or frequency of sexual activity), such problems may occur in up to 64% of cancer patients.[94,95]

A number of things may contribute to sexual dysfunction in this population. They include the type of surgery (lumpectomy, mastectomy, or mastectomy with reconstruction), chemotherapy, and a variety of psychosocial factors. Several studies have compared women's psychological adjustment after mastectomy or breast-conserving surgery. One robust finding is that mastectomy, compared with lumpectomy, more strongly affects women's body image and feelings of attractiveness,[96,97] potentially leading to sexual dysfunction. Research suggests that sexual problems occur in 30% to 40% of women who undergo modified radical mastectomy compared with 5% of women who undergo lumpectomy and radiation. The benefits of less-disfiguring treatments are less alteration of body image, greater comfort with nudity and discussing sexuality with one's partner, and lower incidence of sexual dysfunction.[92] A meta-analysis revealed small but statistically significant effects on body image depending on the type of surgery. Breast-conserving surgery, which involves partial breast removal and lumpectomy, produced more beneficial results than mastectomy did in terms of body image and marital sexual adjustment.[96] Depression and anxiety, which can significantly disrupt aspects of sexual functioning in women generally, occur frequently in cancer patients.[98] Breast cancer also negatively impacts relationship adjustment,[99] which is thought to be a crucial factor in sexual functioning.[93] For instance, some researchers have noted a negative correlation between marital affection and treatment invasiveness, such as mastectomy versus lumpectomy.[100] Cancer-related worries and concerns about health status may distract breast cancer patients from fully engaging in sexual experiences and thereby impair sexual arousal and orgasm.[98] In addition, negative perceived health status may cause survivors to make sexual activity a lower priority, reducing their interest and engagement.[98]

Studies on the psychosexual benefits of breast reconstruction after mastectomy have been equivocal. In a literature review, Schover and colleagues suggested that a restored experience of bodily integrity after reconstruction may have a dramatic impact on a woman's sense of self and sexual pleasure.[93] However, Yurek and colleagues found that women who chose reconstruction experienced greater sexual dysfunction 1 month after surgery than did women whose treatment consisted of either breast-conserving surgery or mastectomy without reconstruction.[101] In another study, longer-term survivors who underwent reconstruction were more likely than those who underwent mastectomy without reconstruction to feel that breast cancer had negatively impacted their sex lives.[97] Clearly, the benefits of reconstruction warrant further research.

Although establishing sexually intimate relationships is an important developmental and maturational milestone for healthy adults, there have been few empirical studies of sexual functioning in lesbians. Little is known regarding rates of sexual dysfunction among them. When lesbians seek services for sexual problems, their most frequent concerns have to do with sexual desire, including less or inhibited desire or partners' discordant desire.[102-104] Preliminary research suggests that rates of sexual dysfunction are lower among lesbians than heterosexual women. In a community sample of women, Matthews and colleagues found that significantly fewer lesbians met criteria for sexual dysfunction than did heterosexual women.[105] More research is necessary.

CANCER SURVIVORSHIP

Cancer survivorship has traditionally been defined as living 5 years beyond diagnosis.[28] Broader definitions have emerged along with the aim of gaining a more holistic understanding of the survivorship experience. By one definition, cancer survivorship is a trajectory that begins with diagnosis and continues through the balance of an individual's life.[106] Within this broader definition, the scope of research on cancer survivorship has expanded from concentrating only on the physical to include the psychosocial and economic sequelae of a cancer diagnosis and treatment.[32,107] Given the rapidly increasing number of cancer survivors, more research looking at the impact that cancer diagnosis and treatment have on quality of life, and at factors that affect the quality of cancer survivorship, is highly warranted.[107]

About 65% of people with cancer can expect to live at least 5 years after their diagnosis.[108] While there has been extensive research on the physical health correlates of a cancer diagnosis and treatment, much less is known about the psychosocial impact of cancer survivorship[32] and even less about outcomes among minority and other medically underserved populations.[29]

Cancer survival may be associated with short- and long-term morbidity secondary to the effects of cancer and related treatment. For example, better coordination of patient care is correlated with lower morbidity and mortality, higher patient satisfaction, better perceived health status, and receipt of preventive health services.[109] According to the Institute of Medicine, all cancer patients should receive a comprehensive care summary and follow-up plan with information about their type of cancer and the treatments they received, follow-up care and health promotion, and psychosocial services.[109]

An online study of lesbian, gay, bisexual, or transgender (LGBT) cancer survivors suggested that they are not receiving systematic follow-up care. Although 60% said they received information about survivorship care, only 35% received a complete copy of their cancer treatment records. Rates were similarly low regarding discussion of a detailed follow-up plan with their clinician (23%) and receipt of any health-promotion or risk-reduction counseling (40% and 55%, respectively). Only 60% felt confident that their posttreatment care was being systematically monitored.[110]

Health promotion counseling is an important component of cancer survivorship care, given survivors' ongoing health-risk behaviors.[111,112] Targets for posttreatment health promotion, according to the Institute of Medicine, are smoking cessation, physical activity, a healthy weight, and a healthy diet and good nutrition.[109] In a study of LGBT cancer survivors, 43% experienced cancer-related morbidity—pain, fatigue, or neuropathy, for example. Morbidities not related to cancer also were high: more than 20% had a current diagnosis of hypertension and high cholesterol. Indicators for future health risks in this study population were high levels of overweight and obesity (mean body mass index = 27.4), alcohol use (69% of participants), low adherence to recommended daily intake of fruits and vegetables (12%), and ongoing tobacco use (15%). Sixty-six percent of participants cited exercise as a posttreatment need; 63%, 49%, and 8% cited nutrition counseling, weight loss, and smoking cessation, respectively.[110]

The Institute of Medicine has highlighted the importance of mental health services for cancer patients and survivors, noting that psychosocial problems are common. These problems may include fear of cancer recurrence and death, anxiety and depression, feelings of alienation and isolation, problems with interpersonal relationships, and economic hardships related to the cost of care, job loss, and employment and insurance discrimination.[1]

Access to and use of support resources may mitigate the negative impact of cancer.[81] The online survey by Matthews and colleagues of LGBT cancer survivors revealed that 62% had participated in counseling since their cancer diagnosis and treatment. However, of those, only 16% had access to an LGBT-specific cancer support group. Another 24% said they would have participated in a cancer support group if a group for LGBT patients had been available. The need for additional emotional support was one of the posttreatment needs participants most often cited.[110]

A number of large urban areas, including Boston, New York, and Washington, D.C., have lesbian-specific cancer support programs. But fewer such resources are available in smaller cities, suburbs, and rural areas where there also is a need for them.

CONCLUSION

Although the prevalence of cancer among lesbians is unknown, evidence suggests that sexual minority status increases the risk of certain types of malignancies. Many factors place lesbians at greater risk and make it especially difficult for them to adjust to the disease. These include behavioral and lifestyle factors, among them obesity, alcohol and tobacco consumption, and lower use of birth control pills; health care disparities as a result of discrimination, homophobia, lack of access to services, and poor communication with physicians; and limited lesbian-specific support during recovery. For all cancer patients, quality of life encompasses physical, functional, psychological, social, spiritual, and sexual well-being. Much more research is necessary to understand how cancer affects lesbians in these realms, the correlation between cancer and sexual minority status, psychosocial factors that impact survivorship, and services necessary to meet this population's unique health care and support needs.

REFERENCES

1. Hewitt, M., Herdman, R., & Holland, J. (2004). *Meeting psychosocial needs of women with breast cancer.* Institute of Medicine and National Research Council of the National Academies. Washington, DC: National Academies Press. Available at books.nap.edu/openbook.php?record_id=10909.

2. Arora, N. K., Gustafson, D. H., Hawkins, R. P., McTavish, F., Cella, D. F., Pingree, S., et al. (2001). Impact of surgery and chemotherapy on quality of life of younger women with breast carcinoma: A prospective study. *Cancer, 92,* 1288–1298.

3. Hirschman, J., Whitman, S., & Ansell, D. (2007). The Black:White disparity in breast cancer mortality: The example of Chicago. *Cancer Causes & Control, 18,* 323–333.

4. National Cancer Institute. (2007). *Cancer trends progress report—2007 update.* Bethesda, MD: Author. Available at progressreport.cancer.gov.

5. Jemal, A., Siegel, R., Ward, E., Murray, T., Xu, J., & Thun, M. J. (2007). Cancer statistics, 2007. *CA: A Cancer Journal for Clinicians, 57,* 43–66.

6. American Cancer Society. (2004). *Cancer facts & figures, 2004.* Atlanta, GA: Author. Available at www.cancer.org/downloads/STT/CAFF_finalPWSecured.pdf.

7. U.S. Department of Health & Human Services. (2000). *Healthy people 2010: Understanding and improving health* (2nd ed.). Washington, DC: U.S. Government Printing Office. Available at www.healthypeople.gov/Document/tableofcontents.htm#under.

8. Brown, J. P., & Tracy, J. K. (2008). Lesbians and cancer: An overlooked health disparity. *Cancer Causes & Control, 19,* 1009–1020.

9. Frisch, M., Smith, E., Grulich, A., & Johansen, C. (2003). Cancer in a population-based cohort of men and women in registered homosexual partnerships. *American Journal of Epidemiology, 157,* 966–972.

10. Gay and Lesbian Medical Association. (2001). *Healthy People 2010. Companion document for lesbian, gay, bisexual, and transgender (LGBT) health.* San Francisco: Author. Available at www.lgbthealth.net/downloads/hp2010doc.pdf.

11. Bigby, J., & Holmes, M. D. (2005). Disparities across the breast cancer continuum. *Cancer Causes & Control, 16,* 35–44.

12. Bouchardy, C., Verkooijen, H. M., & Fioretta, G. (2006). Social class is an important and independent prognostic factor of breast cancer mortality. *International Journal of Cancer, 119,* 1145–1151.

13. Gordon, H. S., Street, R. L., Sharf, B. F., Kelly, A., & Souchel, J. (2006). Racial differences in trust and lung patients' perception of physician communication. *Journal of Clinical Oncology, 24,* 904–909.

14. Guidry, J. J., Matthews-Juarez, P., & Copeland, V. A. (2003). Barriers to breast cancer control for African-American women: The interdependence of culture and psychosocial issues. *Cancer, 97*(Suppl. 1), 318–323.

15. Smedley, B. D., Stith, A. Y., & Nelson, A. R. (Eds.). (2003). *Unequal treatment: Confronting racial and ethnic disparities in health care.* Washington, DC: National Academies Press.

16. Cochran, S. D., Mays, V. M., Bowen, D., Gage, S., Bybee, D., Roberts, S. J., et al. (2001). Cancer-related risk indicators and preventive screening behaviors among lesbians and bisexual women. *American Journal of Public Health, 91,* 591–597.

17. Albarran, J. W., & Salmon, D. (2000). Lesbian, gay and bisexual experiences within critical care nursing, 1988–1998: A survey of the literature. *International Journal of Nursing Studies, 37,* 445–455.

18. Bailey, J. V., Kavanagh, J., Owen, C., McLean, K. A., & Skinner, C. J. (2000). Lesbians and cervical screening. *British Journal of General Practice, 50,* 481–482.

19. Diamant, A. L., Wold, C., Spritzer, K., & Gelberg, L. (2000). Health behaviors, health status, and access to and use of health care: A population-based study of lesbian, bisexual, and heterosexual women. *Archives of Family Medicine, 9,* 1043–1051.

20. Thompson, E. J. (2004). Expressions of manhood: Reconciling sexualities, masculinities, and aging. *Gerontologist, 44,* 714–718.

21. Risdon, C., Cook, D., & Willms, D. (2000). Gay and lesbian physicians in training: A qualitative study. *Canadian Medical Association Journal, 162,* 331–334. Available at www.cmaj.ca/cgi/content/full/162/3/331.

22. Dibble, S. L., & Roberts, S. A. (2003). Improving cancer screening among lesbians over 50: Results of a pilot study. *Oncology Nursing Forum, 30,* E71–79.

23. Koh, A. (2000). Use of preventive health behaviors by lesbian, bisexual, and heterosexual women: Questionnaire survey. *Western Journal of Medicine, 172,* 379–384.

24. Matthews, A. K., Brandenburg, D. L., Johnson, T. P., & Hughes, T. L. (2004). Correlates of underutilization of gynecological cancer screening among lesbian and heterosexual women. *Preventive Medicine, 38,* 105–113.

25. Sanvidge Spinks, V., Andrews, J., & Boyle, J. S. (2000). Providing health care for lesbians. *Journal of Transcultural Nursing, 11,* 137–143.

26. Trippet, S. E., & Bain, J. (1992). Reasons American lesbians fail to seek traditional health care. *Health Care for Women International, 13,* 145–153.

27. Cella, D. F. (1995). Measuring quality of life in palliative care. *Seminars in Oncology, 22*(2 Suppl. 3), 73–81.

28. Ries L. A., Wingo, P. A., Miller, D. S., Howe, H. L., Weir, H. K., Rosenberg, H. M., et al. (2000). The annual report to the nation on the status of cancer, 1973–1997, with a special section on colorectal cancer. *Cancer, 88,* 2398–2424.

29. Giedzinska, A. S., Meyerowitz, B. E., Ganz, P. A., & Rowland, J. H. (2004). Health-related quality of life in a multiethnic sample of breast cancer survivors. *Annals of Behavioral Medicine, 28,* 39–51.

30. Soler-Vila, H., Kasl, S. V., & Jones, B. A. (2003). Prognostic significance of psychosocial factors in African-American and White breast cancer patients: A population-based study. *Cancer, 98,* 1299–1308.

31. Wenzel, L. B., Fairclough, D. L., Brady, M. J., Cella, D., Garrett, K. M., Kluhsman, B. C., et al. (1999). Age-related differences in the quality of life of breast carcinoma patients after treatment. *Cancer, 86,* 1768–1774.

32. Parker, P. A., Baile, W. F., de Moor, C., & Cohen, L. (2003). Psychosocial and demographic predictors of quality of life in a large sample of cancer patients. *Psycho-Oncology, 12,* 183–193.

33. Dean, C. (1988). Psychiatric morbidity following mastectomy: Preoperative predictors and type of illness. *Journal of Psychosomatic Research, 31,* 385–392.

34. Northouse, L. L., Caffey, M., Deichelbohrer, L., Schmidt, L., Guziatek-Trojniak, L., West, S., et al. (1999). The quality of life of African American women with breast cancer. *Research in Nursing & Health, 22,* 449–460.

35. Kornblith, A. B., Anderson, J., Cella, D. F., Tross, S., Zuckerman, E., Cherin, E., et al. (1992). Hodgkin disease survivors at increased risk for problems in psychosocial adaptation. The Cancer and Leukemia Group B. *Cancer, 70,* 2214–2224.

36. Skrzypulec, V., Tobor, E., Drosdzol, A., & Nowosielski, K. (2008). Biopsychosocial functioning of women after mastectomy. *Journal of Clinical Nursing, 18,* 613–619.

37. Holland, J. (1998). *Psycho-oncology.* New York: Oxford University Press.

38. Peled, R., Carmil, D., Siboni-Samocha, O., & Shoham-Vardi, I. (2008). Breast cancer, psychological distress and life events among young women. *BMC Cancer, 8,* 245.

39. George, L. K., Larson, D. B., Koenig, H. G., & McCullough, M. E. (2000). Spirituality and health: What we know, what we need to know. *Journal of Social & Clinical Psychology, 19,* 102–116.

40. Stewart, M., Brown, J. B., Boon, H., Galajda, J., Meredith, L., & Sangster, M. (1999). Evidence on patient-provider communication. *Cancer Prevention and Control, 3,* 25–30.

41. Eliason, M. J., & Raheim, S. (2000). Experiences and comfort with culturally diverse groups in undergraduate prenursing students. *Journal of Nursing Education, 39,* 161–165.

42. Dean, L., Meyer, I. H., Robinson, K., Sell, R. L., Sember, R., Silenzio, V. M. B., et al. (2000). Lesbian, gay, bisexual, and transgender health: Findings and concerns. *Journal of the Gay and Lesbian Medical Association, 4,* 101–151.

43. Millman, M. (Ed.). (1993). *Access to health care in America.* Washington, DC: National Academy Press.

44. Fobair, P., O'Hanlan, K., Koopman, C., Classen, C., Dimiceli, S., Drooker, N., et al. (2001). Comparison of lesbian and heterosexual women's response to newly diagnosed breast cancer. *Psycho-Oncology, 10,* 40–51.

45. Ferrans, C. E., & Powers, M. J. (1985). Quality of life index: Development and psychometric properties. *Advances in Nursing Science, 8,* 15–24.

46. Cooper-Patrick, L., Gallo, J. J., Gonzales, J. J., Vu, H. T., Powe, N. R., Nelson, C., et al. (1999). Race, gender, and partnership in the patient-physician relationship. *Journal of the American Medical Association, 282,* 583–589.

47. LaVeist, T. A., Nickerson, K. J., & Bowie, J. V. (2000). Attitudes about racism, medical mistrust, and satisfaction with care among African American and White cardiac patients. *Medical Care Research and Review, 57*(Suppl. 1), 146–161.

48. Saha, S., Komaromy, M., Koepsell, R. D., & Bindman, A. B. (1999). Patient-physician racial concordance and the perceived quality and use of health care. *Archives of Internal Medicine, 159,* 997–1004.

49. Johnson, R. L., Saha, S., Arbelaez, J. J., Beach, M. C., & Cooper, L. A. (2004). Racial and ethnic differences in patient perceptions of bias and cultural competence in health care. *Journal of General Internal Medicine, 19,* 101–110.

50. Handler, A., Rosenberg, D., Raube, K., & Lyons, S. (2003). Prenatal care characteristics and African American women's satisfaction with prenatal care. *Medical Care, 36,* 679–694.

51. Arora, N. K. (2003). Interacting with cancer patients: The significance of physicians' communication behavior. *Social Science & Medicine, 57,* 791–806.

52. Facione, N. C. (1999). Breast cancer screening in relation to access to health services. *Oncology Nursing Forum, 26,* 689–696.

53. Cooper, L. A., & Roter, D. L. (2000). Patient-provider communication: Effect of race/ethnicity on processes and outcomes of healthcare. In Institute of Medicine (Ed.), *Unequal treatment: Role of social and psychological research in medicine* (pp. 552–593). Washington, DC: National Academy Press.

54. Gordon, H. S., Street, R. L., Sharf, B. F., Kelly, A., & Souchel, J. (2006). Racial differences in doctors' information-giving and patients' participation. *Cancer, 107,* 1313–1320.

55. Johnson, R. L., Roter, D., Powe, N. R., & Cooper, L. A. (2004). Patient race/ethnicity and quality of patient-physician communication during medical visits. *American Journal of Public Health, 94,* 2084–2090.

56. Siminoff, L. A., Graham, G. C., & Gordon, N. H. (2006). Cancer communication patterns and the influence of patient characteristics: Disparities in information-giving and affective behaviors. *Patient Education and Counseling, 6,* 355–360.

57. Madan, A. K., Aliabadi-Wahle, S., & Beech, D. J. (2001). Ageism in medical students' treatment recommendations: The example of breast-conserving procedures. *Academic Medicine, 76,* 282–284.

58. Alter, D. A., Iron, K., Austin, P. C., & Naylor, C. D. (2004). Socioeconomic status, service patterns, and perceptions of care among survivors of acute myocardial infarction in Canada. *Journal of the American Medical Association, 291,* 1100–1107.

59. Solarz A. L. (Ed.). (1999). *Lesbian health: Current assessment and directions for the future.* Institute of Medicine. Washington, DC: National Academy Press. Available at www.nap.edu/openbook.php?record_id=6109&page=17.

60. Stewart, M., Brown, J. B., Donner, A., McWhinney, I. R., Oates, J., Weston, W. W., et al. (2000). The impact of patient-centered care on outcomes. *Journal of Family Practice, 49,* 796–804.

61. Rose, P., & Platzer, H. (1993). Confronting prejudice. *Nursing Times, 89,* 52–54.

62. Brogan, M. (1997). Health care for lesbians: Attitudes and experiences. *Nursing Standard, 11,* 39–42.

63. Stine, K. (1997). Health care for lesbians: Issues and influences. *ADVANCE for Nurse Practitioners, 5,* 60–62.

64. Lynch, M. A., & Ferri, R. S. (1997). Health needs of lesbian women and gay men. *Clinician Reviews, 7,* 85–112.

65. Stevens, P. (1992). Lesbian health care research: A review of the literature from 1970 to 1990. *Health Care for Women International, 13,* 91–120.

66. D'Augelli, A. R., Grossman, A. H., Hershberger, S. L, & O'Connell, T. S. (2001). Aspects of mental health among older lesbian, gay, and bisexual adults. *Aging & Mental Health, 5,* 149–158.

67. Morris, J. F., Waldo, C. R., & Rothblum, E. D. (2001). A model of predictors and outcomes of outness among lesbian and bisexual women. *American Journal of Orthopsychiatry, 71,* 61–71.

68. Boehmer, U., & Case, P. (2004). Physicians don't ask, sometimes patients tell: Disclosure of sexual orientation among women with breast carcinoma. *Cancer, 101,* 1882–1889.

69. Matthews, A. K. (1998). Lesbians and cancer support: Clinical issues for cancer patients. *Health Care for Women International, 19,* 193–203.

70. Boehmer, U., Linde, R., & Freund, K. M. (2005). Sexual minority women's coping and psychological adjustment after a diagnosis of breast cancer. *Journal of Women's Health, 14,* 214–224.

71. Bultz, B. D., & Carlson, L. E. (2005). Emotional distress: The sixth vital sign in cancer care. *Journal of Clinical Oncology, 23,* 6440–6441.

72. Ell, K., Sanchez, K., Vourlekis, B., Lee, P. J., Dwight-Johnson, M., Lagomasino, I., et al. (2005). Depression, correlates of depression, and receipt of depression care among low-income women with breast or gynecologic cancer. *Journal of Clinical Oncology, 23,* 3052–3060.

73. Hinnen, C., Ranchor, A. V., Sanderman, R., Snijders, T. A., Hagedoorn, M., & Coyne, J. C. (2008). Course of distress in breast cancer patients, their partners, and matched control couples. *Annals of Behavioral Medicine, 36,* 141–148.

74. Matthews, A. K., Peterman, A. H., Delaney, P., Menard, L., & Brandenburg, D. (2002). A qualitative exploration of the experiences of lesbian and heterosexual patients with breast cancer. *Oncology Nursing Forum, 29,* 1455–1462.

75. Bowen, D. J., Boehmer, U., & Russo, M. (2007). Cancer and sexual minority women. In I. H. Meyer & M. E. Northridge (Eds.), *The health of sexual minorities: Public health perspectives on lesbian, gay, bisexual and transgender populations* (pp. 523–538). New York: Springer.

76. Rankow, E. J. (1995). Breast and cervical cancer among lesbians. *Women's Health International, 5,* 123–129.

77. Helgeson, V. S., Cohen, S., & Fritz, H. L. (1998). Social ties and cancer. In J. C. Holland (Ed.), *Psycho-oncology* (pp. 99–109). New York: Oxford University Press.

78. Presberg, B. A., & Levenson, J. L. (1993). A survey of cancer support groups provided by National Cancer Institute clinical and comprehensive centers. *Psycho-Oncology, 2,* 215–217.

79. Sleek, S. (1995). Battling breast cancer through group therapy. *APA Monitor, 26,* 24.

80. Spiegel, D., Bloom, J. R., & Yalom, I. (1981). Group support for patients with metastatic cancer: A randomized prospective outcome study. *Archives of General Psychiatry, 38,* 527–533.

81. Hewlitt, M., Greenfield, S., & Stovall, E. (Eds.). (2005). *From cancer patient to cancer survivor: Lost in transition.* Washington, DC: National Academies Press.

82. McGough, K. (1990). Assessing social support of people with AIDS. *Oncology Nursing Forum, 17,* 31–35.

83. Muldoon, M., & King, N. (1995). Spirituality, health care, and bioethics. *Journal of Religion and Health, 34,* 329–349.

84. Hackney, C. H., & Sanders, G. S. (2003). Religiosity and mental health: A meta-analysis of recent studies. *Journal for the Scientific Study of Religion, 42,* 43–55.

85. Brady, M. J., Peterman, A. H., Fitchett, G., Mo, M., & Cella, D. (1999). A case for including spirituality in quality of life measurement in oncology. *Psycho-Oncology, 8,* 417–428.

86. Musick, M., Koening, H. G., Larson, D., & Matthews, D. (1998). Religion and spiritual beliefs. In J. C. Holland (Ed.), *Psycho-oncology* (pp. 780–789). New York: Oxford University Press.

87. Feher, S., & Maly, R. C. (1999). Coping with breast cancer in later life: The role of religious faith. *Psycho-Oncology, 8,* 408–416.

88. Roberts, J. A., Brown, D., Elkins, T., & Larson, D. (1997). Factors influencing views of patients with gynecological cancer about end-of-life decisions. *American Journal of Obstetrics & Gynecology, 176,* 166–172.

89. Yates, J. W., Chalmer, B. J., St. James, P., Follansbee, M., & McKegney, F. P. (1981). Religion in patients with advanced cancer. *Medical and Pediatric Oncology, 9*, 121–128.

90. Kaczorowski, J. M. (1989). Spiritual well-being and anxiety in adults diagnosed with cancer. *Hospice Journal, 5*, 105–116.

91. Jenkins, R. A., & Pargament, K. I. (1995). Religion and spirituality as resources for coping with cancer. *Journal of Psychosocial Oncology, 13*, 51–74.

92. Andersen, B. L. (1990). How cancer affects sexual functioning. *Oncology, 4*, 81–88.

93. Schover, L. R., Schain, W. S., & Montague, D. K. (1989). Sexual problems of patients with cancer. In V. T. DeVita, S. Hellman, & S. A. Rosenberg (Eds.), (3rd ed.) (pp. 2206–2225). Philadelphia: J. B. Lippincott.

94. Ganz, P. A., Rowland, J. H., Desmond, K., Meyerowitz, B. E., & Wyatt, G. E. (1998). Life after breast cancer: Understanding women's health-related quality of life and sexual functioning. *Journal of Clinical Oncology, 16*, 501–514.

95. Thors, C. L., Broeckel, J. A., & Jacobsen, P. B. (2001). Sexual functioning in breast cancer survivors. *Cancer Control, 8*, 442–448.

96. Moyer, A. (1997). Psychosocial outcomes of breast-conserving surgery versus mastectomy: A meta-analytic review. *Health Psychology, 16*, 284–298.

97. Rowland, J. H., Desmond, K. A., Meyerowitz, B. E., Belin, T. R., Wyatt, G. E., & Ganz, P. A. (2000). Role of breast reconstructive surgery in physical and emotional outcomes among breast cancer survivors. *Journal of the National Cancer Institute, 92*, 1422–1429.

98. Andersen, B. L. (1985). Sexual functioning morbidity among cancer survivors. *Cancer, 55*, 1835–1842.

99. Morris, T., Greer, H. S., & White, P. (1977). Psychological and social adjustment to mastectomy. *Cancer, 40*, 2381–2387.

100. Taylor, S. E., Lichtman, R. R., & Wood, J. V. (1984). Attributions, beliefs about control, and adjustment to breast cancer. *Journal of Personality and Social Psychology, 46*, 489–502.

101. Yurek, D., Farrar, W., & Andersen, B. L. (2000). Breast cancer surgery: Comparing surgical groups and determining individual differences in postoperative sexuality and body change stress. *Journal of Consulting and Clinical Psychology, 68*, 697–709.

102. Nichols, M. (1987). Lesbian sexuality: Issues and developing theory. In Boston Lesbian Psychologies Collective (Ed.), *Lesbian psychologies: Explorations and challenges* (pp. 97–125). Chicago: University of Illinois Free Press.

103. Nichols, M. (1987). Doing sex therapy with lesbians: Bending a heterosexual paradigm to fit a gay life-style. In Boston Lesbian Psychologies Collective (Ed.), *Lesbian psychologies: Explorations and challenges* (pp. 242–260). Chicago: University of Illinois Free Press.

104. Nichols, M. (1988). Low sexual desire in lesbian couples. In S. R. Leiblum & R. C. Rosen (Eds.), *Sexual desire disorders* (pp. 387–412). New York: Guilford Press.

105. Matthews, A. K., Hughes, T. L., & Tartaro, J. (2006). Sexual behavior and sexual dysfunction in a community sample of lesbian and heterosexual women. *Journal of Lesbian Studies, 7*, 101–114.

106. National Cancer Institute. (2003). Plans and priorities for cancer research. *Cancer survivorship: Improving treatment outcomes and quality of life*. Bethesda, MD: Author.

107. Aziz, N. M., & Rowland, J. H. (2002). Cancer survivorship research among ethnic minority and medically underserved groups. *Oncology Nursing Forum, 29,* 789–801.

108. Ries, L. A. G., Melbert, D., Krapcho, M., Stinchcomb, D. G., Howlader, N., Horner, M. J., et al. (Eds.). (2008). *SEER cancer statistics review, 1975–2005*. Bethesda, MD: National Cancer Institute. Available at seer.cancer.gov/csr/1975_2005.

109. Adler, N. E., & Page, A. E. K. (Eds.). (2008). *Cancer care of the whole patient: Meeting psychosocial health needs*. Institute of Medicine and National Research Council of the National Academies. Washington, DC: National Academies Press.

110. Matthews, A. K., Masini, B., & Halem, J. (2006, October). *Experiences and needs of LGBT cancer survivors*. Paper presented at the annual meeting of the Gay and Lesbian Medical Association, San Francisco, CA.

111. Pinto, B. M., & Trunzo, J. J. (2005). Health behaviors during and after a cancer diagnosis. *Cancer, 104*(Suppl. 11), 2614–2623.

112. Demark-Wahnefried, W., Aziz, N. W., Rowland, J. H., & Pinto, B. M. (2005). Riding the crest of the teachable-moment: Promoting long-term health after the diagnosis of cancer. *Journal of Clinical Oncology, 23,* 5814–5830.

ABOUT THE AUTHOR

Alicia K. Matthews, PhD is Associate Professor in the College of Nursing at the University of Illinois, Chicago and a clinical psychologist. She has expertise working with cancer patients and their families and with persons at high risk of developing cancer. Her research interests are cancer prevention and control as well as the socio-cultural determinants of health disparities.

CHAPTER 22

"Why Us?"

BREAST CANCER AMONG LESBIANS

MARION H. E. KAVANAUGH-LYNCH, MD, MPH

MELISSA, *38, has no medical problems and no family history of cancer. Her 41-year-old ex-partner, with whom she is very close, was just diagnosed with stage 3 breast cancer. In reading extensively about the disease to learn more, Melissa came across articles stating that one in three lesbians will get breast cancer. She arrives for a doctor visit frightened that she, too, will get breast cancer and wants to know if there is anything she can do about it. What should the clinician tell Melissa? How can the clinician help her?*

■ ■ ■

Breast cancer is the most common cancer diagnosis among women in the United States.[1] It is the leading cause of cancer-related death in women younger than 50 and second only to lung cancer in women older than 50. Although often described as a disease of aging, given that incidence increases with age and 70% of diagnoses occur after age 55, breast cancer also has an enormous impact on younger and middle-age women. Sixty percent of breast cancer cases occur among women younger than 65, who are diagnosed in all younger age ranges, including the teen years.[2] The disease takes a tragic toll in terms of premature death and disability, and causes a huge loss in productivity and income for women of all ages.

BACKGROUND

In the 1980s, awareness of women's health issues and the need for research focusing on women, rather than men only, gradually grew among women and in the scientific community. Awareness turned into activism. In the early 1990s, women adopted the tactics of AIDS activists and launched the lesbian-health and breast-cancer movements, both of which advocated for research. Their efforts prompted new funding. Public programs included the U.S. Department of Defense Breast Cancer Research Program and special initiatives on lesbian health in the Office on Women's Health at the National Institutes of Health (NIH). Private programs included Komen for the Cure and the Lesbian Health Fund.

The two movements collided in 1992 when a NIH scientist hypothesized that the risk of breast cancer was about two to three times greater among lesbians than among heterosexual women.[3] The hypothesis was based on data from rather crude, convenience-sample health surveys of primarily young, White, middle-class lesbians, many of them recruited from bars and other selective settings, suggesting that lesbians had a higher prevalence of some known risk factors for breast cancer. These factors included nulliparity, higher body mass index, and greater alcohol consumption. Given the estimated lifetime risk of breast cancer for heterosexual women of one in nine at that time, the story quickly became that one in three lesbians would develop breast cancer.[3,4]

To this day, the topic of lesbians and breast cancer is hotly debated. Some have labeled breast cancer a lesbian epidemic,[5-9] but others see this as a very stubborn myth.[10] While many questions about the effect sexual orientation has on breast cancer remain unanswered, there is strong evidence that being lesbian can have an impact on every part of the breast cancer continuum—from risk, prevention, and etiology to screening, diagnosis, treatment, survival, mortality, and quality of life.[11-13]

The incidence of breast cancer among lesbians is unknown. The federal government and state governments carefully track breast and other types of cancer, a reportable disease. They collect demographic information, including place of residence, race/ethnicity, occupation, religion, and marital status, which enables calculation of cancer incidence in different populations, but they do not gather data on sexual orientation. Even if the sexual orientation of every person with cancer were known, calculations would still require knowledge of the total number of lesbians in a given population. Estimates of the number of lesbians in the United States vary from 0.6% to 4.0% of the female population[14,15]—a variation that is too wide for meaningfully estimating cancer rates. Accurate estimates will not be possible until the U.S. Census Bureau or some other entity routinely collects data on sexual orientation and assures lesbians that they can report this information without fear of repercussions.

An alternative to calculating actual cancer rates is to estimate risks for lesbians versus heterosexual women. This might be possible through very large and broad studies, such as the Women's Health Initiative or the Nurse's Health Study. Still, estimates would be approximate at best. Data from the Women's Health Initiative revealed a higher age-adjusted prevalence of breast cancer among lesbians and bisexuals: 5.8% among lifetime lesbians, or women who had only female sexual partners throughout their lives; 7.0% among adult lesbians, or women who had only female sexual partners after age 45; 8.4% among bisexual women; and 4.9% among heterosexual women.[16] However, another analysis of the reported prevalence of breast cancer in a different population, based on pooled survey data, did not reveal any differences between lesbians and heterosexual women.[17]

There have been attempts to use alternative research methods to estimate comparable breast cancer risks. According to one study, the relative risk of breast cancer for lesbians compared with women who are not lesbian is 0.84 to 4.91. These results, based on three surrogate correlates of sexual orientation (lifetime sexual history, lifetime marital history, and use of oral contraceptives), suggest an elevated risk for lesbians, but the findings were not statistically significant.[18]

Three other studies yielded lifetime risk estimates using the validated Gail model[19] to calculate individual risk based on known risk factors in a sample of lesbians and a heterosexual control group. In two of the three studies, lesbians scored significantly higher than the controls did.[20,21] The third study found similar elevated risks in both groups due to positive family history.[22] The first two studies had more specific control groups (heterosexual sisters in one and heterosexual friends or coworkers in another) than did the third, which used similarly recruited but unrelated women for the control group.

In summary, although direct observation of breast cancer incidence is not currently possible, evidence based on extrapolation of data from population-based cohort studies, use of available cancer demographics to estimate sexual orientation, and estimates of risk among cohorts of lesbians and heterosexual women strongly suggests a higher risk of the disease among lesbians.

RISK AND PROTECTIVE FACTORS AMONG LESBIANS

TABLE 22.1. BREAST CANCER: RISK, PROTECTIVE, AND UNASSOCIATED FACTORS

RISK	PROTECTIVE	UNASSOCIATED
■ Sex (female) ■ Genetic mutation (BRCA1 or BRCA2) ■ Family history ■ Older age ■ High socioeconomic status ■ Caucasian race ■ Early age at menarche ■ Late age at menopause ■ Postmenopausal hormone replacement therapy ■ Smoking ■ Environmental tobacco smoke (premenopausal breast cancer only) ■ Obesity (postmenopausal breast cancer only) ■ Greater alcohol consumption ■ Previous breast biopsy ■ Chest radiation early in life ■ Occupation (nuns, teachers, flight attendants) ■ Exposure to diethylstilbestrol (DES) (prenatally or as an adult)	■ Younger age at first full-term pregnancy ■ High parity ■ History of breast-feeding ■ Regular physical activity ■ Obesity (premenopausal breast cancer only)	■ Diet ■ Abortion

Sources:
(1) Morris, C. R., & Kwong, S. L. (Eds.). (2004). *Breast cancer in California, 2003.* Sacramento, CA: California Department of Health Services. Available at www.ccrcal.org/PDF/BreastCancer-03.pdf.
(2) American Cancer Society. (2009). *What causes breast cancer?* Available at www.cancer.org/docroot/CRI/content/CRI_2_2_2X_What_causes_breast_cancer_5.asp.
(3) National Cancer Institute. (2009). *Breast cancer: Risk factors.* Available at www.cancer.gov/cancertopics/wyntk/breast/page4.

Given the limitations cited above, one must rely on known risk factors and the available calculation methods to hypothesize about breast cancer risks among lesbians. Many factors influence this complex disease, including sex, age, race/ethnicity, socioeconomic status, geography, and occupation (Table 22.1). Diet and abortion are not risk factors.[23,24]

Individual risk factors vary in terms of how prevalent they are among lesbians. The more prevalent factors prompted the hypothesis that lesbians may be at disproportionately higher risk of breast cancer. Thus, sexual orientation itself may not pose a higher risk; rather, higher overall risk may be a sociological phenomenon arising from aggregated risk factors in the lesbian population. This phenomenon could be a consequence of the influence that shared community characteristics and social determinants of health have on behavior and risk patterns.

Aggregate evidence suggests that lesbians are more likely than heterosexual women to get breast cancer. Counterbalancing this likelihood are certain protective factors that are more prevalent among lesbians, and the fact that known risk factors cannot account for more than half of all breast cancer cases. It may be more helpful to focus on the protective factors instead of the risk factors in learning how to leverage population characteristics to reduce the risk of this disease among lesbians.

SCREENING

Health surveys of lesbians generally show that lesbians are less likely than heterosexual women to undergo routine and preventive screening. Researchers have suggested a number of multifactorial reasons for this: lesbians have less access to health coverage than other women do under a husband's insurance policy, lesbians are reticent about using the health care system due to a history or fear of homophobic reactions on the part of health care providers, and they have less need for annual visits to obtain oral contraceptives.[25–32]

The U.S. Preventive Services Task Force recently issued new guidelines for breast cancer screening,[33] which reduces deaths from the disease by as much as 30% in women older than 50.[34–37] Therefore, any screening deficit among lesbians could lead to higher breast cancer mortality.

Studies examining the rate of breast cancer screening among lesbians have produced mixed results. Some found that lesbians were less likely than heterosexual women to receive screening, some found that they were more likely, and others found no difference. Very few looked at clinical breast exam and mammography combined, but those that did consistently reported lower rates of clinical breast exam among lesbians. Although some researchers have investigated the rates of breast self-exam, any reported differences are questionable because there is no evidence supporting the effectiveness of self-exams. Table 22.2 summarizes the results from appropriately controlled studies of breast cancer screening rates among sexual-minority and heterosexual women. Without more data on clinical breast exams, one can only assume that lesbians are at higher risk of poor outcomes from breast cancer if they do not receive this type of screening.

A number of quantitative and qualitative studies have looked at what motivates lesbians to get screened, what prevents them from doing so, and interventions targeted specifically to lesbians. In focus groups of unmarried women who partner either with men or with women, Clark and colleagues found that the barriers to breast cancer screening were similar for both groups and included lack of acknowledgment or validation of relationships in health care settings, administrative hurdles, pain, and concerns about body image. Barriers unique to lesbians included fears of discrimination based on sexual orientation and gender nonconformity.[38] Similarly, Pearson-Fields and colleagues described greater barriers for androgynous and butch African American lesbians based on gender identity, gender nonconformity, and related discrimination.[39] In a study of lesbians who had a first-degree relative with breast cancer, the only factors related to differences in screening behavior were income/employment status and extent of worry about breast cancer, both of which correlated with more screening.[40] This conflicts with previous research showing an inverse relationship between extent of worry and adherence to mammography screening among older heterosexual women.[41]

In telephone interviews with older lesbians, Lauver and colleagues found barriers to breast cancer screening similar to those for heterosexual women, including cost, discomfort, competing life demands, lack of motivation to get screened, and negative emotions. Barriers unique to lesbians were lack of a good relationship with health care providers and lack of trust in the health care community. Participants said an important facilitator of mammography was social support. They also cited a need for openness and safety for lesbians in the health care system.[42] A national, convenience-sample survey of lesbians revealed that those who were older, had higher incomes, did not smoke, performed breast self-exams, and received regular physical exams were more likely to undergo breast cancer screening.[43]

Fish and Anthony surveyed lesbians throughout the United Kingdom. They expected that previous negative experiences with breast cancer screening would be a barrier to further screening. However, such experiences had no detectable effect on screening behavior, while previous positive experiences increased the likelihood of further screening.[44] This underscores the potential impact of interventions that make breast cancer screening a good experience for women.

Two studies examined interventions to increase breast cancer screening among lesbians. In a randomized trial comprising lesbians at risk for breast cancer, Bowen

TABLE 22.2. BREAST CANCER SCREENING RATES AMONG SEXUAL MINORITY WOMEN VERSUS HETEROSEXUAL WOMEN

STUDY	MAMMOGRAPHY	CLINICAL BREAST EXAM
LOWER SCREENING RATES		
Pooled convenience samples[17]	Lower lifetime rate compared with standardized rates among heterosexual women	N.A.
Risk counseling volunteers in Seattle[45]	Less likely to have mammograms	N.A.
Qualitative study of lesbian/bisexual and heterosexual patients with breast cancer.[46] Participants included Hispanics, African Americans, and Asian Americans.	No difference between lesbian/bisexual women and heterosexual women	Lesbian/bisexual women less likely than heterosexual women to have had a breast exam in the previous 2 years
Sexual behavior and identity[47]	Lesbians less likely than other women to have mammograms (53% vs. 73%)	N.A.
HIGHER SCREENING RATES		
Cohort in the Women's Health Initiative[16]	In the previous year, 70% of lesbians versus 63–67% of other female participants	N.A.
Epidemiologic study of health risks among lesbians[48]	Lesbians more likely to have had a mammogram ever or within the previous 2 years	N.A.
NO DIFFERENCE IN OR SIMILAR SCREENING RATES		
Questionnaire administered by *The Advocate*[49]	No difference in rates among lesbians, bisexual women, and heterosexual women	N.A.
Canadian survey[50]	Similar rates among lesbians and heterosexual women. Much lower rate among bisexual women.	N.A.
Lesbians and their heterosexual sisters[21]	No difference	No difference

and colleagues found that group counseling, education, and skills-building reduced perceived risk, anxiety, and fears of the disease, and increased screening rates.[45] Burnett and colleagues, in contrast, reported a positive association between the degree of breast cancer worry and mammography adherence, suggesting that the education and skills-development components had greater influence on screening than they did on perceived risk and anxiety.[40]

Dibble and Roberts looked at the impact of cancer education on a group of lesbians. In the single-arm pilot study, 73% of participants were receiving recommended breast cancer screening. Among the other 27% who were not, one-third received screening shortly after the educational intervention. There was no long-term follow-up.[51] This relatively modest effect suggests that education alone may not be sufficient to influence behavior and that additional elements, such as skills-building and risk assessment, may be necessary.

DIAGNOSIS AND TREATMENT

There are only two published studies on diagnosis and treatment of lesbians who have breast cancer. This topic warrants further study, given that the health care access and utilization issues for lesbians, and their fear and experiences of homophobia in the health care setting, may be barriers to appropriate diagnosis and treatment.

In a nested survey, Dibble and Roberts compared the diagnosis and treatment experiences of lesbians and heterosexual women diagnosed with breast cancer. The lesbians were more likely to have found their tumor by breast self-exam, reported a significantly longer delay between suspicion/detection and provider visit, and were twice as likely to have received their diagnosis by telephone. Although there were no significant differences between the two groups in terms of surgical or other medical therapy, the lesbians reported significantly more side effects from treatment. What this finding means is unclear; it warrants further investigation.[52]

In retrospective, qualitative research, Boehmer and colleagues explored the decisions lesbians made regarding breast reconstruction after mastectomy and the support they received. The women aligned their lesbian identity with their new identity of not having breasts, and felt that body strength and function were more important than esthetics. Regardless of whether or not they chose mastectomy, the women noted a discrepancy between their values and body image and the values of mainstream society. Overall, women who underwent reconstruction experienced more discomfort and discontentment with, and regrets and doubts about, their choice than did those who decided not to undergo the procedure.[53]

PSYCHOSOCIAL ISSUES

Researchers have focused more attention on lesbian-related psychosocial issues than on diagnosis and treatment, perhaps because psychosocial studies more commonly use qualitative methods and depend less on quantitative methods requiring a firm denominator.

A number of studies have compared lesbians and heterosexual women in terms of their personal responses to breast cancer and coping mechanisms. The findings, which are remarkably similar, suggest that lesbians suffer fewer problems with body image, sexual function, and relationship issues; use less avoidance coping; and more often express anger and vent.[54–56] They also receive more support from their partners and friends and less from family members, and are less satisfied with their health care.[55,56] Awareness of these differences is important when clinicians provide supportive care to lesbians. Overall quality of life for lesbians and heterosexual women with breast cancer appears to be equal.[57]

Boehmer and colleagues found that lesbians with breast cancer most often obtain primary support from a relationship partner. Patients and partners experienced similar levels of distress, but the partners got less perceived social and community support than the patients did.[54] Disclosure of sexual orientation to health care providers reduced patients' and partners' distress equally. Discordance between them in terms of the degree to which they disclosed their sexual orientation (when the partners were more open than the patients) led to greater emotional distress.[58]

Boehmer and Case explored breast cancer patients' disclosure of sexual orientation to health care providers more thoroughly. In their sample, no providers inquired about sexual orientation; rather, patients instigated all disclosures, and sexual orientation was not actively concealed by those who did not disclose. Many women who disclosed had prepared for this in order to ensure a positive reaction from providers.[59]

McGregor and colleagues examined the relationships among internalized homophobia, disclosure of sexual orientation, social support, self-esteem, and distress in lesbian women participating in a study of adjustment to breast cancer. They found links between internalized homophobia and less health care, and between internalized homophobia and psychological distress. The latter correlation was consistent with two possible models: (1) internalized homophobia and distress are related to low self-esteem and a perceived lack of social support, and (2) internalized homophobia arises primarily from a lack of self-esteem. The researchers did not find a relationship between distress and extent of disclosure of sexual orientation.[60] Thus, disclosure is a complex issue, one that clinicians and patients must carefully negotiate. Considerations include patients' and partners' comfort with, and health care providers' attitudes about, disclosure.

In the scenario at the beginning of this chapter, Melissa's clinician could best help her by providing thorough and accurate information about lesbians and breast cancer. The clinician should encourage Melissa to adopt or maintain protective behaviors, such as exercise and less alcohol consumption, and work with her to determine the best mammography schedule based on her history, family history, and ethnicity. Referrals for mammograms should be to professionals who know how to serve lesbians in a culturally appropriate manner. The clinician told Melissa she is welcome to include others in their discussions about her health.

CONCLUSION

There is substantial evidence that the incidence of breast cancer is higher among lesbians than heterosexual women. Research also suggests this is partly due to different risk factor patterns. However, because these patterns may be changing across generations, so might breast cancer incidence. Some protective factors are more prevalent among lesbians. Accompanying the differential risk is less access to and appropriate use of health care, including screening. More quantitative research on diagnosis and treatment of breast cancer in lesbians, as well as outcomes, is necessary. Qualitative psychosocial studies provide robust evidence of lesbians who face breast cancer with incredible courage and strength.

REFERENCES

1. Ries, L. A. G., Melbert, D., Krapcho, M., Stinchcomb, D. G., Howlader, N., Horner, M. J., et al. (Eds.). *SEER cancer statistics review 1975–2005.* Bethesda, MD: National Cancer Institute. Available at seer.cancer.gov/csr/1975_2005/accessible_contents.html.

2. American Cancer Society. (2008). *Cancer facts & figures 2008.* Available at www.cancer.org/docroot/stt/content/stt_1x_cancer_facts_and_figures_2008.asp.

3. Haynes, S. (1992, July). *Are lesbians at high risk of breast cancer?* Paper presented at the annual meeting of the National Lesbian and Gay Health Foundation, Los Angeles, CA.

4. Haynes, S. (1994, December). *Risk of breast cancer among lesbians.* Paper presented at an online conference regarding cancer and cancer risk among lesbians.

5. Brandt, K. (1993, September–October). Lesbians at risk. *Deneuve, 3,* 34–37.

6. Brownworth, V. A. (1993, February–March). The other epidemic: Lesbians and breast cancer. *Out,* 60–63.

7. Denenberg, R. (1995). Report on lesbian health. *Women's Health Issues, 5,* 81–91.

8. Gallagher, J. (1997, September 30). Lesbians and breast cancer. *The Advocate, 30,* 20–27.

9. Gessen, M. (1993, February 9). Lesbians and breast cancer. *The Advocate, 26,* 45–48.

10. Rochman, S. (2007, September 25). Doctor, doctor: Two amazing minds take on two deadly diseases. *The Advocate.* Available at www.thefreelibrary.com/Doctor, +doctor:+ two+amazing+minds+take+on+two+deadly+diseases.+David+...-a0169134185.

11. Bigby, J., & Holmes, M. D. (2005). Disparities across the breast cancer continuum. *Cancer Causes & Control, 16,* 35–44.

12. Brody, J. G., Kavanaugh-Lynch, M. H. E., Olopade O Shinagawa, S. M., Steingraber, S., & Williams, D. R. (Eds.). (2007). *Identifying gaps in breast cancer research: Addressing disparities and the roles of the physical and social environment.* Oakland, CA: California Breast Cancer Research Program.

13. Brown, J. P., & Tracy, J. K. (2008). Lesbians and cancer: An overlooked health disparity. *Cancer Causes & Control, 19,* 1009–1020.

14. Black, D., Gates, G., Sanders, S., & Taylor, L. (2000). Demographics of the gay and lesbian population in the United States: Evidence from available systematic data sources. *Demography, 37,* 139–154.

15. Mosher, W. D., Chandra, A., & Jones, J. (2005). Sexual behavior and selected health measures: Men and women 15–44 years of age, United States, 2002. *Advance Data, Sep 15,* 1–55.

16. Valanis, B. G., Bowen, D. J., Bassford, T., Whitlock, E., Charney, P., & Carter, R. A. (2000). Sexual orientation and health: Comparisons in the Women's Health Initiative sample. *Archives of Family Medicine, 9,* 843–853.

17. Cochran, S. D., Mays, V. M., Bowen, D., Gage, S., Bybee, D., Roberts, S. J., et al. (2001). Cancer-related risk indicators and preventive screening behaviors among lesbians and bisexual women. *American Journal of Public Health, 91,* 591–597.

18. Kavanaugh-Lynch, M. H. E., White, E., Daling, J. R., & Bowen, D. J. (2002). Correlates of lesbian sexual orientation and the risk of breast cancer. *Journal of the Gay and Lesbian Medical Association, 6,* 91–95.

19. Gail, M. H., Brinton, L. A., Byar, D. P., Corle, D. K., Green, S. B., Schairer, C., et al. (1989). Projecting individualized probabilities of developing breast cancer for White females who are being examined annually. *Journal of the National Cancer Institute, 81,* 1879–1886.

20. Brandenburg, D. L., Matthews, A. K., Johnson, T. P., & Hughes, T. L. (2007). Breast cancer risk and screening: A comparison of lesbian and heterosexual women. *Women & Health, 45,* 109–130.

21. Dibble, S. L., Roberts, S. A., & Nussey, B. (2004). Comparing breast cancer risk between lesbians and their heterosexual sisters. *Women's Health Issues, 14,* 60–68.

22. McTiernan, A., Kuniyuki, A., Yasui, Y., Bowen, D., Burke, W., Culver, J. B., et al. (2001). Comparisons of two breast cancer risk estimates in women with a family history of breast cancer. *Cancer Epidemiology, Biomarkers & Prevention, 10,* 333–338.

23. American Cancer Society. (2009). *What causes breast cancer?* Available at www.cancer. org/docroot/CRI/content/CRI_2_2_2X_What_causes_breast_cancer_5.asp.

24. National Cancer Institute. (2009). *Breast cancer: Risk factors.* Available at www.cancer. gov/cancertopics/wyntk/breast/page4.

25. Bradford, J., & Ryan, C. (1988). *The National Lesbian Health Care Survey: Final report.* Washington, DC: National Lesbian and Gay Health Foundation.

26. Bybee, D., & Roeder, V. (1990). *Michigan Lesbian Health Survey: Results relevant to AIDS. A report to the Michigan Organization for Human Rights and the Michigan Department of Public Health.* Lansing, MI: Michigan Department of Health and Human Services.

27. Cochran, S. D., & Mays, V. M. (1988). Disclosure of sexual preference to physicians by Black lesbian and bisexual women. *Western Journal of Medicine, 149,* 616–619.

28. Durfy, S. J., Bowen, D. J., McTiernan, A., Sporleder, J., & Burke, W. (1999). Attitudes and interest in genetic testing for breast and ovarian cancer susceptibility in diverse groups of women in western Washington. *Cancer Epidemiology, Biomarkers & Prevention, 8*(4, Pt. 2), 369–375.

29. Lehmann, J. B., Lehmann, C. U., & Kelly, P. J. (1998). Development and health care needs of lesbians. *Journal of Women's Health, 7,* 379–387.

30. Mathews, W. C., Booth, M. W., Turner, J. D., & Kessler, L. (1986). Physicians' attitudes toward homosexuality—survey of a California county medical society. *Western Journal of Medicine, 144,* 106–110.

31. Stevens, P. E., & Hall, J. M. (1988). Stigma, health beliefs, and experiences with health care in lesbian women. *Image, the Journal of Nursing Scholarship, 20,* 69–73.

32. Warchafsky, L. (1992). *Lesbian health needs assessment.* Los Angeles: Los Angeles Gay and Lesbian Community Services Center.

33. U.S. Preventive Services Task Force. (2009). Screening for breast cancer: U.S. Preventive Services Task Force recommendation statement. *Annals of Internal Medicine, 151,* 716–726. Available at www.annals.org/content/151/10/716.full.

34. De Koning, H. J. (2003). Mammographic screening: Evidence from randomised controlled trials. *Annals of Oncology, 14,* 1185–1189.

35. Dean, P. B. (2002). The rationale and current controversies of mammographic screening for breast cancer. *Scandinavian Journal of Surgery, 91,* 288–292.

36. Otto, S. J., Fracheboud, J., Looman, C. W., Broeders, M. J., Boer, R., Hendriks, J. H., et al. (2003). Initiation of population-based mammography screening in Dutch municipalities and effect on breast-cancer mortality: A systematic review. *Lancet, 361,* 1411–1417.

37. Sasieni, P. (2003). Evaluation of the UK breast screening programmes. *Annals of Oncology, 14,* 1206–1208.

38. Clark, M. A., Bonacore, L., Wright, S. J., Armstrong, G., & Rakowski, W. (2003). The Cancer Screening Project for Women: Experiences of women who partner with women and women who partner with men. *Women & Health, 38,* 19–33.

39. Pearson-Fields, C., Gaston, A., Raiser, K., & Fischer, L. (2004, November). *Diversity within diversity: Understanding the impact of gender identity on cancer screening adherence among African American lesbians.* Paper presented at the annual meeting of the American Public Health Association, Washington, DC.

40. Burnett, C. B., Steakley, C. S., Slack, R., Roth, J., & Lerman, C. (1999). Patterns of breast cancer screening among lesbians at increased risk for breast cancer. *Women & Health, 29,* 35–55.

41. Lerman, C., Daly, M., Sands, C., Balshem, A., Lustbader, E., Heggan, T., et al. (1993). Mammography adherence and psychological distress among women at risk for breast cancer. *Journal of the National Cancer Institute, 85*, 1074–1080.

42. Lauver, D. R., Karon, S. L., Egan, J., Jacobson, M., Nugent, J., Settersten, L., et al. (1999). Understanding lesbians' mammography utilization. *Women's Health Issues, 9*, 264–274.

43. Grindel, C. G., McGehee, L. A., Patsdaughter, C. A., & Roberts, S. J. (2006). Cancer prevention and screening behaviors in lesbians. *Women & Health, 44*, 15–39.

44.. Fish, J., & Anthony, D. (2005). UK national Lesbians and Health Care Survey. *Women & Health, 41*, 27–45.

45. Bowen, D. J., Powers, D., & Greenlee, H. (2006). Effects of breast cancer risk counseling for sexual minority women. *Health Care for Women International, 27*, 59–74.

46. Mays, V. M., Yancey, A. K., Cochran, S. D., Weber, M., & Fielding, J. E. (2002). Heterogeneity of health disparities among African American, Hispanic, and Asian American women: Unrecognized influences of sexual orientation. *American Journal of Public Health, 92*, 632–639.

47. Kerker, B. D., Mostashari, F., & Thorpe, L. (2006). Health care access and utilization among women who have sex with women: Sexual behavior and identity. *Journal of Urban Health, 83*, 970–979.

48. Aaron, D. J., Markovic, N., Danielson, M. E., Honnold, J. A., Janosky, J. E., & Schmidt, N. J. (2001). Behavioral risk factors for disease and preventive health practices among lesbians. *American Journal of Public Health, 91*, 972–975

49. Diamant, A. L., Schuster, M. A., & Lever, J. (2000). Receipt of preventive health care services by lesbians. *American Journal of Preventive Medicine, 19*, 141–148.

50. Tjepkema, M. (2008). *Health care use among gay, lesbian, and bisexual Canadians.* Toronto: Statistics Canada.

51. Dibble, S. L., & Roberts, S. A. (2003). Improving cancer screening among lesbians over 50: Results of a pilot study. *Oncology Nursing Forum, 30*, E71–79.

52. Dibble, S. L., & Roberts, S. A. (2002). A comparison of breast cancer diagnosis and treatment between lesbian and heterosexual women. *Journal of the Gay and Lesbian Medical Association, 6*, 9–17.

53. Boehmer, U., Linde, R., & Freund, K. M. (2007). Breast reconstruction following mastectomy for breast cancer: The decisions of sexual minority women. *Plastic and Reconstructive Surgery, 119*, 464–472.

54 Boehmer, U., Linde, R., & Freund, K. M. (2005). Sexual minority women's coping and psychological adjustment after a diagnosis of breast cancer. *Journal of Women's Health, 14*, 214–224.

55. Arena, P. L., Carver, C. S., Antoni, M. H., Weiss, S., Ironson, G., & Durán, R. E. (2006). Psychosocial responses to treatment for breast cancer among lesbian and heterosexual women. *Women & Health, 44*, 81–102.

56. Fobair, P., O'Hanlan, K., Koopman, C., Classen, C., Dimiceli, S., Drooker, N., et al. (2001). Comparison of lesbian and heterosexual women's response to newly diagnosed breast cancer. *Psycho-Oncology, 10*, 40–51.

57. Matthews, A. K., Peterman, A. H., Delaney, P., Menard, L., & Brandenburg, D. (2002). A qualitative exploration of the experiences of lesbian and heterosexual patients with breast cancer. *Oncology Nursing Forum, 29,* 1455–1462.

58. Boehmer, U., Freund, K. M., & Linde, R. (2005). Support providers of sexual minority women with breast cancer: Who they are and how they impact the breast cancer experience. *Journal of Psychosomatic Research, 59,* 307–314.

59. Boehmer, U., & Case, P. (2004). Physicians don't ask, sometimes patients tell: Disclosure of sexual orientation among women with breast carcinoma. *Cancer, 101,* 1882–1889.

60. McGregor, B. A., Carver, C. S., Antoni, M. H., Weiss, S., Yount, S. E., & Ironson, G. (2001). Distress and internalized homophobia among lesbian women treated for early stage breast cancer. *Psychology of Women Quarterly, 25,* 1–9.

ABOUT THE AUTHOR

Marion H. E. Kavanaugh-Lynch, MD, MPH is an oncologist and Director of the California Breast Cancer Research Program at the University of California Office of the President. She guides priorities for $200 million that California has invested in breast cancer research. She is past president of the Lesbian Health Fund and active in the Gay and Lesbian Medical Association.

CHAPTER 23

"Is This Bleeding Normal?"

LESBIANS AND GYNECOLOGIC MALIGNANCY

KATHERINE A. O'HANLAN, MD

WITH *pollen season approaching, Maria, a 55-year-old lesbian, called her nurse practitioner's office and requested that a new prescription for her allergy inhalers be called in. The office told her she would first need an annual physical exam, pelvic exam, and Pap smear. Frustrated, Maria reminded the secretary that, as a lesbian who did not have sex with men, a Pap smear was unnecessary. But the secretary politely insisted, so Maria made an appointment for the following week.*

During the visit, the nurse practitioner seemed to talk about everything but the inhalers. She asked Maria about her exercise and eating habits, noting that her weight was beyond the healthy limit for her height; about her family's medical history; and about many different heart, digestive tract, and urinary symptoms. When they got to the topic of Pap smears, Maria again explained why she thought them unnecessary but confided that she was having a little spotting from her vagina, even though her last normal period was 5 years ago. The nurse told her that, according to the latest research on Pap smears, women who are having sex with women do need the tests, even if they have never had sex with men. More questions from the nurse about Maria's sexual history revealed that she had been in four serial monogamous relationships with other women since coming out at age 16. She was nulliparous and postmenopausal, had very few problems with hot flashes, and, aside from the asthma, considered herself healthy.

The nurse practitioner thoroughly examined Maria and obtained a Pap smear. Everything seemed normal except for some old blood at the opening of Maria's cervix. The clinician explained that because Maria was still bleeding well past menopause, there might be a problem inside her uterus—one that a Pap smear could not detect, as the test only assesses the cervix, and not the inside of the uterus, the endometrium. She said she needed to biopsy the endometrium using a tiny tube that would take a tissue sample from much higher up in the uterus. Maria would feel strong cramps for a few minutes, which would taper off after the procedure. Bleeding that occurs long after menopause is not normal, the nurse practitioner explained, and the cause of such bleeding in about 20% of women is cancer or a cancerous precursor. She reassured Maria that even if cancer were found, it would probably be curable.

In 2009, an estimated 80,720 women—some of them lesbians—will be diagnosed with gynecologic cancers, and an estimated 28,120 will die.[1] Women with suspected or diagnosed gynecologic cancers are typically referred to gynecologic cancer specialists, who have received 3 additional years of training in this field and know how to avoid surgery if possible or perform all surgery necessary to comprehensively stage each type of malignancy. To take advantage of such expertise, many women patients must travel, as there are only about 1,000 gynecologic oncologists in the United States.[2] State-of-the-art care can significantly increase the length of survival.

This chapter reviews the three major types of gynecologic cancers—ovarian, cervical, and endometrial—and discusses risks, diagnostic tests, treatments, prognoses, and preventive measures, and why these cancers may pose a greater danger for lesbians.

OVARIAN CANCER

About 1.7% of American women will develop ovarian cancer in their lifetime,[3] a subset that may include a disproportionate number of lesbians.[4] In 2009, there will be an estimated 21,550 new cases and 14,600 deaths.[1] Risk factors include older age, high body mass index, having had few or no babies, smoking, endometriosis, and family history. Oral contraceptives can reduce the risk of ovarian cancer by about 50% if women take them for 5 to 10 years.[5]

There are no data on cancer rates among lesbians specifically, but risk factor analysis based on findings from high-quality surveys provides clear insight into strategies for early diagnosis and prevention of ovarian cancer in this population.

DIAGNOSIS

Ovarian cancer is rarely detected in the early stages because symptoms, including pelvic pressure or intestinal problems such as gas pains and early satiety, are few and subtle. Frequently, women with such symptoms notice that their pants do not close because their abdomen is swollen even though they have not concurrently gained weight. A thorough annual gynecologic exam and questions for the patient about intestinal function and pelvic symptoms can lead to a diagnosis. Unusual exam findings or unusual symptoms in the pelvis typically warrant a vaginal ultrasound and a cancer antigen 125 (CA 125) blood test, the two tests most likely to detect ovarian cancer early. Transvaginal ultrasound can cause a great deal of discomfort, especially for lesbians who may be uneasy about penetration of the vagina. In this highly accurate procedure, the inserted sonographic transducer is angled to view all parts of the pelvis to assess each reproductive organ very precisely. Alternatives for women who cannot tolerate transvaginal ultrasound are abdominal ultrasound, computed tomography (CT), and magnetic resonance imaging. CA 125 and ultrasound are not appropriate tools for annual screening of otherwise healthy women because overdiagnoses can result in too many unnecessary surgeries.

Effective communication between clinicians and patients could facilitate earlier diagnosis of ovarian cancer and possibly save lives, as patients would be more likely to report even vague symptoms and undergo testing.

Treatment

The first step in treatment is to get an accurate tissue sample, which requires surgery. Laparoscopy is appropriate when ovarian cancer is diagnosed early. However, because the disease is usually diagnosed in advanced stages, an open laparotomy is typically necessary for staging and debulking. Surgery includes hysterectomy, bilateral oophorectomy, appendectomy, omentectomy, para-aortic and pelvic lymphadenectomy, and removal of all cancerous implants so no visible, residual cancer remains. Additional procedures to eradicate all cancerous implants may include bowel resection, splenectomy, and cholecystectomy. The highest probabilities of cure are associated with zero visible residual cancer after the first operation followed by intraperitoneal chemotherapy.[6] Radiation does not play a role in treatment. The 5- and 10-year survival rates for ovarian cancer are 45% and 38%, respectively.[2]

First-line chemotherapy usually takes 5 to 6 months. Despite total baldness, patients can usually maintain quality of life. Their energy returns within days after chemotherapy, but they typically must postpone travel and strenuous activity. Sexual activity, while encouraged, may be uncomfortable due to temporary skin sensitivity resulting from chemotherapy. Normal sexual activity often resumes about a month after the end of treatment.

CERVICAL CANCER

About 11,270 women in the United States will be diagnosed with cervical cancer in 2009 and about 4,070 of them will die unnecessarily.[1] The primary cause of this cancer is certain types of sexually transmitted human papillomavirus (HPV). There are more than 50 reported HPV subtypes, but two high-risk subtypes cause about two-thirds of cases and around 10 other high-risk subtypes cause the remaining third. Risk factors for progression to cervical cancer when HPV infection is present include smoking, being immunocompromised, high parity, and long-term use of oral contraceptives.[2]

Diagnosis

Pap smears can detect early, precancerous forms of the disease. Smears involve swabbing the cervix through a speculum placed in the vagina to get an endocervical sample and an exocervical sample for placement in the same container. The procedure is slightly uncomfortable, but most women do not feel pain.

The cells are usually placed in a liquid medium for transport to a lab where they are put on a glass slide for examination by computer and then a cytologist. Under the microscope, surface cells of the cervix may look atypical, which signals the need for continued close observation with follow-up Pap smears and/or biopsies, or for treatment. Finally, viral DNA detected by a molecular test can identify high-risk viral particles.

Treatment

Clinicians may be able to eradicate cervical precancers in the office by cauterizing or excising the lesion. If a lesion is not detected and develops into cancer, either chemo-radiation therapy or radical hysterectomy and node dissection offers the highest probability of cure. Both radiation and laparoscopic radical hysterectomy are associated with shortening of the vagina, but the latter less so, making it the treatment of choice for younger women. Women retain clitoral and vaginal sensation after therapy for cervical cancer, although libido may be low during therapy. Some may feel quite unenergetic during pelvic radiation and chemotherapy, but afterward their energy level soon returns to normal. Follow-up pelvic exams and Pap smears—every 3 months initially, then less frequently until a cure is declared at 5 years—seek to detect recurrence of cervical cancer very early so life-saving surgery can be performed.

■ ■ ■

In the scenario at the beginning of this chapter, visual inspection of Maria's cervix and normal Pap smear results would rule out cervical cancer as the cause of her bleeding episode.

ENDOMETRIAL CANCER

Endometrial cancer is the most common gynecologic cancer. In 2009, an estimated 42,160 women will be diagnosed with it and an estimated 7,780 will die.[2] However, endometrial cancer is also the most curable gynecologic malignancy because women see and usually report the earliest and most prevalent symptom: vaginal spotting. They also may report pain on urination, pain during penetrative sex, or just vague pain.

Unopposed estrogen, due either to estrogen replacement therapy without progestin or due to the effects of obesity, is the major risk factor for endometrial cancer. Estrogen alone causes the uterine lining to grow continuously, and constant overgrowth leads to thickening of the lining, bleeding, and discharge. Progestin counteracts this effect. Therefore, women who have a uterus and take estrogen also need progestin, which in some cases causes a premenstrual mood disorder that makes them not want to take the hormone combination. Like estrogen, obesity causes the uterine lining to grow continuously; an enzyme in fat cells converts inactive hormones secreted by the adrenal glands into active estrogens that enter the bloodstream.

Diagnosis

If a menopausal or perimenopausal patient reports irregular bleeding, the clinician typically biopsies her endometrium in the office. Although the soft plastic tube used for this purpose is only one-sixth of an inch in diameter, it can cause labor-like cramps that do not resolve immediately. Another approach is to measure the thickness of the uterine lining via ultrasound, which, in the few women whose lining is sufficiently thin, precludes biopsy. A third method is dilatation and curettage of the uterus under anesthesia in the operating room.

A chest x-ray and CA 125 blood test are necessary when endometrial cancer is diagnosed. An x-ray determines if the cancer has spread to the lungs. If the CA 125 results are elevated or microscopic analysis reveals a virulent subtype of uterine cancer, then a CT scan of the abdomen and pelvis is warranted to determine if or to where the cancer has metastasized.

■ ■ ■

In performing an endometrial biopsy on Maria during her visit, the nurse practitioner aspirated about a teaspoon of gray-tan granular tissue. The resulting cramps lasted about 5 minutes during and after the procedure, but Maria left the office feeling fine. She had vaginal spotting for a few more days.

Maria returned a week later with her partner for the biopsy results, which revealed she had endometrial cancer. This time she met with both the nurse practitioner and the doctor, who gave them two informative hand-outs: one about the disease and another about the surgery Maria needed. In addition, the doctor answered all of the couple's many questions about hysterectomy and removal of the ovaries and associated lymph nodes, and assured them that the probability of cure was quite high and that removal of the uterus would not impact sexual function in any way. Indeed, one of the hand-outs cited research showing that hysterectomy does not compromise sexual enjoyment, frequency of sexual activity, frequency and intensity of orgasms, and partner satisfaction.

Treatment

Patients without enlarged lymph nodes or ovaries typically undergo a total laparoscopic hysterectomy and removal of the ovaries and associated lymph nodes. Some gynecologic oncologists have not learned how to perform these minimally invasive, state-of-the-art surgical techniques, which result in less pain, less blood loss, a shorter hospital stay, and quicker return to work or usual activities. Comprehensive laparoscopic staging entails four to eight incisions in the abdominal wall, each about one-half inch long. The appearance and location of cancer in tissues and nodes indicate how virulent the cancer is and the likelihood of recurrence.

For maximum probability of cure, about 15% of women with early-stage endometrial cancer need pelvic radiation therapy after surgery. Women in advanced stages receive chemotherapy. Five-year survival rates for local, regional, and distant metastatic disease are 95%, 67%, and 23%, respectively.[1]

■ ■ ■

Maria underwent a total laparoscopic hysterectomy during which the surgeon also removed her ovaries. The endometrial cancer was superficially invasive and had not spread to the lymphatic channels or cervix. With a cure probability of 98%, Maria did not need radiation therapy. The nurse practitioner and doctor both strongly advised Maria to begin an exercise regimen and to join a program, such as Weight Watchers, that would teach her how to change her eating habits and consume fewer calories.

RISK FACTORS FOR GYNECOLOGIC CANCERS IN LESBIANS

Several factors pose a greater risk of gynecologic cancers in lesbians than heterosexual women. Smoking, which increases the risk of cervical, lung, colon, stomach, and bladder cancer, is more prevalent among lesbians, so those who smoke need to be educated about cessation techniques. High body mass index (BMI) places women at risk for ovarian and endometrial cancers. The Nurses' Health Study II and Women's Health Initiative found that lesbians have higher BMIs than heterosexual women do, although both groups exercise similarly.[7,8] Although beauty standards in popular lesbian culture do not mandate thinness, lesbians accurately perceive they are overweight and often have a health condition that limits their ability to exercise.[9]

Women who have not given birth are at significantly greater risk of endometrial and ovarian cancers. Among respondents in the Nurses' Health Study II (ages 31 to 49) and those in the Women's Health Initiative (ages 50 to 79), nulliparity rates were 51% to 76% for lesbians, 19% to 49% for bisexual women, and 8% to 22% for heterosexual women.[7,8] These data may have become outdated in recent years, as more lesbians are becoming pregnant through donor insemination.

Lesbians usually do not need birth control pills for contraception, but doctors often recommend them to control the irregular, heavy, or painful periods that are common in younger women. More lesbians should consider taking oral contraceptives, especially if they have other risk factors for ovarian and uterine cancers, because doing so over 5 to 10 years can reduce the incidence of these two diseases by 50%.[5]

PREVENTION

The Nurses' Health Study II and the Women's Health Initiative examined data for 21,000 nurses and 27,000 women, respectively, who had received hormone therapy. Data from these and other pooled national surveys, stratified by sexual orientation, showed that lesbians of all ages were more obese, had lower parity, were more likely to be smokers, and were less likely to have used oral contraceptives compared with heterosexual women, thus supporting the hypothesis that ovarian cancer may be more prevalent among lesbians.[7,8] These risk factors provide clear guidance for prevention.

Prevention of gynecologic cancers begins with an annual gynecologic exam. During these visits, the clinician should focus on modifying patients' lifestyle risks— offering advice about weight loss, smoking cessation, and appropriate hormone use—and reviewing family history to look for genetic risks. A survey of women in the Boston area found that lesbians underwent fewer annual routine exams than heterosexual women did.[10] In other studies, lesbians of all ages were significantly less likely than heterosexual women to have had an exam in the previous 2 years and less likely to be insured.[7,8,11]

Another preventive measure, for cancers of the cervix, uterus, and ovaries, is extirpative surgery. Lesbians with pelvic pain, dysmenorrhea, fibroids, pelvic masses, or a family history of breast and gynecologic cancers may elect hysterectomy and/or removal of the ovaries. Both procedures address symptoms and reduce cancer risk. Annual visits and a good clinician-patient relationship can motivate women to modify their lifestyles, reduce the risk of ovarian and uterine cancer, and save lives.

Preventing HPV infections helps prevent cervical cancer. A starting point is education about HPV transmission. Blake and colleagues found that lesbian and bisexual female youth whose schools offered gay-sensitive health instruction reported fewer sexual partners, less recent sex, and less substance use during sexual activity than did lesbian youth in other schools.[12] As early as 1993, pediatricians expressed concern that lesbian and gay youth "are severely hindered by societal stigmatization and prejudice, limited knowledge of human sexuality, a need for secrecy, a lack of opportunities for open socialization, and limited communication with healthy role models"[13] (p. 632).

To reduce the risk of HPV transmission, some lesbian health groups have advocated the use of barriers such as dental dams, gloves, the female condom, and even plastic kitchen wrap. However, no prospective studies have evaluated these barriers. HPV vaccination of females between 9 and 26 years old reduces the incidence of precancerous cervical and vaginal lesions by 95%; such lesions account for two-thirds of cervical cancer cases.[14,15] The American Academy of Pediatrics, American College of Obstetricians and Gynecologists, and American Cancer Society have endorsed HPV vaccination recommendations by the Centers for Disease Control and Prevention. Some lesbians may not benefit from the availability of this effective vaccine due to cost—about $130 for each of the three required doses. In the absence of routine medical care, they do not receive advice to get vaccinated and may be unaware that their sexual orientation is not protective. The vaccine also might protect all women older than 26 who risk contracting HPV from their partner, although there is currently no formal recommendation regarding this age group or lesbians whose partners are being treated for HPV.

FOLLOW-UP FOR GYNECOLOGIC MALIGNANCIES

Women who have undergone treatment for gynecologic cancer face new challenges. Clinicians can once again encourage them to eat properly and exercise, recommend cancer screening for other malignancies, and recommend pelvic exams every 3 months. For virtually all gynecologic malignancies, a woman's cancer is deemed cured if it has not recurred within 5 years of therapy. Most recurrences happen in the first and second years; these are generally incurable. However, chemotherapy can slow most recurrent gynecologic cancers for awhile, although resistance may develop and hospice may be necessary. For patients unlikely to survive beyond 5 years, hospice can help alleviate suffering by making them comfortable. In a survey of attitudes about end-of-life care, lesbian and gay respondents were more likely than heterosexual women to have completed advance directives, to support legalization of physician-assisted suicide, and to prefer a palliative approach to end-of-life care.[16]

CONCLUSION

Ovarian, cervical, and endometrial cancer in lesbians warrants special consideration. Treatment is the same regardless of women's sexual orientation, but lifestyle factors—a higher prevalence of smoking, obesity, and nulliparity—place lesbians at greater risk of developing malignancies. Furthermore, lesbians are less likely than heterosexual women to undergo annual gynecologic exams, which can detect cancer early and enable effective treatment. This and other preventive measures, such as prescribing oral contraceptives and educating young women and their parents about the vaccination to lower the risk of HPV transmission, will help decrease the incidence of gynecologic cancers in lesbians.

REFERENCES

1. American Cancer Society. (2009). *Cancer facts & figures 2009*. Available at www.cancer. org/downloads/STT/500809web.pdf.

2. Gynecologic Cancer Foundation. (2008). *2008 state of the state of gynecologic cancers. Sixth annual report to the women of America*. Available at www.wcn.org/downloads/ 2008_gcam_state_of_the_state.pdf.

3. Edwards, B. K., Brown, M. L., Wingo, P. A., Howe, H. L., Ward, E., Ries, L. A., et al. (2005). Annual report to the nation on the status of cancer, 1975–2002, featuring population-based trends in cancer treatment. *Journal of the National Cancer Institute, 97*, 1407–1427.

4. Dibble, S. L., Roberts, S. A., Robertson, P. A., & Paul, S. M. (2002). Risk factors for ovarian cancer: Lesbian and heterosexual women. *Oncology Nursing Forum, 29*, E1–7.

5. Collaborative Group on Epidemiological Studies of Ovarian Cancer, Beral, V., Doll, R., Hermon, C., Peto, R., & Reeves, G. (2008). Ovarian cancer and oral contraceptives: Collaborative reanalysis of data from 45 epidemiological studies including 23,257 women with ovarian cancer and 87,303 controls. *Lancet, 371*, 303–314.

6. Bhoola, S., & Hoskins, W. J. (2006). Diagnosis and management of epithelial ovarian cancer. *Obstetrics & Gynecology, 107*, 1399–1410.

7. Case, P., Austin, S. B., Hunter, D. J., Manson, J. E., Malspeis, S., Willett, W. C., et al. (2004). Sexual orientation, health risk factors, and physical functioning in the Nurses' Health Study II. *Journal of Women's Health, 13*, 1033–1047.

8. Valanis, B. G., Bowen, D. J., Bassford, T., Whitlock, E., Charney, P, & Carter, R. A. (2000). Sexual orientation and health: Comparisons in the Women's Health Initiative sample. *Archives of Family Medicine, 9*, 843–853.

9. Yancey, A. K., Cochran, S. D., Corliss, H. L., & Mays, V. M. (2003). Correlates of over-weight and obesity among lesbian and bisexual women. *Preventive Medicine, 36*, 676–683.

10. Roberts, S. J., Patsdaughter, C. A., Grindel, C. G., & Tarmina, M. S. (2004). Health-related behaviors and cancer screening of lesbians: Results of the Boston Lesbian Health Project II. *Women & Health, 39*, 41–55.

11. Cochran, S. D., Mays, V. M., Bowen, D., Gage, S., Bybee, D., Roberts, S. J., et al. (2001). Cancer-related risk indicators and preventive screening behaviors among lesbians and bisexual women. *American Journal of Public Health, 91*, 591–597.

12. Blake, S. M., Ledsky, R., Lehman, T., Goodenow, C., Sawyer, R., & Hack, T. (2001). Pre-venting sexual risk behaviors among gay, lesbian, and bisexual adolescents: The benefits of gay-sensitive HIV instruction in schools. *American Journal of Public Health, 91*, 940–946.

13. Committee on Adolescence, American Academy of Pediatrics. (1993). Homosexuality and adolescence. *Pediatrics, 92*, 631–634.

14. Garland, S. M., Hernandez-Avila, M., Wheeler, C. M., Perez, G., Harper, D. M., Leodolter, S., et al. (2007). Quadrivalent vaccine against human papillomavirus to prevent anogenital diseases. *New England Journal of Medicine, 356*, 1928–1943.

15. The FUTURE II Study Group. (2007). Quadrivalent vaccine against human papillomavirus to prevent high-grade cervical lesions. *New England Journal of Medicine, 356*, 1915–1927.

16. Stein, G. L., & Bonuck, K. A. (2001). Attitudes on end-of-life care and advance care planning in the lesbian and gay community. *Journal of Palliative Medicine, 4,* 173–190.

ABOUT THE AUTHOR

Katherine A. O'Hanlan, MD is a gynecologic oncology surgeon in private practice in Portola Valley, California. She has consulted on lesbian health issues for the National Institutes of Health, President's Cancer Panel, and Office of Research on Women's Health, and has authored numerous journal articles and book chapters. She is past president of the Gay and Lesbian Medical Association.

CHAPTER 24

"How Could I Have Colon Cancer?"

COLON AND RECTAL CANCER AMONG LESBIANS

USHA MENON, PhD, RN   LISA B. WEISSMANN, MD

JESSIE, *52, reluctantly comes in for a colonoscopy at the insistence of her friends, who argued that, given her age, she should be tested. She relented even though she is more comfortable with complementary or alternative medicine and rarely uses Western medicine. According to Jessie's family history, her mother died at 58 from colon cancer. The physical exam is unremarkable: Jessie has normal blood pressure and a body mass index of 24. The clinician orders a complete blood count and schedules a colonoscopy.*

In discussing preparations for the procedure, the clinician tells Jessie that if she is taking St. John's wort or other herbal supplements, she must stop 2 weeks before. Ten days before, she must stop taking products containing aspirin, ibuprofen, and naproxen/naproxen sodium or vitamin E. Tylenol is OK. After explaining the bowel prep and providing written instructions, the clinician informs Jesse that someone will have to take her home after the procedure and stay with her for 24 hours. Jessie says a friend, Kelly, will be with her. When the clinician asks if Kelly should also know the test results, Jessie gives permission.

■ ■ ■

Colorectal cancer (CRC), or cancer of the colon, rectum, or both, is the third leading cause of cancer deaths in the United States.[1] In 2009, there will be an estimated 54,090 new cases of colon cancer and 17,290 new cases of rectal cancer among American women.[2] The American Cancer Society estimates there are 24,680 female deaths from CRC annually.[2] Between 1992 and 2005, CRC incidence in people 20 to 49 years old increased 1.5% per year among men and 1.6% per year among women. In contrast to the overall declining incidence of the disease in the United States, rates are increasing among men and women younger than 50.[3] About 20% of CRC cases among females and males occur in those with a family history or a predisposing illness.[4]

This chapter reviews the causes, potential risk and protective factors, screening methods, treatment, and other issues related to CRC, and briefly discusses its possible impact on lesbians.

CAUSES

Complex interactions between inherited susceptibility factors and environmental factors cause CRC.[5] There is convincing evidence that adenomatous polyps (adenomas) are the precursors in most cases.[6] Most of the adenomas are flat, depressed lesions that may be more prevalent than previously thought. Large flat and depressed lesions are more likely to be severely dysplastic and may require special tests to enable identification, biopsy, and removal.[7] About 72% of CRCs begin in the colon and 28% in the rectum; the vast majority (96%) are adenocarcinomas that evolve from glandular tissue.[1] Rare types of colon and rectal cancers include stromal cell tumors, sarcomas, and melanomas.

Results from multiple studies looking at four main infectious agents as potential CRC causes have been inconclusive. These agents are *Helicobacter pylori, Streptococcus bovis,* John Cunningham virus (a type of human polyomavirus), and human papillomavirus. While there is strong evidence that they are present in the gastrointestinal tract and may be associated with CRC, the causal relationship is a much-debated topic.[8] Different methodologies and limitations, such as small sample sizes, make it difficult to compare research findings. For example, although the John Cunningham virus is present in more than 80% of all colon and rectal cancers, the correlation is not direct, as a virus can cause genetic and cytogenetic alterations in several genes. The possible relationship between infectious agents and CRC is complex and perhaps mediated or moderated by unknown factors.

Genetic mutations also cause CRC. The oncogene c-K-ras is mutated in half of colon cancers.[9] Among the important tumor suppressor genes in colon cancer are TP53 (on chromosome 17), the "deleted in colorectal carcinoma gene" (on chromosome 18), and the adenomatous polyposis coli gene (on chromosome 5).

RISK AND PROTECTIVE FACTORS

Unalterable Risk Factors

Unalterable CRC risk factors include a family history, a personal history of colorectal polyps or inflammatory bowel disease, and advancing age.[1] However, only about 5% to 10% of all people who develop CRC have an inherited genetic susceptibility to the disease.[4] For about 10% to 15% of colon cancer patients, there is a family history of colon cancer in a first-degree relative.[2] The two most common inherited syndromes linked to CRC are familial adenomatous polyposis and familial nonpolyposis colon cancer.[10] Additional risk factors are a history of ulcerative colitis or Crohn's disease.[11]

Among all racial groups in the United States, the highest incidence and mortality are among African American women and men.[2] One of the most at-risk ethnic groups in the world is Ashkenazi Jews, due to several gene mutations. The most common of these—the I1307K familial adenomatous polyposis mutation—is present in about 6% to 8% of American Jews and increases CRC risk by 1.5 to 2.0 times.[12]

Alterable Risk Factors

Researchers have found links between CRC and a number of usually modifiable lifestyle factors.[5] Six case-control studies and two cohort studies in the 1990s and in 2000 explored the potential risk of colorectal adenomas as a result of diet.[13,14] Three of the eight reported a correlation between greater risk and high fat consumption, which also is associated with a greater risk of adenoma recurrence after polypectomy.[15] However, in a multicenter, randomized, controlled trial, a diet low in fat (20% of total calories) and high in fiber, fruits, and vegetables did not reduce the risk of recurring colorectal adenomas.[16]

Recent studies have shown a more definitive relationship between CRC and diet. Red meat (beef, lamb, or liver) and processed meat (hot dogs, bologna, and luncheon meat), substantial consumption of alcohol (for example, three or more drinks per day), and higher body and abdominal fat can increase the risk, while foods containing dietary fiber, garlic, milk, and calcium are probably protective.[17] These studies were statistically powered to detect the incidence of adenomas rather than cancer, which contributed to inconsistent results. Another strong risk factor is smoking.[18] Physical activity may reduce CRC risk in postmenopausal women who are not taking hormones.[19]

SIGNS AND SYMPTOMS

Conditions other than CRC, such as infection, hemorrhoids, or inflammatory bowel disease, are more likely to cause most bowel-related symptoms. Signs and symptoms that warrant an evaluation for CRC include:

- A change in bowel habits, such as diarrhea, constipation, or narrowing of the stool, that lasts for more than a few days;
- Sensing the need for a bowel movement but not feeling relieved by having one;
- Rectal bleeding, dark stools, or blood in the stool, which often looks normal;
- Cramping or abdominal pain (in the epigastric area); and
- Weakness and fatigue.[20]

SCREENING

Screening tests can reveal whether an asymptomatic person has colorectal polyps or dysplasia that may lead to CRC. Table 24.1 lists these tests and their advantages and disadvantages. Because adenomas are precursors to most such cancers, measures that reduce the incidence and prevalence of adenomas may lower the incidence and risk of CRC.[22] An adenoma that appears on flexible sigmoidoscopy may warrant a total colonic exam (colonoscopy) to evaluate the more proximal colon for neoplasms.[21] The evolution of a carcinoma from a small adenoma takes 7 to 10 years.[23] Therefore, using one or more of the recommended tests to screen at regular intervals may be the single most important protective factor in detecting CRC early and, in some instances, preventing the disease by removing precursor lesions. A screening colonoscopy, in particular, effectively reduces the risk if it is performed early and often enough.

Some clinicians tout virtual colonoscopy—a high-resolution, computed-tomography scan of the inside of the bowels—as a viable alternative to colonoscopy, the invasive standard. But no large randomized studies have evaluated the effectiveness of virtual colonoscopy. Researchers are working on blood tests to detect early-stage CRC, which sometimes produces substances, such as carcinoembryonic antigen and carbohydrate antigen 19-9, that are released into the bloodstream. Typically, clinicians use currently available blood tests to detect these tumor markers in patients who have already undergone treatment for CRC; the tests can be fairly sensitive in the early detection of cancer that has spread systemically. However, no existing blood test is sensitive enough to detect localized disease before it metastasizes. Furthermore, existing blood tests are not suitable for screening because many other medical conditions, as well as smoking, can elevate tumor markers.

There is a strong correlation between the frequency of screening and a lower incidence of advanced CRC among people who have access to health care.[24] As a result, many public health departments are screening more underserved individuals. Given the prohibitive cost of colonoscopy, the departments rely on stool blood tests, which, while not as effective colonoscopy, are better than nothing. The fecal occult blood test (FOBT) and the fecal immunochemical test (FIT) only detect cancers, not polyps, some of which are precursors to CRC.

Colonoscopy exams for people in the general population should begin at age 50 and for African Americans at age 45.[25] The exam is indicated in patients of any age who, over a 2-week period, have an inexplicable change in bowel habits or rectal bleeding. Those whose symptoms stem from a rather benign anal condition such as hemorrhoids can easily be treated. Patients younger than 50 with first-degree relatives who were diagnosed with CRC or polyps before age 50 also should be screened. First-degree relatives of a person who had rectal bleeding by age 40 and was diagnosed with CRC should begin screening at age 30. The general rule: screening should take place 10 years before the age at which a first-degree relative was diagnosed with CRC.[26]

Insurance Coverage of Colonoscopy

Screening is an integral part of disease prevention and public health promotion. Yet, despite the known benefits of detecting CRC early, screening colonoscopy still is not a standard insurance benefit, unlike the FOBT, FIT, and flexible sigmoidoscopy. A health insurer may not pay if a routine colonoscopy yields positive findings and the exam then becomes diagnostic. A comprehensive discussion of payment issues is beyond the scope of this chapter, as insurers' policies vary.

Medicare coverage of colonoscopy illustrates the confusing aspects of patient responsibility for this important test.[27] Beneficiaries at high risk for CRC, regardless of age, can undergo a colonoscopy once every 2 years. Among the high-risk factors

TABLE 24.1. COLORECTAL SCREENING TESTS: ADVANTAGES AND DISADVANTAGES

TEST	ADVANTAGES	DISADVANTAGES
Fecal occult blood test (FOBT): guaiac test (GT)	■ No bowel cleansing necessary ■ Samples can be collected at home ■ Inexpensive compared with other CRC screening tests ■ Patient may be reluctant to collect stool in the dry state and take a sample with a wooden stick ■ Safe	■ Fails to detect most polyps and some cancers ■ False-positive results possible ■ Dietary restrictions and changes, such as avoiding meat, certain vegetables, vitamin C, iron supplements, and aspirin, and increasing fiber consumption, are often recommended for 72 hours before test ■ Should be performed annually ■ Additional procedures necessary if results indicate an abnormality
FOBT: fecal immunochemical test (FIT)	■ No bowel cleansing necessary ■ Samples can be collected at home ■ No dietary restrictions ■ Detects occult bleeding from the colon/rectum ■ Patient's acceptance of sample collection may be better than in GT—patient only needs to brush stool in the toilet with a special long-handle brush ■ Safe	■ May miss many polyps and some cancers ■ False-positive results possible ■ Should be performed annually ■ Additional procedures necessary if results indicate an abnormality
Stool DNA test	■ No bowel cleansing necessary ■ Samples can be collected at home ■ No dietary restrictions ■ Patient's acceptance of sample collection may be poor—must defecate into a collection cup ■ Safe	■ May miss many polyps and some cancers ■ False-positive results possible ■ More expensive than other stool tests ■ Unclear how often the test, which is fairly new, should be performed ■ Additional procedures necessary if results indicate an abnormality
Sigmoidoscopy	■ Compared with colonoscopy, less extensive cleansing of the colon is necessary ■ Usually quick, few complications ■ Some patients experience minimal discomfort ■ In some cases, a biopsy and removal of polyps during the test may be possible if necessary ■ Does not require a gastrointestinal specialist ■ Performed every 5 years	■ Enables doctor to view only the rectum and the lower part of the colon—cannot detect any polyps in the upper part of the colon ■ Dietary and medication restrictions often necessary before test ■ Very small risk of bleeding, infection, or tearing/perforation of the colon lining ■ May be some discomfort. Females report more discomfort than males do[20] and they are twice as likely to refuse another sigmoidoscopy.[21] ■ Additional procedures, such as a colonoscopy, may be necessary if results indicate an abnormality

(cont.)

TABLE 24.1. COLORECTAL SCREENING TESTS: ADVANTAGES AND DISADVANTAGES *(cont.)*

TEST	ADVANTAGES	DISADVANTAGES
Double contrast barium enema	■ Usually provides a view of the rectum and entire colon ■ Complications rare ■ No sedation necessary ■ Performed every 5 years	■ Thorough bowel cleansing necessary ■ May not detect some small polyps and cancers ■ False-positive results possible ■ Not possible to perform a biopsy and remove polyps during the test ■ Additional procedures necessary if results indicate an abnormality
CT colonography (virtual colonoscopy)	■ Provides a view of the rectum and entire colon ■ Noninvasive—no risk of bleeding or tearing/perforation of colon lining ■ No sedation necessary ■ Performed every 5 years	■ Thorough bowel cleansing necessary ■ May not detect all small polyps, nonpolypoid lesions, and cancers ■ False-positive results possible ■ Not possible to remove polyps during the test ■ Colonoscopy will be necessary if results are abnormal ■ Insurance may not cover cost of test, which is fairly new
Colonoscopy	■ Provides a view of the rectum and entire colon ■ Biopsy and removal of polyps or other abnormal tissue during the test may be possible if necessary ■ Can diagnose other diseases ■ Performed every 10 years	■ Thorough bowel cleansing necessary ■ May not detect all small polyps, nonpolypoid lesions, and cancers, but it is one of the most sensitive tests available ■ Some type of sedation usually necessary ■ Although uncommon, complications such as bleeding, infection, and/or tearing/perforation of the colon lining can occur ■ On a single-use basis, more expensive than other tests ■ Someone must drive patient home ■ Patient may miss a day of work

Adapted from American Cancer Society. (2008). *Can colorectal polyps and cancer be found early?*
Available at www.cancer.org/docroot/CRI/content/CRI_2_4_3X_Can_colon_and_rectum_cancer_be_found_early.asp.

are a close relative (parent, sibling, or child) who has had CRC or an adenomatous polyp, a family history of adenomatous polyposis or nonpolyposis colon cancer, and a personal history of adenomatous polyps, CRC, or inflammatory bowel disease, including ulcerative colitis and Crohn's disease. Medicare covers a colonoscopy every 10 years for beneficiaries who are not at high risk for CRC, regardless of age. In these cases, the co-insurance or copayment applies, but the Medicare Part B deductible may be waived. However, if a colonoscopy results in a biopsy or removal of a lesion or growth, Medicare considers the procedure to be diagnostic and applies the deductible. If the colonoscopy is performed in a hospital outpatient department or ambulatory surgical center, the patient pays 25% of the Medicare-approved amount.

Whether a patient has Medicare or some other type of insurance, the health care provider and patient should determine before colonoscopy if the patient's insurer will cover it. There are few standard guidelines regarding coverage of this test.

TREATMENT

Depending on the stage of CRC, treatment may include surgical resection of the primary tumor and regional lymph nodes; adjuvant chemotherapy; and/or radiation.

Surgery

Among the surgical options for CRC are surgical incision into the abdominal wall (laparotomy) and laparoscopy. Laparotomy requires 5 to 7 days of hospitalization versus 3 to 5 days after laparoscopy. However, laparoscopies take longer and a significant number of them convert to laparotomies.[28]

Compared with laparotomy, laparoscopic resection produces similar oncologic outcomes but fewer postoperative complications when an experienced surgeon performs it.[29] In most laparoscopic resections, surgeons operate through four or five small incisions, each about 1 cm long, using a laparoscope equipped with a tiny camera that relays images of the patient's internal organs to a television monitor. Sometimes the surgeon lengthens one of the incisions to 3 cm or 4 cm to complete the procedure and remove the specimen.[30] Patients who undergo laparoscopic resection can return to normal activity sooner. There is no evidence showing a difference between this procedure and laparotomy in terms of mortality or disease-free survival up to 3 years later.[28]

Robotic laparoscopic surgery can take longer, but it may reduce the length of hospitalization, blood loss, and the number of procedures that convert to laparotomy; short-term complications and outcomes are similar. This new approach could prove to be a promising way to treat more challenging pathologies, including rectal cancer.[31]

Chemotherapy and Radiation

The goal of adjuvant chemotherapy and radiation therapy after surgical resection of an early-stage colon cancer is to destroy any residual microscopic metastatic disease that increases the risk of tumor recurrence.[32] Not every patient with a CRC diagnosis needs adjuvant therapy. Such therapy is unnecessary for small, early-stage colon cancers that do not involve the adjacent lymph nodes, as the risk of metastatic disease is quite low and chemotherapy does not reduce the risk. Colon cancer patients with node involvement, and rectal cancer patients with a tumor that has grown through the bowel wall, benefit from adjuvant chemotherapy, which clearly reduces the risk of dying from advanced colon cancer.[32] A multidisciplinary assessment of the risks and benefits, along with the patient's preference, should guide the decision about whether to administer chemotherapy.

Fluoropyrimidines such as fluorouracil, which first underwent clinical trials in the 1950s, remain an integral part of most adjuvant treatment regimens for CRC. Although many drugs effectively kill advanced or metastatic colon cancer cells, not all of them are effective as adjuvant treatments. For patients with metastatic CRC, there are seven approved drugs: fluorouracil, capecitabine, irinotecan, oxaliplatin, bevacizumab, cetuximab, and panitumumab.[33] According to a meta-analysis, combination therapy leads to significantly higher tumor response rates and better survival.[34] Clinical trials found that adding oxaliplatin to a regimen of fluorouracil and leucovorin improved adjuvant CRC treatment.[35-37]

An emerging strategy for treating rectal cancer is integrating biologically active agents into chemoradiation protocols. Phase I and II clinical trials are incorporating agents such as cetuximab, which targets a specific protein on some colon cancer cells, and bevacizumab, an anti-angiogenesis protein, into preoperative chemoradiation therapy for rectal cancer.[38] Neither of these agents has yet demonstrated it improves the cure rate, but both are very interesting possibilities that could become part of standard treatment in the future.

Treatment of rectal carcinomas often is a bit different. Given the rectum's rich blood supply and contiguous organs (the bladder, vagina, and uterus), completely removing the primary cancer is frequently difficult without first shrinking it. Therefore, after a biopsy confirms the diagnosis and staging has been completed, many rectal cancer patients receive chemotherapy and radiation, then undergo surgery for tumor removal. Orchestrating this treatment process requires the coordinated care of many specialists.

A Combined Approach

Combining standard surgical intervention, directed radiation, and adjuvant or neo-adjuvant (presurgical) chemotherapy is an emerging area of research. Ideally, a coordinated, multidisciplinary team of physicians, nurses, nutritionists, and others skilled in CRC treatment provides this care, tailoring it to individual circumstances. They must balance the type, timing, and aggressiveness of intervention with the patient's goals regarding the quality and length of remaining life.

LESBIANS AND COLORECTAL CANCER

There has been little research on CRC among lesbians. According to one report, the disease may be more prevalent among lesbians than heterosexual women due to an aggregation of risk factors.[39] However, a Danish study of homosexual men and women in domestic partnerships found that the rate of all cancers and the rate of cancers in major individual organ systems among the more than 1,600 women who participated did not differ significantly from rates in the general population.[40]

Two other studies looked at CRC screening and lesbians. In one, CRC screening rates among unmarried women who partner with women and among women who partner with both women and men were not significantly different from rates among women who partner exclusively with men.[41] Whether there were differences between sexual minority groups is unknown because the researchers combined lesbians and bisexual women for statistical analysis. The other study, a pilot intervention to increase CRC screening of lesbians, comprised a 2-hour group educational intervention for 36 lesbians older than 50. In the short follow-up time (6 months), one of the 10 participants without up-to-date colon cancer screenings had a sigmoidoscopy. The other nine lesbians reported three barriers to screening: lack of money, fear of pain, and the fact that their health care provider did not arrange for a colonoscopy.[42] While these studies are a promising first step in research on lesbians and CRC, more research is necessary.

■ ■ ■

In the scenario at the beginning of this chapter, Jessie awoke from the colonoscopy with Kelly at her bedside. Kelly told Jessie that the doctor had taken some tissue biopsies and wanted to see Jessie again in 2 days. During this time, the pair wondered about the test results but were not unduly alarmed, reasoning that the doctor surely would have said something if the situation were serious.

When Jessie returned for follow-up, Kelly initially stayed in the waiting room. The news was bad: invasive colorectal cancer. Jessie asked Kelly to join them in the consultation room because she needed her partner's support and love. The doctor reviewed the biopsy results; recommended additional tests to determine if the cancer had spread to nearby lymph nodes or distant sites; explained that many people—even those with advanced colon and/or rectal cancer—are living with their disease; and said she would refer them to a surgical oncologist. One positive thing, the clinician emphasized, was that the cancer had been detected early.

Later in the week, a computed-tomography scan and blood tests revealed that Jessie's cancer had not spread beyond the colon and was potentially resectable and curable. Surgeons subsequently performed a low anterior resection of a colon lesion that had perforated the colon but not spread to any lymph nodes, making it a stage 2 cancer. Jessie did not need adjuvant therapy, thanks to early detection, and she has an excellent chance of cure. She was still free of disease three years later. Jessie became a staunch advocate of CRC screening and, at every opportunity, pestered family members and friends to get tested.

CONCLUSION

Colorectal cancer is a major cause of cancer death among women in the United States. There are promising trends in early detection and more CRC patients are surviving the disease, but the number of women who get screened is still suboptimal. Further research is necessary to determine if lesbians face a disproportionately higher CRC risk. Future studies may confirm that better nutrition, more exercise, weight loss, and smoking cessation reduce the risk. Meanwhile, clinicians can share this preliminary evidence with patients by way of encouraging them to take preventive steps. Biotechnological advances can improve treatment, outcomes, and survival. Essential ingredients in follow-up care for CRC patients are an interdisciplinary health care team and the support of family and friends.

REFERENCES

1. American Cancer Society. (2008). *Colorectal cancer facts & figures 2008–2010*. Available at www.cancer.org/downloads/STT/F861708_finalforweb.pdf.

2. American Cancer Society. (2009). *Cancer facts & figures 2009*. Available at www.cancer.org/downloads/STT/500809web.pdf.

3. Siegel, R. L., Jemal, A., & Ward, E. M. (2009). Increase in incidence of colorectal cancer among young men and women in the United States. *Cancer Epidemiology, Biomarkers & Prevention, 18,* 1695–1698.

4. Lynch, H. T., & de la Chapelle, A. (2003). Hereditary colorectal cancer. *New England Journal of Medicine, 348,* 919–932. Available at content.nejm.org/cgi/content/full/348/10/919.

5. National Cancer Institute. (2009). *Colorectal cancer prevention*. Available at www.cancer.gov/cancertopics/pdq/prevention/colorectal/HealthProfessional/page4.

6. Winawer, S. J., Fletcher, R. H., Miller, L., Godlee, F., Stolar, M. H., Mulrow, C. D., et al. (1997). Colorectal cancer screening: Clinical guidelines and rationale. *Gastroenterology, 112,* 594–642.

7. Rembacken, B. J., Fujii, T., Cairns, A., Dixon, M. F., Yoshida, S., Chalmers, D. M., et al. (2000). Flat and depressed colonic neoplasms: A prospective study of 1,000 colonoscopies in the UK. *Lancet, 355,* 1211–1214.

8. Burnett-Hartman, A. N., Newcomb, P. A., & Potter, J. D. (2008). Infectious agents and colorectal cancer: A review of *Helicobacter pylori, Streptococcus bovis,* JC virus, and human papillomavirus. *Cancer Epidemiology, Biomarkers & Prevention, 17,* 2970–2979.

9. Allegra, C. J., Jessup, J. M., Somerfield, M. R., Hamilton, S. R., Hammond, E. H., Hayes, D. F., et al. (2000). American Society of Clinical Oncology provisional clinical opinion: Testing for KRAS gene mutations in patients with metastatic colorectal carcinoma to predict response to anti-epidermal growth factor receptor monoclonal antibody therapy. *Journal of Clinical Oncology, 27,* 2091–2096.

10. Strate, L. L., & Syngal, S. (2005). Hereditary colorectal cancer syndromes. *Cancer Causes & Control, 16,* 201–213.

11. Gillen, C. D., Walmsley, R. S., Prior, P., Andrews, H. A., & Allan, R. N. (1994). Ulcerative colitis and Crohn's disease: A comparison of the colorectal cancer risk in extensive colitis. *Gut, 35,* 1590–1592.

12. Locker, G. Y., & Lynch, H. T. (2004). Genetic factors and colorectal cancer in Ashkenazi Jews. *Familial Cancer, 3,* 215–221.

13. Neugut, A. I., Jacobson, J. S., & DeVivo, I. (1993). Epidemiology of colorectal adenomatous polyps. *Cancer Epidemiology, Biomarkers & Prevention, 2,* 159–176.

14. Kampman, E., Giovannucci, E., Van 't Veer, P., Rimm, E., Stampfer, M. J., Colditz, G. A., et al. (1994). Calcium, vitamin D, dairy foods, and the occurrence of colorectal adenomas among men and women in two prospective studies. *American Journal of Epidemiology, 139,* 16–29.

15. Neugut, A. I., Garbowski, G. C., Lee, W. C., Murray, T., Nieves, J. W., Forde, K. A., et al. (1993). Dietary risk factors for the incidence and recurrence of colorectal adenomatous polyps: A case–control study. *Annals of Internal Medicine, 118,* 91–95.

16. Schatzkin, A., Lanza, E., Corle, D., Lance, P., Iber, F., Caan, B., et al. (2000). Lack of effect of a low-fat, high-fiber diet on the recurrence of colorectal adenomas. Polyp Prevention Trial Study Group. *New England Journal of Medicine, 342,* 1149–1155.

17. Nyström, M., & Mutanen, M. (2009). Diet and epigenetics in colon cancer. *World Journal of Gastroenterology, 15,* 257–263.

18. Omata, F., Brown, W. R., Tokuda, Y., Takahashi, O., Fukui, T., Ueno, F., et al. (2009). Modifiable risk factors for colorectal neoplasms and hyperplastic polyps. *Internal Medicine, 48,* 123–128.

19. Mai, P. L., Sullivan-Halley, J., Ursin, G., Stram, D. O., Deapen, D., Villaluna, D., et al. (2007). Physical activity and colon cancer risk among women in the California Teachers Study. *Cancer Epidemiology, Biomarkers & Prevention, 16,* 517–525.

20. American Cancer Society. (2009). *How is colorectal cancer diagnosed?* Available at www.cancer.org/docroot/CRI/content/CRI_2_4_3X_How_is_colon_and_rectum_cancer_diagnosed.asp?rnav=cri.

21. Read, T. E., Read, J. D., & Butterly, L. F. (1997). Importance of adenomas 5 mm or less in diameter that are detected by sigmoidoscopy. *New England Journal of Medicine, 336,* 8–12.

22. Winawer, S. J., Zauber, A. G., Ho, M. N., O'Brien, M. J., Gottlieb, L. S., Sternberg, S. S., et al. (1993). Prevention of colorectal cancer by colonoscopic polypectomy. The National Polyp Study Workgroup. *New England Journal of Medicine, 329,* 1977–1981.

23. Potter, J. D. (1992). Reconciling the epidemiology, physiology, and molecular biology of colon cancer. *Journal of the American Medical Association, 268,* 1573–1577.

24. Hewitson, P., Glasziou, P., Irwig, L., Towler, B., & Watson, E. (2007). Screening for colorectal cancer using the faecal occult blood test, Hemoccult. *Cochrane Database of Systematic Reviews,* CD001216.

25. Shavers, V. L. (2007). Racial/ethnic variation in the anatomic subsite location of in situ and invasive cancers of the colon. *Journal of the National Medical Association, 99,* 733–748.

26. Levin, B., Lieberman, D. A., McFarland, B., Andrews, K. S., Brooks, D., Bond, J., et al. (2008). Screening and surveillance for the early detection of colorectal cancer and adenomatous polyps, 2008: A joint guideline from the American Cancer Society, the U.S. Multi-Society Task Force on Colorectal Cancer, and the American College of Radiology. *Gastroenterology, 134,* 1570–1595.

27. Medicare, U.S. Department of Health & Human Services. (2009). *Colorectal cancer screening—colonoscopy.* Available at www.medicare.gov/coverage/Search/Results.asp?Stat e=CA|California&Coverage=12|Colorectal+Cancer+Screening+-+Colonoscopy&submitSta te=View+Results+%3E.

28. Murray, A., Lourenco, T., de Verteuil, R., Hernandez, R., Fraser, C., McKinley, A., et al. (2006). Clinical effectiveness and cost-effectiveness of laparoscopic surgery for colorectal cancer: Systematic reviews and economic evaluation. *Health Technology Assessment, 10,* 1–141, iii–iv.

29. Van Cutsem, E., Oliveira, J., & ESMO Guidelines Working Group. (2009). Primary colon cancer: ESMO clinical recommendations for diagnosis, adjuvant treatment and follow-up. *Annals of Oncology, 20*(Suppl. 4), 49–50.

30. Society of American Gastrointestinal and Endoscopic Surgeons. (2004). *Patient information for laparoscopic colon resection from SAGES.* Available at www.sages.org/publications/publication.php?id=PI09.

31. Mirnezami, A. H., Mirnezami, R., Venkatasubramaniam, A. K., Chandrakumaran, K., Cecil, T. D., & Moran, B. J. (2009). Robotic colorectal surgery: Hype or new hope? A systematic review of robotics in colorectal surgery. *Colorectal Disease, Jul 6* [Epub ahead of print].

32. Chung, K. Y., & Saltz, L. B. (2007). Adjuvant therapy of colon cancer: Current status and future directions. *Cancer Journal, 13,* 192–197.

33. National Cancer Institute. (2009). *Stage IV and recurrent colon cancer.* Available at www.cancer.gov/cancertopics/pdq/treatment/colon/HealthProfessional/page10.

34. Buyse, M., Thirion, P., Carlson, R. W., Burzykowski, T., Molenberghs, G., & Piedbois, P. (2000). Relation between tumour response to first-line chemotherapy and survival in advanced colorectal cancer: A meta-analysis. Meta-Analysis Group in Cancer. *Lancet, 356,* 373–378.

35. Saltz, L. B., Cox, J. V., Blanke, C., Rosen, L. S., Fehrenbacher, L., Moore, M. J., et al. (2000). Irinotecan plus fluorouracil and leucovorin for metastatic colorectal cancer. Irinotecan Study Group. *New England Journal of Medicine, 343,* 905–914.

36. De Gramont, A., Figer, A., Seymour, M., Homerin, M., Hmissi, A., Cassidy, J., et al. (2000). Leucovorin and fluorouracil with or without oxaliplatin as first-line treatment in advanced colorectal cancer. *Journal of Clinical Oncology, 18,* 2938–2947.

37. Douillard, J. Y., Cunningham, D., Roth, A. D., Navarro, M., James, R. D., Karasek, P., et al. (2000). Irinotecan combined with fluorouracil compared with fluorouracil alone as first-line treatment for metastatic colorectal cancer: A multicentre randomised trial. *Lancet, 355,* 1041–1047.

38. Marquardt, F., Rödel, F., Capalbo, G., Weiss, C., & Rödel, C. (2009). Molecular targeted treatment and radiation therapy for rectal cancer. *Strahlentherapie und Onkologie, 185,* 371–378.

39. Brown, J. P., & Tracy, J. K. (2008). Lesbians and cancer: An overlooked health disparity. *Cancer Causes & Control, 19,* 1009–1020.

40. Frisch, M., Smith, E., Grulich, A., & Johansen, C. (2003). Cancer in a population-based cohort of men and women in registered homosexual partnerships. *American Journal of Epidemiology, 157,* 966–972.

41. Clark, M. A., Rogers, M. L., Armstrong, G. F., Rakowski, W., Bowen, D. J., Hughes, T., et al. (2009). Comprehensive cancer screening among unmarried women aged 40–75 years: Results from the Cancer Screening Project for Women. *Journal of Women's Health, 18,* 451–459.

42. Dibble, S. L., & Roberts, S. A. (2003). Improving cancer screening among lesbians over 50: Results of a pilot study. *Oncology Nursing Forum, 30,* E71–79.

ABOUT THE AUTHORS

Usha Menon, PhD, RN is the Pamela Kidd Distinguished Research Professor in the College of Nursing & Health Innovation at Arizona State University, Phoenix. Her program of research focuses on the reduction of disparity in cancer mortality among underserved and minority populations, including the LGBT community, by developing tailored interventions to increase breast and colorectal cancer screening.

Lisa B. Weissmann, MD is in private practice specializing in Hematology/Oncology in Cambridge, Massachusetts. She is also Assistant Professor of Medicine at Harvard Medical School. She is former president of the Lesbian Health Fund and continues on its Advisory Board. In addition, she is on the professional Advisory Board of BreastCancer.org.

CHAPTER 25

"But I Don't Want Antibiotics."
LESBIANS AND INFECTIOUS DISEASES

DONNA DEFREITAS, MD, MPH   NYONNOWEH GREENE, MD

LOUISE *is a 38-year-old lesbian and store owner in Northern California. In the last 6 months, she has been hospitalized several times for abscesses on her body. Methicillin-resistant* Staphylococcus aureus *grew from cultures of some of the abscesses. For the most recent abscess, in her right axilla, Louise went to a local emergency room with her girlfriend, where the doctor drained and cultured it, and gave her doxycycline. She is frustrated because she has tried unsuccessfully to prevent and get rid of the infections using over-the-counter soaps. Louise recently began taking 1 teaspoon of turmeric powder in half a* *glass of water three times a day as a treatment. Her girlfriend is turned off by the abscesses and the two have stopped being intimate. What should Louise's clinician recommend?*

■ ■ ■

Lesbian health intersects mainstream care for infectious diseases in many ways. Acute infections often drive lesbians to seek help in the health care system.[1] Because risk factors such as tobacco use,[2] poor access to health care,[3] obesity,[4] and depression[5] are more common among lesbians than heterosexual women, the impact on lesbians of a wide range of infectious disease issues may be greater. The allopathic medical model does not address all of lesbians' health care needs; many lesbians also use complementary medicine.[6,7]

This chapter focuses on common types of infections, pathogens, and disease states relevant to lesbian health.

BACKGROUND

Infectious disease medicine involves a large variety of pathogens that impact every organ system. Many people have suffered a sinus infection, acne flair, or infected boils at some point in their lives. Common pathogens include *Staphylococcus aureus*, *Streptococcus pneumoniae*, and *Escherichia coli*. Especially worrisome are bacteria such as methicillin-resistant *S. aureus* and vancomycin-resistant *Enterococcus*. Chronic fatigue syndrome and Lyme disease are among illnesses that have spurred greater interest in infectious diseases. To date, very few studies have looked at the impact on lesbians of various infectious complications unrelated to sexual activity.

BACTERIAL INFECTIONS

Staphylococcus aureus

S. aureus lives in the anterior nares and usually spreads to the skin by casual contact with the nose. These bacteria are responsible for illnesses as diverse as pimples, inflammation of hair follicles (folliculitis), heart valve infection (endocarditis), life-threatening bloodstream infection (septicemia), and toxic shock syndrome. Diseases stemming from *S. aureus* are some of the most common and morbid conditions that infectious disease specialists encounter.

Many lesbians who participate in sports or outdoor activities may develop local infections from *S. aureus*, which typically affect the skin and soft tissue. The infections often present with tenderness and an abscess over the infected body part, redness, swelling, and fever. Aggressive treatment normally consists of draining the abscess and administering oral or intravenous antibiotics.

S. aureus has a long history of becoming resistant to antibiotics. Penicillin-resistant *S. aureus* was a widely recognized phenomenon in the early 1950s. By the 1960s, 80% of *S. aureus* isolates were resistant to penicillin.[8] This led to the development of antistaphylococcal penicillins such as oxacillin and nafcillin in the United States and of methicillin in Europe.

Methicillin-Resistant *S. aureus*

The first cases of methicillin-resistant *S. aureus* (MRSA) were reported in England in 1961. MRSA infections were occurring quite frequently among the sickest patients in hospital intensive care units in the United States as of 1985,[9] and by the mid-1990s, hospital patients outside ICUs were presenting with such infections. Community-associated MRSA (CA-MRSA) began to draw national and international interest in the early 2000s.[10,11] Its clinical, epidemiologic, and bacteriologic characteristics are distinct from those in health care-associated MRSA (HA-MRSA) (Table 25.1), one

TABLE 25.1. EPIDEMIOLOGICAL CLASSIFICATIONS OF INVASIVE METHICILLIN-RESISTANT *STAPHYLOCOCCUS AUREUS* (MRSA) INFECTIONS

CLASSIFICATION	SUBCLASSIFICATION	DEFINITION
Health care-associated/acquired MRSA (HA-MRSA)	Hospital onset	Cases with a positive culture result from a normally sterile site obtained > 48 hours after hospital admission. These patients may also have one or more community-onset risk factors.
	Community onset	Cases with a least one of the following health-care risk factors: (1) Presence of an invasive medical device at the time of admission; (2) History of MRSA infection or colonization; (3) History of surgery, hospitalization, dialysis, or residence in a long-term care facility in the 12 months preceding the culture date.
Community-associated/acquired MRSA (CA-MRSA)	None	Cases without any documented community-onset, health-care risk factors

Source: Klevens, R. M., Morrison, M. A., Nadle, J., Petit, S., Gershman, K., Ray, S., et al. (2007). Invasive methicillin-resistant *Staphylococcus aureus* infections in the United States. *Journal of the American Medical Association, 298,* 1763–1771.

of the most common causes of nosocomial infections, especially invasive bacterial infections. HA-MRSA is now endemic and even epidemic at many U.S. hospitals and long-term care facilities, and in many communities.[12]

Most CA-MRSA infections affect skin and soft tissues—typically in the face, groin, and axillary regions secondary to direct inoculation—in people who do not have risk factors. From July 2004 to December 2005, nearly 9,000 observed cases of invasive MRSA were reported. Most of these (85%) were health care-associated infections: 58.4% were community-onset; 26.6% were hospital-onset; 13.7% were community-associated; and 1.3% could not be classified.[13] In the United States, the most common strain of health care-associated MRSA is USA 100 and the most common community-associated MRSA is USA 300.[14]

Scientists have vigorously evaluated MRSA strains and learned about their epidemiology by using pulsed-field gel electrophoresis, which helps categorize the strains. In addition, researchers have focused in recent years on what seems to make MRSA more severe. Genetic testing reveals that MRSA can carry virulence factors such as Panton-Valentine leukocidin, improved cell-wall adherence, exfoliative toxin A, and exfoliative toxin B.[15] Although these factors are not exclusively associated with or in all MRSA strains, they have played a key role in the growing severity of MRSA-related abscesses and pneumonia.

■ ■ ■

Here is what the clinician might tell Louise and her girlfriend, the couple in the scenario at the beginning of this chapter: "I think your MRSA is back, but I will order a culture to make sure. I understand that this has been a persistent problem for both of you. Let's see if together we can stop this infection and prevent its return. After we take care of the abscess, I want you to see an infectious disease specialist to talk about what you must do on an ongoing basis to prevent the infection from returning, given that you have had it so often in such a short time." In addition, the clinician should instruct them to follow the guidelines on the next page.

Vancomycin-Resistant *S. aureus* and *Enterococcus*

The first case of vancomycin-resistant *S. aureus* (VRSA) was reported in Japan in 1996.[17] Unlike MRSA, nearly all infections related to VRSA and vancomycin-resistant *Enterococcus* (VRE) occur among inpatients, causing mostly nosocomial colonization.[18] VRE refers to infection by either *Enterococcus faecalis*, which is more common and less resistant, or *Enterococcus faecium*, which is less common and more resistant. Researchers have long known that VRE causes bacteremia, line infections, and patient/health provider colonization.[19–21] Because *Enterococcus* is a common colonizer in the gastrointestinal tract, VRE usually occurs when *Enterococcus* acquires a gene

MRSA GUIDELINES FOR LOUISE

General care:

- Take all the antibiotics and continue taking the turmeric, as some anecdotal and scientific evidence suggests it may help prevent further MRSA outbreaks.

- Wash your hands often with warm water and soap, or use an alcohol-based hand sanitizer.

- Refrain from skin-to-skin contact, such as athletic activities or sex, until the wound has healed.

- Use a 1:100 solution of diluted bleach (1 tablespoon bleach in 1 quart of water) to clean all surfaces at home and work that might have come into contact with bandages or wound drainage.

- Do not share exercise or athletic equipment that touches the skin and thus may become contaminated with wound drainage.

- Visit your health care provider in 48 hours for an evaluation of the therapy in light of culture results that will be available then. Ask the provider for a referral to an infectious disease specialist who can further help you with this condition.

Wound care:

- Wash your hands with warm water and soap, or use an alcohol-based hand sanitizer, before and after each dressing change or any contact with wound drainage or bandages.

- Use gloves when changing dressings. The gloves need not be sterile; those available at stores are fine.

- Keep the wound area bandaged and change the bandage three times a day.

- Read the directions for dressing changes. Enlist friends to help with the dressing changes if your partner does not feel comfortable helping.

- Put all used bandages in a plastic bag. Close and secure the bag, then place it in the trash.

Bathroom:

- Do not share washcloths or towels.

- Do not share deodorant or razors, given the infection's axillary location, and get new deodorant bars and razors.

- Do not use deodorant on or shave your right axilla until the infection has totally healed.

- Take daily showers, not baths, and use antibacterial soap.

- Do not share bar soap.

Laundry:

- All clothing, towels, and linens that come into contact with the wound should be handled separately from those of other household members, and should be put in a separate hamper.

- Launder clothing that has come into contact with wound drainage after each use and dry it thoroughly.

- Do not share clothing.

- Wash sheets, towels, and clothes frequently with hot water and laundry detergent. Use a dryer to thoroughly dry them.

Source: Adapted from County of Orange Health Care Agency. (2009). *What is MRSA? Fact sheet for patients.* Available at www.ochealthinfo.com/docs/public/epi/mrsa/MRSA-FactSheet.pdf.

that confers resistance to vancomycin. Plasmids known as "van a" and "van b" carry the genes. There is also a "van d," a term that refers to an inherently vancomycin-resistant organism. Some species of *Enterococcus*, such as *E. gallinarum*, are inherently resistant to vancomycin.

DIARRHEAL ILLNESSES

Diarrheal illnesses can be devastating. Most such illnesses are viral and occur after ingestion of microbes or their toxins, although there are many noninfectious causes.

Norovirus

In lesbian patients who just returned from an Olivia cruise and have a diarrheal illness, the most likely agent is the norovirus. The average incubation period for norovirus-associated gastroenteritis is 12 to 48 hours, with a median of about 33 hours. Most women experience acute-onset vomiting; watery, bloodless diarrhea with abdominal cramps; nausea; and myalgia, malaise, and headache. About half may have a low-grade fever. Dehydration, the most common complication, may require intravenous fluids for correction. Symptoms usually last 24 to 60 hours, although studies suggest that up to 30% of infections may be asymptomatic.[22] The highly contagious norovirus is transmitted primarily through the fecal-oral route by direct person-to-person contact, fecally contaminated food, or emesis droplets.[22]

Rotavirus

The rotavirus is the most likely to blame for diarrheal illness in lesbians who have young children at home. It is the most common cause of severe diarrhea in children.[23] The primary mode of transmission is the fecal-oral route, and the incubation period lasts about 2 days.[23] The rotavirus causes watery diarrhea for 3 to 8 days as well as nausea and fever. Two vaccines are quite effective in limiting or preventing rotavirus-related diarrhea in children.[24]

Bacterial Enteropathogens

The four most commonly reported bacterial enteropathogens in the United States are *Campylobacter*, nontyphoid *Salmonella*, Shiga toxin-producing *E. coli*, and *Shigella*.[25] A discussion of other bacteria that cause diarrhea is beyond the scope of this chapter.

Campylobacter

Campylobacter infection produces acute watery diarrhea, often with fever or dysenteric characteristics, and lasts about a week.[26] Eighty percent of campylobacteriosis cases are associated with eating raw or undercooked poultry or its cross-contamination of other foods.[25,26] Animals can also become infected; some people have acquired their infection from contact with the stool of an ill dog or cat.[26]

Nearly everyone with a *Campylobacter* infection recovers without any specific treatment. Patients should drink extra fluids for as long as the diarrhea lasts.[26] The recommended treatment for adults is 500 mg of azithromycin once daily for 3 days or

500 mg of erythromycin four times daily for 3 days.[25] As with many other infectious diarrheas, *Campylobacter* can be associated with reactive arthritis and postinfectious irritable bowel syndrome.[25] Guillain-Barré syndrome has been associated with Campylobacter jejuni.[27]

Salmonella

Salmonella infections cause abdominal cramps (often with fever) and acute watery diarrhea (occasionally with dysenteric characteristics) about 12 to 72 hours after infection.[25] Ninety-five percent of cases are a result of transmission from contaminated foods such as poultry, peanut butter, and possibly pistachios.[25] The bacteria may also be in the feces of some pets; people can become infected if they do not wash their hands after contact with pets or pet feces. Reptiles such as turtles, lizards, and snakes are particularly likely to harbor *Salmonella*.[28] The illness usually lasts 4 to 7 days and most people recover without treatment.[28]

Appropriate antimicrobial treatment, if necessary, is 500 mg of levofloxacin or another fluoroquinolone once daily for 7 days.[25] Bacteremia complicates the infection in about 8% of normal, healthy persons, and at a higher rate in the very young, the very old, and individuals whose immune system is compromised.[25] Persons in these categories will need more supportive treatment, such as medications for a longer time and perhaps hospitalization and intravenous fluids.

Shiga Toxin-Producing *E. coli*

Shiga toxin-producing *E. coli* (STEC) is a major cause of cramps and watery diarrhea that progresses to bloody diarrhea (hemorrhagic colitis) in 1 to 5 days.[25] The *E. coli* O157:H7 strain of bacteria causes most reported STEC infections in the United States.[29] It is acquired from food (contaminated ground beef or produce in 52% of cases), person-to-person contact (14%), contaminated water and wading pools (9%), contact with animals (3%), and other unknown sources (21%).[25] Gastrointestinal illnesses from *E. coli* O157:H7 infection are among the most feared, given how easily the bacteria can contaminate food and the severe complications they can cause. About 8% of people with a diagnosis of O157:H7 STEC infection develop hemolytic uremic syndrome, a life-threatening condition characterized by thrombocytopenia, hemolytic anemia, and renal failure.[29] Prompt and accurate diagnosis of STEC is important because treatment with parenteral volume expansion early in the course of infection may reduce renal damage and improve outcomes.[29] Management of patients with a STEC infection can be challenging: conventional antibiotic therapy is contraindicated, as it is believed to increase the risk of complications by promoting the release of Shiga toxin in the gut.[29] Finally, treatment of such an infection should not include antimotility drugs, which can increase the length of contact between the enteropathogen and gut mucosa.[25]

Shigella

A *Shigella* infection can result in severe diarrhea (often bloody), fever, and stomach cramps starting 1 or 2 days after exposure to the bacteria.[25] Such an infection has a high risk of person-to-person spread, via the fecal-oral route, due to the low inoculum necessary. Shigellosis usually resolves in 5 to 7 days without antibiotics; however, appropriate antibiotic therapy kills *Shigella* bacteria and may shorten the illness by a few days.[30] Antibiotic treatment is 750 mg of ciprofloxacin once daily for 3 days or 500 mg of azithromycin once daily for 3 days.[25] Infected persons usually recover completely, although their bowel habits may not return to normal for several months.[30] About 2% of persons infected with *Shigella flexneri* develop postinfection arthritis that can last months or years.[30]

HEPATITIS

Hepatitis is inflammation of the liver; the term also refers to a group of viral infections that affect the liver.[31] The most common types of viral hepatitis in the United States are A, B, and C[32] (Table 25.2). All types can have similar symptoms: fever, fatigue, loss of appetite, nausea, vomiting, abdominal pain, clay-colored stool, joint pain, and jaundice.[33] There are no studies to date suggesting that infection rates, diagnosis, or treatment vary between lesbians and heterosexual women. Patients diagnosed with hepatitis should stop consuming alcohol and be aware that medications processed by the liver are possibly toxic or not effective and may need to be adjusted.

INFLUENZA

Influenza is a contagious respiratory illness caused by viruses. No studies have suggested that lesbians might be more susceptible to the flu than heterosexual women. Three types of viruses—A, B, and C—cause most seasonal flu, a mild to severe illness that may result in death. Each year, on average, 5% to 20% of the U.S. population contracts the flu, more than 200,000 people are hospitalized with related complications, and about 36,000 die from flu-related causes. The very old and very young, as well as people with certain chronic illnesses, are at high risk for serious flu complications.[34]

Type A and B viruses cause seasonal flu epidemics almost every winter in the United States. Type C infections, a mild respiratory illness, are not believed to cause epidemics. The two subtypes of type A viruses, based on two proteins on their surface, are hemagglutinin, a substance that enables ribonucleic acid in the virus to bind to cells, and neuraminidase, an enzyme that enables the virus to cleave from infected cells. There are 16 hemagglutinin (H) and nine neuraminidase (N) subtypes. Current

TABLE 25.2. MAJOR TYPES OF HEPATITIS (UNITED STATES)

	HEPATITIS A (HAV)	HEPATITIS B (HBV)	HEPATITIS C (HCV)
Number of infections (2007)	New: 25,000	New: 43,000 Chronic: 800,000–1.4 million	New: 17,000 Chronic: 2.7–3.9 million
Percent of people ever infected	29.1–33.5%	4.3–5.6%	1.3–1.9%
Transmission routes	Fecal-oral: contact with contaminated food, water, stool (e.g. diapers, anal/oral sex)	Contact with infectious blood, semen, and other body fluids via needlestick, injection drug use, sexual contact	Contact with infectious blood via needlestick, injection drug use, sexual contact
Average incubation period (days)	28 (15–50)	120 (45–160)	45 (14–180)
Diagnostic tests	Immunoglobulin M antibody	HBV surface antigen	▪ HCV antibody ▪ HCV recombinant immunoblot assay ▪ Nucleic acid test for HCV RNA
Acute treatment	Supportive care: ~ 2 months	Supportive care: several weeks to 6 months	Supportive care and antiretroviral drugs
Chronic treatment	N.A.	Careful monitoring and, for some patients, antiviral drugs: interferon, lamivudine, entecavir, adefovir, tenofovir, and emtricitabine to control replication of virus	Careful monitoring and, for some patients, antiviral drugs: pegylated interferon with ribavirin
Fatality rates	Rarely fatal	▪ 3,000/year ▪ 1% of people with continuing chronic HBV develop liver cancer	12,000/year
Vaccine	Yes	Yes	No

Sources:

(1) Centers for Disease Control and Prevention. (n.d.). *The ABCs of hepatitis.* Available at www.cdc.gov/HEPATITIS/Resources/ Professionals/PDFs/ABCTable_BW.pdf;

(2) Strader, D. B., Wright, T., Thomas, D. L., & Seeff, L. B. (2004). Diagnosis, management, and treatment of hepatitis C. *Hepatology, 39,* 1147–1171. Available at www.aasld.org/practiceguidelines/Practice%20Guideline%20Archive/ Diagnosis,%20Management%20and%20Treatment%20of%20Hepatitis%20C.pdf;

(3) Sherman, M., Shafran, S., Burak, K., Doucette, K., Wong, W., Girgrah, N., et al. (2007). Management of chronic hepatitis C: Consensus guidelines. Canadian *Journal of Gastroenterology, 21* (Suppl. C), 25C–34C;

(4) Lai, C. L., & Yuen, M. F. (2007). The natural history and treatment of chronic hepatitis B: A critical evaluation of standard treatment criteria and end points. *Annals of Internal Medicine, 147,* 58–61.

subtypes of type A viruses include H1N1 and H3N2. Type B viruses do not have subtypes, but there are different strains.[34]

Flu viruses spread from person to person mainly through large respiratory droplets, such as those from an infected person who coughs or sneezes. Contact with infected respiratory droplets on surfaces is another mode of transmission. One possible contamination source is evaporated droplets containing small particles of residue ($\leq$ 5 μm); these droplets may be suspended in the air for long periods of time. However, data supporting this kind of transmission are limited.[35] The typical incubation period for the flu is 1 to 4 days (2 days, on average); adults shed the virus anytime between the day before symptoms begin until 5 to 10 days after illness begins.[35] (See the accompanying box for flu prevention tactics.)

FLU PREVENTION TACTICS

- Cover your nose and mouth when coughing or sneezing. Dispose of the tissue. If a tissue is unavailable, cough or sneeze into your elbow.

- Wash your hands with soap and water before eating, after using the bathroom, and especially after coughing or sneezing. Alcohol-based hand sanitizers are also effective.

- Avoid touching your eyes, nose, or mouth. The flu can spread via such contact.

- Avoid close contact with sick persons, such as an ill infant. If such contact is unavoidable, wear a face mask.

- Get a flu vaccination.

- If you are sick, stay home until at least 24 hours after a fever has stopped (< 100° F/37.8° C) or signs of a fever have disappeared without the use of fever-reducing medicine.

- Heed the advice of public health authorities regarding school closures, avoidance of crowds, and other social-distancing measures.

Source: U.S. Department of Health & Human Services. (n.d.). *Prevention & treatment.* Available at www.flu.gov/individualfamily/prevention/index.html.

Most patients present with a moderately disabling but treatable upper respiratory tract infection—a cough, nasal congestion, and fever. Many also present with nausea and vomiting[36,37] and, due to the large cytokine cascade, complain of myalgia, arthralgia, and headaches. Typically, experienced practitioners can make the diagnosis based on such symptoms, but viral cultures, bronchoscopy, or rapid detection methodologies may help. Patients usually respond well to hydration, rest, and acetaminophen as needed; for most of them, the flu resolves after 3 to 7 days, although a cough and malaise can persist for more than 2 weeks.*

In spring 2009, a novel influenza H1N1 type A virus, sometimes called "swine flu," emerged and caused a pandemic.[38] The usual type A and type B viruses are included in the seasonal flu vaccine each year, which offers protection against these and related viruses. However, it does not protect against type C viruses. Although seasonal flu vaccines usually protect against type A viruses, they do not protect against the 2009 H1N1; a separate vaccination was required for the 2009 flu season. Table 25.3 lists medications for preventing and treating influenza.†

TABLE 25.3. INFLUENZA MEDICATIONS

NAME	USE
Oseltamivir phosphate (Tamiflu)	All influenza types: prevention and treatment for people ≥ 1 year old
Zanamivir (Relenza)	All influenza types: prevention for people ≥ 5 years old, treatment for those ≥ 7 years old
Amantadine hydrochloride (Symmetrel and generic)	Prevention and treatment of influenza A for people ≥ 1 year old
Rimantadine hydrochloride (Flumadine and generic)	Prevention of influenza A for people ≥ 1 year old, treatment for those ≥ 13 years old

Source: Centers for Disease Control and Prevention. (2009). *Updated interim recommendations for the use of antiviral medications in the treatment and prevention of influenza for the 2009–2010 season.* Available at www.cdc.gov/h1n1flu/recommendations.htm.

URINARY TRACT INFECTIONS

A urinary tract infection (UTI) is defined by the presence of bacteria in the urine. The usual threshold for treatment is ≥ 100,000 bacterial colony-forming units per milliliter.[38,39] Women with symptomatic UTIs may have urgency, frequency, dysuria, cloudy urine, lower back pain, fever, hematuria, and pyuria.[38]

---

* *Updated information on preventing, diagnosing, and treating the various types of flu viruses is available at www.cdc.gov/flu and www.flu.gov.*

† *The latest recommendations for antiviral medications are available at www.cdc.gov/h1n1flu/recommendations.htm.*

The two UTI classifications are lower-tract infections, such as cystitis and urethritis, and kidney infections, or pyelonephritis, which warrants consideration in women who present with fever, dehydration secondary to nausea, and flank pain. Depending on the length of illness, signs of pyelonephritis may also include white blood cells (WBCs) and/or WBC casts in the urine, leukocytosis in the serum, and a mildly elevated creatinine.

UTI risk is 50 times higher in women than men; up to 30% of women experience a symptomatic infection in their lifetime.[39] Given that most UTIs arise from the ascending route, the higher risk in women may be due to their shorter urethra. Bacteria that cause these infections include *E. coli*, *Klebsiella pneumoniae*, *Proteus mirabilis*, and, in nosocomial patients, *Pseudomonadaceae* and MRSA.

For women, a common cause of UTIs is sexual activity, when bacteria from the anal and/or vaginal area ascend into the urethra. Those who change sexual partners or begin having sexual intercourse more frequently may experience UTIs or bladder infections more often than do women who are celibate or in monogamous relationships.

Delayed urination also can lead to UTIs. The bladder is a muscle that stretches to hold urine and contracts when urine is released. Delayed urination can cause it to stretch severely, which, over time, may weaken the muscle. If a weakened bladder does not empty completely, the remaining urine may increase the risk of infection. Military women are particularly vulnerable to genitourinary infections due to long periods between voids.[40] Research suggests that women who work as manual laborers also may be more susceptible due to poor fluid intake and infrequent voiding.[41]

Treatment depends on the infection site, number of previous infections, type of bacteria, and individual patient factors. Most first-time infections can easily be treated with antibiotics for 3 to 7 days. In some cases, 10 to 14 days of antibiotic therapy is necessary to ensure that infection does not recur. Resistant organisms can be a major cause of recurrence because women who have multiple UTIs take antibiotics frequently. For women with severe illness or multiple recurrences, an ultrasound of the abdomen is indicated to check the kidneys and ureters. These women also benefit from hygiene training, voiding schedules, and early antibiotic treatment. In addition, a longer course of treatment—1 to 2 months versus suppressive therapy—is beneficial in many instances[42,43] and so is drinking cranberry juice to acidify urine and thus discourage bacterial growth in the urine.[39] Pregnancy can be associated with a higher UTI risk, often stemming from asymptomatic bacteriuria, which may cause complications later during pregnancy. Pregnant women should undergo a screening urine culture at their first prenatal visit.[44,45] (See the box below for ways that patients can reduce the risk of UTIs.)

HOW TO REDUCE UTI RISK: GUIDELINES FOR PATIENTS

- Drink plenty of fluids, especially water. Cranberry juice may have infection-fighting properties. However, women taking warfarin, a blood-thinning medication, should not drink it, as possible interactions between cranberry juice and warfarin can lead to bleeding.

- Urinate frequently. Do not delay urination when you feel the urge to void.

- Wipe from front to back after a bowel movement. This prevents bacteria in the anal region from spreading to the vagina and urethra.

- Take showers rather than tub baths. If you are susceptible to infections, this can help prevent them.

- Gently wash the skin around the anus and vagina daily. Do not use harsh soap or wash too vigorously, as the delicate skin around these areas can become irritated.

- Empty your bladder as soon as possible after sexual activity and drink a full glass of water to help flush bacteria.

- Avoid using deodorant sprays or feminine products in the genital area, as they can irritate the urethra and bladder.

Source: Adapted from Mayo Clinic. (2008). *Urinary tract infection. Prevention.* Available at www.mayoclinic.com/health/urinary-tract-infection/DS00286/DSECTION=prevention.

CHRONIC FATIGUE SYNDROME

Researchers, health practitioners, and patients have hotly debated chronic fatigue syndrome (CFS) in the last two decades—both its existence and the underlying pathophysiology.[46] The disorder is characterized by persistent and unexplained fatigue resulting in severe restriction of daily activities. CFS does not necessarily occur more often in lesbians than in other populations, but lesbians do suffer from it.[47]

Diagnostic criteria for CFS includes severe chronic fatigue lasting at least 6 months, exclusion of other known medical conditions causing the fatigue, and four or more of the following symptoms, which must be present for at least 6 months:

- Substantial impairment of short-term memory or concentration;
- Sore throat;
- Tender lymph nodes;
- Muscle pain;
- Multijoint pain without swelling or redness;
- Headaches of a new type, pattern, or severity;
- Unrefreshing sleep; and
- Postexertional malaise lasting more than 24 hours.[48]

There are several long-held presumptions about what causes CFS. One is that an unknown virus has escaped detection. Another is that a well-known virus, possibly a virus in the herpes family, causes atypical side effects. The bulk of research evidence shows that CFS symptoms are similar to those stemming from cytomegalovirus, human herpes virus 6, and Epstein-Barr virus, which causes infectious mononucleosis.[49,50] Some scientists hypothesize that CFS is related to depression or other psychiatric problems.[51-53]

The syndrome's impact on patients can be devastating. Many of them report years of crippling fatigue, loss of effectiveness, mental laxity, and debility.[54] Studies have shown that CFS patients are more likely to suffer mild cardiac dysfunction, such as tilt-test, heart-wall and cardioelectrical abnormalities.[55-58]

Studies have not shown broad anti-infection therapies to be effective,[59-61] and research indicates that antidepressants are largely unsuccessful.[62] Cognitive behavioral therapy is very moderately effective, particularly in patients with untreated depression.[63,64] Findings from studies that looked at antiviral medications for patients with a history of Epstein-Barr virus have been controversial.[65,66] Exercise therapy, although very difficult for many patients, has proved moderately successful.[67-71] Finally, results regarding the effectiveness of vitamins and other nutritional supplements have been very mixed.[72-75]

LYME DISEASE

Lyme disease, named after the Connecticut town where the first cases presented, was initially discovered in women who had atypical, nonerosive arthritis with negative rheumatoid factors. The disease can be merely inconvenient or, worse, cause life-threatening complications for people who hunt, fish, and otherwise spend time outdoors.

The spirochete *Borrelia burgdorferi sensu stricto* spreads to humans via deer tick bites, but researchers suspect it also spreads through sexual activity or perinatally.[76] The ticks—*Ixodes scapularis* or *Ixodes pacificus*—must latch on for about 24 hours to transmit the spirochete. The peak time of year for transmission is May to June. Most cases occur in the Northeast or Great Lakes region of the United States, but a related spirochete, *Borrelia afzelii*, causes Lyme-like disease in Eastern Europe.[77] Within a few weeks of a bite, a small, characteristic targetoid lesion—or erythema migrans, a result of direct inoculation of the spirochete into the skin—develops along with flu-like symptoms. *B. afzelii* then spreads throughout the body, causing early disseminated or secondary Lyme disease. The latter usually involves the heart and brain, and often the cranial nerves.

A common treatment for Lyme disease is doxycycline, with amoxicillin as the alternative for pregnant women and children. Three-day prophylaxis with doxycycline, which limits the disease very successfully, should begin within 72 hours after removal of *I. scapularis*.

Lyme meningitis usually presents with cranial nerve abnormalities, headache, nuchal rigidity, and paresthesia. It typically begins a few weeks to months after the erythema migrans disappears. Carditis stemming from Lyme disease causes various forms of heart block,[78] which in most cases is transitory and requires only temporary pacing, aggressive telemetry monitoring, and treatment with ceftriaxone or doxycycline. Ceftriaxone is the treatment for most patients with Lyme meningitis or carditis.

Sixty percent of untreated Lyme disease patients will later develop arthritis.[79] The treatment for arthritis in most women who are not pregnant or lactating is a 2-week course of doxycycline, and in those who have persistent symptoms of joint swelling after treatment, an additional 2 to 4 weeks of doxycycline. Up to 5% of untreated patients may have chronic neurological complaints months to years after infection, including shooting pains, numbness or tingling in the hands or feet, and problems with concentration and short-term memory.[78] About 60% of untreated patients with erythema migrans will ultimately develop monoarticular or oligoarticular arthritis, typically involving the knee; around 10% will have a neurologic manifestation, the most common being facial nerve palsy; and about 5% will have a cardiac complication, usually varying degrees of atrioventricular block.[79] Chronically ill patients should receive a lumbar puncture and, if disease indicators are present in their central nervous system, ceftriaxone or penicillin IV for 2 weeks.

Although one study found that antibiotics are ineffective, this issue is controversial.[80] There is a vaccine that eliminates the spirochete from ticks, but the manufacturer removed it from the market in 2002 due to poor sales and a vaccine-induced autoimmune syndrome.[81]

CONCLUSION

Infectious diseases have a large impact on people regardless of their sexual orientation, gender, race, ethnicity, or socioeconomic status. Diseases ranging from methicillin-resistant *S. aureus* to Lyme disease affect untold numbers of lesbians each day. There has been no epidemiological research to determine if lesbians are particularly vulnerable to some of these infections. However, because smoking, alcohol consumption, excessive weight, and other risk factors are more prevalent among lesbians than heterosexual women, lesbians are more vulnerable to health threats generally.

REFERENCES

1. Diamant, A. L., Schuster, M. A., & Lever, J. (2000). Receipt of preventive health care services by lesbians. *American Journal of Preventive Medicine, 19,* 141–148.

2. Tang, H., Greenwood, G. L., Cowling, D. W., Lloyd, J. C., Roeseler, A. G., & Bal, D. G. (2004). Cigarette smoking among lesbians, gays, and bisexuals: How serious a problem? (United States). *Cancer Causes & Control, 15,* 797–803.

3. Marrazzo, J. M. (2004). Barriers to infectious disease care among lesbians. *Emerging Infectious Diseases, 10,* 1974–1978.

4. Bowen, D. J., Balsam, K. F., & Ender, S. R. (2008). A review of obesity issues in sexual minority women. *Obesity, 16,* 221–228.

5. Koh, A. S., & Ross, L. K. (2006). Mental health issues: A comparison of lesbian, bisexual and heterosexual women. *Journal of Homosexuality, 15,* 33–57.

6. Pisarski, A., & Gallois, C. (1996). A needs analysis of Brisbane lesbians: Implications for the lesbian community. *Journal of Homosexuality, 30,* 79–95.

7. Matthews, A. K., Hughes, T. L., Osterman, G. P., & Kodl, M. M. (2005). Complementary medicine practices in a community-based sample of lesbian and heterosexual women. *Health Care for Women International, 26,* 430–447.

8. Chambers, H. F. (2001). The changing epidemiology of *Staphylococcus aureus*? *Emerging Infectious Diseases, 7,* 178–182.

9. Chambers, H. F. (1988). Methicillin-resistant staphylococci. *Clinical Microbiology Reviews, 1,* 173–186.

10. Eguia, J. M., & Chambers, H. F. (2003). Community-acquired methicillin-resistant *Staphylococcus aureus*: Epidemiology and potential virulence factors. *Current Infectious Disease Reports, 5,* 459–466.

11. Chambers, H. F. (2005). Community-associated MRSA—resistance and virulence converge. *New England Journal of Medicine, 352,* 1485–1487.

12. Klein, E., Smith, D. L., & Laxminarayan, R. (2009). Community-associated methicillin-resistant *Staphylococcus aureus* in outpatients, United States, 1999–2006. *Emerging Infectious Diseases, 15,* 1925–1930. Available at www.cdc.gov/EID/content/15/12/1925.htm.

13. Klevens, R. M., Morrison, M. A., Nadle, J., Petit, S., Gershman, K., Ray, S., et al. (2007). Invasive methicillin-resistant *Staphylococcus aureus* infections in the United States. *Journal of the American Medical Association, 298,* 1763–1771.

14. Klevens, R. M., Morrison, M. A., Fridkin, S. K., Reingold, A., Petit, S., Gershman, K., et al. (2006). Community-associated methicillin-resistant *Staphylococcus aureus* and healthcare risk factors. *Emerging Infectious Diseases, 12,* 1991–1993. Available at www.cdc.gov/ncidod/EID/vol12no12/pdfs/06-0505.pdf.

15. Mertz, P. M., Cardenas, T. C., Snyder, R. V., Kinney, M. A., Davis, S. C., & Plano, L. R. (2007). *Staphylococcus aureus* virulence factors associated with infected skin lesions: Influence on the local immune response. *Archives of Dermatology, 143,* 1259–1263.

16. Faires, M. C., Tater, K. C., & Weese, J. S. (2009). An investigation of methicillin-resistant *Staphylococcus aureus* colonization in people and pets in the same household with an

infected person or infected pet. *Journal of the American Veterinary Medical Association, 235,* 540–543.

17. Hiramatsu, K., Hanaki, H., Ino, T., Yabuta, K., Oguri, T., & Tenover, F. C. (1997). Methicillin-resistant *Staphylococcus aureus* clinical strain with reduced vancomycin susceptibility. *Journal of Antimicrobial Chemotherapy, 40,* 135–136.

18. Ghanem, G., Hachem, R., Jiang, Y., Chemaly, R. F., & Raad, I. (2007). Outcomes for and risk factors associated with vancomycin-resistant *Enterococcus faecalis* and vancomycin-resistant *Enterococcus faecium* bacteremia in cancer patients. *Infection Control and Hospital Epidemiology, 28,* 1054–1059.

19. Sato, K., Oka, H., Utsuki, S., Shimizu, S., Suzuki, S., Yamada, M., et al. (2006). Vancomycin-resistant enterococcal meningitis in patients with ventriculoperitoneal shunt: Two case reports and review of the literature. *No Shinkei Geka, 34,* 203–207.

20. Zirakzadeh, A., & Patel, R. (2006). Vancomycin-resistant enterococci: Colonization, infection, detection, and treatment. *Mayo Clinic Proceedings, 81,* 529–536.

21. Bryant, S., & Wilbeck, J. (2007). Vancomycin-resistant *Enterococcus* in critical care areas. *Critical Care Nursing Clinics of North America, 19,* 69–75.

22. Centers for Disease Control and Prevention. (2006). *Norovirus in healthcare facilities fact sheet.* Available at www.cdc.gov/ncidod/dhqp/id_norovirusFS.html.

23. Centers for Disease Control and Prevention. (2007). *About rotavirus.* Available at www.cdc.gov/rotavirus/about_rotavirus.htm.

24. Cortese, M. M., Parashar, U. D., & Centers for Disease Control and Prevention. (2009). Prevention of rotavirus gastroenteritis among infants and children: Recommendations of the Advisory Committee on Immunization Practices (ACIP). *Morbidity and Mortality Weekly Report, 58,* 1–25.

25. DuPont, H. L. (2009). Clinical practice. Bacterial diarrhea. *New England Journal of Medicine, 361,* 1560–1569.

26. Centers for Disease Control and Prevention. (2008). *Campylobacter.* Available at www.cdc.gov/nczved/dfbmd/disease_listing/campylobacter_gi.html#5.

27. Vucic, S., Kiernan, M. C., & Cornblath, D. R. (2009). Guillain-Barré syndrome: An update. *Journal of Clinical Neuroscience, 16,* 733–741.

28. Centers for Disease Control and Prevention. (2008). *Salmonellosis.* Available at www.cdc.gov/nczved/dfbmd/disease_listing/salmonellosis_gi.html.

29. Gould, L. H., Bopp, C., Strockbine, N., Atkinson, R. Baselski, V., Body, B., et al. (2009). Recommendations for diagnosis of Shiga toxin-producing *Escherichia coli* infections by clinical laboratories. *Morbidity and Mortality Weekly Report, 58,* 1–14.

30. Centers for Disease Control and Prevention. (2008). *Shigellosis.* Available at www.cdc.gov/nczved/dfbmd/disease_listing/shigellosis_gi.html.

31. Centers for Disease Control and Prevention. (2009). *Viral hepatitis.* Available at www.cdc.gov/hepatitis.

32. Centers for Disease Control and Prevention. (2009). Surveillance for acute viral hepatitis—United States, 2007. *Morbidity and Mortality Weekly Report, 58,* 1–27.

33. Centers for Disease Control and Prevention. (2009). *Disease burden from viral hepatitis A, B, and C in the United States.* Available at www.cdc.gov/hepatitis/PDFs/disease_burden.pdf.

34. Centers for Disease Control and Prevention. (2009). *Seasonal influenza: The disease.* Available at www.cdc.gov/flu/about/disease.

35. Centers for Disease Control and Prevention. (2009). *Clinical signs and symptoms of influenza.* Available at www.cdc.gov/flu/professionals/acip/clinical.htm.

36. Rothberg, M. B., Bellantonio, S., & Rose, D. N. (2003). Management of influenza in adults older than 65 years of age: Cost-effectiveness of rapid testing and antiviral therapy. *Annals of Internal Medicine, 139*(5, Pt. 1), 321–329.

37. Rothberg, M. B., He, S., & Rose, D. N. (2003). Management of influenza symptoms in healthy adults. *Journal of General Internal Medicine, 18,* 808–815.

38. Masson, P., Matheson, S., Webster, A. C., & Craig, J. C. (2009). Meta-analyses in prevention and treatment of urinary tract infections. *Infectious Disease Clinics of North America, 23,* 355–385.

39. Jepson, R. G., & Craig, J. C. (2008). Cranberries for preventing urinary tract infections. *Cochrane Database of Systematic Reviews, Jan 23,* CD001321.

40. Lowe, N. K., & Ryan-Wenger, N. A. (2003). Military women's risk factors for and symptoms of genitourinary infections during deployment. *Military Medicine, 168,* 569–574.

41. Su, S. B., Wang, J. N., Lu, C. W., & Guo, H. R. (2006). Reducing urinary tract infections among female clean room workers. *Journal of Women's Health, 15,* 870–876.

42. Brumfitt, W., Hamilton-Miller, J. M., Smith, G. W., & al-Wali, W. (1991). Comparative trial of norfloxacin and macrocrystalline nitrofurantoin (Macrodantin) in the prophylaxis of recurrent urinary tract infection in women. *Quarterly Journal of Medicine, 81,* 811–820.

43. Sandock, D. S., Gothe, B. G., & Bodner, D. R. (1995). Trimethoprim-sulfamethoxazole prophylaxis against urinary tract infection in the chronic spinal cord injury patient. *Paraplegia, 33,* 156–160.

44. Colgan, R., Nicolle, L. E., McGlone, A., & Hooton, T. M. (2006). Asymptomatic bacteriuria in adults. *American Family Physician, 74,* 985–990.

45. Smaill, F. (2007). Asymptomatic bacteriuria in pregnancy. *Best Practice & Research. Clinical Obstetrics & Gynaecology, 21,* 439–450.

46. Prins, J. B., van der Meer, J. W., & Bleijenberg, G. (2006). Chronic fatigue syndrome. *Lancet, 367,* 346–355.

47. Munson, M. (Ed.). (2000). *Stricken: Voices from the hidden epidemic of chronic fatigue.* Binghamton, NY: Haworth Press.

48. Fukuda, K., Straus, S. E., Hickie, I., Sharpe, M. C., Dobbins, J. G., & Komaroff, A. (1994). The chronic fatigue syndrome: A comprehensive approach to its definition and study. International Chronic Fatigue Syndrome Study Group. *Annals of Internal Medicine, 121,* 953–959.

49. Di Luca, D., Zorzenon, M., Mirandola, P., Colle, R., Botta, G. A., & Cassai, E. (1995). Human herpesvirus 6 and human herpesvirus 7 in chronic fatigue syndrome. *Journal of Clinical Microbiology, 33,* 1660–1661.

50. Soto, N. E., & Straus, S. E. (2000). Chronic fatigue syndrome and herpesviruses: The fading evidence. *Herpes, 7,* 46–50.

51. Prins, J. B., Bos, E., Huibers, M. J., Servaes, P., van der Werf, S. P., van der Meer, J. W., et al. (2004). Social support and the persistence of complaints in chronic fatigue syndrome. *Psychotherapy and Psychosomatics, 73,* 174–182.

52. Raine, R., Carter, S., Sensky, T., & Black, N. (2004). General practitioners' perceptions of chronic fatigue syndrome and beliefs about its management, compared with irritable bowel syndrome: Qualitative study. *BMJ, 328,* 1354–1357.

53. Tritt, K., Nickel, M., Mitterlehner, F., Nickel, C., Forthuber, P., Leiberich, P., et al. (2004). Chronic fatigue and indicators of long-term employment disability in psychosomatic inpatients. *Wiener Klinische Wochenschrift, 116,* 182–189.

54. Marcel, B., Komaroff, A. L., Fagioli, L. R., Kornish, R. J. II, & Albert, M. S. (1996). Cognitive deficits in patients with chronic fatigue syndrome. *Biological Psychiatry, 40,* 535–541.

55. De Lorenzo, F., Hargreaves, J., & Kakkar, V. V. (1997). Pathogenesis and management of delayed orthostatic hypotension in patients with chronic fatigue syndrome. *Clinical Autonomic Research, 7,* 185–190.

56. LaManca, J. J., Peckerman, A., Walker, J., Kesil, W., Cook, S., Taylor, A., et al. (1999). Cardiovascular response during head-up tilt in chronic fatigue syndrome. *Clinical Physiology, 19,* 111–120.

57. Sargent, C., Scroop, G. C., Nemeth, P. M., Burnet, R. B., & Buckley, J. D. (2002). Maximal oxygen uptake and lactate metabolism are normal in chronic fatigue syndrome. *Medicine & Science in Sports & Exercise, 34,* 51–56.

58. Naschitz, J., Fields, M., Isseroff, H., Sharif, D., Sabo, E., & Rosner, I. (2006). Shortened QT interval: A distinctive feature of the dysautonomia of chronic fatigue syndrome. *Journal of Electrocardiology, 39,* 389–394.

59. Peterson, P. K., Shepard, J., Macres, M., Schenck, C., Crosson, J., Rechtman, D., et al. (1990). A controlled trial of intravenous immunoglobulin G in chronic fatigue syndrome. *American Journal of Medicine, 89,* 554–560.

60. See, D. M., & Tilles, J. G. (1996). Alpha-interferon treatment of patients with chronic fatigue syndrome. *Immunological Investigations, 25,* 153–164.

61. Vollmer-Conna, U., Hickie, I., Hadzi-Pavlovic, D., Tymms, K., Wakefield, D., Dwyer, J., et al. (1997). Intravenous immunoglobulin is ineffective in the treatment of patients with chronic fatigue syndrome. *American Journal of Medicine, 103,* 38–43.

62. Vercoulen, J. H., Swanink, C. M., Zitman, F. G., Vreden, S. G., Hoofs, M. P., Fennis, J. F., et al. (1996). Randomised, double-blind, placebo-controlled study of fluoxetine in chronic fatigue syndrome. *Lancet, 347,* 858–861.

63. Friedberg, F., & Krupp, L. B. (1994). A comparison of cognitive behavioral treatment for chronic fatigue syndrome and primary depression. *Clinical Infectious Diseases, 18*(Suppl. 1), S105–110.

64. Knoop, H., Prins, J. B., Stulemeijer, M., van der Meer, J. W., & Bleijenberg, G. (2007). The effect of cognitive behaviour therapy for chronic fatigue syndrome on self-reported

cognitive impairments and neuropsychological test performance. *Journal of Neurology, Neurosurgery, & Psychiatry, 78,* 434–436.

65. Kogelnik, A. M., Loomis, K., Hoegh-Petersen, M., Rosso, F., Hischier, C., & Montoya, J. G. (2006). Use of valganciclovir in patients with elevated antibody titers against human herpesvirus-6 (HHV-6) and Epstein-Barr virus (EBV) who were experiencing central nervous system dysfunction including long-standing fatigue. *Journal of Clinical Virology, 37*(Suppl. 1), S33–38.

66. Lerner, A. M., Beqaj, S. H., Deeter, R. G., & Fitzgerald, J. T. (2007). Valacyclovir treatment in Epstein-Barr virus subset chronic fatigue syndrome: Thirty-six months follow-up. *In Vivo, 21,* 707–713.

67. Powell, P., Bentall, R. P., Nye, F. J., & Edwards, R. H. (2001). Randomised controlled trial of patient education to encourage graded exercise in chronic fatigue syndrome. *BMJ, 322,* 387–390.

68. Bentall, R. P., Powell, P., Nye, F. J., & Edwards, R. H. (2002). Predictors of response to treatment for chronic fatigue syndrome. *British Journal of Psychiatry, 181,* 248–252.

69. Wallman, K. E., Morton, A. R., Goodman, C., Grove, R., & Guilfoyle, A. M. (2004). Randomised controlled trial of graded exercise in chronic fatigue syndrome. *Medical Journal of Australia, 180,* 444–448.

70. Cook, D. B., Nagelkirk, P. R., Peckerman, A., Poluri, A. Mores, J., & Natelson, B. H. (2005). Exercise and cognitive performance in chronic fatigue syndrome. *Medicine & Science in Sports & Exercise, 37,* 1460–1467.

71. Moss-Morris, R., Sharon, C., Tobin, R., & Baldi, J. C. (2005). A randomized controlled graded exercise trial for chronic fatigue syndrome: Outcomes and mechanisms of change. *Journal of Health Psychology, 10,* 245–259.

72. Kaslow, J. E., Rucker, L., & Onishi, R. (1989). Liver extract-folic acid-cyanocobalamin vs. placebo for chronic fatigue syndrome. *Archives of Internal Medicine, 149,* 2501–2503.

73. Behan, P. O., Behan, W. M., & Horrobin, D. (1990). Effect of high doses of essential fatty acids on the postviral fatigue syndrome. *Acta Neurologica Scandinavica, 82,* 209–216.

74. Plioplys, A. V., & Plioplys, S. (1997). Amantadine and L-carnitine treatment of chronic fatigue syndrome. *Neuropsychobiology, 35,* 16–23.

75. Dykman, K. D., Tone, C., Ford, C., & Dykman, R. A. (1998). The effects of nutritional supplements on the symptoms of fibromyalgia and chronic fatigue syndrome. *Integrative Physiological and Behavioral Science, 33,* 61–71.

76. Walsh, C. A., Mayer, E. W., & Baxi, L. V. (2007). Lyme disease in pregnancy: Case report and review of the literature. *Obstetrical & Gynecological Survey, 62,* 41–50.

77. Centers for Disease Control and Prevention. (2007). Lyme disease—United States, 2003–2005. *Morbidity and Mortality Weekly Report, 56,* 573–576.

78. Centers for Disease Control and Prevention. (2009). *Learn about Lyme disease.* Available at www.cdc.gov/ncidod/dvbid/lyme/index.htm.

79. Wormser, G. P. (2006). Clinical practice. Early Lyme disease. *New England Journal of Medicine, 354,* 2794–2801.

80. Wormser, G. P., Dattwyler, R. J., Shapiro, E. D., Halperin, J. J., Steere, A. C., Klempner, M. S., et al. (2006). The clinical assessment, treatment, and prevention of Lyme disease, human granulocytic anaplasmosis, and babesiosis: Clinical practice guidelines by the Infectious Diseases Society of America. *Clinical Infectious Diseases, 43,* 1089–1134.

81. Earnhart, C. G., & Marconi, R. T. (2007). OspC phylogenetic analyses support the feasibility of a broadly protective polyvalent chimeric Lyme disease vaccine. *Clinical and Vaccine Immunology, 14,* 628–634.

ABOUT THE AUTHORS

Donna DeFreitas, MD, MPH, is Assistant Clinical Professor of Infectious Diseases and Internal Medicine at the University of California, Davis. Her research focus is HIV prevention. She has written about recruiting and retaining participants in HIV clinical trials.

Nyonnoweh Greene, MD, is a family practice resident at Methodist Hospital in Sacramento, California. Before she began medical school, Nyonnoweh worked as a Natural Therapeutic Specialist teaching yoga and doing massage therapy, energy work, and herbology.

CHAPTER 26

"Oh, My Aching Heart."

CARDIOVASCULAR ISSUES FOR LESBIANS

PAMELA CHARNEY, MD

DANA P. MCGLOTHLIN, MD

ANNA *has lived with Karen for more than 25 years. Both are in their early sixties, overweight, and hypertensive former smokers, and both receive regular medical care. Anna controls her diabetes through diet and takes medication for her hyperlipidemia. Her family had invited the couple to family gatherings many times, but Karen always felt only begrudgingly welcome.*

One evening after dinner, Anna suddenly became short of breath. Karen called 911, but before help arrived, Anna collapsed and Karen began cardiopulmonary resuscitation. At the hospital, Anna was treated for a heart attack. Karen told the admitting physician about the uncomfortable relationship with Anna's family. After reviewing Anna's health care power of attorney, the physician wrote orders that Karen be allowed to make medical decisions for Anna and visit her as next of kin. The next day, the entire extended family was uneasily sitting with Karen outside the intensive care unit when the admitting physician came by after rounds. The tone in the group changed for the better as the physician described how Karen had saved Anna's life.

■ ■ ■

BACKGROUND

Cardiovascular disease is the leading cause of death in the industrialized world. Since the 1980s, the related mortality rate has declined more dramatically among men than women. Many experts believe that this disparity reflects gaps in attention to reducing primary and secondary cardiovascular risk factors in women.[1,2] In 2006, the third in a series of three identical telephone surveys of women revealed that only 57% were aware that heart disease is the leading cause of death among women, although this percentage was significantly higher than the percentages in the previous two surveys in 2000 and 2003. However, Black and Hispanic women were less aware of this fact than White women were, a racial/ethnic gap that has not narrowed.[3]

More women than men die from cardiovascular disease in part because cardiovascular disease—particularly coronary heart disease—begins 10 years later in women on average than it does in men; consequently, women tend to be older and therefore less likely to survive a heart attack.[4,5] Notably, cardiac death is the leading cause of death in women of all ages. Among women, there are substantial racial, ethnic, and other differences in the prevalence of heart disease and related risk factors: prevalence is highest among African Americans and American Indians/Alaska Natives, and lowest among Asian Americans. Prevalence is also higher among women with less education and lower income.[6]

Women and men also differ in terms of cardiovascular risk factors, several of which, including obesity, hypertension, and dyslipidemia, tend to increase after menopause. This clustering of risk factors after menopause may be related to hormone-mediated metabolic disturbances.[7]

LESBIANS AND HEART DISEASE

The number of lesbians who have heart disease is unknown, but some information is available regarding risk factors in this population. The best studies about lesbians and heart disease risks stem from two major investigations: the Nurses' Health Study and the Women's Health Initiative.

For decades, the Nurses' Health Study, a national ongoing survey of female nurses, has provided detailed information about the presentation, risk factors, and outcomes related to major chronic diseases. Participants regularly complete extensive questionnaires and sometimes provide specimens for analysis. Among the initial 90,823 participants, 694 identified themselves as lesbians. Results to date show that the prevalence of tobacco and alcohol use, obesity, depression, and use of prescription medications is higher among lesbian nurses enrolled in the study. More physical activity is correlated with less weight gain as the study participants age, and with lower rates of cardiovascular disease and cancer.[8] Among tobacco smokers, the adverse health effects are dose-related. Although women who smoke one to two cigarettes a day have fewer health problems than those who smoke one pack a day, they still have more problems than nonsmokers do. Also disturbing is that even secondhand cigarette smoke increases cardiovascular mortality significantly; the exposure-mortality relationship is relatively steep at low levels of exposure and flattens out at higher levels of exposure.[9]

The Women's Health Initiative enrolled ethnically diverse women between 50 and 79 years old in three clinical trials and an observational arm. The clinical trials were all randomized, double-blind, and placebo-controlled. Two of them sought to resolve questions about the impact of estrogen and estrogen plus progesterone on the risk of a variety of important health outcomes during the postmenopausal period. The pharmaceutical trials have ended, but the observational study continues. Of the 93,311 women whom researchers queried about sexual orientation, 97.1% were heterosexuals and only 0.6% were lesbians. (The number of lifetime lesbians and the number of lesbians only after age 45 were about equal.) Only 33% of self-identified lesbians, versus 50% of heterosexual women, had never smoked. In addition, lesbians received comparatively fewer health screening services; had a higher prevalence of obesity, smoking, and alcohol use; and consumed fewer fruits and vegetables. These findings suggest that lesbians have unmet health needs requiring more effective interaction between them and clinicians.[10]

A small, population-based telephone survey by Diamant and Wold based on random-digit dialing revealed that lesbian and bisexual women between 18 and 64 years old were more likely than heterosexual women to report a diagnosis of heart disease.[11]

SEX DIFFERENCES

Important anatomical and physiological differences between men and women have a role in cardiovascular issues:

- Women generally have coronary arteries that are smaller in diameter, which, until smaller instruments and stents were invented, caused more complications during invasive procedures;
- To boost cardiac output (stroke volume times heart rate), female hearts beat faster. Male hearts, in contrast, increase the size of the left ventricle (stroke volume). As heart rate increases, the time of cardiac relaxation between beats decreases. Because the left ventricle fills during relaxation, there is a point at which the heart rate is too fast to allow adequate time for ventricular filling. This means females have a lower cardiac output limit compared with men—a major reason why, even among elite athletes, most men perform better than women do during physical exertion; and
- Electrocardiogram evaluation during stress testing is based on male norms. The height of changes in ST waves, a segment of the heart beat, is related to body mass, which is typically higher in men. Some researchers believe that using male norms to evaluate women is inappropriate and have proposed recalibrating stress testing machines based on sex. This could potentially yield more-sensitive and specific results in women.[12]

Researchers are exploring sex-based cardiovascular differences. Evidence suggests there may also be significant differences in sympathetic and parasympathetic function,[13] which may play a role in arrhythmia risk. In addition, using digoxin to treat patients with congestive heart failure and a low ejection fraction has been associated with higher mortality among women but not men.[14]

PRESENTATION OF CARDIOVASCULAR DISEASE

Myocardial Infarction

The presentation of acute coronary syndrome (myocardial infarction and/or unstable angina) varies depending on sex and age. The crushing chest pain associated with profuse sweating most often occurs in middle-age men; women—especially those who are older—and older men are more likely to present with atypical symptoms, including upper abdominal discomfort, shortness of breath, and jaw pain, or no symptoms at all. A recent study in Sweden compared symptoms of a first acute myocardial infarction in women and men 25 to 74 years old: 88.5% of the women and 94.8% of the men experienced chest pain. Four symptoms were significantly more common in women than men: nausea (53.8% vs. 29.5%), back pain (42.3% vs. 14.3%), dizziness (17.3% vs. 7.5%), and palpitations (11.5% vs. 2.9%).[15] After an acute myocardial infarction and during initial hospitalization, women are less likely than men to undergo coronary artery bypass surgery but nearly as likely to undergo catheterization; balloon angioplasty, in which the coronary artery is dilated; and stent placement, to prevent blockage.[16]

Heart attacks not clinically identified initially are categorized as silent myocardial infarctions, which increase the risk of recurrent ischemia and death. In fact, more than 24% of myocardial infarctions are not initially recognized. Follow-up of participants in the Framingham Heart Study over 34 years revealed that 34% of women and 26% of men had had myocardial infarctions their physicians did not identify. Even though clinicians carefully took additional patient histories at the time of new electrocardiogram (EKG) findings, 50% of participants did not retrospectively report any symptoms that would have suggested acute ischemia.[17]

The prevalence of silent myocardial infarction increases dramatically with age. Prevalence is 11% among women between 55 and 64 years old and 22% among those between 65 and 69. It increases more rapidly, to 32%, between 70 and 74 years, reaching 40% between 75 and 79 years, and 43% between 80 and 85 and beyond.[6]

After myocardial infarction, all patients benefit from certain medications that lower the rate of a second myocardial infarction and death. However, before hospitals first started reporting core performance measures, women who had suffered a heart attack were less likely than men to have received such medications upon discharge: aspirin (to reduce the incidence of thrombosis), beta-blockers (to reduce heart rate), angiotensin-converting enzyme inhibitors or angiotensin II receptor blockers (to control congestive heart failure and high blood pressure), and statins (to reduce cholesterol). Even when patients take these medications, blood pressure and cholesterol goals may not be met, as the Heart and Estrogen/Progestin Replacement Study (HERS) demonstrated. Furthermore, the HERS participants who had had a heart attack were less likely than men to have undergone cardiac angiography, cardiac bypass surgery, or rehabilitation.[18]

Although sudden death from myocardial infarction occurs more frequently in men than women, the prevalence is shifting. Between 1989 and 1998, the rate of sudden death increased 21% among women 35 to 44 years old but decreased 2.8% among men. In the Nurses' Health Study, between 1976–1998, there were 1,110 women who died from cardiovascular causes. Most (57.3%) died outside the hospital or in the Emergency Room, and 69% did not have any history of cardiovascular disease. At least one coronary risk factor was present in 94% of those who died. The most prevalent risk factors among the mortalities were cigarette smoking, diabetes, and hypertension.[19]

Angina

In women, angina is the most common initial symptomatic presentation of coronary artery disease. Diagnosing angina requires careful attention to symptom details. Classical symptoms are chest pressure that may radiate to the jaw or upper arms, and shortness of breath lasting up to 10 or 20 minutes. Physical exertion may trigger angina and rest may relieve it. However, women may report other, sometimes minimal symptoms that arise during physical activity or emotional stress, such as shortness of breath; neck, arm, jaw, or abdominal discomfort; nausea; or sweating. The duration of angina is nearly always less than 30 minutes. If ischemic symptoms last longer than 30 minutes, a myocardial infarction usually results. Therefore, the duration of symptoms can help distinguish cardiac from noncardiac chest pain syndromes.

A meta-analysis revealed a similar or slightly higher prevalence of angina in women versus men across 31 countries.[20] A Finnish study showed that "test-positive" coronary artery disease (CAD) based on abnormal invasive or noninvasive test results occurred less often in women versus men with angina, but the lower incidence of abnormal results did not reflect a lower rate of coronary mortality. Among women using nitrates for angina who did not have test-positive CAD, the coronary mortality rate was the same as that among women using nitrates for angina who did have test-positive CAD. The coronary mortality rate was positively correlated with the nitrate dose prescribed.[21] The hypothesis is that, compared with men, women have less "fixed" or obstructive disease in the coronary arteries that yields abnormal test results, but have more arterial spasm/microvascular dysfunction that causes anginal symptoms.

Stroke

Strokes are the third most common cause of death after heart disease and cancer.[6] The etiologies and risk factors are often directly related to the cardiovascular system. More women than men die of stroke. In addition, strokes are twice as common among Blacks as they are among Whites, and Black survivors report more subsequent limitations. Significant risk factors for stroke include transient ischemic attack (TIA), hypertension, inactivity, and hormonal exposure in pregnancy and exogenously. A TIA, or stroke symptoms lasting less than 24 hours, has significant prognostic importance. The highest risk of stroke after a TIA is within the first month. About 15% of strokes begin with TIA symptoms, and the chance of death within a year of a TIA is 25%. The 10-year risk of stroke after such an attack is 18.8% and the 10-year combined risk of stroke, myocardial infarction, or vascular death is 42.8%, or about 4% annually.[6]

A randomized, controlled trial of low-dose aspirin (100 mg) taken every other day to prevent cardiovascular disease in women showed that it lowered the risk of stroke without affecting the risk of myocardial infarction or death from cardiovascular causes. However, in women older than 65, low-dose aspirin did significantly reduce the risk of major cardiovascular events, ischemic stroke, and myocardial infarction. Consequently, many clinicians advise women ≥ 45 years old, especially those with risk factors for cardiovascular disease, to take enteric-coated, low-dose aspirin (81–100 mg) every day.[22]

CARDIOVASCULAR DISEASE IN WOMEN

Diagnostic Challenges

To diagnose cardiovascular disease, clinicians must carefully consider the symptoms, especially in women. As mentioned earlier, women often present with atypical angina; they do not feel right during physical activity. Symptoms may include chest pressure, shortness of breath, lightheadedness, upper abdominal discomfort, discomfort in the jaw or inner left arm, and/or nausea. In the authors' experiences, too many women only reluctantly mention these symptoms, dismissing such signs as "just part of aging" due to their weight and/or lack of exercise. Other women come in for a second opinion after a clinician failed to consider cardiovascular disease. An abnormal EKG can be a clue, but a normal EKG does not rule out the possibility of coronary artery disease. Noninvasive stress-test imaging can identify patients at highest risk for coronary events. In any case, clinicians must be very suspicious when women present with symptoms.

Prevention and Treatment

Historically, physicians and patients have believed that coronary artery disease primarily afflicts men. This has hampered prevention efforts for women and may be a key reason for the dramatic reduction of the disease among men. Aggressively reducing the risk factors for cardiovascular disease, mostly by changing patients' behavior, is necessary in both men and women.

Prochaska and Velicer proposed a theoretical model of health behavior change comprising six stages: precontemplation, contemplation, preparation, action, maintenance, and termination or relapse.[23] Multiple research programs have found that addressing patients' current stage of behavioral change can best facilitate movement toward action. In precontemplation, the health care provider, but not the patient, is focused on behaviors and health outcomes, as if the two were watching different TV channels. In contemplation, the patient often begins to make connections between her behavior and outcomes; now, the two are at least watching the same channel. Action will not occur until the patient has begun preparation, so providers and their patients are better served by focusing on preparation rather than action when the patient is in the contemplation stage. Once the patient has accepted and enacted an action plan, maintenance and continuous monitoring are essential. Reducing cardiovascular risk factors usually requires life-long vigilance and having a plan in place in case of relapse.

Risk Factors

■ TOBACCO

Tobacco exposure is a critical risk factor for coronary artery disease. In 2006, about 24% of men and 18% of women were smokers. Education level inversely correlated with tobacco use: among people with a general education diploma, 51.3% smoked compared with 27.6% of those who had a high school diploma, 10.8% who had completed college, and 7% who also had a graduate degree.[24] Among current smokers, about 64% of deaths were related to cigarette smoking.[25] Secondary exposure to tobacco smoke is a significant risk factor as well.

Nationally, more men than women have stopped smoking, partly because short- and long-term smoking cessation has been less successful among women. The reasons for this are not entirely clear. Many women smokers worry about gaining weight if they quit, which is an unacceptable outcome for them. After quitting, the average cigarette smoker gains 7 to 10 pounds and 10% gain at least 20 pounds.[26]

Multiple studies, including the Nurses' Health Study,[8] have revealed that current smoking is more prevalent among lesbians than heterosexual women. In the California Health Interview Survey ($N = 44,505$), 25.4% of the 343 self-identified lesbians smoked versus 14.9% of heterosexual women.[27] Black smokers have more trouble quitting, partly due to genetics. They lack an enzyme that otherwise breaks down nicotine,[28] which means a higher amount of addictive nicotine by-products remains in their blood even if they only smoke two cigarettes a day. Therefore, more aggressive use of nicotine replacement products is warranted in Blacks even if they consume less tobacco.

■ HYPERTENSION

The ideal blood pressure is less than 120/80 mm Hg.[1] Population and treatment studies show that both systolic and diastolic hypertension are predictors of cardiovascular events. In 1991, Anastos and colleagues reported higher rates of cardiovascular disease among middle-age subjects with elevated diastolic blood pressure and less disease among those with lower readings.[29]

The definition of acceptable blood pressure has become more rigorous over time. Normal systolic blood pressure, previously defined as < 140 mm Hg, is now < 120 mm Hg, and normal diastolic blood pressure, previously < 90 mm Hg, is now

< 80 mm Hg. Persons with a systolic blood pressure between 120 and 139 mm Hg and/or a diastolic blood pressure between 80 and 89 mm Hg are currently considered to have "prehypertension." This enables early intervention—the adoption of a healthy lifestyle—to possibly reduce blood pressure, reduce the rate of progression to hypertension, or prevent hypertension.[29] One possible complication of hypertension treatment that can be avoided with monitoring is orthostatic hypotension—a drop in systolic blood pressure of > 10 mm Hg when the patient stands for more than 3 minutes compared with the patient's baseline blood pressure when she is sitting. This condition can be associated with feeling weak or lightheaded, or with a loss of consciousness. Orthostatic hypotension commonly occurs in the elderly, especially those with autonomic dysfunction (as is the case in some people with diabetes), and in people taking certain antihypertensive medications.[30]

Due to public health efforts, the number of people with hypertension who are aware of their diagnosis has gradually increased. But a substantial number of hypertensive patients still have suboptimal control of their blood pressure. Although public education campaigns have focused on "knowing one's numbers," more patient education is necessary.[31]

Lifestyle modifications can control hypertension. The Dietary Approaches to Stop Hypertension (DASH) diet is the most effective; it lowers hypertension by 8 to 14 mm Hg. The diet is high in fiber, fruit, and vegetables. Daily intake typically includes 7 to 8 servings of grains (1 serving = 1 slice of bread, ½ cup of cooked pasta or rice, or 1 ounce of dried cereal), 4 to 5 servings each of fruit and vegetables, limited protein (less than 6 ounces), and 2 to 3 servings of low-fat or fat-free milk products (1 serving = 8 ounces of milk or 1 cup of yogurt). However, the DASH diet may not substantially reduce weight. Other modifications are weight loss, more physical activity, and limiting the amount of dietary sodium.

There are key sex-related considerations regarding pharmacologic antihypertensive therapy. Given that up to 50% of pregnancies are unplanned, the most important consideration is the potential danger of medication to a developing fetus. Angiotensin-converting enzyme (ACE) inhibitors warrant very cautious use in women of reproductive age, who must be informed of the potential risks. Cooper and colleagues reported that ACE inhibitors can have teratogenic effects in the first and second trimesters. Infants exposed to these medications only in the first trimester had a higher risk of cardiovascular and central nervous system malformations (risk ratio [RR] = 2.71, confidence interval [CI] = 1.72–4.27) compared with infants not exposed to any antihypertensive medications.[32] Angiotensin receptor agonists, a class of drugs similar to ACE inhibitors, may also have teratogenic effects. No other hypertensive drugs increased the risk of congenital abnormalities.

Thiazide diuretics are often a first-choice treatment for hypertension in women as well as men. They lower the risk of coronary heart disease, stroke, and mortality.[33] In a randomized, double-blind, placebo-controlled trial, thiazides were associated with preservation of bone mineral density in the hip and spine.[34] Other medications are beta-blockers, and calcium channel blockers, which are often used in combination to control hypertension and thereby reduce long-term complications.

■ DYSLIPIDEMIA

Dyslipidemia is a major, modifiable risk factor for cardiovascular disease. A variety of available lipid-lowering medications, such as statins, fibrates, bile acid sequestrants, and nicotinic acid, reduce myocardial infarctions and other cardiovascular events by about 30% over a 5-year period.[35,36] However, much needs to be done to increase women's access to dyslipidemia testing and treatment. Of patients in a commercial HMO receiving lipid-lowering medication in the 6 months after an initial diagnosis of coronary heart disease, 61% were not at the low-density lipoprotein goal of < 100 mg/dL.[37] The Lipid Treatment Assessment Project revealed that high-risk women were undertreated compared with men.[38]

■ DIABETES

Although the prevalence of diabetes is increasing, its relationship to mortality especially among women has not received adequate attention. In the last decade, deaths as a result of coronary heart disease have risen 23% among diabetic women and declined by 27% in nondiabetic women. Meanwhile, mortality rates among diabetic and nondiabetic men have fallen 13% and 36%, respectively. Diabetic women also have higher inpatient mortality after myocardial infarction and a higher incidence of congestive heart failure than do diabetic men.[2] More research is necessary to determine the reasons for these patterns.

Lipid abnormalities are common in diabetic patients. When type 2 diabetes is diagnosed, women have substantially less high-density lipoprotein cholesterol than do age-matched, nondiabetic women.[39] Telephone interviews of diabetic patients with cardiovascular disease found that 54.7% of women and 82.7% of men took low-dose aspirin ($RR = 0.81$, 95% $CI = 0.70$–0.90).[40] Aggressive secondary prevention with low-dose aspirin is mandatory for diabetic women to reduce their very high risk of cardiovascular disease.

■ OBESITY

There is an expanding worldwide epidemic of obesity, which begins in childhood. Obesity is associated with cardiovascular events and earlier onset of hypertension, diabetes, and hyperlipidemia.[41] More than 33% of adult women are obese. Incidence varies substantially by ethnicity and race: among women, it afflicts 45% of non-Hispanic Blacks, 36.8% of Mexican Americans, and 30% of non-Hispanic Whites.[42]

Body mass index (BMI) is higher among lesbians than heterosexual women.[8,10,43] Another predictor of coronary events is weight distribution: more such events occur among women with the "apple" shape (greater central or abdominal girth) than among those with the "pear" shape (more weight on the hips and buttocks).[44] Roberts and colleagues studied 324 lesbians ≥ 40 years old and compared waist measurements with those of the lesbians' sisters. The lesbians had a significantly higher BMI, waist circumference, and waist-to-hip ratio, which may reflect greater abdominal/visceral adiposity and thus place them at higher risk for cardiovascular disease.[45]

■ INACTIVITY

In the Nurses' Health Study, a BMI > 25 and physical activity were important predictors of coronary heart disease on 20-year follow-up. The risk was greatest when participants had a BMI > 30 and were minimally active ($RR = 3.44$).[8]

■ ALCOHOL CONSUMPTION

Alcohol in moderate amounts has been associated with a lower risk of cardiovascular disease and death, although not necessarily in African American women.[46] In lesbians, alcohol is a risk factor for breast cancer and other substance use. Clinicians should individualize recommendations about alcohol intake for lesbian patients.

■ LUPUS AND RHEUMATOID ARTHRITIS

Researchers are paying more attention to the higher risk of cardiovascular disease morbidity and mortality that occurs as a result of lupus[47] and rheumatoid arthritis.[48] This focus corresponds with more research on the importance of inflammatory factors in the development of cardiovascular disease. At the point that women with rheumatoid arthritis undergo evaluation, coronary artery disease may have occurred a decade earlier.

■ DEPRESSION

Compared with heterosexual women, lesbians are at greater risk for depression. Furthermore, depression is more prevalent among people with coronary artery disease, and in these people, depression is associated with worse coronary outcomes. Clinical trials have not shown that specific treatments for depression improve cardiovascular outcomes although they modestly improve the symptoms of depression.[49]

■ **LESS ACCESS TO HEALTH CARE**

Surveys show that, compared with heterosexual women, lesbians have less access to health care and are less likely to have health insurance. Of those who do access health care, bisexual women, not lesbians, were less likely than heterosexual women to obtain screening tests, including lipid panels, at regular intervals. This is a barrier to potentially reducing risk factors for cardiovascular disease.[50]

■ ■ ■

In the scenario at the beginning of this chapter, Anna and Karen were "out" regarding their partnership. However, up to 30% of lesbians say they have not revealed their sexual orientation to their physician.[51] Because Anna and Karen were open about their relationship, Anna's physician could become an advocate for her and Karen in the health care system and with Anna's extended family, which would not have been possible had their relationship been a secret.

CONCLUSION

Heart disease is the leading cause of death among women and men. Clinicians should keep in mind that symptoms other than, or in addition to, classic chest pain, such as newly developed exercise intolerance, episodic nausea, abdominal pain, or palpitations, may yield a diagnosis of angina. A key strategy in preventing cardiovascular mortality is to reduce cardiovascular risk factors, especially for women who are already at risk. Lesbians may be at greater risk of heart disease due to their higher prevalence of tobacco exposure, obesity, and depression. Diabetes dramatically increases the risk of heart disease and mortality. Clinicians should consider recommending that lesbians ≥ 45 years old take enteric-coated, low-dose aspirin daily to decrease cardiovascular problems. Health care providers and their lesbian patients must pay greater attention to cardiovascular health and to potential heart disease and its complications.

REFERENCES

1. Mosca, L., Banka, C. L., Benjamin, E. J., Berra, K., Bushnell, C., Dolor, R. J., et al. (2007). Evidence-based guidelines for cardiovascular disease prevention in women: 2007 update. *Circulation, 115,* 1481–1501.

2. Rennert, N. J., & Charney, P. (2003). Preventing cardiovascular disease in diabetes and glucose intolerance: Evidence and implications for care. *Primary Care, 30,* 569–592.

3. Christian, A. H., Rosamond, W., White, A. R., & Mosca, L. (2007). Nine-year trends and racial and ethnic disparities in women's awareness of heart disease and stroke: An American Heart Association national study. *Journal of Women's Health, 16,* 68–81.

4. Lerner, D. J., & Kannel, W. B. (1986). Patterns of coronary heart disease morbidity and mortality in the sexes: A 26-year follow-up of the Framingham population. *American Heart Journal, 111,* 383–390.

5. Centers for Disease Control and Prevention. (2002). State-specific mortality from sudden cardiac death—United States, 1999. *Morbidity and Mortality Weekly Report, 51,* 123–126. Available at www.cdc.gov/mmwr/preview/mmwrhtml/mm5106a3.htm.

6. Rosamond, W., Flegal, K., Friday, G., Furie, K., Go, A., Greenlund, K., et al. (2007). Heart disease and stroke statistics—2007 update: A report from the American Heart Association Statistics Committee and Stroke Statistics Subcommittee. *Circulation, 115,* e69–171.

7. Shaw, L. J., Bugiardini, R., & Merz, C. N. (2009). Women and ischemic heart disease: Evolving knowledge. *Journal of the American College of Cardiology, 54,* 1561–1575.

8. Case, P., Austin, S. B., Hunter, D. J., Manson, J. E., Malspeis, S., Willett, W. C., et al. (2004). Sexual orientation, health risk factors, and physical functioning in the Nurses' Health Study II. Journal of Women's Health, 13, 1033–1047.

9. Pope, C. A. III, Burnett, R. T., Krewski, D., Jerrett, M., Shi, Y., Calle, E. E., et al. (2009). Cardiovascular mortality and exposure to airborne fine particulate matter and cigarette smoke: Shape of the exposure-response relationship. Circulation, 120, 941–948.

10. Valanis, B. G., Bowen, D. J., Bassford, T., Whitlock, E., Charney, P., & Carter, R. A. (2000). Sexual orientation and health: Comparisons in the Women's Health Initiative sample. Archives of Family Medicine, 9, 843–853.

11. Diamant, A. L., & Wold, C. (2003). Sexual orientation and variation in physical and mental health status among women. Journal of Women's Health, 12, 41–49.

12. Mora, S., Redberg, R. F., Cui, Y., Whiteman, M. K., Flaws, J. A., Sharrett, A. R., et al. (2003). Ability of exercise testing to predict cardiovascular and all-cause death in asymptomatic women: A 20-year follow-up of the Lipid Research Clinics Prevalence Study. Journal of the American Medical Association, 290, 1600–1607.

13. Christou, D. D., Jones, P. P., Jorder, J., Diedrich, A., Robertson, D., & Seals, D. R. (2005). Women have lower tonic autonomic support of arterial blood pressure and less effective baroreflex buffering than men. Circulation, 111, 494–498.

14. Rathore, S. S., Wang, Y., & Krumholz, H. M. (2002). Sex-based differences in the effect of digoxin for the treatment of heart failure. *New England Journal of Medicine, 347,* 1403–1411.

15. Berg, J., Björck, L., Dudas, K., Lappas, G., & Rosengren, A. (2009). Symptoms of a first acute myocardial infarction in women and men. *Gender Medicine, 6,* 454–462.

16. Bertoni, A. G., Bonds, D. E., Lovato, J., Goff, D. C., & Brancati, F. L. (2004). Sex disparities in procedure use for acute myocardial infarction in the United States, 1995 to 2001. *American Heart Journal, 147,* 1054–1060.

17. Sheifer, S. E., Manolio, T. A., & Gersh, B. J. (2001). Unrecognized myocardial infarction. *Annals of Internal Medicine, 135,* 801–811.

18. Grady, D., Herrington, D., Bittner, V., Blumenthal, R., Davidson, M., Hlatky, M., et al. (2002). Cardiovascular disease outcomes during 6.8 years of hormone therapy: Heart and Estrogen/Progestin Replacement Study follow-up (HERS II). *Journal of the American Medical Association, 288,* 49–57.

19. Albert, C. M., Chae, C. U., Grodstein, F., Rose, L. M., Rexrode, K. M., Ruskin, J. N., et al. (2003). Prospective study of sudden cardiac death among women in the United States. *Circulation, 107,* 2096–2101.

20. Hemingway, H., Langenberg, C., Damant, J., Frost, C., Pyörälä, K., & Barrett-Connor, E. (2008). Prevalence of angina in women versus men: A systematic review and meta-analysis of international variations across 31 countries. *Circulation, 117,* 1526–1536.

21. Hemingway, H., McCallum, A., Shipley, M., Manderbacka, K., Martikainen, P., & Keskimäki, I. (2006). Incidence and prognostic implications of stable angina pectoris among women and men. *Journal of the American Medical Association, 295,* 1404–1411.

22. Ridker, P. M., Cook, N. R., Lee, I. M., Gordon, D., Gaziano, J. M., Manson, J. E., et al. (2005). A randomized trial of low-dose aspirin in the primary prevention of cardiovascular disease in women. *New England Journal of Medicine, 352,* 1293–1304.

23. Prochaska, J. O., & Velicer, W. F. (1997). The transtheoretical model of health behavior change. *American Journal of Health Promotion, 12,* 38–48.

24. Centers for Disease Control and Prevention. (2007). Cigarette smoking among adults— United States, 2006. *Morbidity and Mortality Weekly Report, 56,* 1157–1161.

25. Kenfield, S. A., Stampfer, M. J., Rosner, B. A., & Colditz, G. A. (2008). Smoking and smoking cessation in relation to mortality in women. Journal of the American Medical Association, 299, 2037–2047.

26. Wee, C. C., Rigotti, N. A., Davis, R. B., & Phillips, R. S. (2001). Relationship between smoking and weight control efforts among adults in the United States. Archives of Internal Medicine, 161, 546–550.

27. Tang, H., Greenwood, G. L., Cowling, D. W., Lloyd, J. C., Roeseler, A. G., & Bal, D. G. (2004). Cigarette smoking among lesbians, gays, and bisexuals: How serious a problem? Cancer Causes & Control, 15, 797–803.

28. Pérez-Stable, E. J., Herrera, B., Jacob, P. III, & Benowitz, N. L. (1998). Nicotine metabolism and intake in Black and White smokers. Journal of the American Medical Association, 280, 152–156.

29. Anastos, K., Charney, P., Charon, R. A., Cohen, E., Jones, C. Y., Marte, C., et al. (1991). Hypertension in women: What is really known? The Women's Caucus, Working Group on Women's Health of the Society of General Internal Medicine. *Annals of Internal Medicine, 115,* 287–293.

30. Chobanian, A. V., Bakris, G. L, Black, H. R., Cushman, W. C., Green, L. A., Izzo Jr., J. L., et al. (2003). Seventh report of the Joint National Committee on Prevention, Detection, Evaluation, and Treatment of High Blood Pressure. *Hypertension, 42,* 1206–1252.

31. Oliveria, S. A., Chen, R. S., McCarthy, B. D., Davis, C. C., & Hill, M. N. (2005). Hypertension knowledge, awareness, and attitudes in a hypertensive population. *Journal of General Internal Medicine, 20,* 219–225.

32. Cooper, W. O., Hernandez-Diaz, S., Arbogast, P. G., Dudley, J. A., Dyer, S., Gideon, P. S., et al. (2006). Major congenital malformations after first-trimester exposure to ACE inhibitors. *New England Journal of Medicine, 354,* 2443–2451.

33. Wright, J. M., & Musini, V. M. (2009). First-line drugs for hypertension. *Cochrane Database of Systematic Reviews, Jul 8,* CD001841.

34. LaCroix, A. Z., Ott, S. M., Ichikawa, L., Scholes, D., & Barlow, W. E. (2000). Low-dose hydrochlorothiazide and preservation of bone mineral density in older adults. A randomized, double-blind, placebo-controlled trial. *Annals of Internal Medicine, 133*, 516–526.

35. Grundy, S. M., Cleeman, J. I., Merz, C. N., Brewer Jr., H. B., Clark, L. T., Hunninghake, D. B., et al. (2004). Implications of recent clinical trials for the National Cholesterol Education Program Adult Treatment Panel III guidelines. *Journal of the American College of Cardiology, 44*, 720–732.

36. Cheung, B. M., Lauder, I. J., Lau, C. P., & Kumana, C. R. (2004). Meta-analysis of large randomized controlled trials to evaluate the impact of statins on cardiovascular outcomes. *British Journal of Clinical Pharmacology, 57*, 640–651.

37. Nag S. S., Daniel, G. W., Bullano, M. F., Kamal-Bahl, S., Sajjan, S. G, Hu, H., et al. (2007). LDL-C goal attainment among patients newly diagnosed with coronary heart disease or diabetes in a commercial HMO. *Journal of Managed Care Pharmacy, 13*, 652–663.

38. Santos, R. D, Waters, D. D, Tarasenko, L., Messig, M., Jukema, J. W., Ferrières, J., et al. (2009). Low- and high-density lipoprotein cholesterol goal attainment in dyslipidemic women: The Lipid Treatment Assessment Project (L-TAP) 2. *American Heart Journal, 158*, 860–866.

39. Prospective Diabetes Study Group. (1997). United Kingdom Prospective Diabetes Study 27: Plasma lipids and lipoproteins at diagnosis of NIDDM by age and sex, UK. *Diabetes Care, 20*, 1683–1687.

40. Persell, S. D., & Baker, D. W. (2004). Aspirin use among adults with diabetes: Recent trends and emerging sex disparities. *Archives of Internal Medicine, 164*, 2492–2499.

41. Wilson, P. W., D'Agostino, R. B., Sullivan, L., Parise, H., & Kannel, W. B. (2002). Overweight and obesity as determinants of cardiovascular risk: The Framingham experience. *Archives of Internal Medicine, 16*, 1867–1872.

42. Ogden, C. L., Carroll, M. D., Curtin, L. R., McDowell, M. A., Tabak, C. J., & Flegal, K. M. (2006). Prevalence of overweight and obesity in the United States, 1999–2004. *Journal of the American Medical Association, 295*, 1549–1555.

43. Boehmer, U., Bowen, D. J., & Bauer, G. R. (2007). Overweight and obesity in sexual-minority women: Evidence from population-based data. *American Journal of Public Health, 97*, 1134–1140.

44. Zhang, C., Rexrode, K. M., van Dam, R. M., Li, T. Y., & Hu, F. B. (2008). Abdominal obesity and the risk of all-cause, cardiovascular, and cancer mortality: Sixteen years of follow-up in U.S. women. *Circulation, 117*, 1658–1667.

45. Roberts, S. A., Dibble, S. L., Nussey, B., & Casey, K. (2003). Cardiovascular disease risk in lesbian women. *Women's Health Issues, 13*, 167–174.

46. Freiberg, M. S., Chang, Y. F., Kraemer, K. L., Robinson, J. G., Adams-Campbell, L. L., & Kuller, L. L. (2009). Alcohol consumption, hypertension, and total mortality among women. *American Journal of Hypertension, 11*, 1212–1218.

47. Asanuma, Y., Oeser, A., Shintani, A. K., Turner, E., Olsen, N., Fazio, S., et al. (2003). Premature coronary-artery atherosclerosis in systemic lupus erythematosus. *New England Journal of Medicine, 349*, 2407–2415.

48. Kaplan, M. J. (2006). Cardiovascular disease in rheumatoid arthritis. *Current Opinion in Rheumatology, 18,* 289–297.

49. Lichtman, J. H., Bigger, J. T., Blumenthal, J. A., Frasure-Smith, N., Kaufmann, P. G., Lespérance, F., et al. (2008). Depression and coronary artery heart disease. Recommendations for screening, referral, and treatment: A science advisory from the American Heart Association Prevention Committee of the Council on Cardiovascular Nursing, Council on Clinical Cardiology, Council on Epidemiology and Prevention, and Interdisciplinary Council on Quality of Care and Outcomes Research. Endorsed by the American Psychiatric Association. *Circulation, 118,* 1768–1775.

50. Koh, A. S. (2000). Use of preventive health behaviors by lesbians, bisexual, and heterosexual women: Questionnaire survey. *Western Journal of Medicine, 172,* 379–384.

51. O'Hanlan, K. A. (2006). Health policy considerations for our sexual minority patients. *Obstetrics & Gynecology, 107,* 709–714.

ABOUT THE AUTHORS

Pamela Charney, MD, is Professor of Clinical Internal Medicine and Associate Professor of Obstetrics and Gynecology at the Weill Medical College of Cornell University, New York City. Her academic interest is the impact of patient characteristics on health and disease, especially coronary artery disease. She was an investigator with the Women's Health Initiative, evaluating data about self-identified lesbians.

Dana P. McGlothlin, MD, is Assistant Professor in the Division of Cardiology, Department of Medicine, at the University of California, San Francisco. She is the Director of the Coronary Care Unit, Associate Director of the Pulmonary Hypertension Program, member of the Advanced Heart Failure and Transplant Program, and attending Echocardiographer at UCSF. Her clinical research interests are pulmonary arterial hypertension and heart failure.

CHAPTER 27

"I Am Filling Up and Spilling Over."

URINARY INCONTINENCE AMONG LESBIANS

LEAH M. KELLEY, MD

LESLEE L. SUBAK, MD

PAMELA, *57, presents to her family physician for a routine physical exam and gynecologic check-up. She is 6 years postmenopausal and healthy except for moderate hypertension, which she treats with a diuretic. Asked about her marital status, Pamela says she is in a long-term relationship with another woman.*

Aside from a body mass index of 37, the physical exam is unremarkable. However, Pamela reports daily involuntary leakage of urine that requires her to wear a pantyliner. "I just can't seem to get to the bathroom on time," she says, "and I leak whenever I cough or laugh. This is just part of getting older, isn't it?"

The doctor replies, "Well, it can be, although there are some risk factors, such as obesity, which is very common among lesbians."

Pamela becomes withdrawn. The doctor recognizes her withdrawal and turns instead to a discussion of Pamela's exercise regimen.

■ ■ ■

Involuntary loss of urine, or urinary incontinence (UI), affects more than 13 million American women, 25% of whom are of reproductive age and up to 50% of whom are postmenopausal.[1-3] The condition is associated with a profound adverse impact on quality of life and a higher risk of falls, fractures, nursing home admissions, and social isolation. Each year, consumers spend more than $30 billion on incontinence, including $20 billion in out-of-pocket costs for incontinence management.[4] Yet UI among adult women is a frequently unrecognized and undertreated problem.

This chapter reviews the definitions and epidemiology of UI, focusing on the associated fixed and modifiable risk factors, and briefly describes clinical evaluation and treatment. Although there are no population-based or clinical data regarding the prevalence or clinical course of UI among lesbians, available epidemiological data regarding their risks for incontinence and its potential presentations enable inferences about the effects this condition may have on them.

BACKGROUND

UI is classified based on clinical presentation and severity. The primary circumstances leading to leakage of urine determine the type of incontinence. Types include involuntary loss of urine as a result of physical stress from coughing, sneezing, straining, or exercise; loss of urine associated with a strong urge or need to void; mixed incontinence (episodes of both stress and urge); overflow of urine from an abnormally full bladder; and leakage unassociated with the urinary tract. Some patients present with overactive bladder syndrome—urinary frequency, urgency and/or nocturia, and possibly urge incontinence.

The prevalence of UI types varies according to age and underlying health status. Stress incontinence is more common in younger, ambulatory women, while urge and mixed incontinence increase with age and other health conditions. Symptoms are characterized by severity, frequency, and impact on quality of life. Researchers have used frequency of incontinence episodes, volume of urine loss, and use of pads or undergarments to categorize symptom severity. Table 27.1 summarizes the differential diagnosis of UI types.

TABLE 27.1. DIFFERENTIAL DIAGNOSIS OF URINARY INCONTINENCE IN WOMEN

TYPE	PRESENTATION	TIMING	VOLUME
Stress	Leakage associated with greater abdominal pressure from coughing, sneezing, straining, or exercise	Immediate	Small to moderate
Urge	Leakage occurs with a strong urge or need to void	Delayed	Large
Mixed	Combination of stress and urge incontinence. One or the other may predominate.	Varies	Varies
Overflow	Leakage resulting from an overflow of urine from an abnormally full bladder	Frequent	Small
Other	Leakage due to factors unassociated with the urinary tract, such as impaired mobility or neurologic deficits	N.A.	Varies

Source: Authors

EPIDEMIOLOGY

The proportion of women with UI varies widely—from 2% to 55%—depending on the definitions researchers used and the populations they surveyed. In a population-based study in Norway, 25% of all women reported symptomatic urinary leakage, and of these, 7% reported severe (daily) leakage. Fifty percent of respondents had stress incontinence, 11% urge incontinence, and 36% mixed symptoms. Among older women, the prevalence of daily UI was 12%.[2] Researchers in the United States followed 64,000 women for at least 2 years in the Nurses' Health Study. The 2-year incidence of UI was 13.7%, but the 2-year remission rate—that is, the percentage of women who reported leaking at least once a month at baseline and no leakage on follow-up—was 13.9%.[5] This surprising result underscores the dynamic nature of UI as a clinical condition.

RISK FACTORS

Among nonmodifiable risk factors for UI in women are age, race/ethnicity, and possibly genetics. Potentially modifiable risk factors include vaginal delivery, other obstetric events, and hysterectomy, and those that are modifiable or preventable include obesity, diabetes, smoking, chronic cough, and constipation.

Age

Participants in the Health, Aging, and Body Composition Study were well-functioning, community-dwelling women between 70 and 79 years old. Ten percent reported severe (daily) incontinence, 12% reported weekly incontinence, and 24% reported incontinence in the prior 12 months.[6] In another study, the prevalence of daily incontinence among women ≥ 69 years old was 14%, and it increased 30% for every 5 years of advancing age.[7] Cross-sectional analysis of data from the Nurses' Health Study II revealed that participants 50 to 54 years old were 1.8 times more likely than women younger than 40 to have severe incontinence. This significantly greater risk increased steadily with age[8] (Figure 27.1).

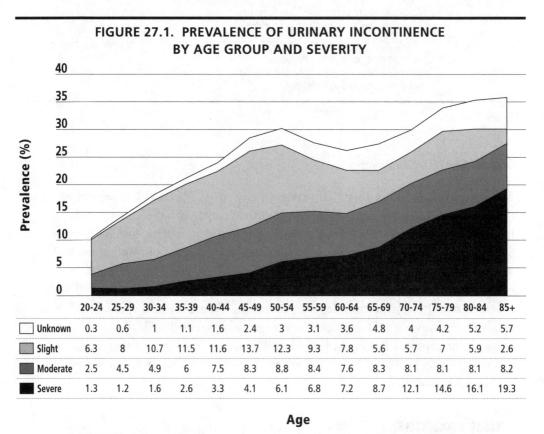

FIGURE 27.1. PREVALENCE OF URINARY INCONTINENCE BY AGE GROUP AND SEVERITY

	20-24	25-29	30-34	35-39	40-44	45-49	50-54	55-59	60-64	65-69	70-74	75-79	80-84	85+
Unknown	0.3	0.6	1	1.1	1.6	2.4	3	3.1	3.6	4.8	4	4.2	5.2	5.7
Slight	6.3	8	10.7	11.5	11.6	13.7	12.3	9.3	7.8	5.6	5.7	7	5.9	2.6
Moderate	2.5	4.5	4.9	6	7.5	8.3	8.8	8.4	7.6	8.3	8.1	8.1	8.1	8.2
Severe	1.3	1.2	1.6	2.6	3.3	4.1	6.1	6.8	7.2	8.7	12.1	14.6	16.1	19.3

Age

Source: Hannestad, Y. S., Rortveit, G., Sandvik, H., & Hunskaar, S. (2000). A community-based epidemiological survey of female urinary incontinence: The Norwegian EPINCONT study. Epidemiology of Incontinence in the County of Nord-Trøndelag. *Journal of Clinical Epidemiology, 53*, 1150–1157.

Race/Ethnicity

Research clearly shows race/ethnicity differences as well. In a population-based cohort of more than 2,000 women, Latinas had an overall higher prevalence of weekly UI (36%) compared with White (30%), African American (30%), and Asian women (19%). The odds of stress UI were lowest among African American and Asian women, while the risk of urge UI was about the same in all ethnic groups, according to multivariate analyses to determine independent risk factors.[9] Another study of a convenience sample of 800 women attending a nonurgent gynecology clinic found that White women experienced significantly more UI symptoms than their Black and Hispanic counterparts did—41% versus 30%. The risk of urge incontinence appeared to be the same for all groups, but the risk of stress UI was still higher among White women.[10]

Reproductive History

UI increases during pregnancy and the postpartum period.[11,12] But results from studies that tried to retrospectively correlate its occurrence in later life with reproductive history have been mixed. In the Nurses' Health Study, the risk of any UI among parous women (those who had given live birth) was 40% higher, and the risk among those who had given three live births was 60% higher.[8] A population-based study found that one or more vaginal deliveries was associated with double the risk of UI compared with women who had not given birth and with those who had delivered by cesarean section only.[13] In a very large population-based study in Norway, researchers stratified women according to the number and mode of deliveries. The prevalence of any UI was 10% among women who had never delivered, 16% among women who had delivered by C-section only, and 21% among those who had delivered vaginally at least once. The risk of incontinence increased significantly as the number of vaginal deliveries increased—from 21% of women with one vaginal delivery to 28% of women with four or more such deliveries. After multivariate analysis adjusted for age, parity, body mass index (BMI), and years since the last delivery, moderate to severe incontinence was 2.6 times more likely in women with any vaginal parity than in nulliparous women, and 1.4 times more likely in women who had delivered by C-section only. The risk of moderate to severe incontinence in women with only vaginal deliveries was 2.2 times greater than it was in women who had delivered by C-section only.[14] Attempts to correlate UI rates with obstetric risk factors, such as weight of the largest infant delivered vaginally, episiotomy, length of the second stage of labor, and operative vaginal delivery, have produced inconsistent results.[12]

Obesity

Obesity is an independent risk factor for UI.[15] More than 50% of American women are obese (BMI $\geq$ 30.0 kg/m^2) or overweight (BMI = 25.0 to 29.9 kg/m^2) and the prevalence of obesity is increasing.[16] Epidemiological studies suggest that obesity is one of the strongest risk factors for UI: each 5-unit increase in BMI is associated with a 60% to 100% higher risk of daily incontinence.[12,17,18] Among older women with incontinence, 65% to 75% are overweight or obese and the prevalence of daily incontinence increases from 10% in those with a BMI < 25.0 to 20% in those with a BMI ≥ 30.0.[7] BMI is also highly correlated with greater leakage in middle-age women. Among participants in the Nurses' Health Study, the risk of prevalent UI was 2.2 times higher in women with a BMI of 30.0 to 34.9 and 3.8 times higher in those with a BMI of at least 35.0. For each 1 kg/m^2 increase in BMI, there was a 7% higher risk of weekly or more frequent incontinence. There also was an association between UI and long-term weight gain, or the change in reported weight since age 18: compared with women who maintained their weight within a 2-kg range, those who gained 5 kg were at significantly higher risk of developing the condition.[19]

■■■

At the end of Pamela's visit, the clinician again raised the issue of weight management and was able to engage Pamela in a discussion of the importance and difficulty of weight loss. The clinician referred her to appropriate resources for weight loss information and to the practice's incontinence class.

Diabetes

Diabetes also is a strong, independent risk factor for UI. In one study, the prevalence of UI in older women who received medication for this disease was 1.8 times higher and, in those who received insulin, 3.5 times higher.[6] Another study showed an odds ratio (OR) of 1.5 for urge incontinence in women with any history of diabetes.[20]

Other Risk Factors

Many studies have investigated modifiable risk factors, such as smoking, exercise/activity level, and caffeine and alcohol consumption. Several of them established a link between smoking and UI.[21] One found that current and former women smokers had a 40% higher risk of severe UI compared with nonsmokers, and those who smoked more than 20 cigarettes a day were at higher risk of all types of incontinence. In addition, low-impact physical activity was associated with less risk of any UI symptoms and severe UI symptoms in women (OR = 0.8 and 0.5, respectively), but high-impact physical activity did not seem to affect UI incidence or prevalence. Caffeine intake from tea was positively correlated with incontinence (OR = 1.5 for severe incontinence in women who consumed three or more cups daily), but there was no evidence that coffee or alcohol had a similar effect.[22]

Certain aspects of patients' histories, such as dementia and poor functional status, are also risk factors.[23] Other factors include postmenopausal oral estrogen and combined estrogen/progesterone therapy, which are associated with a higher prevalence of and more severe incontinence. For example, Jackson and colleagues reported a greater risk of both stress and urge incontinence among older, current users of oral estrogen.[6] In a randomized, blind trial, 39% of women with incontinence at baseline who were assigned to estrogen/progesterone therapy experienced an increase in incontinence severity compared with 27% in the placebo group. They also had an average of 0.7 more weekly incontinence episodes.[24] Finally, a literature review reported a 60% increase in UI risk after age 60 among women who had had a hysterectomy.[25]

The epidemiologic association between depression and incontinence is clear. Bump and McClish found that among elderly women, the risk of urge incontinence in those who also reported depressive symptoms was 2.7 times greater.[21] A population-based study of women 50 to 69 years old demonstrated a highly significant correlation between depression and mild-to-moderate ($OR = 1.41$) or severe ($OR = 1.82$) incontinence symptoms.[26]

INITIAL EVALUATION

Initial evaluation of UI begins with a thorough medical, surgical, obstetric, and gynecologic history and a complete list of the patient's medications. Clinicians can use a three-part screening tool to determine the type of incontinence (Table 27.2). These questions reliably correlate with clinical findings. It is important to carefully note the timing, frequency, and severity of incontinence episodes and the amount and nature of fluid intake. A urinary diary that the patient keeps for 1 to 3 days correlates well with the results of urodynamic testing[27] (Table 27.3). She records each void, each episode of incontinence, and the type and amount of fluid intake. Diary entries can be very useful in planning therapy, such as fluid management and the type and timing of medication. Patient awareness of voiding patterns can also serve as effective behavioral therapy by enabling patients to self-regulate fluid intake and the timing of voids. The clinician should rule out transient causes of incontinence, especially urinary tract infection, and other potentially reversible causes, such as atrophic vaginitis, medication side effects, greater fluid intake or urine production, fecal impaction, and reduced mobility.

A pelvic exam is unnecessary, but it might provide clues to other underlying etiologies. Based on the patient's history, a directed exam may include inspection of the urethra for diverticulum or inflammation, catheterization for postvoid residual urine, and evaluation of vaginal atrophy and the degree and nature of pelvic organ

TABLE 27.2. INITIAL SCREENING FOR URINARY INCONTINENCE

1. **During the last 3 months, have you leaked urine (even a small amount)?**
   ☐ Yes   ☐ No

2. **During the last 3 months, did you leak urine (check all that apply):**
   ☐ a. When you were performing some physical activity, such as coughing, sneezing, lifting, or exercise?
   ☐ b. When you had the urge or the feeling that you needed to empty your bladder, but you could not get to the toilet fast enough?
   ☐ c. Without physical activity and without a sense of urgency?

3. **During the last 3 months, did you leak urine most often (check only one):**
   ☐ a. When you were performing some physical activity, such as coughing, sneezing, lifting, or exercise?
   ☐ b. When you had the urge or the feeling that you needed to empty your bladder, but you could not get to the toilet fast enough?
   ☐ c. Without physical activity and without a sense of urgency?
   ☐ d. About equally as often with physical activity as with a sense of urgency?

TYPE OF URINARY INCONTINENCE ARE BASED ON RESPONSES TO QUESTION 3	
RESPONSES TO QUESTION 3	**TYPE OF INCONTINENCE**
a. Most often with physical activity	Stress only or stress predominant
b. Most often with the urge to empty the bladder	Urge only or urge predominant
c. Without physical activity or a sense of urgency	Other cause only or other cause predominant
d. About equally with physical activity and a sense of urgency	Mixed

Source: Brown, J. S., Bradley, C. S., Subak, L. L., Richter, H. E., Kraus, S. R., Brubaker, L., et al. (2006). The sensitivity and specificity of a simple test to distinguish between urge and stress urinary incontinence. *Annals of Internal Medicine, 144,* 715–723.

prolapse. A bimanual exam may rule out other gynecologic pathology, and a rectal exam assesses anal sphincter tone and the presence of fecal impaction, which may be associated with UI in older women. A screening neurologic exam—of mental status and of sensory and motor function of the perineum and lower extremities—can exclude neurologic disease as the underlying cause. Urodynamic testing measures detrusor function, bladder capacity and compliance, and sensation to void. While

TABLE 27.3. URINARY DIARY

Name: _____

Day/Date: _____

Instructions:

1. In the first column, mark an "**X**" every time you urinate in the toilet.
2. In the second column, mark an "**X**" every time you accidently leaked urine.
3. If an accident occurred, indicate the reason or circumstances surrounding the accident—for example, "*coughed*," "*bent over*," or "*sudden urge*."
4. Under "**Fluid Intake**," describe the type (*coffee, juice, tea,* etc.) and amount (*1 cup, 1 quart,* etc.).
5. Circle the time you went to bed and the time you got up.
6. Record the number and type of pads you used.

TIME	URINATE IN TOILET	LEAKING ACCIDENT	REASON FOR ACCIDENT	FLUID INTAKE	
				TYPE	AMOUNT
6 a.m.					
7 a.m.					
8 a.m.*					

Table continues in this format for 24 hours.

Number and type of pads used in 24 hours: _____

Notes: _____

_____

_____

Source: Assessment and treatment of urinary incontinence. Scientific Committee of the First International Consultation on Incontinence. (2000). *Lancet, 355,* 2153–2158.

such testing may be useful in evaluating patients with complex symptoms or voiding dysfunction, it is unnecessary in all patients with incontinence before proceeding to treatment based on clinical presentation.

NONPHARMACOLOGIC TREATMENT

First-line treatment for all types of UI involves patient education and thorough evaluation and modification of lifestyle factors. Patient education alone significantly improves symptoms. A randomized, controlled trial of 222 women with urge incontinence who received biofeedback, verbal instruction, or a self-help booklet showed that these techniques reduced the frequency of incontinence episodes by 59% to 69%. There was no statistical difference between the modalities of education.[28] Clinicians should encourage all women who present with incontinence to stop smoking and reduce their intake of caffeine and excess oral fluids. The most effective education includes bladder training, pelvic muscle exercises, and urge suppression. These interventions influence function of the bladder and the pelvic floor or bladder outlet.

Bladder training, which helps patients re-establish voluntary bladder control, is primarily for urge symptoms, but it also is effective for mixed symptoms and for patients with reduced voiding sensation. Patients learn how to void on a set schedule, beginning with about 30 to 60 minutes between voids and then slowly increasing the interval to 3 or 4 hours. Relaxation techniques effectively suppress the strong urge to void that is associated with urge UI, and reduce incontinent episodes in older women by 50% to 80%.[29]

Pelvic floor muscle exercises, or Kegel exercises, are sometimes prescribed to strengthen the muscles of the pelvic floor and to improve patient awareness and control of them (Table 27.4). Several randomized, controlled trials have demonstrated

---

TABLE 27.4. PATIENT INSTRUCTIONS FOR PELVIC FLOOR EXERCISES

Begin by locating the muscles to be exercised:

- Squeeze the area of the rectum to tighten the anus as if trying not to pass gas. Feel the sensation of the muscles pulling inward and upward.

- Insert a finger in your vagina and contract the vaginal muscles upward. The squeeze you feel will confirm that you are exercising the correct muscles.

Remember not to tense your stomach, buttock, or thigh muscles. Using other muscles will defeat the purpose of the exercise and slow your progress.

Exercise instructions:

When you have located the correct muscle, set aside a short time each day for three exercise sessions. At breakfast, lunch, or dinner, or before going to bed, are convenient and easy-to-remember times for many women. Make it a habit to exercise at regularly scheduled times each day.

Squeeze your muscle for a slow count of three. Then relax the muscle completely to a slow count of three. Do not "push out" during the relaxation of the muscle. Repeat the exercise 15 times. Fifteen exercises is one set.

Be sure to do three complete sets each day. As you feel your muscle strength growing, increase the count to five for each squeeze and each relaxation.

Source: The Women's Continence Center, University of California, San Francisco.

---

that a regular regimen of pelvic floor muscle training (PFMT) with or without adjunct therapy effectively reduces stress and urge incontinence, with decreases of 50% to 80% in incontinence frequency.[30]

In biofeedback, patients learn pelvic floor muscle exercises through directed instructions and receive feedback from electromyography or manometry that reinforces their actions. This modality can help women isolate pelvic muscles and improve the efficacy of PFMT.[31] Researchers have experimented with direct electrical stimulation of the pelvic floor using external vaginal or anal electrodes to enhance the learning and efficacy of pelvic floor muscle training. However, evidence is mixed on whether adding electrical stimulation to PFMT, compared with PFMT alone, improves outcomes.[32] For patients in whom electrical stimulation is promising, implantable devices for sacral neuromodulation are an option.[33] For stress incontinence, secondary treatment may include a stress-dish pessary—especially one with an incontinence knob—to support the pelvic floor. This shape supports the bladder neck and gently compresses the urethro-vesical junction.

Losing weight also improves incontinence symptoms. One study found that overweight and obese women who lost as little as 3% to 5% of their baseline weight reduced weekly incontinence episodes by 50% to 60%, which was significantly more than the reduction in a control group. The experimental group had maintained this improvement at 6- and 9-month follow-up, with 18% of participants reporting 100% improvement in symptoms and 35% reporting 75% improvement.[34] In a randomized, controlled trial involving 338 overweight and obese women who had at least 10 UI episodes per week, participants in an intensive, 6-month weight loss program that included diet, exercise, and behavior modification lost more weight (8.0% compared with 1.6% in the control group, $p < 0.001$) and experienced a greater reduction in the mean number of weekly incontinence episodes (47% compared with 28% in the control group, $p = 0.01$). Thus, less UI may be another benefit among the extensive health improvements associated with moderate weight reduction in overweight and obsese women.[35]

■ ■ ■

Pamela returned to her primary care provider after attending the incontinence class. They agreed to change Pamela's antihypertensive treatment from a diuretic to a beta-blocker, which controls her blood pressure well and reduces her frequency of urination. She subsequently attended a weight management seminar and had lost 10 pounds by the time of her next visit. Pamela's symptoms became less severe and she only wore a pad during strenuous exercise. She still reports occasional leakage with the urge to void.

PHARMACOLOGIC TREATMENT

Medications are available to treat urge and overflow incontinence as well as nocturia (Table 27.5). Generally, these agents, which inhibit the bladder's contractile activity, have an anticholinergic or antimuscarinic effect. While they provide excellent symptom relief and reduce weekly incontinence episodes by 15% to 60%, they may also cause bothersome side effects, such as dry mouth, constipation, drowsiness, and blurred vision.[36-39] Newer, sustained-release medications may cause fewer side effects.

Medical treatment of stress UI has been largely unsuccessful, although some initial small studies indicate that imipramine may be partially effective. Researchers have not completed randomized, controlled trials to confirm these findings.[40] In the past, clinicians treated stress incontinence with estrogen, which is no longer recommended. Early case series indicated that estrogen reduced incontinence episodes, but subsequent clinical trials contradicted this finding. Two large randomized, controlled trials—the Women's Health Initiative and the Heart and Estrogen Replacement Study—evaluated the effect of estrogen-only and combined hormone replacement therapy on stress, urge, and mixed UI. The prevalence of UI increased 40% to 50% over a 4-year period and 20% to 60% at 12 months.[24,41]

SURGICAL TREATMENT

Surgery can effectively treat stress incontinence but not urge incontinence. Treatments for stress incontinence in the setting of urethral hypermobility are retropubic colposuspension or bladder neck sling suspension. There are a number of surgical techniques for performing colposuspension, which generally require an abdominal incision. Sling suspensions using a vaginal approach have largely supplanted colposuspension, unless it is combined with other necessary surgery. Research comparing Burch colposuspension and fascial sling demonstrated higher success rates with fascial sling but also a higher incidence of minor postoperative complications.[42] Currently, the most common sling procedure is the tension-free vaginal tape (TVT), in which the surgeon places a narrow piece of polypropylene mesh under the mid-urethra and passes it through the anterior abdominal wall behind the pubic bone. A more recent variation on TVT is the transobturator tape; it avoids some of the potential TVT complications. Although initial data suggest that the two techniques have comparable success rates, there has not been a randomized, controlled trial to confirm this.[43] Patients whose stress incontinence results from intrinsic sphincter deficiency may benefit from urethral bulking agents, such as collagen and carbon-coated beads, that are inserted during outpatient surgery. These agents produce excellent results, but retreatment may be necessary.[44]

TABLE 27.5. MEDICATIONS FOR URINARY INCONTINENCE AND OVERACTIVE BLADDER

TYPE	MEDICATIONS	ADMINISTRATION*
Immediate-release (short-acting) oral medication	Oxybutynin (Ditropan), 5.0-mg tablets	½ tablet twice daily to 1 tablet three times daily
	Tolterodine (Detrol), 2.0-mg tablets	1 tablet twice daily. May reduce dose to ½ tablet twice daily.
	Trospium (Sanctura), 20-mg tablets	1 tablet twice daily. Take on an empty stomach 1 hour before eating. In older women, 1 tablet at bedtime.
Extended-release oral medication	Oxybutynin (Ditropan XL), 5.0-mg tablets (also available in 10-mg and 15-mg tablets)	Start with 5.0–10 mg daily, increase by 5.0 mg/day every week to a maximum of 30 mg daily
	Oxybutynin transdermal patch (Oxytrol), which delivers 3.9 mg/day	Twice weekly
	Darifenacin (Enablex), 7.5-mg tablets	7.5 mg daily
	Fesoterodine (Toviaz), 4.0-mg tablets	4.0 mg daily
	Solifenacin (VESIcare), 5.0-mg tablets	5.0 mg daily
	Tolterodine LA (Detrol LA), 2.0-mg and 4.0-mg tablets	4.0 mg daily. If patient is taking a potent CYP3A4 inhibitor, maximum of 2.0 mg daily.
	Trospium (Sanctura XR), 60-mg capsules	60 mg daily. Take on an empty stomach 1 hour before eating.
Topical gel	Oxybutynin (Gelnique), 1.0-g sachet containing 100 mg of active ingredient	About 1 sachet daily

NOTES

Listed doses are maximum dosing regimens. In general, patients should begin with lower doses. Low dosing is essential in the elderly.

Contraindications: narrow-angle glaucoma or severe liver or kidney disease.

Side effects: dry mouth, blurred vision, and constipation are the most common. Elderly persons sometimes become confused or hallucinate. Side effects limit the most tolerable dose.

Alternative: 10 mg of imipramine at bedtime and adjust as often as weekly. Adjust per the patient's urinary diary and symptoms to a maximum of 100 mg at bedtime. Use with caution in the elderly due to hypotension and/or cognitive impairment.

Source: Authors

Success rates for these procedures vary greatly depending on surgeons' experience and the types of patients. One prospective study found significant improvements in patient-reported frequency of incontinence episodes and a satisfaction rate of 91% after TVT.[45] A number of studies have noted that urodynamic and objective cure rates are lower than subjective cure rates, and that patients were satisfied despite incomplete remission of symptoms.[46]

POSSIBLE INCONTINENCE RISKS AMONG LESBIANS

Lesbians may have health needs and risk factors that differ from those of their heterosexual peers. Known risk factors among lesbians, such as higher BMI, substance use, and depression, may make them more likely to experience symptomatic incontinence.

Parity

Lesbians are less likely to be parous. Marrazzo and Stine found that in a convenience sample of women who reported same-sex sexual activity in the preceding year, 25% had been pregnant. Of those who had ever been pregnant, 21% reported a live birth.[47] In contrast, 84% of U.S. women between 40 and 44 years old reported at least one live birth.[48] One study looked at lesbians and their heterosexual sisters. Thirty-two percent of the self-identified lesbians reported having ever been pregnant, compared with 86% of the heterosexual sisters, and consequently had had significantly fewer live births (mean = 0.8 vs. 1.4).[49] While this may increase lesbians' risk of adverse outcomes such as breast and ovarian cancer, it should protect them from developing UI.

Obesity

The greater prevalence of obesity among lesbians and bisexual women may make them more prone to symptomatic incontinence. Analysis of participants in the Women's Health Initiative based on sexual orientation revealed a significantly greater prevalence of obesity among lesbians. Fifty-one percent of lesbians and 48% of bisexuals, compared with 46% of heterosexual women, were obese.[50] In the Nurses' Health Study, 30% of lesbians, 28% of bisexual women, and 20% of heterosexual women had a BMI > 30.0.[51]

Smoking

Many studies show that lesbians are more likely than heterosexual women to be current or lifetime smokers. One of the largest was a subanalysis of participants in the Nurses' Health Study II who self-identified as lesbian or bisexual. Rates of current smoking were significantly higher among lesbians and bisexual women compared with heterosexual women: 19%, 20%, and 10%, respectively.[51] In the Women's Health Initiative, a very large, population-based study of postmenopausal women, 14% of adult lesbians versus 7% of heterosexual women were current smokers.[50]

Depression

Depressive symptoms, which are associated with incontinence, also may be more common among lesbians. The Nurses' Health Study II reported that, based on SF-36 mental health index measurements, 19% of lesbians were depressed—a 40% higher rate than that among their heterosexual counterparts.[51] In the Womens' Health Initiative, 16% of lesbians and bisexual women reported depression versus 11% of heterosexual women.[50]

Other Factors

In a survey of a population-based sample of women, 12% of self-identified lesbians had diabetes, another risk factor for UI, compared with 5% of heterosexual women.[52] Dibble and colleagues reported that hysterectomy rates in these two groups do not appear to be different.[53]

■ ■ ■

In the scenario at the beginning of this chapter, the addition of a low-dose, extended-release anticholinergic medication and daily Kegel exercises enabled Pamela to achieve nearly complete resolution of her UI symptoms. At the suggestion of her physician, Pamela and her partner, who is diabetic, started a hiking club to manage their weight and bring together members of the local lesbian community.

CONCLUSION

To optimally care for lesbians with urinary incontinence, clinicians must discuss sexual orientation with their patients and be willing to ask and answer questions about the condition. Research demonstrates that fewer than half of women with UI discuss their incontinence with a health care provider. Among women who seek care, fewer than a third receive treatment and more than half continue to experience symptoms.[54] Younger age, longer duration and greater severity of UI symptoms, and lack of embarrassment about symptoms are positively correlated with the likelihood of discussing UI with a provider.[55] Clinicians must create a supportive environment so lesbians feel comfortable addressing important issues, including multifaceted treatment of UI.

REFERENCES

1. Anger, J. T., Saigal, C. S., Litwin, M. S., & Urologic Diseases of America Project. (2006). The prevalence of urinary incontinence among community dwelling adult women: Results from the National Health and Nutrition Examination Survey. *Journal of Urology, 175,* 601–604.

2. Hannestad, Y. S., Rortveit, G., Sandvik, H., & Hunskaar, S. (2000). A community-based epidemiological survey of female urinary incontinence: The Norwegian EPINCONT study. Epidemiology of Incontinence in the County of Nord-Trøndelag. *Journal of Clinical Epidemiology, 53,* 1150–1157.

3. Melville, J. L., Katon, W., Delaney, K., & Newton, K. (2005). Urinary incontinence in U.S. women: A population-based study. *Archives of Internal Medicine, 165,* 537–542.

4. Wilson, L., Brown, J. S., Shin, G. P., & Subak, L. L. (2001). Annual direct cost of urinary incontinence. *Obstetrics & Gynecology, 98,* 398–406.

5. Townsend, M. K., Danforth, K. N., Lifford, K. L., Rosner, B., Curhan, G. C., Resnick, N. M., et al. (2007). Incidence and remission of urinary incontinence in middle-aged women. *American Journal of Obstetrics & Gynecology, 197,* 167.e1–5.

6. Jackson, R. A., Vittinghoff, E., Kanaya, A. M., Miles, T. P., Resnick, H. E., Kritchevsky, S. B., et al. (2004). Urinary incontinence in elderly women: Findings from the Health, Aging, and Body Composition Study. *Obstetrics & Gynecology, 104,* 301–307.

7. Brown, J. S., Seeley, D. G., Fong, J., Black, D. M., Ensrud, K. E., & Grady, D. (1996). Urinary incontinence in older women: Who is at risk? Study of Osteoporotic Fractures Research Group. *Obstetrics & Gynecology, 87*(5, Pt. 1), 715–721.

8. Danforth, K. N., Townsend, M. K., Lifford, K., Curhan, G. C., Resnick, N. M., & Grodstein, F. (2006). Risk factors for urinary incontinence among middle-aged women. *American Journal of Obstetrics & Gynecology, 194,* 339–345.

9. Thom, D. H., van den Eeden, S. K., Ragins, A. I., Wassel-Fyr, C., Vittinghof, E., Subak, L. L., et al. (2006). Differences in prevalence of urinary incontinence by race/ethnicity. *Journal of Urology, 175,* 259–264.

10. Sze, E. H., Jones, W. P., Ferguson, J. L., Barker, C. D., & Dolezal, J. M. (2002). Prevalence of urinary incontinence symptoms among Black, White, and Hispanic women. *Obstetrics & Gynecology, 99,* 572–575.

11. Mørkved, S., & Bø, K. (1999). Prevalence of urinary incontinence during pregnancy and postpartum. *International Urogynecology Journal and Pelvic Floor Dysfunction, 10,* 394–398.

12. Thom, D. H., & Brown, J. S. (1998). Reproductive and hormonal risk factors for urinary incontinence in late life: A review of the clinical and epidemiologic literature. *Journal of the American Geriatrics Society, 46,* 1411–1417.

13. Connolly, T. J., Litman, H. J., Tennstedt, S. L., Link, C. L., & McKinlay, J. B. (2007). The effect of mode of delivery, parity, and birth weight on risk of urinary incontinence. *International Urogynecology Journal and Pelvic Floor Dysfunction, 18,* 1033–1042.

14. Rortveit, G., Daltveit, A. K., Hannestad, Y. S., & Hunskaar, S. (2003). Urinary incontinence after vaginal delivery or cesarean section. *New England Journal of Medicine, 348,* 900–907.

15. Hunskaar, S., Arnold, E. P., Burgio, K., Diokno, A. C., Herzog A. R., & Mallett, V. T. (2000). Epidemiology and natural history of urinary incontinence. *International Urogynecology Journal and Pelvic Floor Dysfunction, 11,* 301–319.

16. Mokdad, A. H., Bowman, B. A., Ford, E. S., Vinicor, F., Marks, J. S., & Koplan, J. P. (2001). The continuing epidemics of obesity and diabetes in the United States. *Journal of the American Medical Association, 286,* 1195–1200.

17. Mommsen, S., & Foldspang, A. (1994). Body mass index and adult female urinary incontinence. *World Journal of Urology, 12,* 319–322.

18. Moller, L. A., Lose, G., & Jorgensen, T. (2000). Risk factors for lower urinary tract symptoms in women 40 to 60 years of age. *Obstetrics & Gynecology, 96,* 446–451.

19. Townsend, M. K., Danforth, K. N., Rosner, B., Curhan, G. C., Resnick, N. M., & Grodstein, F. (2007). Body mass index, weight gain, and incident urinary incontinence in middle-aged women. *Obstetrics & Gynecology, 110*(2, Pt. 1), 346–353.

20. Brown, J., Grady, D., Ouslander, J. G., Herzog, A. R., Varner, R. E., & Posner, S. F. (1999). Prevalence of urinary incontinence and associated risk factors in postmenopausal women. Heart & Estrogen/Progestin Replacement Study (HERS) Research Group. *Obstetrics & Gynecology, 94,* 66–70.

21. Bump, R. C., & McClish, D. K. (1992). Cigarette smoking and urinary incontinence in women. *American Journal of Obstetrics & Gynecology, 167,* 1213–1218.

22. Hannestad, Y. S., Rortveit, G., Daltveit, A. K., & Hunskaar, S. (2003). Are smoking and other lifestyle factors associated with female urinary incontinence? The Norwegian EPINCONT Study. *BJOG, 110,* 247–254.

23. Skelly, J., & Flint, A. J. (1995). Urinary incontinence associated with dementia. *Journal of the American Geriatrics Society, 43,* 286–289.

24. Grady, D., Brown, J. S., Vittinghoff, E., Applegate, W., Varner, E., Snyder, T., et al. (2001). Postmenopausal hormones and incontinence: The Heart and Estrogen/Progestin Replacement Study. *Obstetrics & Gynecology, 97,* 116–120.

25. Brown, J. S., Sawaya, G., Thom, D. H., & Grady, D. (2000). Hysterectomy and urinary incontinence: A systematic review. *Lancet, 356,* 535–539.

26. Nygaard, I., Turvey, C., Burns, T. L., Crischilles, E., & Wallace, R. (2003). Urinary incontinence and depression in middle-aged United States women. *Obstetrics & Gynecology, 101,* 149–156.

27. Wyman, J. F., Choi, S. C., Harkins, S. W., Wilson, M. S., & Fantl, J. A. (1988). The urinary diary in evaluation of incontinent women: A test-retest analysis. *Obstetrics & Gynecology, 71,* 812–817.

28. Burgio, K. L., Goode, P. S., Locher, J. L., Umlauf, M. G., Roth, D. L., Richter, H. E., et al. (2002). Behavioral training with and without biofeedback in the treatment of urge incontinence in older women. *Journal of the American Medical Association, 288,* 2293–2299.

29. Fantl J. A., Wyman, J. F., McClish, D. K., Harkins, S. W., Elswick, R. K., Taylor, J. R., et al. (1991). Efficacy of bladder training in older women with urinary incontinence. *Journal of the American Medical Association, 265,* 609–613.

30. Burns, P. A., Pranikoff, K., Nochajski, T. H., Hadley, E. C., Levy, K. J., & Ory, M. G. (1993). A comparison of effectiveness of biofeedback and pelvic muscle exercise treatment of stress incontinence in older community-dwelling women. *Journal of Gerontology, 48*, M167–174.

31. Mørkved, S., Bø, K., & Fjørtoft, T. (2002). Effect of adding biofeedback to pelvic floor muscle training to treat urodynamic stress incontinence. *Obstetrics & Gynecology, 100*, 730–739.

32. Borello-France, D., & Burgio, K. L. (2004). Nonsurgical treatment of urinary incontinence. *Clinical Obstetrics and Gynecology, 47*, 70–82.

33. Brubaker, L. (2000). Electrical stimulation in overactive bladder. *Urology, 55*(Suppl. 5A), 17–23.

34. Subak. L. L., Whitcomb, E., Shen, H., Saxton, J., Vittinghoff, E., & Brown, J. S. (2005). Weight loss: A novel and effective treatment for urinary incontinence. *Journal of Urology, 174*, 190–195.

35. Subak, L. L., Wing, R., West, D. S., Franklin, F., Vittinghoff, E., Creasman, J. M., et al. (2009). Weight loss to treat urinary incontinence in overweight and obese women. *New England Journal of Medicine, 360*, 481–490.

36. Fantl, J. A., Newman, D. K., Colling, J., DeLancey, J. O. L., Keeys, C., Loughery, R., et al. (1996). *Urinary incontinence in adults: Acute and chronic management* (Publication No. 96-0682). Rockville, MD: Agency for Health Care Policy and Research.

37. Anderson, R. U., Mobley, D., Blank, B., Saltzstein, D., Susset, J., & Brown, J. S. (1999). Once daily controlled versus immediate release oxybutynin chloride for urge urinary incontinence. OROS Oxybutynin Study Group. *Journal of Urology, 161*, 1809–1812.

38. Appell, R. A. (1997). Clinical efficacy and safety of tolterodine in the treatment of overactive bladder: A pooled analysis. *Urology, 50*(Suppl. 6A), 90–96.

39. Van Kerrebroeck, P., Kreder, K., Jonas, U., Zinner, N., & Wein, A. (2001). Tolterodine once-daily: Superior efficacy and tolerability in the treatment of the overactive bladder. *Urology, 57*, 414–421.

40. Nygaard, I. E., & Kreder, K. J. (2004). Pharmacologic therapy of lower urinary tract dysfunction. *Clinical Obstetrics and Gynecology, 47*, 83–92.

41. Hendrix, S. L., Cochrane, B. B., Nygaard, I. E., Handa, V. L., Barnabei, V. M., Iglesia, C., et al. (2005). Effect of estrogen with and without progestin on urinary incontinence. *Journal of the American Medical Association, 293*, 935–948.

42. Albo, M. E., Richter, H. E., Brubaker, L., Norton, P., Kraus, S. R., Zimmern, P. E., et al. (2007). Burch colposuspension versus fascial cling to reduce urinary stress incontinence. *New England Journal of Medicine, 356*, 2143–2155.

43. Nygaard, I. E., & Heit, M. (2004). Stress urinary incontinence. *Obstetrics & Gynecology, 104*, 607–620.

44. American College of Obstetricians and Gynecologists. (2005). Urinary incontinence in women (practice bulletin no. 63). *Obstetrics & Gynecology, 105*, 1533–1545.

45. Richter, H., Norman, A. M., Burgio, K. L., Goode, P. S., Wright, K. C., Benton, J., et al. (2005). Tension-free vaginal tape: A prospective subjective and objective outcome analysis. *Urogynecology Journal and Pelvic Floor Dysfunction, 16*, 109–113.

46. Walters, M., & Daneshgari, F. (2004). Surgical management of stress urinary incontinence. *Clinical Obstetrics and Gynecology, 47*, 93–103.

47. Marrazzo, J. M., & Stine, K. (2004). Reproductive health history of lesbians: Implications for care. *American Journal of Obstetrics & Gynecology, 190*, 1298–1304.

48. Wendel, H. F., & Wendel, C. S. (Eds.). (2006). *Vital statistics of the United States: Births, life expectancy, deaths, and selected health data* (2nd ed.). New York: Berman Press.

49. Dibble, S. L., Roberts, S. A., & Nussey, B. (2004). Comparing breast cancer risk between lesbians and their heterosexual sisters. *Women's Health Issues, 14*, 60–68.

50. Valanis, B. G., Bowen, D. J., Bassford, T., Whitlock, E., Charney, P., & Carter, R. A. (2000). Sexual orientation and health: Comparisons in the Women's Health Initiative sample. *Archives of Family Medicine, 9*, 843–853.

51. Case, P., Austin, S. B., Hunter, D. J., Manson, J. E., Malspeis, S., Willett, W. C., et al. (2004). Sexual orientation, health risk factors, and physical functioning in the Nurses' Health Study II. *Journal of Women's Health, 13*, 1033–1047.

52. Diamant, A. L., & Wold, C. (2003). Sexual orientation and variation in physical and mental health status among women. *Journal of Women's Health, 12*, 41–49.

53. Dibble, S. L., Roberts, S. A., Robertson, P. A., & Paul, S. M. (2002). Risk factors for ovarian cancer: Lesbian and heterosexual women. *Oncology Nursing Forum, 29*, E1–7.

54. Harris, S. S., Link, C. L., Tennstedt, S. L., Kusek, J. W., & McKinlay, J. B. (2007). Care seeking and treatment for urinary incontinence in a diverse population. *Journal of Urology, 177*, 680–684.

55. Melville, J. L., Newton, K., Fan, M. Y., & Katon, W. (2006). Health care discussions and treatment for urinary incontinence in U.S. women. *American Journal of Obstetrics & Gynecology, 194*, 729–737.

ABOUT THE AUTHORS

Leah M. Kelley, MD is an obstetrician/gynecologist who is completing a fellowship in breast surgery at the University of Southern California. Since medical school, she has been involved in LGBT health, including both direct patient care and provider education, with special interests in lesbian health and the surgical aspects of transgender care.

Leslee L. Subak, MD is Professor in the Departments of Obstetrics, Gynecology & Reproductive Sciences, Epidemiology & Biostatistics, and Urology at the University of California, San Francisco. She is a urogynecologist at the UCSF Women's Continence Center, a program for pelvic floor dysfunction and incontinence. Dr. Subak directs a research program evaluating treatments for incontinence.

CHAPTER 28

"I Have Fragile Bones?"

OSTEOPOROSIS AMONG LESBIANS

CAROLYN B. BECKER, MD

MARY *is a 50-year-old postmenopausal woman referred because of osteoporosis. After she sustained a wrist fracture in a minor fall, her internist ordered a dual-energy x-ray absorptiometry study that revealed very low bone density in her spine and hip. The wrist fracture was her first clinical fracture.*

Mary's history is notable for tobacco use since age 13 (one pack per day) and binge alcohol drinking on weekends beginning in her teens and extending into her twenties. She "came out" as a lesbian in high school and spent most weekends at bars. This behavior continued throughout college until her senior year, when she developed severe abdominal pains, fever, and diarrhea and was diagnosed with ulcerative colitis. She stopped smoking and drinking at that time, began taking high doses of glucocorticoids (steroids), and went into remission.

Mary lost 20 pounds after the ulcerative colitis began and her periods stopped for 1 year. Although she had always been thin, her body mass index (BMI) fell to 18. She gradually regained some pounds but did not return to her ideal weight. Over the next 20 years, she had occasional flare-ups of her colitis that required short courses of steroids. She remained thin, with a BMI of 20, and her menses ceased completely at age 44.

■ ■ ■

Osteoporosis is a complex skeletal disorder in which compromised bone strength increases the risk of fragility fractures. Appropriate screening and early intervention can greatly prevent fractures in people who are at risk. For those who suffer a fracture, the physical and psychological effects are severe. Although very few studies have examined osteoporosis or fracture risk among lesbians, certain common behaviors and lifestyle choices in this population may place lesbians at higher risk.

BACKGROUND

Osteoporosis can be defined in three ways: as a skeletal disorder characterized by compromised bone strength, predisposing people to a higher risk of fracture[1]; as bone mineral density in the lumbar spine, hip, or wrist that is 2.5 or more standard deviations below the mean for young women[2]; or as a clinical fracture that occurs in the setting of low or minimal trauma, such as falling from a standing height.

Osteoporosis is the most common bone disease in the world and a major public health problem. In 2010, an estimated 9.1 million women living in the United States who are older than 50 will have the disease, and another 26 million will be at risk of fractures due to low bone mass.[3] Worldwide, osteoporosis afflicts 200 million people.[4] Prevalence varies significantly according to ethnicity: among women older than 50, 20% of Asian Americans, 20% of Caucasians, 10% of Hispanics, and 5% of African Americans have osteoporosis.[5]

The annual incidence of osteoporotic fractures in the United States exceeds 1.5 million.[6] The most common fractures are those of the vertebrae, hip, and the distal forearm (wrist). Twenty percent of individuals die within the first year of a hip fracture, 30% must be placed in a nursing home, and up to 60% never regain the same level of prefracture independence. Vertebral fractures also are associated with higher mortality as well as chronic pain, deformity, restrictive lung disease, depression, fear, and loss of self-esteem.[7]

In 2005, osteoporosis-related fractures cost the U.S. health care system $17 billion.[7] Hip fractures account for only 14% of new fractures each year, but they are responsible for 72% of total fracture costs.[8] Given the aging population, the number of hip fractures and associated costs could double or triple by 2040.[6]

PATHOGENESIS

Bone is living tissue that constantly renews itself. Every 10 years, the adult skeleton is totally replaced in a process called bone remodeling. In normal bone remodeling, there is a balance between the amount of bone resorbed (broken down) and the amount of new bone formed. Osteoclasts are cells that remove old or damaged bone, leaving behind small holes, or lacunae, in bone tissue. Osteoblasts fill in lacunae with healthy, new bone tissue, which keeps the skeleton strong. In postmenopausal women, the loss of estrogen releases inflammatory factors called cytokines that greatly stimulate osteoclastic bone resorption and lead to a net loss of bone. Although the rates of bone resorption and bone formation are high after menopause, resorption outstrips formation, resulting in disrupted skeletal architecture and greater bone fragility.[9] Research has demonstrated that rapid bone loss begins well before the last menstrual period, during the late perimenopause.[10]

A major determinant of bone mass in a postmenopausal woman is her peak bone mass—the maximum mass she is biologically and genetically destined to obtain at maturity. Hereditary factors account for 50% to 80% of women's peak bone mass; the rest is related to lifestyle and health factors. Although women gain most peak bone mass during adolescence, they may continue to accrue bone up until age 40.[11] A low peak bone mass may predispose a woman to a higher risk of osteoporotic fracture later in life. Mary's history of early tobacco and heavy alcohol use, for example, probably left her with a peak bone mass well below her genetic potential.

RISK FACTORS

Many factors contribute to a woman's risk for osteoporosis (Table 28.1) and, consequently, fractures. In general, the more factors there are, the greater the risk.

TABLE 28.1. RISK FACTORS FOR OSTEOPOROSIS

GENERAL	SPECIFIC
Family history	Parental history of hip fracture
Demographic factors	▪ Advanced age ▪ Female sex ▪ Personal history of fracture ▪ Low BMI
Lifestyle factors	▪ Low calcium intake ▪ Smoking ▪ High alcohol consumption (three or more drinks per day) ▪ High caffeine intake ▪ Vitamin D deficiency ▪ Diet high in salt or animal protein ▪ Inadequate physical activity or immobilization ▪ Thinness

Endocrine disorders	▪ Hypogonadism
	   Anorexia nervosa
	   Exercise-induced amenorrhea
	   Premature ovarian failure
	   Hyperprolactinemia
	   Hypopituitarism
	▪ Cushing's syndrome
	▪ Diabetes mellitus (types 1 and 2)
	▪ Hyperparathyroidism
	▪ Hyperthyroidism
	▪ Hypercalciuria/kidney stones

Gastrointestinal disorders	▪ Inflammatory bowel disease (Crohn's, ulcerative colitis) ▪ Celiac disease ▪ Primary biliary cirrhosis ▪ Malabsorption syndromes ▪ Postgastric bypass or other intestinal resections
Rheumatologic disorders	▪ Rheumatoid arthritis ▪ Systemic lupus erythematosis ▪ Ankylosing spondylitis
Hematologic disorders	▪ Multiple myeloma ▪ Leukemia and lymphomas ▪ Systemic mastocytosis ▪ Hemoglobinopathies

(cont.)

TABLE 28.1. RISK FACTORS FOR OSTEOPOROSIS *(cont.)*

GENERAL	SPECIFIC
Miscellaneous disorders	▪ Alcoholism ▪ Depression ▪ End-stage renal disease ▪ Chronic obstructive pulmonary disease ▪ Multiple sclerosis ▪ Epilepsy ▪ Posttransplant bone disease
Medications	▪ Glucocorticoids (5 mg or more of prednisone for 3 months or longer) ▪ Anticonvulsants ▪ Aromatase inhibitors ▪ Depo-medroxyprogesterone acetate ▪ Cyclosporine A and tacrolimus ▪ Highly active antiretroviral therapy ▪ Heparin ▪ Cancer chemotherapy ▪ Gonadotropin-releasing hormone agonists ▪ Thiazolidinediones ▪ Antidepressants (selective serotonin reuptake inhibitors)

Source: Adapted from National Osteoporosis Foundation. (2008). *Clinician's guide to prevention and treatment of osteoporosis.* Available at www.nof.org/professionals/NOF_Clinicians_Guide.pdf.

Mary's risk factors included smoking and heavy alcohol use during her formative years, malabsorption, weight loss, nutritional deficiencies, release of inflammatory cytokines from ulcerative colitis, exposure to glucocorticoids, and early menopause.

SCREENING

A careful history and the results of a physical exam focusing on the clinical risk factors in Table 28.1 guide the decision about whether or not to screen a woman for low bone density or osteoporosis using bone densitometry. The gold standard for measuring bone mineral density (BMD) is dual-energy x-ray absorptiometry, or central DXA, at the lumbar spine, hip, and wrist. The BMD reading is compared to a reference population of "young normal adults" who are at their peak bone density. The difference between the patient's BMD in g/cm^2 and the norm is expressed as a standard deviation (SD) above or below the mean. This yields a T-score (Table 28.2). Comparing a patient's BMD to a reference population of women her age yields a Z-score. One SD equals 10% to 15% of the BMD in g/cm^2. For example, a T-score of −1.0 indicates that a woman's BMD is about 10% to 15% below the mean for the young normal reference population.

TABLE 28.2. BONE MINERAL DENSITY CLASSIFICATIONS

CLASSIFICATION	BONE MINERAL DENSITY
Normal	Within 1.0 standard deviation (SD) of that for a young normal adult (T-score = ≥ −1.0)
Low bone mass (osteopenia)	Between 1.0 and 2.5 SD below that for a young normal adult (T-score = −1.0 to −2.5)
Osteoporosis	≥ 2.5 SD below that for a young normal adult (T-score = ≤ −2.5)
Established or severe osteoporosis	≥ 2.5 SD below that for a young normal adult (T-score = ≤ −2.5) and an osteoporotic fracture has already occurred

Source: Kanis, J. A., Melton, L. J. III, Christiansen, C., Johnston, C. C., & Khaltaev, N. (1994). The diagnosis of osteoporosis. *Journal of Bone and Mineral Research, 9,* 1137–1141.

DXA results are useful not only for diagnosing osteoporosis, but also for monitoring changes in BMD over time and for predicting future fracture risk. For every 1 SD below the mean, there is an approximate doubling of fracture risk.[12] Peripheral devices such as heel ultrasound may help screen for and diagnose low bone mass but not monitor it over time.

ELIGIBILITY CRITERIA FOR DXA SCREENING OF ADULT WOMEN

- ≥ 65 years old
- Younger women at risk for osteoporosis or fractures
- In the menopause transition and have additional risk factors, such as low BMI
- Fracture after age 50
- Are stopping hormone therapy
- Have a medical condition associated with low BMD or are taking medication associated with low BMD
- Are considering taking medication for low BMD
- Are considering or already taking medication for osteoporosis
- Loss of BMD would alter the therapeutic approach (e.g., a woman with primary hyperparathyroidism whose loss of BMD would indicate parathyroid surgery)

Source: National Osteoporosis Foundation. (2008). *Clinician's guide to prevention and treatment of osteoporosis.* Available at www.nof.org/professionals/NOF_Clinicians_Guide.pdf.

DXA Screening

There are a number of published guidelines for bone densitometry screening, the most recent being those from the National Osteoporosis Foundation. The above box lists criteria that make adult women eligible for DXA screening.

Fracture Risk Assessment Tool

In 2008, the World Health Organization published its long-awaited Fracture Risk Assessment Tool (FRAX),[*] which can calculate the 10-year probability of a hip fracture or any other major osteoporotic fracture—vertebral, forearm, or humerus—based on femoral neck BMD and clinical risk factors (see box below). Data for the calculator come from numerous large, international epidemiologic studies that correlated these factors with actual fractures. The quick, simple tool is most useful for deciding whether to treat a woman who has low BMD but does not meet the criteria for osteoporosis. It also calculates the 10-year risk of fracture in patients whose BMD measurement is not available or not useful, as in someone who has undergone bilateral hip replacement. The tool is not appropriate when patients clearly qualify for or are already receiving treatment for osteoporosis.

RISK FACTORS IN THE FRAX CALCULATOR

- Age
- Sex
- Personal history of fracture
- Parental history of fracture
- Femoral neck BMD
- Low BMI
- Secondary osteoporosis, such as rheumatoid arthritis
- Use of oral corticosteroids
- Current smoking
- Three or more alcoholic drinks per day

TREATMENT

Clinicians should consider pharmacologic treatment for postmenopausal women if they present with a:

---

* Available at www.shef.ac.uk/FRAX.

- Hip or vertebral fracture;
- Fracture other than a hip or vertebral fracture associated with low BMD (T-score between –1.0 and –2.5 in the hip or spine);
- BMD T-score of ≤ –2.5 in the total hip, spine, or femoral neck after excluding secondary causes;
- BMD T-score between –1.0 and –2.5 and a secondary condition associated with a high risk of fracture, such as immobilization or glucocorticoid use; or a
- BMD T-score between –1.0 and –2.5 and a 10-year probability (3% or more) of hip fracture or a 10-year probability (20% or more) of any major osteoporotic fracture based on a FRAX calculation.[7]

■ ■ ■

Mary's DXA revealed T-scores of –4.0 at the spine and –2.8 at the hip, which, coupled with her wrist fracture, placed her in the category of established or severe osteoporosis. The clinician put Mary on calcium and vitamin D, and referred her to an osteoporosis specialist for evaluation and management.

MODALITIES

In the United States, treatment with a pharmacologic agent is suggested for postmenopausal women and men ≥ 50 years old who have a 10-year risk of hip fracture ≥ 3% or a 10-year risk of any major osteoporotic fracture ≥ 20%.[13]

Before women start any pharmacologic therapy for osteoporosis, they should be counseled about the importance of preventive strategies (discussed below). In addition, they should undergo central DXA and an evaluation for any secondary causes of osteoporosis, such as hyperparathyroidism or vitamin D deficiency.

The U.S. Food and Drug Administration (FDA) has approved a number of osteoporosis medications. The choice depends on a woman's risk factors, overall health status, contraindications, and preferences. Unfortunately, it may also depend on which drugs her health insurance covers. The following sections summarize these therapies.

Bisphosphonates

The "backbone" drugs for osteoporosis are alendronate (Fosamax and Fosamax Plus D), risedronate (Actonel), ibandronate (oral and intravenous Boniva), and zoledronic acid (Reclast, approved for both treatment and prevention). Once these medications are incorporated into the bone matrix, osteoclasts ingest them during bone resorption. The bisphosphonate structure interferes with osteoclasts' cytoskeleton, causing them to die. Consequently, bone resorption slows down dramatically, which enables osteoblasts to fill in and repair holes in the bone, and thus strengthen the skeleton.

Over time, the pace of bone resorption and bone formation slows to premenopausal rates. The body poorly absorbs oral bisphosphonates and, to be effective, patients must take them properly. Their unique mechanism of action allows dosing intervals of once per week or month. The most common side effects are gastrointestinal.

In 2007, the FDA approved zoledronic acid, an intravenous bisphosphonate that patients receive once a year for osteoporosis. Unlike its oral counterparts, zoledronic acid does not pose absorption, compliance, and gastrointestinal intolerance issues. It also significantly increases BMD and reduces hip, spinal, and other nonvertebral fractures.[14,15] However, it is more expensive than the oral drugs and may be associated with an acute-phase reaction, including flu-like symptoms.

Three of the four FDA-approved bisphosphonates reduce the risk of hip, vertebral, and nonvertebral fractures. Ibandronate effectively reduces only spinal fractures. A serious potential side effect of all bisphosphonates is osteonecrosis of the jaw, or jaw bone death, which mostly occurs in patients with cancer who receive frequent and repetitive doses of intravenous bisphosphonate over the long term. The incidence of jaw bone death is extremely low among patients who take either an oral or intravenous bisphosphonate for osteoporosis.[16]

Estrogen

Estrogen is approved for the prevention but not treatment of osteoporosis. It reduces the inflammatory cytokines that increase osteoclastic bone resorption and positively affects calcium absorption and calcium excretion. However, as the Women's Health Initiative revealed, hormone therapy increases the risk of myocardial infarction, stroke, invasive breast cancer, and thrombophlebitis. Therefore, clinicians generally prescribe estrogen to manage postmenopausal vasomotor symptoms and vulvovaginal atrophy, not solely to prevent osteoporosis.

Selective Estrogen Receptor Modulators

In this class of medications, the FDA has only approved raloxifene (Evista) for both the treatment and prevention of osteoporosis in postmenopausal women. Raloxifene's action resembles that of estrogen on the skeleton and that of tamoxifen, an antiestrogen, on the breast. It significantly reduces spinal fractures and the risk of invasive estrogen-receptor-positive breast cancer but is also associated with thrombophlebitis and hot flashes. Compared with bisphosphonates, raloxifene is a weaker antiresorptive agent and does not reduce the risk of nonvertebral or hip fractures.

Human Parathyroid Hormone

Teriparatide, the only truly bone-forming agent, has been available since 2002 for treating osteoporosis. Daily subcutaneous injections via a preloaded pen device directly stimulate bone-forming osteoblasts, a unique action. However, because teriparatide increases osteosarcoma in rats, the drug, which has a number of contraindications, carries a black box warning and may only be used for up to 2 years. Patients tolerate teriparatide very well and it is generally very safe. The drug is most effective in reducing vertebral fractures—the results can be dramatic—but it also significantly reduces nonvertebral fractures. Teriparatide should be reserved for patients with severe or established osteoporosis, particularly those with very low BMD or prevalent vertebral fractures, as it costs up to $1,000 per month and requires subcutaneous injections.

Calcitonin

Calcitonin (Miacalcin, Calcimar, Fortical) is an approved osteoporosis treatment for women who have been postmenopausal for at least 5 years. Delivered as a single, daily intranasal spray or as a subcutaneous injection, it reduces fractures much less effectively than other medications do and therefore is a second- or third-line agent.

■ ■ ■

An endocrinologist found that Mary had profound vitamin D deficiency and secondary hyperparathyroidism, and prescribed vitamin D3 (10,000 IU cholecalciferol weekly) and calcium citrate (1,500 mg daily in divided doses). After these problems were corrected, Mary began receiving annual infusions of intravenous bisphosphonate (zoledronic acid) after a brief trial of oral bisphosphonate (alendronate) caused her ulcerative colitis to flare and therefore had to be stopped immediately.

PREVENTION

Prevention of osteoporosis should begin in childhood and adolescence with healthy nutrition and a healthy lifestyle. The following are general prevention recommendations for virtually all people:

- Lifelong adequate intake of dietary calcium: 1,000 to 1,200 mg per day, including supplements if necessary;
- Adequate vitamin D either from sun, food, or supplements. For women 50 years old or older, vitamin D3 (cholecalciferol): 800 to 1,000 IU per day. Some individuals may need up to 3,000 IU per day. The goal is to maintain serum 25-hydroxy-vitamin D level at 30 ng/ml (75 nmol/L) or higher;
- Weight-bearing exercise three times per week or more often—activities such as walking, jogging, tai-chi, stair climbing, dancing, tennis, and low-impact aerobics. Other beneficial activities are muscle strengthening, stretching and flexibility exercises such as yoga, and pilates. Elderly patients or those with neurological dysfunction also benefit from balance and gait training;

- Not smoking;
- Avoiding excessive alcohol consumption (three or more drinks per day);
- Maintaining an ideal body weight; and
- Preventing falls.[7] (See box for related risk factors.)

FALL RISK FACTORS

- Advanced age
- Environmental factors, such as poor lighting or obstacles on the floor
- Poor vision
- Cardiac arrhythmias
- Orthostatic hypotension
- Frailty
- Neuromuscular disorders, such as poor balance, Parkinson's disease, a cerebrovascular accident, reduced proprioception, or muscle weakness
- Dementia
- History of falls

Source: National Osteoporosis Foundation. (2008). *Clinician's guide to prevention and treatment of osteoporosis*. Available at www.nof.org/professionals/NOF_Clinicians_Guide.pdf.

OSTEOPOROSIS AMONG LESBIANS

A small study by Patton and colleagues is one of the few studies that have addressed skeletal health in lesbians. Their research did not find any differences in calcaneal ultrasound measurements between lesbians and heterosexual women who were 30 to 50 years old and had regular menses.[17] Although these results are encouraging, certain behaviors among lesbians, such as significantly higher rates of smoking[18–21] and high alcohol consumption,[22,23] may place them at greater risk of osteoporosis and fractures. The FRAX calculator includes smoking and heavy alcohol consumption as risk factors because they are such strong predictors of osteoporotic fractures.

Because lesbians are more likely than heterosexual women to be overweight,[22,24] and because low BMI is another potent risk factor for fractures, the fracture and osteoporosis risk among lesbians may be less. The prevalence of severe eating disorders, such as anorexia nervosa, among lesbians is unknown. Researchers have found that depression and chronic use of antidepressants, particularly selective serotonin reuptake inhibitors, are associated with higher rates of osteoporosis and fractures.[25–27] In the Women's Health Initiative, lesbians were more likely than heterosexual women to report depression and use of antidepressants.[22] In the study by Patton and colleagues, lesbians who were taking antidepressants had significantly lower calcaneal ultrasound BMD than did lesbians who were not.[17]

Finally, lesbians are less likely than heterosexual women to access preventive health care.[28,29] It follows that they are less likely to undergo DXA screening for osteoporosis. Without BMD measurement and clinical risk factor assessment, lesbians may not receive counseling about preventive skeletal-health measures nor treatment for osteoporosis. Interestingly, one study found that even older lesbians of relatively higher socioeconomic status and educational achievement and with good access to health care received fewer recommended screening services and had higher rates of smoking, alcohol consumption, and obesity than did their heterosexual peers.[30]

CONCLUSION

Osteoporosis and bone fracture are potentially serious problems for all women. Clinicians should be aware of risk factors that place lesbians at higher risk, including a greater prevalence of smoking, alcohol consumption, depression, and chronic use of certain antidepressants. Furthermore, because lesbians generally have less access to health care, many do not receive screening that otherwise could detect osteoporosis. Clearly, there is a need for much more research on osteoporosis and fractures among lesbians.

REFERENCES

1. Genant, H. K., Cooper, C., Poor, G., Reid, I., Ehrlich, G., Kanis, J., et al. (1990). Interim report and recommendations of the World Health Organization Task Force for Osteoporosis. *Osteoporosis International, 10,* 259–264.

2. Kanis, J. A., Melton, L. J. III, Christiansen, C., Johnston, C. C., & Khaltaev, N. (1994). The diagnosis of osteoporosis. *Journal of Bone and Mineral Research, 9,* 1137–1141.

3. National Osteoporosis Foundation. (2002). *America's bone health: The state of osteoporosis and low bone mass in our nation.* Washington, DC: Author.

4. International Osteoporosis Foundation. (2007). *About osteoporosis: Epidemiology.* Available at www.iofbonehealth.org/health-professionals/about-osteoporosis/epidemiology.html.

5. National Osteoporosis Foundation. (2007) *Fast facts on osteoporosis.* Available at www.nof.org/professionals/Fast_Facts_Osteoporosis.pdf.

6. Office of the Surgeon General. (2004). *Bone health and osteoporosis: A report of the Surgeon General.* Washington, DC: U.S. Department of Health & Human Services. Available at www.surgeongeneral.gov/library/bonehealth.

7. National Osteoporosis Foundation. (2008). *Clinician's guide to prevention and treatment of osteoporosis.* Available at www.nof.org/professionals/NOF_Clinicians_Guide.pdf.

8. Burge, R. T., Dawson-Hughes, B., Solomon, D. H., Wong, J. B., King, A., & Tosteson, A. (2007). Incidence and economic burden of osteoporotic fractures in the United States, 2005–2025. *Journal of Bone and Mineral Research, 22,* 465–475.

9. Seeman, E., & Delmas, P. D. (2006). Bone quality—the material and structural basis of bone strength and fragility. *New England Journal of Medicine, 354,* 2250–2261.

10. Finkelstein, J. S., Brockwell, S. E., Mehta, V., Greendale, G. A., Sowers, M. R., Ettinger, B., et al. (2008). Bone mineral density changes during the menopause transition in a multiethnic cohort of women. *Journal of Clinical Endocrinology and Metabolism, 93,* 861–868.

11. Mora, S., & Gilsanz, V. (2003). Establishment of peak bone mass. *Endocrinology and Metabolism Clinics of North America, 32,* 39–63.

12. Cummings, S. R., Nevitt, M. C., Browner, W. S., Stone, K., Fox, K. M., Ensrud, K. E., et al. (1995). Risk factors for hip fractures in White women. *New England Journal of Medicine, 332,* 767–773.

13. Dawson-Hughes, B., Tosteson, A. N., Melton, L. J. III, Baim, S., Favus, M. J., Khosla, S., et al. (2008). Implications of absolute fracture risk assessment for osteoporosis practice guidelines in the U.S.A. *Osteoporosis International, 19,* 449–458.

14. Black, D. M., Delmas, P. D., Eastell, R., Reid, I. R., Boonen, S., Cauley, J. A., et al. (2007). Once yearly zoledronic acid for treatment of postmenopausal osteoporosis. *New England Journal of Medicine, 356,* 1809–1822.

15. Lyles, K. W., Colón-Emeric, C. S., Magaziner, J. S., Adachi, J. D., Pieper, C. F., Mautalen, C., et al. (2007). Zoledronic acid and clinical fractures and mortality after hip fracture. *New England Journal of Medicine, 357,* 1799–1809.

16. Khosla, S., Burr, D., Cauley, J., Dempster, D. W., Ebeling, P. R., Felsenberg, D., et al. (2007). Bisphosphonate-associated osteonecrosis of the jaw: Report of a task force of the American Society for Bone and Mineral Research. *Journal of Bone and Mineral Research, 22,* 1479–1491.

17. Patton, C. L., Millard, P. S., Kessenich, C. R., Storm, D., Kinnicutt, E., & Rosen, C. J. (1998). Screening calcaneal ultrasound and risk factors for osteoporosis among lesbians and heterosexual women. *Journal of Women's Health, 7,* 909–915.

18. Mercer, C. H., Bailey, J. V., Johnson, A. M., Erens, B., Wellings, K., Fenton, K. A., et al. (2007). Women who report having sex with women: British national probability data on prevalence, sexual behaviors, and health outcomes. *American Journal of Public Health, 97,* 1126–1133.

19. King, M., & Nazareth, I. (2006). The health of people characterized as lesbian, gay and bisexual attending family practitioners in London: A controlled study. *BMC Public Health, 6,* 127.

20. Tang, H., Greenwood, G. L., Cowling, D. W., Lloyd, J. C., Roeseler, A. G., & Bal, D. G. (2004). Cigarette smoking among lesbians, gays, and bisexuals: How serious a problem? (United States). *Cancer Causes & Control, 15,* 797–803.

21. Gruskin, E. P., Greenwood, G. L., Matevia, M., Pollack, L. M., & Bye, L. (2007). Disparities in smoking between the lesbian, gay, and bisexual population and the general population in California. *American Journal of Public Health, 97,* 1496–1502.

22. Case, P., Austin, S. B., Hunter, D. J., Manson, J. E., Malspeis, S., Willett, W. C., et al. (2004). Sexual orientation, health risk factors, and physical functioning in the Nurses' Health Study II. *Journal of Women's Health, 13,* 1033–1047.

23. Gruskin, E. P., & Gordon, N. (2006). Gay/lesbian sexual orientation increases risk for cigarette smoking and heavy drinking among members of a large Northern California health plan. *BMC Public Health, 6*, 241.

24. Boehmer, U., Bowen, D. J., & Bauer, G. R. (2007). Overweight and obesity in sexual-minority women: Evidence from population-based data. *American Journal of Public Health, 97*, 1134–1140.

25. Diem, S. J., Blackwell, T. L., Stone, K. L., Yaffe, K., Haney, E. M., Bliziotes, M. M., et al. (2007). Use of antidepressants and rates of hip bone loss in older women: The study of osteoporotic fractures. *Archives of Internal Medicine, 167*, 1240–1245.

26. Petronijević, M., Petronijević, N., Ivković, M., Stefanović, D., Radonjić, N., Glišić, B., et al. (2008). Low bone mineral density and high bone metabolism turnover in premenopausal women with unipolar depression. *Bone, 42*, 582–590.

27. Spangler, L., Scholes, D., Brunner, R. L., Robbins, J., Reed, S. D., Newton, K. M., et al. (2008). Depressive symptoms, bone loss, and fractures in postmenopausal women. *Journal of General Internal Medicine, 23*, 567–574.

28. Cochran, S. D., Mays, V. M., Bowen, D., Gage, S., Bybee, D., Roberts, S. J., et al. (2001). Cancer-related risk indicators and preventive screening behaviors among lesbians and bisexual women. *American Journal of Public Health, 91*, 591–594.

29. Diamant, A. L., Wold, C., Spritzer, K., & Gelberg, L. (2000). Health behaviors, health status, and access to and use of health care: A population-based study of lesbian, bisexual, and heterosexual women. *Archives of Family Medicine, 9*, 1043–1051.

30. Valanis B. G., Bowen, D. J., Bassford, T., Whitlock, E., Charney, P., & Carter, R. A. (2000). Sexual orientation and health. Comparisons in the Women's Health Initiative sample. *Archives of Family Medicine, 9*, 843–853.

ABOUT THE AUTHOR

Carolyn B. Becker, MD is Associate Professor of Medicine at Harvard Medical School and Master Clinician in the Division of Endocrinology, Diabetes and Hypertension at Brigham and Women's Hospital in Boston. Her major interests are caring for patients with osteoporosis and other metabolic bone disorders as well as teaching medical students, residents and fellows.

CHAPTER 29

"But I Feel OK. How Could I Have Diabetes?"

DIABETES AMONG LESBIANS

CINDY RIPSIN, MD, MPH   PATRICIA A. ROBERTSON, MD

ALICIA, *37, comes to a physician's office to establish care. She divorced her husband when she "came out" as a lesbian; her daughter was 3 years old. She now lives with her female partner of 7 years. As a self-employed commercial artist, Alicia has not had medical insurance for several years. However, her partner just obtained job-based partner benefits, so Alicia is excited about having a full health evaluation.*

Alicia generally feels well but has struggled to keep her weight under control since the birth of her daughter, who is now 10. She thinks she might have a "thyroid problem" because she cannot lose weight and keep it off. Alicia also has a vaginal discharge that she attributes to a yeast infection; it gets better when she uses over-the-counter vaginal creams for yeast infections but always returns.

Even though Alicia received only sporadic prenatal care when she was pregnant, she had an uncomplicated vaginal delivery. Her daughter weighed 9 pounds at birth. Alicia sleeps pretty well, getting up once or twice at night to urinate. She has noticed some increase in urinary frequency during the day but no major urinary urgency or incontinence. Alicia denies depression and anxiety symptoms, and feels happy and supported in her relationship. She does not use tobacco products, occasionally drinks wine with dinner, and sometimes has a beer on weekends. She does not exercise regularly but acknowledges that it would be good to start because both she and her daughter are overweight.

The remainder of a complete review of systems reveals only that Alicia has occasional, unexplained blurred vision that sometimes lasts several hours and then improves. She cannot really characterize the blurred vision when it occurs. There is no associated eye pain, darkening of the field of vision, or headaches. Alicia thinks she might need stronger contact lenses, but the blurred vision does not last long enough that she feels a need to address it. She says that her mother had diabetes and died of a "heart attack" at age 54, and that her 73-year-old father has high blood pressure and has had several "mini-strokes."

Alicia's physical exam is normal except for a body mass index (BMI) of 34 kg/m², blood pressure of 132/92 mm Hg, and vulvovaginal candidiasis. She ate breakfast about 3 hours before the appointment. A random check reveals a blood glucose of 137 mg/dL. A subsequent oral glucose tolerance test with 75 mg of glucola shows a fasting glucose of 118 mg/dL, 267 mg/dL at 1 hour, and 156 mg/dL at 2 hours, confirming the diagnosis of type 2 diabetes mellitus.

In addition, a fasting lipid panel yields these values: total cholesterol, 203 mg/ dL; low-density lipoprotein, 126 mg/dL; high-density lipoprotein, 33 mg/dL; and triglycerides, 220 mg/dL. Her calculated glomerular filtration rate, thyroid stimulating hormone, and urine microalbumin are normal.

■ ■ ■

Fueled by an epidemic of obesity, diabetes has become the seventh leading cause of death in the United States. More than 20 million Americans are diabetic—a figure that, given the 57 million adults who have impaired fasting glucose, is expected to rise. Diabetes is directly responsible for more than 73,000 deaths annually and a contributing factor in more than 233,000.[1] But these estimates are well below the true numbers because death certificates for fewer than half of all decedents with confirmed diabetes cite the disease.[2]

The incidence of type 2 diabetes mellitus (T2DM), the predominant type, is rising rapidly in every U.S. racial and ethnic group, and disproportionately affects racial and ethnic minorities[1] (see box below). Although research on diabetes among lesbians is scant, a population-based telephone survey in Los Angeles did not reveal a significant difference in diabetes rates between lesbians and heterosexual women after adjusting for age, race/ethnicity, education, income, health insurance, cigarette smoking, and obesity.[3] However, the sample included only 43 lesbians. Given the obesity epidemic and the fact that lesbians generally have a higher BMI than heterosexual women do, diabetes among lesbians is likely to increase.[4]

DIABETES IN MINORITY POPULATIONS

- African Americans are 1.4 to 2.2 times more likely than Whites to have diabetes.
- Diabetes is more prevalent among Hispanic Americans than non-Hispanic Americans. The highest rates of type 2 diabetes are among Puerto Ricans and Hispanics living in the Southwest. Cubans have the lowest rate.
- The prevalence of diabetes among American Indians is 2.8 times greater than the overall prevalence.
- Prevalence among major groups in Asian and Pacific Islander communities (Japanese Americans, Chinese Americans, Filipino Americans, and Korean Americans) is higher than among Whites.

Source: Agency for Healthcare Quality and Research. (2001). *Diabetes disparities among racial and ethnic minorities* (Publication No. 02-P007). Rockville, MD. Available at www.ahrq.gov/research/diabdisp.htm.

EPIDEMIOLOGY

There are many types of diabetes (Table 29.1). An absolute lack of insulin characterizes type 1 diabetes mellitus (T1DM). More than 90% of Americans with diabetes have T2DM, in which derangement of glucose homeostasis occurs along a continuum from prediabetes (impaired glucose tolerance and/or impaired fasting glucose) to diabetes with clinical manifestations. Progression along this continuum involves genetic, racial/ethnic, and environmental factors. The three primary defects in T2DM are:

- Insulin resistance. In the early stages, insulin receptors become less sensitive to the action of insulin. Beta cells in the pancreas compensate by increasing production of insulin so blood glucose remains normal or near normal and insulin levels are high;
- Insulin deficiency. Beta cells eventually fail to produce enough insulin to fully compensate for insulin resistance. Consequently, insulin levels decline relative to needs and blood glucose rises above the normal range; and
- Hepatic glucose production, which increases markedly and contributes to elevated blood glucose.[5]

SCREENING

Prediabetes and Diabetes

Screening detects medical conditions in asymptomatic individuals, hopefully early enough to prevent or minimize adverse outcomes.[6] A 3-year study in which subjects who had impaired glucose tolerance (IGT) were randomly assigned to an intensive lifestyle intervention, metformin, or usual care demonstrated that progression from prediabetes to T2DM can be prevented or delayed.[7] Prediabetes entails many of the same risks as diabetes, so identifying at-risk individuals early offers an opportunity to prepare a prevention strategy. Because more than two-thirds of Americans are over-weight and most overweight individuals have at least one additional risk factor for diabetes, screening for this disease should be a part of routine care for most women. The American Diabetes Association recommends screening adult, nonpregnant women for prediabetes and diabetes, regardless of age, if they are overweight (BMI $\geq$ 25) and have one or more of the following risk factors:

- History of gestational diabetes or delivery of a baby weighing > 9 pounds;
- Polycystic ovarian syndrome;
- First-degree relative (mother, father, brother, sister) who has diabetes;
- Member of a high-risk ethnic population (for example, African American, Latino, American Indian, Asian American, Pacific Islander);

TABLE 29.1. TYPES OF DIABETES MELLITUS

NAME	DESCRIPTION	DIAGNOSIS	DETAILS
PREDIABETES			
Impaired glucose tolerance (IGT)	■ Insulin resistance ■ Blood glucose may be normal after a fast of ≥ 8 hours but is abnormally high after a meal.	Blood glucose of 140–199 mg/dL 2 hours after a glucose load	IGT and impaired fasting glucose can coexist.
Impaired fasting glucose (IFG)	■ Insulin resistance ■ Blood glucose is abnormally high after a fast of ≥ 8 hours.	Blood glucose of 100–125 mg/dL after a fast of ≥ 8 hours	IGT and IFG can coexist.
DIABETES			
Type 1 diabetes mellitus (T1DM)	■ Complete absence of insulin ■ Hyperglycemia	Hyperglycemia and absence of C-peptide	Ketoacidosis is often the primary presentation.
Type 2 diabetes mellitus (T2DM)	■ Insulin resistance with continued production of insulin ■ Abnormally high blood glucose	■ Hyperglycemia symptoms and random blood glucose > 200 mg/dL OR ■ Blood glucose ≥ 126 mg/dL after a fast of ≥ 8 hours	■ For asymptomatic patients meeting the glucose criteria, need to repeat the test to confirm the diagnosis. ■ Ketoacidosis is very rare.
Gestational diabetes mellitus (GDM)	■ Develops during pregnancy ■ Most pregnant women are routinely screened with a 50-g load of glucola followed by a blood glucose test 1 hour later. If the value is ≥ 140 mg/dL, a 3-hour glucose tolerance test is indicated.	Two of the following after a 100-g glucose load test = GDM: ■ Fasting glucose ≥ 95 mg/dL; ■ After 1 hour, glucose ≥ 180 mg/dL; ■ After 2 hours, glucose ≥ 155 mg/dL; ■ After 3 hours, glucose ≥ 140 mg/dL.	■ Significant risk of eventual T2DM ■ Need to test at 6–12 weeks postpartum, with a blood glucose test 2 hours after a 75-g glucola load. Glucose > 200 mg/dL = T2DM; glucose of 140–199 mg/dL = prediabetes.
Maturity onset diabetes of the young	Mild	Autosomal dominant genetic defect involving beta cells	Rare
Latent autoimmune diabetes of adults	Slowly progressive beta cell failure in the presence of autoimmunity	Eventual absence of C-peptide. Because the failure of beta cells is gradual, C-peptide is initially present.	Patients often receive oral medications in the early stages, then progress to insulin.

Source: Authors

- History of cardiovascular disease (CVD);
- Hypertension ≥ 140/90 mm Hg or therapy for hypertension;
- High-density lipoprotein cholesterol < 35 mg/dL and/or a triglyceride level ≥ 250 mg/dL;
- Other clinical conditions associated with insulin resistance, such as severe obesity or acanthosis nigricans;
- IGT or IFG (impaired fasting glucose) on previous testing;
- Physical inactivity.[8]

Asymptomatic women who meet these criteria should be screened every 3 years if initial test results are normal. For women who do not meet the criteria, screening should begin at age 45 and take place every 3 years if the initial results are normal.[8]

Gestational Diabetes

The prevalence of gestational diabetes mellitus (GDM) in the United States is 1% to 4%, depending on population characteristics.[9] Clinicians should assess pregnant women for their risk of GDM on the first prenatal visit. Those at high risk should be screened as soon as possible and again at 24 to 28 weeks of gestation if the first result was negative. Any of the following risk factors warrant early screening:

- BMI ≥ 30;
- Glucosuria;
- History of GDM;
- History of polycystic ovarian syndrome;
- History of T2DM in a first-degree relative;
- History of stillbirth;
- Delivery of a baby that was large for gestational age (for example, 4,000 g at term);
- Current corticosteroid medication.[10]

Women at low risk of GDM (10% of the general population) do not need screening during pregnancy. They have the following characteristics:

- Younger than 25 years old;
- Not a member of an ethnic group at higher risk for T2DM. These groups include Hispanic Americans, African Americans, American Indians, and people of Pacific Islands ancestry;
- Healthy BMI (≤ 25);
- No history of abnormal glucose tolerance;
- No history of adverse obstetric outcomes usually associated with GDM;
- No first-degree relative with diabetes.[11]

Women at risk for GDM should be screened at 24 to 28 weeks of gestation with a 50-g glucola load followed 1 hour later by a blood glucose test. Patients whose blood glucose is ≥ 140 mg/dL should undergo a fasting blood glucose test followed by a 100-g glucola load and 1-, 2-, and 3-hour blood glucose tests after the load. For a GDM diagnosis, two of the four values must be abnormal (see Table 29.1). GDM patients can be managed through diet and exercise unless their blood glucose levels are abnormally high, which requires insulin or oral medications; in these cases, special surveillance is necessary to assess for fetal macrosomia and placental insufficiency.[10] Because only 10% of pregnant women are at low risk for developing diabetes, many clinicians screen all pregnant women at 24 to 28 weeks of gestation. It is essential that all women diagnosed with GDM be tested at 6 to 12 weeks postpartum with a 75-g, 2-hour oral glucose tolerance test to rule out T2DM.[12]

DIAGNOSIS

The screening guidelines above are for asymptomatic women who have risk factors. A diagnostic test is warranted if screening results are abnormal or if there is a clinical reason to suspect underlying prediabetes or diabetes, regardless of whether or not the patient meets the screening criteria. See Table 29.1 regarding diagnostic criteria for impaired glucose tolerance, impaired fasting glucose, and T2DM.

Table 29.2 summarizes the evaluation of patients diagnosed with prediabetes or diabetes. Women with prediabetes or diabetes should receive counseling for family planning (if they are of reproductive age), medical nutrition, and diabetes self-management. All patients should be advised not to smoke; if they smoke, a discussion of smoking cessation programs is necessary. The clinician should refer patients to an ophthalmologist for a dilated eye exam, and to a mental health professional if there are symptoms of depression.

MANAGEMENT

Each January in *Diabetes Care*, the American Diabetes Association publishes clinical practice guidelines with detailed information about managing patients who have T1DM or T2DM. Because these updates change depending on the latest research, clinicians should review them annually.

Prediabetes

Prediabetes carries many of the same risks as T2DM, so a diagnosis of impaired glucose tolerance or impaired fasting glucose necessitates a plan to prevent or minimize morbidity and early mortality. Like others who are chronically ill,

TABLE 29.2. EVALUATION OF PATIENTS WITH PREDIABETES OR DIABETES

Medical history	■ Age of onset of diabetes ■ Current and past treatments for diabetes ■ Nutritional habits ■ History of hypoglycemic episodes ■ History of diabetes-associated complications
Physical exam	■ Height ■ Weight ■ BMI ■ Blood pressure ■ Fundoscopic exam ■ Thyroid palpation ■ Comprehensive foot exam (proprioception, monofilament, vibratory sensation)
Lab tests	■ Hemoglobin A1c ■ Fasting lipid panel ■ Urine albumin and spot urine for albumin-to-creatinine ratio ■ Serum creatinine ■ Liver function tests ■ Calculated glomerular filtration rate ■ Thyroid-stimulating hormone for women with T1DM, if there is dyslipidemia, or if the patient is ≥ 35 years old

Source: Authors

prediabetes patients need regular clinical attention. Management guidelines from the American Diabetes Association include:

■ An initial weight loss goal of 5% to 10% of baseline body weight for overweight patients (BMI > 25);
■ A low-fat diet: saturated fats < 7% of total calories and minimal trans fat. Calorie restriction may be necessary to achieve weight loss goals; and
■ At least 150 minutes of aerobic activity per week. Ideally, the activity is on 3 or more days each week with no more than 1 day between sessions.[8]

Losing weight can be very frustrating for patients with impaired glucose intolerance, impaired fasting glucose, or T2DM. Multiple unsuccessful attempts to lose weight are often demoralizing, and providers may mistakenly believe that patients are being noncompliant when they gain, or there is no change in, weight from one visit to the next. The way clinicians interact with overweight patients is as important as the weight loss goals they set for them. Shedding pounds is more difficult for people with insulin resistance because their fat cells take up a larger proportion of circulating glucose. Acknowledging this fact encourages patients to lose weight even if they do not ultimately succeed. In the Diabetes Prevention Program, Knowler and colleagues found that the incidence of T2DM declined 58% even though only 38% of participants in their study achieved and maintained weight loss goals. The researchers prevented one case of diabetes for every seven high-risk subjects who enrolled.[7] Therefore, clinicians should encourage all patients on all visits to diet, exercise, and lose weight.

Exercising regularly also can be challenging. The minimum recommendation is 150 minutes per week, or 30 minutes five times a week, of aerobic activity, such as walking, running, biking, or swimming.[13] This prospect is so daunting for many people that they fail even before they begin. Patients often respond much more positively to "150 weekly," which allows creativity in meeting the exercise goal. For example, a clinician might suggest to a patient that she ride a bike or walk for an hour on Saturdays and exercise for 45 minutes on two other occasions during the week.

Some patients who have impaired glucose intolerance or impaired fasting glucose may benefit from metformin, an oral medication. In the Diabetes Prevention Program, metformin was more effective than usual care, although not as effective as intensive lifestyle changes, in reducing T2DM incidence.[7] The drug primarily lowers hepatic glucose output. It also increases glucose uptake in peripheral tissues and does not contribute to weight gain.

Type 2 Diabetes Mellitus

Weight loss, a low-fat diet, and exercise are no less important in managing T2DM than they are in managing prediabetes. Even if there is no significant weight loss, exercise reduces blood glucose and triglycerides.[13] Clinicians should encourage all patients on every visit to achieve and maintain these lifestyle parameters.

■ CONTROL OF BLOOD GLUCOSE

The United Kingdom Prospective Diabetes Study, a placebo-controlled, 10-year trial of aggressive glycemic control in subjects with newly diagnosed T2DM, demonstrated significant reductions in microvascular complications (retinopathy, nephropathy, and neuropathy).[14] In this classic study, each 1% reduction in glycosylated hemoglobin (HbA1c) reduced such complications by 35%.[15] The American Diabetes Association guidelines recommend maintaining blood glucose as close to normal as possible without risking significant hypoglycemia.[8] The recommended goal for HbA1c is < 7%.[8] Table 29.3 shows the relationship between blood glucose and HbA1c levels.

TABLE 29.3. CORRELATION BETWEEN BLOOD GLUCOSE AND HBA1C

AVERAGE BLOOD GLUCOSE (MG/DL)	HBA1C
135	6%
170	7%
205	8%
240	9%
275	10%
310	11%
345	12%

Source: American Diabetes Association. (2009). Standards of medical care in diabetes—2009. *Diabetes Care, 32*(Suppl. 1), S13–S61. Available at care.diabetesjournals. org/content/32/Supplement_1/S13.full.

Clinicians need to take into account patients' ability to comply with complex monitoring and medication regimens. For people with cognitive, visual, and/or motor difficulties, modifying the HbA1c goal might be reasonable rather than risking serious hypoglycemia. If HbA1c is not consistently well-controlled, it should be checked every 3 months. Checking HbA1c twice yearly is adequate for women with well-controlled diabetes.[8]

The HbA1c test is an excellent way to evaluate overall glycemic control in the preceding 3 months, but it is not always accurate. Conditions that cause accelerated turnover of red blood cells, such as hemolytic anemia, will falsely lower the values; conversely, conditions that increase average circulating erythrocyte age can falsely elevate the values.[16]

■ MODIFIABLE CARDIOVASCULAR RISK FACTORS

In addition to premature and accelerated cardiovascular disease (CVD) attributable to insulin resistance, traditional risk factors for this disease—hypertension, albuminuria, and dyslipidemia—are much more prevalent in people with T2DM. Rates of death as a result of heart disease are two to four times higher among adults with diabetes than among those without diabetes.[17] Interventions that target modifiable risk factors can reduce cardiovascular events by up to 50%,[18] but clinicians are not widely adopting them. In a 2-year study of diabetics, 85% of whom were known to have coronary artery disease, HbA1C was < 7% in only 21%, just 10% had appropriate control of their blood pressure, and only 11% had a BMI < 25.[19] It is crucially important to target and manage these cardiac risk factors in diabetic patients and to avoid focusing narrowly on managing only blood glucose.

Hypertension

Between 20% and 60% of people with diabetes have hypertension, depending on obesity, ethnicity, and age.[20] Hypertension in this population is defined as a blood pressure ≥ 130/80 mm Hg.[8] In T2DM, it often is present as part of the metabolic syndrome of insulin resistance, central obesity, and dyslipidemia.[21] Aggressively managing blood pressure significantly reduces total mortality among diabetic patients.[21-24] Those with a systolic blood pressure of 130 to 139 mm Hg or a diastolic blood pressure of 80 to 89 mm Hg may receive lifestyle therapy alone for up to 3 months; if blood pressure does not decline by then, they will need medication.[8] Patients with more severe hypertension (a systolic blood pressure ≥ 140 mm Hg at diagnosis or on follow-up) should receive both lifestyle and pharmacologic therapy.[8]

Pharmacologic therapy for diabetic hypertensive patients is often an angiotensin-converting enzyme (ACE) inhibitor or an angiotensin receptor blocker (do not use in pregnancy). To achieve blood pressure targets, treatment should include a thiazide diuretic for patients with an estimated glomerular filtration rate (GFR) ≥ 30 ml/minute per 1.73 m² or a loop diuretic for those with an estimated GFR < 30 ml/minute per 1.73 m².[8] ACE inhibitors are superior to amlodipine besylate (a long-acting calcium channel blocker), beta blockers (which slow the heart rate), and diuretics for reducing adverse cardiovascular events, including fatal myocardial infarction in women who have T2DM.[21-24]

Albuminuria

Diabetic nephropathy is the leading cause of end-stage kidney disease in the United States.[8,25] Screening for microalbuminuria should be performed at least annually by measuring the albumin-to-creatinine ratio in a random spot collection.[13] Additionally, it is recommended that clinicians routinely estimate the GFR to enable appropriate screening for nephropathy, as some patients have a lower GFR when urine albumin values are in the normal range.[26] Microalbuminuria is also an independent risk factor for CVD. Compared with the general population, the risk of CVD in people with T2DM and albuminuria is eight times higher.[27] ACE inhibitors and angiotensin receptor blockers can slow the progression of microalbuminuria to macroalbuminuria.[8]

Dyslipidemia

Elevated triglycerides, low levels of high-density lipoprotein (HDL-C), and high levels of low-density lipoprotein (LDL-C) constitute the "lipid triad" associated with T2DM. When blood glucose is poorly controlled, the release of free fatty acids from fat cells increases. This elevates triglycerides and reduces HDL-C levels, and LDL-C particles become even smaller and more dense.[28] Aggressive glycemic control can help manage dyslipidemia but, by itself, does not significantly lower the risk of CVD. Diabetes confers a risk of coronary artery disease (CAD) equivalent to that in pre-existing CAD; in women, the risk is more than twice as high as in men.[29] Dyslipidemia is managed primarily by aggressively reducing LDL-C. Statins, a mainstay treatment, lower LDL-C in diabetics and nondiabetics, and thus reduce cardiovascular mortality. They also reduce CVD events independently of lowering LDL-C.[30] Goals for managing dyslipidemia in diabetic patients include the following:

- Statin therapy (contraindicated during pregnancy) in addition to lifestyle therapy, regardless of baseline lipid levels, for patients with CVD and patients without overt CVD who are > 40 years old and have one or more other risk factors for the disease;
- For patients with CVD, the LDL-C goal is < 70 mg/dL;
- For patients without overt CVD, the LDL-C goal is < 100 mg/dL;
- A triglyceride level < 150 mg/dL is also important, but the primary goal is to maintain optimum levels of LDL-C.[8]

A review of 145 long-term randomized, controlled trials of antiplatelet therapy concluded that low-dose aspirin reduces cardiovascular events by about one-third compared with placebo and that this benefit is similar in diabetic and nondiabetic patients. In this review, a meta-analysis of data for more than 51,000 women and 44,000 men revealed that, while such therapy reduced cardiovascular events in both groups, the primary beneficial effect in women was a lower rate of ischemic stroke and in men a lower rate of acute myocardial infarction.[31]

Low-dose aspirin is strongly recommended for women with T2DM who have a history of myocardial infarction, a vascular bypass procedure, stroke or transient ischemic attack, peripheral vascular disease, claudication, and/or angina. It is also strongly recommended for women with T2DM who are at higher cardiovascular risk, including those older than 40 and those who have additional risk factors—a family history of CVD, hypertension, smoking, dyslipidemia, and/or albuminuria.[32] To date, no research has demonstrated that aspirin benefits patients younger than 30, and its use in patients younger than 21 is contraindicated due to the risk of Reye's syndrome.[32]

■ HYPERGLYCEMIA MONITORING

Excluding patients who receive multiple daily injections of insulin, there are no evidence-based recommendations for the frequency of home monitoring, and studies have questioned its usefulness.[33,34] Home monitoring, compared with no monitoring, minimally improves HbA1c in patients with relatively well-controlled diabetes.[33,34] It can help clinicians adjust medications during the 3-month intervals between HbA1c measurements, but it is expensive, time-consuming, and in some cases uncomfortable. Home monitoring should be used judiciously; clinicians must weigh its utility versus cost.

Assessing blood glucose after an 8-hour fast, usually in the morning, gives patients a general idea of overall glycemic control. If fasting values are elevated, values after a meal will almost certainly be too high. A baseline record of fasting values is very helpful in initially managing hyperglycemia. Daily monitoring is not always necessary, but it should be frequent enough to enable identification of trends in fasting glucose and take place whenever other health conditions fluctuate.

Preprandial glucose monitoring can provide tight control. The main reason for checking blood glucose before a meal is to adjust medication—usually insulin—according to the value obtained. For example, a patient who is taking sliding-scale (rapid-acting) insulin with meals first needs the blood glucose value to determine the appropriate amount of insulin. Because sliding-scale regimens are complex, this type of management is usually reserved for people with T1DM and for those with T2DM who temporarily need tighter control. Patients can transition from these regimens to standard-dose routines once a pattern has been established.

Postprandial glucose monitoring also can help with tight control. One hour after a meal, blood glucose should be ≤ 180 mg/dL, and 2 hours after a meal, ≤ 140 mg/dL.[8] Checking postprandial blood glucose when fasting glucose is normal but HbA1c remains high is especially helpful.

■ HYPERGLYCEMIA MEDICATIONS

The major classes of medications that reduce blood glucose are insulin secretagogues, biguanide, thiazolidinediones, alpha glucosidase inhibitors, incretin mimetics and enhancers, amylin analogs, and insulin and insulin analogs. The following basic principles apply to their use:

- Monotherapy with any oral hypoglycemic agent is superior to diet or placebo in reducing HbA1c values, but no particular class or combination of medications has consistently proved to be better than another[35,36];
- Medications for T2DM target one or more of the underlying defects: insulin resistance, decreased insulin secretion, and increased hepatic glucose output. When clinicians add or change medications, they should aim for balanced glycemic control—a combination of medications that, together, target two or more of these defects;
- In the long term, preventing or delaying morbidity and/or mortality is more important than lowering blood glucose. Oftentimes, there is no evidence that newer medications improve morbidity or mortality;

- Patients with diabetes take many medications and must manage the cost of monitoring their blood sugar. Newer medications and monitoring devices are almost always more expensive but not always the most beneficial. Patients rely on clinicians to help them weigh cost and benefit; and
- Patients who take medications such as insulin and exenatide must manage complex monitoring and drug regimens. An important first step in diabetes management is carefully considering a patient's ability to do this.

Sulfonylureas and Nonsulfonylurea Insulin Secretagogues

Sulfonylureas (SUs), such as glipizide and glimeperide, and nonsulfonylurea insulin secretagogues (nSUs), such as nateglinide and repaglinide, increase insulin secretion by closing K+-gated channels on the surface of pancreatic beta cells.[37] These medications can cause hypoglycemia and they have an unpredictable impact on glucose levels, especially in older adults. Furthermore, SUs—and, to a lesser extent, possibly nSUs— can cause weight gain. SUs neither increase nor decrease cardiovascular morbidity and mortality,[38] and evidence regarding the effect of nSUs in this regard is insufficient to draw any conclusions.[27] These medications are generally not expensive; they cost slightly more than biguanide, which is the most affordable.

Biguanide

Metformin, the only biguanide on the market, reduces hepatic glucose output and, to a lesser extent, sensitizes peripheral tissues to insulin.[39] This very affordable drug slows progression from impaired glucose tolerance to T2DM.[7] To prevent one new case of T2DM in 3 years, 13.9 people would need treatment with metformin.[7] Most importantly, it is the only hypoglycemic agent that reduces total mortality among T2DM patients.[40]

A review representing more than 36,000 patient-years of metformin use found no increase in fatal or nonfatal lactic acidosis.[41] However, clinicians should be cautious when they prescribe metformin for patients with renal dysfunction. An assessment of such dysfunction based on serum creatinine or estimated glomerular filtration rate helps clinicians determine if metformin is the most appropriate medication in these cases.[42]

Thiazolidinediones

Thiazolidinediones (TZDs), such as rosiglitazone and pioglitazone, increase insulin sensitivity in peripheral tissues and, to a lesser extent, reduce hepatic glucose production.[37] They do not cause hypoglycemia when used as monotherapy. A potential side effect is peripheral edema. TZDs are contraindicated for patients with poorly compensated congestive heart failure. The drugs are expensive; no generic equivalents are available.

A review of 18 clinical trials concluded that rosiglitazone is associated with a higher risk of myocardial infarction and death from cardiovascular causes.[43] Another review of four clinical trials concluded that rosiglitazone significantly increases the risk of myocardial infarction and heart failure but, overall, does not affect cardiovascular mortality.[44] The latter review only included trials with 1 or more years of follow-up, while the former included trials with shorter follow-up periods.

In a meta-analysis of 19 controlled trials, pioglitazone was associated with a reduction in composite death, myocardial infarction, and stroke. It increased the incidence of serious heart failure by 40% without increasing cardiovascular mortality.[45]

Alpha Glucosidase Inhibitors

These moderately expensive medications, which include acarbose and miglitol, act at the brush border in the small intestine. They inactivate the enzyme that breaks down complex carbohydrates, thereby slowing absorption and flattening the postprandial glycemic curve.[37] In patients with impaired glucose tolerance and T2DM, acarbose significantly reduces acute myocardial infarction and cardiovascular mortality.[38,46,47]

Incretin Mimetics and Enhancers

Incretin hormones stimulate secretion of glucose-dependent insulin, lower glucagon secretion, slow gastric emptying, and reduce appetite.[37] These expensive therapeutics include exenatide, an injectable incretin mimetic, and sitagliptin, an oral incretin enhancer. No generic equivalents are available. Exenatide lowers blood glucose and stimulates weight loss, perhaps by slowing gastric emptying and producing satiety.[37,48] Sitagliptin also lowers blood glucose but has no effect on body weight.[49] Evidence regarding the impact of incretin mimetics and enhancers on cardiovascular events is insufficient to draw any conclusions.[27]

Amylin Analogs

Along with insulin, the pancreas secretes amylin in response to a meal, which slows gastric emptying and inhibits glucagon secretion. Amylin analogs, such as pramlintide, are indicated for T1DM but rarely for T2DM.[1,37] When therapy begins, the insulin dose should be reduced by 50% to avoid potentially severe hypoglycemia. Evidence regarding the impact of amylin analogs on cardiovascular disease is insufficient to draw any conclusions.[38] The drugs are expensive; no generic equivalents are available.

Insulin and Insulin Analogs

In patients with T2DM, insulin and insulin analogs supplement the body's natural supply; in patients with T1DM, they replace it. Insulin analogs are created by altering amino acid sequences, which changes the hormone's onset and duration of action.

Rapid-acting insulin blunts the hyperglycemic, postprandial peak. Medications include lispro (Humalog), aspart (NovoLog), and glulisine (Apidra). The insulin begins acting in 5 to 15 minutes, has a peak of 1 to 2 hours, and lasts 4 to 5 hours. Patients take it immediately before or a few minutes before meals. Another rapid-acting insulin is human regular insulin (Humulin R, Novolin R, and ReliOn). It begins acting in 30 to 60 minutes, has a peak of 2 to 4 hours, and lasts 8 to 10 hours. Patients must take human regular insulin 30 minutes before a meal.

Intermediate-acting insulin—human neutral protamine Hagedorn (Humulin N and Novolin N)—requires two daily injections for it to be basally effective. It has an onset of 1 to 2 hours, a peak of 4 to 8 hours, and a duration of 10 to 20 hours.

Long-acting insulin meets basal needs. Glargine (Lantus) begins acting in 1 to 2 hours, does not have a peak, and lasts 20 to 24 hours. Detemir (Levemir), administered once or twice daily by injection, has an onset of 1 to 2 hours, no peak, and a duration of 12 to 20 hours.

■ MEDICATION STRATEGIES

The first step in diabetes treatment is to normalize fasting blood glucose through weekly or monthly adjustments in the drug regimen.[50,51] Metformin, a first-line agent, does not increase body weight or cause hypoglycemia, and it reduces total mortality, especially in patients who are overweight or obese. Beginning with a low dose and titrating slowly can minimize the gastrointestinal symptoms that may occur. If a patient increases her dose of metformin to take advantage of its beneficial effects and then develops diarrhea, the most common side effect, she should drop back to the lowest tolerable dose rather than stop the drug altogether.

Clinicians can combine any of the first-line agents—TZDs, SUs, nSUs, and alpha-glucosidase inhibitors—to address the three primary defects in T2DM. Combination products are available, but none is more effective than another, and prescribing combination pills potentially limits flexibility in terms of altering doses.

When fasting blood glucose levels are nearly normal, clinicians can address postprandial glucose by increasing the dose of current medications or adding medications. Second-line agents worth considering after first-line therapeutics have provided maximum benefit include exenatide (approved for use with metformin and/or SUs) and sitagliptin (approved for use with metformin or TZDs).

■ INITIATING INSULIN THERAPY

There is no evidence-based guideline for when to initiate insulin therapy. However, experts recommend starting it if fasting blood glucose is consistently > 250 mg/dL or if random glucose is consistently > 300 mg/dL.[51]

Fewer than 40% of diabetics in the United States successfully achieve a HbA1c of < 7%.[50] One reason is the reluctance of patients and clinicians to start insulin, which they view as an acknowledgment of their inability to otherwise manage diabetes. In fact, progressive failure of beta cells often occurs even when patients follow a proper diet, exercise, and take oral medications. Clinicians need to tell patients that insulin is simply another management tool. Although typically introduced when oral agents can no longer control glucose, insulin is an option when such agents are contraindicated, as in patients who have liver or kidney disease.

Newly diagnosed patients may also benefit from acute insulin use. Prolonged hyperglycemia can cause glucose toxicity, a potentially reversible impairment in glucose-stimulated insulin secretion. Aggressive insulin therapy, followed by the addition of oral medications while insulin is tapered and perhaps discontinued, can correct this.

If an intermediate-acting or long-acting insulin is added to a patient's regimen, she should continue taking oral medications, at least initially. Insulin treatment begins with 10 units/day, or 0.17 to 0.50 unit/kg/day; the dose is titrated in increments of 2 units every 3 days, the goal being to normalize fasting glucose.[50,51] If the patient begins to experience unpredictable, intermittent hypoglycemia, an option is to discontinue insulin secretagogues first. Rapid-acting or premixed preparations can be added when fasting blood glucose is persistently high or when it is under control but, as may occur, HbA1c hits a plateau of around 7.5%, indicating high postprandial glucose. In these cases, adding more basal insulin usually does not enable patients to achieve their glucose target.[51] Combinations of rapid-acting and long-acting insulin are more convenient for patients, but they limit dosing flexibility and typically do not improve tight glycemic control.

■ MEDICATION FOR OLDER ADULTS

The greater prevalence of comorbid conditions in older women requires careful consideration of appropriate diabetes medications. Metformin is often contraindicated due to renal insufficiency or significant heart failure. TZDs can cause fluid retention that may exacerbate or result in heart failure. Sulfonylureas, other insulin secretagogues, and insulin can cause hypoglycemia that is not tolerated well. In addition, patients who use insulin, and their caregivers, must have good visual and motor skills and good cognitive ability. Aggressive management of known cardiovascular risk factors such as hypertension, rather than tight glycemic control, will likely be more beneficial for most of these patients.[8]

In the scenario at the beginning of this chapter, the physician gave Alicia printed information about self-management of T2DM, provided instruction on home glucose monitoring, and scheduled an appointment for medical nutrition therapy. Alicia returned in 2 weeks with the calendar she received on the first visit; it showed the days and times she had checked her fasting 1-hour and 2-hour postprandial blood glucose at home. She had visited the nutritionist and was trying to improve her diet.

Alicia's weight had not changed since the first visit. Based on her glucose diary, she and the physician agreed that she should take a medication to manage her hyperglycemia: 500 mg of metformin with breakfast each day for 2 weeks. Absent gastrointestinal side effects such as loose stools during the first 2 weeks of medication, Alicia was instructed to increase the dose to 500 mg with both breakfast and dinner. She listed the physical activities she enjoys and times during the week when she could fit exercise into her schedule, and said she would begin an aerobic exercise program.

Alicia returned in a month for her third visit. She was tolerating the metformin twice a day, had lost 3 pounds, and was pleased with the improvement in her blood glucose readings at home. Twice each week and on separate days, she was checking her fasting glucose, which varied between 72 and 94 mg/dL, and her two-hour postprandial glucose, which ranged between 105 and 150 mg/dL. She was walking for exercise—at least three times a week with her partner or daughter. The physician congratulated Alicia on her progress, then summarized her particular issues:

- Weight loss: "You're definitely on the right track and have managed to lose 3 pounds in 4 weeks, which is almost a pound a week. We agreed you would try to lose 7% of your initial weight, so you are almost a quarter of the way to achieving your first goal of 13 pounds. Wonderful!"

- Exercise: "You're well on your way to 150 minutes weekly of aerobic exercise. Keep thinking of fun ways to increase your activities and of other ways to stay active, like parking farther away from the grocery store entrance. Most importantly, try not to think of all this as a chore but rather as something that can be fun and will make you feel better."

- Diet: "Diet is difficult when you're planning meals for other people as well as yourself. Keep in mind your overall goals regarding low-fat, lower-calorie eating, and remember that when you limit snack foods, sodas, and juices at home, you're helping yourself and your daughter, who you mentioned is overweight. Because she has many risk factors for prediabetes, you might consider getting her screened."

- Blood sugar: "Your blood sugars are excellent. You've done a great job bringing them under control. You won't need any medicines in addition to the metformin and can cut back on checking your blood sugar to twice weekly—once while fasting and once 2 hours after a meal. About every 3 months, we'll check your hemoglobin A1c, which will tell us if, on average, your blood sugar during the times you're not checking it is staying in the normal range."

- Blood pressure: "Diabetes requires strict control of your blood pressure—more control than in people without the disease—to prevent early heart attacks, strokes, and kidney problems. We'll check your blood pressure regularly and talk about adding a medication if we can't keep the top reading below 130 and the bottom reading below 80 through diet and exercise."

- Albuminuria: "All kidney tests so far have turned out great. We'll check each year to be sure your kidneys remain healthy. If a problem arises, medications can help."

- Cholesterol: "Cholesterol, like blood pressure, also requires stricter control than usual. After checking your fasting cholesterol panel on the next visit, I might talk with you about starting a statin if you need it. Statins are cholesterol-lowering medications that help reduce the risk of early heart attacks."

- Referrals: "Diabetes can affect your eyesight. Although you've taken the first big step toward preventing that by controlling your blood sugar, you need to see a specialist who should closely examine your eyes for early signs of problems. If you decide to get pregnant again, you must first see a high-risk pregnancy specialist, or perinatologist, because there are special, diabetes-related considerations. Each time you come in, I'll ask if you're feeling depressed, overwhelmed, or anxious; many people with a chronic health condition do. If you are, a counselor can help address these feelings."

- Ongoing support: "Call me if you have any questions or any problems arise. If I'm unavailable, another doctor here who has experience treating diabetes will respond. Other types of support are also helpful. The American Diabetes Association Web site, at www.diabetes.org, has lots of good information for patients about a wide range of topics—from diet and exercise to handling the frustrations of living with diabetes."

CONCLUSION

An epidemic of obesity in the United States is fueling an increase in the incidence of diabetes, a major cause of death. Because lesbians are more likely than heterosexual women to be overweight or obese, they and their physicians must remain vigilant for signs of this potentially debilitating and/or lethal condition and for related risk factors. With guidance and encouragement from clinicians, patients can modify some of the key risk factors, including obesity, high blood pressure, poor diet, and lack of exercise, to improve their health. Numerous medications and medication strategies are available to effectively manage diabetes and prevent or minimize adverse outcomes.

REFERENCES

1. National Center for Chronic Disease Prevention and Health Promotion. (2009). *Diabetes: Successes and opportunities for population-based prevention and control.* Available at www.cdc.gov/nccdphp/publications/aag/ddt.htm.

2. Cheng, W. S., Wingard, D. L., Kritz-Silverstein, D., & Barrett-Connor, E. (2008). Sensitivity and specificity of death certificates for diabetes: As good as it gets? *Diabetes Care, 31,* 279–284.

3. Diamant, A. L., & Wold, C. (2003). Sexual orientation and variation in physical and mental health status among women. *Journal of Women's Health, 12,* 41–49.

4. Bowen, D. J., Balsam, K. F., & Ender, S. R. (2008). A review of obesity issues in sexual minority women. *Obesity, 16,* 221–228.

5. Ramlo-Halsted, B. A., & Edelman, S. V. (2000). The natural history of type 2 diabetes: Practical points to consider in developing prevention and treatment strategies. *Clinical Diabetes, 18,* 80–85. Available at journal.diabetes.org/clinicaldiabetes/V18N22000/pg80.htm.

6. Porta, M. (Ed.). (2008). *A dictionary of epidemiology* (5th ed.). New York: Oxford University Press.

7. Knowler, W. C., Barrett-Connor, E., Fowler, S. E., Hamman, R. F., Lachin, J. M., Walker, E. A., et al. (2002). Reduction in the incidence of type 2 diabetes with lifestyle intervention or metformin. *New England Journal of Medicine, 346,* 393–403.

8. American Diabetes Association. (2009). Standards of medical care in diabetes—2009. *Diabetes Care, 32*(Suppl. 1), S13–S61. Available at care.diabetesjournals.org/content/32/Supplement_1/S13.full.

9. Hillier, T. A., Vesco, K. K., Pedula, K. L., Beil, T. L., Whitlock, E. P., & Pettitt, D. J. (2008). Screening for gestational diabetes mellitus: A systematic review for the U.S. Preventive Services Task Force. *Annals of Internal Medicine, 148,* 766–775. Available at annals.highwire.org/content/148/10/766.full.

10. American College of Obstetricians and Gynecologists Committee on Practice Bulletins—Obstetrics. (2001). ACOG practice bulletin. Clinical management guidelines for obstetrician-gynecologists. Number 30, September 2001. Gestational diabetes. *Obstetrics & Gynecology, 98,* 525–538.

11. American Diabetes Association. (2009). Diagnosis and classification of diabetes mellitus. *Diabetes Care, 32*(Suppl. 1), S62–S67. Available at care.diabetesjournals.org/content/32/Supplement_1/S62.full.

12. Committee on Obstetric Practice. (2009). ACOG committee opinion no. 435: Postpartum screening for abnormal glucose tolerance in women who had gestational diabetes mellitus. *Obstetrics & Gynecology, 113,* 1419–1421.

13. Norris, S. L., Zhang, X., Avenell, A., Gregg, E., Brown, T. J., Schmid, C. H., et al. (2005). Long-term non-pharmacological weight loss interventions for adults with type 2 diabetes. *Cochrane Database of Systematic Reviews, Apr 18,* CD004095.

14. Intensive blood-glucose control with sulphonylureas or insulin compared with conventional treatment and risk of complications in patients with type 2 diabetes (UKPDS 33). UK Prospective Diabetes Study (UKPDS) Group. (1998). *Lancet, 352,* 837–853.

15. Implications of the United Kingdom Prospective Diabetes Study. American Diabetes Association. (1998). *Diabetes Care, 21,* 2180–2184.

16. Saudek, C. D., Herman, W. H., Sacks, D. B., Bergenstal, R. M., Edelman, D., & Davidson, M. B. (2008). A new look at screening and diagnosing diabetes mellitus. *Journal of Endocrinology & Metabolism, 93,* 2447–2453.

17. Centers for Disease Control and Prevention. (2008). *National diabetes fact sheet, 2007.* Available at www.cdc.gov/diabetes/pubs/pdf/ndfs_2007.pdf.

18. Gaede, P., Vedel, P., Larsen, N., Jensen, G. V., Parving, H. H., & Pedersen, O. (2003). Multifactorial intervention and cardiovascular disease in patients with type 2 diabetes. *New England Journal of Medicine, 348,* 383–393.

19. George, P. B., Tobin, K. J., Corpus, R. A., Devlin, W. H., & O'Neill, W. W. (2001). Treatment of cardiac risk factors in diabetic patients. How well do we follow the guidelines? *American Heart Journal, 142,* 857–863.

20. Arauz-Pacheco, C., Parrott, M. A., Raskin, P., & American Diabetes Association. (2003). Treatment of hypertension in adults with diabetes. *Diabetes Care, 26*(Suppl. 1), S80–S82.

21. Tatti, P., Pahor, M., Byrington, R. P., Di Mauro, P., Guarisco, R., Strollo, G., et al. (1998). Cardiovascular Events Randomized Trial (FACET) in patients with hypertension and NIDDM. *Diabetes Care, 21,* 597–603.

22. Hansson, L., Hedner, T., Lindholm, L., Niklason, A., Luomanmäki, K., Niskanen, L., et. al. (1997). The Captopril Prevention Project (CAPP) in hypertension—baseline data and current status. *Blood Pressure, 6,* 365–367.

23. Yusuf, S., Sleight, P., Pogue, J., Bosch, J., Davies, R., & Dagenais, G. (2000). Effects of an angiotensin-converting-enzyme inhibitor, ramipril, on cardiovascular events in high-risk patients. The Heart Outcomes Prevention Evaluation Study investigators. *New England Journal of Medicine, 342,* 145–153.

24. Effects of ramipril on cardiovascular and microvascular outcomes in people with diabetes mellitus: Results of the HOPE study and the MICRO-HOPE substudy. The Heart Outcomes Prevention Evaluation Study investigators. (2000). *Lancet, 355,* 253–259.

25. U.S. Renal Data System. (2009). *USRDS 2009 annual data report: Atlas of chronic kidney disease and end-stage renal disease in the United States.* Bethesda, MD: National Institute of Diabetes and Digestive and Kidney Diseases. Available at www.usrds.org/atlas.htm.

26. Zelmanovitz, T., Gerchman, F., Balthazar, A. P. S., Thomazelli, F. C. S., Matos, J. D., & Canani, L. H. (2009). Diabetic nephropathy. *Diabetology & Metabolic Syndrome, 1,* 10. Available at www.dmsjournal.com/content/1/1/10.

27. Colhoun, H. M., Lee, E. T., Bennett, P. H., Lu, M., Keen, H., Wang, S. L., et al. (2001). Risk factors for renal failure: The WHO Multinational Study of Vascular Disease in Diabetes. *Diabetologia, 44*(Suppl. 2), S46–53.

28. Isley, W., & Harris, W. (2004). Lipoprotein abnormalities. In S. P. Marso & D. M. Stern (Eds.), *Diabetes and cardiovascular disease: Integrating science and clinical medicine* (pp. 337–353). Philadelphia: Lippincott Williams & Wilkins.

29. Juutilainen, A., Lehto, S., Rönnemaa, T., Pyörälä, K., & Laakso, M. (2005). Type 2 diabetes as a "coronary heart disease equivalent": An 18-year prospective population-based study in Finnish subjects. *Diabetes Care, 28,* 2901–2907.

30. Goldberg, R. B., Mellies, M. J., Sacks, F. M., Moyé, L. A., Howard, B. V., Howard, W. J., et al. (1998). Cardiovascular events and their reduction with pravastatin in diabetic and glucose-intolerant myocardial infarction survivors with average cholesterol levels: Subgroup analyses in the Cholesterol and Recurrent Events (CARE) trial. The CARE investigators. *Circulation, 98,* 2513–2519.

31. Collaborative overview of randomised trials of antiplatelet therapy—I: Prevention of death, myocardial infarction, and stroke by prolonged antiplatelet therapy in various categories of patients. Antiplatelet Trialists' Collaboration. (1994). *BMJ, 308,* 81–106.

32. American Diabetes Association. (1994). Aspirin therapy in diabetes. *Diabetes Care, 27*(Suppl. 1), S72–S73. Available at care.diabetesjournals.org/content/27/suppl_1/s72.full.

33. Farmer, A., Wade, A., Goyder, E., Yudkin, P., French, D., Craven, A., et al. (2007). Impact of self monitoring of blood glucose in the management of patients with non-insulin treated diabetes: Open parallel group randomised trial. *BMJ, 335,* 132.

34. Welchen, L. M., Bloementhal, E., Nijpels, G., Dekker, J. M., Heine, R. J., Stalman, W. A., et al. (2005). Self-monitoring of blood glucose in patients with type 2 diabetes who are not using insulin: A systematic review. *Diabetes Care, 28,* 1510–1517.

35. Kimmel, B., & Inzucchi, S. E. (2006). Oral agents for type 2 diabetes: An update. *Clinical Diabetes, 23,* 64–76.

36. Bolen, S., Feldman, L., Vassy, J., Wilson, L., Yeh, H.-C., Marinopoulos, S., et al. (2002). Systematic review: Comparative effectiveness and safety of oral medications for type 2 diabetes mellitus. *Annals of Internal Medicine, 147,* 386–399.

37. Brunton, L. L., Lazo, J. S., & Parker, K. L. (2005). *Goodman & Gilman's the pharmacological basis of therapeutics* (11th ed.). New York: McGraw Hill.

38. Uwaifo, G. I., & Ratner, R. E. (2007). Differential effects of oral hypoglycemic agents on glucose control and cardiovascular risk. *American Journal of Cardiology, 99,* 51B–67B.

39. American Society of Health-System Pharmacists. (2007). *Metformin.* Available at www.ncbi.nlm.nih.gov/bookshelf/br.fcgi?book=meds&part=a696005.

40. Effect of intensive blood-glucose control with metformin on complications in overweight patients with type 2 diabetes (UKPDS 34). UK Prospective Diabetes Study Group. (1998). *Lancet, 352,* 854–865.

41. Salpeter, S. R., Greyber, E., Pasternak, G. A., & Salpeter, E. E. (2003). Risk of fatal and nonfatal lactic acidosis with metformin use in type 2 diabetes mellitus: Systematic review and meta-analysis. *Archives of Internal Medicine, 163,* 2594–2602.

42. Warren, R. E., Strachan, M. W., Wild, S., & McKnight, J. A. (2007). Introducing estimated glomerular filtration rate (eGFR) into clinical practice in the UK: Implications for the use of metformin. *Diabetic Medicine, 24,* 494–497.

43. Singh, S., Loke, Y. K., & Furberg, C. D. (2007). Long-term risk of cardiovascular events with rosiglitazone: A meta-analysis. *Journal of the American Medical Association, 298,* 1189–1195.

44. Nissen, S. E., & Wolski, K. (2007). Effect of rosiglitazone on the risk of myocardial infarction and death from cardiovascular causes. *New England Journal of Medicine, 356,* 2457–2471.

45. Lincoff, A. M., Wolski, K., Nicholls, S. J., & Nissen, S. E. (2007). Pioglitazone and risk of cardiovascular events in patients with type 2 diabetes mellitus: A meta-analysis of randomized trials. *Journal of the American Medical Association, 298,* 1180–1188.

46. Chiasson, J. L. (2006). Acarbose for the prevention of diabetes, hypertension, and cardiovascular disease in subjects with impaired glucose tolerance: The Study to Prevent Non-Insulin-Dependent Diabetes Mellitus (STOP-NIDDM) trial. *Endocrine Practice, 12*(Suppl. 1), 25–30.

47. Chiasson J. L., Josse, R. G., Gomis, R., Hanefeld, M., Karasik, A., Laakso, M., et al. (2003). Acarbose treatment and the risk of cardiovascular disease and hypertension in patients with impaired glucose tolerance: The STOP-NIDDM trial. *Journal of the American Medical Association, 290,* 486–494.

48. American Society of Health-System Pharmacists. (2009). *Exenatide injection.* Available at www.ncbi.nlm.nih.gov/bookshelf/br.fcgi?book=meds&part=a605034.

49. American Society of Health-System Pharmacists. (2007). *Sitagliptin.* Available at www.ncbi.nlm.nih.gov/bookshelf/br.fcgi?book=meds&part=a606023.

50. Nathan, D. M., Buse, J. B., Davidson, M. B., Heine, R. J., Holman, R. R., Sherwin, R., et al. (2006). Management of hyperglycemia in type 2 diabetes: A consensus algorithm for the initiation and adjustment of therapy: A consensus statement from the American Diabetes Association and the European Association for the Study of Diabetes. *Diabetes Care, 29,* 1963–1972.

51. Hirsch, I. B., Bergenstal, R. M., Parkin, C. G., Wright, E. Jr., & Buse J. B. (2006). A real-world approach to insulin therapy in primary care practice. *Clinical Diabetes, 23,* 78–86.

ABOUT THE AUTHORS

Cindy Ripsin, MD, is Clinical Assistant Professor in the Department of Family Medicine at the University of Texas Medical Branch, Galveston. Her research interest is management of chronic diseases that affect the cardiovascular system, especially diabetes.

Patricia Robertson, MD, is Professor in the Department of Obstetrics, Gynecology, & Reproductive Sciences at the University of California, San Francisco. She provides medical care to pregnant women with high-risk pregnancies, including those with diabetes.

CHAPTER 30

"Will I Be in Pain?"

PALLIATIVE AND HOSPICE CARE FOR LESBIANS

JANE L. APPLEBY, MD

ANDREA, *47, is a successful graphic artist who has had amyotrophic lateral sclerosis (ALS) for 8 years. She and her partner Victoria, an executive at a local corporation, have been together for 15 years and have a rich network of friends. Andrea's father died 3 years ago. Andrea's mother, who remarried, recently experienced the sudden, traumatic death of her second husband. Victoria has two adult children from a previous marriage to a man.*

Andrea gradually lost function. Bed-bound for the last 4 years, she needed help with all activities of daily living. Progressive bulbar involvement made it difficult for her to chew, swallow, and speak. The progression of disease accelerated in the last month, requiring that she use a percutaneous feeding tube to maintain adequate nutrition and avoid more weight loss. There was also progressive respiratory failure; bilevel positive airway pressure (BiPAP) had been recommended based on the results of overnight oximetry. Andrea is severely claustrophobic, which limited her ability to use the BiPAP ventilator comfortably, and she did not want to use a cough-assist device.

A week ago, Andrea developed a severe loose cough and fever. She was hospitalized with severe respiratory failure and presumed pneumonia. An arterial blood gas test revealed hypercarbia and hypoxemia. Despite her weakness and respiratory distress, Andrea was completely oriented, responded appropriately to cognitive-assessment questions, and could make decisions. She declined intubation and mechanical ventilation. After a period of observation in the intensive care unit, she was transferred to the medical unit, where she responded somewhat to continued treatment with antibiotics, oxygen, intermittent BiPAP, and inhaled bronchodilators. Her physician recommended that she receive nutrition only through a feeding tube.

The physician, Andrea, and her family consulted the palliative care team because Andrea requested comfort care and hospice evaluation. She was determined to stop receiving nutrition through a feeding tube and air through a ventilator after her mother's birthday in 8 days. The entire extended family was distraught and insisted on continuing aggressive care. At Andrea's bedside, clutching her hand and sobbing, the mother repeatedly said she could not bear the thought of Andrea's death and pleaded with her daughter to continue *fighting ALS. Victoria was uncomfortable with this extreme demonstration of grief and unsure how to react. She supported Andrea's decision. Andrea's will was up-to-date and she had given Victoria durable health care power of attorney.*

■ ■ ■

DEFINITIONS

Palliative Care

Palliative care is total care for patients whose disease does not respond to curative treatment. It seeks to alleviate symptoms, be they physical, psychological, social, or spiritual. An interdisciplinary team of professionals provides coordinated medical, nursing, social, and spiritual services, working with patients and families to achieve the best possible quality of life.[1-3] Treatment may include very aggressive measures, such as chemotherapy, radiation therapy, and surgical intervention, to control pain and other distressing symptoms. The choice of treatment is based on how well a therapy can meet the patient's stated goals rather than on its efficacy. Because a patient's symptoms and quality of life evolve as illness progresses, the care goals and selected therapies require frequent reassessment.

Hospice

Hospice provides coordinated, comprehensive palliative care to terminally ill patients and supportive services to families and significant others in the home, hospice units, and other facilities. An interdisciplinary team of health care professionals attends to patients' and families' physical, social, spiritual, and emotional needs in the last stages of illness and during the dying process and bereavement period. The team includes a physician, nurses, certified nursing assistants, a social worker, a chaplain, community volunteers, and secretarial staff, all of whom have received special training in hospice care. Hospice focuses on maintaining the quality of remaining life, helping terminal patients live as fully and comfortably as possible. It recognizes dying as a part of the normal process of living but affirms life and does not hasten or postpone death. By providing appropriate care and promoting a caring community, hospice seeks to free patients and families to prepare physically, mentally, and spiritually for death in a satisfactory and potentially healing way.[1] Cicely Saunders, a physician and nurse who founded modern hospice, developed the following related principles:

- ■ Patients, families, and health care professionals all have important physical, emotional, social, and spiritual needs;

- Each person's beliefs, values, and concerns should be respected regardless of nationality, race, religion, sexual orientation, disability, or financial status;
- Suffering people usually need help from caring, skilled professionals to articulate needs, values, concerns, and fears;
- Suffering people benefit from skilled interdisciplinary interventions that alleviate physical, emotional, spiritual, and social pain;
- Palliative interventions should be based on the results of careful research; and
- Continuous professional and personal growth is important for all.[1]

CURATIVE VERSUS PALLIATIVE CARE

Table 30.1 summarizes characteristics of traditional curative care and palliative care. These two approaches are not mutually exclusive; if necessary, combining curative and palliative treatments is appropriate.

TABLE 30.1. CHARACTERISTICS OF CURATIVE AND PALLIATIVE CARE

	CURATIVE CARE	PALLIATIVE CARE
Goal	Provide a cure	Relieve suffering
Object of analysis	The disease process	The patient and family
Primary value	Measurable data are important, but subjective information is not	Both measurable data and subjective information are important
Indications for therapy	If therapy will slow the progression of or eradicate the disease	If therapy will control symptoms and relieve suffering
Philosophy of care	▪ The patient's body and mind are distinct—physical circumstances overrule mental/emotional experience ▪ Patients are a collection of parts—there is little need to know the whole person	▪ The patient is a complex being with physical, emotional, social, and spiritual dimensions ▪ Treatment is congruent with the patient's and family's values, beliefs, and concerns
Definition of success	Delay progression of the disease, cure the disease, and prolong life	Enable the patient to live fully and comfortably with dignity until death

Source: Adapted from Storey, P., & Knight, C. F. (2003). *American Academy of Hospice and Palliative Medicine UNIPAC 1. The hospice/palliative medicine approach to end-of-life care* (2nd ed.). Glenview, IL: Mary Ann Liebert, Inc.

TOWARD END-OF-LIFE CARE

Preparation for and transition to end-of-life care include assessment of the prognosis, determining when to initiate palliative care or hospice, delivering the bad news, and determining and setting care goals. In addition, clinicians, patients, and families should discuss advance directives, assign durable health care power of attorney, and address legal issues regarding lesbian partnerships.

Determining when to move toward end-of-life care is not always easy. Ideally, this occurs progressively and incrementally rather than suddenly. The patient, family, and care team frequently have divergent views, expectations, and goals about prognosis and treatment. Lesbians may also be concerned about homophobia, feel ashamed, be fearful due to prior discrimination or denial of treatment, want to hide their sexual orientation or be afraid to disclose it, struggle with past or current family discord related to their sexual orientation, and confront issues regarding the custody and care of children. In addition to fearing death, they also often fear the loss of relationships, control, independence, identity, and financial security. For all of these reasons, patients and families might be reluctant to discuss end-of-life care.

Given the variable levels of professional experience and training in end-of-life care, and the inherent difficulty of determining a prognosis, some health care providers are uncomfortable discussing such care. They may not be aware of the lesbian patient's sexual orientation and she may not feel safe disclosing it. Moreover, providers vary in terms of their comfort with and knowledge about lesbian health, culture, and family structure. For some, directing or participating in the care of lesbian patients is personally challenging.

WHEN TO INITIATE CARE

Palliative Care

Palliative care can begin whenever chronic illness is diagnosed. Both palliative and curative care are appropriate during the early course of any disease to treat pain, control symptoms, and foster quality of life. Early collaboration with a palliative care team benefits the patient and family because it establishes supportive and trusting relationships, which may ease the transition to hospice care. The team's multidisciplinary nature also enables early identification of physical, emotional, social, and spiritual factors that may influence the disease process.

The amount of palliative care may be minimal immediately after a diagnosis, when clinicians aggressively treat reversible aspects of a disease. Typically, chronic conditions entail episodic exacerbations and remissions of illness. At some point, despite optimal and maximal therapy, chronic illness continues to progress and may necessitate a primary focus on palliative care to maximize symptom control, quality of life, and end-of-life planning.[2]

Hospice

Patients generally are eligible for hospice care when they have a terminal illness and a life expectancy of less than 6 months, which the physician determines based on the illness's usual course. The patient or her surrogate must understand the hospice philosophy and choose this type of care. Usually the physician makes the initial referral to a hospice program and the program's medical director confirms eligibility for services.

Eligible patients qualify for Medicare Hospice Benefits under Medicare Part A. Coverage of comprehensive, end-of-life care for terminal illness is 100%; for unrelated illnesses, traditional Medicare Part A covers 80% of costs, with patients responsible for the remainder.[*][1] Hospice benefits available from other insurers vary and eligibility for services depends on individual policies. Many hospice organizations are committed to providing end-of-life care to the uninsured and to people with limited means of paying for it.

GUIDELINES FOR PREDICTING PROGNOSIS

Life expectancy is difficult to predict, especially when the patient has a chronic illness such as heart disease, lung disease, or a neurological condition. Prognosis is a little more predictable for cancer. A complete discussion of prognostication is beyond the scope of this chapter, but in general, the criteria that help clinicians predict progressive disease are:

- Increasing frequency of hospitalization or use of other health care services;
- Progression of disease as indicated by serial testing;
- Poor response to optimal therapy;
- An increasing number of comorbid conditions;
- Diminished functional status as measured by tools such as the Karnofsky Performance Status Scale and the Palliative Performance Scale;
- Declining nutritional status as evidenced by weight loss or loss of skin integrity; and
- Other, less measurable factors, such as personal goals, emotional and spiritual state, and the will to live.[4]

---

* *For more information on Medicare Hospice Benefits, see www.medicare.gov/publications/Pubs/pdf/02154.pdf.*

Guidelines from the National Hospice and Palliative Care Organization help predict the prognosis when patients have diseases other than cancer.[†]

FACTORS THAT AFFECT DISEASE PROGRESSION

A number of risk factors among lesbians may influence illness progression. Generalizations based solely on sexual orientation are not possible because personal circumstances vary; consequently, one must consider each individual's social context, emotional resources, spiritual health, and illness experience. Researchers know that prognoses are worse for people who continuously use a significant amount of substances, such as drugs, alcohol, and tobacco; are socially isolated; and lack a social support network. Social support systems and financial and emotional resources influence adherence to treatment recommendations and medications. Lack of trust in the health care system, prior negative experience with the system, and indifferent or hostile providers influence the willingness of lesbians to access care.[5]

Spiritual and emotional well-being affects quality of life and the experience of illness. Spirituality, which refers to an individual's essential nature and life experience, can be an important aspect of well-being. It is different from religion: people may use religious rites and rituals to express spirituality, but spirituality can exist outside of formal or organized religion. Many religions do not accept homosexuality, so lesbians may have a negative view of them. A journey of the spirit often includes searching for meaning and purpose in response to the inevitable challenges of life.[6] Neutral vocabulary when discussing spiritual issues enables patients to express their beliefs and spiritual or religious practices. Health care providers must accept, affirm, and honor a patient's belief system, and offer care congruent with her belief system. Religious rites, rituals, or traditions that a patient and family do not accept are useless during end-of-life care and may cause unnecessary distress.

COMMUNICATING BAD NEWS

Delivering bad news to patients is difficult and stressful for clinicians, who receive little practical training in communication and often prefer to avoid such conversations, which make many of them feel inadequate. Moreover, they must fit this time-intensive task into their busy daily routine. Some clinicians fear they will be blamed or sued.

---

† *See Table 13, pp. 30–32, in UNIPAC 1.* The hospice and palliative medicine approach to life-limiting stress. This is one of nine titles in Storey, C. P. Jr. (Ed.). (2005). Hospice and palliative care training for physicians (3rd ed.). Glenview, IL: Mary Ann Liebert, Inc.

Bad news threatens patients' physical and/or mental well-being. It also significantly and negatively changes their view of the future. How bad the news is depends on the gap between the medical reality and the outcome a patient expects. As this gap widens, the information is likely to have a greater negative impact. Whether the news is "bad" from the provider's perspective, the patient's perspective, or both, it creates a challenge for the clinician, who cannot turn it into good news. Health care professionals are often tempted to soften bad news partly out of fear that it will harm the patient or take away hope. However, poor or vague delivery of critical information may result in ineffective coping, inappropriate treatment, or an inability to do the work necessary to prepare for the end of life. One way to deliver bad news is to follow the six sequential elements in the SPIKES protocol: setting, perception, invitation, knowledge, empathy, and summation.[7]

Setting

Health care providers should deliver the news in a comfortable, private setting and in person, not remotely by phone or electronically. They must prepare for this event by reviewing the medical and social details of the patient's situation. If preparation includes multidisciplinary team members, they should discuss the goals and format of their forthcoming meeting with the patient to ensure effective collaboration. Team members may need to reflect on their own emotional reactions, values, and opinions if the clinical situation is especially difficult. Taking time for personal reflection and self-care enables them to be completely present during the meeting.

Participants in the meeting should be seated if possible, as this puts everyone more at ease, makes the session feel less rushed, and establishes eye contact on an equal level. All cell phones and pagers should be turned off to avoid interruptions. Patients benefit if a spouse, partner, family member, or trusted friend is present.

Perception

The conversation begins by asking the patient open-ended questions about how she perceives her illness and what she already knows, an approach that conveys team members' respect and willingness to listen. Her response guides the subsequent dialog. Most patients know or suspect they have a serious diagnosis. Gauging the extent of a patient's understanding enables the team to discuss the situation at her level; otherwise, they might share information that, while accurate, is overwhelming. Silence is powerful: pausing to give the patient time to reflect and respond generates more information.

Invitation

The next step is to find out how much the patient wants to know, which depends on her personality, culture, emotional capacity, and perhaps religion. Denial is a common initial response to an illness threat. If a patient is not ready to hear bad news, the team should leave open the possibility of future communication. If she indicates a willingness to hear the news, it should be delivered through a simple, short, direct, and compassionate statement. A subsequent pause gives her time to respond and gives team members an opportunity to observe her reaction. By listening to what the patient says, they will better understand what the illness means to her.

Knowledge and Empathy

Knowledge includes information contained in the patient's emotional as well as verbal responses. Empathy means paying attention to and understanding all aspects of a communication—words, body language and other nonverbal messages, and emotional content—and then conveying this understanding to the patient with kindness and authentic presence. Empathetic responses identify and validate her experience.

Summation

The final step is to summarize, in simple language, the information that team members have conveyed and to review the care options. Asking the patient to share her understanding of the information is an excellent way to ensure successful communication or determine if clarification is necessary. Then the group develops a follow-up plan. When the patient and family leave, they must clearly understand this plan and know that the team will continue to be available.

Common Reactions to Bad News

Patients react to bad news in various ways. Among the factors that influence response are her psychological functioning, history of coping with bad news, available social support, and spiritual and cultural beliefs. Some reactions may seem abnormal or extreme when in fact they are absolutely normal, given the new, intense, life-threatening situation. Common and usually helpful reactions include denial, anger, crying, fear, bargaining, hope, and humor. They are coping mechanisms that enable the patient and family to deal with the troubling situation over time. Unhelpful reactions—guilt, severe denial, prolonged rage, and sustained anxiety or severe depression—inhibit emotional acceptance of bad news. They may warrant additional intervention, such as psychiatric evaluation.

■ ■ ■

Communication skills must be learned, cultivated, and practiced. Clinicians who have good communication skills and personal insight can deliver bad news effectively and compassionately, which in turn enables patients and families to adapt to an illness challenge. All multidisciplinary team members play an important role in the care plan;

their patient interaction skills are a critical aspect of providing excellent care. Patients and families do not remember all treatment details, but they often vividly remember how they felt during the course of an illness—for example, whether or not they received respectful care.

REALISTIC GOAL-SETTING

A foundation of palliative care and hospice is careful discussion and determination of realistic goals, which are specific and individualized for each patient and family. Successful care planning depends on obtaining a clear and robust understanding of the experience of illness—including experience in the physical, social, spiritual, and emotional domains—and of the patient's and family's values, interests, fears, needs, goals, and wishes. The role of the hospice team is to assess the medical, social, and spiritual context in which the patient and family functions. Once it does this and understands the patient and family perspective, the team can provide information and facilitate discussion and planning of care for each stage of the final journey.[9]

ADVANCE CARE PLANNING

Advance care planning includes discussion and determination of the type of treatments and care a patient wants at the end of life. Care goals support this process. For example, a patient may express her desires regarding discontinuation of treatment and when to switch from curative efforts to care. To appropriately plan and discuss this and other topics, the clinician must be aware of the patient's culture, family structure (including her family of choice), social support, financial means, and legal designations. Goals and priorities may change as the illness evolves, so it is important to reassess care decisions periodically and allow for modification, including revocation of prior decisions.

Designating a health care proxy through durable health care power of attorney and completing advance directives are particularly relevant for lesbian patients. These steps enable the designated proxy to make health care decisions, prevent conflict between the family of origin and the partner or spouse, and ensure appropriate distribution of the patient's property after death. Without a legally designated proxy, a lesbian patient's partner may be unable to gain access to her personal information, may be prevented from visiting her in the hospital, or may not be legally recognized as next of kin if she is incapacitated. Although some lesbian couples, depending on where they live, can get their relationship legally sanctioned through marriage, civil union, or domestic partnership, not all states recognize such relationships, and in states that do, the legal implications vary.[10]

It is important to discuss the patient's wishes regarding resuscitation in the event of cardiac or pulmonary arrest. Emergency medical technicians cannot honor a living will or durable health care power of attorney; they must do everything necessary to stabilize patients and transport them to a hospital. People who live in an outpatient setting, such as a retirement community or at home, can prepare for this eventuality by executing an out-of-hospital (or pre-hospital), do-not-resuscitate form. The availability of this form and requirements regarding its completion, use, and revocation vary among states. Because each state has specific laws governing advance directives and resuscitation, a patient should complete the form her state provides.[‡11]

Many health care providers worry that discussing end-of-life goals or treatments will take away the patient's hope, defined as wishing for something with the expectation of fulfillment. Hope is important because it may sustain people during difficult times. Appropriate support of hope does not include providing false information or setting false expectations; it requires reframing expectations as illness progresses. One way to support hope is to redefine the meaning of daily life—for example, by substituting the hope of cure with the hope of leaving a legacy.

COMMON SYMPTOMS NEAR THE END OF LIFE

In the last stages of life, many patients deal with symptoms such as pain, dyspnea, fatigue, nausea, anorexia, constipation, weakness, depression, anxiety, and lack of skin integrity. Symptom management for lesbian and other patients is the same.

Uncontrolled pain can cause unnecessary suffering, exhaustion, fear, and an inability to focus on psychological, emotional, and spiritual healing near the end of life. The barriers to adequate pain control are numerous. Health care providers may not be thoroughly knowledgeable about pharmacology or pain assessment. Or they may worry that certain medications will cause addiction, prompt sanctions by regulatory agencies, or unduly hasten or even cause death. Some patients are reluctant to report pain out of fear that doing so would be a sign of weakness or would label them as a complainer or drug seeker, or they believe that suffering is necessary. Others want to save a strong opioid "until I really need it." Uncontrolled pain is more prevalent among women, minorities, and the elderly, probably due to societal or personal biases.[12]

Not all pain is amenable to analgesics. If patients do not respond as expected to the usual medications, their pain might have an emotional or spiritual component. Psychosocial or spiritual experts on the interdisciplinary team may be able to recommend something that will alleviate suffering. For patients, an important tenant of palliative care is the provider's healing presence and explanations of what to

‡ *For more information on advance directives, see www.caringinfo.org/AdvanceDirectives.*

expect, which allay anxiety, uncertainty, and suffering. The gift of attention creates a safe environment for patients and families to attend to necessary, end-of-life tasks.

THE ACTIVELY DYING PROCESS

One to 2 weeks before death, patients typically become progressively weak, lethargic, disoriented, and more dependent on caregivers for help with daily activities. They also sleep more, have a shorter attention span, withdraw from interaction, are restless, have less interest in eating and more difficulty swallowing, and lose continence. Two to 3 days before death, consciousness often is cloudy; patients are minimally responsive to external stimuli, have a glassy or unfocused gaze, and show no interest in food or fluid. Blood pressure drops, heart rate increases, and the extremities become mottled, clammy, and cool. Changes in breathing pattern vary depending on the individual. The upper and lower airways may be congested, after which apnea occurs, the length of apnea periods increases, and respiration eventually ceases. Most deaths are peaceful, but some patients experience pain, severe restlessness, nausea, seizures, or dyspnea before they die. An experienced hospice team can manage these symptoms and thus minimize the patient's suffering and the family's trauma.[13]

BEREAVEMENT AND GRIEF

For health care providers, the first step in bereavement care is to acknowledge the significance of the loss to oneself and the survivors, and to tell them that their feelings of loss are valid. Survivors may experience or express grief in terms of somatic sensations or events, behavioral changes, emotional states, and cognitive dissonance. The loss will oblige them to change socially and spiritually, and to adapt. With adequate support and as time passes, most people can adjust even if the death results in dramatic life changes. During bereavement and grief, survivors often need to reassess personal identity, the meaning of life, and their life purpose.

Complicated grief occurs in up to 25% of survivors.[14] It may include chronic grief due to lack of closure or integration of the loss into life, delay of the grieving process, an inability to acknowledge the loss, or intensified normal responses. The risk of complicated grief is greater for lesbians who have lost their life partner and have not disclosed their sexual orientation to family or friends. These individuals cannot openly acknowledge their grief, mourn publicly, or rely on social support. Furthermore, family or friends who do not accept lesbian relationships as valid or equivalent to heterosexual relationships may minimize the loss of a partner. Bereavement support—grief counseling, support groups, and grief therapy—is a routine part of palliative care and hospice, but the sense of vulnerability and risk that accompanies disclosure of same-sex orientation may make lesbians hesitant to attend group therapy. The judgment of others, be it perceived or real, might reduce the benefit of group support.

ETHICAL PRINCIPLES AND CULTURAL ISSUES

Basic ethical principles of health care, including end-of-life care, include:

- Beneficence—the obligation to always act in the patient's best interest;
- Autonomy—recognizing a capable individual's right to make treatment decisions in accordance with her beliefs, cultural and personal values, and life plan;
- Nonmaleficence—avoiding harm and respecting the inherent worth and dignity of every patient; and
- Justice—the fair allocation and application of resources.[15,16–18]

Ethical care requires careful attention to the values, needs, wishes, and judgments of everyone who participates in care planning. Full exploration of these domains enables shifts from divergent to convergent thinking, which in turn leads to a culturally appropriate, individualized care plan.

Among the ethical issues that frequently arise during end-of-life care are confidentiality, autonomy (making one's own decisions), cultural expectations, independence versus safety (for example, whether the patient can safely get out of bed without assistance), and treatments to comfort the family. Culturally appropriate care—which, for lesbians especially, includes sensitive and accepting care—requires a patient-centered approach and the health care provider's awareness of his or her own cultural perspective and attitude toward other cultures, knowledge of different cultural views and practices, and development of cross-cultural skills.[19,20] Providers must examine their personal biases and how these might affect their interactions with, and medical decisions regarding, lesbian patients. The core of culturally appropriate care is unconditional respect for the patient as an individual and for her beliefs, values, and the meaning she attaches to her illness. These tenets are built into the palliative-care and hospice philosophy and the multidisciplinary model of care.

END-OF-LIFE CARE FOR LESBIANS

No studies have examined lesbians' needs, attitudes, or outcomes in end-of-life care. However, a 64-item survey of lesbians and gay men in the New York City area did assess preferences and other factors. It found that lesbians favored palliative care and generally preferred pain relief over life-extending treatment. In addition, lesbians were likely to be aware of health care proxies and were significantly more likely than gay men to have assigned durable health care power of attorney. These findings are generally consistent with those from other attitudinal studies of U.S. adults, although lesbians' preference for palliative care may be stronger.[21]

While end-of-life care for lesbian patients and their families mirrors that for all people, certain factors highlight the need for care that includes, accepts, and validates the lesbian experience. Lesbians may not fully trust the health care system or may be reluctant to seek care if they have had negative experiences. Those who are conflicted about their sexual orientation or about disclosing it also may not seek care. Elderly lesbians who live in nursing facilities are at risk of social isolation, discrimination, and abuse.[22] In navigating the health care system, lesbian couples face special challenges obtaining personal information, visiting hospitalized loved ones, and negotiating for health benefits before and after death. Lesbian parents may have to deal with complex custody issues in addition to the grief and other issues that accompany terminal illness.[10]

CARE RECOMMENDATIONS

It is difficult to generalize about end-of-life care for lesbians, given their diversity. But the following recommendations may help.

Be Accepting and Appropriately Curious

Health care providers should accept all patients, not just lesbians, as individuals without making any assumptions about who they might be based on prior experience, personal bias, perception, or a patient's appearance. Providers also need to pay special attention to how they use language. For example, an appropriately phrased question would be: "Can you describe your family for me, including if you have a partner or spouse?"

Avoid Labels

It is best to let the patient take the lead in labeling her significant other as a "life partner," "domestic partner," "partner," "spouse," or "wife." Some lesbians self-identify as "butch," others prefer "gay" or "queer."

Respect Diversity

Relationships should be mutually respectful. Respect and trust enable effective communication, the basis of healing. Patients will divulge everything a health care provider needs to know if the provider communicates respectfully and authentically.

Genuine respect for and acceptance of others, regardless of their sexual orientation, gender, race, religion, or social standing, requires courageous self-assessment of values, beliefs, and biases.

Be Sensitive to Shame

Shame is powerful. Deep-seated shame, which some patients do not acknowledge, can amplify illness experiences; inhibit feelings of acceptance, self-worth, and empowerment; and make it difficult to speak up and be heard. Providers may help lesbian patients overcome shame by recognizing and validating their partnered relationship and acknowledging their concerns about discrimination, homophobia, the care they receive, and a partner's access to medical information regarding the patient's diagnosis, care plan, response to therapy, and other issues.

Accept and Acknowledge All Families

Palliative care and hospice focus on the patient and family as a unit. Because a lesbian's family structure may be nontraditional, providers must carefully learn about it in order to understand, accept, and honor family and/or family-of-choice relationships, and to detect and manage potential conflicts. The patient can indicate who in their family of origin and/or family of choice should be included in discussions of treatment and end-of-life care. Providers need to acknowledge and document these participants.

Encourage Legal Protection

Most partnered lesbians do not enjoy the legal benefits of heterosexual marriage, so making funeral arrangements and dealing with insurance companies and other institutions before or after a partner's death can be challenging. Providers should encourage patients to consult appropriate legal counsel for planning and support purposes before their terminal illness becomes incapacitating.

■ ■ ■

In the scenario at the beginning of this chapter, a palliative care team met with Andrea, Victoria, and the extended family. The team helped them explore the benefits and burdens of continuing or discontinuing the use of BiPAP and nutrition through a feeding tube. It also helped Andrea share her illness experience with her family. Andrea explained that even the simplest daily activities, such as conversing and getting dressed, were too exhausting. Her severe fatigue limited her ability to enjoy interacting with Victoria, family, and friends. Although Andrea was no longer able to create art, she expressed satisfaction with her life experience and was confident that Victoria would do fine. She wanted to die with dignity and, in the final days, focus her limited energy on comfort and interacting with loved ones. Andrea said BiPAP and artificial feedings would unnecessarily prolong her predicament. She and Victoria had talked at length about these issues.

Andrea's mother said she was still grieving over previous losses and now faced the loss of her only daughter. Although her relationship with Andrea and Victoria was positive toward the end, in the past she had had difficulty accepting Andrea's sexual orientation and openly resented Victoria. The mother was angry with God about all her suffering. She had not been regularly involved in Andrea's care and harbored unexpressed feelings of guilt and regret. However, the palliative care team helped Andrea's mother express her anticipatory grief and love for her daughter. She became willing to listen to and consider Andrea's illness experience, and was surprised to learn how much effort it took for Andrea to make it through the day.

Andrea signed an out-of-hospital, do-not-resuscitate form and was transferred to the hospice unit. Family members were still struggling with Andrea's decision to halt further treatment, but with the hospice team's ongoing support and guidance, they continued to discuss and evaluate their feelings about Andrea's wishes for end-of-life care. The family spent many intimate, healing moments sharing stories and experiences. Andrea's mom helped with daily care, which enabled her to express love for Andrea and resolve some of her feelings of guilt and regret. About 10 days after admission to hospice, Andrea died peacefully with her partner and extended family present.

Andrea's case illustrates how, as a patient approaches death, palliative-care and hospice professionals can facilitate effective, compassionate, open communication and help the family listen to different perspectives. The professionals honored autonomy (Andrea expressed her wishes regarding end-of-life care and made her own decisions), beneficence (she made it clear that prolonging treatment would not contribute to her well-being), and nonmaleficence (the team created an environment in which Andrea's mother could accept her daughter's wishes rather than insist on aggressive treatment). The team also recognized and validated Andrea's relationship with Victoria and included Victoria in all aspects of her partner's care.

CONCLUSION

Palliative care and hospice are highly appropriate for terminally ill lesbian patients. Although researchers have not studied lesbians' specific needs, attitudes, or outcomes in end-of-life care, a number of factors may affect whether and how lesbians receive such care. These factors include possibly negative past experiences in the health care system, such as hostility or bias on the part of providers; lack of social support due to sexual orientation; and complex child-custody or other legal issues. The gift that health care providers can offer is creation of a safe and accepting environment for terminally ill lesbian patients and their families so patients can complete their story and heal. The challenge for providers is recognizing and understanding their own attitudes toward lesbian patients so beliefs, thoughts, and actions do not interfere with care at the end of life.

ADDITIONAL RESOURCES

- American Academy of Hospice and Palliative Medicine:
  ⚘ www.aahpm.org/index.html
- Doyle, D., Hanks, G. W. C., & MacDonald, N. (Eds). (2010). *Oxford textbook of palliative medicine* (4th ed.). New York: Oxford University Press.
- Hospice Net. *A dying person's guide to dying:*
  ⚘ www.hospicenet.org/html/dying_guide.html
- Hospice Net. *Helping yourself when you are dying:*
  ⚘ www.hospicenet.org/html/help_yourself.html
- Hospice Net. *What does someone dying need?:*
  ⚘ www.hospicenet.org/html/what_you_need.html
- National Cancer Institute. *End-of-life care: Questions and answers:*
  ⚘ www.cancer.gov/cancertopics/factsheet/Support/end-of-life-care
- National Hospice and Palliative Care Organization:
  ⚘ www.nhpco.org/templates/1/homepage.cfm

REFERENCES

1. Storey, P., & Knight, C. F. (2003). *American Academy of Hospice and Palliative Medicine UNIPAC 1. The hospice/palliative medicine approach to end-of-life care* (2nd ed.). Glenview, IL: Mary Ann Liebert, Inc.

2. National Consensus Project. (2009). *Clinical practice guidelines for quality palliative care* (2nd ed.). Pittsburgh, PA: Author. Available at www.nationalconsensusproject.org/Guidelines_Download.asp.

3. Waller, A., & Caroline, N. L. (2000). *Handbook of palliative care in cancer* (2nd ed.). Boston: Butterworth-Heinemann.

4. Kinzbrunner, B. M. (2002). Predicting prognosis: How to decide when end-of-life care is needed. In B. M. Kinzbrunner, N. J. Weinreb, & J. S. Policzer (Eds.), *20 common problems: End-of-life care* (pp. 3–28). New York: McGraw-Hill.

5. Storey, P., & Knight, C. F. (2003). *American Academy of Hospice and Palliative Medicine UNIPAC 7: The hospice/palliative medicine approach to caring for patients with HIV/AIDS* (2nd ed.). Glenview, IL: Mary Ann Liebert, Inc.

6. Storey, P., & Knight, C. F. (2003). *American Academy of Hospice and Palliative Medicine UNIPAC 2: Alleviating psychological and spiritual pain in the terminally ill* (2nd ed.). Glenview, IL: Mary Ann Liebert, Inc.

7. Nguyen, V. D., & Weinreb, N. J. (2002). How to inform the patient: Conveying bad news. In B. M. Kinzbrunner, N. J. Weinreb, & J. S. Policzer (Eds.), *20 common problems: End-of-life care* (pp. 47–56). New York: McGraw-Hill.

8. Buckman, R. (1992). *How to break bad news: A guide for health care professionals.* Baltimore: Johns Hopkins University Press.

9. Emanuel, L. L., von Gunten, C. F., & Ferris, F. D. (1999). *The Education for Physicians on End-of-Life Care (EPEC) curriculum, module 7: Goals of care.* Chicago: American Medical Association.

10. McWilliams, D., Fournier, D., Booth, B. A., Burke, P., & Kauffman, J. (2008). Legal issues of importance to clinicians. In H. J. Makadon, K. H. Mayer, J. Potter, & H. Goldhammer (Eds.), *Fenway guide to lesbian, gay, bisexual, and transgender health* (pp. 443–462). Philadelphia: American College of Physicians.

11. Gomez, D. (2002). Advance directives and CPR. In B. M. Kinzbrunner, N. J. Weinreb, & J. S. Policzer (Eds.), *20 common problems: End-of-life care* (pp. 297–312). New York: McGraw-Hill.

12. Davies, J., & McVicar, A. (2000). Issues in effective pain control. 2: From assessment to management. *International Journal of Palliative Nursing, 6,* 162–169.

13. Nguyen, V. D., & Micklich Ash, J. (2002). The last days: The actively dying patient. In B. M. Kinzbrunner, N. J. Weinreb, & J. S. Policzer (Eds.), *20 common problems: End-of-life care* (pp. 241–256). New York: McGraw-Hill.

14. Bozeman, M. (2002). Bereavement. In B. M. Kinzbrunner, N. J. Weinreb, & J. S. Policzer (Eds.), *20 common problems: End-of-life care* (pp. 275–294). New York: McGraw-Hill.

15. Storey, P., & Knight, C. F. (2003). *American Academy of Hospice and Palliative Medicine UNIPAC 6: Ethical and legal decision making when caring for the terminally ill* (2nd ed.). Glenview, IL: Mary Ann Liebert, Inc.

16. Corr, C. A. (2005). Anticipatory grief and mourning: An overview. In K. J. Doka, B. Jennings, & C. A. Corr (Eds.), *Living with grief: Ethical dilemmas at the end of life* (pp. 12–18). Washington, DC: Hospice Foundation of America.

17. Sofka, C. (2005). Supporting families during the process of death. In K. J. Doka, B. Jennings, & C. A. Corr (Eds.), *Living with grief: Ethical dilemmas at the end of life* (pp. 43–59). Washington, DC: Hospice Foundation of America.

18. Beckwith, S. K. (2005). When families disagree: Family conflict and decisions. In K. J. Doka, B. Jennings, & C. A. Corr (Eds.), *Living with grief: Ethical dilemmas at the end of life* (pp. 144–156). Washington, DC: Hospice Foundation of America.

19. Berlin, E. A., & Fowkes, W. C. Jr. (1983). A teaching framework for cross-cultural health care. Application in family practice. *Western Journal of Medicine, 139,* 934–938.

20. Clarke, M. E., & DeGannes, C. N. (2008). *Cultural competency in healthcare: A clinical review and video vignettes from the National Medical Association* [Continuing medical education]. Medscape.

21. Stein, G. L., & Bonuck, K. A. (2001). Attitudes on end-of-life care and advance care planning in the lesbian and gay community. *Journal of Palliative Medicine, 4,* 173–190.

22. Gross, J. (2007, October 9). Aging and gay, and facing prejudice in twilight. *New York Times.* Available at www.nytimes.com/2007/10/09/us/09aged.html.

ABOUT THE AUTHOR

Jane L. Appleby, MD is Medical Director of Vitas Innovative Hospice and Chief Quality Officer for the Methodist Healthcare System in San Antonio, Texas and Clinical Associate Professor in the Department of Medicine at the University of Texas. Her interests include caring for patients and families dealing with end-of-life issues as well as improving their bedside care.

CHAPTER 31

"Who Will Care for Me?"

OLD AGE IN LESBIAN COMMUNITIES

KELLY KNOCHEL,
ABD, MSW, LGSW

JEAN K. QUAM,
PhD, MSW

ARLENE, 86, *had short-term memory loss but was in good physical health. She lived independently in her own home with the help of Alice (her former partner), Helen (Alice's current partner), neighbors, and friends.*

One early winter morning while walking, Arlene fell on the ice and broke her hip. She awoke from hip surgery to find her son, Ed, arguing with Alice. Ed had disliked Alice during the 23 years she had lived with his mother, blaming Alice for his parents' divorce. Alice and Helen offered to have Arlene move in with them, but Ed insisted that his mother could no longer live without professional assistance. Ed was adamant that, as Arlene's only child, he should be appointed her legal guardian. However, Arlene convinced the social worker that she was capable of making her own decisions. She moved in with Alice and Helen, who drove Arlene to rehabilitation every day.

Late one night, Arlene got out of bed to go to the bathroom. Forgetting that she needed help, she fell on the floor and broke her right arm and wrist. Ed insisted that his mother could not receive proper care in this "strange" household. Over Arlene's objections, Ed was granted power of attorney. He sold his mother's home and placed her in a rehabilitation hospital. Ed made sure that no one other than immediate family members was allowed to visit Arlene.

This scenario raises a number of important questions. Who is part of Arlene's family? How might her identity as a lesbian impact her hospital experience? Should Alice have been granted power of attorney and the right to make decisions on Arlene's behalf? Would Alice have had more rights if she had been a former spouse rather than a former lover?

■ ■ ■

Broadly defined, health includes mental and emotional health as well as social networks and other types of support that affect well-being. This chapter examines the health of old members of lesbian communities, incorporating research on lesbian, gay, bisexual, and transgender (LGBT) people in midlife to better understand the health issues that lesbians 60 years old or older will encounter. Among such women are those who identify as lesbians or as members of a lesbian community, those who may also have sexual relationships with men, transgender people who identified as lesbian before their gender transition, lesbian-identified partners of transgender people, and transgender women who are primarily attracted to other women.[*]

There have been few studies on old lesbians, especially those who are bisexual or transgender, those of color, those who are poor or working class, those who live in

---

[*] *In this chapter, the term "old lesbians" encompasses the broad range of people described here.*

rural areas, and those who hide their sexual orientation or gender identity.[1-4] Most studies have looked at small convenience samples on the East and West coasts of the United States. None were truly randomized, as there is no centralized list of lesbian communities from which to sample.[1] In studies cited in this chapter, participants were predominantly White, urban-dwelling, well-educated, and economically well-off, and they affirmed their sexual orientation. As such, their mental and emotional health represent only certain portions of lesbian communities, leaving gaps for further research.

IDENTITY AND GENDER ISSUES

Some members of lesbian communities narrowly define lesbians as females who only have sexual relationships with other females, yet lesbian-specific research frequently includes female participants who report sexual relationships with men or intimate relationships with women that are not sexual.[5,6] Furthermore, in many lesbian communities, gender identity and expression are contested. Various eras and lesbian spaces have alternately embraced or excluded female-born women who are feminine ("femme") or masculine ("butch"). Although the Michigan Womyn's Music Festival and some other lesbian spaces portray lesbian identity and transgender identity as mutually exclusive, research increasingly shows that a significant number of transgender people and their partners identify with lesbian communities. These people include butch community members who identify as transgender men (female to male) or see themselves inhabiting a space between female and male (genderqueer).[7-10] Intersex people who identify as lesbians have become vocal about claiming membership in lesbian communities.[11]

The Stonewall Rebellion of 1969, which ushered in the modern LGBT movement, often serves as a dividing line between two distinct LGBT identities and public faces. In a study by Rosenfeld, pre-Stonewall lesbians took pride in keeping their sexual orientation confidential and viewed "coming out" as an indication of unsuccessful identity development. The post-Stonewall women, in contrast, equated successful identity development with living visibly as a lesbian.[12] Clunis and colleagues found that old lesbians' age and the age at which they acknowledged their lesbianism shaped how they handled that identity. Those in their fifties and sixties who came out when they were young, before Stonewall, spoke of living a "double life," maintaining a heterosexual façade in public, and privately participating in lesbian communities. Those who came out later in life, during the women's and gay liberation movements, received social support for embracing a visible lesbian identity.[13]

Some studies contradict the finding that lesbians who came out before Stonewall generally hide their sexual identity. In a study by Claassen, for example, four-fifths of lesbian-identified women ≥ 60 years old said they had a visible lesbian identity. Of these, more than three-fourths came out as lesbians before Stonewall.[14] Quam and colleagues reported that more than 85% of lesbian-identified women ≥ 50 years old labeled themselves as out or very out.[15]

Many transgender people, including those who identify with a lesbian community, come out later in life. This may be due to the increasing visibility of the transgender community or to a feeling among transgender people that they have more freedom to explore gender identity after retirement, after their children's transition into adulthood, or after the death of parents, a spouse, or a partner.[7] For some of them, such as male-to-female persons, the gender transition marks their entrance into a lesbian community. For others, such as female-to-male persons, their transition or a partner's transition casts doubt on their long-term membership in a lesbian community.[7]

THE OLD LESBIAN POPULATION

Estimates of the total number of old lesbians vary widely. In 2006, about 28.7 million females were older than 60, according to the U.S. Census Bureau.[16] The Policy Institute of the National Gay and Lesbian Task Force Foundation calculated that, based on available research, 3% to 8% of the elderly U.S. population identifies as lesbian, gay, or bisexual,[17] so the number of lesbian and bisexual women could be between 861,000 and 2.3 million. The population of old lesbians may be larger than this estimate because the calculation does not account for transgender people who are legally male.

The demographics of the old lesbian population are not entirely clear, as studies based on convenience samples do not accurately depict its full breadth. Data from voter exit polls suggest that the racial and ethnic make-up of the lesbian, gay, and bisexual population mirrors the make-up of the general population.[17] Some old lesbians are less well off financially than their age-relative counterparts in the general population as a result of gender bias in the workplace, which affects earnings. Others are less well-off due to denial of benefits, such as survivor benefits under Social Security and private pension plans, for partners in nonheterosexual relationships. However, compared with heterosexual couples in which one member stayed at home and did not work, some older lesbian couples may have achieved higher household earnings if both members were employed, partially offsetting the financial impact of discrimination.

Relationships Past and Present

Statistics vary in terms of the number of old lesbians who have been heterosexually married, have raised children, and are currently partnered, and there has been very little research on bisexual and transgender people in this regard. Studies suggest that 40% to 50% of old lesbians have been married to a man.[1,14] In three studies, between 30% and 47% of participants had raised children who were primarily the result of past marriages.[1,14,15] A review of studies on lesbians across age groups found a broad range (45% to 80%) who were involved in same-sex partnerships at the time.[18] Other research showed rates of partnering among old lesbians ranging from 43% to 65%.[13,14,19,20]

Discrimination and Mental Health

Discrimination experiences affect mental health, including rates of depression and suicide.[21–24] Old lesbians have experienced discrimination for decades. This is compounded for people of color and those who have a physical or mental disability or are not citizens, and for those whose transgender identity leads to marginalization in lesbian communities. Research suggests that homophobic or transphobic experiences harm the mental health of old lesbians but also may help them develop coping strategies that aid in aging.

In one of the earliest studies of old lesbians, Deevey found that 80% of participants had endured discrimination based on sexual orientation, including verbal assault (37%) and family disapproval (31%).[25] A national sample of lesbian and bisexual people ≥ 60 years old reported markedly higher levels of assault, such as verbal and physical assault, threats of violence, and threats to divulge sexual orientation.[19] In another study, nearly one-third of lesbian participants reported serious, negative life experiences as a result of their sexual orientation. Among these experiences were expulsion from home or school as youths, custody battles over children, incarceration after a bar raid, and job loss.[14] More than half of transgender participants in one study indicated they had experienced discrimination based on gender identity, and one-fourth recounted transgender-related violence.[26] Factor and Rothblum reported that transgender people suffered significantly more verbal attacks than their nontransgender siblings did.[8]

Transphobia in lesbian communities affects transgender people as well as their partners. For example, some long-term couples who have been active in a lesbian community are exiled from the community when one partner transitions from female to male.[7,27] Transgender women who identify as lesbians are still considered men by some lesbian communities and may be excluded from "women only" community spaces.[7,27]

The impact of discrimination on rates of depression and suicide among old lesbians is unclear. Grossman and colleagues found that lesbians and bisexual study participants ≥ 60 years old who reported higher rates of victimization scored significantly lower on measures of mental health and self-esteem than did those who were less victimized. In addition, participants in partnered relationships scored significantly higher than did single participants, which suggests that such relationships may mediate the long-term mental health consequences of discrimination. Eighty-four percent of the study participants indicated they had good mental health, and a majority showed high levels of self-esteem.[19]

In the study by Clunis and colleagues, many old lesbians had experienced bouts of adversity, such as alcoholism; attempts by the health care system to "cure" their homosexuality; and serious health problems. While some had not recovered from discrimination experiences, most said they emerged stronger and more aware of their abilities. Indeed, their stories of discrimination focused on their ability to triumph rather than on the pain they had experienced.[13]

This study suggests that old lesbians are highly resilient, a quality in line with Friend's theory of successful aging. According to this theory, self-affirming lesbians and gay men acquire a set of skills and attitudes as they encounter discrimination, such as a flexible definition of gender roles, crisis competence, and self-advocacy, that ease their adjustment to old age.[28] Other research supports the theory. A small study of middle-age lesbians found that they had experienced less emotional turmoil in midlife than their heterosexual counterparts had.[29] In a national study, two-fifths of middle-age lesbians and bisexual women asserted that living as lesbians and bisexual women had prepared them well for aging by helping them develop greater self-reliance, focus more attention on legal and financial matters, and establish strong support systems.[30]

Studies of old lesbians reveal they are aging with an optimism tempered by concerns about discrimination, financial security, and care-taking. In the study by Clunis and colleagues, for example, most of the subjects had settled into old age with few regrets and many characterized the present as the best period in their life because of the freedom it bestowed, although they worried about housing discrimination.[13]

Many lesbians have indicated they fear disclosing their sexual orientation to social service providers and anticipate homophobia in long-term care facilities and in housing for seniors.[4,13,20,25,31–34] Anecdotal evidence of the difficulties lesbians encounter in long-term care is well-documented.[4,25,35] Quam[4] and Deevey[25] identified the negative consequences of not disclosing sexual orientation, which included inaccurate diagnoses, improper care, and prescriptions that may be ineffective or unnecessary. Richard and Brown found that lesbians older than 55 were reluctant to use social services because they perceived bias and lack of connection with other service users.[36]

Old lesbians have made it clear they want lesbian-specific or lesbian-welcoming housing options so they can age without fear of discrimination.[13,20,31,34,37] LGBT-specific aging services have been established in some areas of the United States,[38–40] but such services, especially housing for lesbians or housing that welcomes them, are rare.[37,41]

Lesbians may have earned less income throughout their working lives due to unequal pay or other employment discrimination, leading to fears of economic insecurity in old age. In the MetLife Mature Market Institute's national survey of 1,000 randomly sampled LGBT people between 40 and 61 years old, most lesbians expressed concern about money, 60% feared they will outlive their savings, and nearly one-fifth worried about who would care for them when they get sick. More than one-third of participants without a partner worried about having a caregiver.[30]

OLD LESBIANS' PHYSICAL HEALTH

Research on the physical health of old members of lesbian communities, especially bisexual and transgender people, is sparse and often lacks rigor.[42] This section considers how long-term exposure to risk factors for physical illness and disease affects old lesbians, and how a health care system that is discriminatory, or perceived as such, impacts their physical well-being.

Risk Factors

Some research describes healthy behaviors among lesbians, including good nutrition, routine Pap smears, and moderate alcohol intake, that help prevent chronic and acute health conditions.[43] In addition, although findings on the rates of breast cancer screening among lesbians are mixed, several studies have revealed that lesbians are more likely than females in general to undergo routine mammograms.[43–45] Most research indicates that lesbians, compared with the general female population, are at greater risk of certain serious health conditions, including cardiovascular disease, breast cancer, and reproductive tract cancers.[1,46] Among the risk factors for such diseases are obesity, higher alcohol consumption, and smoking.

Obesity

Yancey and colleagues studied more than 1,200 lesbian and bisexual women in the Los Angeles area, 31.4% of whom were women of color and 23% of whom were older than 50. Most of the participants were overweight and, of these, 48% were obese, compared to an obesity rate of 36% among the general population of women in that region. Participants older than 50 were significantly more likely than younger participants to have a high body mass index.[47] This is consistent with a national study of women 50 to 79 years old: it found that lesbian, bisexual, and asexual participants were more likely than their heterosexual counterparts to be overweight.[46]

Chemical Dependency

Greater alcohol consumption and smoking are risk factors for cancer. A study of a racially diverse group of lesbians found that, unlike the general population of women, lesbians who consumed more alcohol maintained these high levels as they aged.[48] In analyzing data from the California Women's Health Survey, Burgard and colleagues reported that lesbians ≥ 46 years old reported routine and heavy drinking at rates that were significantly higher than those among heterosexual participants.[49] This is consistent with findings from other research on lesbian and bisexual women in the United States, including old lesbians, that suggests they engage in such behaviors at higher rates compared with the general population of women in their age group.[42,46,50]

In the California Health Interview Study, nearly 20% of nonheterosexual women older than 46 smoked tobacco compared with 15% of heterosexual women.[49] Other findings show that lesbian and bisexual women are more likely than heterosexual women to be current or former smokers.[45,46] Despite the prevalence of this risky behavior, there is a dearth of research on smoking cessation in LGBT and older populations.[51]

Sexual Practices

Very little research has been conducted on the sexual activity and desire of elderly women, regardless of sexual orientation.[1] However, while sexual desire, function, and activity may decrease with age,[52] old lesbians continue to have sex, including outside of monogamous relationships and with female and sometimes male partners. Studies reveal that many women older than 50 do not practice safe-sex techniques.[43]

Use of Health Care

Lesbians of all ages may be reluctant to disclose their sexual orientation to health care providers due to real or anticipated discrimination.[1,30,32,53] Ageism and sexism create additional barriers to health care services.[4,20,54] While some studies of old lesbians have revealed good physical health and few serious health problems,[13,19] reluctance to disclose sexual orientation and potential discrimination by health care providers may prevent early detection and treatment of such problems.

Gender-variant appearance is another obstacle to health care. A hospitalized butch lesbian may be forced to wear traditional female clothing and feel uncomfortable with, or hostility from, a female roommate.[7] This vulnerability is greater for transgender people. Health care providers may refer to a transgender person by a birth name he or she no longer uses and manage the patient based on a gender that does not match self-identity. For example, a transgender man may be assigned a female roommate. Furthermore, an overt gender that others accept when a transgender person is clothed comes into question when the patient is naked and scars from gender transition surgeries, incongruent body parts, or other telltale signs are visible, thus exposing the patient to a higher risk of discrimination by a health care provider.[7] Old transgender persons may also face a health crisis that is incongruent with their gender identity, such as prostate cancer in a transgender woman or ovarian cancer in a transgender man.[3] These and other factors may prompt transgender people and butch lesbians to postpone treatment, increasing the potential for more serious health conditions and perhaps causing them mental and emotional suffering when they do seek health care.[7]

Finally, many elderly people seeking to transition to a different gender must contend with standards of care established by the World Professional Association for Transgender Health. Providers and health insurers customarily adhere to these standards when determining if a transgender person should receive hormone therapy or undergo gender confirmation surgery. Elderly people who want to transition to a different gender need help navigating an often-transphobic health care system.

SOCIAL SUPPORT

Loneliness is not a natural consequence of old age. Grossman and colleagues found that old, partnered lesbians and bisexual women were less lonely than those who did not have a partner. These individuals had an average of six to eight people in their social networks; received support from birth relatives, families of choice, and people across a range of genders, ages, and sexual orientations; and were out to most members of their social networks.[19] In the study by Clunis and colleagues, maintaining mutual support in aging was a priority for old lesbians. Social support played a key role in helping them accept themselves and live full lives, whether the support came from a partner, friend, parent, or child, or from within a lesbian, heterosexual, or mixed circle of friends.[13]

Family

Old lesbians have a broad definition of family, one that widens throughout life. The definition may include their current and former partners, their children, members of the family of origin, members of the lesbian community, and nonlesbian members of their social groups.[13]

Clunis and colleagues learned that most aging lesbians want to grow old with a partner.[13] In a study by Quam and colleagues of old, long-term, same-sex couples, lesbian couples had more relationship satisfaction than did heterosexual and gay couples, which were about the same age and in relationships of similar longevity. The lesbian couples also scored higher on measures of communication and conflict resolution.[15] Studies have identified a subset of female partners who maintain separate living arrangements.[15,19]

Support from the family of origin varies. Lesbians may experience estrangement or strained relationships with their family after coming out, but some families eventually resolve this conflict.[13,20,55,56] Participants in one study said their families of origin were a very important source of support, even though family members were aware of their sexual orientation but would not discuss it.[13] Half of female participants in Quam and colleagues' study identified a member of their family of origin as the biggest supporter of their lesbian relationship.[15]

Studies reveal the importance of friends to the well-being of middle-age and old lesbians.[34,58,59] Findings suggest that old lesbians have developed families of choice to compensate for weak ties to families of origin and to complement these ties,[1] and that they have creatively developed informal support networks.[36] A strong sense of social support was not necessarily correlated with being partnered.

A study by Galupo, in which 30% of participants were women of color and working-class women, reported that lesbians derived most of their friends from lesbian, gay, and bisexual communities, and that bisexual women established most of their friendships in heterosexual communities.[59] Claassen found that old lesbians interacted with gay men but were less likely to include them in their families of choice as they aged.[14] According to some researchers, former partners have remained close friends.[20,55] Several small studies of old lesbians chronicled ways in which families of choice took on roles traditionally assigned to families of origin, including care-giving.[35,57,60]

There has been little research on how gender transition affects social support for transgender members of lesbian communities. Many transgender people transition late in life, when their social roles among family, significant others, and friends are more entrenched. Transitioning may cause them to lose significant support, including dissolution of long-term marriages.[7] Furthermore, lesbian communities may expel members who are transitioning from female to male or reject new members who have transitioned from male to female.[7]

SPIRITUALITY

Organized religion has an important role in the health, life satisfaction, and resilience of many older adults,[61,62] but it can also be a source of homophobia.[37] A number of organized religions have branches that welcome and affirm LGBT people. A third of participants in one study of LGBT people said they attended services at an LGBT-affirming church.[34] In three other studies, most lesbians considered themselves spiritual or religious and credited their spirituality or religious beliefs with helping them develop resilience and a sense of purpose.[13-15] In two of the studies, however, a significant minority said religion does not have a role in their lives or has harmed them.[14,15]

FINANCIAL, LEGAL, AND CARE ISSUES

Work and Income

Some research, including Claassen's study,[14] has shown that members of lesbian communities are more financially stable than females in the general population. This may be due to the predominance of well-educated professionals in the study samples. Lower earnings for women, laws precluding unmarried partners from inheriting

Social Security survivor benefits, and similar exclusions in many private pension plans suggest less financial stability in lesbian communities. Grossman and colleagues found that one-fourth of elderly female participants in their study were still working,[19] a markedly higher proportion than the national average for female workers older than 65.[63] Old lesbians in the study by Clunis and colleagues said they earned less than their male or heterosexual counterparts partly as a result of sexism and homophobia.[13] According to lesbians, homophobia and transphobia threaten job security and are reasons not to disclose sexual orientation or gender identity in the workplace.[7,13]

Legal Planning

Studies of middle-age and old lesbians revealed high rates of legal planning for illness and death with instruments such as power of attorney, wills, and trusts.[13-15] The highest rates were among couples, lesbians who expressed a strong relationship commitment, and those who had disclosed their sexual orientation to their families of origin.[14,64] Transgender members of lesbian communities may encounter additional legal issues, such as updating records kept by the U.S. Social Security Administration and the U.S. Department of Veterans Affairs to reflect their legal gender.[7]

Elderly Care

Little is known about the care that old lesbians receive from their families of origin, including children, nieces, and nephews. Middle-age members of lesbian communities who participated in a national study expressed concern about who would care for them.[1] Dorrell described the care that an 84-year-old lesbian received from seven members of her family of choice, a notable case study of alternative care-giving arrangements.[35] Barker and colleagues discussed a care-giving scheme called tontines in which lesbians or gay men make a binding, albeit informal, pact to care for one another in old age.[65]

ELDER ABUSE

Elder abuse occurs when a caregiver or someone else whom a vulnerable elder trusts does something that causes the elder harm or serious risk of harm. The harm may be intentional or unintentional and includes failing to satisfy the elder's basic needs or to protect her from harm.[66]

Few studies have examined abuse and neglect of the elderly, including old lesbians. According to Cruikshank, lesbian elders are an "invisible" population; ageism, sexism, and homophobia converge to keep them hidden away.[67] Between 2% and 10% of the nation's older adult population experiences abuse, neglect, self-neglect, or financial exploitation.[68] For every report that Adult Protective Services

(APS) receives regarding elder mistreatment, an estimated five or more cases go unreported.[69] Teaster and colleagues found that in 65% of APS reports of elder abuse, the victim was a woman. In substantiated reports, self-neglect was the most common type of mistreatment.[70] Predictors of self-neglect include depression, alcohol or drug abuse, and dementia.[71] Old lesbians who remain closeted or do not receive assistance they perceive as safe may be at high risk of self-neglect. The older a person is, the greater the likelihood of abuse or neglect. Other predictors include a history of being abused, a poor family relationship, aggressive behavior, dementia, and isolation.[69]

Although old lesbians may experience various types of abuse, Cook-Daniels has postulated that they are most likely to suffer from domestic violence, self-neglect, or physical or emotional abuse related to sexual orientation or gender identity. Cook-Daniels argued that fear of authorities, shame, self-blame, and legal barriers put old LGBT people at greater risk of abuse and neglect than their heterosexual and gender-conforming counterparts.[72]

Efforts to train health care, social service, APS, and law enforcement professionals regarding elder abuse should focus on helping them extend safe, competent, and appropriate assistance to this population. In addition, APS services need to be demystified and honor the self-determination of the elderly. These steps may help old lesbians feel comfortable reaching out for assistance if they are victims of abuse or neglect, or if they need help living independently at home.

CONCLUSION

Few studies have examined the health and demographics of old lesbians—topics that warrant further research. Available evidence suggests that this population faces a number of identity issues and important challenges in old age that vary depending on sexual orientation and gender identity. Among these challenges are discrimination, lack of financial security, and concerns about who will care for them. Certain risk factors, including obesity, chemical dependency, reluctance to use health care services, and elder abuse, have implications for their mental and physical well-being. Nevertheless, old lesbians are resilient and they create strong support networks.

ADDITIONAL RESOURCES

- CenterLink, the Community of LGBT Centers:
  www.lgbtcenters.org

- Elder Law, National Center for Lesbian Rights:
  www.nclrights.org/site/PageServer?pagename=issue_elderLaw

- LGBT Aging Issues Network, American Society on Aging:
  - www.asaging.org/LAIN
- Old Lesbians Organizing for Change:
  - www.oloc.org
- Services and Advocacy for Gay, Lesbian, Bisexual & Transgender Elders:
  - www.sageusa.org
- Transgender Aging Network:
  - www.forge-forward.org/tan

REFERENCES

1. Barker, J. C. (2004). Lesbian aging: An agenda for social research. In G. Herdt & B. de Vries (Eds.), *Gay and lesbian aging: Research and future directions* (pp. 29–72). New York: Springer.

2. Blando, J. A. (2001). Twice hidden: Older gay and lesbian couples, friends, and intimacy. *Generations, 25,* 87–90.

3. Quam, J. K. (1993). Gay and lesbian aging. *SIECUS Report, 21,* 10–12.

4. Quam, J. K. (1997). *Social services for senior gay men and lesbians.* Binghamton, NY: Haworth Press.

5. Morris, J. F., & Rothblum, E. D. (1999). Who fills out a "lesbian" questionnaire? The interrelationship of sexual orientation, years out, disclosure of sexual orientation, sexual experience with women, and participation in the lesbian community. *Psychology of Women Quarterly, 33,* 537–557.

6. Rust, P. C. (1995). *Bisexuality and the challenge to lesbian politics: Sex, loyalty, and revolution.* New York: New York University Press.

7. Cook-Daniels, L. (2002, August). *Transgender elders and SOFFAs: A primer.* Presentation to the meeting of the American Psychological Association, Chicago, IL. Available at www.forge-forward.org/handouts/TransEldersSOFFAs-web.pdf.

8. Factor, R. J., & Rothblum, E. D. (2007). A study of transgender adults and their non-transgender siblings on demographic characteristics, social support, and experiences of violence. *Journal of LGBT Health Research, 3,* 11–30.

9. Green, E. R. (2006). In another bracket: Trans acceptance in lesbian utopia. In A. Pattatucci Aragón (Ed.), *Challenging lesbian norms: Intersex, transgender, intersectional, and queer perspectives* (pp. 231–248). Binghamton, NY: Harrington Park Press.

10. McDonald, M. (2006). Another space: Between and beyond lesbian-normativity and trans-normativity. In A. Pattatucci Aragón (Ed.), *Challenging lesbian norms: Intersex, transgender, intersectional, and queer perspectives* (pp. 201–214). Binghamton, NY: Harrington Park Press.

11. Pattatucci Aragón, A. (Ed.). (2006). *Challenging lesbian norms: Intersex, transgender, intersectional, and queer perspectives.* Binghamton, NY: Harrington Park Press.

12. Rosenfeld, D. (2003). *The changing of the guard: Lesbian and gay elders, identity, and social change*. Philadelphia: Temple University Press.

13. Clunis, D. M., Fredriksen-Goldsen, K. I., Freeman, P. A., & Nystrom, N. (2005). *Lives of lesbian elders: Looking back, looking forward*. Binghamton, NY: Haworth Press.

14. Claassen, C. (2005). *Whistling women: A study of the lives of older lesbians*. Binghamton, NY: Haworth Press.

15. Quam, J. K., Whitford, G. S., Dziengel, L., & Knochel, K. (2009). *Understanding the nature of long-term same-sex relationships: What contributes to couple satisfaction in older adults?* Manuscript submitted for publication.

16. U.S. Census Bureau. (2006). *S0102. Population 60 years and over in the United States. Data set: 2006 American Community Survey*. Available at factfinder.census.gov/servlet/STTable?_bm=y&-geo_id=01000US&-qr_name=ACS_2006_EST_G00_S0102&-Tables=('ACS_2006_EST_G00_S0102')&-ds_name=ACS_2006_EST_G00_&-redoLog=false&-CONTEXT=st.

17. Cahill, S., South, K., & Spade, J. (2000). *Outing age: Public policy issues affecting gay, lesbian, bisexual and transgender elders*. Washington, DC: Policy Institute of the National Gay and Lesbian Task Force Foundation. Available at www.thetaskforce.org/downloads/reports/reports/OutingAge.pdf.

18. Cohler, B. J., & Galatzer-Levy, R. M. (2000). *The course of gay and lesbian lives: Social and psychoanalytic perspectives*. Chicago: University of Chicago Press.

19. Grossman, A. H., D'Augelli, A. R., & O'Connell, T. S. (2001). Being lesbian, gay, bisexual, and 60 or older in North America. *Journal of Gay & Lesbian Social Services, 13*, 23–40.

20. Kehoe, M. (1989). *Lesbians over 60 speak for themselves*. Binghamton, NY: Haworth Press.

21. Clements-Nolle, K., Marx, R., & Katz, M. (2006). Attempted suicide among transgender persons: The influence of gender-based discrimination and victimization. *Journal of Homosexuality, 51*, 53–69.

22. Díaz, R. M., Ayala, G., Bein, E., Henne, J., & Marin, B. V. (2001). The impact of homophobia, poverty, and racism on the mental health of gay and bisexual Latino men: Findings from 3 U.S. cities. *American Journal of Public Health, 91*, 927–932.

23. Guarnero, P. A. (2007). Family and community influences on the social and sexual lives of Latino gay men. *Journal of Transcultural Nursing, 18*, 12–18.

24. Kessler, R. C., Mickelson, K. D., & Williams, D. R. (1999). The prevalence, distribution, and mental health correlates of perceived discrimination in the United States. *Journal of Health and Social Behavior, 40*, 208–230.

25. Deevey, S. (1990). Older lesbian women: An invisible minority. *Journal of Gerontological Nursing, 16*, 35–39.

26. Lombardi, E. L., Wilchins, R. A., Priesing, D., & Malouf, D. (2001). Gender violence: Transgender experiences with violence and discrimination. *Journal of Homosexuality, 42*, 89–101.

27. Stryker, S. (2008). *Transgender history*. Berkeley, CA: Seal Press.

28. Friend, R. A. (1990). Older lesbian and gay people: A theory of successful aging. *Journal of Homosexuality, 20*, 99–118.

29. Calhoun Howell, L., & Beth, A. (2004). Pioneers in our own lives: Grounded theory of lesbians' midlife development. *Journal of Women & Aging, 16,* 133–147.

30. MetLife Mature Market Institute (2006). *Out and aging: The MetLife study of lesbian and gay baby boomers.* New York: Metropolitan Life Insurance Company. Available at www.asaging.org/networks/LGAIN/OutandAging.pdf.

31. Hamburger, L. J. (1997). The wisdom of non-heterosexually based senior housing and related services. *Journal of Gay & Lesbian Social Services, 6,* 11–25.

32. Johnson, M. J., Jackson, N. C., Arnette, J. K., & Koffman, S. D. (2005). Gay and lesbian perceptions of discrimination in retirement care facilities. *Journal of Homosexuality, 49,* 83–102.

33. Kehoe, M. (1986). Lesbians over 65: A triply invisible minority. *Journal of Homosexuality, 12,* 139–152.

34. Quam, J. K., & Whitford, G. S. (1992). Adaptation and age-related expectations of older gay and lesbian adults. *Gerontologist, 32,* 367–374.

35. Dorrell, B. (1990). Being there: A support network of lesbian women. *Journal of Homosexuality, 20,* 89–98.

36. Richard, C. A., & Brown, A. H. (2006). Configurations of informal social support among older lesbians. *Journal of Women & Aging, 18,* 49–65.

37. Quam, J. K. (2004). Issues in gay, lesbian, bisexual, and transgender aging. In W. Swan (Ed.), *Handbook of lesbian, gay, bisexual, and transgender administration and policy* (pp. 137–156). New York: Marcel Dekker.

38. Croghan, C. F. (2006). LGBT community centers provide services, programming for older adults in North America. *Outword, 12,* 3, 7.

39. Gwenwald, M. (1984). The SAGE model for serving older lesbians and gay men. *Journal of Social Work and Human Sexuality, 2,* 53–61.

40. Slusher, M. P., Mayer, C. J., & Dunkle, R. E. (1996). Gays and Lesbians Older and Wiser (GLOW): A support group for older gay people. *Gerontologist, 36,* 118–123.

41. Lundberg, P. M. (2004). Housing our elders: Snapshots of projects across North America. *Outword, 11,* 1, 6–7.

42. Solarz, A. L. (Ed.). (1999). *Lesbian health: Current assessment and directions for the future.* Washington, DC: National Academy Press. Available at www.nap.edu/openbook.php?record_id=6109.

43. Grindel, C. G., McGehee, L. A., Patsdaughter, C. A., & Roberts, S. J. (2006). Cancer prevention and screening behaviors in lesbians. *Women & Health, 44,* 15–39.

44. Aaron, D. J., Markovic, N., Danielson, M. E., Honnold, J. A., Janosky, J. E., & Schmidt, N. J. (2001). Behavioral risk factors for disease and preventive health practices among lesbians. *American Journal of Public Health, 91,* 972–975.

45. Rankow, E. J., & Tessaro, I. (1999). Mammography and risk factors for breast cancer in lesbian and bisexual women. *American Journal of Health Behavior, 22,* 403–410.

46. Valanis, B. G., Bowen, D. J., Bassford, T., Whitlock, E., Charney, P., & Carter, R. A. (2000). Sexual orientation and health: Comparisons in the Women's Health Initiative sample. *Archives of Family Medicine, 9,* 843–853.

47. Yancey, A. K., Cochran, S. D., Corliss, H. L., & Mays, V. M. (2003). Correlates of overweight and obesity among lesbians and bisexual women. *Preventive Medicine, 36,* 676–683.

48. Hughes, T. L., Wilsnack, S. C., Szalacha, L. A., Johnson, T., Bostwick, W. B., Seymour, R., et al. (2006). Age and racial/ethnic differences in drinking and drinking-related problems in a community sample of lesbians. *Journal of Studies on Alcohol, 67,* 579–590.

49. Burgard, S. A., Cochran, S. D., & Mays, V. M. (2005). Alcohol and tobacco use patterns among heterosexually and homosexually experienced California women. *Drug and Alcohol Dependence, 77,* 61–70.

50. Roberts, S. J., & Sorensen, L. (1999). Health related behaviors and cancer screening of lesbians: Results from the Boston Lesbian Health Project. *Women & Health, 28,* 1–12.

51. Doolan, D. M., & Froelicher, E. S. (2006). Efficacy of smoking cessation intervention among special populations: Review of the literature from 2000 to 2005. *Nursing Research, 55,* S29–37.

52. Tracy, J. K., & Junginger, J. (2007). Correlates of lesbian sexual functioning. *Journal of Women's Health, 16,* 499–509.

53. Bowen, D. J., Bradford, J. B., Powers, D., McMorrow, P., Linde, R., Murphy, B. C., et al. (2004). Comparing women of differing sexual orientations using population-based sampling. *Women & Health, 40,* 19–34.

54. Daniluk, J. C. (1998). *Women's sexuality across the life span: Challenging myths, creating meanings.* New York: Guilford Press.

55. Adelman, M. (1990). Stigma, gay lifestyles, and adjustment to aging: A study of later-life gay men and lesbians. *Journal of Homosexuality, 20,* 7–32.

56. Kimmel, D. C., & Martin, D. L. (Eds). (2001). *Midlife and aging in gay America: Proceedings of the SAGE conference 2000.* Binghamton, NY: Harrington Park Press.

57. Beeler, J. A., Rawls, T. W., Herdt, G., & Cohler, B. J. (1999). The needs of older lesbians and gay men in Chicago. *Journal of Gay & Lesbian Social Services, 9,* 31–49.

58. Dorfman, R., Walters, K., Burke, P., Hardin, L., Karanik, T., Raphael, J., et al. (1995). Old, sad and alone: The myth of the aging homosexual. *Journal of Gerontological Social Work, 24,* 29–44.

59. Galupo, M. P. (2007). Friendship patterns of sexual minority individuals in adulthood. *Journal of Social and Personal Relationships, 24,* 5–17.

60. De Vries, B., & Hoctel, P. (2007). The family-friends of older gay men and lesbians. In N. Teunis & G. H. Herdt (Eds.), *Sexual inequalities and social justice* (pp. 213–232). Berkeley, CA: University of California Press.

61. Koenig, H. G. (1995). Religion and health in later life. In M. A. Kimble, S. H. McFadden, J. W. Ellor, & J. J. Seeber (Eds.), *Aging, spirituality, and religion: A handbook* (pp. 9–29). Minneapolis, MN: Augsburg Fortress.

62. Ramsey, J. L. (2001). Spiritual intimacy in later life: Implications for clinical practice. *Generations, 25,* 59–63.

63. Rix, S. E. (2000). *Update on the older worker: 1999.* Washington, DC: AARP Public Policy Institute. Available at assets.aarp.org/rgcenter/econ/dd48_workers.pdf.

64. Riggle, E. D. B., Rostosky, S. S., & Prather, R. A. (2006). Advance planning by same-sex couples. *Journal of Family Issues, 27,* 758–776.

65. Barker, J. C., Herdt, G., & de Vries, B. (2006). Social support in the lives of lesbians and gay men at midlife and later. *Sexuality Research & Social Policy, 3,* 1–23.

66. Bonnie, R. J., & Wallace, R. B. (Eds.). (2003). *Elder mistreatment: Abuse, neglect, and exploitation in an aging America.* Washington, DC: National Academies Press. Available at www.nap.edu/openbook.php?isbn=0309084342.

67. Cruikshank, M. (1991). Lavender and gray: A brief survey of lesbian and gay aging studies. In J. A. Lee (Ed.), *Gay midlife and maturity* (pp. 77–88). Binghamton, NY: Haworth Press.

68. Lachs, M. S., & Pillemer, K. (2004). Elder abuse. *Lancet, 364,* 1263–1273.

69. National Center on Elder Abuse. (1998). *National elder abuse incidence study: Final report.* Washington, DC: American Public Human Services Association.

70. Teaster, P. B., Dugar, T. A., Mendiondo, M. S., Abner, E. L., Cecil, K. A., & Otto, J. M. (2006). *The 2004 survey of state Adult Protective Services: Abuse of adults 60 years of age and older.* Washington, DC: National Center on Elder Abuse.

71. Dyer, C. B., Goodwin, J. S., Pickens-Pace, S., Burnett, J., & Kelly, P. A. (2007). Self-neglect among the elderly: A model based on more than 500 patients seen by a geriatric medicine team. *American Journal of Public Health, 97,* 1671–1676.

72. Cook-Daniels, L. (1997). Lesbian, gay male, bisexual and transgendered elders: Elder abuse and neglect issues. *Journal of Elder Abuse & Neglect, 9,* 35–49.

ABOUT THE AUTHORS

Kelly Knochel, ABD, MSW, LGSW is a doctoral candidate at the University of Minnesota School of Social Work. Kelly conducts research on issues of LGBT aging, with a focus on the old transgender population. Kelly and research partners developed Training to Serve, a program that helps service providers give appropriate and competent care to the aging LGBT population.

Jean K. Quam, PhD, MSW is Interim Dean of the College of Education and Human Development at the University of Minnesota and Professor in its School of Social Work. Her research focus has been on LGBT aging. She is a founding member of the Editorial Board of *Outword*, the newsletter of the American Society on Aging's LGBT Information Network.

Index

Page numbers followed by t *denote tables; those followed by* f *denote figures*

Alcohol abuse *(continued)*
  risk factors, 158
  screening, 15, 15*t*, 152, 153*t*
  self-help programs, 150
  sexual abuse, 332
  social support, 150
  trauma-related causes, 149–150
  treatment, 152–157
  women with disabilities, 356
Alcohol consumption
  adolescents, 148
  breast cancer, 11
  cardiovascular disease risks, 453
  coronary heart disease, 14
  depression, 280–281
  older lesbians, 543–544
  patterns, 14, 281
  prevalence, 103
  smoking, 131
  social contexts, 151–152
  studies, 145
Alcoholics Anonymous, 143,146, 150,250, 294, 299
Alpha glucosidase inhibitors, 507
Amantadine hydrochloride, 431*t*
Amenorrhea, 257–260, 482
American Diabetes Association, 500
Amylin analogs, 507
Anal intercourse, 34*t*, 250
Angina, 446, 448, 449, 454
Angiotensin-converting enzyme inhibitors, 451, 503
Anilingus, 34*t*, 37
Antenatal care, 101*t*, 102–104
Anterior cruciate ligament injuries, 220–222
Anticonvulsants, 209, 230*t*, 285, 483*t*
Antidepressants
  chronic pain, 209
  depression treatment, 285, 289
  hot flashes treatment, 261
  osteoporosis, 489
  sexual dysfunction, 242
Arthritis
  Lyme disease-related, 435
  osteoarthritis, 227–229
  rheumatoid, 453
Arthroscopic surgery, 225
Aspirin, 448–449, 504
Assisted reproductive technology, 86
Athlete stereotype, 184, 193
Atrophic vaginitis, 249, 465
Attractiveness, 176–177

B

Back pain
  age-related factors, 204–205
  causes, 203–206, 204*t*
  depression, 203
  economic costs, 203
  educational level, 205–206
  epidemiology, 203
  evaluation, 206–207
  exercise, 206, 213
  gender risks, 204
  genetic factors, 205
  magnetic resonance imaging, 206–207
  obesity, 205
  prevention, 213
  risk factors, 203–206
  smoking, 205
  treatment, 207–213
  types, 204*t*
Bacterial enteropathogens, 426–428
Bacterial infections, 422–425
Bacterial vaginosis, 37, 46–47, 61, 247–248
Bad news, 523–526
Barrier methods used during sexual activity, 37–38, 63
Barriers to physical activity, 188, 190
Barriers to health care, 5, 8, 56–57, 352–354, 358, 454
Bars, 151
Battering, 312
Behavioral Risk Factor Surveillance System, 186
Bereavement, 528–529
Bias-related victimization, 329–330
Biguanide, 506
Biofeedback, 212, 469
Biphobia, 310*f*
Bipolar disorder, 300
Birth Control. *See* Contraception
Bisexual, 26*t*
Bisphosphonates, 264, 486–487
Black cohosh, 261–262
Bladder neck sling suspension, 470
Blood glucose
  control, in type 2 diabetes mellitus, 501–502
  glycosylated hemoglobin, 502*t*
  postprandial monitoring, 505, 508
  test, 6*t*
Blood pressure, 6*t*, 450–451
Body mass index
  obesity parameters, 8, 167, 453
  studies, 9
Bone mineral density, 6*t*, 483, 484*t*, 486, 490

Boniva. *See* Ibandronate
Borderline personality disorder, 300
Borrelia burgdorferi, 434
Breast cancer
 age of patient, 382
 background, 382
 coping, 389
 diagnosis, 388
 disclosure of sexual orientation to health care
  providers, 389
 incidence, 383–385
 nulliparity, 11
 psychosocial issues, 389–390
 risk/risk factors, 10, 384*t*
 screening, 10–11, 385–388, 387*t*
 treatment, 388
Breastfeeding, 104
Breast self-examination, 10
Bunion, 226–227
Bupropion, 285
Butch, 26*t*, 43, 74, 77–78, 100, 176–177, 315–316,
  386, 530, 539, 544

C

CA-125, 244, 397
Calcitonin, 208–209, 488
Campylobacter, 426–427
Cancer
 breast. *See* Breast cancer
 cervical. *See* Cervical cancer
 colorectal. *See* Colorectal cancer
 depression, 368
 distress, 368
 endometrial, 13, 399–401
 morbidities, 372
 ovarian, 13, 397–398, 401
 prevalence, 365
 quality of life affected, 365–371
 reproductive tract, 12–13
 risk factors, 373
 survivorship, 371–373
 types, 365
Cancer screening
 breast cancer, 385–388
 colorectal cancer, 410–414, 412*t*–413*t*
 women with disabilities, 355
Candidiasis, vaginal, 248
Capsaicin, 209
Cardiovascular disease
 alcohol consumption, 453
 angina, 448

deaths, 444
depression, 453
diabetes mellitus, 452
diagnosis, 449
gender differences, 446
hypertension, 450–452
lesbians, 445
lupus, 453
myocardial infarction, 446–447
obesity, 9, 452–453
physical inactivity, 453
presentation, 446–449
prevention, 449–450
rheumatoid arthritis, 453
risk factors, 444, 450–454
smoking, 450
stroke, 448–449
treatment, 449–450
Cervical cancer, 12–13, 56, 62, 398–399
Chemotherapy, 363, 370, 398–399, 401, 403,
  414–415, 483*t*, 519
Chicken pox. *See* Varicella
Childhood abuse
 physical, 103–104, 284, 327–328
 sexual. *See* Sexual abuse
Children of lesbian parents
 assumptions, 115
 burdens, 116–117
 disclosure effects, 112–113
 health care providers, 117–119
 nondisclosure effects, 112–113
 stigmatization, 116–117
 studies, 115–116
 supports, 116–117
 verbal harassment, 116
Chiropractic, 211–212
Chlamydia
 prevalence, 60–61
 testing, 6*t*
 transmission, 37
Chlamydia trachomatis, 60–61
Cholesterol screening, 6*t*
Chondromalacia, 223
Chronic fatigue syndrome, 433–434
Chronic pelvic pain, 243
Cigarette smoking. *See* Smoking
Civil union, 73–75, 90, 91, 97, 156*t*, 353, 526
Clinical breast examination, 6*t*, 10, 387*t*
Clinical space, 27–29
Clonidine, 261
Clotrimazole, 248
Cognitive behavioral therapy, 287

Dietary supplements, 171
Diet pills, 171
Digital-anal sex, 58–60, 59*t*
Digital-vaginal sex, 58–60, 59*t*
Disabilities
    alcohol abuse, 356
    attitudinal barriers, 353–354
    burdens associated, 352
    cancer screening and therapy, 355
    challenges associated, 349, 350*t*–351*t*
    definition, 349
    health care barriers, 352–354, 358
    health risks, 354–357
    obesity, 355
    primary care needs, 354
    protective factors, 357
    risk factors, 352
    social support, 357
    substance abuse associated, 355–356
    violence, 356–357
Disclosure of sexual orientation
    adolescents, 27
    alcohol abuse, 151
    children of lesbian parents, 112–113, 118
    consequences, 542
    depression, 16
    family, 147
    grieving, 528
    health care providers, 8, 98, 367, 389, 544
    older lesbians, 542, 544
    safety, 146
    stages, 146
    substance abuse treatment, 152, 146
Discrimination, 282–283, 541
Ditropan. *See* Oxybutynin
Diuretics, 452, 503
Domestic partner, 75, 90, 97, 99, 100, 189, 238, 476, 526, 530
Domestic violence, 16, 154, 306, 308, 312, 317–319, 358, 548
Donor insemination
    description, 86–87, 97
    infertility, 90
    intrauterine vs. intracervical, 90
    recipient counseling and testing, 89
    sperm donor, 86–88
Do-not-resuscitate form, 527
Double contrast barium enema, 7*t*, 413*t*
Doula, 98
Drug use. *See also* Alcohol abuse; Substance abuse
    adolescents, 46*t*
    risk factors, 158

screenings, 152, 153*t*
smoking, 131
social contexts, 151–152
Dual-energy x-ray absorptiometry, 483–485, 490
Duloxetine, 285
Dying, 528
Dyslipidemia, 452, 503–504
Dysmenorrhea, 30, 241, 243, 246, 402
Dysthymia, 276

E

Eating disorders, 168–169
Elderly. *See also* Older lesbians
    abuse, 336, 547–548
    nursing facilities, 530
Electroconvulsive therapy, 285–286
Emergency contraception, 33, 250
Enablex. *See* Darifenacin
End-of-life care. *See also* Hospice; Palliative care
    acceptance of lesbian family, 531
    advance care planning, 526–527
    bereavement, 528–529
    communicating bad news, 523–526
    culturally appropriate, 529
    disease progression, 523
    dying process, 528
    ethical principles, 529
    grief, 528–529
    lesbian-specific needs, 529–530
    pain management, 527
    preparation, 521
    prognosis predictions, 522–523
    recommendations, 530–531
    resuscitation issues, 527
    symptoms experienced, 527–528
    when to initiate, 521–522
Endometrial biopsy, 239
Endometrial cancer, 13, 399–401
Endometrial ultrasound, 239
Endometriosis, 241, 243–244, 397
Enterococcus, 424–425
Epidural steroids, 210
Escherichia coli, 427
Estradiol, 242, 257–259, 264
Estrogen
    endometrial cancer risks, 400
    hot flashes treatment, 261
    osteoporosis treatment, 487
    vaginal dryness, 262
Estrogen/progestin, 264
Estrogen replacement therapy, 264

Exenatide, 507–508
Exercise.See Physical activity
Eye examination, 7t

F

Facet injections, 210
Falls, 489
Family
  acceptance, 39, 42t
  disclosure of sexual orientation, 147
  older lesbians, 545
  rejection, 40–41, 42t, 330
  step-family,14
  support, 150
Family of choice, 99, 101t, 105–106, 150, 317, 333,
    526, 531, 547
Fatigue, 433–434
Fecal immunochemical test, 412t
Fecal occult blood test, 7t, 411, 412t
Feminism, 78, 175–176
Femme, 26t, 74, 77–79, 100, 176–177, 315, 539
Fertility
  assisted reproductive technologies, 86
  donor insemination. See Donor insemination
  rates, 96
Fesoterodine, 471t
Fibroids, 244–246
Flexible sigmoidoscopy, 7t
Flu. See Influenza
Fluconazole, 248
Flumadine. See Rimantadine hydrochloride
Fluoropyrimidines, 415
Follicle-stimulating hormone, 257–258
Follicular cysts, 246
Foot disorders, 226–227
Fracture(s)
  hip, 229–230, 230t, 481, 485
  osteoporosis-related, 480–481
Fracture Risk Assessment Tool, 485, 489
Frozen shoulder, See Adhesive capsulitis

G

Gabapentin, 261
Gastric banding, 172t, 174
Gastric bypass, 173t
Gay affirmative psychotherapy, 286–287
Gay men
  definition, 26t
  lesbian coparenting, 113
  older lesbian interactions, 546

Gender identity, 78, 286, 539
Gender identity disorder, 25
Gender roles, 176
Gender variance, 26t
Genital herpes. See Herpes simplex virus
Genital-to-genital contact, 59t
Gestational diabetes mellitus, 497t, 498–499
Glomerular filtration rate, 503
Gloves, 37
Glucose. See Blood glucose
Glycemic control, 505
Glycosylated hemoglobin, 501, 509
Gonorrhea, 37, 61
Grief, 528–529
Group-mediated cognitive behavioral interventions,
    191–192
Guaiac test, 412t
Gynecologic cancers
  cervical cancer, 12–13, 56, 62, 398–399
  endometrial cancer, 13, 399–401
  extirpative surgery for, 402
  follow-up, 403
  ovarian cancer, 13, 397–398, 401
  prevention, 402–403
  risk factors, 401–402
Gynecologic disorders
  abnormal uterine bleeding, 239–241
  adnexal masses, 246–247
  chronic pelvic pain, 243
  dysmenorrhea, 241
  endometriosis, 243–244
  fibroids, 244–246
  polycystic ovarian syndrome, 240, 242–243
  sexual dysfunction, 241–242
  vaginal bleeding, 240
  vaginal candidiasis, 248
  vaginitis, 247–249
Gynecologic examination, 42–43
Gynecologic history, 238

H

Hallux valgus, 226
Hate crimes, 282, 330
HbA1c. See Glycosylated hemoglobin
HEADSS medical interview, 45, 46t
Health care
  barriers, 5, 8, 56–57, 352–354, 358, 454
  end-of-life. See End-of-life care
  older lesbians' utilization, 544–545
  reasons for avoidance, 8
  reluctance to seek, 544

transgender people, 544–545

Health care power of attorney, 97, 100, 101t, 105, 107–108, 444, 519, 521, 526–7, 530

Health care providers
children of lesbian parents, 117–119
communicating bad news to patients, 523–526
confidentiality, 28
disclosure of sexual orientation, 8, 98, 118, 367, 389, 544
gender preferences, 98
identity promotion, 44
inclusive language use, 28, 34t–35t, 118
office environment, 27–29
physical examination considerations, 42–43
smoking prevention, 134

Health promotion counseling, 372

Health-related quality of life. *See* Quality of life

Health screenings, 6t–7t. *See* Screenings

Hearing test, 7t

Hepatitis, 17t, 428, 429t

Herbal remedies, 171, 212, 257, 261–262

Herpes simplex virus-1, 37, 56, 60

Herpes simplex virus-2, 63–64

Herpes zoster, 17t

Heterosexism
definition, 97, 148
intimate partner violence, 310f
remarks or behavior, 28
substance abuse treatment barriers, 158
victimization studies, 333

Heterosexual marriages, 76–77

High-density lipoprotein, 452, 503–504

Hip fractures, 229–230, 230t, 481, 485

History
gynecologic, 238
intimate partner violence, 315
medical, 29–31
sexual, 57–58
social, 32–41

HIV. *See* Human immunodeficiency virus

H1N1 type A virus, 431

Homelessness, 40–41

Homophobia
description, 40
health care delivery, 97–98
internalized, 16, 142, 146, 148–149, 154, 274, 282–283, 287–288, 389
minority stress, 148
substance abuse treatment, 154

Hormone therapy, 263–265

Hospice. *See also* End-of-life care
advance care planning, 526–527
definition, 519
realistic goal-setting, 526
resuscitation issues, 527
team-based approach, 519
when to initiate, 522

Hot flashes, 259–262

Human immunodeficiency virus, 56, 63, 311f

HPV. *See* Human papillomavirus

Human papillomavirus
cervical cancer, 12, 56, 62, 398, 402
definition, 62
immunization, 17t, 403
prevention, 402–403
screening, 62–63
transmission, 37, 60, 62, 102, 402

Hyperglycemia
medications, 505–507
monitoring, 504–505

Hypertension
cardiovascular disease, 450–452
diabetes mellitus, 503

I

Ibandronate, 486–487

Immunizations, 17, 17t, 47, 403

Impaired fasting glucose, 497t

Impaired glucose tolerance, 496, 497t

Inclusive language, 28, 34t–35t, 99, 118

Income, 542–543, 546–547

Incontinence. *See* Urinary incontinence

Incretin mimetics and enhancers, 507

Infectious diseases
bacterial, 422–425
diarrheal, 426–428
hepatitis, 17t, 428, 429t
influenza, 428, 430–431, 431t
Lyme disease, 434–435
urinary tract infection, 30–31, 431–433

Infertility, 90, 244

Influenza, 17t, 428, 430–431, 431t

Informed consent, 89, 288

Insemination. *See* Donor insemination

Instability, shoulder, 224–225

Insulin, 508–509

Insulin analogs, 508

Insulin resistance, 230, 496

Internalized homophobia, 16, 142, 146, 148–149, 154, 274, 282–283, 287–288, 389

Intimate partner violence
assessment, 312–317, 314f
battering, 312

Pelvic pain, chronic, 243
Pessary, 469
Physical abuse. *See also* Intimate partner violence;
  Violence
  behaviors, 327
  childhood, 103–104, 284, 327–328
  developmentally disabled patients, 356
  health consequences, 331–332
Physical activity
  back pain, 206, 213
  barriers, 187–193
  benefits, 184
  clinician guide, 196*t*–197*t*
  ecological barriers, 189*t*
  studies, 184–187
  types, 194*t*–195*t*
Physical examination, 41–45
Physical inactivity, 453
Physical well-being, 366
Pioglitazone, 507
Pneumococcal vaccine, 17*t*
Polyamory, 79
Polycystic ovarian syndrome, 240, 242–243
Polymenorrhea, 239
Postmenopausal women
  depression, 279
  estrogen loss, 481
  obesity, 11
Postpartum care, 101*t*, 105–107
Postpartum depression, 106–107, 276, 279
Postprandial glucose, 505, 508
Posttraumatic stress disorder, 301, 332
Power of attorney, 97, 526
Preconception counseling, 100, 101*t*
Prediabetes, 496, 498–499, 500*t*
Pregnancy
  abnormal uterine bleeding, 240
  antenatal care, 101*t*, 102–104
  conception methods, 97
  delivery preparations, 101*t*, 104
  donor insemination. *See* Donor insemination
  intimate partner violence, 103
  labor and delivery, 101*t*, 105
  legal issues, 105
  non-pregnant partner, 99
  office visits, 98–99
  postpartum care, 101*t*, 105–107
  preconception counseling, 100, 101*t*
  prenatal classes, 104
  psychosocial risks, 103
  recommendations, 108
  sexually transmitted infection screening, 64

  testing, 240
  unintended, 32–33, 41
  urinary incontinence, 463
  urinary tract infection risks, 432
Prenatal education, 104
Progestin, 261
Psychotherapy, 286–288

Q

Quality of life
  cancer effects, 365–371
  domains, 366–371
  factors, 366
  functional well-being, 366–368
  physical well-being, 366
  psychological well-being, 368
  sexual well-being, 370–371
  social well-being, 369
  spiritual well-being, 369–370

R

Radiation therapy, 415
Raloxifene, 264, 487
Rapid Alcohol Problems Screen, 15, 15*t*
Reclast. *See* Zoledronic acid
Referral, 29
Rejection, 40–41, 42*t*, 330
Relationships
  changes, 78
  closeted, 77
  legal considerations, 74–76
  older lesbian, 540–541
  partnered. *See* Partnered relationships
  polyamory, 79
  power imbalances, 316
  support during alcohol abuse treatment, 150
  variations, 79–80
  violence risks, 308
Relenza. *See* Zanamivir
Religion, 73, 369, 520, 523, 546
Reparative therapy, 287–288
Reproductive tract cancers, 12–13
Revictimization, 328
Rheumatoid arthritis, 453
Rimantadine hydrochloride, 431*t*
Rimming, 59*t*
Rosiglitazone, 507
Rotator cuff tears and disease, 225–226
Rotavirus, 426
Roux-en-Y gastric bypass, 173*t*, 174–175

S

Sadomasochism, 59*t*
Safer sex, 33, 37–38
Salmonella, 427
Same-sex attraction and behavior, 32
Same-sex marriage
  ceremonies, 74
  countries that recognize, 75
  history, 74
  media, 74–75
  states that permit, 70, 75
Sanctura. *See* Trospium
Schizoaffective disorder, 301
Schizophrenia, 295–296, 301
Screenings
  adolescent, 45–47
  alcohol abuse, 15, 15*t*, 152, 153*t*
  breast cancer, 10–11, 385–388
  colorectal cancer, 410–414, 412*t*–413*t*, 416
  depression, 16, 276
  diabetes mellitus, 496, 498–499
  drug use, 152, 153*t*
  gestational diabetes mellitus, 499
  herpes simplex virus-2, 63–64
  human papillomavirus, 62–63
  intimate partner violence, 312–317
  osteoporosis, 483–485
  schedule, 6*t*–7*t*
  sexually transmitted infections, 7*t*, 46–47
  substance use, 103
  urinary incontinence, 466*t*
Second-parent adoption, 91
Self-acceptance, 148–149
Self-identity, 44, 238, 286, 334
Serious mental illness
  community services, 299
  considerations, 297–298
  definition, 295
  epidemiology, 296–297
  patient characteristics, 295–296
  schizophrenia, 295–296, 301
  services, 298–299
  sexuality issues, 297
  types, 300–301
Sex toys, 58–60, 59*t*
Sexual abuse
  adult revictimization, 328
  alcohol abuse risks, 149, 332
  behaviors, 327
  childhood, 283–284, 328
  depression risks, 283–284
  developmentally disabled patients, 356

  health consequences, 331–332
  intimate partner violence susceptibility, 315
  pelvic examination considerations, 238–239
  pregnancy issues, 103–104
  prevalence, 298, 328
  relationships, 311*f*
  reporting, 336
  sexual identity development, 333–334
Sexual activity
  cervical cancer, 12
  men, 40, 57, 249
  number of partners, 58
  older lesbians, 544
  partnered relationships, 73
  protective methods, 37
  risk taking, 40
  urinary tract infections, 432
Sexual assault, 329, 331–332
Sexual dysfunction, 241–242, 262, 370
  lesbian bed death, 241
Sexual health, 60
Sexual history, 57–58
Sexual identity, 333–334, 539
Sexual ideologies, 75–76
Sexual intercourse, 40, 250
Sexuality
  definitions, 26*t*
  development, 25
Sexually transmitted infections
  adolescent screening, 46–47
  bacterial vaginosis, 37, 46–47, 61
  cervical cancer risks, 12
  chlamydia, 6*t*, 37, 60–61
  counseling of patients, 33, 37
  data sources, 57
  education, 60
  gonorrhea, 37, 61
  human immunodeficiency virus, 56, 63, 311*f*
  human papillomavirus. *See* Human
    papillomavirus
  overview, 56–57
  pregnancy screening, 64
  prevalence, 56
  screening, 7*t*, 46–47, 65, 102
  sexual practices, 59*t*
  Treponema pallidum, 64
  Trichomonas vaginalis, 62
Sexual minority youth. *See* Adolescents
Sexual orientation
  confidentiality, 27
  depression, 16
  disclosure. *See* Disclosure of sexual orientation

Tetanus, diphtheria, pertussis vaccine, 17t
Thiazide diuretics, 452, 503
Thiazolidinediones, 506–507, 509
Tobacco use. *See also* Smoking
  cardiovascular disease, 450
  risk factors, 127, 130–131
  targeted advertising, 127, 155
Tolterodine, 471t
Tomboys, 330
Tontines, 547
Total knee replacement, 229
Toviaz. *See* Fesoterodine
Tramadol, 208
Transgender, 26t, 540, 544–545
Transient ischemic attack, 448
Transphobia, 310f, 541
Trauma
  alcohol abuse, 149–150
  coming-out, 147
Treponema pallidum, 64
Tribadism, 59t
Trichomonas vaginalis, 62, 248–249
Trichomonas vaginitis, 248–249
Trospium, 471t
Tubo-ovarian abscess, 246–247
Type 2 diabetes mellitus
  blood glucose control, 501–502
  cardiovascular risk factors, 502–504
  characteristics, 497t
  dyslipidemia management, 503–504
  epidemiology, 496
  glycemic control, 505
  hyperglycemia. *See* Hyperglycemia
  hypertension, 503
  incidence, 495
  medication strategies, 508–511
  treatment, 501–511

U

Urethral bulking agents, 470
Urge incontinence, 460, 461t, 468
Urinary diary, 465, 466t
Urinary incontinence
  age of patient, 462
  depression, 465, 473
  diabetes mellitus, 464
  economic costs, 460
  epidemiology, 461
  ethnicity, 463
  evaluation, 465–467
  menopause-related, 263

mixed, 460, 461t
nonpharmacologic treatment, 467–469
obesity, 463–464, 472
overflow, 460, 461t
pelvic floor exercises, 468t, 468–469
pharmacologic treatment, 470, 471t
pregnancy-related, 463
prevalence, 460
race, 463
risk factors, 461–465, 472–473
screening, 466t
smoking, 464, 472–473
stress incontinence, 460, 461t, 470
surgical treatment, 470, 472
treatment, 467–472
types, 460, 461t
weight loss benefits, 469
Urinary tract infection, 30–31, 431–433
Urodynamic testing, 465–466
Uterine cancer, 13
Uterus
  abnormal bleeding, 239–241
  fibroids, 244–246

V

Vaginal bleeding
  abnormal, 240
  menopause transition, 259–260
Vaginal candidiasis, 248
Vaginal dryness, 262
Vaginitis, 247–249
Vancomycin-resistant *Enterococcus*, 424–425
Vancomycin-resistant *Staphylococcus aureus*,
    424–425
Varicella vaccine, 17t
Vasomotor symptoms, 260–263
Venlafaxine, 285
VESIcare. *See* Solifenacin
Victimization
  assessment, 334–335
  depression, 541
  description, 282–283
  follow-up, 335
  pathways, 329–330
  revictimization, 328
  safety considerations, 335–336
  stereotypes, 335
  stress, 332
Violence
  bias-related pathways, 329–330
  domestic, 16

W

X

Y

Z

Also available from
UCSF NURSING PRESS

Culture & Clinical Care
Juliene Lipson and Suzanne Dibble and 35 contributors
2005 | $33.95

Women's Primary Health Care: Protocols for Practice
Winifred L. Star, Maureen T. Shannon, and Lisa L. Lommel and 37 contributors
Second Edition | 2004 | $100.00

Surgery: A Patient's Guide from Diagnosis to Recovery
Claire Mailhot, Melinda Alves Brubaker and Linda Garratt Slezak
1999 | $20.00

Nurse Practitioner/Physician Collaborative Practice:
Clinical Guidelines for Ambulatory Care
Geraldine M. Collins-Bride and JoAnne M. Saxes
1998 | $27.47

Assessing and Managing Common Signs and Symptoms:
A Decision-Making Approach for Health Care Providers
Lisa Lommel, Patricia Jackson, and 11 contributors
1997 | $27.47

Managing the Side Effects of Chemotherapy and
Radiation Therapy: A Guide for Patients and Their Families
Marylin J. Dodd
Third Edition | 1996 | $20.00

SCHOOL OF NURSING
UNIVERSITY OF CALIFORNIA, SAN FRANCISCO
UCSF NURSING PRESS

521 Parnassus Avenue, Room N505, Box 0608
San Francisco, CA 94143-0608
Phone: 415-476-4992   Fax: 415-476-2373
Web: www.ucsfnursingpress.com